The 96th]
Volunteers in the
Civil War

41/00   University Drive

The 96th Pennsylvania Volunteers in the Civil War

DAVID A. WARD

Foreword by Edwin C. Bearss

For Sherm Barker,
Historian, colleague, friend...
Three cheers for The Civil War!,
With all best wishes of Thank Rou
David A. Ward
2 Oct. 2018

McFarland & Company, Inc., Publishers
Jefferson, North Carolina

Frontispiece: Colonel Henry Lutz Cake. He was the only officer to command
the 96th Pennsylvania Volunteers with the rank of colonel of volunteers.
He was a coal operator, an infantry colonel, and a congressman (Library of Congress).

LIBRARY OF CONGRESS CATALOGUING-IN-PUBLICATION DATA

Names: Ward, David A., 1957– author. | Bearss, Edwin C., writer of foreword.
Title: The 96th Pennsylvania Volunteers in the Civil War / David A. Ward ;
foreword by Edward C. Bearss.
Description: Jefferson, North Carolina : McFarland & Company, Inc.,
Publishers, 2018 | Includes bibliographical references and index.
Identifiers: LCCN 2018004070 | ISBN 9781476668512 (softcover : acid free paper) ∞
Subjects: LCSH: United States. Army. Pennsylvania Infantry Regiment, 96th
(1861–1864) | United States—History—Civil War, 1861–1865—
Campaigns—Virginia. | United States—History—Civil War,
1861–1865—Regimental histories.
Classification: LCC E527.5 96th .W37 2018 | DDC 973.7/448—dc23
LC record available at https://lccn.loc.gov/2018004070

BRITISH LIBRARY CATALOGUING DATA ARE AVAILABLE

ISBN (print) 978-1-4766-6851-2
ISBN (ebook) 978-1-4766-3011-3

On the cover: officers of the 96th Pennsylvania Volunteers at Camp
Northumberland circa February 26, 1862 (Library of Congress)

Printed in the United States of America

McFarland & Company, Inc., Publishers
Box 611, Jefferson, North Carolina 28640
www.mcfarlandpub.com

For Jean Ann, Jon & Ryan

Contents

Acknowledgments	ix
Foreword by Edwin C. Bearss	1
Introduction	3
I. "Attention: young, sober, active men"	7
II. "We always respond with three cheers"	22
III. "My God! The ninety-sixth has never been under fire!"	38
IV. "The enemy … fought like devils"	60
V. "Now, Pennsylvanians, do your duty"	84
VI. "Colonel, your coal-heavers did well!"	109
VII. "Our soldiers are very much discouraged"	128
VIII. "Try and gobble some of them"	151
IX. "The Sixth Corps has come!"	176
X. "O how I do wish that them Irish drunkerts would get drafted"	192
XI. "The skirmishers were sent out ahead"	212
XII. "Forward, double quick! Charge!"	227
XIII. "O God, what a sight"	245
XIV. "There was hope in the air"	260
Appendix: Roster and Muster Roll Sources	279
Chapter Notes	281
Bibliography	318
Index	328

Acknowledgments

In the course of researching and writing the history of the 96th Pennsylvania Volunteers, the author received gracious and courteous assistance from a variety of people. It is only fitting, therefore, that they be recognized for answering inquiries, suggesting research leads and in many instances for providing copies of letters, diaries and memoirs written by their ancestors who served in the regiment. In many cases, a host of individuals expedited research, offered encouragement and inspiration and, at times, went beyond the call of duty thus insuring that the story of the 96th Pennsylvania Volunteers would indeed be told.

For anyone researching and writing about military history, the United States Army Heritage and Education Center at Carlisle Barracks, Pennsylvania, is a most rewarding port of call. It was the good fortune of the author, at the outset of this project, to meet Dr. Richard J. Sommers, who served for four decades as the archivist at the Army Heritage Center. Dick not only pointed me toward pertinent letter and diary collections, at Carlisle Barracks, but he also provided encouragement and inspiration to the author throughout my undergraduate and graduate studies. It is therefore a pleasure to thank Dick for his support all these many years, his professional courtesy and most of all his friendship.

It is also a pleasure to recognize the assistance and friendship of the dean of Pennsylvania Civil War studies, Dr. Richard A. Sauers. The author first met Rick when he was acting as the military historian for the Pennsylvania Capitol Preservation Committee. Rick was instrumental in providing research leads and for sharing his bibliographies concerning Pennsylvania Civil War regiments. For all of his support it is a pleasure to thank him not simply for his help or generosity with sources but to recognize our friendship which spans more than three decades.

Other professional historians, too, offered assistance, and in many instances forwarded research leads or source material, relative to the 96th Pennsylvania Volunteers. Chief among those historians who have spent their careers on the canon ball circuit is Bobby Krick of Richmond, Virginia. Bobby has my enduring gratitude for always keeping a sharp eye for anything related to the author's project and often placed significant source material at my disposal. In addition, Don Pfanz, and Bob Krick, Sr., formerly of the Fredericksburg-Spotsylvania National Military Park, both offered research assistance in one form or another throughout the course of this project. I am especially indebted to Bob for reading several chapters of the manuscript and for making valuable suggestions toward improving the manuscript. The author would also like to thank the dean of Civil War historians, Edwin C. Bearss of Arlington, Virginia, for reading an early draft and for all of his suggestions which greatly enhanced the finished manuscript. Most of all, however, the author would like to thank Ed for his friendship these many years and all that he has done—both personally and professionally—in the course of the author's career as a historian. In addition, the author extends his gratitude to Jeff Wert and Ted Alexander for reading a draft of this manuscript.

Librarians and archivists also played a vital role in the research process. It is a pleasure to recognize and thank these folks for their expertise and professional courtesy. Linda A. Reis and John E. Shelly, Pennsylvania Historical and Museum Commission; Catherine T. Engel, Colorado Historical Society; Galen R. Wilson, Clements Library, University of Michigan; Carolyn Autry, Indiana Historical Society.

Two of the author's college professors also deserve recognition. Dr. Louis Athey, Franklin & Marshall College, Lancaster, Pennsylvania, and Dr. Hugh Davis, Southern Connecticut State University, New Haven, Connecticut. In addition, the author would like to express his gratitude to Dr. David Valuska, Kutztown, Pennsylvania, for reviewing an early draft of this manuscript and for his friendship and encouragement in the course of writing the history of the 96th Pennsylvania Volunteers.

Other historians, too, provided the author with copies of source material or pointed the way toward important historical material pertinent to this study. Dr. Keith Bohannon, University of West Georgia, Carrollton, Georgia; Dr. Grace Palladino, University of Maryland; Dr. J. Tracy Power, South Carolina Department of Archives & History; Sal Cilella, Atlanta History Center; and Ronald G. Griffin, Jackson, Michigan.

The author would also like to extend his gratitude to George Faison, former colleague at The Hotchkiss School and life-long member of Red Sox Nation for his considerable editorial talents. In addition, George Skoch developed a handsome portfolio of maps to accompany the narrative.

The various descendants of the 96th Pennsylvania Volunteers who the author met, in person or through correspondence, during the long research phase of this project can be formally acknowledged for the help and hospitality. At the head of the role call is James F. Haas, formerly of Harrisburg, Pennsylvania. It was Jim Haas, through his passion and enthusiasm, who encouraged the author to undertake this study. The author recalls fondly too the many research visits to Jim's home in Harrisburg and the field trips undertaken in order to follow in the footsteps of the "boys from Schuylkill County." The author will always be grateful to Jim, a fellow of boundless energy, for his support and encouragement. Sadly, Jim passed away thirty years ago but the author can at least thank him posthumously for everything he did to bring this manuscript to publication.

Another descendant who provided initial encouragement, source material and contacts was Michael Cavanaugh of New Jersey. He demonstrated a genuine interest in the author's project and offered his enthusiastic support throughout the research and writing of the manuscript. Most of all, the author would like to thank Mike for his long and abiding friendship and his continued interest in Schuylkill County and the 96th Pennsylvania Volunteers. Other descendants, too, brought forth photo copies or typescripts of letters, diaries and memoirs written by their ancestors who endured camp and battlefield with the 96th Pennsylvania Volunteer. Ron Keiser, Baltimore, Maryland; Mrs. Mary Filbert, Pine Grove, Pennsylvania; Mrs. Marion Fernsler, Pottsville, Pennsylvania; Carl Madison, Marshall, Virginia; Michael T. Snyder, Pottstown, Pennsylvania; Maria R. Allen, Watertown, Connecticut; William Dick, Girard, Pennsylvania; Rev. Emil C. Oestreich, Philadelphia, Pennsylvania; Randy Treichler, Three Springs, Pennsylvania; Randy M. Brandt,

Vineland, New Jersey; and George H. Kain, Emigsville, Pennsylvania, collectively form the 96th Pennsylvania descendant reserve corps.

Finally, there are a number of Ward family members who deserve the enduring gratitude of the author. Margaret Ward-Toussaint, the author's grandmother, photocopied and transcribed documents in the course of her association as a research volunteer at the Historical Society of Schuylkill County. She was a constant source of inspiration and supported the author's project from inception. Leo L. Ward, the author's father, as president of the Historical Society of Schuylkill County, offered encouragement, too, during the research and writing of this manuscript. Dad took me to visit the battlefields and introduced me to the study of the Civil War. He always offered his support and for that I will always be grateful. It is unfortunate that my grandmother and my father passed away before the publication of this manuscript. And last, the most important person throughout the course of this project is the author's wife, Jean Ann Ward. For all that she has done for me I can never repay her. Thanks for your patience, your encouragement and most of all your friendship and love these many years.

Foreword by Edwin C. Bearss

I was introduced to David Ward in the early 1990s at the New England Civil War seminar he had organized at The Hotchkiss School—one of the most prestigious independent preparatory schools. As chief historian of the National Park Service with primary interest in the Civil War, I was impressed with David's academic credentials. At Hotchkiss since 1987 he has served as assistant library director of the Edsel Ford Memorial Library, with a collection of books and access to sources usually unattainable even at small city or private college libraries.

In discussing his educational background, I learned he was a 1980 graduate of Franklin & Marshall College in Lancaster, Pennsylvania, with a B.A. in history. Better yet, because of my position as NPS chief historian for thirteen years, I was pleased to learn he was familiar with Gettysburg National Military Park. Equally important, while earning advanced degrees in 1988 in history and library science from Southern Connecticut State University, he had authored his master's thesis, "Amidst a Tempest of Shot and Shell: A History of the Ninety-Sxith Pennsylvania Volunteers." In addition he later published several book reviews and an article: "Of Battlefields and Bitter Feuds " in *Civil War Regiments*. To me more pertinent was the *Gettysburg Magazine* of which I was senior editor, as I recalled his fine article published in issue number 22, "Sedgwick's Foot Cavalry: The March of the Sixth Corps to Gettysburg."

Upon my September 1995 retirement from the NPS I became a free-lance battlefield guide. This built upon my experience gained through my forty-one years with the NPS. My second career proved enlightening and educational. It reintroduced me to David Ward. In the intervening years, while still librarian at Hotchkiss School, he had established a popular and highly successful weekend business, Civil War Tours. Because of mutual interest, he asked me to join him as one of the principal tour leaders, and I said, count me in.

During the next fourteen years as guide and lecturer I traveled extensively with David and his tour company, averaging about half dozen different battlefields annually. Several years ago David told me of his plans to sell his company, retire from Hotchkiss and relocate, along with his lovely wife, Jean Ann, to the Scottsdale area of Arizona. Like many historians he also planned to revisit the subject of his thesis, which traced the history of the 96th Pennsylvania Volunteers and extensively expand his previous work. I readily agreed to review the final draft and write a foreword to the revised manuscript.

Although a native of the hard coal region (Schuylkill County) where the 96th Pennsylvania was organized, David has resided most of his life in Connecticut. Because of his professional position at Hotchkiss he was able to acquire microfilm, hard-to-find books and use the internet to locate manuscript collections pertinent to his study. As a result, he was able to find previously unknown sources, thus adding new voices to his colorful narrative.

During the years that I led tours, most of them focused on engagements and battles associated with the Army of the Potomac and the eastern campaigns. While a tour operator, David did not remain on the bus during a battlefield tour but accompanied the group as they walked in the footsteps of history. As a seriously wounded Marine combat veteran of World War II I have learned through experience that the only way to read a battlefield and understand and appreciate the terrain is to walk the ground. During our time together on the battlefields, David and I tramped Eltham's Landing, Gaines' Mill, Crampton's Gap, Salem Church, Spotsylvania and Cold Harbor.

David's book meets the criteria of a "scholarly study" of a Pennsylvania unit that Civil War readers need to know more about. Unit histories were rediscovered after a hiatus of more than a half century in 1957 with the publication of John Pullen's *The Twentieth Maine: A Volunteer Regiment in the Civil War*. This new regimental history relies upon previously unused accounts by participants, providing new information not available in standard works, to tell the story of the 96th Pennsylvania Volunteers. Now Ward's tour-de-force adds to the significant shelf of regimental histories and fills a gap in the historiography of the Army of the Potomac and Pennsylvania history.

Edwin C. Bearss is chief historian emeritus of the National Park Service and lives in Arlington, Virginia.

Introduction

In the preface to his influential book, *Richmond Redeemed: The Siege at Petersburg*, Richard J. Sommers stated:

> There is no truth to the old canard that every aspect of the conflict [the American Civil War] has already been fully covered. To the contrary, the war is rich with scores of commanders, hundreds of units, thousands of operations that have never received full treatment. Nor are these untapped areas confined to obscure officers, inactive outfits, and inconsequential encounters. Many of the greatest campaigns of the war remain without modern scholarly study.[1]

The 96th Pennsylvania Volunteers, one of Colonel William Fox's "Fighting Three Hundred Regiments," remains an infantry regiment in need of modern scholarly analysis and interpretation. The 96th Pennsylvania served a three-year enlistment as an infantry unit in the Second Brigade, First Division of the Sixth Corps in the Army of the Potomac. The regiment served in the Civil War's principal theater of operation, Virginia, against the Confederacy's most formidable fighting force, the Army of Northern Virginia. When the 96th Pennsylvania Volunteers left the Keystone State for Washington in November 1861, the regiment numbered some 1,139 effectives. Three years later, when the regiment's term of service expired, only a steadfast 100 veteran volunteers could answer morning roll call.[2]

How, in the course of three years of service did this infantry regiment—referred to by Bell Wiley as the "common soldiers" of the Civil War—come so close to extinction? What role did the regiment play in the evolving tactical operations of its brigade in particular and the ongoing strategic combinations of the Sixth Corps in general? Why did these men from the anthracite coal region of eastern Pennsylvania respond quickly and patriotically to Lincoln's call for volunteers? Did they mirror the political and social norms of their region, Schuylkill County, Pennsylvania? What motivated them to sustain their commitment to Union victory during their three-year period of service? How did they cope with health problems, the long separation from their families, inclement weather, the boredom of camp life and the harsh living conditions they encountered during active operations? Finally, how would the fury, trauma and destruction of a Civil War battle affect the citizens-turned-soldiers of the 96th Pennsylvania Volunteers?

Such questions suggest useful avenues of inquiry for the modern historian. Yet, the 96th Pennsylvania Volunteers has received scant attention from Civil War scholars and professional historians. Bruce Catton mentions the unit in *Mr. Lincoln's Army*, and Stephen Ambrose affords the regiment coverage in his book *Upton and the Army*. More contemporary campaign and battle studies, such as Brian Burton's *Extraordinary Circumstances*, Timothy Reese's *Sealed with Their Lives*, and Stephen Sears' *Chancellorsville* along with Gordon Rhea's *Spotsylvania*, explore the tactical role of the 96th Pennsylvania Volunteers within the context of some of the Civil War's most dramatic battles.[3] Collectively, these modern studies have essentially forged the combat history of the 96th Pennsylvania Volunteers. But the story of the 96th Pennsylvania cannot be written simply by recounting the handful of battles the unit participated in from the spring of 1862 until the spring of 1864. To produce a modern, scholarly history of the unit, contemporary sources, written by participants, should form its foundation.

Unlike many Civil War regiments, whose service was memorialized by a comrade who served in the ranks, the 96th Pennsylvania never found a member of the unit to chronicle its history. The most thorough history of the 96th Pennsylvania Civil War service can be found in Samuel P. Bates' massive compilation, *History of Pennsylvania Volunteers, 1861–5*. In addition to the short history of the unit in Bates, the regiment's service was briefly reviewed by John T. Boyle, former captain of Company D, in his fine article, "An Outline Sketch of the Ninety-Sixth Pennsylvania Volunteers," published in the "Annals of the War" series in the Philadelphia *Weekly Times*. Finally, Henry Boyer penned three long columns under the title "At Crampton's Pass," published in the Shenandoah *Evening Herald*, recounting the regiment's participation in the Battle of South Mountain. In addition, there is a brief history of the regiment's service outlined in Henry Royer's address delivered at the dedication of the unit's monument at Gettysburg and published in *Pennsylvania at Gettysburg*. These four brief histories constitute fine pioneering studies of the regiment's service. Since the publication of these pieces in the 1880s, however, a collection of official and personal papers, written by junior officers and enlisted men, have become available to form the corpus of material necessary to produce a long overdue history of the regiment.[4]

The value of regimental histories, especially those that are well-executed, is beyond question. In her recent book, *A Broken Regiment*, historian Lesley Gordon argues that "the regimental history as a genre or as a form of storytelling can be an especially fruitful way of thinking about and exploring war and its lasting impact." Regimental histories have evolved significantly since the appearance of John Pullen's classic chronicle of the 20th Maine Volunteers. These works not only offer insights concerning particular regiments, but they also collectively afford the reader a view of the Civil War from the bottom up. Recent contributions such as Warren Wilkinson's definitive study of the 57th Massachusetts Volunteers and Salvatore Cilella's history of the 121st New York Volunteers underscore the value of comprehensive regimental histories.[5]

Because Civil War regiments were usually composed of men from a specific region, generally a state county or several closely connected counties, regimental histories offer the modern historian an excellent lens through which to study the people and events of the early 1860s. Further, and most significantly, regimental histories present the Civil War from the perspective of the participants—the citizen volunteers who became the common soldiers. The format of a regimental history also provides a convenient forum for re-examining accepted truths about the role of individual soldiers in the broader context of the war. According to Leslie Anders, a thoroughly researched, carefully documented narrative of one Civil War regiment will

> afford the reader a clearer view of what moved the men of the sixties from their civilian pursuits to the perils of the battlefield, what changes of mind and mood came over them, what it was like to organize and manage a typical organization of citizens-turned-soldiers, and the wide range of

experiences that came to the average soldier in cantonment and campaign. These are hardly to be glimpsed from biographies of officers.[6]

The Civil War inspired an outpouring of unit histories documenting the service of infantry, artillery and cavalry units that fought the War for the Union. With only a few exceptions, regimental histories were written by members of the unit—surgeons, adjutants, junior officers, chaplains, enlisted men or a small committee composed of veterans who served with the regiment. Unfortunately, the regimental histories produced after the war suffered from a number of shortcomings. Often the volumes were compiled hastily and were riddled with factual errors. In many cases, regimental histories were authored quickly for aging veterans, their widows, descendants and relatives and were often works of piety. The regimental histories written in the decades following the war often eulogized comrades who fell in battle, exaggerated the role of the unit in the outcome of the war, and often ignored unpleasant aspects of a particular regiment's term of service. In sum, regimental histories produced during this period served as memorial volumes rather than interpretive monographs examining critical issues relevant to academic historians.

Not until after the final roll of the soldiers who served in the 96th Pennsylvania regiment was called, and their diaries, letters and pertinent personal papers became available in libraries, historical societies and manuscript repositories, did the possibility of writing a unit history present itself. Although several members of the unit were well qualified to write a history of the regiment, none of the veterans ever produced a substantive history of the regiment's service. The task of researching and writing a unit history has waited for a modern historian. The author is hopeful that a thoroughly researched regimental history and an interpretive narrative will broaden our understanding of the common soldier of the Civil War and add to our sum knowledge of what James McPherson referred to as "the central event in the American historical consciousness."[7]

The Keystone State forged a distinguished record during the Civil War. Pennsylvania raised over two hundred regiments of infantry and cavalry, along with a substantial number of artillery batteries. Since the Civil War Centennial, however, only about twenty of these units have received comprehensive study and analysis by amateur and professional historians. According to Wayne Smith, "No historian has attempted to prepare a comprehensive review of the 360,000 Pennsylvanians who defended the republic. The Pennsylvania soldier awaits the attention of some historian."[8] Such a daunting project, however, has not, and perhaps never will be, undertaken. For that reason, individual regimental histories of units from Pennsylvania will most likely continue to be produced by independent researchers and professional historians. For a sampling of such histories, the interested reader should consult Edwin Glover, *Bucktailed Wildcats*, John Rowell, *Yankee Cavalrymen*, Edward Hagerty, *Collis' Zouaves,* or Dennis Brandt, *From Home Guards to Heroes.*[9] These studies stand as sentinels to the largely ignored yet fertile field of study concerning the soldiers from Pennsylvania who participated in the War of the Rebellion.

This work will examine the organization, operations and character of the 96th Pennsylvania Volunteers. Emphasis will be placed on the social life and customs of the enlisted men and the military campaigns and battles in which the regiment experienced the hardships and horror of combat. A principal goal is to examine this regiment of infantry as a subset of the Pennsylvania community they represented in the early 1860s and to document the war's effect on the lives of some of its participants. Only by examining the common soldier of the Civil War, during campaigns and combat, on fatigue or guard duty, in camp or on the march, can we gain better insight and fulfill the purpose of all historical study: "contributing to knowledge and enhancing understanding of the human experience."[10] Perhaps Bell Wiley stated it best in the preface to his landmark study, *The Life of Billy Yank*, when he said that many Americans are drawn to the study of the Civil War in order to develop portraits of the faceless soldiers who comprised the rank and file of the Union armies.

> I wanted to know what sort of men they were, what caused them to fight, how they reacted to combat, what they thought about the land and the people of Dixie, how well they stood up under strain of prolonged conflict, what they thought of their leaders, and how they compared to their opposites in gray. All this and more I wanted to learn.[11]

As such, one facet of Clio's discipline that this work encompasses falls into the realm of classical military history. The study of battlefield combat, coupled with the decisions of the regiment's commanders and the subsequent responses by the soldiers of the 96th Pennsylvania are a significant aspect of the unit's military history. Minor tactics and the leadership of the regiment as they related to the brigade, division, corps and army will be afforded analysis and interpretation. It is the intention of the author, however, to relate more than merely generalized information concerning the principal military engagements of the 96th Pennsylvania. The hope is that the following narrative, based on extensive research and analysis, will contribute to the evolving interpretations of these battles in particular and the broader field of the military history of the Civil War.

The Civil War affords an unusually good opportunity to study the common citizen of the era. Volunteer soldiers who were far from home, and absent from their families for extended periods, regularly wrote informative letters describing their experiences and often kept pocket diaries where they recorded daily observations. Thus, there is a rich recorded heritage of thoughts and deeds from the soldiers who served in the 96th Pennsylvania infantry regiment. Using these documentary sources, the author hopes to develop for the rank and file of the 96th Pennsylvania what the historian John Keegan termed a "face of battle."[12] In addition to drawing heavily from the letters, diaries, memoirs and writings of the soldiers the author chose, in many instances, to present their words in the narrative without editing and spelling corrections.

This study is based upon research in manuscript repositories, archives and libraries from Maine to Colorado. Whenever possible, excerpts from original letters, diaries or memoirs are used to enhance both the narrative and give the reader a sense of immediacy. The author hopes to demonstrate, through the use of original sources, that the rank and file of the 96th Pennsylvania were devoted volunteer soldiers, unashamedly patriotic, dedicated to their regiment, and to the cause in which they believed and for which many died. It is a story of human suffering and tragedy but also of the triumph of the spirit to overcome adversity.

I

"Attention: young, sober, active men"

Attention: young, sober, active men wanted to enlist with a company now forming at Pine Grove in service of the United States for three years or the duration of the war. The company will be attached to a regiment now forming in Schuylkill County and to be mustered into service of the United States before they leave the county and from that day draw pay. Will be armed with the most approved rifles.[1]

On a sultry day in August 1861, Peter A. Filbert, former second lieutenant of Company D, 10th Pennsylvania Volunteers—mustered out of active service at the close of Maj. Gen. Robert Patterson's Shenandoah Valley move-

ments—distributed the above captioned handbill to the patriotic men of Pine Grove, a sleepy little hamlet in the southwest corner of Schuylkill County. Filbert recently learned that Col. Henry L. Cake, former commander of the disbanded 25th Pennsylvania Volunteers, was recruiting a regiment of infantry in Pottsville to serve an enlistment period of three years, or the duration of the war. Filbert planned to organize a company of infantry and then join Cake's regiment. Within two weeks Filbert raised a full company, comprised mostly of men with militia background, as well as the veterans who served under Gen. Patterson during "Granny" Patterson's Shenandoah Valley Campaign. The troops immediately decided on a company nickname, unanimously choosing to call themselves the "Pine Grove Sharpshooters," and they elected Filbert captain, and Ernest T. Ellrich the first lieutenant. After the unit completed that necessary bit of business, Filbert dressed his ranks and marched the "Sharpshooters" to Pottsville, where the company presented itself for duty to Colonel Cake.[2]

At the outbreak of the war, Peter Filbert

Lt. Col. Peter A. Filbert. Originally the captain of Company B. Discharged from United States service on December 22, 1862 (courtesy Mary E. Filbert).

was twenty-eight years old, and a relative newcomer to the art of war. His family, old line Whigs, was active in local politics and had a history of military service. Filbert attended the common school in Pine Grove, and later studied at the Business College of Baltimore, Maryland. After completing his studies, Filbert found employment in York, Pennsylvania, as an apprentice machinist. After a short time he returned to Baltimore. Soon thereafter he was offered a clerk position with the Ashland Furnace, which he accepted, as it allowed him the opportunity to return to his native state. Filbert later moved to the Swatara Furnace, near Outwood, and at the firing upon Fort Sumter was acting as a clerk for the firm of Graeff & Nutting in Pine Grove. In response to President Lincoln's initial call for volunteers, Filbert enlisted with the Washington Light Infantry, one of the militia companies of Pine Grove. He served with that unit, which subsequently formed Company D of the 10th Pennsylvania Volunteers, as a second lieutenant, completing a three month term of service. The 10th Pennsylvania regiment participated in General Patterson's Shenandoah Valley Campaign, but saw no active duty. Now Filbert was a three-year, or duration of the war, volunteer and would become embroiled in a conflict that would be the most dramatic event of his lifetime.[3]

On August 13, 1861, Cake received permission from the War Department to raise and organize a regiment of three-year volunteers. Originally Cake wanted to reorganize his disbanded three-month command, the 25th Pennsylvania Volunteers, but the War Department refused his request, as they decided to renumber the new three-year volunteer units. Cake therefore opened a recruiting station in Pottsville and established an encampment site atop Lawton's Hill, overlooking the borough.[4]

Henry Lutz Cake, thirty-three years old at the start of the War of the Rebellion, was born near Northumberland, Pennsylvania. After learning the printing trade in Harrisburg, he moved to Pottsville in 1847 and established a weekly newspaper, the *Mining Record*. Shortly after adjusting to life in Schuylkill County and becoming a familiar face at political gatherings, Cake became active in a militia company, the National Light Infantry. In 1852, when the company was in desperate need of financial backing, Cake stepped forward and revived its sagging fortunes by purchasing Continental style uniforms for the unit. Edmund McDonald, a member of the company, correctly stated that from that time until Lincoln's call for volunteers in April 1861, "the National Light Infantry owed its

Col. Henry L. Cake. Recruited and organized the 96th Pennsylvania Volunteers. Commanded the regiment at the battles of Eltham's Landing, Gaines' Mill and Crampton's Gap. Resigned from United States service March 12, 1863 (author's collection).

continuation and existence to him." In addition to his financial backing, Cake provided an armory for the militia company, paid all of its expenses and often hired men to parade to meet the requirements of the law.

As Cake's influence with the militia grew, he also developed interests in the anthracite coal industry, which was booming during the pre–Civil War era. After acquiring a share in the St. Nicholas Colliery, Cake emerged as an innovative and powerful coal operator in Schuylkill County. At the outbreak of the Civil War he was one of the county's most powerful figures, with lofty ambitions. In 1861, he turned away from his entrepreneurial interests and elected to go on duty as a colonel of volunteer infantrymen. Cake's experience with the Pennsylvania militia and his field command of the 25th Pennsylvania in the summer campaign prompted Governor Andrew G. Curtin to commission him a colonel of a three-year regiment of volunteers, the 96th Pennsylvania regiment. He accepted the appointment and set about the task of raising, organizing and training a volunteer infantry regiment.[5]

The rank and file of the 96th Pennsylvania was recruited principally from Schuylkill County. Situated in eastern Pennsylvania, Schuylkill County, was in the midst of an economic boom. The discovery of anthracite coal in 1790 turned the region into a desirable place for immigrants to fulfill their dreams of economic freedom, steady employment and perhaps the accumulation of wealth. From the coal miners in England and Wales, to the illiterate, landless peasants of Ireland, and the disenchanted Germans, the anthracite region of Pennsylvania presented an appealing land of opportunity. In 1840, according to the United States Census, 29,053 people inhabited Schuylkill County. By the outbreak of the Civil War, an additional 60,000 immigrants had settled in the southern coal fields. This enormous influx of foreigners sought to work in the coal mines or forge a living through the many service businesses which developed to support the colliery operations. At the center of the southern anthracite coal field was the rapidly growing city of Pottsville, the civic and commercial seat of Schuylkill County. By 1860, Pottsville was well established as the economic hub of the southern coal region, the center of manufacturing, the social center and the place where everyone met for news and entertainment. As such, it was only fitting that Pottsville would be established as the rendezvous site for the newly recruited 96th Pennsylvania Volunteers.[6]

The first company to join Colonel Cake's new command at Camp Schuylkill, the name given to the rendezvous site, was a reorganized unit from Cake's old three-month command. After learning that Cake was actively recruiting a regiment of infantry, Lewis J. Martin, a former member of the National Light Infantry and second lieutenant of Company D, 25th Pennsylvania Volunteers, recalled the troops of his old command and reported for duty. Upon arriving at Camp Schuylkill, Cake promoted Martin to the rank of major, thus filling an important position on his staff. In turn, Lamar S. Hay, who served as first sergeant of the National Light Infantry during the three-month campaign, was appointed captain of Company A. In recognition of being the first company to enroll in the newly formed regiment, Hay's command was designated as one of the regiment's flanking companies.[7]

On the afternoon of September 2, Captain Filbert's Pine Grove Sharpshooters tramped up Lawton's Hill and reported to Colonel Cake. Filbert's command was designated Company B, and along with Martin's unit constituted the flanking companies of the regiment. Soon thereafter Capt. Beaton Smith brought his company, a unit of infantry raised in Luzerne County, into Camp Schuylkill. Smith's command was designated Company C. Almost simultaneously two more companies of infantry arrived atop Lawton's Hill. The first, designated Company E, composed of recruits from Schuylkill County and Luzerne County, was commanded by Capt. James E. Russell, a long-time member of the National Light Infantry and former first lieutenant of Company D, 25th Pennsylvania Volunteers. The second unit, raised in Schuylkill County, which formed Company F of the 96th regiment, was under the command of Capt. Joseph Anthony. By the end of the first week in September, fifty percent of Cake's regiment was in camp.[8]

Soon after Anthony's company pitched its shelter tents atop Lawton's Hill, companies D, G, H, I and K reported for duty to Cake. Company I, Capt. Isaac M. Cake commanding, Company K, under Capt. Richard Budd and Company D, led by Capt. John T. Boyle, contained virtually all Schuylkill County men. Charles D. Hipple's Company H, and Capt. James N. Douden's Company G, "The Hamburg Light Infantry," included men from Berks, Dauphin, Montgomery and Schuylkill Counties. By the close of the third week in September, ten full companies of infantry were assigned positions and quartered at Camp Schuylkill. The line officers of the 96th regiment, unlike their counterparts in other Schuylkill County regiments, were not a collection of inexperienced amateur soldiers. Many had a long history of militia service. All served previously with Pennsylvania units during the three-month's campaign; some holding the rank of captain, while most were mustered out as junior officers.[9]

After the regiment was completely recruited, the line officers of the ten companies elected Jacob G. Frick to serve as lieutenant colonel. After Frick's election, and the promotions of Lewis Martin and Lamar S. Hay, Captain Filbert of Company B was recognized as the senior captain—the next line officer to receive a promotion should a staff officer vacancy develop. Colonel Cake appointed Mathias E. Richards to serve as the regiment's adjutant—a post he previously held under Cake during the three-month service with the 25th Pennsylvania Volunteers. Finally, the Pottsville Cornet Band was attached to the 96th Pennsylvania to serve as the regimental musicians.[10]

Lieutenant Colonel Frick was a welcome addition to the regiment. A native of Northumberland, Pennsylvania, he was thirty-six years old when he joined the 96th Pennsylvania. Before the war he was a prominent citizen of Pottsville who established a moderately successful business which manufactured wire coal screens. His business background, however, was not the reason why he loomed as such an attractive officer candidate. Frick, unlike the other volunteers, had been previously exposed to the din of battle and the hardships of military campaigning as a second lieutenant in the Army during the Mexican War, initially in the 3rd Ohio Infantry, under Col. Samuel R. Curtis and then in the 11th United States Infantry. Eventually, he was transferred to Fort McHenry, where he served as assistant instructor of infantry tactics before being discharged in August of 1848. Certainly Frick's military experience—one contemporary biographer described him as being "of Saul like stature" and "well proportioned"—coupled with his knowledge of the art of war made him a coveted commodity.[11]

To the rank of major, Cake appointed old friend and colleague Lewis Martin. Prior to the war, Martin, a civil engineer by profession, served as the county surveyor. He was a Republican in his politics and a Presbyterian in his religious beliefs. At the outbreak of the war, he enrolled in the National Light Infantry, one of the first organized companies of volunteers to respond to Lincoln's call for citizen-soldiers. He served as a corporal and

later received promotion to first lieutenant during his ninety-day service with
the 25th Pennsylvania Volunteers. Cake
held the rank of colonel during the 25th
Pennsylvania's three month period of
active duty. During that time, he recognized Martin's character and considerable
talents as an officer of volunteer soldiers.
Francis Wallace described Martin as "a
gallant officer and strictly conscientious in
the discharge of his duties. With cultivated
mind he possessed amiable qualities that
rendered him a great favorite" among the
men of his regiment. Another contemporary observer stated that "his manners
were remarkably modest and unobtrusive.
[He] was a hard worker at whatever he
undertook. In point of morals, no better
young man could be found … his deport-
ment was highly exemplary and reflected
the evidence of careful, religious training
at home." Now, in the late summer of 1861,
he was preparing to join the second wave
of patriots to suppress the rebellion. Enlisting for three years, he would leave behind
his widowed mother, young wife and three
children.[12]

Lt. Col. Jacob G. Frick. Former Army officer with
the 3rd Ohio and 11th United States Infantry.
Appointed colonel of the 129th Pennsylvania
Volunteers July 29, 1862 (MOLLUS Mass. Collection, United States Army Heritage and Education Center).

Throughout early September, as the
96th regiment assembled on the eastern
slope of Lawton's Hill, civilians visited the
encampment to witness first-hand the excitement associated with Camp Schuylkill. Captain Boyle, of Company D, described the scene which greeted the citizens from Pottsville
and nearby towns. "As the regiment expanded," wrote Boyle, "people from all parts of the
county drawn thither through curiosity or to visit their friends or relatives continually
thronged its spacious avenue, or sauntered through its commodious streets, and the scenes
within its boundaries on a gala day, once seen, was not likely to be forgotten." During this
period, as new companies reported to Camp Schuylkill, Major Martin assigned the incoming units to their respective positions on the eastern slope of Lawton's Hill. In addition to
recording the impression Camp Schuylkill made on the local citizenry, Captain Boyle also
described the sights which the new volunteers experienced as they ascended the hill toward
Camp Schuylkill. "Upon their arrival in camp the men were assigned their quarters, and
supplied by their officers with blankets, knife, fork, tin spoon, plate and cup. Having thus
identified themselves with the regiment, they entered immediately upon the duties of their
new vocation, and day after day, responded … to the … commands of the drill sergeants,
and the orders of their line officers." Gradually, over the course of the autumn months,
the untrained, unseasoned and untested volunteers would be turned into soldiers.[13]

On September 23, the volunteer soldiers at Camp Schuylkill were drawn up in parade ground formation and mustered into the service of the United States Army. This was the last rite of passage for the volunteers, who had already cleared several other obstacles. Before being mustered, each Bluecoat was required to sign a "volunteer enlistment" form which stated the period that the soldier would legally bear arms against the Confederacy. This form required the signatures of three people. Along with the soldier, the enlistment form was signed by the examining surgeon. In this case, Dr. D. Webster Bland, the regimental surgeon, who certified that he had carefully examined each volunteer and that in his professional opinion each Bluecoat was "free from all bodily defects and mental infirmity which might disqualify him from performing the duties of a soldier." Most importantly, the examining surgeon carefully inspected each recruit's teeth, to insure that the volunteer could tear open a paper cartridge, which was required in order to load a Civil War era rifle musket. The recruiting officer also certified that he too had "minutely examined" the volunteer and that the prospective soldier was "entirely sober when enlisted," of lawful age and qualified to perform the duties of a fighting man. The Pennsylvanians were mustered into United States service by a Regular Army officer, 2nd Lt. H. L. Taliaferro, attached to the 5th United States Artillery Regiment. After he administered the oath of Allegiance to the gathered Bluecoats, and the reading of the *Articles of War* was completed, the volunteers began learning the rudiments of military drill and discipline under the command of Lieutenant Colonel Frick.[14]

While a number of soldiers enrolled in the new regiment had previously served in the Pennsylvania militia, or responded to Lincoln's call, many were relatively young men unaccustomed to military life. The average age of the enlisted soldiers in the 96th Pennsylvania was 24 years old. The youngest soldier was Private John Haley, just 16 years old, who served in Company F. Three soldiers, each 50 years old, were the oldest men to serve in the regiment. Two of them, Thomas Jones and Daniel Wolf, served in Company D, while Capt. James Russell commanded Company E.[15] The average age of the soldiers filling the ranks of the 96th Pennsylvania is very close to the average computed by Benjamin Gould in his extensive study published in 1869. Gould concluded in his survey that the average age of the Union soldier in July 1862 was 25 years old. Young, enthusiastic men, but inexperienced volunteer soldiers, filled the rolls of the 96th Pennsylvania.[16] In age, the volunteers who joined Cake's 96th regiment, conformed to the typical Union regiment of infantry raised in the late summer of 1861.

Maj. Lewis J. Martin. Killed in action at Crampton's Gap September 14, 1862 (Heber Thompson, *The First Defenders*, 1910).

As Colonel Cake readily recruited a full complement of volunteers, the diverse ethnic backgrounds of the citizen-soldiers posed challenges for the officers charged with training them. Illiterate Irish, non–English speaking Germans, and other immigrants of different European backgrounds complicated the training. Cake and his subordinates found the initial training to be tedious and the ability of the green volunteers to master the intricate maneuvers was slower than desired. While secession and the issue of slavery galvanized the Irish and Germans alike to enlist, the question which remained concerned their ability to emerge victorious upon the tactical field.[17]

The ethnicity of the rank and file of the 96th Pennsylvania corresponded to the population change which the region experienced prior to the outbreak of the war. The population growth coincided with a rapidly improving economic situation. The late 1840s proved to be financially disastrous to the coal trade. In addition, an abnormal amount of rainfall caused flooding which curtailed production in the 1850 and 1851. The coal trade rebounded in 1852, a boom year, allowing the region to boast 10,000 miners compared to 3,500 a decade before. Throughout the 1850s, however, the anthracite coal industry continued to suffer economic uncertainty while the region experienced continued demographic changes.[18]

The ethnic profile of the regiment, compiled after the war by Capt. John T. Boyle, reflected the rapid growth of immigrants entering the anthracite coal fields during the first half of the nineteenth century. Of the original body of troops comprising the 96th regiment, 605 were native Pennsylvanians. Sixteen were born in other states. Two hundred seventy-nine volunteers were natives of Ireland—comprising twenty-four percent of the regiment. Sixty men were from Germany, fifty-nine from England, forty from Wales, ten from France, six from Scotland, four from Bavaria, two from Canada and one member each from Austria, Hanover, Poland and Switzerland. An examination of the native Americans reveals that the majority were of Irish ancestry. The Germans and the English comprised the next largest block of recruits, while the men of Welsh heritage were not far behind.[19]

By examining the coal industry it is easy to establish why the Irish came to the anthracite fields. The Schuylkill County coal mines offered work to any Immigrant, particularly the Irish, who wished to risk life toiling in the dangerous shafts of the collieries. Many from Ireland knew of the dangers in mining, as they had practiced the trade in the old country. In fact, the 96th regiment listed 282 coal miners on its rolls in 1861. Two hundred eighty-five were coal miners' laborers who ranked just below a miner on the anthracite industry hierarchy. Statistically, the Schuylkill County coal mines supplied one half of the 96th Pennsylvania's rank and file. One hundred two of the regiment were iron workers, sixty-eight farmed for a living, fifty-nine were carpenters, forty-five worked on the railroad, forty-three were in the leather craft trade, sixteen were cloth makers, twenty-two held professional occupations and eleven were students. The balance of the regiment—some one hundred and nine volunteers—worked at a variety of trades and occupations.[20]

There was considerable doubt whether or not these outsiders would volunteer to suppress the rebellion. Within the ranks of the 96th Pennsylvania was a contingent of Germans, Company G, recruited in Berks County. The Pennsylvania Germans, stereotyped as "the Dutch," developed communities which reinforced social, language and cultural features which kept them distinct from other immigrant groups in eastern Pennsylvania. The Germans enrolled in the 96th Pennsylvania leaving behind their family farms in Berks County to join Colonel Cake's regiment. They would continue to speak in their native tongue and read the German newspapers published in the region. They also preferred to receive their drill and command instructions on the parade ground in German.[21] Unlike the Germans, the Irish were prominent in number, active in community affairs and social organizations within a growing class particularly in the anthracite coal region. For the Germans and the Irish, enlisting to restore the Union was an opportunity to accelerate the process of becoming an American, change nativist prejudices and through their service, reduce discrimination against their respective communities. The question remained: could the German recruits and the illiterate Irish be trained to become effective combat soldiers?[22]

To the citizen-turned-soldier, military drill, when it was taken seriously, was but a necessary evil. Military discipline, a fundamental building block in the training of infantry soldiers, was perceived by the rank and file of the 96th Pennsylvania as an infringement upon personal freedoms.[23] Although the Bluecoats from Camp Schuylkill complained about what they felt was an excessive amount of drilling, they really did not receive intensive military instruction. After training in the facings, they were taught the School of the Soldier, which consisted of instruction in the handling of weapons, various alignments, and, of course, marching. After the volunteer was properly drilled to the point of maneuvering, he was introduced to the School of the Company, the foundation of movement for the regiment. All of this instruction sought to get the soldiers into a formation which would allow them to fire a volley at the enemy or advance in unison against the foe.[24]

After the foot soldiers gained a degree of competency in the School of the Company the volunteers were introduced to battalion drill. With a comprehensive program of instruction, the ten companies of the 96th Pennsylvania could learn to maneuver as a unit rather than as a loose aggregation of semi-independent commands. The tactical proficiency of the Schuylkill County Bluecoats depended upon how well the officer corps of the regiment could impart to the volunteers the difficult drill regulations outlined in William J. Hardee's *Rifle and Light Infantry Tactics*.[25]

During the training period at Camp Schuylkill the line officers benefited greatly from the presence of Lieutenant Colonel Frick. His schooling of the company officers made the transfer of tactical maneuvers from paper to movements on the parade ground a much easier process. The unfortunate aspect of all of this training was that no matter how proficient the 96th Pennsylvania became in close order drill and parade evolutions, they would soon find that their training was inadequate for battle. Eventually they would learn that the mere act of marching across a smooth drill ground, free of the din of war, did not approximate the confusion and stress of an actual engagement.[26]

As the soldiers trained in marching and maneuvering skills, they also had to be schooled in the use of their muskets. Instruction was given at Camp Schuylkill in the proper procedure for loading a smooth-bore musket, which entailed the following: extracting a paper cartridge from the cartridge box, biting off the end of the cartridge, inserting it in the gun barrel, drawing the ramrod, ramming the charge home, returning the ramrod, and placing the percussion cap on the nipple of the musket. The soldier had to complete all of these tasks before he could discharge his weapon. Consequently, all of this required a great deal of practice and repetition. After familiarizing themselves with the *Manual of Arms*, the soldiers were also given instruction in the use of the bayonet.[27]

Although the work to produce competent infantrymen seemed hard, it could not emulate the stress of a battlefield situation. When a Bluecoat neglected to withdraw the ramrod from the barrel of his musket and accidentally fired the weapon, only to hear a "twang" not to mention the laughter of his company mates, as the ramrod flew through the air, the soldier could also chuckle at his forgetfulness. But if his company, while under fire, had to move on a diagonal to support a hard-pressed battery, the Bluecoat had better not make the same error with his ramrod. Lessons not properly learned on the drilling ground would eventually haunt a volunteer. In short, the parade ground of Lawton's Hill did not approximate the battleground; the two would prove to be vastly different.[28]

While the soldiers trained on Lawton's Hill, learning the intricacies of military drill and discipline, local political battles, waged with words, overshadowed the upcoming combat action that would be fought with rifles and bayonets. Despite the resounding Republican victories of Abraham Lincoln and Pennsylvania Governor Andrew Curtin in the 1860 election, the lower anthracite region demonstrated a long allegiance to the Democratic Party. Both Lincoln and Curtin won majorities across Pennsylvania and reversed the usual trend of Democratic victories in Schuylkill County. According to labor statistics in 1860, almost half of Schuylkill County's miners were Irish, voted democratic and dominated the coal towns, hamlets and patches. The agricultural towns, characterized by the German community, also represented a solid Democratic voting block.[29]

The Republican victory in 1860 indicated a significant political shift in national as well as local elections. Despite the continuation of anti-immigrant sentiment, nativism which characterized Schuylkill County politics in the 1850s, the issue of slavery eclipsed other national as well as local political matters. The outbreak of the Civil War insured that the issue of slavery would be resolved on the battlefield. In Schuylkill County, although both the Irish and the Germans responded to Lincoln's call for volunteers in significant numbers, local political matters would lead to unrest and violence in the anthracite region. The rise of the Molly Maguires in 1862, a secret society known for their activism among Irish immigrant coal miners, led to coal mine strikes and subsequently the intervention of the Pennsylvania militia. Implementation of the draft the following year insured that Schuylkill County would be embroiled in its own regional civil war.[30]

While Lieutenant Colonel Frick carefully molded the 96th regiment into a cohesive military unit, Colonel Cake was preoccupied with local politics. Through the late summer and into the early autumn Cake was frequently absent from Lawton's Hill attempting to secure the necessary political backing which would enable him to gain a seat in the Pennsylvania State Senate.[31] Cake was the senatorial candidate of the Schuylkill County Union Ticket party. He achieved his nomination by soundly defeating a prominent and powerful Pottsville attorney, Charlemagne Tower, by a wide margin on the second ballot. Cake's easy victory over the popular Tower caused the editor of the *Miners' Journal*, Benjamin Bannan, to issue a halfhearted endorsement of the aspiring senatorial candidate.

> Colonel Henry L. Cake was fairly nominated for the senate. It is known that we have here-to-fore always opposed him politically; and under other circumstances we will in all probability, oppose him again. In forming a Union ticket, we can not expect in every case, to obtain such a candidate as we desire…. Under these circumstances we waive political feelings and heartily accord our support for the Union ticket for the vast Principles involved in its success. We consider at this time the great national cause of infinitely more importance, than the election or defeat of this or that man.[32]

Clearly Colonel Cake, turned candidate Cake, was a man who had strong political connections as well as powerful detractors. Although editor Bannan was not one of Cake's most ardent supporters, the Pennsylvania colonel had ample political backing throughout the community. Cake was a formidable political candidate and a prominent, highly visible personality in the local community. His newspaper editorial columns allowed him to publicly air his views on a variety of local and national issues. His affiliation with the National Light Infantry prior to the war and the 25th Pennsylvania after the firing on Fort Sumter further enhanced his image in Pottsville as a man of courage and boldness.[33] Now, at the same time that he was spearheading a political campaign, he was also preparing a regiment of three-year volunteers to journey to the field of battle. Cake would need all of those credentials in order to defeat his adversary for state senate, Bernard Reilly.

The Schuylkill County Union Ticket, a coalition of Whigs, Know-Nothings, Free Soilers and dissatisfied Democrats, failed miserably at the polls. A product of the turbulent political fallout of the campaigns of 1859 and 1860, the ticket was not able to unite the diverse political elements in the county to defeat the powerful and popular Bernard Reilly. Judge Reilly, a Democrat, on the support of the large block of Irish who populated the region, polled fifty-five percent of the popular vote to Colonel Cake's respectable forty-five percent. Although Cake was able to secure the sizable block of votes cast by the members of the various volunteer military regiments forming at staging areas throughout Schuylkill County that fall, it was not enough to insure victory. After this bitter setback, Cake devoted his energies to the 96th regiment, convinced that a strong war record would prove a boon should he attempt another campaign for political office. But for now he was a colonel of volunteers with important responsibilities.[34]

Colonel Cake's failed attempt at political life seriously affected his military relationship with Lieutenant Colonel Frick. The former Regular Army officer could not condone Cake's political activities, which kept him away from Camp Schuylkill during the initial training period. After the October election, Frick's relationship with Cake began to deteriorate. In time two factions would develop within the field and staff officer ranks of the 96th. Frick would lead one contingent, while Cake would control the other. The factions would eventually wage a desperate fight for control of the regiment. Whichever faction controlled the unit could manipulate officer promotions and in effect govern the daily affairs of the regiment. The seeds of officer factionalism were sown while the regiment was at the Camp Schuylkill staging area. They would not sprout, however, until spring.[35]

The cornerstone of the impending political machinations was laid in mid–October. At that time a light battery of infantry, organized by Capt. William H. Lessig, joined the 96th Pennsylvania at Camp Schuylkill. This battery was originally the Good Intent Light Artillery militia company, whose membership was drawn from a volunteer fire brigade in Pottsville. The same day that Lessig's light battery of infantry reported for duty at Camp Schuylkill, Colonel Cake transferred Beaton Smith's Company C, by order of Governor Curtin, to the 52nd Pennsylvania, where it was attached as Company I.[36] Lessig's unit subsequently assumed Smith's vacant Company C designation. The addition of Lessig's light battery to the 96th Pennsylvania completed the regimental alignment. Although the replacement of Smith's company with Lessig's unit might at first seem to be of minor importance, the presence of Captain Lessig would have a profound effect upon the officer corps of the 96th. Within eighteen months the light battery captain, who at this time was the lowest ranking line officer on the seniority roster, would rise to command the 96th Pennsylvania. But before Lessig could become embroiled in regimental politics, he had a light battery of infantry to train.[37]

Through the balance of October life at Camp Schuylkill was defined by drill, leisure time and a few singular events. Lieutenant Colonel Frick drilled the regiment daily and continued with line officer instruction in the evening. Volunteers devoted their spare time to the pursuit of the amenities of camp life. A favorite game of the Bluecoats was called "running the guards," which was usually played out after sunset. Soldiers who could not secure a pass to leave camp often chose to sneak out of the encampment past the sentries.[38] Judging from the numbers who successfully slipped into Pottsville and avoided detection, the Bluecoats on outpost duty were either asleep at their posts or simply looked the other way when one of the regiment unofficially left camp. Reverend Samuel F. Colt, the regimental chaplain, was also quite busy throughout the month, but with more important matters. He devised a cooking stove for the regimental mess which allowed the cook to perform the operations of boiling, stewing and baking simultaneously.[39] An event which broke the monotony of camp life was the presentation of an American flag to the 96th regiment by A. L. Gee of Pottsville. Prior to the ceremony the regiment was drawn up in a line, facing the flag staff. Captain Boyle made a speech after which he presented the flag to the regiment "amid the cheers of the men, the inspiring strains of a national air, and the roar of the Good Intent's cannon."[40] It was a spirited affair attended by local citizens. After the ceremony, Lieutenant Colonel Frick sent the 96th Pennsylvania through a series of parade ground evolutions for the dignitaries and citizens and much to the delight of the ladies in attendance.

As the nights became cooler, the days shorter and frost became visible on the ground at morning, soldier life continued to be an ordered affair. The dozen daily activities of the regiment were sounded out by a bugler or tapped out by a drummer. The day began with reveille about five o'clock. Failure to answer the signal usually resulted in a Yank performing extra duty or spending time in the guardhouse. As the Bluecoats stood in line, the first sergeant of each company called the roll, after which the men were allowed to return to their quarters while the sergeant prepared the morning report. Thirty minutes after reveille came the breakfast call. A short time later the sick call for the ailing and fatigue call for the stout and hearty were sounded. Fatigue duty usually consisted of policing the company grounds, digging sills or drainage ditches for the latrines, cutting wood, and other physically exhausting activities. At approximately 8 a.m. the Pottsville Cornet Band sounded the call for guard mounting. After hearing that signal, the first sergeant of each company turned out his detail for the next twenty-four hours' duty, inspected the troops carefully and then marched them out from their quarters to the regimental parade ground. After the adjutant inspected the company details, the Bluecoats were sent to their respective posts, each man to stand guard only two hours out of every six.[41]

Once the camp guards were properly deployed, the next call was for drill, which commonly lasted until the noon meal. After dinner the soldiers were given a period of free time, but most of the afternoon was devoted to more drill. Late in the afternoon the companies were dismissed and the Bluecoats retired to their quarters. After a short period the volunteers returned to the drill ground for retreat exercises which consisted of roll call, inspection and dress parade. The dress parade, a most impressive ceremony, was the climax to the day's activities. A colorful pageant, it combined military precision and marching music calculated to inspire the Bluecoats as they stepped lively through the various maneuvers. It was also a good occasion for reading orders, such as the findings of courts martial and other official orders, since the entire regiment was drawn up in formation.

Shortly after retreat came supper call, which was followed by another roll call and an order sending the volunteers to their quarters. The final call of the day was taps, after which "all lights must go out." This was the typical daily routine of a regiment of infantry not involved in active campaigning. Naturally the events of a Sabbath day differed greatly from the routine of the regular week days.[42]

Every Sunday was a day of inspection. After a hearty breakfast the Bluecoats busied themselves policing the regimental camp. Company streets were cleaned, quarters were swept, bunks were properly arranged and the accouterments of each soldier received "spit and polish" treatment. Civil War volunteers were required by regulation to scrub the buttons of their tunics and their buckles with any tool they could find to accomplish the chore. Mess equipment was also cleaned—often by plunging the knives and the forks into the ground a few times. After the camp was cleaned and the Yanks had attended to their personal equipment, there was a preliminary inspection of the troops by the first sergeants and captains. After the company examinations the Bluecoats marched to the drill ground and formed by company—Company A on the right, B on the left of the line, and the others in between—to conduct the inspection of the regiment.

Once the field officers were inspected, the examining officer, beginning with Company A, walked down the open column and scrutinized the arms, equipment and dress of each member of the regiment. Then, each captain barked out the order to his command for the company to stack arms, unsling and open their knapsacks and lay them on the parade ground to be examined by the inspecting officer. After the last company was examined the inspecting officer made the rounds of the regimental hospital, guardhouse, sutler's shop, kitchens and any other facility that he chose to view. Finally, the examining officer checked the company quarters, paying close attention to note anything not in accordance with the prescribed regulations. It was a process that consumed most of the Sabbath morning.[43]

For the next three weeks, Lieutenant Colonel Frick patiently drilled the raw volunteers in battalion movement intent upon turning the military novices into parade ground veterans. Captain Boyle, in a postwar sketch, recalled vividly this period in the regiment's history. "Having thus identified themselves with the regiment," recalled the captain, "day after day, [the soldiers] responded with alacrity to the … commands of the drill sergeants, and the orders of their line officers."[44] The daily training regimen, repeated over the coming weeks and months, reinforced the lessons of parade ground drill and prepared the civilians for combat. The transformation of the green volunteers would take time and patience by the regiment's principal drill instructor Lieutenant Colonel Frick. According to Captain Boyle, "The great majority of the men and some of the officers were entirely ignorant of even the rudiments of a soldier's education, and many and laughable were the mistakes made and blunders committed, as, under the orders of some finished veteran of the 'three month's service,' they essayed to attain the correct position of the soldier, to master the mysteries of the facings, the puzzling of 'hayfoot,' 'strawfoot,' or to unravel the intricacies of the march."[45] Along with the soldiers, the officers, too, received command instruction and training in the evening from Lieutenant Colonel Frick.

Finally, in early November, after weeks of instruction in the School of the Soldier, learning how to "load in nine times" and spending uncounted hours on the parade ground, Colonel Cake received the order to transfer the 96th Pennsylvania Volunteers to Washington. On November 6, Governor Curtin traveled to Pottsville in order to present the Schuylkill County regiment with the state colors. At 2 p.m. the 96th regiment marched out of Camp Schuylkill and formed in front of the American House hotel, where the flag presentation took place. The "War Governor," flag in hand, then addressed the regiment.

> Colonel Cake and men of the 96th regiment, Pennsylvania Volunteers:—I am here today in obedience to the call of this Commonwealth to perform the last act which you deserve at the hands of your fellow citizens, before you leave to take part in the great struggle which now agitates this once happy and prosperous country.
>
> And I am here today, recognizing you as a regiment of Pennsylvania Volunteers, about to go into the service of the country, to present to you this beautiful standard. I deliver to you the honor of the State.[46]

At the conclusion of his remarks, Curtin handed the flag to Colonel Cake, who received the standard on behalf of the officers and men of the 96th regiment. Cake, never one to dismiss the opportunity presented at a public gathering, offered some patriotic remarks to the attentive regiment and the gathered crowd.

> Governor: You have done us great honor in coming here to Pottsville in order to present to us, in person, the banner of our country.
>
> In the field or at home, in war or peace, our motto shall ever be, "Our country right or wrong, our country."[47]

At the conclusion of the flag presentation ceremony, the officers and men of the 96th Pennsylvania heartily cheered Governor Curtin and Colonel Cake. The band, in turn, struck up "The Star-Spangled Banner," closing the festivities for the day. The regiment then marched back to Camp Schuylkill where the flag was hoisted for everyone to see. The standard, measuring eight feet across by six feet, was an impressive banner to the Bluecoats who watched the flag flapping in the breeze atop Lawton's Hill. One proud volunteer described the physical appearance of the flag this way: "It was made of silk and bound round the edge with yellow or golden colored silk fringe, about one and a half inches wide. In the azure field was the Pennsylvania State coat-of-arms, with thirty-four stars encircling it. The inscription on the flag was: 'NINETY-SIXTH REGIMENT, P.V.'" After marveling at their flag, the soldiers began the arduous chore of dismantling their camp.[48]

During the final week of the 96th Pennsylvania's encampment upon the grounds atop Lawton's Hill, the soldiers received overcoats, bibles and needle books, along with a gift for each volunteer from the local ladies of Pottsville. Line officers, too, received personalized gifts from their families, friends, local community groups or dignitaries to show their support for the service of the soldiers. Colonel Cake received a handsome field glass from a "few friends," while Captain Budd, of Company K, was presented with a handsome sword, belt and sash by a select group of local citizens.[49] As the warm October afternoons gave way to the windswept days of November, the soldiers of the 96th Pennsylvania prepared to leave Schuylkill County for the long trip to Washington and the Union camps dotting the countryside around Alexandria, Virginia. The day after Curtin's visit to Pottsville, all of the shelter tents upon Lawton's Hill were struck by the rank and file of the regiment. Virtually all that remained to be done was to receive their baptism under fire. That sacrament, however, would not be conferred upon them for some time. For the immediate moment family and friends gathered along the streets of Pottsville to offer their respective farewells to the volunteers.

On November 7, after the flag presentation ceremony, the 96th Pennsylvania, numbering some 1,139 officers and men, prepared to leave Camp Schuylkill and embark on the long journey to Washington.[50] As the column of Bluecoats filed through the streets of Pottsville, a torrential downpour forced a halt to the march, causing the soldiers to find shelter for the night at the Schuylkill County Court House. The next morning the unit resumed its march and proceeded to Westwoods, where a train was waiting to convey them to Washington.[51] As the regiment reached Westwoods a young fellow named George Foltz stood mesmerized on Fisher's Hill watching the military procession—the regimental flags fluttering in the breeze with the column of soldiers winding along the dirt road and the Pottsville Cornet Band playing an inspirational marching tune. Unable to contain himself any longer the sixteen-year-old youth rushed down from his vantage point and cried out as he approached the 96th's column, "I, too, will be a member of this regiment. I, too, will be a soldier."[52] One of the men in the ranks outfitted Foltz with a military cap, signifying his acceptance into the Schuylkill County regiment. Eventually Foltz was assigned to Company C, carried the flag, and served his country admirably.

The issues which compelled George Foltz to join the Schuylkill County regiment were also prominent in the recruitment of the regiment in the late summer of 1861. Clearly the most distinctive force behind volunteer enlistments was old fashioned patriotism. National origin or wage earning were not the primary factors motivating the men who passed through Schuylkill County recruiting stations almost six months after the first shot at Fort Sumter. The Irish miners of the 96th Pennsylvania tossed aside their picks and shovels for smoothbores simply because they did not approve of the Secessionists' firing upon Fort Sumter. Recruitment, mobilization and regimental formation in Schuylkill County in the late summer of 1861 demonstrated that the citizenry was overwhelming in its desire to exchange the tools of the coal mine for the weapons of the battlefield.[53]

Nevertheless the reaction to the outbreak of the war in Schuylkill County, as a case study in mobilization, runs contrary to recent his-

Sgt. George W. Foltz. Color bearer, Company C. Promoted from corporal May 5, 1863. Mustered out with company October 21, 1864 (Ronn Palm collection).

torical findings which concluded that "a powerful rhetoric of patriotism urged citizens to become soldiers, yet in Pennsylvania, many residents were pulled in conflicting directions by obligations to self, family, and community." Captain Hipple, of Company H, described the patriotic beliefs of the soldiers when stated in a letter, "We are determined to conquer in the name of God and our country, or die in the defence [sic] of that religion, that flag, and that Constitution handed down to us by a noble parentage."[54] Along with patriotism, other factors too, such as adventure, heroism, travel, new scenery and the excitement of life in the army, motivated local men of Schuylkill County to sign the volunteer enlistment form in 1861. Thus it was that only by going to war could the North maintain its national honor. That was the only motivation that the young men of the Schuylkill County needed in order to make a decision to enlist in the growing ranks of the 96th Pennsylvania Volunteers. Finally, they were ready to travel to meet the foe.

II

"We always respond with three cheers"

After a great deal of fanfare the volunteers of the 96th Pennsylvania marched two miles from Pottsville to Westwood where they boarded specially commissioned trains on the Mine Hill Railroad bound for Harrisburg. The trains consisted of "sixteen passenger, freight and truck cars drawn by one and pushed by two locomotives," and a seventeen car train. After passing over Broad Mountain, which the volunteers hiked over because of the inability of the engines to negotiate the steep grade, the train was divided into two separate trains. Companies A, F, D, I and Lessig's battery, with their cannon on board, occupied the first set of cars. The balance of the regiment traveled on the second train. As the trains chugged along the rolling hills of Pennsylvania, a member of the regiment described this initial part of the journey. In a letter to the *Miners' Journal* he recalled that "each town, village and hamlet, as we passed turned out its population to greet us, and many were the endearing expressions of regret which the winds wafted to our ears."[1]

The two trains steamed into Sunbury that evening, where the transports halted to allow the troops to have supper. One of the soldiers described the reception of the 96th Pennsylvania at Sunbury. In a letter to the *Miners' Journal*, "Ninety-sixth" marveled that "we were attended by crowds of people who expressed their Union feelings by doing all in their power to make our short stay as agreeable as possible."[2] Approximately one hour later the trains started onward again and plunged into the autumnal darkness toward Maryland. One of the volunteers, who had an eye for natural beauty, lamented in a letter home that he was unable to view, "the splendid scenery of the Susquehanna … and the beautiful surroundings," because of the late hour.[3] Throughout the night many of the soldiers passed the hours of the train ride by swapping stories as the rattle of the cars prevented the volunteers from sleeping. The officers of the regiment were entertained throughout the trip, according to one witness, by "listening to the piquant witicisms [sic] of Martz … the poignant allusions of Boyer, of Company D, the eccentricities of Haas, of Company G, and the promiscuous small talk of others of the party."[4] Throughout the night frequent peals of laughter rang out in the coaches, muffling for a short time the constant clatter of the rails.

By morning the trains had passed through Harrisburg and York and were steaming toward Baltimore. At first light the members of the 96th were startled to see squads of Union soldiers along the railway and extra guards standing watch at bridges. As the two troop trains chugged through Maryland past farmhouses and through villages the Schuylkill Countians "were universally greeted with cheers, waving of handkerchiefs and Union flags." As the volunteers passed one palatial home they noticed "the ladies of the house ... assembled on the green, surrounded by 'contrabands,' all waving American flags." According to one Bluecoat the "scene drew from our men three rousing cheers and a 'tiger,' heard high above the puff of the iron horse and the rattle of the ... cars."[5]

At 2:30 a.m., after considerable delays along the railway, the troop trains, full of weary volunteers, lumbered into Washington and stopped in front of a temporary shelter for newly arrived regiments. The soldiers vacated the cars and trudged into their overnight quarters. After a hearty breakfast of coffee, bread and beef at the Soldier's Retreat, the regiment, under the command of Lieutenant Colonel Frick, marched to their assigned quarters located one and one quarter miles from the Capitol, near the first toll-gate, on the Bladensburg Turnpike. Once at Kendall Green, the unit pitched their tents and began to adjust to life at Camp Wilder, the name given to their new home in honor of Rufus Wilder, superintendent of the Mine Hill Railroad. While at Camp Wilder, Colonel Cake was appointed to the command of the First Provisional Brigade, which consisted of the 54th New York Volunteers, two other regiments from the Empire State and the 96th Pennsylvania Volunteers. Cake received his promotion from Brig. Gen. Silas Casey, who was already more famous for his book on tactical military training than he was for his generalship.[6]

The Pennsylvanians spent two weeks at Camp Wilder waiting to be permanently assigned to a Federal infantry brigade. Before that assignment could be made, however, the soldiers still needed the accoutrements associated with an infantry soldier. A few days after arriving in Washington, referred to by some members of the regiment as "the seat of war," the Schuylkill County men were issued regulation infantry overcoats. According to Captain Hipple, of Company H, the greatcoats were "dark in color—some are made of pefersham and some are a good strong camel net. I wish you could see the regiment in line," Hipple continued, beaming with patriotism, "it makes my heart swell with joy."[7] Soon after the regiment was properly outfitted with infantry clothing, the unit marched to the Washington Arsenal where they were issued muskets. According to one observer, the regiment received Harpers Ferry muskets, but could take them if they promised to use the arms only for drill. Later, the Schuylkill County volunteers could exchange the weapons for "the latest approved" muskets. After the regiment was properly clothed and armed, the troops received a portable two-hundred volume Harper's family library. The library was a gift from the pupils of a ladies' seminary in Pottsville. Many women's aid societies were active throughout Schuylkill County during the Civil War.[8] Acts of kindness and simplicity such as this were greatly appreciated by the troops. One volunteer remarked that the library was "nicely arranged in a portable case," and proved to be the "means of rescuing many an hour from weariness."

Soon after arriving in Washington the Bluecoats wrote letters home, describing the sights and communicating how they felt being so near the Secessionists. Francis Boland, a private in Company K, related to his family what he saw in Washington:

> I walked around all the principal streets of Washington on yesterday. It is a very fine place. The Potomac River surrounds it on both sides almost a semi-circle. The country all round is level and fine. The weather is warm by day but cool at night. The whole face of land is covered with camps forty miles in length and twenty in breadth. It is the grandest sight imaginable to look upon the scene.
>
> [There are] two hundred and eighty regiments here. Thirty cavalry and twelve artillery reaching from ten miles below us to thirty above us along the River Potomac.[9]

Another soldier, Pvt. Clement Potts of Company A, a lad of eighteen years, told his relatives about an unauthorized, but exciting, trip he made into Washington:

> I went into the Capital and seen the Senate chamber and House of Representatives. The floors are covered with the finest of Brussells carpet and the seats and chairs are covered with red silk velvet. The floors and stairways are of a white and colored marble. They are splendid. I also went over to see the Smithsonian Institute.
>
>   I also took a trip out to see.... Fort Lincoln. They say that fort is the finest and strongest one about the District.[10]

A fortnight after the 96th regiment established Camp Wilder the Pennsylvanians received orders to join a brigade encamped near Alexandria, Virginia. On November 25, the Schuylkill Countians packed up their belongings at Camp Wilder and tramped over the Long Bridge, crossing the Potomac River and moving onto the often talked about "Sacred Soil" of Virginia. The regiment joined General William B. Franklin's division, to which they had been assigned and went into bivouac near Fairfax Seminary, naming their new home Camp Pottsville.[11] Four days later the regiment moved again, quickly establishing Camp Franklin in honor of their new divisional commander, Brig. Gen. William Buel Franklin. The 96th Pennsylvania was assigned to Brig. Gen. Henry Warner Slocum's brigade. To make room for the Schuylkill County regiment in Slocum's command, the 26th New York Volunteers were transferred to another brigade. Slocum's brigade, as it was known, consisted of the following units: the 16th and 27th New York Volunteers, and the 5th Maine Volunteers, all veterans of the Battle of Bull Run.[12]

General Franklin, a native of York County, Pennsylvania, graduated from the United States Military Academy in 1843 at the head of his class. While at West Point he forged a friendship with Ulysses S. Grant, who graduated twenty-first out of a class of thirty-nine cadets. After West point, Franklin served in the topographical engineers and later under Gen. John Wool during the Mexican War. He commanded a brigade in Col. (later Maj. Gen.) Samuel P. Heintzelman's division at the First Battle of Bull Run. In May of 1862 he was appointed to command the Sixth Corps of the Army of the Potomac. Early in the war Franklin was regarded "as an officer of brilliant promise in the 'Old Army,'" and as "an officer of great ability."[13] General McClellan, the army commander, praised Franklin in his memoirs and regarded him as "one of the best officers I had." Further, McClellan added, "He was a man not only of excellent judgment, but of a remarkably high order of intellectual ability. His moral character was of the highest, and he was in all respects an admirable corps commander."[14] One regimental historian even suggested that Franklin "served throughout the war as a subordinate, where his commanding abilities and usefulness were minimized by the fact that, except under General McClellan, he was the superior in capacity and military skill of every commander to whom he reported."[15]

Maj. Thomas Hyde, the historian of the Sixth Corps, stated that "as a commander of troops, [Franklin] proved himself cool and brave, and of great ability. No one then serving in the army could have commanded it better."[16] He was one of the senior officers of the Army of the Potomac who had forged important friendships with other officers who would distinguish themselves in the war. During the winter of 1861–1862 he would organize his command and prepare to lead the soldiers in his division, such as the 96th Pennsylvania Volunteers, when the Army of the Potomac embarked on transports down Chesapeake Bay and joined the campaign that everyone believed would end in the capture of Richmond and the capitulation of the Confederacy.

While the soldiers of the 96th Pennsylvania would initially serve in General Franklin's division, their first glimpse of a West Point trained soldier was their brigadier general, Henry Warner Slocum. Born in Onondaga County, New York, Slocum graduated seventh in the West Point class of 1852.[17] In the judgment of the historian Harry Pfanz, "Slocum was one of those numerous important Union generals who were deservedly prominent in their time but whose fame has paled with the passing years."[18] According to a contemporary, "Slocum is a small, rather spare, with black, straight hair and beard, which latter is unshaven and thin, large, full, quick, black eyes, white skin, sharp nose, wide cheek bones, and hollow cheeks and small chin. His movements are quick and angular, and he dresses with a sufficient degree of elegance."[19] In 1856, Slocum resigned from the United States Army, relocated to Syracuse, New York and established a law

Maj. Gen. William B. Franklin. Commanded VI Corps and later Left Grand Division of the Army of the Potomac (author's collection).

practice. After the firing upon Fort Sumter, he raised the 27th New York Volunteers. He commanded that unit, which formed part of Andrew Porter's brigade, in David Hunter's division, at the First Battle of Bull Run. An officer in the Army of the Potomac offered the following opinion of Slocum, "I like our new corps commander very much so far, though he does not strike me as of wonderful capacity."[20] The men in the ranks, however, held a different opinion of the New Yorker. Naturally, the Empire State volunteers idolized Slocum. One volunteer stated that "General Slocum is revered and loved as ever. When he makes a brief and stirring address to his brigade ... we always respond with three cheers."[21]

The chaplain of the 5th Maine Volunteers stated that Slocum, "served with so much distinction," and "inspired us with confidence and ambition."[22] Another New Yorker proclaimed boldly that the soldiers of Slocum's brigade were "determined to go where General Slocum would lead."[23] Newton Curtis, the historian of the 16th New York Volunteers and himself a famous fighting general, concluded that "Slocum's record was exceptional," and "that he possessed the essential qualities of a great commander."[24] Several officers serving with the 96th Pennsylvania Volunteers also offered descriptions of Slocum in their correspondence form camp. Capt. John Boyle, Company D, reported that a visit by Slocum resulted in "great cheering, much enthusiasm." Adding further, Boyle wrote, "I like him. He has a soul."[25] Dr. Washington Nugent, in a letter to his wife, stated that "our present Brig. Gen. Slocum is a gentleman and thorough soldier."[26] During the winter of 1861–1862, though, Slocum was a relatively unknown brigadier general charged with a command composed of Bull Run veterans, the 16th and 27th New York regiments and the 5th Maine Volunteers. In addition, he was responsible for training and preparing an untested and untried regiment of Pennsylvania volunteers from the anthracite coal region.

At Camp Franklin, when they were not on picket duty or drilling, the soldiers visited friends in nearby regiments and inquired into the local way of life. Private Boland, in a letter from Camp Franklin, described the military sights and the opportunities for civilian employment:

> I have visited the forts and inquired into the civil and local way of living around this city. Tell any man you see out of employment [that] he ought to come here. He can get plenty of work. Ninety cents a day together with board. The government wants thousands yet of laborers. They are paid monthly and do not enlist at all. They get the best of board free. It is a good change for a single man.[27]

The most discussed event in the early Camp Franklin letters, however, had nothing to do with the local economy. Virtually all of the Bluecoats of the 96th Pennsylvania lamented in letters home their genuine disappointment at not being able to participate in Maj. Gen. George B. McClellan's Grand Review, held on November 20, in the vicinity of Bailey's Cross Roads. This military spectacle was McClellan's way of showing the Washington politicians the mighty fighting machine he had shaped from the 50,000 troops, which he described as "a mere collection of regiments cowering on the banks of the

Maj. Gen. Henry W. Slocum. Originally served as colonel of the 27th New York Volunteers. Subsequently promoted to command 2nd Brigade and later 1st Division of the VI Corps (author's collection).

Potomac" when he arrived in Washington after the debacle at Bull Run.[28] One correspondent from the 16th New York Volunteers stated that McClellan's review "was the most important event which took place between the Battle of Bull Run and the beginning of the spring campaign."[29] The review featured seven full divisions totaling some 70,000 soldiers of foot, cannoneers and troopers, fully armed and equipped.

As the Bluecoats tramped forward through ankle deep mud past the reviewing stand where Abraham Lincoln stood, the officers of the 96th Pennsylvania watched in awe from Munson's Hill as the scene unfolded before them. In a letter home, Maj. Lewis Martin stated that the review "was one of the grandest sights ... ever witnessed in my life."[30] Indeed, the Schuylkill Countians perched on high ground above the reviewing stand, swelled with pride as the troops filed past Lincoln, McClellan and the other assembled dignitaries. All who watched the grand review from Munson's Hill agreed that the day's events dramatically illustrated the panoply of war.

Shortly after McClellan's spectacle, the Pennsylvanians found out how cruel a military life could be. On December 13, the Schuylkill County unit, along with the balance of Franklin's division, was drawn up in line to witness the military execution of Pvt. William Johnson, Company D, 1st New York Lincoln Cavalry. Johnson had been taken prisoner while attempting to escape to the Confederates. He was subsequently court-martialed and sentenced to be put to death by a firing squad.[31] In 1861 the Federal high command elevated executions from the level of obscure shootings to public spectacles, requiring entire brigades and divisions to witness the event. Union officers hoped that the gruesome nature of the execution would have a dramatic impact upon any witnesses who harbored thoughts of leaving the service before fulfilling their term of service. In many instances an execution achieved the effect that the high command desired. Pvt. Henry Keiser, of Company G, was convinced not to desert after he witnessed Private Johnson's fate:

> At three o'clock, the escort, with the prisoner on a wagon, sitting on his coffin, made their appearance on the east side of the square. He shook hands with his executioners, after which the minister offered up a prayer. The executioners [twelve in number] then made ready, took aim, and as the signal was given by Col. Boyd [by raising of a white handkerchief], nine of the executioners fired. He sat on the coffin about four seconds after they had fired, and then fell backward over it.... The troops were all marched by him so as to have a good view. I seen one hole in his forehead above the left eye, one in the mouth and four in his breast.[32]

The execution of Private Johnson received considerable coverage by the soldiers of the 96th Pennsylvania in their private letters and diaries. Regimental surgeon Washington Nugent described the event as a "gloomy and sad spectacle to look upon." He added that the execution of a soldier "witnessed last Friday.... I have no particular desire to see again. It was a and solemn sight to see a poor mortal sent ... into Eternity. He richly deserved his fate and his Execution, I have no doubt, will have a salutary effect upon our soldiery."[33] Major Martin reported in a letter that he was surprised to learn that the regiment was marched out of camp and drawn up in formation to witness an execution. Martin believed that the 96th Pennsylvania Volunteers were advancing "for the purpose of resisting an unexpected attack from the enemy."[34] Clement Potts, a private in Company A, recorded the gruesome execution in great detail for his brother in a letter written several days after the event.

> Before he was shot, he was hauled in [and] marched around for all the regiment to see him but I did not look. As he passed our regiment our [Pottsville Cornet] band played the Dead March. He went all around until he arrived in the centre. After he fell ... we were marched around to see him. It was the most horrible sight I ever seen. It was the first time I ever seen a man shot and hope the last. I did not think that their were such hard hearted men to shoot another in cold blood. I would rather be shot myself than shoot another man.[35]

Approximately four weeks after the Pennsylvanians arrived at Camp Franklin, they packed up their equipment once again and moved to Camp Northumberland, their permanent winter quarters. The new encampment was situated along the Loudoun and Hampshire Railroad, near the Four Mile Run crossing. One of the members of the regiment described the physical layout of the camp in a letter to the *Miners' Journal*:

> The streets are laid out with mathematical precision, and the tents of the men are, in their way, models of comfort. They are placed on good log foundations, the later-spaces plastered with clay, and are, as a general thing, floored. Each tent contains a fire place built of brick, which our efficient

Regimental Quarter-Master was so fortunate as to obtain for the hauling, at so great distance from the grounds. Altogether we have one of the handsomest, best regulated, and cleanest camps on this side of the Potomac.[36]

Other members of the regiment informed family members back in Pennsylvania about the winter campsite, named Camp Northumberland in honor of Colonel Cake's native county, and the quarters they would call home until the Army of the Potomac moved to meet the Confederates in battle. In a letter to his "dear friend," James Augustine of Company A stated that "we are camped on a nice little hill … about 4 miles from Alexandria." He described the living quarters constructed by the soldiers to withstand the Virginia winter. "We live very comfortable here we build a log cabbin—and put our tents on the top of the logs … and now we are as happy as pigs in the pen."[37] Fireplaces were built, according to Lt. John Fernsler, for each hut with bricks hauled from a "Reb brick kiln at Bailey's Crossroads."[38] Washington Nugent, one of the regimental surgeons, wrote to his wife informing her about the "comfortable quarters … good floored tents" and other luxuries the soldiers enjoyed at camp Northumberland.[39] Another soldier reported that "we have comfortable warm tents fires and plenty of wood and clothing."[40] Maj. Lewis Martin was also pleased with the winter quarters at Camp Northumberland. No doubt Martin spoke for all of the soldiers of the 96th Pennsylvania when he wrote to his wife about the relocation of the regiment from Camp Franklin to the new camp grounds. "You have no idea," wrote Martin, "what an improvement has been effected by the change in almost every respect at least as far as looks, comfort and convenience are concerned." Finally, Martin concluded that "Camp Northumberland is entirely differently located. It is one of the finest spots for a camp, and at the same time one of the most favorably located that I ever saw in my life."[41]

Aside from the excitement generated by the Grand Review and the execution of Private Johnson, the winter encampment was a dreary affair. The Bluecoats primarily had to contend with long hours on picket duty, brigade drills in ankle deep mud, the boredom and monotony of camp life, and diarrhea and dysentery, the greatest killers of the Civil War. More cases of flux—as bowel disorders were referred to in those days—were reported than of any other disease. According to medical records, no malady caused more deaths. The best available figures show 57,265 Union soldier deaths from diarrhea and dysentery.[42] A fundamental factor in death from disease was the state of medical science at that time. A veteran of the Union Medical Corps, contrasting the medical practices of the Civil War and of World War I, stated in 1918: "In the Civil War we knew absolutely nothing of 'germs.' Bacteriology—the youngest and greatest science to aid in the conquest of death— did not exist … sanitation … was crude and satisfactory … research had not discovered any of the antitoxins nor the role of the insect world in spreading disease."[43]

Although diarrhea, dysentery and typhoid were frequently mentioned in the letters of Federal soldiers, the letters of the 96th Pennsylvania, for the Camp Franklin and Camp Northumberland period, were remarkably silent where bowel disorders, or the "quickstep" as the Bluecoats called it, were concerned. In fact, the missives written by the soldiers during the winter encampment attested to the robust health of the men in the regiment. A soldier using the *nom de guerre* "Ninety-Sixth" reported to the *Miners' Journal* that "the health of the men is most excellent."[44] In letters to John Brislin, Private McGlenn stated that he was in good health, "and also all the boys."[45] Writing to his mother, Clement Potts proudly proclaimed that one of the New York soldiers mentioned to him "that we had the healthiest regiment in the field."[46] In early January, surgeon Nugent related to his wife that "the health of the Regiment is still good."[47] The Schuylkill Countians experienced a great deal of sickness during the Peninsula Campaign, but their letters and diaries during the Camp Northumberland residency, repeatedly spoke, or more precisely bragged, about the good health of the regiment while in winter quarters.

Perhaps one reason why the regimental hospital had so many vacancies can be linked to the reputation that Dr. Bland established among the rank and file of the camp. Clement Potts characterized surgeon Bland's hospital tent as "the killing pen" and stated that the doctor was "not at all liked" by the volunteers. According to the young private, "not one of the men that went in there [the hospital tent] sick ever came out alive."[48] Private Potts, how-

Dr. Daniel Webster Bland. Surgeon, 96th Pennsylvania Volunteers. Mustered out with regiment October 21, 1864 (author's collection).

ever, greatly exaggerated the shortcomings of Dr. Bland's medical skills. In fact, Bland, a graduate of Bucknell University in the class of 1857, would prove to be an innovative and accomplished surgeon. Gaining the attention of senior officers, Bland would eventually be appointed to the staff of Maj. Gen. John Sedgwick and serve as Medical Inspector of the VI corps.[49]

While Potts ridiculed the sanitary conditions of the hospital tent and derided Bland's bedside manner, members of other regiments in the 96th's brigade envied the health of the Pennsylvanians throughout the winter encampment. One day, a Bluecoat of one of the New York regiments asked Potts, after several companies of the Schuylkill County unit had been on picket duty for five days in constant rain and muddy conditions, how many sick volunteers the 96th Pennsylvania had sent back to camp. The young private proudly told the Empire State man that the regiment had sent no one back to the hospital tent. The stunned New Yorker responded by telling Potts that his regiment "never went out unless they sent a dozen or more sick ones home."[50]

Throughout the winter, described by one of the meteorologists of the regiment as a mild one, the Pennsylvania Bluecoats endured incessant rain. Soldiers' letters from Camp Northumberland universally complained of the intolerable rain and muddy conditions in camp. After a tour of picket duty in the vicinity of Benton's Tavern, some ten miles from Camp Northumberland, one volunteer had this to say about the tramp back to quarters:

> On Sunday morning our pickets were relieved, and after a weary march of ten miles, through mud up to your knees, and if you were so unfortunate as to step into an old post hole, up to your neck, we reached camp.
>
> The mud is very deep, and the roads are impassable. The soldiers say this country has no bottom. It holds water remarkably well, whether it has or not. Water won't even run down hill, and stays on the surface of the ground until dried up by the sun and the wind.[51]

During January and February the volunteers plodded along, coping with the harsh camp life and generally feeling miserable at not being allowed to return home for a short furlough, as all leaves were stopped. A few events, however, generated a degree of excitement and raised the spirits of the troops. During the first month of 1862, the Schuylkill Countians exchanged their old Harpers Ferry smoothbores for new Austrian made rifled muskets. The soldiers were issued .58 caliber 1854 Lorenz infantry rifles. An Illinois soldier described the Lorenz rifle as a "wicked shooter" due to its hard kick when fired. In a report to a Congressional committee, Ulysses S. Grant stated, "Men would hold them very tight, shut their eyes, and brace themselves to prepare for the shock." No doubt a few of the soldiers, like Pvt. Thomas Houck, who thought that the 96th Pennsylvania would be equipped with a "Springfield Rifle with the sword bayonet," were surprised to receive an infantry weapon manufactured in Europe.[52] Although the men liked the appearance of the new weapons, they believed that only a test in battle would prove their worth. Lt. John Fernsler recorded in his diary that the entire regiment was outfitted with "our new Austrian rifled musket with a Spring Diamond Bayonet."[53] Erasmus Reed, in a letter to his family in Schuylkill County, wrote that "we used to have the old muscat until … we received the new rifles the other day. They are a bully gun."[54]

Officers of the 96th Pennsylvania Volunteers. This iconic photograph depicts the field and staff and the line officers of the regiment. Featured are two interesting light artillery pieces. The cannon on the left could be the locally manufactured artillery piece brought to Camp Northumberland by Company C, the light battery commanded by Capt. William H. Lessig. The artillery piece to the right is an excellent example of an Ager Rapid-Fire Coffee Mill gun. To the right of the "Coffee Mill" gun are Lt. Col. Frick (his hand appears to be on the gun) and Col. Henry Cake (to the right of Frick, his hand on his hip). The photograph was most likely composed the same day that the entire regiment was photographed in column at Camp Northumberland, February 26, 1862 (Library of Congress).

With the newly issued Austrian rifles, the 96th Pennsylvania resumed drilling on their muddy parade ground. One soldier opined that "all we do now is repeat and go over the same exercises every day. 'School of the Soldier' 'Manual of Arms' 'light Infantry' and 'Heavy Infantry' 'Skirmish Drill' 'Bayonet Exercises' 'Company Drill' 'Battalion Drill' 'Brigade Drill' 'Division Drill.'"[55] Through the soldier correspondent using the *nom-de-guerre* "Ninety-Sixth," the readers of the *Miners' Journal* learned that "our men begin to drill well and ... rival the crack regiments of the Reserve. Our band ... is improving rapidly and is considered by those judges who know the *second best* on this side of the Potomac."[56] Clement Potts informed his brother that camp life for the Pennsylvania soldiers that winter was centered on drilling the volunteers for battle. "I must tell you about our drill. "First we have roll call at six in the morning until half past six breakfast seven drill eight while half past nine division drill which is very hard at ten until twelve come in after dinner go out at two come in at half past two go out at three stay out until five have supper at six roll call eight lights out fifteen minutes after."[57] In addition to daily drilling, the soldiers occasionally fired their new Austrian rifles at targets. According to Captain Filbert, Company B, the soldiers also "drilled before breakfast in skirmish and bayonet exercise."[58] The regiment also participated in a significant number of reviews, conducted by senior officers, during the winter encampment.

Although the soldiers of the 96th Pennsylvania were unable to participate in the Grand Review of Union troops in November, other opportunities to march in formation arose. From late December through early March, the soldiers drilled in the intricate infantry movements under the command of Lieutenant Colonel Frick. During the winter, Colonel Cake was often absent from Camp Northumberland due to illness and other administrative business.[59] As winter turned to spring, senior officers in the Army of the Potomac reviewed and inspected the Pennsylvania volunteers. Slocum, Franklin and the army commander, General McClellan, reviewed the soldiers of the 96th Pennsylvania. The officers used the reviews not simply to admire the well formed ranks of the volunteers but also to build *esprit de corps* and unit morale with the soldiers. "Ninety-Sixth," in a letter to the *Miners' Journal,* reported that "Brig. Gen. Slocum ... has won the hearts of the men by his humane and soldierly bearing, honored the regiment a short time ago with his special attention saying that they did honor to the brigade."[60] Surgeon Nugent, in a letter to his wife informed her that "General McClellan reviewed the whole of our division. The day was fine and the command looked well."[61] In late March, Captain Filbert noted in his diary, "Ordered to be reviewed by Franklin, McClellan and McDowell."[62] The volunteers from Schuylkill County decided, too, that the endless hours of training were forging the men into competent combat soldiers. Erasmus Reed noted in a letter that "our regiment is getting along fine. We have got the finest Regiment in our Division."[63]

While Lieutenant Colonel Frick prepared the soldiers for combat, Rev. Samuel Colt, a Presbyterian minister from Pottsville, tended to the spiritual needs of the Pennsylvania volunteers. Colt was very popular with the officers and men of the 96th Pennsylvania. Diaries and letters penned during the winter encampment at Camp Northumberland attest to Colt's positive influence. Surgeon Nugent believed that "it is in the power of the Chaplain to do a vast deal of good, and I feel that Mr. Colt is just the man for his position and an earnest and good Christian."[64] In addition to preaching and ministering to the spiritual needs of the soldiers, Colt also sought to contribute to their physical welfare.

To help the Bluecoats through the difficult winter conditions, the ladies of the German Reformed Congregation sent a large box containing caps, comforters, and dozens of pairs of woolen mittens.[65] Upon receipt of this parcel, Reverend Colt stated that "many a poor fellow will bless the tender forethought which has provided in anticipation of this sore need."[66] The women of the German Lutheran Church of Pottsville also made a considerable donation to the 96th Pennsylvania for the care of the regiment's sick. Upon receiving the gift, Surgeon Bland responded to the ladies:

> Let me assure you all, that the donations that you have seen proper to make, shall be appropriately and economically used; and that, in the silent hour of night, the prayers of our men shall go up to High Heaven, for blessings upon each and every one of your.[67]

Another nicety which was highly valued at Camp Northumberland and caused great excitement among the men was the arrival of a packages of food from home. When the citizens of Pottsville sent three barrels of sauerkraut, the Bluecoats' spirits soared. Captain Filbert's company also enjoyed the pleasure of home style cooking when they received a shipment of pepper sauce from Pennsylvania. In a letter home, Filbert told his father how much the boys from his company enjoyed the home cooked present:

> The pepper sauce of which we had heard so frequently duly came to hand and you may well imagine the expressions of elation of the boys as they returned to their tents with for each tent a half mess pan of as they termed Pine Grove Sauce. Many thanks go forth on behalf of the donor.[68]

Beside the pleasantness of a home cooked meal, the Bluecoats also found other diversions to pass the time. Virtually all of the volunteers took great pride in having a roving photographer take their "likeness" in their "regimental clothes." The folks at home welcomed the receipt of the small *carte-de-visite*, as they were called, from the "seat of war." The soldiers also foraged for small game in the vicinity of their camp in order to add to their meager diet. The officers of the regiment found that a good party with lots of singing and toasting was an ideal way to turn their attention away from the hardships of camp life.[69]

One of the most festive parties was held on Washington's birthday. Lessig's light battery ushered in the day by firing a national salute. The Pottsville Cornet Band played all of the appropriate national airs, after which the officers enjoyed a sumptuous dinner, prepared and served in "sovereign style" by "Honest Lou" Louis Bocam, Lieutenant Colonel Frick intended to read Washington's farewell address to the Bluecoats, a typical gesture of the period, but inclement weather forced that portion of the program to be postponed. That evening the officers of the regiment enjoyed a night of song, laughter and spirits. The line captains gave toasts to "The charge of the 96th" and to the "Schuylkill County Volunteers." One line officer even proposed a toast to Lieutenant Colonel Frick, uttering, "may he be in Heaven three days before the devil knows he is dead." The soldiers closed the night's entertainment with songs such as, "Hurry Up the Cakes," "Drink it Down," "Halla-loo-ja-rum," "Dixie Land," "Pop Goes the Weasel," and "Bold Sojer Boy."[70]

Although the gala Washington's birthday celebration suggested that the officer corps of the 96th Pennsylvania was a harmonious lot, nothing could have been more misleading. Like the foul weather, officer relations, especially in the upper echelon regimental staff, turned stormy and then muddy throughout the winter encampment. During the long stay at Camp Northumberland Captain Filbert, like Lieutenant Colonel Frick, experienced personal as well as military procedural differences with Colonel Cake. In time, Filbert

This famous photograph, often reproduced to illustrate books pertaining to the events of the Civil War, is often misidentified as featuring the 1st Minnesota Volunteers. Composed at Camp Northumberland on February 26, 1862, the photograph depicts the 96th Pennsylvania arrayed in column by companies. On the right, clustered in a small square, are the regimental musicians known as the Pottsville Cornet Band. In the foreground, on horseback, in front of the musicians, are Col. Cake (front) and Lt. Col. Frick (behind). The identity of the photographer is unknown (National Archives).

emerged as a harsh critic of Colonel Cake and aligned himself with the officer faction developing under Lieutenant Colonel Frick. Further straining the Filbert–Cake relationship was a personality conflict. The tone of the Filbert letters during the Camp Northumberland period indicates that the young line captain viewed Cake with utter disdain. Filbert spent a great deal of his time during the winter documenting his complaints concerning Colonel Cake.[71]

In detailed letters to his father Filbert repeatedly stated that Colonel Cake had committed frauds upon the regiment.[72] According to him, eight companies of the regiment had been illegally mustered into service at Camp Schuylkill in that those units did not have the required minimum number of men in their ranks required for mustering. In order to muster the under strength companies of the regiment, Cake transferred men from over strength companies to those that were not at the minimum muster requirement. This procedure violated Section 1642 of the *Revised Regulations for the Army of the United States*: "Officers mustering in troops will be careful that men from one company or detachment are not borrowed for the occasion, to swell the ranks of others about to be mustered."[73] Therefore, if Filbert's allegation were upheld, it would have a profound impact upon the regimental seniority roster. Line captains of illegitimately mustered companies would lose the positions they currently held on the seniority roster. Filbert's charges raised serious questions concerning the ability of Colonel Cake to follow military procedures and posed a grave threat to the internal structure of the regiment.

Filbert also complained to his father about the deficiencies among the rank and file of the 96th Pennsylvania concerning military practices and procedures. As the senior line captain and as the officer of the day throughout most of the winter, Filbert constantly found fault with the camp guard of the regiment. Compared to the other regiments in Slocum's brigade, Filbert contended that the Pennsylvanians were sub-par in such exercises and training as the manual of arms. In checking the camp outposts, Filbert found that the regiment's sentries failed to challenge him as he approached their posts. On finding a guard from the 96th Pennsylvania sitting down at his post, Filbert drafted a special dispatch to General Slocum, outlining his findings: "Having been Field Officer of the day I herewith give a report after visiting the camp several times. I found the guard well instructed, with the exception of the 96th Penna. Vol., in the Manual of Arms. I noticed and found a man [one of the sentries] who was taken up [with] intoxicating liquors."[74] Filbert also reported that the color signals, used for identification purposes, had not been given to the Color Sergeant.

When Filbert was not enumerating the shortcomings of the 96th Pennsylvania on outpost duty, he criticized the regiment's poor habits regarding sanitation removal.[75] The duty of disposing of garbage was simply not carried out at Camp Northumberland. The camp streets, the spaces or lanes between the tents, became littered with refuse, including food in various states of foul-smelling decomposition. This effused nauseous odors throughout the winter. A further complication was the improper maintenance of the latrines, or "sinks" as the soldiers called them. These shallow trenches located close to the quarters of the rank and file, according to military regulations, were to be covered with fresh earth on a daily basis. This practice, however, went neglected in the 96th regiment. All of this inefficiency disturbed Captain Filbert.

Filbert was also appalled at the gross disregard for military law and regulations by the regimental staff and officers of the 96th Pennsylvania. He found officer drunkenness and absenteeism from Camp Northumberland especially troublesome. In his letters and daily diary entries he made constant references to the regimental adjutant and other line captains who were "drunk in their tent."[76] At one point in February, Filbert noted in his diary that he was virtually the only officer in camp. "Colonel Cake, Captain Lessig, Lieutenant Haas and Adjutant Richards were all in Washington in violation of General Order No. 11—which prohibited the issuance of passes to visit the city."[77] Although these issues rankled Filbert, they proved to be less important when compared to the problem the Pine Grove man faced with the regimental sutler, A. L. Gee.

According to historian Henry Anson Castle, the Civil War sutler "ranked a trifle higher than a corporal; a fraction lower than an army mule. His was always the post of danger, in the rear during an advance; in front while on retreat. Suspicion, not affection, was the sole sentiment distinguishing the volunteer warrior and the sutler."[78] Although Civil War sutlers never planned military strategy, never led a battle charge, issued no policies concerning the conduct of the war, they were always involved in the daily camp activities. In most regiments the sutler's store was a meeting place where soldiers gathered to share innocent camp gossip. The sutler was, in fact, a civilian who was appointed to serve a particular regiment by selling provisions to the troops not furnished by the government. In theory sutlers were authorized to sell only articles approved by the government; in fact, they sold anything that promised a profit. One historian stated that "with luck and shrewd management, a sutler, serving a regiment from three hundred to a thousand men, could acquire a small fortune."[79] Little wonder that sutlerships, which were advertised heavily in newspapers like the New York *Herald*, were eagerly sought after.

Each regiment was allowed one sutler, who obtained his position in a variety of ways. Ostensibly, sutler appointments were made by a regimental administrative council, consisting of the lieutenant colonel, the major and the first captain. A study conducted in 1861 by the United States Sanitary Commission, however, revealed that only fourteen of 188 sutlers had been appointed. Of the remainder, 103 received appointments from regimental colonels, sixty-three by the Secretary of War, five by state governors, and three others by unknown means.[80] To prevent the sutler from charging exorbitant prices for their goods, Congress passed legislation in 1862 designed to regulate the business of sutling. Known to the soldiers as "Mr. Wilson's Bill," prompted by Senator Henry Wilson of Massachusetts, this legislation sought to eliminate common abuses by sutlers. The bill prescribed the means by which appointments were to be made, detailed the articles which sutlers would be authorized to sell, and established machinery for fixing prices.[81] In the field, military authorities imposed certain other regulations.

The sutler was inextricably linked to the economy of the Civil War regiment. While the sutler might reap a tidy profit, due mostly to his inflated prices and his ability to "corner the market" on items coveted by the Bluecoats, he was required to pay a percentage of his monthly business, in effect an operating tax, to the unit he served. Regulations allowed an assessment on sutlers for the regimental or post fund. Article XXII, Section 198, of the Army Regulations, provided that "a Post Fund (later referred to as a regimental fund) shall be raised at each post by imposing a tax on the sutler, not to exceed ten cents a month for every officer and soldier of the command."[82] Originally the post fund was established to defray the expense of the bake house and support the regimental band. To ensure that the sutler complied with the monthly assessment, the regimental Council of Administration was empowered to hold the sutler accountable and to regulate the prices of the goods available at the sutler's tent.

Further, the Council of Administration saw to it that the sutler did not abuse troops who were temporarily out of money and in need of credit. Regulations allowed the sutler a lien of no more than one-sixth of the monthly pay of any officer or enlisted man in the regiment. Early in the war, sutlers often claimed all, or nearly all, of some volunteers' pay, but this abuse was largely corrected by the passage of Wilson's legislation. The Council of Administration, the regimental watch dog of the sutler's economic activities, also disbursed monies from the post fund to the companies of the regiment. These allotments and the savings from the various company rations, constituted the company fund; each company in the 96th regiment had its own fund. The money was to be disbursed by the captain of each company for the benefit of the enlisted men of the command, pursuant to the resolves of the company council.[83] During the first winter of the war many volunteer companies depended heavily upon receiving money from the regimental fund. Many line officers depleted their savings from the company rations and needed money from the post fund to feed their command often because sutlers dodged paying their tax to the post fund. Every Civil War regiment was faced with the dilemma of the sutler: He was perceived as a necessary evil, he supplied the volunteers with welcome goods of all kinds, and he provided the Bluecoats with a camp social center, yet by not paying his tax to the post fund he posed a serious threat to the economy of a Civil War regiment.

During the winter encampment at Camp Northumberland, sutler Gee became the scourge of the line officers by refusing to contribute to the regimental fund. Gee contended that he was exempt from the operating assessment by virtue of a private agreement with Colonel Cake. As the winter winds whipped through the company streets, a bitter feud developed between the regimental sutler and the officers of the 96th Pennsylvania on the Council of Administration who attempted to force Gee to comply with the obligatory tax. Gee's defiance of the military mandate crippled the finances of the line captains, who struggled to meet their monthly expenses under adverse economic conditions. Further exacerbating the volatile sutler issue was Colonel Cake's refusal to acknowledge the decision of the Council of Administration—that Gee pay the requisite tax to the post fund. Presumably, Cake blocked the recommendation of the Council of Administration because he was accepting gifts, perhaps not always in the guise of money, from sutler Gee. Superficial evidence suggests that Cake was indeed receiving delicacies, otherwise unobtainable at the front, or sharing a portion of Gee's profit. In return, Cake provided Gee with a first-rate tax exemption. By March the sutler matter was a point of such unrest

Companion scene features the 96th Pennsylvania regiment drawn up in formation at Camp Northumberland. Note that the mounted officers have moved slightly and that the man wearing the white shirt, in the doorway of the structure immediately to the left of the regiment, is no longer visible. The wagon on the left is most likely the photographer's darkroom (National Archives).

among the line officers that it further polarized Captain Filbert and Lieutenant Colonel Frick—the latter being the chair of the Council of Administration—from Colonel Cake.[84]

Actually, the seeds of dissent, directed at sutler Gee, were not sown at Camp Northumberland. Rather, the source of the animosity had its origins at Camp Schuylkill, where Gee had been appointed the regimental sutler. Gee was an old political ally of Cake's, who was heavily involved in town meetings and county elections for public office. While atop Lawton's Hill, Colonel Cake had cast the first stone, perhaps unknowingly, in the sutler controversy. Cake ordered the line captains to purchase caps for their respective commands from Gee. This transaction netted the sutler a handsome profit, but it provoked resentment among the line officers because they had to pay for the headgear from their company funds, a very limited account to begin with. Captain Filbert alleged that the kepi hats had a retail value of only 25 cents, not the 63 cents that Gee called the government price. Although this deal caused unrest among the line officers of the regiment, they did not act to oppose Cake's order. Then in February, when company funds were low and needed to purchase food, Cake ordered each company to purchase leggings from the sutler. That mandate so angered the line captains that they actively opposed Cake's mandate.[85]

But before the line officers could organize themselves, formulate a plan of action, and present Colonel Cake with their grievances concerning the sutler, the army assembled under George Brinton McClellan began to awaken from its winter slumber, flex its unflexed muscles, and come to life. The Bluecoats knew that a spring campaign was not far off; the signs were all around them. First, shelter tents arrived in camp, followed by new sky-blue trousers for each enlisted man. Then rumors about a movement, what the soldiers called a "big thing," swirled like the March winds through the Unionist camps nestled in the Virginia countryside. Finally, one brisk morning the 96th regiment was ordered to assemble on its parade ground. All of the men in the ranks believed that they were going to receive the order to march against the Butternuts. Instead of moving against the Graycoats and meeting a brigade of Secessionists in battle, the Pennsylvanians were "shot" by a local photographer![86]

In early March, the line officers of the 96th regiment were ordered to reduce their personal stores to one carpetbag and be prepared to move at any moment. The long awaited spring campaign was about to begin. At dress parade on March 9, orders were read confirming Peter Filbert as the senior line captain and assigning the 96th Pennsylvania to Franklin's division, which formed the First Division, of Maj. Gen. Irvin McDowell's I Corps.[87] The Yankees were also informed that a movement would commence the next morning.[88] That evening Camp Northumberland was a beehive of frenzied activity. The next morning, as the Pennsylvanians tramped toward Fairfax Court House, the comforts enjoyed at Camp Northumberland quickly became fond memories.

III

"My God! The ninety-sixth has never been under fire!"

On a bleak March day, amidst a drenching rainstorm, the 96th tramped out of its winter quarters at Camp Northumberland destined at last to meet the Confederates. As the Pennsylvanians marched west along the Fairfax Turnpike, their newly issued sky-blue trousers soon became covered with red Virginia mud. Muddy pantaloons, however, could not discourage the soldiers as they marched with Franklin's division to meet the Secessionists in battle. The men in the ranks had been informed, prior to the commencement of the march, that the Confederates were "in strong force at Fairfax and Manassas."[1] Although the wild enthusiasm of Sunday's dress parade, where the order "Prepare to move at once" sent up cheer upon cheer throughout the regiment's camp, died down during the weary march, the Pennsylvanians were still eager to meet the Rebels. In a post-war memoir, James Treichler of Company H recalled the *esprit de corps* which swept through the regiment as the soldiers trudged through the mud toward Fairfax Court House. "With their heads up and shoulders thrown back marching with perfect step and rhythm to the shrill music of the fife and drum. This was not playing soldier. It was real service."[2] Clement Potts stated that he hoped the regiment saw "a little fun" while away from the comfortable quarters of Camp Northumberland.[3] Others in the regiment pondered what it would be like when they engaged the enemy in battle. Late in the afternoon, the Schuylkill County regiment reached Fairfax Court House, where the soldiers pitched shelter tents and established Camp Slocum. As they settled into their new camp, they whispered about the excitement of battle. The Bluecoats thought that the Confederates were close at hand, but they soon learned that "the bird had flown."[4]

Major Lewis Martin summarized the situation in a letter to his family. "The evacuation of that stronghold [Manassas] seems to have nonplussed all the Generals and there is now no telling what the next move will be or where the destination."[5] Realizing that the Confederate withdrawal offered no opportunity for attack, General McClellan allowed his army to rest for a few days while he finalized the York-James peninsula invasion plans.[6] Although the evacuation of the Graycoats meant that a battle was not imminent, the Schuylkill Countians, at least, were not happy. The long march, conducted in the rain, followed by a night of picket duty served as their introduction to active campaigning. The boys had enjoyed the military spectacle of the army tramping to Fairfax Court House, but no one was pleased with the night spent on the picket line. It was, however, a memorable event and afforded the soldiers an opportunity to see the Virginia landscape. James Treichler recalled the sights: "I distinctly remember how the landscape appeared in our immediate front the first night. We were on duty [near] the court house, in a sparsely wooded country. It was a clear moonlight night and objects could be seen at an unusual distance. The land sloped gradually ... to the Valley of bull-run, where eight months previous the disastrous battle took place."[7]

The bivouac at Fairfax also afforded the Pennsylvanians their first opportunity to pursue activities that amused Civil War soldiers. Small raiding parties foraged throughout the countryside, even stopping to plunder the homes and farms of the local inhabitants. According to one eyewitness, Lewis Luckenbill, the tired, wet, hungry soldiers coming in from picket duty, quickly "made preparation to have something to eat." According to Luckenbill, they "killed three hogs. They ... shot at them with muskets, some ran after them with swords and knives until they had all three of them killed. The soldiers are ... [came] in [to] camp from all directions. Some with sheep on their shoulders, some calves, hogs, chickens, others with half a beef, anything they ... [could] get a hold of. A squad of our men started out today and killed a heifer, weighing about 4 hundred pounds and fetched her in camp. We had plenty of beef."[8] Perhaps the most notorious plundering at the Fairfax encampment occurred when a long train of army wagons, loaded down with beer destined for Blenker's division of Germans, passed through the camp. The Bluecoats gathered along both sides of the road, watching the train creak past them in review. Their mouths watered "for the good stuff, that was so near, and yet so far!" As the train ascended a small hill, one Yank managed to cut the straps that held up the tail-gate, of one of the wagons, causing barrel after barrel of the German's lager to roll off the wagon. The heads of the barrels were quickly knocked in, and several thousand "men could be seen running to the train, all anxious to get a taste of the booty."[9] Soon a cavalry squadron was called in to drive off the raiders and escort the train over the rest of its journey.

When the troops were not out plundering or foraging, they actively discussed the empty Rebel fortifications at Centreville. Virtually all felt that McClellan, who had kept the Bluecoats from assaulting the Rebel entrenchments around Manassas, had done them a "good turn." Although the Keystoners were eager to go into action, they probably trembled at the thought of charging the Graycoat fortifications lined with gun emplacements. They laughed, however, when they learned that a large number of the Butternut guns were harmless wooden cannon—trimmed logs, painted black and upended over wagon wheels—known to the troops as "Quaker guns." When the newspaper men learned of the "Quaker guns," left in the Rebel emplacements to mock the Yankees, public opinion concerning McClellan's generalship turned impatient. The soldiers, too, including many in the 96th Pennsylvania, as well as surgeon Washington Nugent, wondered how McClellan would respond to the citizens and newspaper editorials all urging him to move the army rapidly and advance "On to Richmond!"[10]

People were collectively mortified and humiliated with his slow pursuit of the Rebels surmising that his reputation was somewhat in jeopardy, McClellan made a speech to his troops, which had two intentions. First, McClellan did not want his soldiers to become dispirited. Second, he wanted to communicate to the public, through the press, how he planned to win the war in a quick, decisive campaign. In a spirited address at Fairfax Court House in mid–March, McClellan told his soldiers that he was about to take them "where I know you wish to be—on the decisive battlefield." Concerning the army's inaction McClellan stated:

The Army of the Potomac is now a real Army,—magnificent in material, admirable in discipline and instruction excellently equipped and armed;—your commanders are all that I could wish. The moment for action has arrived.... I am to watch over you as a parent; ... It shall be my care, as it has ever been, to gain success with the least possible loss; but I know that if it is necessary, you will willingly follow me to our graves for our righteous cause.... I shall demand of you great, heroic exertions, rapid and long marches, desperate combats, privations perhaps. We will share all these together; and that when this sad war is over we will return to our homes, and feel that we can ask no higher honor than the proved consciousness that we belonged to the ARMY OF THE POTOMAC.[11]

After McClellan's stirring speech, the Federal columns began the march back to Alexandria, where transports waited to ferry them to Fort Monroe. The 96th Pennsylvania, however, along with Slocum's brigade, straggled back to Camp Northumberland in the rain and awaited orders.[12] Rumors circulated through the ranks about the deployment of Slocum's Brigade, but the balance of McClellan's grand army was beginning to move to the intended theater of operations, the York-James peninsula. The Bluecoats at Camp Northumberland knew that other troops were being loaded on transports and steamers to be sent down the Potomac River and wondered why they were not included in the movement of men and materiel. The reason they remained inactive at Camp Northumberland, was a complicated one. Lincoln was worried that the departure of some 100,000 Unionist troops from the vicinity of Washington would leave an inadequate defense in case of a Rebel invasion. The President was particularly concerned about the Secessionists reoccupying their abandoned works in the Manassas area. In order to reassure the President that Washington was properly garrisoned, McClellan decided to alter his plan of operations.[13]

McClellan's original proposal called for McDowell's corps—approximately 38,000 troops—to be brought down to the Peninsula last of all. This corps was to remain in the Washington area, as McDowell explained the scheme to President Lincoln, "until it was ascertained that the whole of the enemy's force was down below." McClellan, however, never got an opportunity to commit McDowell's troops to battle. Just as McClellan was landing at Fort Monroe, President Lincoln decided to retain McDowell's corps near Washington. The President was especially wary of the success "Old Blue Light," General Thomas Jonathan "Stonewall" Jackson, was enjoying against Banks' forces in the Shenandoah Valley. To guarantee that McDowell's force would provide protection for the capital, the President informed McClellan that McDowell would receive his orders directly from Washington. This action was given emphasis by a supplementary order creating what was called the Department of the Rappahannock, to be commanded by McDowell. All of this meant that the 96th Pennsylvania might miss the first attempt to capture Richmond. If McClellan's operation succeeded, the war would be over. The Pennsylvanians responded like veterans, disappointed but resigned, when they realized that they might not bask in the glory of crushing the rebellion. Their disappointment, however, was premature.[14]

Although the 96th Pennsylvania was detached from McClellan's Peninsula operations, there were still orders to carry out and military matters to attend to. In particular, daily drilling and reviews, the routines that had characterized the winter at Camp Northumberland, once again comprised the central features of military life. Most notably, on March 19, the regiment marched, with knapsacks, to the brigade drill ground where they were reviewed by General Slocum. Then, in the afternoon, the entire division was reviewed by Generals Franklin, McDowell, and McClellan. For the volunteers of the 96th

Pennsylvania, this was their first glimpse of the magnetic McClellan. One soldier recalled, "Our division was reviewed by General McClellan who was received with enthusiasm … this was his first appearance to us as a division. He sat his horse well and rode with great speed. While his appearance and address were pleasing, there seemed in his smooth face and mild eye nothing to indicate a man of brilliant genius or great purpose."[15] Surgeon Nugent informed his wife, "I had seen 'Little Mack' before but never had so fair a chance of scrutinizing the gentleman. He is not very much like the photographs I have seen, less like the pictures of Napoleon than I had expected to find him and not near so heavy in person as his pictures represent him. He looked well, very well, but I admired his horsemanship and his horse."[16]

Maj. Gen. George B. McClellan, commander Army of the Potomac (author's collection).

After McDowell's review of the "Corps de Armee," he issued a general order congratulating the soldiers for their splendid marching and military precision. "The review of yesterday was all that could be wished. The troops did themselves and the country credit." In addition, McDowell commended the soldiers for their "steadiness … in line and on the march … America has, in her volunteers of a few months, troops on which she may rely."[17] By the end of March, however, the war was gathering momentum. McClellan's mighty Army of the Potomac was beginning the "On to Richmond" campaign intent upon ending the rebellion. Private McGlenn noted in a letter that "the cavalry men are all gone to Richmond. We feel lonesome these few days just as two thirds of the army are gone away. We are not yet moved away in fact all the Army of the Potomac is gone to Richmond and Fortress Monroe…. Times are very busy in Alexandria every day. There is no doubt but we will be off in a few days."[18] As the blustery winds of March, which swept through the company streets of Camp Northumberland subsided. and the muddy streets became firm, the drilling, reviews, and inspections came to an end. On April 4, McDowell's corps was ordered to march to Alexandria. The soldiers believed that at last they were going to join the main body of the Army of the Potomac. Instead, they would be disappointed. Rather than boarding transports for a trip down the Chesapeake, they were loaded on freight cars and began a rail journey that would take them through Manassas Junction to Catlett's Station—a whistle stop on the Orange and Alexandria Railroad.[19]

Arriving at Manassas Junction, late in the afternoon, after a journey of twenty seven miles, the 96th Pennsylvania established a temporary camp near the abandoned Confederate winter quarters. The soldiers were approximately five miles from Centreville, two miles from Manassas Junction, and a short distance from the famous battlefield of

Bull Run. Once again in the field, the soldiers proclaimed confidence in their cause and informed friends and family at home about the advance of McDowell's corps. The regimental adjutant, Mathias Richards informed his brother that morale within the regiment was building to a fever pitch. "They [the soldiers] say 'Wait till the 96th commences then you will see the fur fly!!'" In another letter Richards proudly proclaimed that "Franklin's Division ... is the crack division of the army."[20] Private Edward Henry, of Company D, also commented on the regiment's readiness for battle. "Our general [Slocum] says there is not a better regiment in the service and we soon hope to prove it, which will be before long, if I am not mistaken."[21]

After arriving in the Manassas vicinity, a few curious Schuylkill Countians made the short trip to survey the famous Bull Run battlefield. Lieutenant John Fernsler, Company H, found a guide to lead him over the terrain of the fight. After visiting the hallowed ground, Fernsler recorded in his diary the sights that greeted him:

> Plenty of our soldiers lying on the ground that were never buried. I judged that they were wounded and dragged their bodies, to where I found them, to die. Their skulls were gone. Nothing but arms and legs could be seen. I uncovered several where the drawers could be seen tied around their legs. The legs had been decayed off their bones.[22]

Lewis Luckenbill recorded in his diary, "The next morning I started out to see the great Battlefield Bull Run. After I got away from camp about one mile I found a place where

1st Lt. John K. Fernsler. Promoted from sergeant, Company H, to 2nd lieutenant on March 5, 1862, and to 1st lieutenant September 1, 1862. Resigned from United States service February 24, 1863 (courtesy Alice Fernsler Lopez).

there was two hundred soldiers buried at one place. I seen some men that were buried with their arms sticking out, others with their legs and many that had not been buried at all."[23] Other soldiers who visited the Bull Run field also commented upon the dead. One Bluecoat noted that "war is indeed terrible," while another stated, "My heart bleeds for their weeping friends at home."[24] Four days after arriving at Manassas Junction, McDowell's command began advancing further south, electing to march along the tracks of the Orange and Alexandria Railroad. On April 7, after the column had covered eleven miles, the command to halt and pitch shelter tents was given. Just as the Pennsylvanians began to erect their tents, torrents of rain fell. The soldiers, unable to get their temporary shelters raised before the deluge, were drenched and their blankets soaked. This caused Private Keiser to conclude "we [were] in a nice predicament."[25]

The torrential rain at Catlett's Station, which caused such terrible flash flooding, was followed by howling winds and several inches of wet snow. Later, the snow turned back to rain, and the Yanks sought shelter in nearby farm houses, barns and blacks' cabins. For three days the rain continued, turning the area into a quagmire. Major Martin did not exaggerate in a letter home, when he referred to the regiment's bivouac as Camp Misery. To his folks he wrote, "Our present camp is a perfect mud hole. We can not step two steps from the tent without getting ankle deep into mud."[26] To the joy of the Bluecoats the order was given on April 12 to return to Alexandria. The regiments of Slocum's brigade, except for the 5th Maine—perhaps victims of logistical failure—who had to march, were loaded onto platform cars drawn by two wheezy old engines, and transported back to Alexandria.[27] There the Pennsylvanians learned that their division, some 12,000 strong, was being sent to McClellan. One soldier noted that "our march through the city was accompanied by quite an ovation; our reception being quite enthusiastic, and the citizens seemingly wishing us Godspeed."[28] At last, the Schuylkill Countians were going to meet the Secessionists.

On April 17 the men again packed their knap-sacks, folded their shelter tents, and marched to the huzzahs of enthusiastic citizens into Alexandria where a variety of vessels would transport them to the peninsula. While they waited to be loaded onto the transport vessels, some of the Pennsylvanians in Colonel Cake's command seized the opportunity to have their "likenesses" taken at a nearby daguerreotypist's studio. Company H, for example, had themselves photographed in a group.[29] Finally, after a three hour delay, they were loaded onto three separate transports. Companies A, B, C and D, under the command of Colonel Cake, boarded the steamer *S.R. Spaulding.* Lewis Luckenbill recalled the overcrowded conditions on board the *Spaulding.* In his diary he wrote, "on board the steam ship *S. R. Spaulding* numbering 12 hundred soldiers our four companies and three companies of the 27th [New York] were put in to the lower deck of the steamer. Making about six hundred in the lower deck."[30] Under the command of Lieutenant Colonel Frick, companies G, H, I and K boarded the steamer *John Brooks.* The last two companies, E and F, under Major Martin, boarded the *Daniel Webster, No. 2.*[31] After the troops were loaded, each transport proceeded down the Potomac River about three miles, where the ships dropped anchor for the night. By morning the flotilla was ready to embark on the voyage to McClellan's theater of operations.[32]

Early the next morning, the armada of steamships, schooners, transports and barges began the trip down the Potomac toward Chesapeake Bay and Fort Monroe. The Bluecoats agreed that water travel was a welcome change from plodding up and down Virginia hills, along roads thick with mud. Then the splendid sights along the Potomac leg of the journey gave way to a violent storm as the flotilla navigated Chesapeake Bay. As the wind whistled across the decks, and the vessels rolled with the choppy waves, seasick Unionists wished they could exchange the "ocean wave for the red mud again."[33] For the next two weeks, McClellan deliberated how best to employ Franklin's division. Meanwhile, many Pennsylvanians were quartered on the open-air upper decks of the transports, without shelter from the rain and devoid of cooking facilities. About these hardships one volunteer complained: "We ate salt pork raw, and sometimes (by paying the cook), we could get enough hot water from the galley to make a cup of coffee."[34] Captain Filbert, however, recorded in his diary, "Gay times. Had strawberries [and] canned peaches."[35] Adjutant Richards, in a letter penned on board the *Spaulding,* informed his sister that "we are very comfortable.... This steamer, the S. R. Spalding is an elegant, large boat."[36] Another soldier reported that "the upper saloon was the quarters of the officers, who were about as snugly stowed as the men below."[37] Upon reaching the Fort Monroe vicinity, Franklin's armada was instructed to steam toward the mouth of the York River, and drop anchor near Ship Point and Cheeseman's Creek; there the Bluecoats awaited orders.

As the southern days grew warmer the troops remained on board the transports, living in cramped, crowded conditions. Col. Joseph Howland, commanding the 16th New York onboard the *Daniel Webster*, lamented, "The boat is so crowded and dirty that life is becoming intensely disgusting."[38] The Pennsylvanians, however, did not express similar sentiments in their letters or diaries. A few of the soldiers mentioned that the tight quarters on the vessels, however, were becoming a problem. But they all agreed that conditions on the *Spaulding* were considerably better than what their comrades endured on the other vessels, the *John Brooks* and the *Daniel Webster*. Surgeon Nugent recalled, "Our vessel is a fine sea boat and the accommodations on board are much better than any other in the fleet."[39] Major Martin, quartered on the *Daniel Webster*, wrote in a letter that he found "the Spaulding a magnificent Ocean Steamer and contrasts so favorably with our crowded up craft."[40] Edward Henry noted that "there are fifteen hundred troops aboard this ship in a very crowded condition and all are anxious to be set ashore."[41] On April 24, to alleviate the crowded and unsanitary conditions, Franklin received permission to order his regiments to establish camps ashore.

The Pennsylvanians bivouacked in a grove of pine trees, named Camp Martin in honor of the regiment's major, along the shore of Cheeseman's Creek. There they enjoyed the oysters, clams and eels of tidewater Virginia. Perhaps the "big thing" of the Cheeseman's Creek layover was the re-coaling of the fleet. In order to take on fuel, the steamships had to go down to Fort Monroe. Upon reaching the coaling station, Lieutenant Fernsler was excited to see "Monitor … lying there keeping a look out for the Merrimac [*C.S.S. Virginia*]."[42] Adjutant Richards, also recorded his observations, in a letter to his sister, concerning the *Monitor*. "The rebel description of 'a cheese box on a raft' is a very good one of its appearance."[43] Erasmus Reed also mentioned the trip to Fort Monroe and the excitement which captivated the soldiers upon seeing the famous naval vessel. "We were taken down to Fortress Monroe but General Wool would not allow us to land. I had a good view of the Monitor and also seen the smoke of the Merimack laying beyond Sewell's Point. The fort is a grand old structure. I was sorry we could not get off the ship to see the inside of it."[44] For the soldiers of the 96th Pennsylvania, the *U.S.S. Monitor* and Fort Monroe constituted not just exciting sights but important symbols of power. The *Monitor* represented advanced naval technology while the old fort, the "Gibraltar of Chesapeake Bay," symbolized, in its oversize guns, the military might of the industrialized North.

Many of the Schuylkill Countians were confident that the war would soon end. Edward Henry believed that "victory is shure to crown our efforts. There is nothing like retreat known. The men have confidence in their officers and in themselves and we are shure to win."[45] Another member of the 96th stated, "The Army will fight if we are only handled right. All the talk of the Army being demoralized is all nonsense."[46] Erasmus Reed believed that "the rebels are nearly played out and cannot hold out against George B. [McClellan] much longer. I should not be surprised if he would bag them at Yorktown. That would end the rebellion at the same place the Revolution was ended."[47] As April gave way to May, and McClellan pushed the Confederates back toward the old colonial town of Williamsburg, the soldiers of the 96th Pennsylvania became increasingly eager to confront the foe. As Surgeon Nugent observed on the return trip from Fort Monroe, "the 'old flag' is waving and the dogs of war look grimly forth as waiting for a foe."[48] After the evacuation of Yorktown by the Confederates, Franklin's division re-embarked the transports, and awaited further orders. The Bluecoats knew that McClellan was driving the Butternuts. The Yanks clearly heard the "music" of the Union artillery batteries playing their tunes in the vicinity of Yorktown. The Pennsylvanians knew, too, that the Confederates were withdrawing up the peninsula toward Richmond. For the soldiers of the 96th Pennsylvania, it was time to steam up the York River and seek the Secessionists.

The plan called for Franklin, regarded by some as an accomplished soldier, by others as a circumspect commander, to take his flotilla up river, as far as Yorktown and await further orders from McClellan.[49] Early in the morning on May 5, Franklin's task force embarked for Yorktown. Several hours later, the vessels anchored opposite the old colonial town. Throughout the day, the soldiers appeared in the rain on the decks of the transports to view the extensive Confederate field fortifications. While the fighting at Williamsburg raged nearby, Private McGlenn remarked in a letter, "We saw all the Rebel forts [and the] cannon and ammunition which they left behind. It was a very strong place."[50] Private Boland also commented on the impressive Confederate earthworks at Yorktown. "We saw all the Rebel forts [and] cannon; 70 of them being left behind. The Rebels left the works filled with torpedoes." Another soldier recalled, "It almost seemed strange that they should leave there without at least a terrible resistance. But it seemed so ordered, and off they went, leaving behind them a large number of splendid guns, besides an immense amount of ammunition, etc."[51] While at Yorktown, McClellan awaited information concerning the outcome at Williamsburg. Patiently, Franklin remained idle anticipating orders from his commander.

Finally, McClellan instructed Franklin to steam up the York River, disembark his command at Brick House landing and "to hold his position until reinforced sufficiently to justify an advance."[52] In a letter to his wife, Franklin quoted McClellan's orders. "Please push your movement as rapidly as possible, securing the landing beyond all doubt and being cautious though bold in your advance."[53] Although McClellan was acting boldly in sending Franklin and his division up the York River, he was not intending to strike the retreating Confederate column. During the night of May 5, the soldiers of the 96th Pennsylvania heard rumors concerning their mission. "Don't know where the Rebels have gone to," wrote Major Martin, "but our forces are supposed to be in hot pursuit … all kinds of reports are current as to what is going on up River, and conjecture is rife as to what we are to do."[54] Lieutenant Fernsler simply noted in his diary, "We leave here for West Point in order to cut off about 15,000 of the rebels, who are retreating towards Richmond."[55]

On the morning of May 6, convoyed by a handful of Flag Officer Louis Goldsborough's gunboats, the steamships, transports and barges, left Yorktown and proceeded cautiously up river to the vicinity of West Point, located at the confluence of the Mattapony and Pamunkey Rivers.[56] In the afternoon, as the lead ships reached Brick House Landing on the York River, the soldiers spotted Confederate cavalry scouting the presence of the Yankee intruders. Using pontoons to ferry the soldiers ashore, the 27th New York Volunteers were the first to disembark and establish a skirmish line under Colonel Bartlett. Quickly, the New York regiment secured a perimeter, thus preparing the landing zone for the balance of Franklin's division. According to a member of the 27th New York, the Union position was on "a peninsula formed by two creeks which empty into the York at this point, which flow through swamps and marshes, overgrown with pine and dense underbrush."[57] To support Bartlett's command, a few shells from the 100-pounder Parrott rifles on board the Union gunboats were hurled toward the stray Confederates, scattering the cavalry videttes. Before the soldiers could establish a regimental camp for the evening, four companies of the regiment "were ordered to go out and protect our pioneers, who were obstructing several roads, to prevent the enemy from coming in on us."[58] Near dusk, the four companies were recalled and the regiment pitched shelter for the night. As the soldiers from Schuylkill County rested and prepared for the combat engagement which might develop the next morning, General Franklin spent the night making preparations to "prevent the success of an [enemy] attack."[59]

As Franklin's division massed at Brick House Landing, Confederate Maj. Gen. Gustavus W. Smith, charged with protecting the path of Johnston's retreating columns, made preparations to thwart the approach of the enemy. At last report, Johnston's trains and rear guard were still wallowing through the mud somewhere below Barhamsville, about six miles from the Federal position, and would need at least a full day to pass through that threatened sector. After assessing the tactical situation, Smith refrained from contesting the debarkation of Franklin's command, primarily because he feared the fire power of the heavy ordnance on board the gun-boats. The wiser course of action for Smith on May 6 seemed to be to permit the Bluecoats to move inland, out of range of naval support, and then to assail them. The sole objective of the operation, at least from the point of view of the Confederates, would be to keep the Unionists from interdicting the Secessionist trains and rear guard until the Confederate column moved through this threatened sector.[60]

While Smith prepared for several contingencies, Franklin pondered his situation. That evening the Federal commander had misgivings concerning the deployment of his troops at the Brick House beach-head. The landing place was a clearing about a square mile in area with dense woods on three sides. Several roads, or more precisely country lanes, entered the clearing, but it was uncertain just where they came from. Complicating matters further, Franklin's maps bore little resemblance to the terrain he faced, and the presence of Confederate cavalry and infantry in the surrounding woods convinced him to wait until day light before beginning any forward movement of his forces.[61] That night, tension was thick along the picket line for the Unionists charged with that perilous duty. Eerie shadows, cast along the outposts by a bright moonlight, caused further anxiety. Several hours before daybreak, Franklin ordered the Yankees to form battle lines, to prepare for the impending attack by the Confederates. Shortly after 3 o'clock, according to Major Martin, the 96th Pennsylvanian was "under arms, rolls all called and [the] men ordered to lay on their arms till daybreak."[62] About 7 o'clock, an officer of the 96th Pennsylvania recalled that "after breakfast our pickets were attacked, and we were formed in line of battle again. Presently word came in that a brigade of rebels was advancing on our right, and that they were also in great force on our centre."[63] The threat posed by the Confederates compelled General Franklin to examine the Union position and perhaps issue orders to probe the forest in his front to ascertain enemy strength.

While General Franklin and Brig. Gen. John Newton, commanding the Third Brigade, inspected the Union position, Confederate Major General Smith met with his subordinates, and decided that one of his divisions, commanded by Brig. Gen. William H.C. Whiting, should advance against the Yankee force at the landing. At 7 a.m., after realizing that the Federals were not going to advance to meet him, Whiting decided to move forward, clear the woods in front of Brick House Landing, and then, if practicable, push up field artillery to a position where it could bombard the beachhead and the transports. After examining the Yankee line on foot, Franklin and Newton were satisfied that the flanks were protected by creeks and the terrain was well suited to guarding against the approaching Confederates. The most vulnerable point along the Union line appeared to be where one of the interior roads bisected the position held by Newton's brigade. To shore up this weak point Franklin ordered an artillery battery to support that sector. Convinced that the Federal line was secure, Franklin returned to the transports to supervise the disembarkation of Brig. Gen. Napoleon J. T. Dana's brigade to the landing place. As Franklin departed Brick House Landing, the Secessionists advanced through the pine woods toward the Bluecoat picket line.[64]

As Whiting's Graycoats neared the Federal position, the Mississippian directed General John Bell Hood's Texas brigade to spearhead the attack.[65] Near 9 a.m., the lead elements of Hood's brigade drove the Federal skirmish line back through the dense forest surrounding Brick House Landing with "considerable loss."[66] The Confederate attack initially struck two companies of the 16th New York Volunteers under the command of Col. Joseph Howland. As the Bluecoats retreated, Hood's line of Texans rolled forward, continuing a lively musketry fire.[67] As the Federal skirmishers withdrew, Newton moved his forces forward—the 18th, 31st, 32nd New York and the 95th Pennsylvania—and formed a battle line along the edge of the wood road. He then requested that Slocum, commanding the center and left of the Union position, send him reinforcements. Slocum immediately ordered forward the 5th Maine, additional companies of the 16th New York and elements of the 27th New York Volunteers in support of Newton's advanced line.[68] As the reinforcements moved forward, Colonel Cake of the 96th Pennsylvania approached the officer who had charge of the brigade and requested that his regiment be ordered into action. Cake wanted desperately to shed the label that the other veteran regiments in the brigade had bestowed upon his troops during the winter at Camp Franklin: "The regiment that had never been under fire."[69] Throughout the winter, Cake waited for this opportunity. Now, at long last, was his chance to prove the mettle of his command to the "Heroes of Bull Run." With the possibility of demonstrating their fighting courage looming large in their front, the Pennsylvanians, however, were denied entry into the battle.

While Hood's Texans engaged the center and right of the Federal position, Wade Hampton's South Carolina "Legion" and the 6th North Carolina, supported by the Rowan (1st North Carolina) Artillery, menaced Dana's brigade, which anchored the left of the Union line. As the Hampton Legion drove the Bluecoats back toward Brick House Landing, Dana requested that Slocum push forward additional infantry to reinforce his line. Slocum subsequently dispatched the 96th Pennsylvania to support the far left flank of the Unionist line. As the Pennsylvanians took up their line of march, General Slocum intercepted Dana's staff officer, who was escorting them, and asked, "What did you tell Colonel Cake?" The young officer told Slocum that the 96th Pennsylvania was not going to wait for the enemy to "come up," but was going to seek the Graycoats. To that Slocum exclaimed, "My God! The ninety-sixth has never been under fire!"[70]

Throughout the morning the volunteers of the 96th Pennsylvania could hear the sounds of the battle. Now, perhaps, they would have the opportunity to see the enemy and fire their first volley against the foe. Initially, the Pennsylvania soldiers moved into position on the Union left to support General Newton's brigade. Six hundred yards behind the 96th Pennsylvania, Captain Josiah Porter, commanding Battery A 1st Massachusetts Artillery, unlimbered his six guns; four 10-pounder Parrotts and two 12-pounder How-itzers.[71] Major Martin, in a letter written a day after the engagement, described the scene as the soldiers of the 96th Pennsylvania formed their first line of battle. "Orders then came for all hands to fall in to the support of our Pickets who were being driven back on us. Line of battle was formed at once. Word came the rebels were retreating. Our reg-iment … [was] ordered across a marshy swamp to the edge of the woods and to get as far into the woods as we could. We went over to the woods and formed in line of battle but before we had time to advance we were ordered to stand still till we received further orders."[72] In a letter to the *Miners' Journal*, an officer of the Schuylkill County regiment wrote, "We took position at the edge of a wood and a covering out of fence rails. Very soon the regiment, which was in front of us, was attacked. It was volley after volley for some ten minutes. We thought we would get it very soon, but the firing stopped. By this time one of our Batteries on our right opened and shelled the woods for some time. The firing on both sides was soon stopped. In about a quarter of an hour, a rebel battery opened on our left and directed its fire on the vessels in the [York] river. Two of our field batteries and gunboats opened on them, the shells of both sides going over our heads."[73]

According to Major Martin, for nearly two hours Porter's battery and the Union gunboats exchanged artillery fire with the Confederate battery commanded by Capt. James Reilly.[74] A correspondent with the Philadelphia *Press* reported that the guns of Capt. Porter's battery opened fire and "in a few minutes the shells were flying through the air at the rate of about ten a minute. This soon compelled the rebels to make a move more on our left, where the shells flew less thick than upon the ground they were then occupying. But there evidently is not rest for the wicked; for no sooner had the rebels moved their forces upon our left than our gunboats, which up until that time had been unable to have a hand in the affair, opened their batteries upon the foe, with so much effect that, when I commenced to write, they had completely driven the enemy out of sight and hearing."[75] As the artillery rounds shrieked above the heads of the soldiers, Major Martin recalled that "our position now was rather an unenviable one for we were directly between the Rebel Batteries and our Batteries and Gun Boats and shells some-times fall very carelessly."[76] Despite the dramatic artillery duel, and the crackling of mus-ketry in the woods, perhaps 300 yards in front of their line, the 96th Pennsylvania merely held their position and did not fire a volley against the Confederates. At four o'clock, they were relieved by the 19th Massachusetts. As the 96th Pennsylvania withdrew an offi-cer noted, "We were on our way to camp when we saw a rebel regiment down near the river. Our batteries opened on them and they left very suddenly."[77] Returning to the orig-inal landing area at Brick House point, the soldiers quickly ate supper and moved to the far right of the clearing to support another Union battery should the Graycoats mount a night attack upon the Yankees.

For the men in the ranks, although not directly involved in the combat action, the day had been full of anxious moments and uncertainty, creating vivid memories for the young Pennsylvania volunteers. Writing almost one month after the battle, Private McGlenn recounted the dramatic events of May 7 to his friend John Brislin back in Pottsville.

We had only Franklin's command 12,000 men without any cavalry.... We now had to fight a battle against great odds five to our one. At 8 o'clock in the morning the 95th Pennsylvania went into the woods as skirmishers.... This commenced the battle. Our picket informed us that the whole rebel columns was coming in on our left wing.

We had 3 generals present Franklin, Slocum & Newton. Our ... regiments fought on bravely ... at noon the Rebels drove us in three times at the point of the bayonet.... There was continual firing of musketry all day.... The 96th has to protect the batteries but other regiments calling for reinforcements. We were then sent into the woods along with the others. We were not placed in the front but behind the others in case that they were all driven in with orders not to fall back until a dozen would be killed out of each company then to fall behind the [Baker's] creek two hundred yards to the rear still to fight on.... The Rebels were pouring their shells over our heads and in fact the branches of the trees were all shot away.... The dead and wounded were brought in during the day. It was an awful sight.

Next morning after I had slept soundly I went to see all the dead and wounded. I saw a great number with whom I was acquainted as we lived together near Alexandria all winter.... Our Division got great praise the next Sunday before all the Generals and McClellan himself came and thanked them.[78]

The price that the Confederates paid, at the Battle of Eltham's Landing, for the passage of Johnston's trains was slight in the six-hour battle: forty wounded and eight killed. A soldier in Wade Hampton's South Carolina Legion recalled the battle in a postwar memoir. "For about ten minutes the cracking of rifles was quite lively, then, suddenly, there was a tremendous crash and roar of small arms, sounding like the beating of many drums. In the midst of this there was sent up through the woods a great cheer, really the rebel yell, and then the noise of battle seemed to be receding."[79] One of Hood's men, a member of the 1st Texas, recalled the exciting events of the battle in a letter published in the Galveston *Weekly News*. "The regiments were formed in line of battle in the following order: the 5th Texas on the extreme right, next the 4th Texas, then the 1st Texas. The 'Yanks' line of battle was composed of the 31st and 32nd N. York or 1st Cal., the 95th and 96th Pennsylvania regiments being first on the left and then on the right where they were into a swamp, from which they soon retreated.... We charged them three times, and the fourth charge left us in possession of the field, the 'Yank' taking the 'Bull Run quick step' out of the woods into an adjoining field."[80] For the soldiers of the 96th Pennsylvania, Eltham's Landing was an opportunity to form a line of battle and advance against the foe. Instead, the day resulted in a futile attempt to receive their baptism under fire.

As soon as the guns cooled and the blinding smoke from the musket and artillery fire cleared, the Pennsylvanians took pens in hand to write their homefolk regarding the dramatic events they witnessed at Eltham's Landing. The Yanks of the 96th Pennsylvania rendered accurate, detailed and graphic accounts of the battle, but with little mention of the psychological impact of battle on untested volunteer soldiers. In fact, the soldiers of the 96th Pennsylvania heard the sounds of battle, and perhaps the rebel yell, but they had not experienced destruction and death first hand. More importantly, only one Yank, Clement Potts, devoted commentary to his thoughts and impressions of the "din of war," but these were superficial. "I can tell you we had a lively time of it. I was just as near to the shells and bullets as I care about getting.... I heard the bullets whiz a past me but none near enough to hurt me.... Of the battle you can see a better account in the papers as I did not take time to look at much only to keep myself behind a tree [to gain protection] from the bullets that were flying past me."[81] Aside from reporting the events of the battle, and the movements of the various regiments, the letters from the camp of the

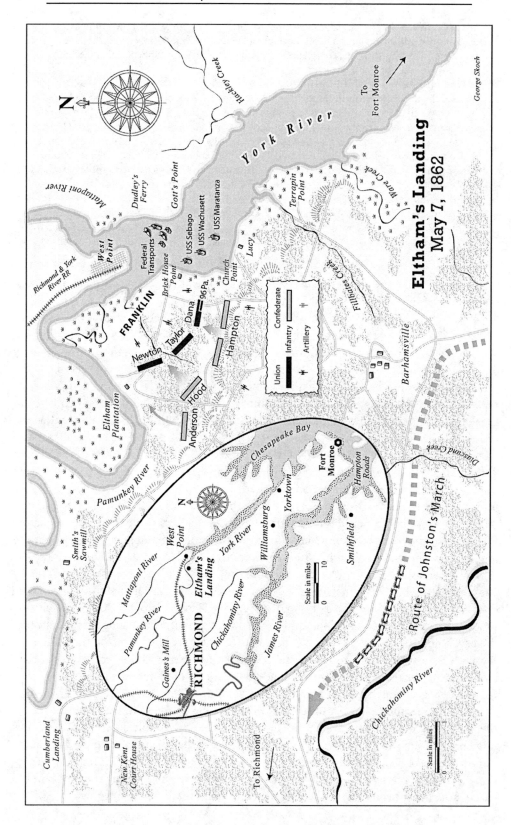

Eltham's Landing
May 7, 1862

George Skoch

96th Pennsylvania Volunteers revealed little about the ultimate in soldiering: the closing of opposing forces in warfare. What captured the attention of the soldiers most was the fallen Secessionists littering the battle zone. The sight of the dead dotting the woods near Eltham's Landing was a main topic of conversation around the regimental campfires and in letters sent home to Pennsylvania.

Indeed, the most exciting aspect of the Eltham's Landing battle concerned the apparent throat slashing of wounded Unionists by one or more of the Graycoats. One soldier reported that the Yankee "wounded lay on the battle field from five to seven hours and one of our men had his throat cut from ear to ear after being wounded."[82] A letter published in the New York *Times* also told a similar story. "Here the rebels were guilty of barbarous atrocities. Many of the dead ... presented a horrible spectacle."[83] In his after action report, General Newton also mentioned the grim discoveries made by the Bluecoats. "The enemy committed inhuman barbarities upon some of the wounded. One was found with his throat cut, and the other bore the marks of eight bayonet stabs in his body."[84] Francis Boland of the 96th Pennsylvania also mentioned the gruesome sights in a letter written several weeks after the battle. "They mutilated our dead and stripped them naked. They bayoneted our wounded ... in cold blood."[85] Private Potts, in a letter to his mother, also described the carnage: "Today I seen a number [of] dead rebels who were concealed in the woods. I tell you ... it [was] such a sight. I hope I will never see [it] again."[86]

According to a casualty report in the New York *Times*, 22 men were killed in the battle while 29 were reported wounded and 34 missing.[87] General Franklin's list of casualties, however, reported 48 killed, 100 wounded and 28 captured or missing.[88] Francis Boland of the 96th Pennsylvania stated that "the Union lost in killed 122, wounded 250 and 50 prisoners in the hands of the Rebels."[89] In the same letter, Boland described the scene he witnessed upon visiting the hospital established within the camp of the 5th Maine. "I went to visit the killed and wounded the next day where they lay. The guard an Irishman of the 5th Maine ... allowed me to go in where they were and examine all the dead and wounded. It was really a poor scene." Another correspondent recalled that all of "the buildings on the plantation are all used for hospitals. I went through one of them this morning; and although some were dying, and all were severely wounded, I heard scarcely a single groan."[90] Lewis Luckenbill and Patrick McGlenn also noted that many wounded and dead soldiers were carried to the hospital sites during the engagement and throughout the next day.[91] Chaplain Adams of the 5th Maine described the scene at the hospital:

> As the dead were brought into our camp, which was the general Hospital, it was known from the position of the troops in the skirmishes, to which regiment the dead belonged.... Our inquiry was, who from the respective regiments can identify these men. Sometimes it was easily done ... [but often] the wounds were so ghastly and the bodies so disfigured that it was difficult for the most intimate friend to recognize them. As we learned the name, Mr. Colt [chaplain of the 96th Pennsylvania] wrote it down, with the number of the regiment, and I pinned the paper on the clothes of the dead. It was a sad office to do this to 41 men ... and to look upon ghastly wounds and upon the strange and distorted features of the dead.[92]

While the soldiers gasped at the sight of the wounded, they also prayed over the graves of the fallen and buried them with the "Honors of War."[93] One Bluecoat described the somber burial of several comrades. "The six men were buried side by side, in one grave beside two large shade trees near the encampment. The funeral took place at dark … the whole regiment attending as mourners. A fervent, heartfelt prayer was offered by the Chaplain…. It was a most impressive ceremony."[94] For the Yankees who saw their dead comrades, the deceased Bluecoats revealed a great deal about the skills of their foemen. According to one soldier, "The dead showed that the enemy were good marksmen, nearly everyone being shot through the head, and many who survived the battle must eventually die from the mortal nature of the wounds they received."[95] Another stated that "the enemy … fired low," while a comrade who spoke with a surgeon recorded that the doctor amputated five legs but no arms at the hospital.[96] Commentary also focused on what the Unionists believed was the unchivalrous style of warfare enacted by the Secessionists. Clement Potts noted that the Confederates tended to use the bayonet in the battle.[97] Another soldier reported that "in this melee bushwackers were in their element, and the rebels had a decided advantage in this respect besides being acquainted with the ground."[98] One Yankee also referred to the Confederates as "black villains."[99] While the 96th Pennsylvania did not fire a volley at the engagement at Eltham's Landing, the sounds of battle and the horrific sights of the wounded at the hospital, proved to be important elements for the Schuylkill Countians as they developed from green volunteers into combat veterans.

While the Battle of Eltham's Landing gave the soldiers of the 96th Pennsylvania some experience regarding the chaos of combat, the engagement also brought them into contact with Southern slaves. In fact, the appearance of slaves, during the battle, was alarming and confusing. Several soldier correspondents reported that they were confronted by "battalions of niggers."[100] Francis Boland of the 96th Pennsylvania stated, "The Rebels had two regiments of negroes. They advanced against us…. It was wrong to bring negroes into battlefields."[101] A letter in the New York *Times* reported that that "one of the flank companies became separated from the rest of the regiment in the difficult ground, and *found they were engaged with negroes, who called upon them to surrender*, but the captain said 'he would be d___d if he would surrender to niggers."[102] Another soldier correspondent reported the presence of "black Confederate troops": "The rebels had a number of blacks, probably a company, armed in the fight, the truth of which is attested by the finding of several of their bodies in the woods."[103]

After the engagement, Franklin's division remained in the vicinity of the battlefield for several days. While Franklin's command rested and awaited marching orders, they were treated to the sight of General McClellan galloping through their camp. The troops cheered McClellan as he rode along the ranks. In his diary, Lewis Luckenbill jotted the following entry. "McClellan and staff paid a visit soon after we had arrived at our camping ground. He was cheered by the soldiers as he passed the different regiments."[104] Although Franklin failed to cripple the Confederate retreat, McClellan was not discouraged. In fact, at this point in the campaign he was delighted with the performance of his troops. A New York soldier recalled McClellan's unanticipated visit with General Franklin and his subordinates. "Here we received McClellan, who … had just arrived from Yorktown, bringing the glorious news of the fall of Norfolk, and the destruction of the Merrimac, and he seemed overjoyed at the prospect of affairs. He gave the news from his saddle, telling the bystanders to spread it through the camps…. Meeting Generals Franklin, Slocum, Newton and others, [McClellan] leaped from his horse and slapping Franklin on his shoulders, exclaimed: 'Franklin we have got the whole rebel crew, Jos. Johnson

This photograph, composed May 14, 1862, at Cumberland Landing, Virginia, features the commanding officers of the VI Corps. Front row from left: Col. Joseph J. Bartlett, Brig. Gen. Henry W. Slocum, Maj. Gen. William B. Franklin, Brig. Gen. William F. Barry and Brig. Gen. John Newton. The men in the back row are unidentified (Library of Congress).

[sic], G. W. Smith and all!' … During the conversation he complimented Franklin for the part his division took at West Point, [Eltham's Landing] saying, 'that it had glory enough for one day.'"[105]

Franklin's end run, resulting in the affair at Eltham's Landing, "served its purpose," according to the army commander "in clearing our front to the banks of the Chicka-hominy."[106] In accordance with plans made prior to the Peninsula movement, when Urbanna was the intended place of debarkation, McClellan established a base of operation at West Point, the terminus of the 35-mile-long Richmond and York River Railroad. At West Point the York River, formed by the convergence of the Mattapony and Pamunkey Rivers, afforded a deep draft supply line all the way back to Chesapeake Bay. McClellan envisioned regiment after regiment, division after division, landing at the West Point staging area ready for the decisive movement against Richmond. While McClellan attended to logistical matters pertaining to his campaign, he also formally organized and appointed commanders to the Fifth and Sixth Corps of the Army of the Potomac. In that regard, two old friends received those coveted appointments. William B. Franklin received the appointment as chief of the VI Corps, and Fitz John Porter was promoted to command the V Corps.[107]

Franklin's promotion cleared the path for General Slocum's promotion to command the First Division. Slocum was virtually idolized by his soldiers. One Bluecoat, in a letter written at Camp Franklin in late December 1861, observed that Slocum was "revered and loved as ever."[108] The appointment of Slocum to divisional command subsequently opened an opportunity for Bartlett, of the 27th New York, to assume the position of brigadier general. Like his mentor Slocum, Bartlett was an impressive soldier with combat experience and command potential. Bartlett, a lawyer from Binghamton, New York, was highly regarded by the soldiers he commanded. Serving initially with the 27th New York Volunteers as major, Bartlett was conspicuous in the 1st Battle of Bull Run.[109] A veteran of the Sixth Corps, writing after the war, penned the following description of Bartlett. "General Bartlett was a splendid specimen of a soldier. He was nearly six feet tall, straight as an arrow, of powerful build, with black eyes and hair, and sat in his saddle as though horse and man were one. He dressed in a tight fitting uniform, low cap with straight visor. As he rode by on his fine black horse, he gained the admiration of his command and he deserved it, for he was ... skillful and brave, and there was not a man of our regiment who would not have followed him anywhere at this time."[110]

By May 15, while Johnston continued his retreat toward Richmond, McClellan advanced his base to a large southern mansion called the White House, fifteen miles along the railroad line from West Point. In preparation for the big push on Richmond, and quite possibly the grand battle which would end the war, the Young Napoleon sent

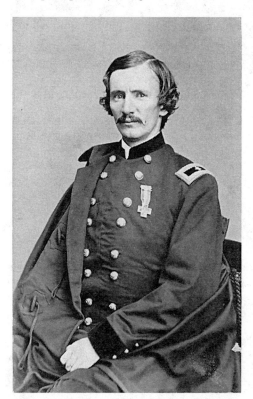

Brig. Gen. Joseph J. Bartlett, photograph by C. D. Fredericks Company, New York (author's collection).

Fitz-John Porter's corps to drive the Rebel infantry away from Hanover Court House. With McClellan's right flank firmly anchored by Porter's forces, and McDowell's command poised for a southern advance, Johnston realized that not even evacuation would assure the salvation of his army. He had only one choice: He had to strike a blow at once. After studying McClellan's position, Johnston decided to attack against the Bluecoat forces along the north bank of the river. Rather than attacking the weaker southern Union wing, keeping Richmond covered as he did so, the Graycoat commander sought to cripple the Bluecoat forces north of the Chickahominy and block McDowell's advance at the same time. It was a bold plan for the conservative Confederate commander, but one factor weighed heavily in its favor. Because the Chickahominy was greatly swollen as a result of the heavy spring rains, it might isolate the Union wings, preventing their mutual support and giving the Graycoats a chance to move against one or the other with equal, or perhaps superior, numbers.[111]

While Johnston finalized his plans to advance against the Bluecoats, Franklin's corps slowly worked its way toward Mechanicsville. As the men of the VI Corps tramped along the plantation lanes of tidewater Virginia great numbers of blacks flocked to the roadside to welcome the Union army. One soldier in Franklin's corps described the reception that the troops received this way: "The Negroes, gathering in crowds along the wayside, would grasp the hands of the Union soldiers, calling down all manner of blessings upon them, and leaping and dancing in their frantic delight. All hoped we would shortly overtake and destroy the Rebel army, their own masters included."[112] A soldier in Bartlett's brigade, while encamped near Mechanicsville, recalled his first encounter with a group of Virginia slaves. "A holiday among the slaves took place last week, and the first intimation the soldiers had of such a thing, was … a large number of negroes … coming from the plantations … to see the wonders of camp. In many cases the slaves outdress their masters and on this occasion was all the display of darky finery."[113] Another Sixth Corps soldier related that "they were dirty and ragged and probably as a perfectly natural result were ignorant and degraded, but they seemed to understand, as nearly all the negroes here do, that somehow all this commotion has a connection with them and will bring about their freedom in the end."[114] While the interactions with the slaves made a singular impression upon the soldiers, the Bluecoats also related in their letters observations concerning the Virginia countryside, the farms and plantations.

By the end of the third week in May, Franklin's corps was encamped near Mechanicsville. According to one historian of the Second Brigade, Mechanicsville "was a lovely spot, five miles from Richmond, and, in ante-bellum days, a favorite resort for people riding out from the capital, to spend a pleasant afternoon or evening."[115] An infantry soldier remarked that Mechanicsville, "like all Virginia villages … is a small affair, and takes its name from one wagon and two blacksmith shops, that stand on five corners crossed by roads converging at this place."[116] The men of the 96th Pennsylvania, however, never received an opportunity to rest along the banks of the Chickahominy and enjoy "the pleasure" of Mechanicsville on a warm Virginia evening. They divided their time between picket duty and labor at nearby Gaines' grist mill. General Slocum detailed work crews from the division to collect wheat and corn from the nearby farms within the Union lines. A detail from the 96th Pennsylvania was kept busy shelling the corn brought in from the fields.[117] On May 27 the Pennsylvanians, along with the rest of Bartlett's brigade, left their camp in the vicinity of Gaines' Mill and established a new camp near Hogan's House.[118] Four days later Joseph Johnston launched his long delayed attack. Rather than attacking north of the Chickahominy, as originally planned, but against the isolated Union left wing posted south of that stream.

After the Battle of Fair Oaks, also known as Seven Pines, the 96th Pennsylvania, along with Bartlett's brigade, moved to within seven miles of Richmond. Still a short distance from Mechanicsville, the Schuylkill County regiment established Camp Richards, named in honor of the regimental adjutant Mathias Edgar Richards. A New Jersey officer, in a letter home, graphically described the campsite:

We are in a nice grove of trees close by this village [Mechanicsville], a beautiful spot but the dirtiest place I have ever seen. Language could hardly give you a picture of it. We are cleaning it up and hauling the dirt and filth away and will soon have a very nice camp. When we came here the 96th Pennsylvania Regiment was encamped on it. But some of our regiments, I am sorry to say, don't police as much as they should. The 96th squatted down right on top of the Rebel dirt, a thing you won't get the 1st New Jersey to do. We police first and pitch tents afterwards. The 96th Pennsylvania had a large sick list. No wonder. I am sick now looking at the filth.[119]

Although Camp Richards might have been "filthy," it was very near Richmond—linchpin of strategy. For the first two weeks of June, McClellan pondered how he would break through the heavily entrenched Confederate position. The Confederate Army had a long line to hold. It ran from Chaffin's Bluff on the James, crossed all of the main roads coming into Richmond from the east, touched the Chickahominy a little above New Bridge, and ran along the southern side of that stream to Meadow Bridges. Meanwhile, the 96th Pennsylvania performed picket duty, and sent letters home reporting their impressions of being in "Dixie Land."[120]

Very few references to the character of the Virginia countryside can be found in the letters of the Pennsylvania volunteers. The theme running through these observations was the general backwardness of the region. The consensus was that the land below the line of Mason and Dixon "suffered considerably" when contrasted to the hills of Pennsylvania. Major Martin espoused this point of view:

> I have not seen any place in Virginia where I would move to from Pottsville. And as for Alexandria, I have seen no place that deserved the name of a town. There are many pretty plantations in the state, places that might be made magnificently beautiful if their owners possessed the least energy or enterprise whatever. The location of this place is delightful. But the general appearance of things such as the buildings, fences, etc. show a wonderful want of industry and ambition.[121]

Other soldiers, too, offered descriptions of the region and the farms of Virginia which focused on the buildings and fields. "Since leaving West Point," stated a Second Brigade soldier, "we have marched through the most beautiful country I ever saw. Extensive plantations, on perfectly level land, are covered with wheat, clover and corn; large pine woods offer their dense shade at intervals along the dusty road to the weary soldier."[122] Another soldier remarked that "the country … is very fertile…. Wheat, barley and corn were the principal grains sown this year. The farms are very large and in good order; well watered and well timbered. The farm houses are large and comfortable not as palatial as I imagined. The negroes' quarters are always separate."[123] In general the Schuylkill Countians concluded that the country had tremendous potentialities. They continually found that Southern deficiencies could be overcome by Northern energy and enterprise. Perhaps the conclusion can be drawn that the Yanks from Pennsylvania, developed a singular view of the Old Dominion—born of ignorance, nurtured by years of sectional controversy.[124]

Expressions of opinion concerning the Southern people were also grist for the soldiers' letters. The privileged class had abandoned their plantations east of Richmond prior to the arrival of the Army of the Potomac. Consequently the plain folk, who comprised the overwhelming majority of the population, received infrequent, but at times disparaging, comment in diary entries and letters written from camp. One observer noted the following about poor whites: "All the white men capable of bearing arms, and every able-bodied negro, had been swept along by the rebel army in its retreat, and none but women and children and aged negroes were now left along the route. At every house the alarmed white people threw out the white flag in token of submission, as though their protection from injury depended upon this symbol of peace."[125] Another soldier simply stated, "But very few white person were to be seen."[126] Private McGlenn of the 96th Pennsylvania remarked that "the farmers left all behind them … to the care of … the negroes.

You could scarcely see a white man here. They are all gone in the Rebel army."[127] It was the common folk of Virginia whom the Pennsylvania Yanks observed; and hence the Bluecoats developed a distorted view of life in Virginia. The absence of Unionist contact with the plantation class inevitably led to an incomplete picture of the social culture and inhabitants of Dixie Land.

For the first two weeks of June the Pennsylvanians divided their time between picket duty and building corduroy roads across the swollen Chickahominy bottoms. During this time, McClellan continually informed the Washington authorities of his difficulties as he planned his final assault on Richmond.[128] While McClellan completed his plans, Franklin's corps crossed the Chickahominy and went into camp near Garnett's Farm. One Bluecoat remarked that they were encamped "so close to the enemy's lines that

Adj. Mathias E. Richards. Served as adjutant of the 96th Pennsylvania Volunteers until promoted A.D.C. to Gen. Bartlett June 14, 1862. Mustered out with regiment October 21, 1864 (collection of James F. Haas, United States Army Heritage and Education Center).

when on picket, in the still morning, we could hear roll-call in their camp."[129] Lewis Luckenbill scribbled in his pocket diary, "we can see the Rebels quite plain from our camp. We can see there Pickets."[130] Adjutant Richards informed his father that "our pickets are in speaking distance almost along the whole line, and of course in easy musket range, but do not fire at each other. I must say we have rather gentlemanly secesh opposite to us, who carry on the war according to Hoyle and not as savages as they do in some other places."[131]

In fact, throughout most of June, the war along the Chickahominy River was a gentleman's affair. Neither the Army of the Potomac nor the Army of Northern Virginia mounted an operation to disrupt the status quo. For more than three weeks after the Battle of Fair Oaks, the armies watched each other, engaged in dialogue while on picket duty and prepared for the next battle which many of the soldiers believed would decide the fate of the Confederacy. Occasionally camp life was sometimes punctuated by a squad of rebel sharpshooters or Confederate artillery fire.[132] In his diary, on June 21, Lewis Luckenbill described his experience coming under fire from Secessionist artillery. "When the rebels commenced shelling the camp their first shell went into the camp, but did not burst. The second went right over our heads and into the ground the other side of us. The 3rd one came the same direction and burst 10 paces the other side of us and took two pine trees smack off. None of us were hurt because of us lying flat on the ground."[133] These episodes were reminders that the war, while quiescent for most of the month, was not far from their camp. Near the end of the month, however, General McClellan informed Secretary of War Stanton that "all things very quiet on this bank of the Chickahominy. I would prefer more noise."[134] The calm, which characterized the first three weeks of June along the Chickahominy, was about to be shattered. McClellan's Army of the Potomac was about to be swept from the Chickahominy by a Confederate tidal wave. By the end of the month, Robert E. Lee's Army of Northern Virginia would successfully drive McClellan and his Bluecoats from the gates of Richmond and push the Army of the Potomac back to the banks of the James River.[50]

While McClellan completed his preparations, the soldiers of the 96th Pennsylvania readied themselves for the climactic campaign. A crucial factor in combat readiness was the physical health of the rank and file. Throughout the recent winter at Camp Northumberland, while the other three regiments in the brigade suffered significant health issues, the 96th Pennsylvania avoided overcrowding at the regimental hospital tent. During the methodical movement of the Army of the Potomac toward Richmond, while many Bluecoats contracted the "Chickahominy fever," the Schuylkill County volunteers continued to exhibit robust health. During the third week of June, Major Martin made the following statement: "Last Fall and Winter while we were permanently encamped near Alexandria we were the largest Regiment [in] Franklin's whole Division and our sick list was smaller than that of any other."[135] In late May, Erasmus Reed reported, "There are not very many sick in our Regiment."[136] Actually, many of the soldiers disregarded minor maladies, preferring to carry out their assigned duties. In their letters and diaries of late spring, they stated emphatically that they preferred to remain on picket duty with their comrades rather than spend time receiving rest and medical treatment in the hospital. At the end of the third week of June, the 96th Pennsylvania Mustered slightly more than 800 soldiers ready for duty.[137]

Along with enjoying good health, the volunteers of the 96th Pennsylvania were eager to confront the Confederates in combat. Beginning at Camp Northumberland and continuing through the advance of the Army of the Potomac to the outskirts of Richmond, morale continued to grow. Throughout the spring campaign, the letters home expressed confidence in their commanders and in their cause. In a letter to his brother, Adjutant Richards proclaimed that the soldiers of Franklin's "Division idolize McClellan, and he has the confidence of the men—blind and unreserved—McClellan has only to say the word and they will crawl into the muzzles of the enemy's artillery."[138] Major Martin informed his family members that he had "every confidence in McClellan and so has every man under his command; no one complains, every one waits till he is ready, when he says the word no man will hesitate."[139] John Madison of Company A in a missive to

Pvt. John Madison, Company A. Died at Harrison's Landing, Virginia, July 23, 1862 (courtesy Carl Madison).

his family boasted that he "saw a rebel prisoner ... that was taken yesterday. He looked heard for they have poor clothing to ware.... They think that they can whip us which I think they can not for they do not stand and fight for they know that they are whipped.... I think in about a month it will be right again so we must trust to one that is mighty to save and strong to deliver. So in God is our trust and union is our motto. So connker we must for our caus it is just and vicketery is ours."[140]

Although June was filled with a host of military assignments, such as picket duty, at times performed in unrelenting rain, building roads and constructing bridges, some soldiers also engaged in activities that diverted their attention from the business of war.[141] The most interesting adventure, and perhaps the most exciting of their careers, involved Lieutenant Colonel Frick and Major Martin. While the two officers were riding to find acquaintances in other Pennsylvania regiments, they stumbled upon Professor Thaddeus Lowe, referred to by Major Martin as the "Balloon man." According to Martin, Lowe was descending after conducting an observation of the Confederate position. "Col. F[rick] immediately dropped a hint to the Prof.," related Martin in a letter to his family, "which he *immediately* took and in less than a jiffy the Col. and I were in the Basket and on our way upwards. We were *let up* between eight hundred and a thousand feet. Col. F. had his glass and with it we saw the whole of Richmond and acres of Rebel camps. I consider it one of the greatest adventures of my life. Would not have missed it for a fortune."[142] The view of the sprawling Confederate camps, which highlighted the balloon adventure for Frick and Martin, also served notice that the Army of Northern Virginia stood ready to thwart the Bluecoats in their quest to seize Richmond. An enemy army in their front, and the nearby Fair Oaks battlefield in their rear, visited by many members of the 96th Pennsylvania, served as visible signs that that the war along the Chickahominy was beginning to build rather than subside. Adjutant Richards, in discussion with Colonel Cake, opined that the pair "were struck with the circumstance that we have both been in this war nearly a year ... and neither of us has yet seen an armed rebel."[143] Unknown to both officers, and to the soldiers of the 96th Pennsylvania, the relative calm which had characterized the war along the Chickahominy for the first three weeks of June was about to change.

IV

"The enemy … fought like devils"

Finally, on June 25, McClellan pushed forward elements of Brig. Gen. Samuel Heintzelman's III Corps, posted on the left of his line, toward the Confederates. His objective was the seizure of Old Tavern, situated on high ground along the Nine Mile Road, a mile and a half in advance of the existing Federal lines. The army commander sought to plant his siege artillery upon the high ground, breaching the enemy's defenses and clearing the road to Richmond for his infantry. A mild engagement in the vicinity of Oak Grove, however, failed to alter the lines east of Richmond.[1] By nightfall the Blue-coats of the 96th Pennsylvania took their ease in Camp Bland, named for the regimental surgeon, located near the Fair Oaks battlefield. Some of the soldiers lolled about the freshly dug gun emplacements or under the trees still standing in the area. Other members of the regiment took the opportunity to pen a letter or scribble an entry in their diary. Major Martin, like many of his comrades, was confident that the Bluecoats would "obtain possession of Richmond with less loss of life than has been sustained in any of the skirmishes that have taken place in advancing thus far upon the City."[2] Sergeant Boland and Private McGlenn believed that they would each write their next letter from Richmond. They believed, too, that "the great battle may come off at any time."[3] Neither soldier knew that the battle for Richmond would begin the next day. It would be the Confederates, however, and not the Unionists, seizing the initiative.

That night, while the Army of the Potomac rested, Robert E. Lee, now the Confederate commander, finished his plans to launch a bold counterattack against McClellan's army. In a postwar memoir, 2nd Lt. John Saylor of Company A recalled that the rival bands of both sides filled the June night with patriotic melodies. "No sooner had the Johnnies sent the challenge of 'Dixie,' than all the Yankee bands gave them a taste of 'Hail Columbia,' and the 'Star Spangled Banner,' in which every northern soldier within hearing, joined the full power of his lungs, almost drowning the brass instruments. It was like an anthem sung by many thousand voices. Both sides played until long after dark, then, thinking of the sadder music set for the stage tomorrow, they laid aside the bugle and took up the gun."[4]

The next day, late in the afternoon, the volunteers from Schuylkill County became aware that a "fearful engagement" was raging on the Federal right flank, two or three miles off in the distance along Beaver Dam Creek. The Pennsylvanians were told "the rebels fell upon our lines like a thunderbolt; that our men stood the shock nobly; that ultimately our boys charged, drove the rebs over the river, and put them to perfect route."[5] By nightfall, after the guns along Beaver Dam Creek fell silent, the soldiers on both sides went back to their respective camps fully expecting to renew hostilities the next day.

Lewis Luckenbill noted in his pocket diary, "They kept the fight up until 8 o'clock at night. After the firing ceased we heard great cheering by the rebels. Then our fellows commenced to cheer. We [also] heard the rebel bands playing."[6] Morale was exceptionally high that evening throughout the camps of the Army of the Potomac. The soldiers were confident that within a short time they would enter Richmond and end the war. One soldier recalled the mood of the volunteers: "Bands played, joy seemed to almost illuminate the night.... *Richmond was to be ours*."[7] Reverend Colt, the regimental chaplain recalled, "The regimental bands all along our lines, for more than an hour were discoursing national and favorite airs, and the midnight hours were winged with gladness pervading the whole army."[8] While many of the Bluecoats relaxed and rested that evening, enjoying the regimental bands, most of the volunteers comprising the 96th Pennsylvania spent the night on picket duty. One soldier later informed Colt that their picket line was in such close proximity to the Confederate camps that they could "plainly discern *negroes* doing duty in the rebel lines."[9] In addition, they could "distinguish many of the names called off during their evening roll call."[10] The next day they would hear the rebel yell and the ringing noise of the Confederate artillery. The calm that characterized the evening of June 26 would turn to chaos the next day.

During the night, while many of the soldiers rested from the events which had unfolded along Beaver Dam Creek, a contingent of the 96th Pennsylvania was hard at work. McClellan, fearing an attack from John B. Magruder's command and Benjamin Huger's division against his left flank, ordered entrenched positions to be prepared along the south side of the Chickahominy. Subsequently, a detail of 350 men from the 96th Pennsylvania, along with a like detail from the 7th Maine, under command of Lieutenant Colonel Frick, advanced in the direction of Old Tavern, where the soldiers erected a three-fronted redoubt near the enemy's line.[11] According to an eyewitness, "The work was to be done with great secrecy.... Our farthest advanced pickets were ... on the crest of the hill and the rebel advanced posts were in the bottom."[12] Erasmus Reed, with some measure of bravado, stated that the soldiers "worked all night, digging a long entrenchment ... under the very nose of the rebel pickets."[13] Relieving the detail from the 7th Maine near midnight, the Schuylkill Countians labored three and a half hours completing the redoubt some four hundred yards in length. After finishing their work, the Bluecoats garrisoned the earthwork until the first streaks of gray light enabled the soldiers to discern the proximity of the Secessionists. A correspondent for the Philadelphia *Press* quipped that "for five hours and a half, in the very face of the enemy and within a hundred yards of his pickets, these six hundred men handled their picks and shovels and spades, as they were wont to do in potato digging at home."[14] Another Yankee correspondent recalled seeing "squads of rebels ... gazing in astonishment at this second Bunker Hill bristling with Yankee bayonets."[15]

At early dawn the Pennsylvanians, along with the Maine men, retired, unassailed, to their old camp in the vicinity of Strong Courtney's House. A number of the soldiers in the 96th, exhausted from digging the redoubt at Old Tavern, had time in camp only for a cup of coffee. At 7 o'clock, the regiment, along with the rest of Bartlett's brigade, was ordered to move up the right bank of the Chickahominy to the vicinity of Duane's Bridge. The soldiers received light marching orders, two days' cooked rations and knapsacks. According to Lieutenant Colonel Frick the regiment initially received orders to cross the Chickahominy at Duane's Bridge but the order was countermanded.[16] At noon, the Union and Confederate artillery erupted, the Yankee gunners along the Chickahominy exchanging fire with a rebel battery posted near Dr. Gaines' house. Shortly after the artillery barrage commenced, Frick, Adjutant Richards and Dr. Bland, crossed Duane's bridge on horseback and rode toward the Confederate battery. According to Lieutenant Colonel Frick, the Confederate battery commander, an "audacious rebel," upon spotting the Yankees, "discourteously prevented us … the pleasure from … witnessing the display of fireworks before us."[17] Within moments, Frick's party was spattered by mud from the Chickahominy swamp as the artillery fire landed within feet of the three Yankees. Quickly they withdrew to the safety of the south side of the river.

Throughout the afternoon, the Pennsylvanians endured the accurate artillery fire from the Confederate batteries on the north side of the Chickahominy. Finally, at 3 o'clock, a detail from the 96th and the 3rd Vermont was ordered to destroy Duane's Bridge.[18] Shortly afterwards, Bartlett's brigade, along with Slocum's entire division, was ordered by General Franklin to cross the Chickahominy at Woodbury's Bridge and report to General Porter for further instructions. In his after action report, Colonel Bartlett recalled that he was told by General Slocum to "hasten to the assistance of General Porter's forces, who were at the time being severely pressed." Erasmus Reed, writing after the battle, recalled that once the 96th received the order to cross the Chickahominy that the Schuylkill Countians "knew what was coming."[19]

Long before dawn on June 27, McClellan determined that General Porter and the V Corps would hold the bridges spanning the Chickahominy while he superintended the Army of the Potomac's change of base to the James River. General Lee, however, was determined to turn the right flank of the Union army. The Confederate commander recognized that he held the initiative after the encounter at Beaver Dam Creek. A bold attack on June 27, conducted while the Army of the Potomac was most vulnerable, might yield decisive results. Lee intended to force Porter's corps beyond the ridge overlooking Beaver Dam Creek, which the Yankees were holding. About noon, Ambrose Powell Hill sent the South Carolinians of Maxcy Gregg's brigade forward, unsupported, and engaged the Federals in a short fire-fight near Gaines' Mill. After the initial assault, the Federals withdrew to a new line behind Boatswain's Swamp. McClellan, with his engineer's skill, selected the position along the front by boggy Boatswain Swamp. The new position was stronger than the Union line of the previous day at Beaver Dam Creek. McClellan had found a natural fortress, ready-made for the Unionists.[20]

By mid-afternoon the battle was raging up and down the tangled slopes and marshes of Boatswain's Swamp. While the V Corps dug in to prepare for the impending attack, Lee's forces probed the Union line to develop potentially weak points along Porter's line. Early in the afternoon, Confederate artillery and infantry exploited the weakest part of Porter's position, the far right flank held by the United States Regular division commanded by Gen. George Sykes. While the Confederates attempted to outflank the Unionists, Porter and Sykes sought to strengthen this sector of the line with artillery to support the two brigades of Regulars deployed in the farm fields near the McGhee house.[21] A correspondent for the New York Times described the early afternoon action where Sykes' Regulars were deployed.

> About 10 o'clock the pickets on our right were driven back from the woods skirting the field, and
> shortly afterward those stationed on the Cross Roads toward the Coal Harbor road, were also
> driven in. The enemy were silently creeping up to the right. Simultaneously he made his appear-

ance in a green field, directly in front, drawn up in line of battle, and in five minutes their batteries opened on our lines with shell.... The whi-z-z of Minie bullets, and scream of shell and shot from a dozen different directions now showed that the work had begun in earnest.... By 2 o'clock, the woods covering the hill were thronged by the two contending armies.... It was apparent that the rebels were constantly bringing fresh troops upon the field, and there was literally no end to their number.[22]

At 2 p.m., Porter observed that the Union artillery, sent to support General Sykes, was not stopping the Confederate advance on the far right flank. Infantry support in that threatened sector was desperately needed. Recognizing the crisis, Porter signaled McClellan's headquarters, "If you can send Slocum over please do so."[23]

Alerted that a Confederate assault was about to fall on Porter's beleaguered divisions, McClellan ordered Slocum's Bluecoats to move to the north side in support of the embattled V Corps veterans. Leaving the far right of the Union line, anchored by a formidable earthwork known as Fort Davidson, shortly after 2 o'clock "under a galling fire," the command reformed in a nearby woods, from which, preceded by Newton's and Taylor's commands, Bartlett's brigade crossed to the north side via the Woodbury-Alexander Bridge.[24] In many of the after-action reports, and in other contemporary accounts, there is considerable confusion identifying the bridge use by Slocum's division. An assessment of the existing evidence indicates that the soldiers used the Woodbury-Alexander bridge downstream from the Duane's and Woodbury bridges.[25] After crossing to the north side, Slocum ordered Newton's brigade to the support of McCall's division, which was wavering under the weight of a Confederate assault. Taylor's brigade was instructed to move to the left of the Union line, where they were to support Morell's division. While Slocum assigned Generals Taylor's and Newton's brigades to threatened sectors of Porter's line, Bartlett's brigade was still marching across the river and starting to ascend the hill leading to the plateau where the battle was beginning to develop into a significant engagement.

Bartlett's brigade reached the high ground above the Chickahominy shortly after 3 o'clock.[26] As the soldiers crested the hill, the Schuylkill Countians saw the first ghastly sights of a Civil War battle. According to Lieutenant Saylor, "Soon we reached the house and grounds of Dr. Gaine's and here the sight that met us was most appalling. The ground, in and around the house, was literally covered with wounded, and a long string of stretchers, coming up from where the battle raged, all filled with wounded, dying, and dead!"[27] The vivid scene was still fresh in Saylor's memory when he wrote his memoir many years after the war: "We saw the Doctors with knives and bandages, and the cries of the suffering boys followed us.... We filed past the dreadful scene..., with bowed heads looking neither to the right or left, but wishing we were well out of it."[28] Erasmus Reed also described the gruesome scene which greeted the Pennsylvanians. "The first sight that drew our attention was the bringing of wounded out of the field, some shot in the head, others in the legs and arms, and wounds of every description."[29] Upon reaching the battlefield an officer of Porter's staff instructed Slocum to deploy Taylor's and Newton's brigades but did not deliver orders to the divisional commander concerning Bartlett's brigade. Subsequently, Slocum directed Bartlett to position his brigade on the extreme left of the line, "near the new road leading through the valley from Doctor Gaines' house to Alexander Bridge."[30] About four o'clock, Bartlett moved his command to support General Butterfield's brigade, which appeared to be in danger from a concerted Confederate attack upon the Union left flank.

Subsequently, an aide-de-camp of Porter ordered Bartlett to report with his brigade to the extreme right of the Union position where Sykes and his gallant United States Regulars were struggling to hold that end of the line. At approximately 4:30 p.m., Bartlett reoriented his brigade and set the soldiers in motion across the field to find Sykes.[31] While conducting this dangerous flank march, at the double quick, several soldiers of the 96th were wounded as the long column presented a splendid target for Confederate artillery. One veteran recalled that the flank march was made "under a hot fire of iron and lead that pitched into [our] ranks right and left, for more than two-thirds of the entire distance."[32] An officer in Company H stated that the regiment "passed to the extreme right under a galling fire, in which four of our men were wounded."[33] Exhausted from the long summer day under arms and the frightening trek across the field, Colonel Cake sought to shelter and rest his command before the Schuylkill Countians were ordered into combat.[34] At this point, many of the soldiers were in need of water, fatigued from the march made under the stress of grape and canister fire, and their exposure to the elements. Clement Potts of Company A volunteered to fill the canteens of his comrades.[35] While many of the soldiers sought refuge from the Confederate artillery missiles, an officer in Company H reported that "the balls flew all around, tearing up the ground at my feet. Indeed, I was so tired that I felt not the least danger."[36] Reaching the far right flank of the Union line, Bartlett issued orders to shelter the Bluecoats in a ravine where the men could rest and reorganize before being called forward by General Sykes.

Utilizing the sloping terrain to his advantage, Bartlett sheltered his brigade and Captain Porter's Battery A, 1st Massachusetts Artillery, from the incessant Confederate rifle and artillery fire.[37] According to an officer in Company H, the 96th "rested in a ravine, while a perfect shower of shot, shell and balls passed over our heads. It was intensely hot and dusty, and the fatigue of the men rendered this rest necessary."[38] Meanwhile, Colonel Cake observed that the Confederate artillery was trained on the farm lane leading down the center of the ravine. Although Cake tried to shield his regiment from the deadly artillery rounds, the rank and file suddenly sent up a tremendous cheer attracting the attention of the Confederate gunners. Within moments, "a shower of spherical case ... [tore through] the Brigade, the 96th occupying nearly the whole of a section of a small valley that was enfiladed by the enemy's battery a shell fell into the closed masses of the Regiment, but thank God! It did not explode, but bounding from the ground, flew hissing down the ravine."[39] Subsequently, recognizing that his regiment was vulnerable to enfilading fire, Cake reformed the 96th in double columns, and massed his command closely behind the 16th New York Volunteers, near the crest of the hill, at the head of the brigade.[40] At 5 o'clock, as the Regulars slowly gave ground to the oncoming Graycoats, General Sykes ordered Bartlett to bring his brigade forward. As Bartlett prepared to advance in support of the Regulars, "who were unable longer to withstand the fierce attacks and withering fire of the enemy," the 96th Pennsylvania continued to endure the murderous artillery fire.[41] According to Erasmus Reed, the cannon balls whizzed, "within a few feet of our heads." As Reed recalled, "There was a perfect rain of iron balls. Then we knew we were in the fight."[42]

During the afternoon, while Bartlett's brigade rested from the rigors of moving into position on the Union right, the Confederates developed a tactical plan to sweep Sykes's division from the field and crush the right flank of Porter's line. Confederate Gen. Daniel Harvey Hill, commanding five brigades on the left flank of the Graycoat line, ordered an assault against Sykes's Regulars. Determined to achieve a signal success, Harvey Hill sent forward the five regiment Alabama brigade commanded by Robert Rodes and a brigade of North Carolinians under Samuel Garland. Rodes's brigade struggled through the swampy ground and became fragmented as the Alabamians moved forward. Garland's brigade, however, fared much better as the Tarheels passed through a cornfield before forming for a final push against the Union troops posted along the crest of a hill in front of the McGhee farm house. As Hill's infantry closed on the Unionists, the North Carolina regiments inclined toward the artillery pieces of Lt. Horace Hayden's guns, part of Capt. John Edwards's 3rd U.S. Artillery. Only one regiment, the untested 20th North Carolina with 850 Tarheels under the command of Col. Alfred Iverson, found the courage to surge forward and capture the two artillery pieces.[43]

In the struggle for Hayden's artillery, the 20th North Carolina suffered heavy casualties. The Tarheel regiment lost 70 killed, 202 wounded and several others who were taken prisoner in the action. Colonel Iverson was seriously wounded and Lt. Col. Franklin Faison was killed, while rejoicing in the Confederate triumph. Nevertheless, according to Major Toon of the 20th North Carolina "the charge was completely successful—the enemy were driven off and the battle flag of the regiment waved over their guns. One of these was turned on the retreating columns."[44] During the battle, according to Captain Edwards, Lieutenant Hayden "threw double rounds of canister" into the ranks of the oncoming Tarheels.[45] Despite the gallantry displayed by the gunners of Hayden's section of the battery, the North Carolinians could not be stopped. Thomas Evans, serving in the 12th United States Infantry, described the desperate encounter for the artillery pieces near the McGhee house. "The enemy attempt[ed] to cross the road [and] take this battery in rear, but two regiments have reformed to the right of the house and hold them in check. Our artillerymen are straining every nerve to keep back the enemy columns, who are rushing on in frantic masses and trying to sweep the whole crest."[46] At this moment, Sergeant Reed of the 14th United States Infantry "saw what I took to be gray coats coming on the right of the line.... I ran back and gave the alarm of our right being turned."[47] Informed of the danger, and recognizing the threat to his right flank, General Sykes rode to Colonel Bartlett and ordered him to reinforce the exhausted brigade of Buchanan's Regulars holding perilously to their position near the McGhee farm house.[48]

At 5 o'clock, upon receiving the order from Sykes to advance his brigade, Bartlett, ordered Col. Joseph Howland, commanding the 16th New York Volunteers, to move his regiment forward. According to Bartlett, the New Yorkers, "with the calmness and precision of veteran soldiers," formed in lines of battle, gave three cheers long and loud, and rushed at the double quick to support the wavering Federal line.[49] Howland's regiment, sporting their new bright yellow straw hats—a gift from Colonel Howland given in honor of his wife—advanced 150 yards where they halted behind a rail fence.[50] Lieutenant Charles Bentley of Company K described the exciting assault in a letter written shortly after the engagement. "We marched forward in line of battle over the hill. We then changed front forward on first company, and then we changed by the right flank, halted, fronted and dressed. [We] were ordered up and to charge bayonets upon the enemy double-quick, which was done splendidly, the men in perfect line, amidst a shower of bullets. We drove the enemy out of their position in the road, [and] captured two artillery pieces."[51] The 16th New York continued to press forward and successfully drove off the 20th North Carolina. Realizing that Howland's regiment would need to be reinforced if

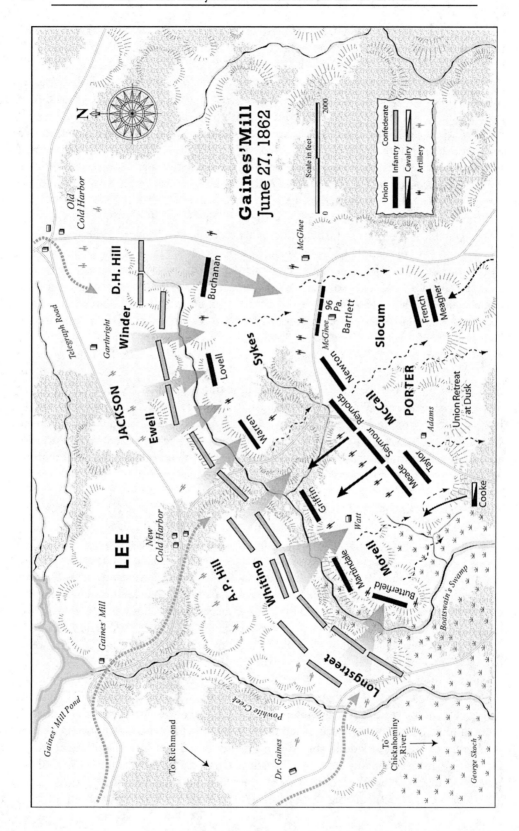

Gaines' Mill
June 27, 1862

they were to hold their position, Bartlett ordered the 96th Pennsylvania forward to support the beleaguered New Yorkers.

After positioning the 16th New York, Bartlett returned to the ravine, where his other three regiments awaited orders. The 96th Pennsylvania occupied the position vacated by the New York men and were the next regiment in line. Under heavy musketry and artillery fire, Bartlett ordered Colonel Cake to deploy his regiment from column into line of battle and move forward to support the 16th New York. The murderous fire sweeping across the plain, however, rendered it impossible for the gallant colonel, aided by Lieutenant Colonel Frick and Major Martin, to align the soldiers for battle. In his official report Bartlett noted that the "noble exertions" of Cake and his staff "were not in many instances seconded by some of the line officers, who lacked that impulsive enthusiasm and cool determination required of them under such trying circumstances."[52] Consequently, Bartlett was forced to lead forward the third regiment in line, the 5th Maine, to support the 16th New York. With a battle shout the Maine men rose up in unison and advanced across the field amidst "a storm of iron and leaden hail."[53] Next the 27th New York Volunteers, Lieutenant Colonel Alexander D. Adams commanding, were ordered to the front. After giving three cheers, they too, rushed forward at the double quick toward the enemy. Bartlett, at last confident that his battle line was firmly established, returned to the ravine and ordered the 96th Pennsylvania into the fight.

In the process of changing front forward, an officer in Company H later recalled that the 96th "received a terrible fire which fortunately, mostly passed over our heads."[54] Amidst a shower of ball and bullets, Cake calmly dressed his lines.[55] Colonel Bartlett, in person, directed Cake to advance at double-quick and move the 96th into line between the 5th Maine and the 16th New York.[56] In his report, Bartlett vividly described the moment that the Pennsylvanians formed their line of battle and advanced toward the Confederates "The Ninety-sixth Pennsylvania Volunteers being in line and eager for the fight, I ordered them to the front, and most nobly now did they respond to the command. No officer or man faltered, and their solid unwavering line pressed forward to their position and completed the front."[57] Just before Cake issued the command forward, an officer in Company H recalled that the regiment's "line was formed as straight as at any dress parade we ever had."[58] Amidst the chaos of battle, Lieutenant Saylor also remembered the moment as the soldiers prepared to advance against the Graycoats. "We formed in line of battle on the Plain above us not hurriedly, but as though we were forming for Dress Parade."[59]

Commanding nearly 800 volunteers, Cake, twenty yards in front of the regiment on horseback, waved his hand and ordered the Pennsylvanians "Forward! Double quick!"[60] As the regiment surged forward 1st Lt. Ernest Ellrich was shot through the brain while gallantly encouraging his comrades in Company B to press forward.[61] As the regiment advanced, Erasmus Reed described his reaction to the artillery and small arms fire which the soldiers encountered. "About this time we were ordered up and went on top of the hill. My God, but there the bullets flew, a perfect rain of them."[62] With the determination of veterans, the Pennsylvanians advanced across the open ground to join the desperate fire fight developing around the McGhee farm house.

Advancing toward the Secessionists, Cake later stated, "The charge across the field was made in fine style, the men coming up square, cheering as they advanced. The firing was heavy in front, a shower of lead and iron falling around us."[63] A mounted officer of one of the U.S. Regular regiments described the charge of the 96th as one of the most magnificent moments of the action.[64] As the Pennsylvanians pressed forward, Lieutenant Saylor later wrote that Confederate "cannon were raking the field like a sweeping tornado!"[65] As the regiment surged across the field the soldiers involuntarily "bent forward their heads as they breasted the terrible torrent of death-dealing missiles, but not one wavered or hesitated."[66] Advancing against the Confederates, Cake steadfastly guided the men toward the right of the line established by Bartlett. As the Pennsylvanians charged across the field, one eyewitness related the following account of Cake's bravery and leadership:

> From the beginning of the fight the colonel was grand, cool, thoughtful; [and] careful of his men. "Listen to the bullets," said [one Schuylkill Countian]. "What of that," [replied another]. "Look! They don't hit the Colonel!" "That's so," [responded the latter] and they [both] went in.[67]

Near the McGhee house, Cake halted his regiment and ordered the men to lie down behind a rail fence. Lewis Luckenbill noted in his diary, "After we got to the fence the balls coming down on us like hail, the fighting was kept up till dark … [when] we had to fall back to the brow of the hill."[68] As soon as the Schuylkill Countians went to ground, a rattling volley passed harmlessly over the heads of the prone soldiers. At this point,

1st Lt. Ernest T. Ellrich, Company B. Killed in action at Gaines' Mill, Virginia, June 27, 1862 (Ronn Palm collection).

during a momentary lull, the smoke lifted, revealing the enemy's line, a mere one hundred yards in front of the Pennsylvanians. John Saylor recalled the scene: "Massed behind a broken down rail fence lying flat on the ground, with the impossible protection of a rail or two, what looked like a long gray serpent trailing across the field about fifty yards in front of us spitting fire at every joint."[69] Exhibiting extraordinary personal courage, Cake, amidst a scathing fire rode quickly to the right flank of the regiment to determine the best course of action in this mounting emergency.[70]

Sensing the crisis developing in front of him, Cake ordered the soldiers to stand and deliver a volley against the oncoming Graybacks. James Hollister, in Company A, simply recounted, "The Col. at last told us to get on our feet and pitch in."[71] Another Pennsylvanian related that "the men rose promptly, and delivered it so efficiently as to silence the rebels for a short time."[72] The engagement around the McGhee house intensified. Private Hollister later described the action in a letter published in the

Miners' Journal. "Our company was under a cross fire for the whole time we were in. We lost 24 killed, wounded and missing. I never felt better in my life than when standing up there and firing at the rebels. I hope that every one of the 41 cartridges I fired took effect. We could only see the rebels once in a while, for the smoke, but they were only 150 yards off."[73] According to Cake's official report, the volley fired by the 96th Pennsylvania brought a brief respite in the action.[74]

As the Pennsylvanians fought on bravely, the regimental commanders realized that the Confederates were reorganizing for a final push to break the position held by Bartlett's brigade. In his after-action report, Bartlett recalled that "the enemy now hurled fresh troops in double numbers against my line, directing his heaviest fire upon my left, and the Twenty-seventh New York Volunteers and Fifth Maine staggered back under the fearful fire."[75] Both of these regiments, composed of veterans of the great summer battle at Bull Run, encountered the furious assault of the 5th and 26th Alabama against the embattled left of Bartlett's line. A rifleman of the 5th Alabama described the exhilarating charge in a letter to the Greensboro *Beacon*. "The word 'Forward!' was given, and with a ringing cheer our men rushed onward … the regulars retreating before them, and both sides loading and firing as they hurried on. The enemy wheeled other regiments so as to give us a flanking fire from two directions from infantry and artillery, and the field was swept with a hailstorm of shot, shell, grape, canister and bullets…. After scattering the regulars, the 5th and 26th dashed across a public road in their front, routed another regiment drawn up there to receive them, and pushed against the others. The 5th charged a battery of cannon, whose artillerists fled before the bayonets reached them, and just before as the guns fell into the hands of our men, a Federal regiment actually charged them."[76] The New Yorkers and Maine men met the two Alabama regiments head on resulting in a deadly, destructive exchange of rifle fire.

Upon reaching the left flank of his regiment, posted near some of the McGhee farm buildings, Cake "found about 50 officers and men, who assured me that their several regiments were posted directly in front of us."[77] Orlando Dunning, serving with the 5th Maine, described the scene: "Looking toward the right we could see the 16th N. Y. and the 96th Pa. already engaged, so [we] commenced firing into the smoke in our front, where the enemy were posted. In a few moments word was passed along the line from one to the other, for we could hear no orders for the horrid din, to cease firing, that we were firing into our own men."[78] Recognizing that the left wing of the 16th New York had possibly advanced beyond the right of the 96th Pennsylvania, and suffered from friendly fire, Cake sought to investigate the situation. Riding to the right flank of the 96th Pennsylvania, Cake noticed a gap of fifty feet between his regiment and the 16th New York. From his vantage point, Cake also "discovered the enemy fearfully close, and momentarily expected to be charged." Under the impression that the Confederates in his front were preparing to mount a final assault, Cake dispatched a messenger to Bartlett for further orders. He then returned to the center of the 96th and cautioned his officers to insure that the rifles of at least one rank were loaded should the Confederates attempt a sudden advance.[79]

As Cake awaited orders from Bartlett, the 96th continued to exchange rifle fire with the Graycoats. Unexpectedly, Major Joel Seaver of the 16th New York appeared and informed Cake that he was seeking Colonel Bartlett. Seaver further advised Cake that the 16th New York had sustained heavy casualties, that their guns were dirty and therefore misfiring, and the regiment was nearly out of ammunition.[80] Unable to communicate directly with Bartlett, therefore, Seaver urged Colonel Cake to push his right wing to join the left of the beleaguered New Yorkers. Initially, Cake hesitated to comply with Seaver's desperate plea for assistance. Upon receiving a second request, Cake relented and shifted his regiment to support the exhausted men of the 16th New York. According to Cake, Seaver "strenuously urged it, begging me for the 'love of God' to close in on their left."[81] Shortly after 7 p.m., Colonel Howland of the 16th New York rode to the center of the 96th's line in order to confer with Cake. The New Yorker advised Cake that his soldiers were in need of ammunition. After further discussion, the two regimental commanders agreed to maintain their respective positions and withdraw from the battlefield under the cover of darkness. Although Confederate rifle fire abated in their immediate front, Cake reported that "an ugly cross-fire of round shot and musketry … cut us obliquely from the right."[82] From that moment until darkness cloaked the battlefield, the Schuylkill Countians continually fired toward the enemy, the men emptying their cartridge boxes of sixty rounds.[83] Out of ammunition, with the Confederates pushing around the left flank of the 27th New York, Bartlett personally superintended the withdrawal of his brigade from the battlefield.[84]

The chaos and confusion which swirled around the McGhee mansion left a ghastly scene of death and destruction to the survivors of the fight. An observant soldier in the 27th New York recorded a detailed word picture of the carnage for his readers at home.

> The yards were strewn with the dead, while the house and every out-building was crowded with the wounded of both parties. Some who received their death wounds crawled under the buildings for safety, and in their agony had torn off their clothing and lay almost naked in their gore.

But the scene beyond the house beggard all description.

> Crowds of the enemy's wounded lay piled under every tree and bush, where they had crawled to escape the hot rays of the sun, and now the poor fellows lay between the firing of the opposing forces, flinging and tossing their arms and legs, begging not to be fired upon. Horses riderless were galloping about or standing over some body, unable to stir from shot wounds, or true to their training in war, standing near their dead masters. It was evident from the beginning that regiments were fighting brigades, and how could men stand such odds? The enemy, too, fought like devils incarnate, but it was under the effects of liquor, for every prisoner taken had his canteen full of the fiery drink.[85]

As darkness cast its shroud over the battlefield, Bartlett ordered his brigade to disengage and retreat from the firing line. The 16th New York withdrew first, followed by the 96th regiment. An officer in Company H recalled that "the men seemed to go reluctantly. When we fell back the enemy advanced beyond the fence we had occupied, evidently with the intention of driving us across the river in confusion."[86] During the withdrawal the 27th New York and the 5th Maine acted as a rear guard. The brigade retreated to the ravine where they had launched their attack earlier in the day. During the retreat the 96th Pennsylvania "came to an about face twice, firing two volleys" at the enemy.[87] Finally, at 8:30 p.m. Bartlett positioned his brigade "in front of the [field] hospital on the second hill from the bridge," forming a final line of battle. In this last position, Lewis Luckenbill reported in his diary that the soldiers "fell back to the brow of the hill, there we made another stand where all [of] us would go down the hill and load and then advance and fire on them. After all of them have left … our company gave them three good heavy volleys. We then fell back to our camp."[88]

For some unexplained reason, however, the Pennsylvanians failed to strictly comply with Bartlett's withdrawal orders. Although Cake reformed the 96th on the crest of the hill above the Chickahominy, he ordered the Pennsylvanians to cross the river to the south side without instructions from Bartlett. There, several officers of the 3rd United States Regulars "were eulogistic in their praises of the Ninety-sixth," according to one witness. The Regulars stated that the 96th "had done nobly ... in this ... [their] ... first general engagement ... [and] ... had established a reputation for coolness and gallantry, which was only accorded to veteran troops." Lieutenant Penrose, embraced Colonel Cake, who was dismounted, "and showered on him and his command a wealth of praise."[89]

After the engagement Colonel Bartlett, also praised Colonel Cake and his Pennsylvanians for their performance in the battle. In the New Yorkers' official report, he stated, "I would particularly mention Colonel Cake, Ninety-sixth Pennsylvania Volunteers, who exhibited rare traits of military excellence. Cool, energetic, fearless, and decided, with the assistance of Lieutenant-Colonel Frick and Major Martin, he has won an enviable name for his regiment, which will always be sustained while the command rests in its present hands."[90] Bartlett, perhaps, expected strong battlefield performances from the two Empire State regiments and the Maine men, seasoned veterans of the battle at Bull Run the previous summer. The good showing of the 96th under fire assured the New Yorker that he did indeed have a fine fighting brigade. Although the Keystone men encountered problems forming their initial line and failed to reform on the hill near the field hospital during the withdrawal, Bartlett was particularly pleased with their combat performance. In addition to Colonel Bartlett, other officers and men in the ranks praised Cake for his courage and leadership. Lieutenant Fernsler of Company H noted in his diary that "Col. Cake behaved most heroic, riding up and down the line while engaged in the fight."[91] Another officer simply stated that "Col. Cake acted with great bravery."[92] But before the rank and file of the Schuylkill County regiment could take a bow for their efforts at Gaines' Mill, there was still hard marching and fighting ahead.

In the aftermath of the battle, the soldiers entered accounts of the engagement in their diaries or wrote letters to their family members in Schuylkill County describing the harrowing experience of combat. In particular, the correspondence of the soldiers of the 96th Pennsylvania reflected several closely related themes. First, the volunteers, described the sensation and dramatic experience of combat. To illustrate the danger they encountered on the battlefield many recounted how close the Confederate artillery and rifle fire had been. John Fernsler wrote that "the balls passed so close to my body, and plenty of them, that I do not wish to have the same show."[93] Clement Potts of Company A noted that "there is not a man in our company who has not a hole in his coat or pants or hat."[94] Other soldiers struggled to understand how any of them survived the deadly encounter near the McGhee farm house. Martin informed his family that "I for one always hooted at the idea of 'Lead + Iron hail' but I saw and heard on that day what I have no longer any curiosity to hear and see."[95] Matt Richards related that "the battle was fought by our Brigade under the fiercest shower of grape and canister crossfire ever poured on a battle field and how anyone escaped is a mystery to me."[96] Finally, each soldier correspondent carefully noted the names of the killed and wounded in their respective companies, after providing a capsule description of the injuries. In addition to describing the traumatic experience of combat and remembering the killed and wounded of the regiment, they also offered evaluations of the regiment's performance in the engagement and critiqued the effectiveness of their commanding officers.

Emerging from the horrific experience at Gaines' Mill, the Pennsylvanians recounted the heroism of their commanding officers and also commented on the regiment's role in the engagement. An officer in Company H offered the following appraisal of his command and the leadership of Cake during the action. "I am proud of the company," wrote the officer, "they fought nobly, and obeyed commands, and kept the best order, and I am sure made many a rebel bite the dust. Col. Cake acted with great bravery; in fact, the whole Regiment, officers and men, behaved nobly."[97] Clement Potts reported that "our regiment fought like tigers and we got a great deal of praise for it from the ... [Colonel Bartlett]."[98] Adjutant Richards opined, to another officer that "the Brigade did nobly, and the 96th covered themselves with glory. It was their first regular battle, but they fought as if they had been in a hundred, and as if fighting was their business."[99] Every member of the 96th Pennsylvania who recorded details and descriptions of their participation in the battle, took enormous pride in stating and emphasizing that the Schuylkill Countians were the last regiment to fire a collective volley and leave the battlefield that evening.[100] Almost immediately, the Pennsylvanians understood that Gaines' Mill was a stinging defeat for the Army of the Potomac. But for the soldiers of the 96th, Gaines' Mill represented a significant achievement in a singular moment of unimagined adversity. On that deadly evening near the McGhee farm house, Colonel Cake forged his reputation as a competent commander of volunteers and the 96th Pennsylvania demonstrated its ability to overcome harrowing combat conditions.

Entering the engagement at Gaines' Mill, the 96th Pennsylvania numbered approximately 800 soldiers ready for duty. By the end of the battle, 13 men were dead, 61 were wounded and 13 were either captured or missing.[101] A preponderance of the casualties was concentrated in Companies A, F and I. It is unclear why Company I sustained two men killed and fifteen wounded. Companies A and F, however, were posted on the extreme right flank of the regiment's line of battle and exposed to a deadly cross-fire during the encounter. Untested, untried yet undaunted, they exceeded expectations in their initial trial by fire. For over one hour the soldiers exchanged rifle fire with their counterparts in gray. Called to action at a pivotal moment in the battle, and deployed at a critical sector on the field, they responded admirably to the chaos and stress experienced in combat. As a result, the Pennsylvanians emerged from the battle, as the other units in Bartlett's brigade did after 1st Bull Run, as veteran volunteers. Cake's successful debut in command, witnessed by many officers and the rank and file of the 96th Pennsylvania, validated him as a rising colonel of volunteers.

Cake's command performance at Gaines' Mill, while not entirely unanticipated, no doubt surprised Colonel Bartlett and other Union officers unfamiliar with the Pennsylvania colonel. Although Cake could draw upon his militia service prior to the war and his tenure as commander of the 25th Pennsylvania in the spring of 1861, those experiences could not adequately prepare him for the combat conditions he encountered at Gaines' Mill. At the outset of the battle, after moving his command out of the ravine, Cake was confronted with the inability of the green Pennsylvania volunteers to adroitly form a tactical line of battle. In his report, Colonel Bartlett stated that "the murderous fire across the plain rendered it almost impossible for their gallant colonel [Cake], aided by Lieutenant Colonel Frick and Major Martin, to form his line of battle."[102] Soon after the 96th Pennsylvania moved forward to support the beleaguered 16th New York, he recognized the fragmented alignment of the 5th Maine on his left flank and moved the Pennsylvanians forward forming a combat line along a fence in front of the McGhee house. While posted along the fence line, the Schuylkill Countians exchanged deadly volleys at short range with the advancing Graybacks. According to an officer, the Pennsylvanians "within forty yards of the enemy's line ... were ordered to lay down and load, and fire."[103] A cease fire order was subsequently issued along the line as it was ascertained that Colonel Howland's regiment, the 16th New York, had surged forward and fell prey to friendly fire from the Pennsylvanians. The chaos of the battlefield, and the smoke limiting visibility, reduced the combat performance of the Pennsylvanians at Gaines' Mill.

For his performance in the battle, Cake received praise from his superiors as well as from his subordinates.[104] Despite his problems getting the Pennsylvanians into the fray and issues associated with the 16th New York, his leadership proved to be more than many expected from an untried commander. A factor which contributed to Cake's success at Gaines' Mill, and the regiment's resolute discharge of its duties, can be attributed to the mission assigned to the Pennsylvanians by Colonel Bartlett. Standing on the defensive, as the regiment did, with very little movement upon the tactical field, as opposed to executing intricate movements, enabled the Schuylkill Countians to stand fast in the face of heavy Confederate pressure. In sum, a static line of battle, with no movement, enabled the soldiers to maintain a tight formation and concentrate on loading and firing their weapons. For Cake, this approach on the field of battle relieved him of possible command and control problems and enabled him to gallantly lead the regiment through its first significant combat experience.

No doubt, too, after the battle Cake was delighted with the splendid performance of his regiment. While many soldiers praised his debut in field command others in Bartlett's brigade wrote derisive comments about him. The historian of the 5th Maine described Cake as a commander "who had before manifested his consummate (?) ability as a military man, by getting his command into tough and needless trying positions."[105] The Bluecoats of the 27th New York referred to the colonel of the 96th Pennsylvania as "Col. John Cake, a jolly fellow of about 200 pounds; whom the boys dubbed 'Johnny Cake.'"[106] And Cyrus Stone of the 16th New York regarded him as "the old Cake that was not half baked."[107] A soldier serving with the 27th New York, however, mentioned in a letter, written in early September 1862, the source of the animosity several regiments in Bartlett's brigade exhibited toward the Schuylkill Countians. "Pennsylvanians do not come up to the *fighting* estimate. There is probably no sheet among army news dealers that, aside from Pennsylvanians, so detested as is the Philadelphia Inquirer, and all on account of its eternally extolling the war like deeds of Pennsylvanians to the exclusion of all others."[108] Perhaps, too, the association of Joel Cook, a correspondent from the Philadelphia *Press*, imbedded with the 96th Pennsylvania during the campaign further alienated them from other officers and soldiers in the brigade. For the commander and men of the 96th Pennsylvania, the Battle of Gaines' Mill was much more than a test of courage for untried volunteers. Their service at Gaines' Mill earned the respect they sought from Bartlett's Bull Run veterans. They emerged with enhanced reputations, forged under fire, as dependable Union soldiers led by a capable regimental commander.

After reaching the south side of the Chickahominy, Cake's regiment, along with Bartlett's brigade, returned to their camps and rested for the night. The following morning the command moved back to its old position near Fort Davidson.[109] During the morning an artillery round from the enemy landed in the vicinity of Colonel Cake's marquee and the regimental hospital. Consequently, Bartlett moved his brigade out of range from the Graycoat missiles. As the Bluecoats moved their camps to elude the barrage, the Yanks speculated about the future of the campaign. Perhaps one foot soldier put it best when he stated, "All seemed shrouded in mystery."[110] In fact, the Young Napoleon was in the process of abandoning his campaign to seize the Confederate capital.[111] Robert E. Lee, on the other hand, was just beginning his offensive, fully intent upon redeeming Richmond.

As the two commanders made preparations to move their respective armies, a brigade of Georgians attacked the far right of the VI Corps line at Goulding's farm. This sudden thrust by the Graycoats interrupted the soldiers of the 96th who had just finished pitching their tents. Henry Keiser of Company G noted in his diary, "We were barely through with our tents when the Rebels opened on us with a battery at short range and made us 'git.'"[112] At 7 a.m. the Schuylkill Countians were sent to the support of Gen. William F. Smith's division and the day proved to be a busy one. The regiment changed positions several times, but most of the time it endured Confederate artillery fire which passed close to their heads and burst all around them. That night, soldiers from the 96th, who had endured artillery fire during the day, were set to work felling trees to obstruct the local roads. Recognizing that his men needed food, Cake sent his adjutant to find the regiment's commissary train which was parked in a grove near McClellan's old head-quarters. An officer recalled this incident, which was characteristic of Cake's leadership. "At nine o'clock Saturday night he took the responsibility of recalling a portion of the [commissary] train ... [and] had three days' meat rations cooked for his men. So they were fed while some [of the] other regiments near us ... sadly lacked [provisions] on our weary marching to the James River. Indeed Colonel Cake was enabled to share [rations] with one of the [other] regiments [of the brigade] that had entirely run out of provisions."[113] Later in the evening of June 28, General Slocum received orders to move his division to Savage's Station. Many in the ranks realized, upon receiving marching orders, that the campaign for Richmond was taking an unforeseen change of direction.[114]

McClellan's change of base, once known to the soldiers, provoked widespread criticism of the Young Napoleon's generalship. In Bartlett's brigade, a New Yorker wryly remarked that "the men had been told in the morning that all this was but the beginning of some great strategic movement on our part, but no one could so far penetrate the design of our General as to ease his mind of the fearful suspense that bore it down.[115] A Sixth Corps veteran recalled the response to McClellan's movement: "It was, for the first time, told them that the army must *retreat* in all haste to the James River! ... Now, they felt that all was lost.... And now the siege of Richmond was to be abandoned, and the men who but two days before had exulted in the glad hope of a speedy entrance into the city, which even now lay just within our grasp, were to turn their backs as *fugitives* [on] their enemies! It was a time of humiliation and sorrow."[116] Some soldiers, however, applauded McClellan for the military skill he displayed in successfully changing the army's line of supply from the York to the James River. Major Martin of the 96th Pennsylvania observed that "the Army of the Potomac is now on the James River, the Grand 'change of front' has been successfully accomplished." Martin later added: "So far as our recent retreat from the Chickahominy to the James River is concerned I believe that after it is properly understood and the different circumstances connected with it rightly appreciated it will be considered by all to have been *the* greatest military feat on record."[117] Whether or not the Bluecoats agreed or disagreed with McClellan, the army was on the move.

At 1 a.m., Sunday, June 29, the 96th Pennsylvania began its march. By dawn Slocum's division, of Franklin's corps, had reached Savage's Station, a frightening scene of destruction. Scores of mangled men—the wounded from the fight at Gaines' Mill—lying upon the ground around the hospital tents, greeted the Pennsylvanians. A soldier in Bartlett's brigade recalled seeing "men [lying] upon the ground around the hospital tents: their wearied, haggard and smoke-begrimed faces, which looked up to us, appealed not less strongly than their words, that they should not be left to fall into the hands of the enemy."[118] Another Bluecoat remarked, "God grant I may never witness another such sight. Arms and legs lay here and there upon the ground, some severed below the elbow and knee, others nearer the body."[119] Many in the ranks wondered what would happen to the wounded who could not be evacuated via ambulance. Near the field hospital were huge piles of commissary and quartermaster stores which were burned to prevent the Graycoats from acquiring magazines of cartridges, shells and kegs of powder. In addition, a VI Corps veteran remembered seeing "boxes of hard bread, hundreds of barrels of flour, rice, sugar, coffee, salt and pork" burning in large piles.[120] Adding to the confusion at Savage's Station was the destruction of a railroad train filled with ordinance stores. The train was set ablaze and put in motion down the tracks toward a burned-out trestle to splash into the Chickahominy. As the cars thundered down the rails a terrific explosion sent shell fragments shrieking through the air.

In the midst of the smoke and noise, McClellan appeared in person and ordered Slocum to continue across White Oak Swamp, without waiting for the rest of the corps.[121]

Wounded soldiers, 2nd Brigade, 1st Division, VI Corps at Union field hospital, Savage's Station, after the Battle of Gaines' Mill. The soldiers in the straw hats served with the 16th New York Volunteers. Photograph by James Gibson (Library of Congress).

A line officer of the 96th Pennsylvania reported that "the men suffered terribly" during the march. Some of the Bluecoats, exhausted and thirsty, "were compelled to drink the muddy water along the road."[122] This first phase of the retreat to the James River proved to be a debilitating march of fifteen miles. Lewis Luckenbill noted in his journal, "We [have] been marching all this time with nothing to eat but crackers and half of the time with no water. Some of the boys were dipping water out of the mudholes off the streets."[123] The next day, June 30, Slocum's division was posted, by direct order of McClellan, on the Charles City Road. The Pennsylvanians were situated about one mile from the junction with the Long Bridge road and an equal distance from Brackett's Ford. Anticipating an advance by the Secessionists down the Charles City Road, Slocum ordered the approach barricaded as thoroughly as possible. To stave off the impending attack, Slocum ordered the batteries of Emory Upton, Josiah Porter and William Hexamer into position in the line. During the day, the Union artillery blazed away at the oncoming Graycoats of Maj. Gen. Benjamin Huger's division.[124]

The cannon fire, coupled with abatis, caused the Graycoats to advance slowly and cautiously. In fact, they spent most of the day chopping through the obstructions that blocked the road. Late in the day Bartlett's brigade moved to the left of Slocum's division to contest an advancing body of Confederates. Upton's battery of light 12-pounder Napoleons, belching canister, caused the formidable Graycoat lines to disappear. In his diary Henry Keiser later recorded that the 96th "supported a battery of 18 guns.... The rebels were mowed down like grass with ... [spherical case shot] and canister."[125] Adjutant Richards boasted that "we had things as we wanted them, and made a 'nice little arrangement' for the Rebs with eighteen pieces of cannon and quietly laid down with our infantry behind the 'arrangement.' The Rebs came along in great force, thought they had a 'soft snap' and came within rifle range when our 'brass band' opened on them with grape and canister for about half an hour without stopping. When the smoke cleared away I could not see anybody where the Rebs had been!"[126] Watching the destructive fire of the VI Corps artillery, Richards added further "that on the field raked not a rat could find a place to live."[127]

Another member of the 96th Pennsylvania stated that "the exposure of our officers and men during the afternoon's fight were much less than on Friday [at Gaines' Mill], but I can feelingly testify that the rebels threw their shot without any care for our safety, since they whistled over my head from *three* different directions."[128] Watching the panoply of war unfold before his eyes, another soldier in the 96th Pennsylvania recorded his observations of the engagement raging up and down the Charles City Road. "The enemy charged on our batteries three or four regiments deep. They were swept away by the grape shot, as they advanced, without our losing any men. Throughout the whole fight, the rebels were all mad drunk.... None but drunken men would have charged in the face of ... [spherical case shot] and canister, which was sweeping away the trees in its very course.... Richmond, to be sure, was not taken; but what of that? We have fought the villains, and have gained a most signal victory."[129] As the fighting subsided the Bluecoats prepared to renew hostilities on the morrow. The soldiers of the 96th Pennsylvania, however, did not know it, but for them the worst of the campaign was over.

Fortunately for the Bluecoats of Slocum's division, the main Confederate thrust during the Battle of White Oak Swamp, or Charles City Road, had fallen on the left of the Federal line. Longstreet's assault in that sector had suffered from poor staff work and was repulsed by a determined lot of Yanks.[130] In a very real sense, the skillful crossing of White Oak Swamp was a victory. The Bluecoats successfully overcame a threat to their rear and a most dangerous obstacle along their line of march. At nightfall on June 30, Franklin withdrew his corps from White Oak Swamp and began the final march to Malvern Hill.[131] An officer of the Schuylkill County regiment described the night tramp this way in a letter to the *Miners' Journal*:

> It was painful to see the suffering connected with this celebrated retreat. Half of the wounded were compelled to walk all the way. It was a common sight to see men with broken arms (unset) walking. We found a man of Co. A, away beyond the Chickahominy Swamp. He had his arm shot off, and had trudged along about fifteen miles, and sunk down in the road unable to go further.[132]

Erasmus Reed recalled that the march from the Charles City Crossroads to Malvern Hill was a difficult arduous affair conducted during the darkness of night. "The suffering I seen that night was enough to make me tired of war. We had been suffering much for water all along. But that night beat all. I shudder when I think of it. Many of the wounded had to walk. They cried for a drop of water. Others begged and threatened. It was awful."[133]

Arriving near Malvern Hill at daybreak of July 1, Slocum's division was ordered to the right and rear of the Federal line, where Franklin's VI Corps was posted. According to Henry Keiser, the 96th Pennsylvania "marched until nearly noon, when we arrived at Malvern Hill ... but soon the rebels were there and commenced shelling us. Our division then packed up and went to the rear a short distance and pitched tents."[134] During Lee's final attempt to break the Union line, much to the pleasure of the regiment, the 96th Pennsylvania was held in reserve.[135] In his memoir, James Treichler recalled that during the Battle of Malvern Hill, the 96th Pennsylvania supported Hexhamer's Battery A, 1st New Jersey Artillery. "The battery in our front was commanded by Captain Hexheimer [who] swore like a german also, he was Gruff and Austeer. It was comical at times to see him galavanting around among his men —He was a thorough Artilleryman. He knew how to shoot, when to shoot and where to shoot…. The slaughter was tremendecys. Great gaps were torn in their ranks, and they were compelled to fall back."[136] Disjointed Confederate assaults, coupled with a lack of coordination among Lee's subordinates, enabled the Unionists to stand fast while holding the high ground on Malvern Hill.

Sgt. Maj. James M. Treichler. Promoted to corporal on October 15, 1862, to sergeant on February 8, 1863, then to sergeant major on July 25, 1864. He transferred to 95th Pennsylvania on October 18, 1864 (courtesy Randy M. Treichler).

By nightfall the Seven Days were over. Lee had failed in his final attempt to stop McClellan from reaching the safety of the James River. After the battle the Federal soldiers prepared to start yet another session of stumbling through the darkness, the rain and the mud. The men of the 96th Pennsylvania were dispirited, hungry, and haggard. Most of them were worn out from marching rather than fighting. Victorious at last upon the tactical field, but strategically defeated in the campaign, the Army of the Potomac withdrew during the night and made its camp at the new base of Harrison's Landing. Warships in the James River covered the movement. The Army of the Potomac was exhausted. The soldiers needed rest.

At 2 o'clock in the morning as Pennsylvanians left their position along the Malvern Hill line, rain began to fall. The march to Harrison's Landing was made on roads that were, in the words of one Sixth Corps veteran "rivers of … fathomless mud."[137] As the Yanks tramped along to the landing many in the ranks began to fall out and straggle. According to one foot soldier, the drenching rain, coupled with the obstructions along the roadway caused by ambulances, wagons and artillery stuck in the mud, interrupted the march. As the Bluecoats reached Harrison's Landing, officers stood like hotel porters at a steamboat landing, calling out, "This way for the Third Corps; this way for the Fifth Corps; this way for Slocum's division."[138] After changing campsites several times, the Pennsylvanians finally established Camp Haeseler, named in honor of the regimental surgeon, near the Berkeley estate.[139] Writing to his mother on July 3, at the end of the campaign, Clement Potts informed her that "where we are encamped the mud is knee deep and I am covered with mud up to my waist and no way of cleaning it off." Henry Keiser jotted the following in his pocket diary: "At daylight it commenced raining and continued most all day…. About 5 o'clock this afternoon I got to Harrison's Landing where all of the troops are encamped. I had a great time in finding the Regiment, but at last found it encamped in a wheat field and in the mud up to the knees. A miserable place, I was wet to the skin."[140] The campaign for Richmond was over.

On the 4th of July, General McClellan issued a congratulatory order commending the soldiers for their gallant effort during the campaign. "*Soldiers of the Army of the Potomac*! Your conduct ranks you among the celebrated armies of history. Your Government is strengthening you with the resources of a great people. On this our Nation's Birthday we declare to our foes, who are rebels against the best interests of mankind, that this Army shall enter the Capital of their so-called Confederacy."[141] At noon an artillery round was fired to signal the celebration. The regimental bands "struck Hail Columbia and several other memorial airs in the afternoon," according to Lewis Luckenbill.[142] Maurus Oestreich equated the firing of the cannon "to remember the freeing of America. I, too, must be free and strong, for, as I was a joiner journeyman working under the orders of another I understand how one feels … about his independence and freedom."[143] But the soldiers of the 96th Pennsylvania did not join the festivities in the Union camp. They were assigned to swing axes and cut down trees. Major Martin informed his family in Pottsville, "I spent [the day] building roads and bridges with 500 men, wasn't that a celebration for you?"[144]

During the rest of July and into August, the regiment was involved in picket and fatigue duty. In mid–July the regiment moved their camp behind the newly erected breastworks ringing the Federal camps at Harrison's Bar. There the Schuylkill Countians exchanged their Austrian muskets for new Enfield Rifles.[145] The Yanks also received new uniforms. The Pottsville Cornet Band, due to an act of Congress, was mustered out of service and the musicians returned home.[146] Lieutenant Colonel Frick resigned, to take command of a nine-month regiment, the 129th Pennsylvania Volunteers. Captain Anthony, of Company F, left the 96th regiment to become the major of Frick's new unit. Captain Isaac Cake, of Company I, also resigned. The heat was oppressive, and the mosquitoes seemed even worse on Harrison's Landing than they had been around Richmond. The camp stank horribly and the regimental sick list kept lengthening. According to one VI Corps veteran, "Sickness became almost universal."[147] With leisure time in abundance the homesick Schuylkill Countians informed their friends and relatives about the campaign and their well being.

At Harrison's Landing, the Unionists reflected upon the failed campaign to seize Richmond, and analyzed McClellan's generalship. The Yanks were not discouraged

Capt. Joseph Anthony, original captain of Company F. Resigned July 31, 1862 (author's collection).

by their "change of front" nor disenchanted with General McClellan. The Pennsylvanians learned much about warfare during the months of May and June. The Federals could not comprehend exactly why the campaign ended in a retreat to the James River. When the Unionists looked back on the battles, they seemed to have done no worse than a draw. They reaffirmed their faith in the Young Napoleon. Indeed Bruce Catton captured the feeling of the Bluecoats in the ranks after Malvern Hill when he wrote, "McClellan's name still had the old magic."[148] The Army of the Potomac believed that Malvern Hill would be followed up by an advance against Richmond. One of the Bluecoats in Bartlett's brigade noted that McClellan still held the confidence of the soldiers. "Probably no general has had the study of Virginia," opined Marker of the 27th New York, "more at heart or is better acquainted with the nature and necessities of a campaign in its borders than George B. McClellan, and certainly thus far he has proved himself the only man able to cope with a Johnson [sic], a Lee or a Jackson. Take the rebel estimate of our generals, and McClellan stands at the head of the list in ability and esteem."[149] Captain Filbert of Company B, a strong supporter of McClellan, did not want the army commander to resign. In his diary Filbert noted, "Our gallant McClellan seems in good spirits again with a smile on his face."[150] When the Pennsylvanians were not praising the Young Napoleon at Harrison's Landing, they proclaimed that victory would eventually crown their banners.

In addition to supporting McClellan, the Schuylkill Countians continued to believe in their cause. Matt Richards assured his folks in a letter that "the capture of Richmond is a fact that is regarded as a matter of course, which will follow the regular train of events."[151] Indeed morale was quite high within the ranks of the 96th Pennsylvania in the weeks after the battles for the possession of Richmond. Erasmus Reed, now a seasoned soldier, was "confident we will whip the rebels this fall."[152] Edward Henry, a private in Company D, also commented on military strategy and the ultimate success of the Union army. Writing from Camp Nugent in late July he stated, "It is expected the army will quarter here until September, or such time as General [John] Pope is prepared to cooperate with us from the opposite direction and then a grand rush will be made for the rebel capital.... It cannot be denied that we were whipped in the crippled state in which the army was at that time, but they will find the next a bitter pill for them to swallow, and then good bye to secession."[153] Filbert, however, recognized that disease and health were equal to the enemy confronting them on the battlefield. "I am afraid this rebellion will never be put down from present appearances. Men die off faster than they are enlisted."[154] In fact, many of the soldiers discovered that tidewater Virginia could be more deadly than the battlefields of the Old Dominion.

The incessant action of the Seven Days' battles, coupled with the swampy conditions in Virginia and the unsanitary conditions of their camp along the James River ravaged the health of the Pennsylvanians. Upon reaching the James River, John Fernsler visited the hospital to see the sick and wounded soldiers. He noted in his diary that "the doctors were busy amputating and the poor fellows were groaning and hollering during the operation."[155] Taking care of the wounded was a priority for the officers of the 96th Pennsylvania. Filbert informed his father, "The men are getting sick daily. It is [an] awful hot climate."[156] In late July Major Martin mentioned to his folks that "diarrhea is quite a common complaint in our Regiment. Very few have escaped it and many have it now more or less severely."[157] By the middle of August, Erasmus Reed observed that "we have not got quite so many deaths as we had a week ago. The men were dying whole sale for some time."[158] Clement Potts noted that "the health of our regiment is none of the best." Attending to the sick and wounded required the assistance of many men from the regiment. In

mid–July Potts, while writing a letter from the regimental hospital, informed his mother that he was "attending to John Madison a member of our company who is lying very ill. ne [soldier] every day is detailed out of the company to attend to him."[159] John Madison never left Camp Haesler. He died shortly after Potts penned his letter. While the soldiers of the 96th dealt with illness and declining health during the Harrison's Landing encampment, the line officers revisited the unfinished business from Camp Northumberland concerning the post fund.

Capt. Isaac M. Cake, original captain of Company I. Resigned July 12, 1862 (collection of James F. Haas, United States Army Heritage and Education Center).

On July 13, while bivouacked in the glue-like mud of Camp Haeseler, the line captains confronted Colonel Cake on the fiery sutler issue. Ever since the winter

This scene, composed at Brandy Station, Virginia, depicts the sutler tent operated by A. Foulke (Library of Congress).

at Camp Northumberland the line officers had been upset with Cake's inability to control the prices of the sutler's goods. Now they were prepared to have a show-down with the regimental commander. The officers submitted a signed petition to Cake, demanding that the Schuylkill County colonel order sutler Gee to reduce the prices of his wares to a reasonable cost. Upon receipt of the petition, Cake confiscated the swords of the line captains and ordered all of them to be placed under arrest. At a meeting in his tent, Cake informed them that their swords would be returned after they apologized for the insulting language of their petition. To the tongue lashing at Cake's tent Captain Filbert remarked, "He then placed us under arrest but asked for an apology, which has not been given and far from giving."[160] The next morning Cake summoned the line officers back to his tent. Cake reprimanded them for their unkind language towards him and then stated "You can now take your swords and go to your quarters and until you apologize I can not respect you as officers of this regiment."[161]

After the confrontation, three line captains apologized to the colonel. Captain Filbert, however, maintained an attitude of disdain towards Colonel Cake. Cake alleged that Filbert, as senior line captain, was responsible for influencing the other officers. Cake considered him "disgraced in his sight."[162] On July 26, during a discussion at the colonel's tent, Filbert and Cake aired their grievances. Filbert resented the fact that Cake, throughout the encampment at Camp Northumberland, had not ordered the regimental

Council of Administration to enforce the Army Regulations requiring the collection of the ten percent tax upon the sutler to be allocated to the Post Fund. Cake responded to Filbert's request by allowing the senior line captain to convene the Council of Administration. Filbert decided that the only way to make any gains with the sutler would be to examine Gee before the Council of Administration. The senior captain planned to question him about the contract with Colonel Cake. Filbert believed that agreement would determine whether or not Gee was liable for the tax payable to the Post Fund.

Before the Council of Administration could convene, however, one of the members of the panel resigned from the Pennsylvania regiment. On July 25, Lieutenant Colonel Frick, a close ally and friend of Filbert's, tendered a letter of resignation to Brig. Gen. Seth Williams, Adjutant General of the Army of the Potomac. Frick's letter revealed much about the friction between the Schuylkill County colonel and the Regular Army veteran.

> I have the honor of tendering my resignation as Lt. Colonel of the 96th Pa. Vols. In addition I desire to say that I cannot consent to serve another day in the 96th Pa. Vols. Under its present commander, and that I can not any longer be useful there. Certainly the best interests of the service will be better subserved relieving me from my present position.[163]

By virtue of his resignation, Frick became the first political casualty of the 96th Pennsylvania Volunteers. The historical evidence documenting their discord, although fragmentary, supports the theory of a personality clash. Specific problems or differences between Cake and Frick, however, cannot be pinpointed, but a paragraph written on Frick's resignation recommendation by the commander of the Second Brigade, Colonel Bartlett, reflected the gravity of the Frick-Cake relationship.

> Respectfully forwarded acceptance recommended. The feeling existing between Col. and Lt. Col. as such is to have a demoralizing effect upon the officers of the rgt. I trust this resignation may be accepted believing it to be in the best interest of the service.[164]

Thursday, July 31, was the day that sutler Gee was to meet with the Council of Administration. The wily sutler, however, claimed that he had a steamboat on the James River laden with fresh produce and other goods coveted by the soldiers and would need to postpone the meeting. Finally, on August 1, the Council of Administration met with sutler Gee in attendance. Late in the afternoon the panel of officers adjourned from its hearing and informed Colonel Cake of its findings. The Council, chaired by Captain Filbert, determined that Gee was indeed a sutler of a regiment, rather than a Post, as Gee had argued. Consequently the Council resolved that the sutler was subjected to the Post Fund assessment. In order to conclude their conflict with Gee, the Council agreed that a seven percent tax per man, payable from November 1861 through the present, would be imposed upon Gee.[165]

After learning of the Council's decision, Colonel Cake interpreted that resolution as a challenge to his authority and an infringement upon his privilege to command. Cake also considered the whole affair to be a personal affront from his junior officers. He set the tone of his future relationship with Filbert by telling the senior line officer that he would get rid of him and four other officers whom he disliked.[166]

But before Filbert and Cake could begin to reconcile their differences, the grand Army of the Potomac began to evacuate the Harrison's Landing encampment. The war planners in the Lincoln administration had decided to transfer the Army of the Potomac back to the vicinity of Washington. Once there McClellan's forces could be united with the growing command of Maj. Gen. John Pope, the Army of Virginia. The new General-in-Chief Henry W. Halleck, wanted to insure that Lee could not drive his army between the forces of Pope and McClellan: the fear in Washington being that Lee's Army of Northern Virginia could hold off one army and crush the other. The war was shifting quickly from the suburbs of Richmond to the countryside of Maryland.

V

"Now, Pennsylvanians, do your duty"

At Harrison's Landing, August 10 dawned hot and humid. The war on the peninsula, however, was not as sultry as the weather. Along the banks of the James the days rolled by like the river, with only an occasional picket discharging his musket. Since the end of McClellan's campaign to capture Richmond, the battleground had shifted to northern Virginia, where the fighting would turn white hot. For the 96th Pennsylvania, however, camp life at Harrison's Landing, afforded the soldiers an opportunity to recover from the rigors of active campaigning. Bartlett's brigade initially moved to a position on the Westover road, near Herring Creek, approximately two miles from the handsome mansion of former president William Henry Harrison.[1] Major Martin informed his mother that he did not have any news but prospects were bright that the regiment might remain in their camp for a period.[2] Captain Filbert, too, took advantage of the inactivity to correspond with his family in Pine Grove and to update his diary. While the war moved slowly that summer along the tidewater region, interrupted only by inspections and picket duty, the military situation in northern Virginia was moving rapidly.

As the Army of the Potomac began to change its base, from Harrison's Landing to the environs of Washington, morale among the Bluecoats was beginning to wane. With the first big boom of battle excitement ebbing, people in the North were getting tired of the war. They had been prepared, in fact the citizenry had expected, a short, sharp and decisive conflict. By the end of the summer, the soldiers in the Army of the Potomac, were also weary and critical of the direction of the war in Washington. Uncertainty, too about the General McClellan began to gather momentum. According to Surgeon George Stevens of the VI Corps, in late August "a gloom hung over the minds of all. The army was satisfied that General McClellan would be removed from command."[3] Major Martin of the 96th, however, was less worried about McClellan's future and more concerned about the life of the army. "One thing I believe is certain and that is the 'Grand Army of the Potomac' will soon be numbered among the things that were. It will no longer be 'The Army.' McClellan of course will resign if he has not already done so. The Army will be divided and distributed ... and as they can not please McClellan under any other commander he will see his only alternative when his command dwindles away."[4]

In addition to the confusion concerning McClellan's tenure, the Bluecoats also sought to understand the administration's commitment to the armies in the field. Writing from camp near Harrison's Landing, Erasmus Reed commented favorably concerning the enlistment of new volunteer soldiers in Pennsylvania. "The army is quite jolly to hear that enlisting progresses so finely. I heard this morning that the Old Keystone State had her quota in the field.... I do not believe that there will be a man drafted for the six hundred thousand men. The boys are all glad to see our government is waking up and taking things in earnest."[5] Perhaps Captain Haas spoke for the Federal foot soldiers about the Northern war effort:

> I am afraid that this war will end by the South obtaining their independence; it will serve us Right, too. For if we had used but half the energy and means the Rebels used, we could have put them down long ago—but as it [the war] is conducted on the principle of "not hurting anybody" and "milk and water" system. I do not feel ashamed to say so.[6]

The Union needed a decisive victory against the Graycoats in order to restore confidence in the men on the battle line and to suppress growing discontent on the home front. The Bluecoats had hoped that McClellan could lead them to such a decisive battlefield. For now, however, they were going to join forces with John Pope's army.

By mid–August, the wharves along the James River witnessed a surge in activity. Wounded soldiers were loaded onto transports for the journey back to Washington. Supplies, which could not be moved, were ordered to be destroyed. Tents were struck compelling the Bluecoats to sleep out in the open air without protection from the elements. On the morning of August 14, six weeks after arriving at Harrison's Landing, the soldiers of the 96th Pennsylvania were notified that the army was moving. Returning to camp from picket duty, the men procured rations and made final preparations to march.[7] Throughout the next day, the 96th awaited the order to "fall in," but the soldiers remained in camp where they learned that Slocum's division would form the rear guard of the VI Corps' marching column.[8] On August 16, the 96th regiment turned its back on Harrison's Landing and at 3 o'clock in the afternoon, under an intensely hot sun, the soldiers tramped at route step toward Charles City Court House.[9] According to Lewis Luckenbill, "this part of the [country] was the prettiest and richest we have travelled since we are in the service."[10] Marching until 9 o'clock, along a dusty road, and past impressive mansions surrounded by extensive plantations, the exhausted soldiers rested in a field near the court house.[11] The morrow would bring more marching.

The third week of August for the Pennsylvanians proved to be a series of grueling marches conducted under difficult conditions. On the morning of August 17, the 96th broke camp at 7 o'clock in the morning, never halted for lunch, and marched steadily to the Chickahominy River. At the Chickahominy, the soldiers crossed an impressive bridge, 2,000 feet in length, constructed upon ninety pontoons.[12] The following day, they were on the move at 4 o'clock in the morning. Early in the afternoon, the Schuylkill Countians passed through the old colonial town of Williamsburg. Severe heat and humidity coupled with little water caused significant straggling as the regiment toiled along the dusty roads of Virginia. Sergeant Luckenbill recalled that the 96th Pennsylvania "marched into a field [and] when we went to stack our arms our company [B] only had 12 men left [and] the regiment was reduced down to about 100 men. The day was very warm and dusty [and we] suffered terribly from [lack of] water. We were half starved and near dead from [no] water and tired out."[13] That night, encamped near Williamsburg, the exhausted soldiers cooked coffee and roasted green corn, which was plentiful that summer. Early the next morning, the soldiers found themselves, yet again, in column trudging under a scorching sun along the roads of tidewater Virginia.[14]

Marching all day, the regiment covered fourteen miles under a "hot burning sun and dust and hardly any water." That afternoon, when the 96th Pennsylvania encamped near Yorktown, many of the men headed to the York River. Captain Filbert noted in his diary, "Had a grand wash after a march through dust."[15] The next morning, August 20, the Schuylkill Countians broke camp at 5 o'clock and marched until early in the afternoon. The Pennsylvanians moved a total of fifteen miles, half of which was conducted at the double quick. At Yorktown, Filbert commented on the "line of fortifications," and noted that the "Confederate Army [built] winter quarters of 1st class." The following day, the soldiers, according to Lewis Luckenbill, "left at 6 and marched as hard as any yet and this was the hottest day of all."[16] Early in the afternoon, the 96th, after covering twelve miles with little food or water, reached Newport News. Almost immediately, the exhausted soldiers made a "grand rush to the landing" in search of cooked rations. Throughout the balance of the day and well into the night, stragglers continued to arrive at the regiment's camp site. Henry Keiser related in his diary that he "procured a good mess of oysters out of the James River."[17] Upon reaching Newport News, Major Martin informed his folks at home about the grueling movements which challenged the Pennsylvanians during the third week of August. "Our regiment left our camp near Harrison's Landing on Saturday last the 16th and after six days hard marching we reached this place yesterday. A more tired, dirty and hungry set of fellows than you ever saw in your life."[18]

Late in the afternoon on August 22, after drawing cooked rations, the Schuylkill Countians boarded the steamship *New Brunswick*.[19] Major Martin was uncertain of the regiment's destination. Some in the ranks believed the regiment was headed to Aquia Creek landing. About 8 o'clock that evening, a tug boat towed *New Brunswick* from the

landing and positioned the steamer in the York River. Early the next morning the vessel, after weighing anchor, passed Fort Monroe and steamed up the Chesapeake. The following day, amidst great cheering from the soldiers, *New Brunswick* reached Alexandria about noon. Upon disembarking the steamer, the 96th regiment encountered Colonel Frick and his newly recruited nine-month regiment, the 129th Pennsylvania Volunteers.[20] On August 26 the 96th, along with the balance of Bartlett's brigade, reached Alexandria. The Bluecoats quickly disembarked the transports and went into camp near Fort Ellsworth. The next day, the 96th Pennsylvania left the immediate environs of Alexandria and encamped near Fort Lyon.[21] For three days the soldiers engaged in regimental and battalion drills while awaiting further orders. Finally, on August 29, the regiment marched to Fairfax Court House via the Little River Turnpike. The following day, according to Henry Keiser, the 96th "left camp at eight a.m.,

Capt. Jacob W. Haas, Company G. Promoted from first lieutenant March 5, 1862. Mustered out with company October 21, 1864 (collection of James F. Haas, United States Army Heritage and Education Center).

and marched through Fairfax Court House and Centreville in the direction of 'Bull Run.' Heavy cannonading ahead of us. There is hard fighting ahead."[22] That evening the seasoned veterans of the 96th Pennsylvania slept on their arms. Perhaps in the morning the Bluecoats would march toward the sound of the guns.

The original plan called for General Franklin to disembark his corps at Aquia Landing. Upon arriving there, the Sixth Corps commander found that the wharves were encumbered with the artillery and stores of Porter's and Burnside's commands. He informed McClellan of that logistical problem, and the army commander directed him to land his corps at Alexandria. For two days the Unionists remained in the vicinity of Alexandria. During this time Franklin was scurrying about attempting to find horses to pull his artillery to the front. Without transportation for the cannon, the artillery could not be used. As the Pennsylvanians remained in camp along the Little River Turnpike, John Pope realized that his campaign was beginning to unravel. Pope sent word to General-in-Chief Halleck that Lee had taken position northwest of the Bull Run mountains, and had even sent "a strong column" forward to Manassas. Consequently, Pope decided to retire from the Rappahannock and re-deploy his army on a line running from the hamlet of Gainesville, five miles east of Thoroughfare Gap, to the vicinity of Warrenton Junction. Pope suggested that reinforcements coming up from the Alexandria-Washington area should march toward Gainesville. While Pope prepared to fight a "general engagement," McClellan sought to withhold reserves from the inexperienced commander of the Army of Virginia.[23]

As Franklin prepared to advance his corps in support of Pope, Little Mac bombarded Halleck with a host of reasons why the VI Corps, and Sumner's Corps, should not go to Pope. McClellan claimed that Franklin's Corps lacked the necessary equipment to fight, and could not join Pope's army in time.[24] Furthermore he contended that the Bluecoats ought to be held back to protect Washington or to protect Pope's forces during a retreat, in case of a defeat. Halleck, who was operating under extreme pressure because of the uncertainty surrounding Pope's situation, acceded to McClellan's suggestions. In fact, as Halleck got more panicky, he wrote to McClellan advising him to "dispose of all troops as you deem best."[25] In response to Halleck's telegram McClellan sent four infantry regiments out to the works at Upton's and Munson's Hills, covering the main highway in from Centreville, and instructed the Bluecoats to hold the lines there at all hazards. On the evening of August 28 the two armies collided in the darkness beyond Centreville. The next day, McClellan ordered Franklin to move forward, telling him: "Whatever may happen, don't allow it to be said that the Army of the Potomac failed to do its utmost for the country."[26]

That morning, Franklin's Bluecoats tramped along the Fairfax Turnpike under orders to communicate with and support General Pope's command. In the distance, beyond Centreville, the Unionists could hear the muffled booming of the guns. Upon the arrival of the vanguard of Franklin's corps at Annandale, it was reported to the VI Corps commander that there was a large force of the enemy posted near Fairfax Court House. As a result, McClellan directed Franklin to stop for the night. The next day, as the second Battle of Bull Run raged to a climax, Franklin's Corps marched to support Pope's beleaguered troops. In the afternoon Franklin reached the head of his column, where he deployed his soldiers across the road, in front of Cub Run "stopping what seemed to be an indiscriminate mass of men, horses, guns and wagons, all going pell-mell to the rear."[27]

The valley below Cub Run and the nearby fields were soon filled with Pope's Bluecoats "retreating in every direction." Slocum ordered his command to form in line and arrest any stragglers.

On Sunday, August 31, after marching and stopping several times, Henry Keiser noted in his diary, "Our army has again been whipped on the 'Bull Run' battlefield. Too bad."[28] That night the 96th Pennsylvania encamped behind the fortifications erected at Centreville by the Confederates the previous year. The following evening, as the rain began to fall, the Bluecoats headed back toward Alexandria. Major Martin recalled that it "rain[ed] nearly all night and mud nearly three and four inches deep owing to the number of troops on the road."[29] Both Henry Keiser and Lewis Luckenbill recorded in their diaries that "they were in mud up to their knees."[30] The next night, at 10 o'clock the 96th Pennsylvania went into camp near Fort Lyon. The 96th was essentially back where it had started from in April. The soldiers found themselves less than a mile from their old winter quarters at Camp Franklin. The Second Bull Run campaign was over. The Unionists were tired, weary and discouraged.

On September 3 the sun finally came out and the roads dried enough so that the Bluecoats coming in on the Fairfax Road, near the forts on Munson's Hill, stirred up a lazy cloud of dust along their line of march. During the day, the 96th moved from Fort Lyon to another camp ground near Episcopal Seminary. Although they were wet and fatigued from the recent marches, it was not the exhaustion or demoralization from losing the battle that concerned the Schuylkill Countians and the rest of the Army of the Potomac. What became clear to the Unionists was that the Republic's finest army had been badly mishandled throughout the campaign and battle. One captain in the 96th Pennsylvania was especially dissatisfied with the apparent selfishness displayed by McClellan during the critical point in the campaign. John T. Boyle, writing more than two decades after the battle, chastised the Young Napoleon for not moving his army vigorously to Pope's assistance.

> The prejudiced student can scarcely arrive at any other conclusion than that General John Pope, and with him the seeming best interests of the country, were sacrificed at the shrine of selfish ambition…. Pope was the unselfish victim of fortuitous circumstances over which he had little or no control.[31]

Although not strong enough to attack the Army of the Potomac after defeating Pope's forces, Lee was determined to invade the North and retain the initiative. In early September Lee's troops marched into northern territory singing "Maryland, My Maryland."[32] At the same time, McClellan was reappointed to command the army and assumed confident and energetic control of the Bluecoat forces. Hastily reorganizing the Army of the Potomac, he moved the Unionists north and west through Maryland, sending his cavalry deep into the countryside in search of Lee's army. Morale within McClellan's army grew steadily as the Bluecoats marched through the Maryland countryside.[33] On the evening of September 6, after crossing the Potomac via the Long Bridge, Bartlett's brigade marched past McClellan's headquarters in Washington. Lewis Luckenbill later recalled that as the 96th passed "through the city our company [B] was cheered by the citizens of Washington."[34] In turn, the soldiers cheered the return of Little Mac. The adjutant of the 5th Maine described the scene that evening as the Bluecoats tramped through Washington. "The streets were crowded with people who seemed to receive us very enthusiastically. In our march the whole force passed by General McClellan's residence; and, as he had then been restored to the command of the army since Pope's disaster and the complete overthrow of his 'headquarters,' as regiment after regiment passed by the abode of their idolized chieftain, they caused the air to ring with the wildest cheers, thus demonstrating that the army of the Potomac had not lost its confidence in its general."[35] Lee's army lay on the western side of South Mountain, a high ridge that runs north and east for about sixty-five miles from the Potomac, a part of the Blue Ridge. To locate the Confederates, McClellan divided his army into three parts. Slowly the Army of the Potomac began to fan out into the Maryland countryside in pursuit of Lee's Graycoats.

At one o'clock on the morning of September 7, after marching past McClellan's headquarters, the 96th regiment encamped on Georgetown Heights. Later that day, the Pennsylvanians marched through Tennallytown, finally resting for the night after tramping fifteen miles. The following day, the regiment moved a mere five miles camping for the night near Rockville. Jacob Haas, of Company G, noted in his pocket diary that he "stole plums and corn and cooked coffee in a large cornfield."[36] The next morning, the regiment marched through Darnestown, rested for a few hours in a large woodlot and bivouacked for the night near a cornfield. On September 10, the Pennsylvanians moved in the morning tramping through Dawsonville and camped for the night near Barnesville.[37] That night, after covering thirteen miles, the Schuylkill Countians performed picket duty in the vicinity of Sugar Loaf Mountain. Captain Haas remarked that "the 'Reb' pickets were within gunshot of us."[38]

The next day, September 11, while still on outpost duty, Henry Keiser recalled that in the "morning the pickets advanced in a skirmish line and drove the Rebel pickets. A few shots were exchanged."[39] Early the next morning, wet and tired, from the rain and picket duty, the 96th spent yet another day marching through Urbana and camping for the night at Licksville Crossroads. The following morning the regiment passed through Buckeystown, crossed the Baltimore and Ohio Railroad at noon, and went into camp at 4 o'clock in the afternoon. Captain Haas recorded in his journal that he "walked three miles to wash. Met a nigger, said the 'Rebs' were not far off."[40] Captain Filbert remarked that he could hear "heavy cannonading toward the [South] mountain, about 8 miles distant."[41] That night, camping in the woods near Buckeystown, the soldiers rested from a week of strenuous marching through the Maryland countryside. The next day, a Sabbath, would not be a day of rest. September 14 would prove to be a day of more marching followed by another deadly encounter with the vaunted Army of Northern Virginia. Once again the soldiers of the 96th Pennsylvania would hear the piercing sound of the rebel yell.

By late afternoon, on the thirteenth of September, McClellan's plans were complete. The Maryland terrain and the network of roads leading to South Mountain gave the Young Napoleon an opportunity to move swiftly and defeat Lee's army. He proposed to force Turner's Gap and descend on Boonsboro with his right and center wings, smashing Longstreet and D. H. Hill, while Franklin pushed his command through Crampton's Gap and down to Maryland Heights to relieve the Union garrison at Harpers Ferry. There, the VI Corps commander would strike the rear of Anderson and McLaws, thereby opening the back door for the escape of more than 12,000 Federals trapped there by Stonewall Jackson.[42]

Shortly after 6 p.m., McClellan sent Franklin his instructions. "You will move at daybreak in the morning.... Having gained the pass [Crampton's Gap] your duty will be first to cut off, destroy, or capture McLaws' command and relieve [Harpers Ferry]. My general idea is to cut the enemy in two and beat him in detail…. I ask of you, at this important moment, all your intellect and the utmost activity that a general can exercise."[43] Franklin was assured that his force if, well managed, would be "sufficient for the end in view." McClellan went to some effort to tailor Franklin's instructions for a subordinate he considered of "so little energy" whose "efficiency is very little."[44] Yet, for all of McClellan's planning, little was said of haste in making any movement. That day, Franklin bivouacked twelve miles from Crampton's Gap. Little Mac, however, did not urge Franklin to march his Bluecoats those dozen miles that afternoon, or evening, so as to be ready to assault Crampton's Gap at first light. Nor did Franklin leave evidence of contemplating such a maneuver. As author Stephen Sears said of Franklin, "Independence of mind was not his forte."[45] So the afternoon and evening hours of the thirteenth slipped quietly away as the VI Corps settled into camp for the night near Buckeystown.[46]

As the sun rose on Sunday, Franklin had 12,300 men under his command in two divisions commanded by Henry Warner Slocum and William F. "Baldy" Smith, almost all battle tested veterans of the Peninsula and Seven Days' fighting.[47] Obeying McClellan's orders, Franklin broke camp at Buckeystown early on the morning of the 14th and sent his corps westward toward Catoctin Mountain. According to Captain Haas, at 5:30 a.m., as the Bluecoats crested the mountain, they were greeted with a magnificent panorama of the Middletown Valley and in the distance South Mountain.[48] Colonel Bartlett, in a memoir written after the war, described the scene. Bartlett recalled that "as we filed down the opposite side of the mountain we could occasionally get a view of the troops in front of us … with the morning sun shining brightly upon their arms and accoutrements,

This image depicts the scene of the VI Corps' advance at the Battle of Crampton's Gap September 14, 1862. The Confederate infantry was posted behind the stone wall running from left to right. The 96th Pennsylvania crossed the fields farther to the right of this image. The name of the photographer is unknown (*Slocum and His Men,* 1904).

winding down and stretching far out in the beautiful valley toward [South Mountain]. Such scenes, which look tame upon canvas, are glorious to the young and enthusiastic soldier, who feels a thrill of pride as he looks upon the magnificent and real picture of war his comrades are presenting."[49]

At 8 a.m., according to Captain Filbert's pocket watch, upon reaching the village of Jefferson, the VI Corps commander stopped to wait for Darius Couch's division of the IV Corps, temporarily attached to the VI Corps, to join him.[50] A VI Corps artilleryman stated that Franklin waited two hours while Bartlett recalled that "a considerable halt was made. To allow General Couch's Division ... to come up."[51] Couch, however, never appeared. Finally, realizing that his corps would not be augmented by Couch's division, Franklin ordered Slocum's division to lead the march to the village of Burkittsville at the base of South Mountain. Colonel Bartlett instructed Colonel Cake to lead the VI Corps march with his regiment. To the music of fifes and drums, the 96th Pennsylvania tramped toward South Mountain where the Confederates were preparing to defend the pass over the mountain known locally as Crampton's Gap.[52]

Meanwhile, on the morning of September 14, Lee's chief of cavalry Jeb Stuart rode from Boonsboro to inspect Confederate readiness at Crampton's Gap. Stuart believed that Crampton's Gap was "the weakest point of the line" in the Confederate front which ran, from south to north, starting at Brownsville Pass extending to Turner's Gap.[53] Given his grasp of the tactical situation, Stuart further reasoned "that the enemy's efforts would be [directed] against [Lafayette] McLaws[,] probably by the route of Crampton's Gap." Subsequently, Stuart ordered Col. Thomas Munford, commanding the 2nd and 12th Virginia Cavalry regiments, as the senior officer, to hold Crampton's Gap " against the enemy at all hazards."[54] To support Munford's troopers, Stuart also ordered Roger P. Chew's Virginia horse battery to Crampton's Gap. In addition he sent the 16th Virginia of Col. William Parham's brigade, temporarily commanding the brigade in place of Gen. William Mahone who was wounded at 2nd Manassas, along with two naval howitzers of the Portsmouth (Virginia) artillery. Upon reaching Crampton's Gap, George Neese, serving with Chew's Battery, recalled the sight of the advancing VI Corps column in his postwar memoir. "At about 10 o'clock we saw the first of the Yankee host, about three miles away, approaching our gap cautiously and slowly. As they drew nearer the whole country seemed to be full of the Bluecoats. They were so numerous that it looked as if they were creeping up out of the ground."[55] An hour later Stuart rode up to and urged McLaws to reinforce the inadequate Confederate command preparing to defend Crampton's Gap from the Bluecoats, who were advancing slowly toward South Mountain.

Upon assuming command at Crampton's Gap, Munford elected to undertake the defense of the pass over South Mountain at the eastern base of the mountain. He immediately deployed the artillery approximately halfway down the eastern slope of South Mountain and posted the infantry—three Virginia regiments—behind a stone wall at the base of the mountain. He also dismounted the cavalry and sent them to protect the left and right flanks of his line of Virginia infantry. Subsequently, the 10th Georgia, of Paul Semmes' brigade was transferred from the vicinity of Brownsville Pass and sent to reinforce Munford's combined command of Virginia infantry, artillery and cavalry. In conjunction with Munford, Col. Edward Montague, commanding the 32nd Virginia at Brownsville Pass, advanced a contingent of 200 soldiers to the base of the mountain and established a skirmish line connecting with Munford's right flank at Crampton's Gap.

About noon, Munford's thinly held line of battle was established at the foot of the mountain. At the southern end of his line was the 2nd Virginia Cavalry. To the left of the 2nd Virginia was the 16th Virginia, positioned astride Burkittsville's Main Street. Extending the Confederate battle line farther north, along the stone wall bordering Mountain Church Road was the 12th Virginia. Next in line was the 16th Virginia and then the lone regiment from Semmes' brigade the veterans of the 10th Georgia. Finally, the 12th Virginia Cavalry anchored the extreme left flank of Munford's position. While these Confederate soldiers awaited the Yankee onslaught, McLaws ordered Brig. Gen. Howell Cobb, a noted Georgia politician and former Secretary of the Treasury under President Buchanan, to march his brigade to Brownsville. Once there, General Semmes was to instruct Cobb to take his command to Crampton's Gap and assume field command. Through his assistant adjutant general, McLaws relayed an order to the portly Georgian to hold Crampton's Gap even "if he lost his last man doing it." While Cobb hastened to Crampton's Gap, with approximately 1,350 Georgia and North Carolina infantry, Munford would need to hold off the entire VI Corps with about 800 battled tested veterans.[56]

Leaving the bivouac near Jefferson, the 96th Pennsylvania was ordered to support a squadron of troopers, Company F of Col. Richard H. Rush's 6th Pennsylvania Cavalry, clearing the road to Burkittsville of mounted Virginia cavalry videttes. As the Schuylkill Countians tramped toward South Mountain they could distinctly hear the thunder of artillery at Turner's Gap which "told the battle was on again." As the Lancers of Company F and the infantry of the 96th Pennsylvania marched cautiously toward South Mountain, the Confederates patiently watched the VI Corps column wind its way toward Burkittsville. Before noon, the lead element of the 96th Pennsylvania crossed Catoctin Creek "amid the smiles and well-wishes of a number of pretty females whom curiosity and patriotism had enticed to the spot."[57]

When the 96th was within two miles of the picturesque village of Burkittsville, the cavalry escort retired behind the Pennsylvanians, and reported to Colonel Cake that they had encountered "a superior force of the enemy's cavalry."[58] Upon learning about the enemy in his front, Cake deployed Companies A and F as skirmishers and pushed forward the balance of the regiment, moving the soldiers steadily, and within close support of his *voltiguers*. Writing nine years after the battle, the captain of Company D, John T. Boyle, recalled the initial contact between the Confederate skirmishers and Companies A and F. "After exchanging shots the enemy's skirmishers retired, closely followed by the regiment, over grounds much broken by hill and ravine."[59] During the Union advance, several of the soldiers performing skirmish duty halted momentarily and filled their haversacks with apples and potatoes from a nearby orchard and potato patch. About 1 p.m. the skirmishers carefully advanced to a rise of ground overlooking Burkittsville, and seeing no enemy in their front "advanced with boldness" to within one thousand yards of the base of South Mountain. Cresting this hill, the skirmishers continued into the village drawing the fire of the Confederate artillery posted on the mountain.[60]

In his after-action report, General Slocum observed that "Colonel Bartlett, deployed the Ninety-sixth Regiment Pennsylvania Volunteers as skirmishers, who drove in the enemy's pickets and advanced to the village."[61] Colonel Bartlett, in his report of Crampton's Gap remarked that "the enemy's pickets retired from the town and opened an artillery fire from two batteries upon my line of skirmishers."[62] During this opening phase of the engagement at Crampton's Gap, the 96th Pennsylvania did not sustain causalities from artillery fire as it did prior to the combat action at Gaines' Mill. But reminiscent of the regiment's march across the farm fields at Gaines' Mill, moving east of the village of Burkittsville, toward the Union right flank, resulted in a number of injuries, especially in Company H.[63]

While the other eight companies of the 96th Pennsylvania filed into position along the Knoxville Road, Company A was ordered down the road to take position at Samuel Ahalt's grist and saw mill. While Company A performed picket duty protecting the left flank, Lt. John Dougherty of Company F led a squad of a dozen soldiers past the fine brick mansion of Otho Harley to the edge of the village while the rest of his company deployed to the right of Harley's house. Using Harley's as regimental headquarters, Cake and Major Martin, the only mounted officers with the 96th Pennsylvania, rode to the eastern end of Burkittsville to survey the tactical situation. Subsequently, Cake ordered Martin to push forward the skirmish line with intervals of twenty feet between the men and if possible, establish a position along the western edge of the village. Cake stationed himself at Harley's where he could observe Company A on the left, and the advance of the skirmish line under Major Martin. As the operation unfolded, Colonel Cake sent Henry Boyer of Company A to Harley's mansion to interview the inhabitants and perhaps develop some intelligence about the position and strength of the Confederates defending Crampton's Gap.[64]

Veterans of Company F. This photograph, dated October 25, 1864, features the soldiers at the expiration of their term of service. This unique portrait reveals the average number of men in each company of the 96th Pennsylvania upon their formal mustering out in Philadelphia October 21, 1864. The soldiers in the image are, back row, left to right, Capt. Edward J. Philips, Sgt. Robert Borland, Corp. Michael Carroll, Pvt. Michael Kavanaugh and Pvt. Patrick Powers. Front row, left to right, Pvt. Hugh Glacken, Pvt. William Smith, Pvt. John O'Donnell, Pvt. Philip Goulden and Pvt. William Manalis. The photographic firm was Wenderoth and Taylor 912, 914 & 916 Chestnut Street, Philadelphia, Pennsylvania (collection of Douglas Sagrillo).

In a lengthy memoir Boyer recalled the meeting and exchange between Cake and Harley. "Finally a gentleman came forth and went immediately to the Colonel. He began at once to beg that the battle might not take place there. He declared the town to be Union almost to a man—that all the Secessionists were off in the Southern army. He was assured that there would be no fight there—that if the enemy had men enough to make a stand it would be beyond the town, at the stone fence that appeared to run along just at the foot of the mountain. He said they intended to fight and did not dream of defeat."[65] While Cake listened to Harley's pleading and awaited the return of Martin with his report, several of the Pennsylvanians raided the nearby farm house "to procure eatables from the inhabitants, many of whom openly expressed their delight … at the arrival of our forces." According to Captain Haas, "the men of B and G Companies stole milk, hams and preserves out of a house."[66]

Major Martin soon returned from the skirmish line, dodging artillery rounds coming from a rifled gun planted to the left of the gap, and reported his field observations to Cake.[67] The "skirmish line of the enemy was posted behind a stonewall only about a thousand feet beyond" (the position of Lt. Dougherty's squad). In addition, Martin related that he could only see one gun, but Confederate cavalry was visible on the mountain side. Inexplicably, Martin informed Colonel Cake about the length of the Confederate line which "indicated more than 4,000 infantry."[68] As Martin finished his report, an aide from General Slocum approached the two officers and demanded to hear the details concerning the Confederate strength and deployment. Subsequently, Colonel Cake was ordered to meet with the VI Corps commanders at the Martin Shafer farm, where Franklin had "established his headquarters in the edge of the little wood, at a point from which he could overlook the intervening valley, which stretched up to the base of the mountain, and had the road leading to the Pass and the Pass itself plainly in vision."[69]

As Bartlett reached Franklin's headquarters he "found grouped there, resting upon the ground, in as comfortable positions as each one could assume, after lunch, smoking their cigars," the divisional commanders and many of the VI Corps brigadiers.[70] After discussing various tactical options, General Slocum, who sarcastically claimed the Confederate force consisted "of four cavalrymen, two guns and no infantry," turned command of the field operation over to Colonel Bartlett. Aston-

Pvt. Henry C. Boyer, Company A. Discharged on surgeon's certificate December 4, 1862 (MOLLUS Mass. Collection, United States Army Heritage and Education Center).

ished by the decision of Franklin and his subordinates, Bartlett informed the West Point-
ers that he intended to attack to the right of the road.[71] In addition, he elected to use a
formation "of the three brigades [of Slocum's division] in column of regiments deployed,
two regiments front, at 100 paces interval between lines (that would give us six lines)."[72]
Finally, Bartlett stated that he would "attack at the point in the manner indicated, take
the crest of the mountain and throw out a picket-line for the might."[73] By 3 p.m. the meeting was over. By that time, however, Bartlett was facing two foes: the Confederates at the
foot of Crampton's Gap and the Sun which was beginning to wane in the western sky
beyond South Mountain.

About 4 p.m. Bartlett ordered his old regiment, the 27th New York, "to deploy as
skirmishers, advance on the pass, and develop the enemy's position, which was all in all
at least a mile long."[74] In a postwar account, George Kilmer, who served with the 27th
New York, recalled the initial action of the engagement. "Along the base of the mountain
the valley road is terraced and provided with a stone wall half a mile each side of the
gap, and there is no connection here between this road and the one passing through the
gap, but instead a heavy forest and limestone ledges block the passage. A strong force lay
behind the stone wall and another remained at the cut and between ... was a battery
commanding the interval. Here the Twenty-seventh deployed and went at double-quick
through orchards and gardens, terrifying beast and fowls and even dogged by spiteful
mastiffs and terriers."[75]

As the New Yorkers advanced across the farm fields "in [a] splendid line" Bartlett
neatly arrayed the 5th Maine and the 16th New York in formation for battle. Following
200 paces behind the 27th New York, the two regiments "advanced in the line of battle
side by side through three or four open fields under fire of shell, [canister] and bullets
from the enemy on the heights, unaided by a single piece of artillery. We advanced till
within twenty rods of the enemy's line, only a level plowed field between us, halted here,
and coolly went to work under every disadvantage of numbers and position."[76] Smith
Bailey, serving in the 5th Maine, recalled that "the 16th N.Y. and 5th M[ain]e was formed
in a line of battle and moved forward while the other Regts. of the Division were formed
in the rear and on the right. The skirmishers [27th New York] were ordered to advance
and were soon engaged. The 16th N.Y. and 5th M[ain]e moved rapidly [double-quick]
across a broad field which was a corn field, amid[st] a raking fire from the rebel artillery,
which was in an advantageous position and engaged the rebel infantry. Our artillery did
but little execution not being able to get into a good position. The steadiness of our Regts.
while advancing for a distance of half a mile under a galling fire was splendid."[77] As
Bartlett led forward the two New York regiments and the Maine men to open the operation, Colonel Cake with the 96th Pennsylvania maintained a stout skirmish line fronting
the Confederate right.

After Colonel Bartlett deployed the New York and Maine men, Cake was ordered
to recall the advance elements of the regiment performing picket duty near Ahalt's saw
mill and the line of skirmishers extending toward the village of Burkittsville.[78] Before
Captain Lamar Hay's Company A could rejoin the regiment, Cake moved the Pennsylvanians from the Knoxville Road into a small valley in rear of the village thus sheltering
the Schuylkill Countians from the deadly Confederate artillery. While awaiting the return
of Company A, General Slocum conferred with Cake. Upon seeing Slocum, Cake quipped,
"Well, we have more than four cavalrymen and two guns before us." Slocum replied, "Yes,

we are going to have a fight."[79] Cake informed Slocum that he was awaiting Captain Hay's return from the mill before advancing farther. As the officers continued their conversation, Confederate artillery fire to their right startled everyone and brought the soldiers to their feet.[80]

While the Bluecoats observed the impact of the Confederate artillery fire, Company A rejoined the regiment. Turning to Slocum, Cake simply said, "Well?" Slocum quickly snapped, "Well, follow [Col. Alfred A.] Torbert, and if you find anything to do, do it!"[81] About 5 o'clock in the afternoon, according to Henry Boyer, "the Jerseymen were quite out of sight, their trail was very plain to view and we followed it easily and quickly. We came upon them just as they had formed their two lines of battle and as they moved forward a third of their rear and continued to follow. Our officers ... reformed our right wing, so that we were debouched from the corn field. We were 100 yards to the right and about halfway between the first and second lines of our friends. In this order we marched until we came in full view of the enemy."[82] As the 96th moved forward in close supporting distance of Torbert's Jersey Brigade, Colonel Bartlett ordered the Schuylkill Countians to advance to the far right of the Union line.[83]

Initially, Cake was ordered by General Slocum to position the 96th Pennsylvania in rear of Torbert's New Jersey Brigade. Subsequently, Bartlett ordered Cake to move his regiment to the extreme right flank of the Union position. As he did at Gaines' Mill, Bartlett personally posted the 96th on the Union line of battle. In his memoir he recalled that "the 96th Pa., Col. Henry L. Cake who had been skirmishing on the extreme left, near Burkittsville ... now came up, and I extended my line with it to the right."[84] Crossing the farm fields, however, proved to be a perilous flank march. According to 2nd Lt. Samuel Russell of Company C, "The enemy had every advantage and we every disadvantage; we were finally ordered forward and after advancing about half a mile, the rebels poured a tremendous fire of shell and grape upon us."[85] It was the converging artillery fire from the two aforementioned gaps which wounded a number of men in Company H as the 96th traversed the field. In addition to the artillery fire raking and harassing the marching column, fence lines, thickets, gullies and rolling terrain added to the difficulties in moving the regiment to the right flank of the Union line.

As they did at Gaines' Mill, the Pennsylvanians once again passed behind the Bluecoat battle line in order to form on the right flank of the Union position. Captain Haas of Company G recalled in his pocket diary the harrowing march across the field. "We marched through a cornfield to the rear and then behind the hills to the brigade, the Enemy shelling us as we retired."[86] In crossing the farm fields, a Confederate artillery round exploded in the ranks of Company H, killing and wounding several of the men. Rifle fire from the Confederate infantry, too, harassed the Pennsylvanians as they crossed the farm fields. This bold movement across the field was recognized as a worthy feat of arms by their Confederate counterparts. In a postwar memoir, Captain James A. Toomer of the 16th Virginia graphically recalled the moment. "One of the prettiest sights I ever saw was the charge of one of their regiments against the lines just to our left. It was a large regiment, with very full ranks, and was supposed by us to be the 'Pennsylvania Bucktails.' They came over the field grandly, the officers all in place and cheering the men onward, the men well aligned on the colors, with the Stars and Stripes floating proudly above them and born aloft by a stalwart sergeant, who bore himself every inch a soldier. Half way across the field the fire upon them was so deadly that they halted and threw themselves upon the ground to avoid, as much as possible, the destructive rain of Minie balls poured into their ranks."[87]

As the 96th reached the right flank of the Union line, Bartlett, as he did at Gaines' Mill, personally superintended the position and deployment of the Pennsylvanians. Arrayed for battle, the Union commanders made final preparations for a coordinated assault by Slocum's division upon the formidable Confederate position along the Mountain Church Road. In order to anchor the right flank of the assault, Cake moved the regiment forward, passing through a screen of dense vegetation and reformed the regiment in a field a considerable distance in advance of the main Union line. Using the rolling terrain of the farm fields to his advantage, Cake moved the 96th Pennsylvania to a slight elevation within five or six hundred yards of the left of the Confederate line anchored by the 10th Georgia Volunteers. As the Pennsylvanians held their advanced and unsupported position, it was becoming increasingly apparent to the soldiers that only a concerted infantry charge would deliver a Union victory. The line officers thus were instructed to resupply the soldiers with ammunition taken from fallen comrades. In addition, the officers instructed the men to examine their weapons, to see that the rifle discharged properly, after the initial volley was fired. Now that the Schuylkill Countians were combat veterans, they not only carried the regulation number of rounds in their cartridge boxes, but they also loaded their pockets with additional rounds in case a stand up fire fight should develop. While the soldiers of the 96th awaited the order to charge, Bartlett and Torbert conferred briefly to finalize the destruction of the Confederates defending the base of the mountain.[88]

Once in position on the Union right, Cake and his Pennsylvanians were sent forward to draw the concentrated fire of the enemy in order to identify the left flank of the Confederate position.[89] In addition, once the enemy's position was determined, Cake was to lead the 96th Pennsylvania forward and turn the Confederate left flank held by the 10th Georgia.[90] Breaking the Confederate position, defined by a formidable stone wall running along Mountain Church Road, was an ambitious and challenging operation for Cake and his band of Pennsylvanians. Crossing the fields of the Goodman farm, unfamiliar terrain with additional obstacles, further complicated the hazardous mission for the Schuylkill Countians. Finally, after the Pennsylvanians closed on the Confederate position they would need to summon their courage in order to execute the bayonet charge and dislodge the Georgians from behind the stone wall. Colonel Cake and Major Martin, both on foot, exhorted the soldiers at each step and actively encouraged the Pennsylvanians as they advanced toward the climactic clash of the battle.

According to Bartlett, he "sought Colonel Torbert on his line and held a hurried consultation with him to the effect that we would separate in the center, each riding down his own line, and order the men to cease firing, load, and be ready for a charge at double-quick."[91] As the Pennsylvanians waited for the signal to begin the assault, they studied the terrain in their front. Henry Boyer believed that the Confederates would reserve their fire until the Pennsylvanians debouched from the corn field in their front perhaps because the soldiers "felt sure that that is just what we would have done under the same circumstances."[92] During the final moments of the brief cease fire, final instructions for the assault were issued to the Schuylkill Countians. The advance was to be conducted at quick-time, which meant one hundred ten steps per minute. The soldiers were to move forward deliberately and "to fire at will when we reach the corn, but only to fire at something we thought we could hit."[93] In addition, recalled Henry Boyer, "Each man was to feel his next file, keep in his place and when we reached within two paces of the open field beyond the corn we were to break into double-quick with a cheer and take the road at all hazard."[94]

Moving forward in two ranks, all of the officers on foot, the left flank would be commanded by Martin while Cake would lead the right flank. Finally, the flags were brought forward. Company C, commanded by Capt. William H. Lessig, would serve as the color company and proudly carry the flag presented to the regiment in Pottsville by Governor Curtin. On this day, too, the 96th Pennsylvania would also follow an old flag previously carried by Colonel Cake's three-month command of the 25th Pennsylvania Volunteers. As the tension mounted, an officer approached the left flank of the regiment. "Just then," recalled John Boyle of Company D, "Colonel Bartlett, his face flushed with the excitement of battle … rode up to the command waving his sword and crying at the top of his voice 'Now, Pennsylvanians, do your duty.'"[95] With a ringing cheer the men advanced intent upon driving the Confederates from behind the stone wall at the point of the bayonet.

As the regiment surged forward, the soldiers stepped over the prone picket reserve of the 27th New York. Moving across the farm fields of Jacob Goodman, the 96th's advance was impeded by several stone walls and worm fence. Cake, who was on foot, as were the other field officers, leaped over a fence, waved his sword and called upon the soldiers to follow him forward. Some of the Pennsylvanians, perhaps overwhelmed with stress, discharged their muskets at random. Most of the men, however, advanced through the fields with their muskets at "Trail arms." Some of the soldiers moved forward with their ramrods in the barrel of the rifle in the act of loading the piece.[96] According to Colonel Cake, "The fields through which the Ninety-sixth charged presented many obstacles, and, in order not to meet the enemy with broken lines, I twice halted momentarily, with a stone fence for a cover, for a great portion of the regiment to form."[97] As the 96th surged across the farm fields, Confederate artillery and rifle fire from the dismounted cavalry, infantry and sharpshooters posted behind the stone wall and within the local farm houses, also interrupted the advance of the Schuylkill Countians. Moving across the fields, the line officers continually urged the soldiers forward shouting, "Trail arms," and then "Steady now!"[98] The last one hundred yards proved to be the most difficult for the Pennsylvanians, numbering between 500 and 525 in the assault, as they advanced toward the stone wall held by the 10th Georgia Volunteers.[99]

As they crossed the fields of the Goodman farm, anxiety gripped many of the soldiers as they converged on the Confederate battle line. The Confederates, sheltered behind the stone wall, held their fire intent upon delivering a thunderous volley as the 96th Pennsylvania emerged from the corn field in their front. In his after-action report, Colonel Cake recalled that "brisk musket firing was in progress on our left, but the good cover in possession of the enemy, and the distance at which we stood rendered it quite certain that we would gain nothing at a stand off fight while the artillery posted in the mountain was punishing us severely."[100] Captain Boyle, writing nine years after the battle, recalled the emotions that the soldiers experienced that afternoon as they closed on the 173 Graycoats of the 10th Georgia.

> At every step some poor soul escaped through a bullet-hole into eternity, or some brave body fell forward, or sank to earth, with [an] agonizing shriek or cry of pain. The excitement was now at fever heat. All fear had fled from the minds of the men, and their pale faces begrimed with powder,

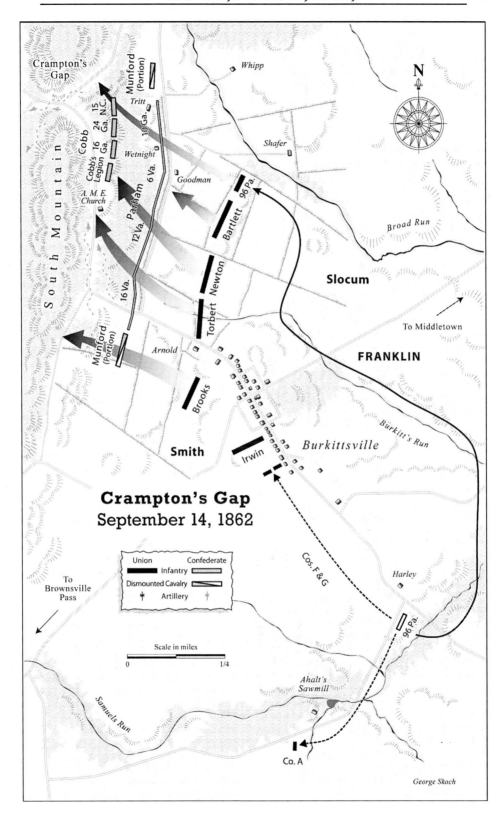

Crampton's Gap

Whipp

Munford (Portion)

Tritt

15 Ga.

24 Ga.

N.C.

Cobb

Shafer

16 Ga.

Cobb's Legion Ga.

10 Ga.

Wetnight

6 Va.

Goodman

A. M. E. Church

Panham

96 Pa.

Bartlett

S o u t h   M o u n t a i n

12 Va.

16 Va.

Newton

Torbert

Broad Run

Slocum

Munford (Portion)

Arnold

Brooks

FRANKLIN

To Middletown

Smith

Irwin

Burkitt's Run

Burkittsville

Crampton's Gap
September 14, 1862

Union	Confederate
■ Infantry	▨
Dismounted Cavalry	⧄
⚔ Artillery	⚔

Cos. F & G

Harley

To
Brownsville
Pass

Scale in miles

0   1/4

96 Pa.

Samuels Run

Ahalt's
Sawmill

Co. A

George Skoch

and lit by frenzied, bloodshot eyes, wore the expressions of demons. The sight of blood seemed to stir some to desperation, while others moved forward with a reckless abandon perfectly surprising. Only one, here and there, yielded to that irresistible feeling of dread which sometimes possesses the breast of the bravest and which is perfectly uncontrollable, sought refuge behind a rock, in the recess of a gully, or behind a favoring tree."[101]

While Cake and his command executed their charge, the veteran soldiers of Maj. Willis Holt's 10th Georgia patiently awaited the arrival of the Schuylkill Countians. As the 96th Pennsylvania emerged from the corn field, forty paces away, the 10th Georgia delivered a volley which temporarily halted the advance of the Unionists.[102] Stopping the 96th momentarily enabled the Georgians to concentrate their rifle fire against the center three companies of the 96th Pennsylvania. It appears that Holt's Georgians sought to disrupt the combat cohesion of the 96th by eliminating the color bearers. By wounding or killing the standard bearers there was a high probability that the regiment, lacking the guidance of the colors, might remain fixed in place. In Captain Boyle's opinion, this proved to be the decisive moment of the battle. "The situation was critical. The moment one of terrible apprehension—enough to appeal [to] the stoutest heart. If allowed to front face in line of battle, one volley from them would annihilate the command or scatter it to the wind. The officers and men were equal to the emergency."[103] Rather than recoiling from the deadly fire, Colonel Cake reformed the ranks of the 96th Pennsylvania and dramatically led the soldiers forward routing the Georgians at the point of the bayonet.

Lt. Col. William H. Lessig, original captain of Company C. Promoted to major September 15, 1862, and lieutenant colonel December 23, 1862. Commissioned in the rank of colonel March 13, 1863, but never mustered. Lessig subsequently mustered out with the regiment on October 21, 1864 (collection of Douglas Sagrillo).

As the regiment neared the Mountain Church Road the Confederates at the stone wall could see the battle flags of the 96th Pennsylvania, bobbing up and down, as the Schulykill Countians advanced across the farm fields. The soldiers of the 10th Georgia could not see the color bearers, Solomon McMinzie, of Company C, a Scotsman who faithfully served twelve years in the Royal Artillery, and Sgt. Thomas Oliver of the color company who carried the national colors, as they were hidden from view by the corn stalks. While most of the 96th was screened by the corn field, the left and right flank companies of the 96th advanced without the benefit of concealment.[104] As soon as the 96th Pennsylvania emerged from the corn field, by one account only twenty paces from the stone wall, the Georgians fired a murderous volley into the on-coming Schuylkill Countians. According to Capt. James Russell, Company E, "Just before we reached the fence, we received a terrible fire; our men fell fast."[105] Henry Keiser noted in his diary, "The Rebels were in line at the foot of the mountain behind a stone fence and when we were within a short distance of them, they gave us a deadly volley, and a great many of our poor boys fell."[106] At this moment, in close quarters combat, the soldiers needed to draw upon their training in camp and their previous combat experience at Gaines' Mill in addition to summoning their courage in order to survive this ordeal by fire.

The Pennsylvanians who survived this deadly encounter with the 10th Georgia recounted the engagement in vivid detail in their diaries and post battle letters. Captain Boyle recalled the moment of the initial volley in a lengthy postwar narrative. "It was here that the regiment met with its heaviest

Capt. James Russell, original captain of Company E. Mustered out with regiment October 21, 1864 (courtesy James Reed).

loss. Scarcely had it entered the corn patch than the companies were thrown into charging disorder and their further progress momentarily stayed by a tremendous reserved fire from the enemy behind the stone wall."[107] James Treichler also recalled the initial fusillade: "A corn field thru which we were passing hid the enemy from view until we were close upon them. They held their fire until we appeared on the edge of the field, within Fourty feet, when they saluted us with a continuous shour of leden Bullets…. It is hardly necessary to say that we were, staggerd and completely surprised, probably stupefied for we did not return the fire for a minute or two."[108] As the Pennsylvanians recoiled from the deadly volley, Cake, Martin and the line officers sought to stabilize and reform the regiment's battle formation. Captain Royer, commanding Company H, adjacent to the color company, ungraciously believed that the color bearers "broke and left colors" upon the opening salvo by the Georgians. In fact, Sergeant McMinzie, according to Captain Boyle "who was bravely upholding the [Pennsylvania] State ensign received a mortal wound in the breast." Adding further, Captain Boyle of Company D recalled that McMinzie exclaimed "I am shot," and as he staggered forward the sergeant cried out "and again." Upon the second wound, recalled Boyle, the "flag staff slipped from his nerveless grasp, and, with shattered thigh, he sank with a sigh into the arms of death." Almost simultaneously with McMinzie's mortal wounding, Sgt. Thomas Oliver of Company C, bearing the national flag, was wounded in the foot and dropped the sacred banner. When the two color bearers fell, "a cry of exultation … [was sent] up from the Rebel line and a chill of dismay shivered through the frames of those of the regiment who saw the occurrence."[109]

As McMinzie fell to the ground, Captain Royer of Company H ordered William Ortner to seize the banner from the stricken color bearer. Subsequently, and in rapid fire sequence, Ortner was wounded by a musket ball, causing the private to relinquish the flag. Seeing Ortner fall, Color Sergeant Johnson raised the standard aloft. Almost immediately, he too was wounded, sustaining a ghastly head injury. Pvt. Charles Ziegler of Company H rushed from his position in line, grasped the flag staff and raised the standard for his comrades to follow. As he did so, another Confederate volley "deprived him of life and he fell forward to the earth," staining the silken folds of the flag with his blood.[110] As the 10th Georgia concentrated its rifle fire upon the flags borne by the color bearers, Cake, Martin and the field officers sought to regroup the shattered ranks of the regiment for a final charge upon the stone wall.[111] Cake labored under fire to reform the regiment in order to undertake a decisive charge to overwhelm the Georgians by sheer weight of numbers. According to Captain Boyle, "The situation was critical; the moment one of terrible apprehension."[112] The Pennsylvanians, peering through the smoke from the rifle fire, believed they saw additional Confederates streaming down the mountain to support the Georgians. Fixing bayonets "the command girded itself for the final rush." Stepping in front of the Pennsylvanians, Cake issued the order, "Forward into the road and give them the bayonet—it is death for all to hesitate now!"[113] "After firing a volley," Captain Boyle wrote, "into the newly arrived troops before they had time to face and fire, the men rushed forward at a charge, and with the force of a whirlwind."[114]

After the battle, many of the Schuylkill Countians recorded the impact the dramatic encounter with the Georgians had upon the soldiers. Captain Royer of Company H recalled that "it was while making the charge that we suffered."[115] Lieutenant Russell of Company C, later wrote that "just before we reached the fence, we received a terrible fire; our men fell fast."[116] In his graphic memoir, Captain Boyle described the sights and sounds of the decisive moment of the bayonet charge. "Instantly, those … who had not yet crossed the fence, commenced scrambling over, and with a shout which sounded high over the din of conflict, rushed forward to the feast of death. The cheers thus started were caught up by the other regiments, who, now, en echelon away off to the left were double quicking it across the fields to the sound of the bugle. The shrill Randolphish yells of the Confederates were completely drowned out, but their firing increased in intensity."[117]

As the Pennsylvanians surged forward against the foe, driving the Secessionists from behind the stone wall at the point of the bayonet, another fusillade from the gallant 10th Georgia tore through the oncoming Schuylkill Countians. As the musket balls riddled the ranks of the 96th Pennsylvania, Major Martin on the left flank was struck in the head as he urged the Pennsylvanians forward. According to Captain Boyle, Martin was "urging on some laggards to the left of the regiment … [when he] was hit by a ball in the back part of the head."[118] Mortally wounded, Martin died while being carried to the rear for medical attention. Almost simultaneously with Martin's mortal wounding, 1st Lt. John Dougherty, commanding Company F, a few paces in front of his company, waving his sword in the air encouraging the soldiers to follow him, received a grievous wound in his chest. Colonel Cake, in close proximity to Dougherty, recalled the lieutenant's wounding in his after action report. "I had seen Lt. Dougherty, one of my best officers, fall….

Shot through the breast, while bravely leading his company to the final struggle at the road."[119] Subsequently, Sergeant Casey seized Dougherty's sword valiantly raised it over his head and dashed forward leading Company F toward the Georgians.[120] Within moments, the Pennsylvanians were over the stone wall, surging past the Confederates, enveloping both flanks of the 10th Georgia, and in the process cutting off the retreat of the Secessionists.[121]

Charging forward the Pennsylvanians engulfed the steadfast soldiers of the 10th Georgia who gallantly held their position under the crushing weight of the Bluecoat bayonet attack. In his lengthy memoir, Captain Boyle recalled the scene along the Mountain Church Road as the Confederate battle line collapsed

Capt. Charles Dougherty, Company F. Promoted from second lieutenant July 31, 1862. Resigned February 28, 1863 (Ronn Palm collection).

under the crushing weight of the Union bayonet assault. "Nothing human could withstand the fury of the onset and ... the enemy immediately in front, seized with a sudden panic, threw down their arms, tore off their accoutrements and fled up the steep side of the mountain like deer before the chase. Instantly their whole line gave way, and ... they poured upward through the deep ravines toward the Pass."[122] In his official report, Colonel Cake described the dramatic charge across the Mountain Church Road toward the Georgians. "It was here [that] we met our great loss. Shocked but not repulsed, the men bounded forward, determined, to end it with the bayonet. The last of the several fields through which we had to charge was meadow and standing corn. As we emerged from the corn [field] the enemy met us with a murderous fire. The road was gained in a twinkling, the enemy leaving for the mountain. Those of the enemy who were [taken prisoner] begged lustily for mercy."[123]

After the battle, Major Holt, commanding the 10th Georgia, described the terrifying situation his regiment confronted at this point in the engagement. "The commander of the 10th Georgia informed me," recalled General McLaws in a postwar memoir, "that looking to his rear when in line of defense to the left of Mahone [Parham], he, much to his astonishment saw that they were behind him, and that facing his men to the rear they fought their way out as best they could, and that finally there was nothing to do but run for it."[124] Charging on the Georgians, Captain Haas leading forward Company G, made a narrow escape. The top of his canteen was shot off knocking him to the ground. Upon regaining his footing, Haas recalled that "one 'Reb' shot at me out of a house [widow Susan Tritt's] as I crossed the fence. I had him in tight papers. I took him prisoner."[125] As the Pennsylvanians clambered over the stone wall, the right wing of the regiment came under fire from a detachment of Georgia sharpshooters posted in the nearby home of the widow Susan Tritt. Captain Boyle, of Company D, later wrote that the Confederate sharpshooters "kept up a galling fire on our force. Several of these [soldiers] unable to make their escape, after vainly endeavoring to hide themselves in the cellar or garret, were captured or bayoneted."[126] As the Bluecoats of the 96th swarmed the gallant men of the 10th Georgia an amusing incident unfolded at this pivotal moment in the battle.

According to Captain Boyle, as the 96th cleared the Tritt house of sharpshooters "an ancient dame ... showed herself at one of the windows waving her old calico sun-bonnet with both her hands, and with loud cries and frantic endeavors, strove to prevent our men from firing."[127] Another Bluecoat, in a New York regiment, also recorded the same scene in a lengthy memoir penned after the war. "A very amusing incident took place at this moment. There was quite a substantial stone house on the opposite side of the road where we came out, and a lady came out on the balcony in a state of great excite-ment, and fairly screamed "I told them they would run, and they did run, for I saw them run." She, no doubt, was not in sympathy with them."[128] As the Georgians fled up the mountain, Colonel Cake sought to reform his battered regiment with the intent of pur-suing the "flying foe" and driving the Confederates from the summit of Crampton's Gap. Cake, in his after-action report, stated that he "hastily formed line, Major Maginnis of the Eighteenth New York promising to form on my left and follow and dashed on up the hill, keeping the line formed as well as possible, to guard against a probable stand of the enemy at the crest of the hill I let the men advance nearly as fast as they could and wanted too."[129]

At this juncture, Cake was compelled to confront the grim realities of Civil War combat. The action had exacted a heavy toll in casualties. The 96th Pennsylvania had lost almost twenty percent of its effective force. The initial volley from the Georgians had also killed Major Martin who was commanding the left wing of the regiment. As a result, Colonel Cake would assume command and control of the regiment for the final ascent of the mountain. Without a lieutenant colonel, having lost Major Martin and a new adjutant—Lieutenant George Boyer—Cake seized the moment and exercised com-mand leadership when it was most needed. Cake's after-action report clearly reveals his thoughts at this important point in the battle. "I hastily formed my line, Major Meginnis of the Eighteenth New York promising to form on my left, and dashed on up the hill."[130] Upon reforming the regiment in the Mountain Church Road the Pennsylvanians girded themselves for the final rush up the mountain. In his detailed memoir Colonel Bartlett recognized that this advance might determine the outcome of the battle. "The 18th N.Y. and the 32nd N.Y. were nearly out of ammunition, but they, together with the 96th Pa., on their right, were directly in front ... of the enemy, and if they faltered the victory would be lost."[131]

As the 96th Pennsylvania and the balance of Slocum's division prepared to ascend South Mountain, Howell Cobb's brigade was moving into position to stem the rising tide of Bluecoats. Various sources, when examined together, reveal that Cobb's Brigade aligned as follows from left to right: 15th North Carolina, 24th Georgia, 16th Georgia and finally Cobb's Legion on the far right.[132] Once deployed for battle, the Confederates of Cobb's brigade were confronted with a series of obstacles which ultimately compromised their combat performance. The Secessionists, although eager for fight, entered the fray as dark-ness was descending. The loss of daylight coupled with the challenging terrain of Cramp-ton's Gap fractured the cohesion of the four Confederate regiments as they made their way down the mountain to engage the Bluecoats. As a result, each Confederate regiment fought its own battle with the opposing elements of Slocum's division. The 24th Georgia numbering less than 300 men and armed principally with inferior smooth bore muskets, moved down the mountain, perhaps halfway, to slow the advancing Unionists.[133] To the left of the Georgians, the 15th North Carolina, also pushed down the eastern slope of the mountain, determined to anchor the flank of the Confederate line. The Georgians, however, were quickly overwhelmed leading Lt. Col. Christopher Sanders to retreat to the summit in order to reform at a better defensive position. The withdrawal of the 24th Georgia created the void in the Confederate line that the 96th Pennsylvania exploited in its advance toward the mountain's summit.

Capt. Henry Royer, Company H. Promoted from first lieutenant February 12, 1862. Resigned January 13, 1863 (author's collection).

In his magisterial study of Lee's Army of Northern Virginia, Douglas Southall Freeman stated that Slocum's division of the VI Corps "came up the mountain like a rain cloud."[134] In squads and broken companies the soldiers of the 96th Pennsylvania ascended the mountain intent upon routing the Confederates hastily reforming for a last stand at the summit of Crampton's Gap. Captain Boyle recalled that the Pennsylvanians "pushed straight on up the steep slope, firing at and capturing the enemy at almost every step."[135] Leading the advance up the mountain was Sgt. Andrew Anderson of Company K. As he struggled through the tangled underbrush, Anderson suddenly encountered the standard bearer of the 16th Georgia. The Georgia color bearer, upon spotting Sergeant Anderson, dropped the flag he was carrying and turned to flee. Anderson, more intent upon capturing the Georgia flag bearer "brought the retreating foeman to earth."[136] While Anderson shot the color bearer, Sgt. Henry Fisher of Company C captured Captain Thompson of the 16th Georgia. After capturing a number of soldiers of the 16th Georgia, Cake sought to reorganize and reform the disjointed elements of his command.

After pushing up the mountain a short distance, in relative disorder, Cake realigned the regiment, formed a new line of battle, deployed skirmishers and continued the advance up the steep slope toward the summit. This final ascent of the mountain, according to Captain Henry Royer of Company H "was a terrible undertaking. Think of it, charging up a mountain steeper and more rugged than Sharp Mountain, and covered with timber and heavy undergrowth."[137] Colonel Cake later reported that "it was a most exhausting charge. By time we had ascended half way the cannon had ceased firing on our left, and the enemy seldom replied to our fire with their muskets. We made captures at every step."[138] As the soldiers of the 10th and 16th Georgia respectively retreated in the face of the oncoming Yankees of the 96th Pennsylvania, James Treichler described the pursuit of the Confederates toward the top of the mountain. With some amusement, he recalled that the Georgians "did not stop to return greetings, or extend compliments at a distance, but scaled these heights with alacrity. We could have avenged our fallen comrades had we been blood thirsty, but it was sufficien[t] to see them climb the rough and rugged hillside.

Writing less than two weeks after the battle, Eli Landers of the 16th Georgia told his mother about the "bad nuse" concerning the fate of his regiment at Crampton's Gap. "We went in[to] the fight with 30 men in our company and lost 18 of them though we can't tell who was killed for it was every man for himself. First they fell back on our right and let the enemy flank us. They come in near taking all of our regiment prisoners."[140] As the 96th swept up the mountain, the Pennsylvanians, according to Cake, "sent during the charge, 42 prisoners to the rear."[141] And yet, as darkness descended on the mountain, after routing the 10th Georgia and capturing many men from the 16th Georgia, the Pennsylvanians found another foe in their front blocking their climb toward the crest of Crampton's Gap.[142]

As the 96th Pennsylvania and the other elements of the VI Corps overwhelmed the Confederates along the Mountain Church Road and began their ascent of Crampton's Gap, a Confederate brigade under General Cobb formed for battle just below the summit of the mountain. On the Confederate left was a lone Tarheel regiment the 15th North Carolina. To their right was the 24th Georgia, the 16th Georgia and finally Cobb's Legion.[143] With the Arnoldstown Road in their rear, the Tarheels moved down the mountain, reformed for battle and waited for the oncoming Pennsylvanians. Elijah Sutton of the 24th Georgia, who stood in line with the 15th North Carolina stated that "the enemy [was] hidden in the undergrowth below us and we could not see them except now and then as they moved. Our line being above them was more easily seen and the men falling on all sides."[144] Continuing up the steep slope toward the summit, Lieutenant Russell of Company C, informed his father after the battle that the 96th Pennsylvania as "not to be kept back." Adding further he related "on we went … we kept on and drove the enemy to the top of the mountain with terrible loss, completely routing them."[145] In his diary, Lewis Luckenbill of Company B, recorded that "we got orders to charge and … ran them clear off the mountain. Going up the mountain our [Orderly Sgt. John Von Hollen] was wounded the only one in our company."[146] Captain Haas described this final phase of the battle best when he noted in his diary, "We gave them hell after we had them on the jump up the mountain."[147]

The breach created by the retreat of the 24th Georgia exposed the left flank of the 16th Georgia and the right flank of the 15th North Carolina. According to Private Boyer the Pennsylvanians "observed [that] his bullets flying high over our heads, which gave us renewed courage, while our aim, being up-hill, was doing deadly work."[148] As a result, the soldiers were able to advance up the mountain, virtually unscathed, clambering over the rocks and capturing Georgians and Tarheels at virtually every step.[149] The 16th Georgia numbered 368 muskets at Crampton's Gap, but 107 soldiers of the regiment were counted as missing, most likely captured at South Mountain.[150] Lieutenant Kearney of the 15th North Carolina, and the author of a history of the regiment, reported that 124 Tarheels were captured by the Sixth Corps at Crampton's Gap. Prior to the battle, the effective strength of the 15th North Carolina was 402.[151]

David Chandler, a young private serving with the 15th North Carolina, in a letter written after the battle, informed his father and wife about the deadly engagement at

Crampton's Gap. Although seriously wounded in the fierce combat action at Crampton's Gap, Private Chandler penned a lengthy account of the deadly engagement to his family in Person County, North Carolina "our Regiment got shot up very badly." Chandler also added that the "Yankees [had] taken about half of the Regiment prisoners.... They ran us over the other side of [South] mountain clear down to the foot of the mountain right among the Enemy and they fought us both wings. And we had to retreat back to the top of the mountain and they had a good shot at us."[152] As the Pennsylvanians clambered up the mountain, the three Georgia regiments of Cobb's Brigade were either shattered or in full retreat under the weight of the Yankee onslaught. Pushing past the 16th Georgia, soldiers of the 96th Pennsylvania not taking prisoners, continued up the mountain bypassing the recoiled right flank of the 15th North Carolina. Lt. H.C. Kearney of Company E, described the final moments of the Confederate defense of Crampton's Gap. "Being engaged with the enemy in front and confident of the strength of our position, the first knowledge we had of the situation on the right was a terrible volley of musketry from the rear and right flank, which was at first thought to be from our own troops, who had mistaken us for the enemy, but soon such thoughts were dispelled by seeing the federal flag in the rear."[153] As the 96th swept past the right flank of the Tarheels, Henry Keiser of Company G later recounted that "the survivors pushed on, routed the Rebels and drove them up over the mountain, but darkness prevented us from following them further than [the] top of the mountain."[154]

Surging to the summit by squads and small groups, the survivors of the 96th Pennsylvania reached the crest of Crampton's Gap as darkness descended upon South Mountain. Recollections of the climactic charge made against the 16th Georgia and the 15th North Carolina varied widely among the veterans of the 96th Pennsylvania. According to James Treichler, the Schuylkill Countians "followed up leisurely gathering Prisoners from behind rock and other hiding places."[155] Henry Boyer in his detailed memoir recalled that the Pennsylvanians "moved up the steep side of the mountain, horribly killing and wounding all we could ... and mercifully a disposition to surrender."[156] In a letter written four days after the battle, Henry Royer of Company H, informed his father that "once we got them going up the hill we murdered them by the hundreds."[157] While personal accounts of the charge up the mountain distorted the actual achievement of the 96th at Crampton's Gap there was universal agreement concerning singular success of Slocum's division of the Sixth Corps. A veteran of Bartlett's brigade recorded the events and significance of the battle with the following passage in his pocket diary. "The Rebels themselves say that our charge was the most brilliant thing they ever saw. The success of this engagement did much to give the men confidence in the Genls. especially Slocum, in each other, and in themselves and to give the Genls. confidence in the men."[158] Captain Boyle later proclaimed the victory at Crampton's Gap to be "one of the cleanest little fights on the war, and had the night not intervened the capture of the greater part of the Rebel forces engaged must have been inevitable."[159]

In the darkness, on the summit of Crampton's Gap, Colonel Cake sought to reform and reorganize the exhausted companies of the 96th. At this juncture, Captain Russell of Company C related that "on reaching the top of the mountain we formed our line again, but it was too dark to follow further. Here we halted for about three quarters of an hour, when we came down some distance and remained for the night. We had no blankets and it was quite cold."[160] Captain Filbert's company was ordered, along with a detachment from Captain Lessig's company, to establish a perimeter and reconnoiter the mountain toward Fox's Gap. Another contingent of thirty men, however, was ordered down the eastern slope of the mountain with candles and torches to locate soldiers wounded at the stone wall running along the Mountain Church Road. In a letter to his father, Henry Royer stated, "We slept among the dead and wounded. I say we, but I slept little. I was busy all night in hunting up my own poor fellows and getting the wounded to the hospitals."[161] Lewis Luckenbill noted in his diary that the 96th "remained in a line of battle until nine o'clock at night when we got orders to fall back to [the] foot of the mountain ... to rest as well as we could. That night we laid down and rested. In the morning dead and wounded men were laying [all] around us."[162] For the soldiers of the 96th the night of September 14 proved to be a bivouac among the dead.

VI

"Colonel, your coal-heavers did well!"

Daylight the following morning afforded the soldiers an opportunity to assist their wounded comrades and bury the dead; whether they hailed from Pennsylvania or Georgia. Unlike the battlefield at Gaines' Mill, where the Unionists retreated under the cover of darkness, at Crampton's Gap the Sixth Corps slept on the ground where they had been victorious. Morning, however, after the Battle of South Mountain revealed to the soldiers the deadly carnage wrought on the Sabbath. In his pocket diary Lewis Luckenbill described the scene. "After I had some coffee kooked I went over the field. It was a great sight to see, it made me feel sick to see so many dead persons lying around over the ground and not buried."[1] Henry Royer "buried the dead in one grave, so that any of them can be taken up if desirable, without difficulty."[2] Captain Haas of Company G recorded in his diary that he "walked down over the battle ground, plenty of dead and wounded 'Rebs' laying around mostly the 16th Georgia and the 15th North Carolina." The following day Haas brought grapes and tea for the injured men of his company and "sent grub down to the wounded."[3] Francis Boland related that "we buried the Union and Rebel dead next day, Monday Sept. 15th. Also we took the wounded on both sides to Burkettsville a mile distant. We filled all the churches with the wounded. This was a shocking scene."[4] For the 96th Pennsylvania, the number of soldiers killed and wounded was similar to the losses they sustained at Gaines' Mill. Nineteen men killed or mortally wounded. Seventy were wounded in the spirited charge upon the 10th Georgia.[5] The loss of Major Martin, Lieutenant Dougherty and several color bearers was a significant toll to pay for the passage over Crampton's Gap. Despite the heavy casualties, Private Boyer stated that "our work was fortuitous, but none of our officers and men ever thought they had done more than their simple duty." While the soldiers collectively understood that they had achieved a dramatic victory, and many were recognized for valor and bravery in Colonel Cake's report of the battle, the finest compliment was delivered by General Slocum. Passing near the regiment a day or two after the battle, General Slocum nodded pleasantly to Cake and quipped, "Colonel, your coal-heavers did well!"[6]

For the survivors, the post-battle accounts focused on the deadly bayonet encounter with the 10th Georgia and the stark reality of the bloated and mangled corpses littering the battlefield. Courage under fire, bravery, valor and the leadership of Colonel Cake, which highlighted soldier accounts after Gaines' Mill, once again were central themes in the descriptions of the engagement at Crampton's Gap. The day after the battle Captain Haas, with some measure of satisfaction, noted in his diary, "Where we advanced, they laid the thickest. Our loss in killed and wounded was heavy."[7] Captain Royer, in a graphic letter to his father paid tribute to "my brave and gallant Company. Oh! How they did fight, and how they did fall! It was no fault of mine. It required no skill. Our course was plain, straight, onward and forward. The only wonder is that we were not annihilated."[8] Private Henry Boyer, of Company A, in his lengthy memoir recounted the climax of the bayonet charge against the 10th Georgia. After crossing the Mountain Church Road, Boyer recalled that the 96th Pennsylvania immediately formed "ranks in the road, every company in its proper place and every individual firing at will at the retreating foe…. We thought we had bayoneted a hundred-fifty in that road, but when we returned to bury them we found but twelve."[9] Unlike the aftermath of the Battle of Gaines' Mill, capturing 40 Georgians at Crampton's Gap brought the Pennsylvanians into close contact with their Confederate counterparts. Finally, Captain Royer noted that the Confederate prisoners were "discouraged with their losses and cool reception in Maryland, besides, in starving condition."[10]

For the soldiers of the 96th Pennsylvania, the Battle of Crampton's Gap proved to be an exhilarating victory. Regimental reunions after the war would be held in September and the veterans of South Mountain would reminisce about their service and commemorate the dramatic events of the battle. Entering the engagement with no more than 525 effectives, Cake had been assigned to spearhead the advance of the Sixth Corps toward Burkittsville on the morning of the battle. It is possible, that the 96th was given this mission as a result of Cake's performance at Eltham's Landing and his handling of the regiment, holding the right flank of Bartlett's brigade at Gaines' Mill. It should be noted, too, that Cake's reputation was further enhanced prior to Gaines' Mill when he led the 96th Pennsylvania, under orders from General. Slocum, to conduct a reconnaissance operation along the Chickahominy River. The newspaper correspondent for the Philadelphia *Press*, Joel Cook, recorded in his narrative of the Peninsula Campaign that "Colonel Cake was highly commended for the successful manner in which he executed his difficult commission."[11] Finally, the opening sequence of the battle, which featured elements of the 96th Pennsylvania clearing the village of Burkittsville of Munford's Virginia cavalry, was conducted under the direct observation of Slocum and Bartlett.

Crampton's Gap proved to be the greatest military success of the 96th Pennsylvania during its three year term of service. The Battle of Antietam, however, fought three days later overshadowed the victory of Slocum's division at South Mountain. Despite the dramatic day at Sharpsburg, on September 17, the Sixth Corps pointed with pride toward its decisive victory at Crampton's Gap. Captain Boyle later wrote that although the newspaper correspondents neglected the action at South Mountain, because the events along Antietam Creek captured the imagination of the public, the soldiers of the 96th Pennsylvania knew that they had achieved a "splendid success—the storming of Crampton's Pass."[12]

The summer battles of Gaines' Mill and Crampton's Gap forged the soldiers of the 96th Pennsylvania into steadfast combat veterans.[13] The patriotic citizens of Schuylkill County who had enlisted in September of 1861 as untried and untested volunteers were skilled and competent combat veterans by September of 1862. Colonel Cake, a veteran of state militia service and colonel of the ninety-day 25th Pennsylvania, was now an accomplished regimental commander with aspirations toward gaining a brigadier's star. Active campaigning and two deadly battles decimated the ranks of the 96th Pennsylvania. Leaving Schuylkill County in early November 1861 with almost 1,140 officers and men, the 96th now numbered approximately 435 muskets.[14] Combat with the Confederates at

Gaines' Mill and Crampton's Gap resulted in 32 killed in action, 131 wounded and 13 missing or captured. The deaths of Major Martin and Lieutenants Ellrich and Dougherty deprived the regiment of the leadership of three highly respected and capable officers. The loss of his trusted subordinate Lewis Martin at Crampton's Gap and the reassignment of Lieutenant Colonel Frick after Gaines' Mill, and the appointment of Adjutant Richards to Colonel Bartlett's staff, meant that Cake would need to rebuild his staff and undertake a significant recruiting effort in the coal region to refill the depleted ranks. But before he could undertake these pressing matters, the armies were concentrating along a narrow creek situated in the valley of the Antietam at Sharpsburg, Maryland. While Crampton's Gap yielded a substantial harvest of death, the bloodiest day was yet to come.

After the Battle of the Blue Ridge, the name used by some of the Schuylkill Countains to refer to the engagement, the 96th remained encamped for two days at Crampton's Gap.[15] The soldiers spent their time searching the nooks and crannies of the heights for discarded Secessionist valuables. As the Bluecoats rested, the war steadily boomed away in the vicinity of South Mountain. During this interlude McClellan continued to maneuver his army against the Confederates. Franklin's troops, however, remained in the vicinity of Crampton's Gap in order to watch for any flank movement by the Confederates, who were positioned in Pleasant Valley, on the western side of South Mountain. While Franklin's Unionists watched Pleasant Valley, the Confederates captured Harpers Ferry. On September 16 Lee gathered his forces and formed marching columns. The Virginian advised his subordinates, via courier, to conduct a forced march to Sharpsburg during the night. That evening, as the Secessionists tramped through the misty darkness, Captain Haas noted in his diary that "it commenced to rain."[16]

During the evening of September 16, Franklin received orders to move his command toward Keedysville in the morning. That night, in the distance, the Bluecoats could hear that an engagement was in progress near Sharpsburg. At 5:30 the next morning, the VI Corps marched toward the stone bridge spanning Antietam Creek near Pry's grist mill.[17] As the long column of Unionists lurched forward, one Maine veteran, writing several years after the war, recalled the mood of the Federal troops: "Inspired by the success which, during the last few days, had attended our arms, our noble boys marched out from their camp ground with light and cheerful hearts, and with quick step. There were no stragglers on that march."[18] Captain Haas recorded hearing "heavy cannonading at Sharpsburg."[19] At 8 o'clock in the morning, the 96th joined the VI Corps column and marched westward over South Mountain, through Crampton's Gap, and struck the road running north through Pleasant Valley toward Rohrersville. Before noon, Franklin's corps reached Keedysville where the Bluecoats tramped across the first of two stone bridges to reach the battlefield. A veteran of Slocum's division described the scene that greeted the VI Corps veterans:

> At Keedysville we ... found many of the houses in possession of our surgeons, and fast being filled with our wounded. The streets were almost blocked with ambulances, waiting to unload their mangled, suffering burdens, while the surgeons and assistance, with coats off and sleeves rolled up; with hands and amputating instruments covered with blood, looked more like butchers in the shambles, than like professional men in hospitals.[20]

After crossing the first bridge, spanning a tributary of Antietam Creek, the soldiers of the VI Corps marched across the second bridge, near Samuel Pry's mill, where Franklin was ordered to deploy his two divisions. Quickly, however, the order was countermanded and the VI Corps marched to support Sumner's battered II Corps positioned in the vicinity of a belt of woods on the eastern edge of the D. R. Miller farm.[21] The 96th, along with the balance of Bartlett's brigade, reached the battlefield about noon. In his splendid memoir, Captain Boyle stated that the regiment formed a line near "the edge of the Miller woods, opposite the Dunker Church, between which and the woods stretched a great corn field."[22] After resting for an hour, the artillery of the VI Corps opened fire upon the woods near the Dunker Church.[23] Confederate counter battery fire quickly erupted in response. Shortly after 2 o'clock, General McClellan reached the area of the Miller woods— now known as the East Woods. He ventured on to the battlefield from his headquarters at the Pry house to personally resolve a dispute between Sumner and Franklin concerning the latter's desire to mount an attack with his two divisions. Henry Keiser, of Company G, recalled that the appearance of McClellan and his cavalcade drew the attention of the Confederate gunners. "General McClellan and General Franklin, with their staffs, rode along our front, and the rebels seeing them, opened on them with a whole battery."[24]

The sight of McClellan, and his retinue of mounted officers, no doubt alerted the Confederate artillerists to the significance of the Bluecoats conferring near the Miller woods.[25] Suddenly, the exposed left wing of the 96th was bombarded with solid shot. Henry Keiser recalled that the Secessionist artillery rounds "flew around us thick as hail."[26] Moments later, Frank Treon of Company G, and McCoy Sargent, were struck by a deadly projectile from the enemy artillery. Captain Haas recounted the scene in his pocket diary. "We at length came into position at the cornfield and laid down behind the Batteries as a support. Our cannon blazed away finely. The enemy sent solid shot, one of which struck two of my boys taking the two hands and leg of Frank Treon, and leg of McCoy Sargent. I had them carried off the field midst a perfect tempest of shot and shell."[27] Later that evening, both men succumbed to their grievous wounds. Subsequently, the regiment was shifted to the right, out of range of the deadly missiles. That night, as they did after the Battle of Crampton's Gap, the Pennsylvanians slept on the field, close to where the unfortunate soldiers fell earlier in the morning.[28]

As the sun rose over the battlefield the next morning, the sounds of rifle and artillery fire gave way to the sights of massive carnage. Captain Royer, in a letter to his father, described the grim scenes the Pennsylvanians observed upon the battlefield. "We slept last night mid the dead and wounded, mutilated in every shape and form. One rebel General, two Colonels, and a Major lie dead about fifty yards from me. Right in front of me lies a Company, I judge, of dead Georgians, some still hanging on the worm fence where they were killed."[29] In his memoir, James Treichler recalled that "the dead of both armies are lying thickly upon the ground of both sides of the fence, making it possible to walk a long distance on the bodies of dead soldiers without stepping upon the ground."[30] Henry Keiser noted in his diary that "the field in our front is literly covered with dead Rebels and Union men. The stench is something awful, the bodies all being buried in long trenches thirty and forty in one trench."[31] According to Captain Haas, "Such ghastly sights were never before seen. Whole lines of dead men lay blackening in the sun as if they had fallen in line of battle."[32] And finally, the young musician Erasmus Reed told his family about the aftermath of the battle. "Believe me you can hardly pass through a field or woods that does not lay full of dead rebels still unburied, and I fear can never be buried. The corpses are bloated and the smell is dreadful. The very air we breathe around here is tinted with the dead smell."[33]

The desperate summer battles of 1862, dramatic events producing unprecedented casualties, caused the volunteers of the 96th come to terms with the issues of death and dying on an enormous scale. Many of the soldiers saw themselves in the faces of the wounded and dead around them as they constantly struggled to come to terms with their own mortality. In nineteenth century America, the concept of the "Good Death" was at the center of Christian religious practice. The shared experience of camp ground and battle ground brought the notion of a Good Death to the forefront of the soldier's military experience. How a soldier died, therefore, epitomized his life to that point and offered a glimpse of life beyond the grave. Most importantly, the moment of death required witnesses, scrutiny, interpretation and a narrative—and careful preparation by a sinner who sought eternal salvation. Hence the deaths suffered by the soldiers, especially those sustained in battle, were characteristic of Good Deaths. Furthermore, all Union deaths supported a righteous cause. Men killed, or mortally wounded in the chaos of combat, sanctified their death almost making it a sacrifice rather than just another Bluecoat losing his life in battle. In sum the soldiers almost sought to construct a Good Death—amidst the carnage of the battlefield—by adding the missing elements of those comrades in arms who perished in combat in order to attain the quality of a Good Death.[34]

While the battlefield indoctrinated them in combat it also served to introduce the soldiers to the grim human wreckage associated with Civil War engagements. In the immediate aftermath of battle, many of the soldiers privately compiled unofficial lists of the dead and wounded in their respective companies. Henry Keiser of Company G not only listed the names of the wounded but he also indicated the nature and severity of each soldier's injuries: "Our Second Lieutenant Sourbeer, [Sauerbrey] wounded in heel; Edwin Moyer, slightly wounded above left eye; Lewis C. Romick in the head, just grazing scalp; William Strausser wounded in the leg, and George Nester wounded in both feet."[35] James Hollister, a private in Company A, compiled a similar list which was published in the weekly *Miners' Journal*.[36] Pennsylvania newspapers such as the Philadelphia *Press*, Philadelphia *Inquirer* and the Harrisburg *Telegraph* published casualty rolls annotating the wounds of the soldiers.[37] Documenting the soldiers killed in battle, mortally wounded, missing or slightly injured was an important aspect of the soldier's experience in the aftermath of a battle. It was his first opportunity to chronicle the loss of his comrades, many of whom were neighbors or relatives. In addition, the soldiers also sought to understand how they managed to survive the deadly battles which swirled around them. After Gaines' Mill, Adjutant Richards wrote, "How I escaped I can't understand…. Providence protected me."[38] Erasmus Reed simply stated, "Thank God I am still well…. I cannot see how so many escaped."[39] Writing after Crampton's Gap, Captain Royer started his letter with the words "I am still alive."[40]

In addition to counting and chronicling the dead and wounded after a battle, soldiers penned descriptions of the heroic deaths of their comrades and composed eulogies and letters of condolence to inform family members in Schuylkill County of the loss of their relative. In his after-action report, written a day after the Battle of Gaines' Mill, Colonel Cake alluded to the Good Death: "While it may be impossible to particularize where the conduct of all is entirely satisfactory, the heroism of the dead may be recorded."[41] In particular he noted the devotion to duty and commitment to the Union displayed by two sergeants. "First Sergeant Boland of Company F, mortally wounded, refused to be carried off the field until after the fight, and First Sgt. Jonas M. Rich, of Company A, also mortally wounded, after being carried a few paces to the rear, ordered his companions to place him at the foot of a tree to die, and return to the conflict."[42] The most poignant description of a Good Death upon the battlefield, however, was described by Francis Boland in a letter written shortly after the VI Corps victory at Crampton's Gap. "Barney McMichael was wounded on Sunday I had to take him in my hands. He [had been hit] … by a round ball. He threw up all blood. I had to give him water many times as his thirst was getting intense. He died in my hands and told me to let his father know how he died. There was none of the regiment near when he died. He is buried in a cornfield. You may let his father know all this. The rest I will tell when I go home."[43] Such heroic Good Deaths to preserve the Union, served to strengthen the commitment of the volunteers to achieve ultimate victory. Despite the heavy casualties suffered at Gaines' Mill and Crampton's Gap, the soldiers remained confident in their cause. Captain Royer earnestly stated to his father that "my brave boys planted our tattered and blood-stained flag triumphantly on the summit of the Blue Ridge. If necessary to avenge the fallen, we will do the like again…. One thing is certain, it can result only in victory for us."[44]

After compiling the casualty rolls and burying the dead, the officers of the regiment offered testimonials to their fallen comrades in official reports, letters to friends and condolence missives to grief stricken families in Schuylkill County. The death of Lieutenant Ellrich at Gaines' Mill, the first officer of the regiment to fall in battle, was a significant event which made a lasting impression upon the soldiers of the 96th. On July 5, shortly after the Pennsylvanians reached Harrison's Landing, an officer sent a brief letter to the *Miners' Journal* describing the events of Ellrich's death. In this case, the letter informed everyone at home that although he died on the battlefield, in so doing he achieved a Good Death. Writing from Camp Haesler an officer stated that "Lt. Ellrich, of Company B, fell in the commencement of the Battle of Friday, 27th June, from the effect of a musket ball entering his brain above his left ear. His last request was, that his body should be sent home, but as the hospital in which the body was placed, fell subsequently, into the hands of the rebels, it was impossible to comply with the wish."[45] After the Battle of Crampton's Gap, Colonel Cake devoted a paragraph of his report to the heroic deaths of Lieutenant Dougherty and his trusted friend and military comrade Major Martin.

Although he recognized the bravery and courage of many officers in his report of Crampton's Gap, Cake proclaimed that "there was no better or braver soldier than Lt. John Dougherty."[46] In regard to Major Martin, however, Cake not only graphically described his mortal wounding but added that "he was an accomplished and brave soldier; an unassuming and perfect gentleman, beloved by all the regiment, and regretted beyond expression. One of the first to volunteer in this war, he has at last laid down his life while gallantly and bravely fighting for his country." In his letter of condolence to Martin's widow, Cake lamented the loss of "his brother, friend, constant companion—the bravest and most gallant soldier of the regiment—*my Major*—The country has lost a *soldier,* I a friend, but oh! Who can describe *your* loss." Finally, in closing, Cake offered particulars of the battle to Martin's widow. "The storming of the Blue Ridge will be memorable and will render memorable Sunday, the 14th of Sept. 1862. It is seven miles to Harpers Ferry, near the village of Burkittsville, Md. It was here you laid your sacrifice upon the altar of your country."[47] In addition, a long column in the *Miners' Journal,* presented biographies of Dougherty and Martin, informing the readers of the weekly newspaper about their lives. The last paragraph ennobled the two fallen heroes and emphasized the symbolism of their Good Deaths. Perhaps written by the newspaper's famous editor Benjamin Bannan, the column concluded with the following sentence: "Thus two more of Schuylkill's brave sons have laid their lives upon the altar of our country's liberties—noble martyrs in a glorious cause."[48]

After the bloody Battle of Antietam the armies rested for a few days in the Maryland countryside. During this interlude the burial details began their grim work. The surgeons at the field hospitals also plied their trade, until they were overcome with exhaustion conducting amputations.[49] The Pennsylvanians took advantage of this inactivity to record their impressions of the battle and inform their families that they had survived the deadly affair. Captain Haas wrote letters to his brother-in-law, and of course to his wife, assuring both that he was uninjured and offering details of the two battles.[50] Samuel Russel and Frank Simpson informed their friends and families about the battles and also indicated that the Army of the Potomac was eager to mount an aggressive pursuit of the Army of Northern Virginia. Simpson informed his friend that "I would sooner keep after them gray backs while we have them going and keep them going until we get them back to Richmond, for I think the time has come now that our army ought to do something in the way of cleaning out this Rebellion."[51] After nightfall the Unionists could hear the creaking and rumbling of the wagons of the Army of Northern Virginia as the Confederates withdrew from the battlefield. Several days later the Bluecoats conducted a feeble pursuit of the Butternuts. It was a slow march that ended in the Williamsport-Bakersville area. There the army encamped while McClellan pondered his next movement.

As McClellan considered his strategy, Bartlett's brigade went into camp on the Rush estate, near Baker's grist mill.[52] While encamped near Bakersville, the nasty business of regimental politics once again took center stage. Cake received a mandate from VI Corps headquarters to fill two field officer vacancies within his command.[53] On the surface the whole matter of promoting the two senior line officers of the regiment to the positions of lieutenant colonel and major, respectively, seemed a routine matter.[54] Military regulations clearly stated the procedure for promoting commissioned officers. It seemed that all that needed to be done was promote the two senior candidates to the vacant positions. This apparently simple matter, however, became a complicated affair within the field and staff officer ranks of the 96th Pennsylvania.

Captain Filbert, as the senior officer, was excited at the prospect of advancing to the rank of lieutenant colonel. Throughout the summer the young line captain maintained a lively correspondence with his father. It is clear from the tone of Filbert's letters that he believed he had a legitimate claim to Frick's old post, even though Major Martin ranked him in seniority. Filbert based his claim on Martin's illness during most of the winter at Camp Northumberland and the post Richmond Campaign encampment at Harrison's Landing. Filbert told his father about the relationship between Colonel Cake and Major Martin: "He [Colonel Cake] now controls the Major [Martin] who does as he says. He swears at him, and the Major is afraid to resent it."[55] Filbert disliked Cake's outbursts, and he had little respect for Major Martin because he failed to rebuke Cake. Consequently, in August, Filbert asked his father to utilize any political leverage he might have with Governor Curtin to secure the lieutenant colonelcy position for him. The company commander knew he would have difficulty gaining the promotion over Martin, but believed fervently that his military service record made him a viable candidate. The death of Martin, at Crampton's Gap, however, significantly altered the promotional picture within the regiment.

By the end of September, his path to the lieutenant colonelcy unencumbered, Filbert felt that he would receive the promotion to the field officer slot. Although Filbert viewed Cake with disdain and stated to his father that the "Cake faction" was intent only on "elevating and favoring Pottsville men of the regiment," he believed that Frick's transfer and Martin's death would end the political machinations within the regiment.[56] Filbert remained wary of any potential intervention on the part of Colonel Cake to block his promotion. Filbert constantly reminded himself that Cake preferred to promote his friends to vacant positions and arrange the dismissal of his enemies. Cake's reputation among the line captains, concerning the colonel's ability to depose his subordinate officers, was well known. The colonel enjoyed telling the story of how he "was rid of two of his officers and would follow the other to the Gates of Hell."[57] Filbert knew that he was not endeared to Colonel Cake, and therefore needed to maintain a constant vigil of the colonel's movements. Although Filbert knew of Cake's past injustices, he seriously underestimated the malevolence of the Pennsylvania colonel.

During the evening of September 29, while Filbert was in his tent working on company muster rolls, Colonel Cake summoned all of the line officers to his tent. At that meeting the colonel informed the line captains that he had received an order from Sixth Corps headquarters instructing him to execute the necessary regimental promotions and forward the names of the new lieutenant colonel and major. Cake informed the officers that he did not want to conduct the promotions in accordance with the military regulations, based on the seniority standard. The colonel proposed that the line officers elect the lieutenant colonel, while allowing him to appoint the major. Cake's motive for suggesting this scheme, which deviated from the accepted seniority promotional system, is unclear. Perhaps he felt that the only way he could maintain his political leverage within the regiment would be to appoint an officer he could intimidate and control. Obviously Cake was willing to concede the lieutenant colonelcy to Filbert, but wanted to retain authority over the officer assigned to the vacant slot of Major Martin.[58]

After meeting with Colonel Cake, Filbert and the line captains unanimously agreed to elect Filbert as the lieutenant colonel of the regiment. They also decided to deny Cake the authority to appoint the new major. In a letter home Filbert stated that Cake planned to advance "a junior lieutenant who would have been promoted over eight captains and four other lieutenants," constituting a serious violation of the seniority system. After reflecting upon the situation, Filbert told the line captains that "he would stand by the officers and prefer to remain a captain [than] to act dishonorable." In a letter to his father, Filbert, torn by his passionate desire for both promotion and honor, exposed his inner thoughts:

> The dye is cast. The Colonel does me injustice, but honor first, I came not altogether for honor but I know promotion is due me and shall try to make things uncomfortable for him [Colonel Cake].
> It is this that after facing death that we have to fight Col.'s to remain in place.
> No, I can't submit. I shall try and act just, honorable and upright.
> Col. Cake attempts to change the seniority of officers but doubt whether he can. I think after all has been done he will find some trouble but it is hard to tell about those wise working politicians. It is very unpleasant and were it not the relation of my Company I would urge a resignation at once, and enlist as a private in a new regiment.

Filbert ended his letter by stating the maxim that would govern his actions throughout the conflict with Colonel Cake, "Honor is my motto."[59]

On September 30, Filbert delivered the following message to Colonel Cake on behalf of the line officers: "Sir, In filling the vacancies now existing in the regiment we respectfully suggest that our preference is that it be done in regular line of promotion according to seniority."[60] Cake responded to this declaration by issuing regimental order number thirty-nine, which altered the order of the seniority roster. Thus, Captain Lessig, of Company C, became the ranking line officer, followed by Lamar Hay, the captain of Company A. Captain Filbert was placed below Hay under the revised seniority alignment. Upon learning of this change, Filbert sent copies of his muster rolls to Governor Curtin and Oliver Duff Greene, Assistant Adjutant General of the VI Corps, to support his claim to the senior captaincy.[61]

Filbert's lengthy letter to Greene documented why his was the only valid claim to the position of senior captain and why the others—Lessig and Hay—should be excluded. He stated that at Camp Northumberland Cake issued Regimental Order 14, designating him as the senior line officer. Filbert carefully refuted Cake's recent Regimental Order 39—which countermanded Regimental Order 14—citing Lessig and Hay as holding seniority over the Company B captain. In his letter Filbert also informed Greene that Lessig had acted as a mail agent on the Philadelphia and Reading Railroad well into October of 1861, which was sometime after the mustering of the 96th Pennsylvania regiment. Further, Filbert indicated to Greene that Lamar Hay had been elevated to the captaincy of Company A after Lewis Martin was promoted to major at Camp Schuylkill. Filbert was determined not to allow what he perceived as "wise working politicians" to unseat him from his position as senior captain without a struggle.[62]

Two weeks after Filbert sent his letters and supporting documents to Governor Curtin and O.D. Greene, he forwarded a recommendation to the "War Governor's" office, proposing that John T. Boyle, captain of Company D, be promoted in line of seniority to the rank of major. (Filbert had already informed the Governor of his desire to be elevated to the position of lieutenant colonel.) These promotions, if approved, would have remained consistent with the 96th Pennsylvania's regimental seniority roster at that point in time. Certainly Filbert's recommendation signified his contempt for Cake's manipulation of the seniority roster and indicated that the young line officer intended to impede Colonel Cake's control over regimental promotions. At this juncture, from Filbert's point of view, the matter of seniority had become more than just regimental politics. Clearly the young line captain and Cake were locked in a power struggle, from which neither could loosen his grip. In a letter home Filbert stated that he would try to "make things uncomfortable" for the "old war horse."[63] This was a clear signal of things to come.

On October 23 Filbert received word from home that his father's influence in Harrisburg had proved successful; his lieutenant colonels' commission had been approved. On the last day of October an optimistic Peter Filbert, believing that at long last he and Colonel Cake could lay aside their grievances, strode toward the colonel's tent to be formally recognized as the 96th Pennsylvania's lieutenant colonel. Cake, however, astonished Filbert by refusing to honor the senior captain's commission, stating that he had a policy of not recognizing officers who did not obtain their commissions through him. He refused to acknowledge Filbert's commission, even though he was risking a potential court-martial. After snubbing the senior captain, Cake told Filbert why he would not recognize his lieutenant colonel's commission. He stated to Filbert that the reason Captain Beaton Smith was transferred to another regiment, while the 96th Pennsylvania was at Camp

Schuylkill, was because Smith had not received his captain's commission through him. Further, Cake told Filbert that he could not consent to serve with officers who did not obtain their commissions through him. In short, contrary to Filbert's expectations, the Filbert-Cake feud was not over, it was just beginning.[64]

Failing to be recognized as lieutenant colonel by Cake, Filbert gathered his muster rolls and his commission and on November 2 reported to 2nd Lt. William Borrowe, the mustering officer of the First Division, VI Corps.[65] Borrowe, after examining the documents, mustered the senior captain in the grade of lieutenant colonel. Cake, upon learning of the newly commissioned lieutenant colonel's maneuver, told Filbert that "he [Cake] had been beaten in his object."[66] Further, the Pennsylvania colonel threatened the newly mustered lieutenant colonel, stating that "he would get rid of [Filbert] in some way" and have him dismissed from the service of the United States.[67] Cake was so infuriated with Filbert that the colonel told the new lieutenant colonel "to take his [Cake's] commission" as he intended "to resign at once or as soon as his resignation is accepted."[68] Cake, however, was not planning to resign. He was too intent on setting a trap with which to snare Lieutenant Colonel Filbert.

On the same day that Filbert was mustered by Second Lieutenant Borrowe, Cake put into motion a plan to dismiss Filbert from his new position as lieutenant colonel. Cake wrote a letter to VI Corps headquarters, requesting that Filbert be ordered to appear before a military board of examination, which would determine whether or not the newly commissioned lieutenant colonel was competent to command troops in the field. On November 11, while the 96th Pennsylvania and the VI Corps were in the vicinity of Thoroughfare Gap, Filbert had received orders from the new commander of the First Division, Gen. William T. H. Brooks, to appear before a military examination board later that day.[69] Captain John T. Boyle, Filbert's recommendation for major, was also ordered to appear before the review board. Filbert hoped that his appearance before the military review board would end his problems with Colonel Cake and firmly establish him as the regiment's lieutenant colonel.

During the Civil War, a system of examining boards was established to determine an officer's fitness for command. The examining boards were instituted to weed out commissioned officers deemed "unfit for their positions." The examining board system, according to Stanley Swart, was established so that the "army could by-pass regular court-martial proceedings in ridding itself of unqualified volunteer officers through the rank of colonel, using instead a faster and more informal procedure."[70] It was directed to review "the capacity, qualifications, propriety of conduct, and efficiency of any commissioned officer of volunteers," and was to consist of from three to five officers appointed by generals commanding departments or detached armies. If the board's report was adverse, the commission of the examined officer was vacated on approval of the President.[71]

The examining boards were rigid in their standards when reviewing the qualifications of field grade officers. The examinees were required to demonstrate a thorough knowledge of Casey's *Tactics*. Also, all officers, regardless of rank, were to be questioned on "their knowledge of military tactics," "the rules and regulations pertaining to the duties of their command," and "their character and moral physical fitness to discharge the duties of their grade."[72] Field officers were supposed to know the entire "School of the Battalion," the duties of the regimental adjutant and quartermaster, how to keep a regiment's books, the duties of Field Officer of the Day, and the "modes" of encamping a regiment and conducting a march. In addition, the applicant had to have a good knowledge of history, geography, arithmetic, algebra and geometry. Officers under examination were also subjected to a thorough physical examination, which, if not passed, resulted in an adverse report from the board.[73] Obviously, to be deemed "competent," an officer had to be physically fit and knowledgeable about an extensive range of military issues and functions.

Although a transcript of Filbert's testimony before the board has not been located, it is certain that he underwent a rigorous oral examination. Modern studies of the procedural operation of a military examination board conclude that the questions posed by the examiners generally fell into two categories. The first set of questions tested the examinees knowledge of Casey's *Infantry Tactics*.[74] In the case of Peter Filbert, a lieutenant colonel, questioning along the tactical line would have concluded with a thorough investigation of the regimental maneuvers of the School of the Battalion.[75] For field grade officers the tactics portion of the exam was the most important, at least from the point of view of the examination board members. Over one-half of the questions posed during the examination session focused on tactics. The second portion of the exam concerned military duties, as described in the *Revised Regulations for the Army of the United States, 1861*.[76] Filbert emerged from his session before the board believing that all of this business concerning his commission could finally be laid to rest. Now he could concentrate on his duties as the 96th Pennsylvania's new lieutenant colonel. It was a challenge he was eager to meet.

Perhaps the word "politics" best describes the activities within the ranks of the Army of the Potomac during the relative quiescence of the post–Antietam period. From the camp of the 96th to the headquarters tent of General McClellan it was politics as usual. As Filbert and Cake brought their political duet to a crescendo, McClellan and Lincoln debated the delicate balance between politics and military operations. Specifically, Lincoln had become concerned about McClellan's political attitudes. Ironically, the Federal victory at Antietam—McClellan's most important military success—gave Lincoln an opportunity to publicly issue his preliminary *Emancipation Proclamation*. McClellan, however, was bitterly opposed to the policy outlined in that document. Everyone knew of McClellan's sympathy for Southern institutions. About a fortnight after the battle, the President visited McClellan in the Maryland countryside. Lincoln wanted to prod McClellan into initiating a forward movement of the army, and to clarify for him that the "game" was not to "prolong the war until both sides were worn out, when the Union might be saved with slavery intact."[77] Lincoln was not going to accept a compromise settlement and wanted some assurance that McClellan would not, either.

After visiting with McClellan for three days, Lincoln returned to Washington satisfied that the Bluecoats were rested and well equipped, and issued an order directing McClellan to "cross the Potomac and give battle to the enemy."[78] Rather than move the army swiftly against the Graycoats, McClellan continued his policy of procrastination. McClellan elected, for a variety of military factors, not to advance the Army of the Potomac: he reasoned that he needed to wait until the Potomac rose to be sure Lee would not re-cross it, and he wanted to finish drilling the new recruits, reorganizing his forces, and procuring sufficient supplies of blankets, shoes and uniforms. Finally, in late October he began moving his army across the Potomac at Harpers Ferry and Berlin. By early November McClellan's army was east of the Blue Ridge, in the New Baltimore-Warrenton area, while Lee was west of the mountain range in the vicinity of Winchester. From a military standpoint, McClellan's position was strategically sound. At this time McClellan had the inside line to Richmond. Unfortunately, he was an ordinary general and failed to exploit his advantage of interior lines. Lee, leaving Jackson's force in the Shenandoah, crossed the Blue Ridge and interposed his Army of Northern Virginia between McClellan and the Confederate capital at Richmond. Upon learning of this latest delay, Lincoln, on November 5, relieved McClellan and replaced him with a corps commander who openly admitted that he did not want the position. All that remained for McClellan was to say goodbye to the Army of the Potomac.[79]

On November 10 McClellan confirmed the rumors that had swirled through the Bluecoat camps during the previous three days. That day he rode through the camps and bid farewell to his troops. The various corps were drawn up in line for a final exchange of salutes. One VI Corps veteran remarked that "the men were wild with excitement. They threw their hats into the air and cheered their old commander as long as his escort was in sight."[80] Another Bluecoat recalled that "almost everybody was disappointed. Officers and men, who never blanched before a cannon's mouth, could not repress the tear when their beloved general waived them a last adieu."[81] Peter Filbert of Company B described the final meeting between General McClellan and the VI Corps. "Our loved

and adored Genl. passed here three times to be greeted by his friends once more. The idol of the Army. Many tears wetted the cheek of old veteran troops, who faced the muzzle of the cannon. What is all this to come to?"[82] Henry Keiser of the 96th Pennsylvania recorded in his diary that "General McClellan and General Burnside rode through the different camps today and were lustily cheered at all points. It is reported that Burnside takes command of the Army, which the boys do not like."[83]

McClellan's departure, and the promotion of Ambrose Burnside to army command, was just the climax of a series of changes that autumn within the Army of the Potomac. After the Battle of Antietam, Henry Warner Slocum, commander of the First Division, VI Corps, was promoted to lead the XII Corps. In Slocum's place stepped "Bully" Brooks, a veteran of the Seminole and Mexican wars, and most recently commander of the Vermont brigade of the VI Corps. Born in Lisbon, Ohio,

Sgt. Henry Keiser and wife, Sara. He was promoted to sergeant May 11, 1864, and transferred to 95th Pennsylvania Volunteers October 18, 1864 (courtesy Carol Holochuk).

Brooks graduated from West Point forty-sixth in a class of 52 cadets in 1841.[84] A member of Brooks' old Vermont brigade stated that "Gen. Brooks is a strict disciplinarian and knows what a soldier's life is, as he first shouldered a musket as a private, and served in the Florida war. But after all we rather like the old General, notwithstanding he is rather rough and rigid."[85] George Foltz, a color bearer with Company C of the 96th Pennsylvania, related an eyewitness account of his first glimpse of "Bully" Brooks. "We have a change in our Division," wrote Foltz to his brother John. "General Slocum has left us & now a general from Smith's Division by the name of Brooks has commanded & he had the Division out yesterday to a Grand Review. He looks like an old farmer and they say he is a good man."[86]

While "Bully" Brooks was assigned to command the First Division of the VI Corps, William F. "Baldy" Smith was subsequently appointed to lead the VI Corps succeeding William B. Franklin. "Baldy" Smith was a native of St. Albans, Vermont, and graduated fourth in the

Maj. Gen. William T. H. "Bully" Brooks. Commanded 1st Division of the VI Corps (National Archives).

West Point class of 1845.[87] At the outbreak of the Civil War he served as colonel of the 3rd Vermont Volunteers and later that summer was a staff officer with General Irvin McDowell. Subsequently, Smith was promoted to the rank of brigadier general and appointed to command the 1st Vermont Brigade in the VI Corps. Thomas Hyde of the 7th Maine, and one of the historians of the VI Corps, opined that "'Baldy' Smith was a kind man to his subordinates, and had the soul of a great soldier in him. He was, at times, a perfect Ishmaelite to his superior officers, as they found out to their cost. I have seen him handle his division in a way that Napoleon would have loved ... he ranks yet in my mind among the greatest commanders of the war."[88] Surgeon Stevens of the 77th New York described General Smith as being "tall, well dressed, his regulation coat buttoned closely about him, [and having an] easy and graceful manner and conversation."[89]

Upon assuming the reins of command of the Army of the Potomac, Ambrose Burnside told the War Department of his plans. Burnside proposed an immediate move to the southeast, massing his army as though intending a move against Culpeper, where a segment of Lee's army was encamped, while stockpiling supplies for a quick march down the northern bank of the Rappahannock River to Fredericksburg. This operation had the dual effect of keeping the Army of the Potomac between Lee's Graycoats and Washington and appeasing the war directors in the Lincoln administration. From Fredericksburg

Burnside intended to advance along the Richmond, Fredericksburg and Potomac Railroad, compelling Lee to fight a pitched battle near the Confederate capital. After some hesitation Lincoln approved Burnside's program. The President urged the field commander to move rapidly, for autumn was slowly slipping into winter.

After planning his strategy Burnside restructured his chain of command, reducing the number of generals who reported directly to him. Burnside did this by grouping the several infantry corps into wings that he called "grand divisions," each having two corps of three divisions. Maj. Gen. Edwin Vose Sumner commanded the Right Grand Division, Maj. Gen. Joseph M. Hooker the Center Grand Division, and the old McClellanite, Maj. Gen. William B. Franklin, was assigned command of the Left Grand Division. Franklin's new command consisted of the I Corps under General John Reynolds and the VI Corps led by General William F. "Baldy" Smith. "Bully" Brooks, noted for being a strict disciplinarian and a courageous soldier, headed the First Division under General Smith. General Albion P. Howe, a native of Maine and a West Point graduate with the class of 1841, assumed duties at the head of the Second Division. Prior to joining the VI Corps, Howe served under General Couch in the IV Corps. And finally, John Newton, a native of Virginia and a graduate of West Point in 1842 was appointed to command the Third Division. All of these men were professional soldiers with considerable experience. On the field of battle, however, they proved to be unspectacular tacticians and at best average combat soldiers. Like Franklin above him and Brooks and Bartlett under him, Smith was a staunch supporter of the departed McClellan. Now, however, they were commanded Burnside, a man who planned to do things differently than their old chief.[90]

Maj. Gen. William F. "Baldy" Smith. Commanded VI Corps (author's collection).

On November 16 the soldiers of the VI Corps struck their shelter tents at New Baltimore and marched fourteen miles to Catlett's Station. The troops of the 96th Pennsylvania all recalled the torrential rain that plagued them when they spent several days at Catlett's Station the previous spring. This time, however, "Camp Misery," became famous for the herd of "little gray rabbits" that inhabited the area. During the stay at Catlett's Station rabbit pot-pie was a favorite. On December 4, after performing picket duty for several days in extremely cold weather, the 96th along with the VI Corps, tramped sixteen miles and encamped near White Oak Church. In his pocket diary Captain Haas described the harsh weather conditions and the long march. "Rose at 4 a.m. Very cold. Broke up camp and moved at 6:30 a.m. Passed through Stafford Court House—a hell of a place (one tavern, one jail and one court house)— and by Belle Plain Landing. Camped three

Catlett's Station, Virginia. Situated on the Orange & Alexandria Railroad, Catlett's Station was a prominent Union supply depot. The photograph was composed by Timothy O'Sullivan in August 1862 (Library of Congress).

miles from the Rappahannock at 4 p.m. Distance marched 17 miles. I suffered very much from rheumatism. Slept badly."[91]

The next day, after only several hours of sleep, the Bluecoats embarked on another march. This one, although shorter than the first two, was perhaps twice as rigorous. By the time the vanguard of the VI Corps column began to move in the afternoon, the rain that started falling in the morning had turned to snow. According to one veteran, "The wind blew terribly, snow and hail filling the air. The roads were very heavy, the mud being at least six inches deep."[92] After a march of five miles Bartlett's brigade reached Belle Plain Landing, described by one eyewitness as "a cold, bleak, barren place."[93] The historian of the 16th New York described Belle Plain as "a barren and dreary spot exposed to the winds from all quarters, without a single tree to shelter or furnish fuel."[94] A facetious soldier, with chattering teeth, said "Belle Plain is it called? The first and last letter of the descriptive word should be dropped, then a cockney would pronounce it correctly."[95]

In fact, the Bluecoats were "wet to the skin." Captain Haas recalled that the short march to Belle Plain Landing started at 1 o'clock. The soldiers tramped slowly "through rain, snow and mud until 4:30 p.m. when we halted and camped without tents or fire (no wood to be got.) Cold terrible. I suffered severely with pain."[96] The wind swept across the proposed encampment site, a wide-open plain, like a hurricane. After stacking their arms Colonel Cake, the senior colonel now in command of the brigade while Bartlett was on furlough, instructed the troops to pitch their tents. According to one Bluecoat "scarcely a man moved" and the troops "stood looking at each other, hardly knowing what to do. The whole movement was an outrage upon humanity."[97] All of the field commanders were upset with the location of the camp site. There was no wood for camp fires and the hollows of the corn rows were full of rain water. Cake, perhaps sensing that his judgment concerning the location of the camp site was in error, allowed the troops to spend the night in the wooded heights beyond the desolate plain.

This exodus to the adjacent woods embarrassed Colonel Cake. He realized that he had made an error in regard to the location of the camp site. His pride wounded, he was not going to succumb to the comfort of the nearby tree line. Probably, too, Cake wanted to show the soldiers that he could endure the elements. As one VI Corps veteran put it, "it was always a fact that his heart was infinitely bigger than his dignity, though when required, he was by no means deficient in the latter article."[98] So Cake procured an officer's tent, had it pitched, and used the shelter as the quarters for the camp guard who were to watch over the stacked arms. Cake and four or five officers remained to perform the guard duty. After organizing the detail Cake alluded to the various regiments in the nearby woods. He looked upon his half-frozen companions and stated, "The boys have had it tough, and we must do guard duty. We need the exercise."[99] So the colonel shouldered a musket and for two and a half hours maintained a vigil over the gun stacks.

For five days the Pennsylvanians remained at Belle Plain Landing. During this time they endured extremely cold temperatures, foraged for wood to keep themselves warm and hunted small game to supplement their meager rations. The intensely cold weather of December 6 prompted Henry Keiser to proclaim that it was the most "miserable night since I am in the Army. I was nearly frozen.... I could not put on my shoes until Jacob Alvord thawed them at a small fire which some of the boys had succeeded in starting."[100] From Belle Plain Matt Richards informed his sister Sophia of the difficult conditions the soldiers were encountering as winter was closing in on the Army of the Potomac. "I pity the poor men who have not the opportunity of carrying as many blankets as I do, and last night no doubt caused much suffering and will swell the sick lists fearfully.—This winter campaigning will cost the lives of more men than two such battles as Antietam."[101]

While the soldiers of the 96th battled the elements, other less fortunate Bluecoats performed fatigue duty at the landing, unloading boats. Burnside ordered his three grand divisions to cross the Rappahannock River on the morning of December 11. (The pontoons that were supposed to arrive at Falmouth as Burnside's columns reached that place had finally met the troops. The late arrival of the pontoons, however, allowed Lee to get his army down to Fredericksburg. Hence by December 9 Burnside's initial advantage was lost.) Burnside planned to cross the Rappahannock simultaneously at three points, as soon as the engineers finished laying the pontoon bridges. Two bridges were to span the river north of the town while another was to be thrown across the Rappahannock just below the southern extremities of Fredericksburg. Another set of pontoon bridges was to be erected one mile south of the town, just below the mouth of Deep Run Creek. The assault was to be a two pronged operation, with Sumner's Right Grand Division to take Fredericksburg and then attack the Confederate forces posted on the ridge beyond the town. Franklin's Left Grand Division was instructed to occupy the plain south of Fredericksburg, then maneuver the Butternuts off of the high ground near Hamilton's Crossing. Hooker's Center Grand Division was to be held in reserve, ready to intervene wherever the attack needed support.[102]

According to Lieutenant Colonel Filbert, December 11 dawned as a "fine day."[103] By 7 o'clock in the morning the Bluecoats of the 96th Pennsylvania started marching toward the Rappahannock River. Henry Keiser noted that as the column trudged forward the soldiers could "hear cannonading all day in the direction of Fredericksburg."[104] About 2 o'clock the Pennsylvanians reached the left bank of the Rappahannock where they enjoyed "a fine view of Fredericksburg and the fortified hills in rear." As Cake's brigade reached the Rappahannock, the soldiers enjoyed a warm December sun bathing the Virginia countryside. As the Pennsylvanians waited for the orders to cross the pontoon bridge, the Union batteries opened fire. One New Yorker remembered the bombardment this way:

> Sixty shells a minute went whizzing through the air, and crashing through buildings while the earth fairly shook beneath the terrific cannonade. The scene was one of awful grandeur. A dark column of smoke rose heavenward from the doomed city, showing that the explosives were doing effective work.[105]

At dusk, Cake's brigade was ordered to cross the river on the hastily assembled pontoon bridge at what would become known as "Franklin's Crossing." Looking upriver, Filbert noticed that "the Rebs burned the Railroad bridge near Fredericksburg."[106] In his diary Captain Haas wrote, "God help my dear wife and darling children if I should fall."[107] Three of Cake's regiments, the 27th and 121st New York Volunteers and the 96th Pennsylvania, crossed the Rappahannock that evening only to withdraw and recross the river a few hours later. These units, however, were quickly recalled because the advance at Franklin's Crossing was supposed to be executed in concert with the movement of Sumner's grand division at the upper bridges. The failure to coordinate the movements of the respective wings of the army caused the senior generals to recall the Pennsylvanians who went into camp near the Rappahannock. The inability of Sumner's lead elements to cross the Rappahannock simultaneously with Franklin's vanguard resulted in the recall of all Union forces, except for a few Bluecoat units who were to hold the bridgeheads on the Fredericksburg side of the river. The attack, therefore, was delayed yet another day.

Early the next morning Franklin's Left Grand Division received authorization to advance across the pontoon bridges. The movement to the river was concealed from the view of the Confederates by a heavy, thick fog. As the Bluecoats crossed the bridges south of town, one veteran noticed "that the surface of the bridge was carpeted with playing cards ... that had been thrown away. It was evident to all that a bloody battle was to be fought and few men wanted to go to certain death with gambling devices in their pockets."[108] As Smith's VI Corps reached the south side of the Rappahannock the fog lifted, revealing to the Confederates the grand procession of Bluecoats. Immediately, the Butternut batteries opened, the missiles humming their deadly tunes as they whirred through the atmosphere. The 96th Pennsylvania left camp at 9 o'clock and crossed the Rappahannock an hour later via the bridges at "Franklin's Crossing."[109] According to Captain Haas, "About 12 noon, we advanced and went forward as skirmishers. Entered a ravine and lay against the bank, the Jersey Brigade following us. The Enemy, who kept ominously silent, then opened his batteries on us and for three hours we were shelled tremendously."[110]

"Bully" Brooks' First Division, the lead element of the VI Corps, was instructed to relieve Newton's skirmishers upon crossing to the south side of the river. Before beginning his advance, however, Brooks formed his command into three lines. The first was composed of Gen. David A. Russell's brigade, followed by Cake's command, and the last line was Alfred Torbert's Jerseymen. Gradually Brooks advanced his three lines. Russell's Third Brigade moved beyond Deep Run, while Cake's command took position behind the old Richmond Stage Road, also known as the Bowling Green Road. Torbert's Jersey brigade, supporting the first two lines, formed in the valley of Deep Run. By noon the troops were in position; most of the day still remained to assault the Graycoat lines.

While Cake's brigade, aligned along the old Richmond Stage Road, and awaited further orders the position soon became untenable. The Confederate artillery fire from the heights raked their lines with savage fury. Henry Keiser noted in his diary that "the skirmishers are firing occasionally. Were shelled this afternoon while lying in a ravine [near Deep Run Creek]."[111] While resting in the safety of the ravine, as they did at Gaines' Mill, some of the Bluecoats leisurely cooked their dinner, while others reflected on their families. In his diary, Captain Haas described how he wanted his belongings disbursed if he was killed in the battle:

> I want Freddy [his brother] to have my silver dollar, and John to have my watch, while to my dear wife and darling Mary, I leave them to select what they may choose of all my effects as a remembrance of me. My fervent love to them all. God bless them. My body I would like to have buried in Pottsville if possible.[112]

Maurus Oestreich, a hospital steward with Company A, confided in his diary that "the bombs and shells come flying with a terrific noise from all directions, not to mention a constant rifle fire which could be heard over the sound of the heavy guns. It didn't take much for anyone of us to realize that all of us were separately and individually in danger of getting killed or wounded in this infantry battle."[113] According to the ailing Captain Haas, picket duty proved to be a perilous proposition that evening. "Shells exploding over our heads all the time," recalled the captain, "some dozen men hit close by. Our batteries exploding some shells near us.... Cold was very intense. We almost froze."[114] The anticipated assault, however, never materialized. Franklin was unsure of his orders and decided to await clarification from Burnside. While Franklin waited the 96th Pennsylvania withdrew from the ravine and performed picket duty along the old Richmond Stage Road.

About one hour after the guns roared back to life on December 13, Torbert's Jersey brigade relieved the 96th Pennsylvania from picket duty.[115] For protection from Graycoat musket fire the Schuylkill Countians took refuge behind the high banks that lined the old Richmond Stage Road. Throughout the day the Pennsylvanians remained in that position, enduring accurate fire from the Graycoat batteries. While the 96th Pennsylvania remained inactive, as did most of the VI Corps, Reynolds' I Corps launched an assault against the Butternuts near Hamilton's Crossing. For most of the day Franklin allowed the I Corps to hurl their lines against the Secessionists with deadly results. The Left Grand Division commander did not utilize any element of the VI Corps to exploit the initial breakthrough of Reynolds' troops.[116] During the night, Lieutenant Colonel Filbert received authorization to straighten the line of the 96th Pennsylvania. According to Filbert the Schuylkill Countians were "within talking distance of their line."[117] He also rode in front of the line to locate a favorable point where the Unionists could mount an advance against the Secessionists. In his diary, Lieutenant Fernsler noted that "this morning all was quiet along the lines. The men had run out of provisions. I had to do without eating for two meals."[118] While Fernsler went hungry, Captain Haas witnessed the fury and grandeur of the Battle of Fredericksburg. In his diary he wrote, "The flash of guns was awful grand—shells bursting at night look pretty but a person must be some distance away 'to see it.'"[119]

Daybreak on December 14 heralded another day of small arms fire along with the thunderous roar of Confederate artillery hurling shells at the cold and tired Bluecoats. A newly assigned regiment to the Second Brigade, the 121st New York Volunteers, lost three killed and six wounded while performing picket duty.[120] The Confederate sharpshooters preyed upon the unsuspecting and uninitiated troops from Herkimer County. Captain Haas noted in his diary, "We relieved the Jerseys, 121st [New York] lost three killed, six wounded on picket (green troops)."[121] Maurus Oestreich wryly remarked in his diary that "today, Sunday, was unusually quiet, disturbed only by a little rifle fire. Either the rebels do not want to fight because it's Sunday, or else it's one of their tricks not to answer our rifle fire."[122] Under cover of darkness, the 96th withdrew from the established picket line, replaced by the unseasoned 121st New York, and went back in to position along the Richmond Stage Road. That night Haas jotted in his diary, "Living very hard. No blankets and half starved."[123] For the next two days the Pennsylvanians performed picket duty and dodged the shells of the Graycoat batteries.

About 5 o'clock on the morning of December 15, alerted by the human telegraph line of the 121st New York on picket duty, Filbert, Cake and Captain R.P. Wilson went in front of the outposts to observe any movement of the enemy. Monday, however, passed relatively quietly. That evening, the soldiers received orders to "fall in without noise."[124] The army was preparing to withdraw from the right bank of the Rappahannock. Captain Haas later recorded in his diary, "Marched at 1 a.m. [December 16] Recrossed the river and marched into the woods and camped at 3 a.m. It commenced to rain. I covered myself with my gum blanket and sat against a tree until daylight. Enemy shelled us with their Whitworth guns. I was very unwell."[125] The Unionists quietly retreated from their positions and retired across the pontoon bridges to the safety of the bluffs on the north side of the river. The next morning, Cake's brigade went into camp close to the river. The guns of the Confederates, however, forced the Bluecoats to gather their belongings and move out of range of the artillery rounds.[126] Three days later Cake moved the brigade back to the vicinity of White Oak Church. Here the soldiers were ordered to build winter quarters. The troops were glad that the winter campaign along the Rappahannock was over. After all, Christmas was less than a week away.

VII

"Our soldiers are very much discouraged"

Dissatisfaction with military service, army high command, and the politicians who managed the war effort reached its nadir during this second winter of the war. The morale crisis of the winter of 1862–1863 can be traced in the letters and diaries of the Schuylkill Countians. First, and foremost, was the accumulation of Unionist losses on the battlefields of the Old Dominion and Maryland. In the Eastern Theater of operations, the failure of the Army of the Potomac to take Richmond was followed by the humiliation of Pope's army at Second Manassas, the "escape" of Lee's Army of Northern Virginia after an auspicious beginning to the Maryland Campaign, and then the futile sacrifice of veteran Bluecoats at the stone wall during the Battle of Fredericksburg. These reverses became more depressing in the absence of an overwhelming victory to offset the loss of trained volunteers, and the discouraging outlook for the future. The gloom which permeated the Federal camps was enhanced by signs at home of declining support of the war, dwindling confidence in political leadership, and outbursts levied against incompetent military commanders. Letters home contained lengthy editorials, by many of the Schuylkill Countians, concerning their dissatisfaction with military and political leadership.[1]

Early in the morning, on December 19, after camping for three days along the Rappahannock River, the 96th Pennsylvania received orders to march to White Oak Church, a few miles east of Fredericksburg, find a suitable camp ground and establish winter quarters. A veteran of the Second Brigade recalled that the soldiers set about removing timber and undergrowth midst the rocks and bushes to clear the ground selected for the camp site. Another soldier stated that "the men made excavations in the earth of some three or four feet in depth and five or six feet square, erecting over them their shelter tents, making the interior … six or seven feet in height. Many built hot fires in the excavations for a day or two, thus hardening the sides and the bottom of the ground … which protected them … from the cold and dampness of the ground."[2] Along with constructing their winter huts, the soldiers informed their families in Schuylkill County about the Battle of Fredericksburg and resumed the usual camp routines of company drill, inspections and picket duty.[3] Christmas, however, brought a welcome interlude to the typical camp duties, including military drills and reviews which characterized daily soldier life. The cold weather which had caused so much suffering during the recent campaign, turned mild as the soldiers prepared to celebrate their second Christmas in camp.[4]

Lt. Col. Peter Filbert lamented in his pocket diary entry of December 25, "Christmas morning on picket. Oh how gloomy!"[5] While some soldiers no doubt spent the day taking advantage of the mild weather by working on their cabins, others foraged for food in order to prepare Christmas dinner. Captain Haas noted that it was a "fine day. Looked at my tree but the Kriss Kringle did not bring me anything. Had potatoes and meat for dinner."[6] Col. Cake procured a couple of barrels of apples and presented them to the soldiers as a Christmas present. According to Tom Houck "the line officers [received] 2 and the Privates 4 Barrels. So today we each received 4 splendid Apples. Christmas passed off and we hardly thought of it. Dinner at 12 as usual consisting of Hard tack good bean soup and potatoes."[7] Maurus Oestreich recorded in his journal that "today, Christmas, we had Mass in camp. There isn't much to a holy day in war time, and that meant that Christmas didn't mean anything to us. In the army one day is like another. No difference between Sunday and weekday."[8] Daniel Faust informed his mother that the weather on Christmas "was like summer."[9] In addition, he related that he had purchased dried apples, crackers and sugar which became his Christmas dinner. Finally, Captain Haas also reported that he issued whiskey to the men who endured the elements while on picket duty. While the pious practiced their religious beliefs, in the spirit of the season, others in camp over indulged in the whiskey ration. Captain Haas noted that a "good many men drunk in camp. A couple of fights."[10] The following day, however, would bring the resumption of soldiering, and the return of camp monotony.

The mild weather which marked the last week of December enabled the soldiers to establish their camp routines and complete construction of their log and canvas huts for the upcoming winter. While many Union regiments sought to cope with the horrific losses of comrades within their ranks after the fiasco at Fredericksburg, the soldiers of the 96th reflected upon the poor leadership of the Union high command, especially on the incompetence of General Burnside. The staggering casualties sustained by the Unionists at Fredericksburg, along with the ignominious defeat, plunged morale within the Army of the Potomac.[11] Veteran soldiers of the army confronted their gloom in an odd way. Writing several decades after the war, one Pennsylvanian recalled the emotions of the Schuylkill Countians after Fredericksburg. "Discontent in the ranks of the Army during the winter following this disastrous campaign was quite common [sic] and many of the rank and file were open in their conversation, declaring that they were tired of the war, and if they had their way would do no more fighting."[12] On the retreat from Fredericksburg there was a snatch of a doggerel, sung to the tune of the sea chantey "Johnny,

Pvt. Daniel Faust, Company H. Transferred to 95th Pennsylvania Volunteers October 18, 1864 (Grand Valley Special Collections & University Archives).

Fill Up the Bowl," making the rounds of the Union camps. The ditty was a cynical response to the plight of the Bluecoats in the aftermath of Fredericksburg:

> Abraham Lincoln, what yer 'bout?
>   Hurrah! Hurrah!
>   Stop this war. It's all played out.
>   Hurrah! Hurrah!
>   Abraham Lincoln, what yer 'bout?
>   Stop this war. It's all played out.
>   We'll all drink stone blind:
>   Johnny, fill up the bowl![13]

Captain Haas, in a letter to his brother Fred, aired his views on the generalship of Burnside and the "abolitionists at home."

> As regards Burnsides, you mistake me, if you believe that I will controvert your saying that he "is a brave and gallant soldier, or a good General," but that he stands second to none that ever lived in this country, is all nonsense. Why, he says himself that he cannot run the Machine that nobody but "Our George" can.
>   I say now that I do not blame "Sides" for the Fredericksburg disaster, but I do blame you Abolitionists at home for crying out "On to Richmond" until at last he succumbed to your cries and didn't go to Richmond.
>   But, instead [he] crossed back again like a sensible man would have done, when he found that the "toll gates" were closed.[14]

Along with Captain Haas, Tom Houck also decried Burnside's inability as an army commander in a long letter to his brother Joe. Writing three days before Christmas, Houck stated:

> We all predicted of Burnside that he was not capable of commanding a large Army. But for what we know he may be had his own way but old Halleck must have his way. I think they had better put him out of Washington. He knows to [sic] much from the day he was made Commander-in-chief. We knowed he and McClellan could not work on the same plans. It was Through him McClellan was removed and I suppose he urged Burnside to move. They had better give General George B. McClellan command over all. Give him his Army of the Potomac and we will then know we have a General that will fight his men not Slaughter them.... The men are getting tired of being slaughtered for Nothing.... I know if McClellan had command of us he Would not have attacked them but we would had nearly one month of rest and try and Settle with peace and if it dont work at em again.[15]

In addition to his criticism of the abolitionists, Captain Haas also indicted the Northern policy makers for underestimating the strength of the Secessionists and accused the administration of mismanagement.

> I think sometimes we will never be able to conquer the "Rebs." Our men do not fight with the same vim and elan that they do. I believe about one half of our Army fight for the money that is in it and not for patriotism. They fight for Nationality and for (as they term it) freedom.
>   I must confess they do fight well and worthy of a better cause. How fearfully the South was underrated before this war. Had our public men comprehended the magnitude of the rebellion at the first outset, it would have been crushed by this time but, alas, there was too much of "if John Brown scared Virginia, one regiment ought to be able to meet the rioters, and they won't fight." However, by this time, all such illusive views are dispelled.
>   I do wish I could think that we can end this war fighting, but am afraid that our blood and treasure has been lavished in vain.[16]

A recurring theme in the letters of the Pennsylvanians written in the morale crisis of the conflict's second winter, was the loss of confidence in military leadership. Charges of incompetence, mismanagement, and inept leadership were freely hurled at general officers commanding Union field armies. Captain Boyle, of Company D, sadly proclaimed:

> I am heartsick at what I see around me. In the present state of our forces, I fear for the result. My heart is with the cause but I fear that if there is not a radical change in Army officers, that success will not perch on our banners. The men have caught the infection from the officers and seem to have lost much of their fire and energy.[17]

Private Patrick McGlenn expressed his dissatisfaction with the military commanders in a letter to his friend at home, John Brislin.

> Our officers are very poor even our Colonel has made this regiment a poorhouse system for his old and broken down hacks and friends for all and every office in it. In fact, they can not be beat for cowardice. You will hear some story soon about such villains. The newspapers we get do not state half the truth.

In the same letter McGlenn also commented on the tactical incompetence of the field grade officers and of certain major generals.

> We have very bad officers. They do not know what to do but they will get us all cut off in the field.
>   Our officers make mistakes in the battlefield. I could mention hundreds of serious mistakes. I however must put up with ignorance for a while. We hear [that] General Banks [was] defeated and routed. Banks was never anything but a political hack.[18]

The soldier letters of the post–Fredericksburg period also reacted to the impact that Lincoln's *Emancipation Proclamation* had on the Bluecoats. The Pennsylvanians regarded the *Emancipation Proclamation* as hard evidence that the radicals at home were corrupting the government and converting the war into an abolitionist crusade. The issuance of Lincoln's *Emancipation Proclamation* served to elicit strong responses from the Pennsylvanians, both on the intent of the document and the reasons for waging war against the Southern Confederacy. Only a small percentage of Bluecoats were primarily interested in freeing the slaves. A larger group, however, wanted no part in a war of emancipation because they thought the effect would be to prolong the conflict. At the outset of the war they had as their primary goal the restoration of "the Union and the system of government that it represented."[19] The devotion to the Union was strong among immigrant groups, such as the Irish and the Germans, in the 96th. Also, they associated the Union with the ideal of freedom and the opportunities that awaited immigrants in America. In a sense the Civil War imperiled those beliefs.[20]

Lincoln's *Emancipation Proclamation* certainly aroused opponents of a "Negro War" to high levels of bitterness.[21] The thought of fighting a "nigger war" was abhorrent to some soldiers in the 96th; others viewed the edict as a war policy which might prove to be a decisive step toward ending the rebellion. Captain Haas offered his views on the emancipation issue in a letter to his brother Fred.

> I suppose you are all in high glee because Abe had set 3 million Niggers free (on paper). Well, I am too if anything comes out of it. I care not if the Niggers eat the Whites or the Whites kill the Niggers, just so that the war be ended. But alas-a-lack-a-day, the Proclamation will not even go as far as our bullets.[22]

Daniel Faust, a private in Captain Haas' company, offered another view concerning the black question.

> I hope this rebellion may be crushed before long ... our soldiers are very much discouraged about this slavery business. They all say they would not fight for the slaves. All the [regimental] colonels ... were ordered to make a speech to their soldiers and encourage them again.[23]

In time, however, the phlegmatic attitudes of the Pennsylvanians toward Lincoln's decree, began to change. A growing belief that emancipation was essential to victory appears to have permeated the Schuylkill County volunteers.

Unlike the opinions expressed by Captain Haas and Private Faust, the young erstwhile musician of Company B, Erasmus Reed, offered a different perspective. Writing from camp at White Oak Church, Reed offered his opinion regarding use of free blacks and "contrabands" to end the rebellion. He suggested that the soldiers should accept emancipation as a war measure and allow blacks to participate in the outcome of the war upon the battlefield. "Let our government now do their duty. Let them arm the Nigers [sic] as fast as they come into our lines, form them into regiments and make them fight for the freedom which our government has offered to them.... The war is now for the Union and the freedom of the slaves. I for my part say let the Nigers [sic] be put in the active field where they can be made useful.... If they don't fight let them go back into slavery. What is the use of risking our lives if they do not want to do something for themselves?"[24]

In another letter, written later in 1863, Faust expounded further on slavery, emancipation and the evolving attitudes of the soldiers towards Lincoln's *Proclamation* and the change in war policy toward ultimate Union victory.

> You also asked me what I thought of this war. My opinion is this, that this war is sent by our Lord and if the People are punished enough once for their National sins then it will soon be settled and another thing it is for destroy slavery which must be fulfilled and will be. Do you or anyone else call this a free Country where they keep human beings as slaves or beasts to [be] used for to keep slavery where it was but not further. But I am just now seeing the wickedness of the thing which gives me a different opinion. A great many of our soldiers are cursing the negroes and that we was fighting for them but that is nothing that will be freed any how and any man that has a feeling for others souls must be to put it down.[25]

Clearly, Lincoln's *Emancipation Proclamation* elicited bold responses from the Pennsylvania volunteers: No longer would talk of a peaceful settlement to the war swirl through the camps of the Army of the Potomac. The *Proclamation* gave the war a deeper meaning. It ensured that the tangled issues underneath the war—slavery, the permanence of the Union, and the concept that a powerful central government was intended to protect people's freedom rather than endanger it—would be settled on the battlefield and not through negotiation in a political forum. Bruce Catton summarized this grim point of view in *Mr. Lincoln's Army*:

> The war now was a war to preserve the Union and to end slavery—two causes in one, the combination carrying its own consequences. It could not stop until one side or the other was made incapable of fighting any longer; hence, by the standards of that day, it was going to be an all-out war—hard, ruthless, vicious.[26]

But before the Pennsylvanians could do their part to end the war there was a long encampment of inactivity to endure.

The winter at White Oak Church, was made more difficult by low morale because of the refusal of furloughs home for soldiers of all rank, significantly affected morale. Policies governing leave, which were notably haphazard throughout the conflict, were especially unsatisfactory during the first half of the war. Apparent hopelessness of visiting home in the foreseeable future contributed significantly to a high desertion rate throughout the winter encampment of 1862–1863. In his comprehensive study of the Chancellorsville campaign, John Bigelow cites various official reports to confirm that "one man in every ten on the rolls was in desertion or absent without leave"[27] during the winter spent in Stafford County. In a letter to his family in late January, Erasmus Reed informed them that "the furlough business is stopped on account of so many reenlisted being absent from the army."[28] In fact, many soldiers completed their three years of military service, or enlistment period, without ever getting an official leave. If soldiers could not get furloughs, many tried to obtain medical leaves of absence.

White Oak Church, Virginia. Also known as White Oak Baptist Church. Located at Famouth, Stafford County, this clapboard church was located near the 1862–1863 winter camp of the 96th Pennsylvania Volunteers. Today the church still stands as a silent sentinel to the wounded soldiers and to those who worshipped in the small rustic structure. It is a Virginia Historic Landmark (Library of Congress).

If they were officers, they usually attempted to resign from the service, citing medical problems. Captain Haas, for example, applied for a medical discharge in late December but his "paper came back disapproved by Dr. [Charles] O'Leary,"[29] the medical director of the VI Corps. During the winter at Fredericksburg, so many Bluecoats tried to obtain honorable discharges that the army initiated a policy to reject all resignations.

Although furloughs and medical leaves of absence were infrequent during the winter at White Oak Church, some Bluecoats of the 96th Pennsylvania managed to find avenues to escape completion of their terms of military duty. In a letter to his sister, Edward Henry mentioned that "the Boys are all tired of the service. They are discharging at the rate of 75 per day for the last 4 weeks."[30] During the winter encampment, any Unionist who could gain an honorable discharge gladly accepted his leave from the misery of the army. In a letter to Lieutenant Colonel Filbert, Captain Boyle opined that "demoralization is rampant amid all the old officers. [They] would gladly leave, if they could, with honor."[31] Captain Haas, Adj. John Hannum, Lieutenant Oberrender, Lieutenant Fesig and others pursued honorable discharges while encamped at White Oak Church. While many of the officers sought discharges throughout the winter none of their applications met with approval.

A few soldiers, however, did not want to leave the service of the United States under any circumstances. Lieutenant Colonel Filbert was just such a soldier. He had worked hard for a leadership position within the regiment and was not about to give it up. Unlike other Bluecoat volunteers, Lieutenant Colonel Filbert was not given a choice whether or not he wanted to remain on active duty. The military board of examination, which had scrutinized him in November, had finally rendered a decision concerning his case. On December 29, he received a shattering dispatch from VI Corps headquarters notifying him that the board of examination rendered an adverse decision in his case: effective immediately he was dismissed from the service of the United States.[32]

On December 31, Filbert left the encampment near White Oak Church for his home in Pine Grove.[33] Perhaps he felt degraded and humiliated in losing his struggle with Colonel Cake, but like his predecessor, Jacob Frick, he left with honor. Filbert's short tenure as lieutenant colonel, in the final analysis was only a pyrrhic victory. In the end Colonel Cake made good on his earlier threat that he could "control the military department," and eventually his powerful political connections proved Filbert's undoing. With Filbert gone, Cake turned his attention to regimental politics. Filling the vacant posts of lieutenant colonel and major required Cake's attention. But before he could influence a series of promotions to fill the vacancies, illness forced him to accept a medical furlough.

On January 4, 1863, after reading the *Emancipation Proclamation* to the Pennsylvania regiment, Colonel Cake called a meeting of the line officers at his quarters. After the group assembled he informed them that he was returning to Pottsville for three weeks on a medical leave of absence. During McClellan's Peninsula Campaign, while the 96th was encamped at Harrison's Landing, Cake contracted chronic diarrhea. He was advised by his personal physician that a convalescent period at home would restore his failing health.[34] During his three-week absence Maj. William Lessig, the colonel's "bosom friend and confidant," held temporary command of the regiment.[35] Upon his return to Pottsville, Cake was presented with a "beautiful sword" along with a sash, shoulder straps and a pair of white buckskin gloves. The sword was a gift from the officers and men of the 96th Pennsylvania "to our worthy and beloved colonel."[36] The presentation was made at town hall by a local attorney on behalf of the committee headed by Captains Royer and Dougherty, along with quartermaster John Schweers, who made the arrangements to honor Cake for his service and devotion to duty and, perhaps most importantly, to acknowledge the respect the men in the ranks had for Cake and his leadership. Although Cake would regain his fragile health, he would never return to Virginia to resume his duties as colonel of the 96th Pennsylvania Volunteers. His return to Pottsville closed his military career. The battlefields were now behind him, business ventures and politics were in his future.

While most Civil War soldiers could successfully battle against illness and sickness, many could not overcome the great enemy of the winter encampment: boredom. Battles and campaigns were marked by long intervals of relative inactivity, reorganization and reconnaissance. Active campaigning comprised only a small fraction of Civil War operations. Between November and April both sides usually suspended active campaigning and spent the cold weather months in winter encampments. The question of what to do during the long periods between operations, when homesickness and despondency threatened the fabric of the army, resulted in a variety of solutions. Civil War officers did not believe that their positions required them to plan activities for the rank and file. The net result, therefore, was to allow the soldiers to find their own form of relaxation. The Bluecoats, in fact, displayed remarkable ingenuity in combating the weariness of camp life.[37]

Of the diversions enjoyed by the Yanks, reading was perhaps the most common. Among the Pennsylvanians newspapers seemed to be the most sought after print medium. According to Bell Wiley, the historian of the common soldier, local weekly newspapers enjoyed a wide circulation among the Federal camps.[38] A great favorite of the Schuylkill Countians was, of course, their hometown weekly, The *Miners' Journal.* Readers in the 96th and other regiments from the anthracite coal region forwarded letters to the newspaper editor, Benjamin Bannan. In letters home, the soldiers frequently made comments such as "The newsboys bring round all the papers every morning. So you see I am posted on all the news."[39] The soldiers were anxious about life back home, especially where their families were concerned. The arrival of the weekly newspaper in camp, with its stories

John A. Schweers, sergeant, Company B. Promoted to regimental quartermaster July 15, 1862. The photographic firm was Wenderoth and Taylor, 912, 914 & 916 Chestnut Street, Philadelphia, Pennsylvania (collection of Douglas Sagrillo).

about community events, reassured them that daily life remained tranquil and calm in Schuylkill County. In short, the weekly newspaper was somewhat symbolic to the Pennsylvania volunteers. The timely arrival of the weekly, with its columns of local news, demonstrated to the soldiers that calm still prevailed at the home front. Through weekly publication and delivery, he *Miners' Journal* reaffirmed to each man that the ravages of war had not reached, nor affected, their communities.

The 96th volunteers also eagerly sought metropolitan dailies such as the Philadelphia *Inquirer*, Philadelphia *Press*, New York *Herald* and New York *Tribune*. They obtained newspapers from the regimental sutler and newsboys, or they asked relatives at home to forward newspapers to them. After the Battle of Fredericksburg, Captain Haas wrote to his brother Fred and asked the following: "Please send me the Philadelphia Inquirer of the following dates–13, 14, 15, 16, 17, 18, 19, 20th. I have not seen a paper for ten days past and I can assure you I am desirous of reading the papers of the above dates."[40] The young line officer was curious to learn how the war correspondents of the Philadelphia *Inquirer* described the fight at Fredericksburg. One newspaper usually served many readers. Newspapers, like most other reading material, frequently passed from one Unionist to another until the paper was literally worn out.[41]

A close second to reading among camp diversions was music. Whether on the march, around the campfire, on trains or river transports, the strains of popular tunes were sure to be heard. Captain Haas, of Company G, was quite a banjoist, and frequently entertained his comrades with his plucking.[42] Impromptu affairs were supplemented by concerts from the Pottsville Cornet Band. The regimental musicians usually featured patriotic selections and sentimental melodies.[43] On some evenings the band serenaded Colonel Cake.[44] On holidays and other festive occasions, such as the Fourth of July, the band offered a special program to the soldiers. The music most enjoyed by the Civil War soldier, however, was the song of their own voices. Second Lieutenant John Fernsler, of Company H, related an incident in his diary concerning entertainers to the Federal camp in early April of 1862.

> There were two young ladies in our regiment today. One was dressed like a Lt. General. They sang for the regiment. The officers paid them $1.00 apiece, making about $30.00. They travel from regiment to regiment. They are splendid singers.[45]

Captain Filbert noted in his diary that one of the entertainers was Miss Laura Keene.[46] Three years later the famous British stage actress entertained the Lincolns at Ford's Theatre in the comedy *Our American Cousin*, on that fateful, frightening evening. The Bluecoats sang mostly for the sheer joy of making music. But mostly they sang to combat homesickness and forget the weariness of daily camp life.[47]

Sports and games also proved to be popular camp diversions for the soldiers. Wrestling, boxing, free-for-all scuffles, cards, dice, dominoes and backgammon all helped the Yanks pass away the tedious hours spent in camp.[48] In winter, snowball sham battles were a favorite activity. Another officer described such an affair in his diary. "[We] had a big snowball battle [today]. Dr. [John] Shamo [the assistant regimental surgeon] got hit in the eye."[49] Some of these battles were highly organized, complete with lines of battle, led by mounted officers, with bugles sounding and flags waving. Fishing and hunting also enjoyed robust followings among soldier sportsmen. The Pennsylvania Bluecoats enjoyed fishing for eel while encamped along Cheeseman's Creek, prior to their landing at Eltham's Landing—the beginning of the Peninsula Campaign for the Schuylkill Countians. On the march to Fredericksburg they hunted rabbits to fill their supper pots. In the evening, by candlelight inside a tent, or on a stump by daylight, checkers or "gammon" were popular past times. Poker, too, usually played for stakes, provided entertainment. The soldiers occasionally found diversion in calling on friends in other regiments, with eating, drinking and talk of home providing the principal activity.[50] Once in a great while life at the front was brightened by a visit from a spouse, a relative, a minister or a politician from the home community. Although special visits sometimes broke the monotonous routine of camp life, it still remained the responsibility of the volunteer soldier to contrive his own recreation.

Perhaps personal letter writing to the folks back home was the most pervasive camp diversion. Letters were composed under all sorts of conditions. In winter quarters desks and other writing surfaces were usually available. But during a march or military operation, correspondents had to improvise. Daniel Faust told of the difficulties in letter writing: "We have a very poor way to write here. We have to use our knees for our writing desk."[51] Captain Haas once composed a letter during a skirmish with Secessionist

Assistant Surgeon Samule B. Light. Mustered out with regiment October 21, 1864 (author's collection).

pickets. "A lovely skirmish is going on the right and working this way. I think one of our boys just got himself a sharpshooter. I wish you were here to see the fun. All over—no one hurt on our side."[52] Stationery varied from fancy sheets adorned with patriotic emblems and verses (with matching envelopes) to ruled pages. Ink was the preferred writing medium, but during active campaigning pencils often were employed. The form and content of soldier letters varied as greatly as the character of the writers.

The great majority of the letters from the various camps of the 96th were not models of literary excellence. In some instances they reflected limited education, but they proved informative, rich in humor, striking in their honesty and replete with original and colorful phrases. Favorite topics included battles, health, the weather, the land and people of Dixie, camp news, rumors of future operations, food and officers. Sin was also a topic of discussion. Daniel Faust told his brother that he was "still trying to serve the Lord," and hoped that he would "never turn off from the narrow path."[53] Mortal illnesses, battlefield fatalities and fatal accidents were reported at length.

Unpopular officers inspired some of the most expressive phrases in the letters. Francis Boland suggested that the captain of his company, Richard Budd, whom he accused of habitual drunkenness, "ought to be drawing mules at home."[54] Second Lieutenant Fernsler, of Company H, upon being asked to exchange commands with a brother officer, declined the offer as the captain of the other company (Isaac Cake of Company I) was "a regular tyrant."[55] For most Yanks, though, letter writing was a difficult chore. The Bluecoats did not want to tell their loved ones at home about the dullness of camp life. If they could not relate a strange, unusual or exciting incident, they usually closed their letters with phrases like "No more at present." Daniel Faust ended one of his missives this way: "I think I will close [at] this time. I do not know much to write. If I was with you [his sister] I could talk a great deal more than I can write."[56] Far more exciting was receiving mail from relatives or families. After waiting for a letter from home Clement Potts decided to write to his mother to express his disappointment in not receiving any communication from home.

> I have been waiting patiently for a letter from you but all in vain. Perhaps you have forgotten that you have a son away from home who is going to offer up his life for his country. If you knew how much a letter cheered me you would write two or three times a week. The day I received the four I was so glad that I read them over about a dozen times.[57]

Perhaps one of the more prolific letter writers within the regiment was Private Henry Keiser. In 1862 Keiser wrote eighty-two letters and received eighty-three. He usually exchanged, on average, at least four letters per month with his girlfriend "Miss Sallie," two per month with his father, and one per month with his mother.[58]

The letters of the commissioned officers of the regiment differed from those of the privates in content and structure. The missives of Lieutenant Colonel Filbert, Maj. Lewis Martin and Capt. Jacob Haas were graphic, grammatical letters. Their correspondence related detailed reports of military operations, lengthy passages concerning regimental politics and their personal opinions concerning emancipation and the conduct of the war. Very little of their correspondence focused on the daily routine of camp life. Of the three, Captain Haas was probably the most provocative correspondent, at least where decorum was concerned. In part Captain Haas' outspoken attitude can be traced to his correspondent. Many of his letters were written to his brother Fred.

I do not write as I have not had a passage in the last 4 days. I cannot see why you folks do not write to me and I am d___d if I pen another line to you until I hear from you.[59]

Filbert's correspondence reveals the problems of a Civil War officer. His letters are cluttered with details concerning regimental politics, and talk little of the daily camp routine.[60] Also, he devoted little space to battlefield operations. His letters, however, demonstrate an honest concern for the health of the men under his command. Of the three officers, the images of the South and the people of Virginia, contained in the Martin letters, proved to be of greatest interest. Martin expressed concern with a wide range of social questions. In particular he devoted passages to the plight of the people of the South who had their lives disrupted by the war. Most of his letters were written to his mother, and perhaps her readership, at least in part, explains Martin's preoccupation with social issues.

> On our return ... to camp we stopped at a farm house [located] ... within ... six miles [of] Richmond. We found the place deserted by everyone except a few of the slaves. And from them we got a very fine mess of strawberries. I don't think I have met six white natives of Virginia since we left Alexandria. Such as were left were either too poor or too feeble to get away and were impressed with the idea that as soon as the Northern soldiers came along they would eat them alive. Many of the Negroes too believed the same thing, and, the majority of those who were not taken away by their owners before we arrived were driven into the woods upon our approach.[61]

Letter writing, despite its difficulties, made tolerable a life that most Bluecoats found to be monotonous while in camp and full of hardships when on campaign.

On January 16, the monotony of winter quarters was broken when the regiment marched to Belle Plain Landing, where for three days the troops unloaded barges laden with coal. Four days later the Pennsylvanians returned to their winter quarters where the regiment received marching orders. Ambrose Burnside issued a general order announcing that "the auspicious moment seems to have arrived to strike a great and mortal blow to the rebellion, and to gain the decisive victory which is due to the country."[62] The commander of the Army of the Potomac was determined to atone for the slaughter at Fredericksburg. He believed that a winter campaign would uplift the waning spirits of his Bluecoats. To many generals, however, Burnside's plan was dangerous and risky. But the Rhode Islander believed differently. The weather that January was unseasonably warm. The ground was dry and firm and the air was balmy. All seemed right for a winter campaign.[63]

Instead of crossing the Rappahannock and retesting the deadly Butternut entrenchments at Fredericksburg, Burnside proposed to march swiftly upriver around the enemy's fortifications, throw pontoon bridges across the Rappahannock at Banks' Ford, and cross his troops to the south side of the river. Accomplishing that movement, without detection from Graycoat videttes, Burnside believed, would cause Lee to evacuate Fredericksburg because the Confederates would be outflanked. To Burnside the plan of the operation, at least on paper, was appealing. This time, however, to insure success, Burnside was going to proceed cautiously. By January 19 his logistical plans were complete. All that remained was to carry out the operation.[64]

As soon as the Bluecoats finished dinner on January 20, the troops dismantled the canvas roofs of their winter huts to use as a shelter tent during the campaign.[65] After the Pennsylvanians packed their knapsacks, they fell into line by squads. General Bartlett, prior to marching, read to the soldiers Burnside's directive. *General Order Number 7* stated "that if the gallant soldiers of so many brilliant battle fields [could] accomplish this achievement, a fame the most glorious awaits them."[66] Morale, however, within the Army of the Potomac, from the Union high command down through the rank and file, virtually doomed the operation before it started. One soldier proclaimed that "we have but little faith in the movement, and less faith in the leading Generals than we once had."[67] Another Yankee related that "although Bartlett's reading of Burnside's order was couched in the most cheering and reliant tone, it did not elicit a spark of enthusiasm ... so often had their fondest hope of success been crushed on more promising occasions, that now the voice of their General met no hearty response."[68] One Bluecoat, however, noted that the winter campaign, simply because it portended action, seemed temporarily to lift the spirits of the men. Just after noon, the Unionists tramped out of their respective camps and started on a long, march along the Rappahannock destined for the river crossing at Banks' Ford.[69]

Maj. Gen. Burnside, commander, Army of the Potomac (author's collection).

At first the march went well. It was a splendid day. One Bluecoat stated that "although the morning was somewhat mild, the day was very cold."[70] The mounted troops and foot soldiers moved briskly over the firm roads.[71] Each infantry soldier was carrying forty or fifty pounds of equipment, several days' rations and sixty rounds of ammunition.[72] Passing Falmouth and marching up the left bank of the Rappahannock lifted spirits as the soldiers realized that Burnside was undertaking a tactical movement designed to outflank the Army of Northern Virginia. If executed without being detected, this maneuver was not going to culminate in another series of bloody assaults against an impregnable position. A member of Bartlett's brigade summarized the mood of the soldiers in the following passage. "The great theme of the talk among the men was the probable result of the present movement. We could advance with much firmer steps and with bolder hearts upon any new scene of action, than to revisit any old positions, especially where we had been compelled to exhibit to the foe our capacity for retreat."[73] Another Bluecoat opined that "auspices were favorable, and [the] rank and file were hopeful of a favorable result."[74]

Then, late in the day, an ominous gray sky covered the Virginia countryside. By evening it was raining. What started as a slow drizzle quickly turned into a steady downpour, with a howling wind whipping the rain down the country roads. The Yanks tried to pitch their shelter tents for protection, but the frozen ground resisted the tent-pins. Failing to erect their tents, many tried to build fires. The green pine wood, however, smoldered rather than burned. Evan Gery noted in his diary, "We are camped in the woods, one mile from the Rappahannock river. Rain started in the evening and continued all night."[75] Another soldier in Bartlett's brigade vividly recalled the hardships of that night.

Scarcely had night arrived when a storm arose. The wind blew a gale and rocked the trees spite-fully. The night was very dark…. Our blankets were wet through and we found ourselves lying in a pool of ice-cold water. No one got a wink of sleep, and all, in that cheerless wilderness, of trees and mud, agreed that it was the most tedious night that we had ever passed.[76]

By dawn the rain was cascading down in torrential fashion, then slowed to a dripping in the gray daylight. At 8 o'clock the Bluecoats again commenced marching toward Banks' Ford.[77] One soldier recalled the increasing challenge of moving the army along the muddy roads during a driving rain storm. "The artillery that had camped in the fields for the night could not move that morning, and we left them behind floundering in the mud, the wheels sunk to the axle, while all the horses in the battery could not drag out a single piece. The roads were given up entirely to the artillery, baggage and pontoon trains, while the column pursued the fields."[78] Lieutenant Fernsler recorded in his pocket diary that "the artillery could not move for the mud."[79] As the troops resumed marching, the soldiers quickly discovered that the firm crust which covered the road the day before, had been transformed into a spongy mass of red muck and mire. Although nature seemed to be turning against them, the soldiers plodded on toward the river crossing. By noon, though, after moving a mere three miles, exhaustion overcame the troops, many of whom sought shelter in the nearby woods. The rain continued to fall during the afternoon and on through the night, ruining the plans of the Yanks. Evan Gery scribbled in his diary that it was "still raining … plodded along three miles, through mud almost to our knees. We are now encamped on a high bluff in the woods."[80] To lift morale that night, a gill of whiskey was issued in lieu of rations.[81] For one exhausted Yankee, the incessant rain and impassable roads led to "the conclusion … that we had made another stupendous move-ment, and had consummated a most gigantic fizzle."[82]

Ironically, Burnside's winter campaign afforded the soldiers of both sides a unique opportunity to socialize and exchange sundries across the river. A member of the 16th New York recorded such an interaction in a letter written shortly after the conclusion of the "Mud March." "On Thursday our men wandered up the river, and on the opposite bank the Rebel pickets were seen, and at one of the fords, a large board was stuck up with 'Burnside stuck in the mud' painted on it. The pickets, however, manifested a very friendly feeling toward us, none of them firing at our men, and one of them offering to come over and help us haul back our pontoons and wagons. We did not accept their services."[83] A soldier with the 5th Maine recalled a similar encounter with his Confederate counterparts. "We went into camp in plain sight of the rebel camps on the opposite bank of the river. Many of our boys went down and entered into conversation with the rebel pickets, who were not more than one hundred yards distant, and were very sociable." The following dialogue took place between some of the 8th Alabama and two men from the 3rd Maine.

Union soldier.—What do you think of Burnside?
Secesh.—We are not afraid of him—he is not much of a General.
Union.—What do you think of McClellan?
Secesh.—He is a perfect brick—first rate for getting out of a tight place.
Union.—How are you off for salt?
Secesh.—Oh, we have plenty of it; old Stonewall Jackson supplies us with everything we need!
Union.—Aint you fellows sick of this war?
Secesh.—We don't care a darn how long it lasts.

Union and Secesh then agreed to meet at 4 o'clock, p.m., and exchange newspaper, coffee for tobacco, &c.[84]

While socializing across the Rappahannock characterized one aspect of Burnside's winter campaign, the torrential rain and the deep Virginia mud compelled the Bluecoats to refer to the operation as the "Mud March." The ambitious campaign featured knee-deep mud and fatigue duty extricating the pontoon trains and artillery pieces from the sticky red Virginia clay. While the first two days of the flank march were devoted to moving the Bluecoats to the river crossing at Banks' Ford, the next two days were spent—both by the officers of all rank and the enlisted men—pulling on ropes to haul the trains laden with pontoons out of the mud which imprisoned them. The intractable logistics, created by the elements, offered Burnside no alternative to his original plan. As a result, he aborted his planned offensive before it became another military debacle.[85]

On January 23, as most of the First Division of the VI Corps started back toward White Oak Church, Gen. Bartlett's brigade was ordered up the Rappahannock a mile further to assist in the recovery of the pontoon train stuck in the mud along the river. One Bluecoat noted that the order aborting the winter campaign was cheerful news to the wet, hungry soldiers in Brooks's division.[86] Another soldier in Bartlett's brigade stated that "the troops are returning to camp and at present only Brooks' division remains as a guard over the pontoons and artillery that are still fast in the mud or being removed as steadily as possible."[87] A soldier from Maine observed that "in the afternoon, the sun came out bright, and we were advanced to the extreme front … when we were assigned to the arduous labor of helping the poor brutes pull off the wagons."[88] As the veterans of Bartlett's brigade reached the banks of the Rappahannock, where the wagons carrying the pontoon train were mired in the thick mud, the soldiers noticed that their Confederate adversaries in Gray were watching the Yankees struggle through the muddy conditions. A New York soldier in the Second Brigade described the scene which greeted the Blue-coats. "Looking across the river, we could see a big tent fly, which the rebs had put up early Wednesday morning, on which they had written with charcoal: 'BURNSIDE STUCK IN THE MUD!' They were greatly elated at the discomfiture of our army, and amused themselves by offering to come over and extricate our men from the mud; to aid them in crossing and to show them around on the other side."[89]

The next day, Brooks's entire division set about the strenuous process of hauling the pontoon wagons out of the mud. According to one eyewitness, "Every wagon and gun was down to the axle in the mud, and it was vain to try and draw them with mules."[90] Captain Huber recalled that the Union "artillery teams [were] all stuck in the mud. Pieces of artillery with 32 horses attached had to be pulled out by from 50 to 100 men with long ropes."[91] James Treichler stated that "the horses could not budge them neither could we leave them.—Some one among us a private or General conceived the idea of securing a rope long enough so that 100 men could lay hold and this proved successful. This was fun for the boys, and they entered into it with a zest.—It soon became contagious and Officers and enlisted men for the time being were on an equal, and the boys took advantage."[92] Just before the soldiers began hauling on the long ropes, everyone received a whiskey ration.[93] Throughout the morning the Bluecoats tugged and grappled with the ropes to pull the pontoon wagons up the hill to higher ground. Hauling the wagons out of the mud was a duty shared by the lowest private up to the senior officers of the VI Corps.

Even a general officer joined the rank and file to share in the fatigue duty. As James Treichler recalled after war, "Brigadier General Bartlett took a notion that he would take a hand and be one of the boys. He succeeded for some time nicely and was having quite a lot of enjoyment, when all at once one of the boys saw a good chance to trip him and down he went with his broad cloth uniform and almost buried in the mud. Someone undertook to console him but he would not, and the next boat that came along he secured a hold laughingly remarking that he was one[e] of them and he intended [to] se[e] it t[h]rough."[94] Another soldier related a similar incident involving a VI Corps officer. A well uniformed officer, in command of the engineers, in a rather peremptory tone commanded the soldiers, struggling to overcome the elements, to pull harder on the ropes attached to the pontoon wagon. Suddenly, a man pulling on one of the ropes, dressed plainly in an old blouse with a slouch hat, looked over his shoulder and asked, "Who are you anyway?" The officer, dressed in a clean, bright blue uniform wearing white gauntlets, replied, "I am Lt. Hunter of the engineers." To that, the mud stained soldier replied, "Well, I am Major-General Brooks, in command of the division, and I order you to get down from that horse and take hold of the rope with these men."[95] Immediately, Lieutenant Hunter, saluted by a derisive cheer from the men, dismounted and joined the soldiers toiling in the mud.

By noon, according to the accounts of several participants, the Bluecoats succeeded in recovering the pontoon wagons from the mud. According to a veteran of Bartlett's brigade, the march back to White Oak Church "was slow, tedious moving, mud half way to our knees, terrible severe for both man and beast."[96] Evan Gery recorded in his diary that "at 11 o'clock we started on the march back to Camp White Oak. We drew rations along the road. It was awful muddy. Half of the men couldn't keep pace with the column."[97] James Treichler recalled the arduous return to camp in his graphic memoir. "Oh what a mud march we had back to camp; I lost both my shoes in the mud that was knee deep to an elephant.—I tell you we were a tired lot of boys.—About a mile out of camp a barrel of whiskey was dropped along the line of march, with the head removed and a couple of tins for drinking; a soldier was on detail to issue rations but what could he do; a jolly lot we had in camp that night."[98] Clearly, "spirits" were high as the soldiers returned to their old winter quarters camp that evening. Captain Huber later wrote that the soldiers of the 96th Pennsylvania reached camp "on Sunday evening ... exhausted and 'played out,' after marching 11 or 12 miles through mud—such as they can only get up in Virginia."[99]

The return march to the White Oak Church encampment was a cheerless march. Many of the soldiers made the trek without their shoes, which had been swallowed up by the quagmire.[100] The Schuylkill County regiment straggled back to their camp, many of the men at the point of exhaustion. The gloom that prevailed in the Unionist camps after the "Mud March" was much greater than the post–Fredericksburg depression that swept through the Bluecoat regiments.[101] The failure of the winter campaign, coupled with the receipt of the news that Colonel Cake planned to seek a medical discharge and resign from the army, plunged the morale of the regiment to new depths.[102] This time the reaction was not limited to the rank and file. Criticism of the army in general and of Burnside in particular was voiced by men in high positions. In a letter to ex-Lieutenant Colonel Filbert, Captain Boyle described the mood within the 96th Pennsylvania regiment: "In the present state of our forces, I fear for the result. My heart is with the cause but I fear that if there is not a radical change in Army Officers, that success will not perch on our banners."[103]

Desertion, too, emerged as a prominent problem in the Army of the Potomac. Tom Houck informed his brother Joe that "when the last move was made the desertions were awful. Some 20 or 30 alone out of the 96th. The Men are downhearted and dispirited tired of fighting without anything being accomplished."[104] Another member of Bartlett's brigade also addressed the issue of desertion in a letter to his friend Stebbins. "You have probably received a list of deserters from the regiment. They are not very many, so that you will probably forget them and their foolish deed soon. The facts in the case are that at least one half of them are the best soldiers in the regiment, or so accounted formerly. A still more significant fact than this is that those deserters had the good wishes of the whole regiment, almost without exception. Men here attach no disgrace to desertion."[105]

On January 26, in an attempt to boost the morale of Bartlett's brigade, the troops were reviewed by their old, but beloved, commander Maj. Gen. Henry W. Slocum, now commanding the XII Corps. Evan Gery recorded that in his brief

Maj. Gen. "Fighting" Joe Hooker, commander, Army of the Potomac (author's collection).

address to the brigade Slocum told the Bluecoats "he would sooner Command his old Brigade than the 12th Army Corps."[106] Upon Slocum's appearance, the men "gave nine cheers for him…. He made a speech … and we gave another three cheers."[107] Certainly in the aftermath of the "Mud March," what was needed at this crucial time to stem the tide of low morale was inspirational leadership. Burnside, however, opted to advise Lincoln that several of his lieutenants should immediately be dismissed from the army, as he believed these individuals were more intent upon undermining his image and authority than in winning victories on the battlefield. Lincoln, upon learning of Burnside's desire, decided that it would be best to retain his lieutenants and relieve the ruff-whiskered general.[108] While Lincoln dealt with frustrated generals, similar sentiments emerged within the officer corps of the 96th. Many of the officers sought discharges due principally to demoralization at the results of the Battle of Fredericksburg and the failure of the "Mud March."[109]

In late January 1863, command changes came quickly. After the departure of General Burnside, Lincoln conferred the command of the Army of the Potomac on Maj. Gen. Joseph Hooker. After Hooker assumed command he effected several leadership changes at the corps level in an attempt to alleviate friction and tension among the major generals. First, he orchestrated the removal of W. B. Franklin, commanding the Left Grand Division, who held seniority over him. "Baldy" Smith, a staunch McClellanite, was also relieved of his VI Corps command and put in charge of the IX Corps. To fill the vacancy created by Smith's removal as head of the VI Corps, Hooker selected "Uncle" John Sedgwick. Although Sedgwick, too, was a disciple of McClellan, he was not as outspoken as his predecessor. Hence, Sedgwick's uncontroversial nature and professional military qualities made him an attractive replacement for the opinionated, but well liked, "Baldy" Smith. Also, "Uncle" John Sedgwick would emerge as perhaps the most beloved soldier in the Army of the Potomac.[110]

Unlike the bold and brash army commander Joe Hooker, the new chief of the VI Corps, John Sedgwick, was a quiet, unassuming soldier who was, according to U.S. Grant, "brave and conscientious."[111] Born in Cornwall Hollow, Connecticut, in 1813, Sedgwick graduated from West Point, with classmate Joe Hooker, in 1837. During the Mexican War he served under generals Zachary Taylor and Winfield Scott, earning brevets of captain and major. He later served in the 1st United States Cavalry commanded by Edwin V. Sumner. During the Civil War, Sedgwick established himself as a capable division commander under Sumner in the II Corps of the Army of the Potomac. Sedgwick's chief of staff, Martin McMahon, stated that "as a soldier he had few equals; for in all the duties of his profession, whether they involved the fate of great armies or concerned the merest question of etiquette or routine he was wholly faithful."[112] Another contemporary biographer noted that "though slow in council he was quick in action, and the roar of battle seemed to sharpen all his faculties. His soldiers cheerfully endured his rigid discipline, had unbounded confidence in his judgment, and willingly followed wherever Faithful 'Uncle John' led. He was always a favorite in the Army."[113] Surgeon Stevens, the historian of the Sixth Corps, described Sedgwick as "modest and retiring in his ordinary intercourse with his fellows, he exhibited the most brilliant qualities in time of battle. The dignity of his bearing fitted him to command, and he needed not the insignia of rank to command the deference of those about him…. No soldier was more beloved by the army or honored by the country than this noble general."[114] That was "Uncle John" Sedgwick, the beloved, lionhearted leader of the VI Corps.

Maj. Gen. John Sedgwick, commander, VI Corps, Army of the Potomac. Killed at Spotsylvania, Virginia, May 9, 1864 (author's collection).

Initially the advent of Hooker and Sedgwick had little impact upon the Pennsylvania 96th regiment. Even the disbanding of Burnside's old grand divisions elicited little comment from the Pennsylvania veterans. They knew that there was still a long winter to endure at the White Oak Church encampment. In early February the mundane routine of camp life was broken by the transfer of the regiment to Windmill Point. At that bleak place the 96th was charged with guarding the hospital and wharf.[115] After four weeks the regiment rejoined the brigade at White Oak Church. After returning from Windmill Point, the rank and file learned that Colonel Cake, for medical reasons, was resigning as colonel of the 96th Pennsylvania. The void created by Cake's retirement opened anew the political wrangling within the field and staff officer corps of the regiment.

In the spring of 1863, William H. Lessig, then holding the rank of major, commanded the 96th Pennsylvania. Lessig, formerly the captain of Company C, was Cake's hand-picked successor. According to Captain Boyle of Company D, Lessig received his promotion to major "over the head of Captain James Russell of Company E, who was justly entitled to it."[116] In fact, Boyle, along with Russell and the captain of Company K, Captain Richard Budd, held seniority over Lessig. To insure that Lessig would receive his commission as major, Cake, prior to his departure from military service, issued regimental order thirty-nine confirming the former captain of Company C as the ranking senior line officer.[117] Clearly, Lessig was a member in good standing of the Cake faction and received the appropriate reward for his loyalty.

Lessig was also highly regarded by the soldiers of the 96th Pennsylvania. In the late summer of 1861, he recruited and organized the Good Intent Light Artillery, composed of men from a local fire company in Pottsville.[118] Lessig's light artillery unit formed Company C, the color company, of the 96th Pennsylvania Volunteers. Due to illness, he missed the Battle of Gaines' Mill but returned to active duty in August, and led his company at the Battle of Crampton's Gap.[119] In his report, Colonel Cake recognized Lessig's leadership and gallantry under fire. "Captain Lessig, Company C, deserves especial mention for brave conduct. The prospect of a fight in the wood and among the rocks on the side of the mountain stimulated him to great exertions to gain that point, and he cheered on his fine company most bravely."[120] After being firmly established as the regimental commander, Lessig next sought to garner his colonel's eagle. He also wanted, through his influence, to fill the vacant posts of lieutenant colonel and major. Like his mentor, Lessig was not going to find his new lieutenant colonel and major at the top of the seniority roster. His plan was a simple one. He proposed to discredit captains Boyle and Russell and elevate two other officers to the open regimental staff vacancies. Edgar "Matt" Richards, the former regimental adjutant and an aide-de-camp to General Bartlett and Jacob W. Haas, the captain of Company G, were to be the beneficiaries of Lessig's scheme. In a letter to his brother Fred, Captain Haas revealed the details of the plot.

> Today, Lessig forwarded my name for Major; Matt Richards for Lt. Colonel and his own for Colonel, to the Governor.... How it will result can not say. I may fail in securing that which is dear to every soldier, "Promotion." I might have been Lt. Colonel, but I did not choose, although Gen. Bartlett urged me to take it, but I prefer that Richards shall rake the chestnuts from the fire for me.
>
> If you can get some influence to bear upon the Governor it may materially aid me; of course, I jump three other captains, but they can't win the way we have it put up. If they win we will bust the regiment up.[121]

Lessig's bold gambit, however, did not receive the blessing of the "War Governor." Obviously, Curtin realized that Lessig was trying to discredit two capable and loyal volunteer line officers in order to advance the military careers of two friends. Although Lessig's plan failed, it was a clear signal that he, like Colonel Cake, was going to manipulate regimental promotions. Favoritism and factionalism, common practices in the Union volunteer army, would continue to be the primary criteria for promotional advancement within the regiment.[122]

Meanwhile, Joseph Hooker initiated sweeping changes within the Army of the Potomac. Upon assuming command of that army, he was shrewd enough to realize that its plight looked worse than it really was. "Fighting Joe" recognized that if he could reestablish *esprit de corps*, he could restore the loss of morale. To accomplish that objective, Hooker began by shaking up the army's housekeeping services, quartermaster, commissary and medical departments. Other reforms reduced desertions. Believing that idleness was "the great evil of all armies," Hooker kept his troops busy at drills, reviews and inspections. Periodically there were spectacular parades, with "Fighting Joe" riding his horse, evoking cheers from the troops. All of this made the Unionists feel like soldiers once more. Hooker also abolished Burnside's Grand Divisions, considering them cumbersome. He expanded upon the use of the so-called Kearny patch. He ordered the adoption of corps insignia of various shapes, cut from red, white or blue cloth, indicating the First, Second or Third Division, and stitched to the crown of the caps. Arguably Hooker's most significant administrative decision was the consolidation of the army's cavalry into one corps of three divisions.[123] All of this led a newspaper reporter for the New York *Times* to comment: "The name of McClellan has vanished from the minds of the soldiers, and the army today ... is about as much Hookerized as it was at one time McClellanized."[124]

St. Patrick's day was a festive occasion within the Greek Cross Corps. Orators delivered speeches while other soldiers engaged in horse racing, foot races, wheelbarrow races and other parade ground activities. Members of the 6th Vermont conducted a spirited game of football, while other regiments of the VI Corps played a game of baseball.[125] Thomas Houck informed his brother Joe that the soldiers in camp "have a good bit of sport playing ball."[126] After this brief respite the Bluecoats returned to their daily programs of regimental drill, grand reviews and inspections, all designed to tighten discipline and restore morale.[127] According to entries recorded in the pocket diaries of Henry Keiser and Evan Gery, Company G was inspected three times by Captain Haas throughout March and April. In that period, too, Company G participated in one battalion drill, seven company drills, and nine dress parades.[128] In addition to preparing for the upcoming campaign on the drill ground, Dr. Bland reported that the men of the regiment were in excellent health. A soldier writing under the pen name "*Amicus Curae*," noted that "during the past five months only three deaths have occurred in camp hospital; at present the number of serious sick is reduced to one."[129]

Thus the reforms instituted by "Fighting Joe" Hooker, had begun to return dividends by early April. In a relatively short period, he successfully restored morale, improved the health of the soldiers and demonstrated leadership qualities, reminiscent of McClellan. All of this served to inspire the Bluecoats to follow him to victory in the next battle. Writing from White Oak Church, just prior to the opening movement of the Chancellorsville campaign, *Amicus Curae* summarized the mood of the army in general and the soldiers of the 96th Pennsylvania in particular. "The Army of the Potomac is in splendid condition in all departments—morally, physically, and in a military view surpasses any army of modern times. The health is astonishing. The Sixth Army Corps I understand has the least sick of any." *Curae* also offered the following assessment of Hooker: "No one really appreciates the real worth of the army as much as Hooker.... He considers it the 'best army on the planet' and is sanguine of success when we shall meet the rebel horde."[130]

In early April, Hooker held a series of grand reviews to further boost morale for the upcoming campaign. On April 3, General Hooker reviewed "Bully" Brooks' First Division of the VI Corps. Erasmus Reed described the scene and the resurgence in morale within the ranks in a letter to his family. "Today our division was reviewed by Major General Hooker. The troops looked splendid, if anything better than last spring when we started out. They are well clothed and well disciplined."[131] In addition, the young musician described the temperament of the soldiers and Hooker's influence on the Army of the Potomac. "There has been a great change in the army. The army has again got the old spirit and the enthusiasm of last spring is surely returning, and Hooker is getting to be a second McClellan. He has a fine army to back him. If it be God's will he must be successful."[132] An unknown soldier in the 96th Pennsylvania proclaimed that "old Joe Hooker's army is in bully fighting trim."[133] While Tom Houck informed his brother that "the Army will fight if we are only handled right. All talk of the Army being demoralized is all nonsense."[134] Five days after the divisional review, the entire Army of the Potomac was paraded past President Lincoln. According to surgeon Stevens, the historian of the VI Corps, this grand review, which spanned four days, "was a most imposing spectacle, never to be forgotten by those who were actors or spectators."[135]

Soldier diaries, which often yield interesting observations and details not available elsewhere, in some cases reveal very little about significant events. The enormous grand review of April 6–9, encompassing the entire Army of the Potomac, was a magnificent military display. Yet, the soldiers recorded modest entries in their respective pocket diaries concerning this singular event. On April 8, Lincoln reviewed the II, III, V and VI Army Corps, and the artillery reserve.[136] Parading as many as 75,000 Bluecoats past the President was a major logistical undertaking and a significant martial ceremony. Strangely, the daily diary entries recorded by the Pennsylvanians paid scant attention to the magnificent grand review before Lincoln and Hooker. Evan Gery merely noted in his diary that "we were reviewed by Abe Lincoln."[137] Henry Keiser recorded a slightly longer recollection when he wrote, "We marched about five miles when the Army was reviewed by President Lincoln and Gen. Hooker."[138] Jerome Miller stated, "Today our Corps was reviewed by the President + Gen. Hooker. The review came off near Falmouth at Hookers Hd Qrs"[139] In his lengthy memoir, James Treichler devoted a mere sentence to the review. "President Lincoln had the visited the Army and reviewed same; he had expressed his satisfaction and thrilled the men with his inspiring presence and personality."[140] Other soldiers in the VI Corps and the 96th Pennsylvania, however, wrote vivid impressions of this exciting and dramatic meeting between Lincoln and the rank and file of the Army of the Potomac.[141]

According to a number of eyewitnesses in the Second Brigade, the entire day was a grand affair. The army bands played patriotic tunes while the soldiers marched across the parade ground, a plateau two miles from the Rappahannock River in full view of the Butternut forces. Writing after the war, a veteran of Bartlett's brigade described the dramatic army review conducted near General Hooker's headquarters. "Never did troops present a grander spectacle than upon that occasion. The marching was superb, and everything moved like clock-work. The men's bright muskets, their neat and clean uniforms, and their white gloves, made the review appear imposing.... To look upon that army, they appeared invincible."[142] Another Bluecoat recorded in his journal that the day was "cloudy and still. The regiment formed at 8 o'clock in the morning, and started on a grand review by President Lincoln, who was to review the Army of the Potomac near Falmouth. It passed off pretty well, and our 'Uncle Abraham' looked better than when I saw him last."[143] The most detailed narrative of the review, however, was authored by *Amicus Curae* of the 96th Pennsylvania. In a letter to the *Miners' Journal*, he captured the drama of the moment and the significance of the review in the minds of the soldiers.

> The scene was most grand—the day all that could be desired for the auspicious occasion. President Lincoln reviewed the troops, in company with Major General Hooker, with his staff, attaches, and cavalcade of Lancers as a body guard. The scene could be compared to none other than when the French were massed and Napoleon appeared upon the field of Mars to accept the crown. It was one of the memorable days of the war. Everything passed off with the most complete success. The troops never appeared to better advantage, and their marching was like veterans of old.... The men are eager for the coming engagement, and I assure You that we will give a respectable account of ourselves.[144]

Captain Haas captured the essence of the event, at least from his vantage point, when he remarked that the review before "'Uncle Able' [was a] great display of military."[145] From the point of view of the soldiers, though, especially a number of Bluecoats in Bartlett's brigade, the Presidential review was not the highlight of the spring. The big news swirling through the camps concerned the appointment of Joseph Bartlett to the rank of brigadier general.[146]

On April 14, while the Bluecoats at White Oak Church cheered the appointment of Bartlett, Hooker was planning the destruction of Lee's mighty Army of Northern Virginia. "Fighting Joe" proposed to send his cavalry around Lee's left flank with instructions to

Franklin's Crossing, Rappahannock River, Fredericksburg, Virginia. Depicts the pontoon bridges spanning the Rappahannock at a point known as Franklin's Crossing, associating the river crossing established by Gen. Franklin in the December 1862 battle at Fredericksburg. The photograph is attributed to Timothy O'Sullivan and most likely composed in May 1863 (New York Public Library).

disrupt Confederate communications with Richmond. In concert with the cavalry movement, "Uncle" John Sedgwick was to cross his oversized command, the I, III and VI Corps, at Fredericksburg to attack Lee's right flank. While the cavalry galloped behind the Confederate army and Sedgwick assaulted Marye's Heights, Hooker planned to cross the V, XI and XII corps in Lee's front and force the Confederates to abandon their fortifications and fight a pitched battle. The plan, at least on paper, looked splendid. Its execution, however, posed serious obstacles. The success of his plan hinged on the ability of Hooker's troops to coordinate their movements with Sedgwick's forces. Because Hooker hoped to crush Lee's Graycoats between his forces and Sedgwick's wing, clear communication and dry roads would be of paramount importance to the Unionists during this operation. Unfortunately for Hooker he received neither of these necessities. He was a general in a hurry. Muddy plantation lanes and vague messages were not going to slow his campaign.[147]

On the evening of April 26, 1863, Hooker issued marching orders for the next day. Well before first light the Bluecoats tramped out of their camps around Falmouth. Optimism abounded within the ranks. Not only were the Union regiments completely refitted and well rested, they were also at fighting trim. The Unionists, too, had a new general with a warlike reputation. Almost as soon as the Yanks marched out of their winter quarters, however, a cold rain set in, drenching the soldiers. Although the troops were carrying sixty pounds apiece in their knapsacks—the gumbo like mud must have made the load seem double that—the inclement weather did not dampen the spirits of the troops. Upon seeing Hooker along the lines, the men cheered "Fighting Joe" in song:

> Joe Hooker is our leader
> He takes his whiskey strong.

The weather, though ominous, did not cause the marching columns to fall behind schedule. Two days later the Army of the Potomac began crossing the Rappahannock at Kelly's Ford, several miles above Fredericksburg. Meanwhile, Sedgwick glared across the river at the Butternuts, who were viewed by Major Lessig and Captain Haas to be "as thick as lice" along the south bank of the Rappahannock.[148]

Early on the morning of April 28, the bell in the Episcopal Church in Fredericksburg, rang out the alarm that the Federal columns were marching. Later that rainy day the 96th Pennsylvania received orders to draw eight days rations, consisting of crackers, sugar, coffee and salt.[149] The soldiers also exchanged their winter quarters tents for the small campaign shelter tents. By 3 o'clock in the afternoon Sedgwick had his columns moving toward the river, headed for the area known to the Unionists as "Franklin's Crossing"—the area used by General Franklin to construct pontoon bridges spanning the Rappahannock in December. By nightfall General Bartlett had his regiments positioned behind General David Russell's Third Brigade, near the river bank.[150] Captain Haas later remarked that his "load was very heavy. 8 days rations is much too much to lug along."[151]In a letter to his brother Fred, the captain further expressed his frustration about carrying a full pack while on the march. "Need I tell you after several miles had been marched over, our loads began to be heavy—curses loud and deep were vented freely by the men upon the heads of those that got up the idea of making men asses."[152]

William Lessig noted that as the 96th Pennsylvania arrived at the Rappahannock and went into bivouac, the rain stopped and a dense fog enshrouded the river's banks, causing the major to conclude that the conditions were perfect that night "for making a dash" across the river. Unfortunately, the pontoon boats, that were supposed to meet the troops at the river bank were still en route. As Lessig prepared to order his troops into camp for the night, he was summoned to a meeting with General Brooks, commanding the first division. Lessig quickly mounted his horse and galloped off to meet with "Bully" Brooks. In a letter to a friend, Lessig related the particulars of the evening rendezvous with Brooks.

> When I came up to the General, I found him under a tree with General Bartlett and all the commanders of [the] regiments in our Brigade. He [Brooks] soon explained his plans to us. The Third Brigade and our Brigade ... were ordered to cross [the Rappahannock River] first; the other Divisions of our Corps were to convey the boats down to the river, when we were to get in them, forty-five men in each boat, with five men to pull the oars. Our orders were to take possession of the rifle-pits which commanded the river, and hold them until the bridges could be built. We were ordered to be ready to move at 11 o'clock; the watchword was Troy, and we were to shoot the first of our men who made any noise, or sabre them if possible.[153]

With the operation for the crossing set, Lessig returned to his unit and told the line officers of Brooks' plan.[154] At midnight, after trying to nap on the cold, wet ground, the Pennsylvanians were ordered to march to the river. Once there they assisted in hauling the pontoon boats to Franklin's Crossing.[155] As the blackness of the night reluctantly gave way to the gray dawn of a new day, the soldiers made their final preparations for the river crossing and the anticipated clash with the Lee's veterans.

VIII

"Try and gobble some of them"

As dawn broke across the Rappahannock on the morning of April 29, Russell's Third Brigade set off in the pontoon boats for the south side of the river to secure a bridgehead. Quickly Bartlett's brigade crossed the Rappahannock and went to the aid of Russell's brigade, which was engaged in front of the Butternut rifle pits.[1] Both brigades then formed strong skirmish lines, with Russell pushing out his voltigeurs on a sweeping front extending from Deep Run on the right, running south and parallel with the Bowling Green Road, and swinging back to the Rappahannock near the ruins of Mansfield, the Bernard mansion, on the left flank. During this operation, the 96th Pennsylvania occupied vacant Secessionist works on the Bernard farm, near Deep Run where they had been posted in December.[2] According to several soldiers of the 96th, the Pennsylvanians spent most of the day prone in line of battle.[3] After Russell's and Bartlett's brigades secured their positions in abandoned Confederate rifle pits, the business of constructing the pontoon bridges began in earnest. Major Lessig later recalled that throughout the day, "the rebs were seen in our front, but showed no disposition to molest us…. At dark we commenced and threw up a line of works along our front, expecting to be attacked by the evening."[4] By early evening one division of Sedgwick's VI Corps was deployed on the plain held by Franklin's troops the previous December.[5]

For the last two days of April Sedgwick's VI Corps did very little. At Fredericksburg, a strange calm prevailed in that sector of Hooker's ongoing Chancellorsville operation. The 96th established a line of battle along Deep Run; ground familiar to the Pennsylvanians from Burnside's battle in December.[6] For the most part, however, "quiet reigned supreme" along the lines on the last day of April.[7] The Pennsylvanians, after being mustered for pay, listened to a dispatch from Hooker, *General Orders No. 47*, praising the accomplishments of the XI and XII Corps.[8] As the new May dawned, the military situation began to crystallize. Hooker had approximately 50,000 men at Chancellorsville, with 22,000 more on the way. At Falmouth and Fredericksburg there were 47,000 more Bluecoats under "Uncle" John Sedgwick. Captain Haas reported that the 96th was assigned picket duty along their sector of the line. He observed that "the neutral ground between the pickets was only about 40 yards."[9] Despite the close proximity to the Secessionists on the last day of April the day passed quietly.

For some of the soldiers of the 96th Pennsylvania, May 1 began long before sunrise. Captain Haas and the men of Company G spent the early morning hours performing advanced picket duty. Throughout the day, details from the 96th regiment, composed of twelve soldiers, a sergeant and an officer, rotated outpost duty. After sunrise, Capt. Haas noted that the "'Rebs' [are] very thick this morning. I think they are advancing."[10] At 7

151

p.m., Bartlett's brigade was relieved and the tired, famished soldiers retired to the banks of the Rappahannock. Some of the Bluecoats spent the evening fishing while others enjoyed the national airs such as "Hail Columbia," "Red, White and Blue" and "Yankee Doodle" played by a Union brass band.[11] In addition, the Bluecoats heard loud cheering from the nearby rebel camps and the music of their brass band. In the morning, however, the "brass bands," on both sides poured deadly tunes of artillery at each other. Captain Haas described the rude awakening the soldiers received on the morning of May 2 in a letter to his brother. "We were aroused by a furious shelling of our camp at 5 a.m. Several shells fell in our camp but did no damage. We quickly packed up and moved to our left … then clambered up the high banks of the bluff and laid in line of battle."[12]

According to Captain Haas, Saturday, May 2, proved to be a "fine day."[13] To Joseph Hooker it was a crucial day for the Union army. The relative calm of the past few days in Sedgwick's sector was broken by increased activity on the part of the skirmishers. Early in the morning Sedgwick received a message from Hooker to send Reynolds' I Corps to him. (Sickles' III Corps had been previously sent to Hooker.) Seeing heavy troop concentration on the pontoon bridges, the Secessionist batteries shelled the departing Bluecoats. During the afternoon, Sedgwick and his forces heard the din of battle to their right. At 6:30 p.m., as Sedgwick received orders from Hooker, "Stonewall" Jackson was routing O.O. Howard's XI Corps. The message from Hooker instructed Sedgwick to "capture Fredericksburg with everything in it, and vigorously pursue the enemy."[14] After receiving Hooker's dispatch, which did not reveal the military situation in "Fighting Joe's" sector, Sedgwick prepared to advance against the foe.

While Sedgwick planned the seizure of Fredericksburg, Confederate artillery fire raked the Pennsylvanians. In order to protect his regiment from Secessionist missiles, Major Lessig used terrain between the river and the Bowling Green Road to shield the soldiers from the incoming shells. Although the cannonade stopped at 10 o'clock, rifle fire between the advanced picket posts intensified. Witnessing the additional Confederates deployed along the line in their immediate front, Lessig noted that "it became evident that a battle could not be longer delayed."[15] For the 96th the day was hot but quiet, until three o'clock. At that time the still air of the clear blue sky was broken by a Confederate band playing *Dixie*, a favorite tune of the Butternuts. As the notes drifted across the Rappahannock, a Federal band sent back a reply in the form of "The Star-Spangled Banner."[16] Suddenly, however, the national melodies were drowned out by the crackling of picket fire along the lines. A regiment of Russell's brigade advanced against the Graycoats in the Deep Run ravine area. The 31st New York, acting as voltiguers, successfully pushed back the Secessionists to the bed of the Richmond, Fredericksburg & Potomac Railroad, (RF&P) and established a skirmish line beyond the Bowling Green Road.[17] The forward movement of the New Yorkers, according to Captain Haas, caused "the pickets … to shoot at each other and kept it up until about 5 p.m. when General Brooks ordered the whole line to advance and drive the 'Rebs' into their rifle pits, which was very handsomely executed."[18] That evening, the 96th Pennsylvania passed the night in the ravine formed by Deep Run.[19] As the soldiers tried to make themselves comfortable, one Bluecoat confided in his diary, "We expect hard work to-morrow."[20]

After assessing his situation, Sedgwick decided, "to move by the flank in the direction of Fredericksburg, on the Bowling Green Road [old Richmond Stage Road]."[21] The night sky was illuminated by bright moonlight, but a ground fog created visual problems for the Bluecoats. Other issues, too, such as unfamiliar terrain, Confederate pickets and false alarms, caused by a night march conducted in the presence of the enemy, contributed to the slow, deliberate advance of Sedgwick's Unionists. With the Bowling Green Road secured, Sedgwick started the VI Corps toward Fredericksburg in order to unite with General Gibbon's Second Division of the II Corps. On the march to Fredericksburg, Newton's division took the lead, followed by Burnham's Light Division (a provisional unit) and then Howe's division. Brooks' division remained at Deep Run, as rear guard, protecting Sedgwick's left from any incursion by Confederates along the line from Deep Run to Hamilton's Crossing.[22]

Before dawn, as Sedgwick's divisions (the Second under Albion Howe and the Third commanded by John Newton) marched into Fredericksburg, General Jubal Early was convinced that the principal Federal assault would be directed against his line at a point below the town between Hamilton's Crossing and Howison's Hill. As a result, Early positioned Brig. Gen. Robert Hoke's North Carolina brigade across Deep Run, and extended his line farther south, parallel and behind the RF&P Railroad, with Gen. John B. Gordon's Georgia brigade and finally Brig. Gen. "Extra Billy" Smith's brigade of Virginians anchoring the Confederate right terminating at Hamilton's Crossing. Substantially because of the deployment the previous day, when the Bluecoats had driven the Secessionists beyond the rail line, thereby securing the Bowling Green Road and controlling the open farm fields below Deep Run, Early believed the Yankee attack would concentrate along this part of his line. Furthermore, Early was aware that the ravine cut by the Deep Run water course afforded the Bluecoats an avenue which they could use to penetrate his thinly held front. Early also observed that "the heaviest force in view was in front of the crossing below the mouth of Deep Run, and there were at that point a number of pieces of artillery."[23] While Sedgwick completed his preparations in Fredericksburg, "Bully" Brooks attracted the attention of Old Jube with an infantry probe along Deep Run ravine toward the sector of the Confederate line held by elements of Hoke's Tarheels.

As Sedgwick finalized his plan of attack in Fredericksburg, "Bully" Brooks informed him that "the enemy kept a large force … in our front … and appeared to be receiving re-enforcements … of both infantry and artillery."[24] In fact, as darkness gave way to early morning, the men of Brooks' division could see Confederate pickets, most likely three Virginia regiments from "Extra Billy" Smith's brigade, moving through the farm fields and threatening the left of Brooks's position. According to General Bartlett, "The enemy on our left caused the general commanding the division to make such disposition of his command as to be ready to repel an attack of infantry or to cover them from the artillery fire which was opened on our left and rear."[25] About 4:15 a.m., in response to the Confederate presence, Bartlett's brigade moved forward and formed a line of battle. According to Captain Haas, the 96th "entered the ravine [Deep Run] in front of us, running parallel with the Turnpike [Bowling Green Road] and [the] Hills. We had scarcely entered it before we were shelled horribly. The 'Rebs' had a Battery to our left, near the railroad, which enfiladed the ravine and did some fine shooting."[26] The 96th Pennsylvania was under fire from a brilliant young cannoneer, Maj. Joseph Latimer, commanding several sections of Early's artillery battalion. At 6:30, Bartlett called upon Major Lessig and ordered him to lead the 96th down Deep Run Creek, using the ravine to screen his movement, drive the Tarheels beyond the railroad and secure the open ground and eliminate the possibility of a threat to Brooks' rear.[27]

Intent upon turning back the advancing Confederates, Brooks deployed two batteries of artillery (Rigby's and McCartney's) along the Bowling Green Road to silence the Confederate artillery and prevent the Secessionist skirmishers from harassing the movement of the Yankee column marching toward Fredericksburg.[28] After positioning the artillery, Bartlett shifted the two New York regiments and the 5th Maine, to support the batteries.[29] Shortly after Bartlett repositioned the infantry regiments, "Bully" Brooks directed him "to send forward one regiment to take the railroad on the right of the ravine, in order to develop more fully the enemy's position and numbers." Between 6:30 and 7 o'clock, Bartlett rode over to the 96th Pennsylvania and ordered Major Lessig "to move down the ravine and 'try and gobble some of them.'"[30] Specifically, Bartlett instructed Lessig "to move down the ravine until we got near the Railroad when we were to swing the right of our Regiment round and "gobble some prisoners."[31] According to Lessig, he quickly realized that the operation would be a difficult undertaking. He would need to advance the Schuylkill Countians forward, approximately 700 yards, seize a section of the rail line and endeavor to draw out the Confederate infantry to develop enemy strength in this sector.[32] For Major Lessig, this reconnaissance operation, conducted under the watchful eyes of his immediate superiors—Generals Brooks and Bartlett—afforded him an opportunity to showcase his command skills under combat conditions. Lessig, a fiery, intrepid leader, was ready to seize the moment.

Maj. William H. Lessig with his horse. This intriguing image is a half-plate tintype. Most likely it was composed at Fairfax Court House June 25, 1863. The photographer is unknown (collection of Douglas Sagrillo).

Immediately, Lessig mounted his horse and reconnoitered the terrain between his regiment and the line of Confederate pickets visible in the fields. In particular, he ascertained how he could use the ravine of Deep Run to advance the 96th Pennsylvania toward the railroad in order to minimize casualties. He understood, too, that as he guided his regiment toward the rail line, he would not only need to shelter the soldiers from the deadly accuracy of the Confederate artillery fire, but also to form a battle line, move forward and sweep the Graycoat skirmishers and sharpshooters from their front. Returning to his regiment, after conducting a thorough visual inspection of the ground, Lessig dismounted and ordered the men to unsling their knapsacks and fix bayonets. Then, "with a cheer (for which the old Regiment is famous)," the 96th advanced against the foe at double-quick time.[33] As the Pennsylvanians moved forward, "The rebs opened a heavy fire of grape, canister, musketry and shell," on the gallant band numbering perhaps slightly more than 350 soldiers.[34]

Emerging from the relative safety of Deep Run ravine, Lessig deployed Company B as skirmishers, formed a battle line with the balance of the regiment and drove the North Carolinians in this area back across the railroad. According to Captain Haas, the right flank of the 96th quickly pushed the Secessionist skirmishers beyond the rail line and into their rifle pits. On the regiment's left flank, where Haas was with his company, the men encountered "a more difficult job as the ravine moved down parallel with the left flank … which was timbered so that the Rebs had a good shelter."[35] Captain Haas recalled that "we charged them and pressed on and took the railroad. The enemy had a Battery in a rifle pit on the other side of the railroad. The firing was lively and exciting."[36] Subsequently, Haas was ordered "to skirmish the woods with Co. B and G. We moved in and deployed. The enemy fired grape and canister at us for about an hour doing much execution."[37] As the Pennsylvanians reached the railroad, Confederate artillery attempted to break their position and compel them to relinquish the rail line and withdraw from the field. In his after-action report, Lt. Col. Richard Snowden Andrews recounted the engagement from the vantage point of his Confederate gunners. "The enemy shortly after appeared at a point on the run nearer. Captain Dement [1st Maryland Battery] was ordered to open upon them, which he did promptly and effectively, but was unable to prevent a body of them (about two regiments) from reaching a point on the railroad opposite a barn to the left of the Run…. They were so well protected that we could not readily dislodge them."[38]

From their vantage point along the Bowling Green Road, Brooks and Bartlett carefully observed the progress of Major Lessig and his "gallant band" of Pennsylvanians. According to an eyewitness, "Gen. Brooks and Bartlett came up to the line, to reconnoiter the position. They stood with their field glasses to their eyes, and though the shells were bursting all around them, not a muscle was seen to move, while staff and line officers were hugging the ground or trying to dodge the shells."[39] Through his glass, General Bartlett saw that Major Lessig successfully fulfilled the initial part of his mission: clearing the Confederates from the fields and seizing a section of the rail line. In his report, Bartlett recorded the scene he witnessed. "Maj. Lessig … in a splendid and dashing manner developed a long line of battle, formed under cover of rifle pits, about 100 yards in rear of and completely controlling the railroad."[40] Recognizing the exposed position of the 96th Pennsylvania, Bartlett ordered Col. Clark Edwards, commanding the 5th Maine, to advance up the ravine to support the Pennsylvanians.[41]

According to Colonel Edwards, as soon as he started to carry out the order from Bartlett, "the movement was discovered by the enemy, they opened a rapid fire from a battery with shrapnel or grape and canister upon us at a range of 200 yards, thinning our ranks at every discharge."[42] Pushing boldly forward, up the ravine of Deep Run, through thick undergrowth and broken ground, the Maine men reached the position tenaciously held by the Pennsylvanians. Lessig stated that "twelve pieces of cannon were playing on us the whole time."[43] In an attempt to keep his vulnerable left wing from collapsing, Lessig ordered Company B to shift its position further to the left, across the ravine, to prevent the Tarheels from outflanking the regiment.[44] Captain Haas also shifted his Company G to the imperiled left wing to strengthen the left flank. In a letter to his brother, Haas recalled the tense situation on the regiment's left flank. "After firing for some time, the Enemy made a move as if he intended to outflank us on the left…. After a few minutes had elapsed—Bang Bang came grape and canister from two pieces in the rifle pits which swept the ravine, tearing trees down and kicking up thunder generally."[45]

For ninety minutes, the Pennsylvanians steadfastly held a section of the RF&P Railroad. During this time, recalled Captain Haas, "an incessant fire of musketry was kept up but both sides kept hid under cover of Railroad and rifle pit."[46] Major Lessig, pointing proudly to the combat prowess of his men, later reported that the Confederates "made several efforts to retake [the railroad] from us, but in vain."[47] The Secessionists in this sector, five North Carolina regiments under General Hoke, made several attempts to dislodge the 96th Pennsylvania from the railroad.[48] Immediately in front of the Schuylkill Countians was the 1st North Carolina Sharpshooter Battalion and to the right the 57th North Carolina. One Tarheel recorded, in his memoir, his impressions of this action. "It was in the morning and we were firing 'at will' at every Yankee that showed himself to us. Our *gun* [cannon] was worked with rapidity for hours we succeeded in keeping them back from capturing the gun though we were exposed to their sheltered riflemen. The firing was sharp."[49] Another North Carolinian, offered the following recollection of the fighting at the railroad in a letter written soon after the engagement. "We soon discovered a large force advancing to our left on our regt. [We] was ordered to reinforce some higher but they being too fast for us we was ordered back on our same position. They charged the works on our right and taken some prisoners."[50] According to Captain Haas, "At 8 1/2 our ammunition getting low we were relieved by another regiment [27th New York] and we retired to our old place in the ravine—and that is the way we took the prisoners."[51]

Finally, as the 96th Pennsylvania and the 5th Maine struggled to maintain their respective positions, Confederate artillery fire intensified, causing the Pennsylvanians to relinquish their grip on the rail line and withdraw from the field.[52] As the 96th Pennsylvania and the 5th Maine withdrew, Col. Alexander Adams deployed his regiment, the 27th New York, to cover the retreat and prevent the Confederates from reoccupying the railroad while the Bluecoats disengaged and evacuated their wounded.[53] Major Lessig, in a graphic letter written after the battle, described the harrowing withdrawal of his regiment: "I was ordered to retire with my command, a thing not so easily done in the face of an enemy with his artillery in full play at us; but I succeeded in getting my men out by twos and threes, until I was the last man to leave it. How I escaped I cannot say, for the enemy's sharpshooters kept popping away at me all the time."[54] Captain Haas, perhaps exhibiting too much bravado, opined that "if we had been supported … we could have driven the Rebs out of their rifle pits and taken their battery." Realistically, however, he confided to his brother Fred, "I do think of all the hot places I have been in (and I have been in a few) this was the warmest."[55]

This deadly engagement, along a section of railroad cut by Deep Run, resulted in substantial casualties for the three Bluecoat regiments. Major Lessig reported that the 96th lost five men killed and eighteen wounded in the early morning encounter.[56] When the 96th reached the safety of the Union line along the Bowling Green Road, General Brooks sought out Major Lessig and complimented him and his regiment for their performance in the battle. "Brooks said he thought that was the last of the Ninety-sixth, and congratulated me on the successful manner in which I retired with my command."[57] Captain Haas echoed Lessig's recollection of Brooks' comment in a letter to his brother Fred. "Old Brooks told Gen. Bartlett when we charged upon the Railroad 'Good bye 96th, that's the last you'll see of them.'"[58] As the engagement unfolded in the valley of Deep Run, Bartlett sitting on his horse, observed the bold advance of the 96th and the tenacity of the Pennsylvania men bravely holding the rail line against Hoke's Tarheels and the withering effects of the Confederate artillery. He proclaimed the Schuylkill Countians to be "noble men, noble men."[59]

As the soldiers of the 96th Pennsylvania withdrew to the safety of the Bowling Green Road, the vanguard of "Bully" Brooks' division reached Fredericksburg just before noon. Many of the soldiers in Bartlett's brigade cheered the success of the Bluecoats who had gallantly stormed Marye's Heights earlier in the morning. One soldier recalled the grand scene: "It was a splendid sight to see our troops charge with fixed bayonets, from where we were."[60] Another soldier, serving with the 96th Pennsylvania, using the pen name *Amicus Curae,* described the action as the Yankees seized possession of Marye's Heights. "The Heights were gained in fine style, being carried at the point of the bayonet. At the storming of the Heights our artillery firing was the most accurate I ever witnessed; every shell exploded within the fortifications. I saw two caissons explode, several limbers broken and the crack company of Washington Artillerists of New Orleans put *hors de combat.*"[61] Watching the singular success of the Unionists, Captain Haas simply remarked, "At 12 M., our troops carried the heights behind the town and the 'rebs' skedippered from all around us."[62] As the Secessionists fled from Fredericksburg, "Bully" Brooks' division marched into the old colonial town, receiving their first glimpse of the stately dwellings and the destruction that the recent battles had inflicted upon the city.

Upon reaching Fredericksburg, Maurus Oestreich recorded that the city "looked like the destruction of Jerusalem."[63] Another Bluecoat recalled the grim scene which greeted the soldiers as they marched through the city. "Our line of march lay through the heart of the city passing a fine mansion with red cross on its observatory, occupied as a hospital for our division, in the suburbs, through streets of dilapidated and shot pierced dwellings, until reaching the neighborhood of the churches, with their spires showing the same effect of Burnside's bombardment, where fine buildings and paved streets attested the residence of the Fredericksburg aristocracy."[64] *Amicus Curae* stated that the Unionists "received orders to occupy the town and use the houses for hospital purposes. The First Division took possession of the large mansion owned by Mr. Slaughter, brother of the Mayor. The building is very commodious, and owing to the very free ventilation caused by the shelling of the town, was most admirably adapted for the purpose."[65] As the 96th tramped through the city, Maurus Oestreich, of Company B, and the young musician, Erasmus Reed, were detailed to the army's Medical Department to care for the battlefield wounded.

Medical care for the wounded, and in many instances surgical intervention for traumatic wounds, was an important issue for regimental commanders. Previously, following the Battle of Antietam, Colonel Cake had appended this observation in his official report: "I regret being compelled to report that our surgeons invariably leave upon the bursting of the first shell near the regiment. This has always heretofore deprived us of their services on the field, though I believe it is the custom to report for duty at the hospitals."[66] Cake's statement and subsequent suggestion was already being considered, unknowingly perhaps to the Pennsylvania colonel, by Dr. Jonathan Letterman, the Medical Director of the Army of the Potomac. In fact, prior to the Battle of Antietam, Letterman was instituting reforms and completely reorganizing the Medical Department, in order to deliver "prompt and efficient care of the wounded."[67] Central to Letterman's reorganization was the establishment of "Field Hospitals," per each division of the army, further development of the Ambulance Corps and appointing skilled surgeons to conduct operations on the wounded soldiers at the earliest moment—even while the battle was still being fought.[68]

Writing after the Chancellorsville campaign, Erasmus Reed described his duties at the divisional hospital.

> In order to give you a correct idea what a division hospital is during a battle I must explain. It is only a temporary affair, stationed in the rear of the corps, where the wounded get their first dress-

This photograph depicts houses on Hanover and Liberty Streets in Fredericksburg, Virginia, destroyed by artillery fire during the December 1862 Battle of Fredericksburg. Possibly photographed by James Gardner. The original photograph is dated circa May 19, 1864 (Library of Congress).

ing. From there they are shipped off as fast as possible. The hospital moves as the army moves. If they advance the hospital advances, so in falling back it is the same. Our duty was to put up tents and take care of the wounded. We were not in much danger. A few shells came over our heads now and then, but that was nothing. It merely reminded us that there was a battle being fought. The doctors are nine of the pluckiest men and you see, we were under their command. Whenever a place would be pretty warm, they would move back and we would, of course follow.[69]

Most importantly, however, Dr. Letterman clearly established procedures for evacuating the wounded from the battlefield to a field hospital where the soldiers could receive immediate treatment. From the forward field hospital, the Ambulance Corps conveyed the wounded to the divisional hospital. According to surgeon Stevens, the VI Corps historian, "By the new system, the surgeons were enabled to accomplish a far greater amount of work, and in much better order than under the old; and the wounded men were better and more quickly cared for."[70]

After crossing over Marye's Heights, and advancing perhaps a mile along the Plank Road, the tired soldiers of the 96th were afforded a brief rest period. While they rested, they viewed the fluid military situation unfolding before them. A VI Corps staff officer recalled that "upon reaching the summit of the sharp hill after passing through the extensive and well-wooded grounds of the Marye House, an exciting scene met the eye. A single glance exhibited to view the broad plateau alive with fleeing soldiers, riderless horses, and artillery wagon-trains on a gallop."[71] Surveying the situation, too, Captain Haas believed that it was "a 'sure thing' now that all we had to do was to move down toward Richmond and pick up prisoners."[72] At this moment the young captain was, however, uncertain about the operational mission of the VI Corps. In a letter to his brother Fred, he wondered "Whether our orders were to form a junction or not with Hooker I cannot say, but at any rate I think we should have remained on the heights."[73] Before 1 p.m., after a rest of just fifteen minutes, Brooks' division was again marching west, along the Orange Plank Road in order to rendezvous with the divisions of Newton and Burnham near the Guest House, which temporarily served as Sedgwick's field headquarters.[74]

As the afternoon of May 3 began to slip away, the fate of Hooker's campaign rested upon Sedgwick's shoulders. "Uncle John," with Hooker's timetable etched in his mind, decided to push Brooks' division against the Alabamians of Brig. Gen. Cadmus Wilcox hoping that his soldiers could achieve a breakthrough against the Confederates blocking the road to Chancellorsville. As Sedgwick lost precious time reuniting the separated divisions of the VI Corps, Wilcox, a North Carolinian commanding five Alabama regiments, sought to stop "Uncle John's" advance to relieve the beleaguered Hooker. In his after-action report, Wilcox stated his understanding of the situation confronting him earlier in the morning. "Finding myself alone on the left of the Plank road with the enemy in full view on the crests of the first range of hills in rear of Fredericksburg, and with three times my own force clearly seen and in line, I felt it a duty to delay the enemy as much as possible in his advance, and to endeavor to check him all that I could should he move forward on the Plank road."[75] Later in the morning, Wilcox learned that the Yankees successfully seized Marye's Heights and that the Confederates who gallantly held Fredericksburg were retreating down the Telegraph Road. It would be up to General Wilcox, and his veteran brigade, to stop the steady advance of the VI Corps.

Cautiously and conservatively, "Bully" Brooks' division advanced toward Wilcox's Alabamians arrayed for battle at Salem Church. About 4 p.m., Brooks deployed Col.

Henry Brown's New Jersey brigade to the right (north) of the Plank Road and General Bartlett's Brigade, including the 96th Pennsylvania, to the left (south) of the road, and made final preparations to attack Wilcox's Alabamians. Brig. Gen. David Russell's brigade, detached earlier in the morning to perform rear guard duties below Fredericksburg, was trailing the column and would eventually move into line on Brown's right flank. Leading Brooks' advance, fanned out on both sides of the Plank Road, were six companies of the 2nd New Jersey, acting as skirmishers. Moving through the farm fields, the Jerseymen were conspicuous for the white canvas knapsacks slung across their backs. With the skill of veterans, the men of the 2nd New Jersey pushed the Confederate skirmishers back into the thick belt of woods just east of Salem Church.[76] Bartlett, in his official report, described the events of the engagement unfolding at approximately 5 p.m. "Our skirmishers pressed those of the enemy steadily back, while the batteries of our division drove the three pieces [of artillery] which were used upon us from successive positions until we arrived in front of a dense thicket, crossing the [Plank] road at right angles and partially concealing the heights of Salem Church. Here our skirmish line was checked, and it became evident our farther advance was to be contested with all the forces of the enemy."[77]

Moving forward from the toll gate in line of battle, approximately one half mile from Salem Church, the most prominent landmark in the area, General Bartlett made some final dispositions for the assault.[78] To the left of the Plank Road, he positioned the 23rd New Jersey, a nine-month regiment 550 men strong, commanded by Col. E. Burd Grubb.[79] To the left of the Jerseymen, was another untested, regiment, the 121st New York Volunteers with 500 muskets present for duty.[80] This regiment, raised principally in Otsego and Herkimer Counties, although unscarred by battle, was well trained and expertly led by a dynamic West Point graduate, Col. Emory Upton. On the left of the 121st New York, who called themselves "Upton's Regulars," was the 96th Pennsylvania, one of the veteran regiments of Bartlett's brigade, under their new commanding officer, Maj. William H. Lessig. After the morning skirmish with Hoke's North Carolinians, 330 Schuylkill Countians prepared for battle that afternoon.[81] On the left flank of the 96th was the 5th Maine, numbering approximately 300 ready for action.[82] Col. Clark Edwards, also new to regimental command, would lead the 5th Maine in battle. Finally, trailing the formation, behind the 23rd New Jersey, was another veteran unit, the 16th New York, 410 present for duty, featuring another commander with significant experience in combat, Col. Joel J. Seaver.[83] The 27th New York, a regiment with considerable service and led by a seasoned officer, Col. Alexander Adams, would not see action at Salem Church. In sum, Bartlett's initial line of battle was composed of three combat tested regiments and two untried but eager volunteers. Of the five regimental commanders, four were inexperienced in their current leadership roles. For Bartlett, command and control issues in this engagement would be further complicated by local terrain features in the vicinity of Salem Church and the inability to see the elements of his brigade due to the belt of timber east of the church.

W. A. Johnson serving with the 2nd South Carolina of Brig. Gen. Joseph Kershaw's brigade, reported that "Salem Church is, or was, a Hardshell Baptist meeting house situated on the [Orange Plank] road between Fredericksburg and Chancellorsville.... A road crossed the main road at the church and on the north side of it. The church was situated in the southeast angle of the intersection and was a small building."[84] While the red brick church was the most prominent building in the area, the belt of timber, just to the east of the building, would prove to be a major obstacle for the advancing Bluecoats. The woods, referred to by some of the soldiers "as a dense thicket of second growth and brush, about 30 yards in width, through which men could advance but slowly and [with] the utmost difficulty," significantly handicapped the Union field commanders and the infantry in the course of the battle.[85] First and foremost, the belt of woods concealed the Confederate defenders from view and prevented the officers from accurately ascertaining the position and approximate strength of the enemy.[86]

The initial fighting at Salem Church, unlike the previous engagements which were fought in open farm fields, would develop in the woods in the "tangled brush" and "dense undergrowth." A soldier with the 16th New York remarked that "the brush was so tangled that we could not see three rods or keep the line." The belt of woods extended on both sides of the Plank Road broken only by the roadway. The depth of the line of timber, from east to west, varies considerably in the official reports and contemporary accounts of the battle which describe the terrain. Several soldiers stated that the depth of the woods was 30 rods while two Union officers, in their respective after-action reports, observed that the timber was only 30 yards deep. Three other participants estimated the depth of the woods to vary between 200 and 300 yards. While observations, concerning the depth of the belt of woods differ among the various eyewitnesses, the line of second growth timber proved beneficial to the Confederate defenders and a major hindrance to the attacking Federals.[87]

About 5 p.m., after the Unionists advanced cautiously across the fields and woods in line of battle, "it was ascertained by our pickets," according to a New York soldier, "thrown out in front that the rebels had made a stand in rear of a narrow strip of woods directly in our front."[88] Meeting sharp resistance from the Confederate skirmishers at the edge of the woods, coupled with brisk firing on the right, General Brooks ordered Bartlett "to follow the skirmishers up closely and drive the Rebels from their Rifle Pits, if possible."[89] Upon reaching the eastern edge of the woods, known today as the Salem Church ridge, Bartlett halted his brigade, and made some minor realignments to his attack formation. He waited for Colonel Brown's New Jersey brigade, advancing parallel to but north of the Plank Road, to move into supporting position on his right. Upon seeing this delay, "Bully" Brooks immediately ordered Bartlett to push his men forward rapidly against the foe. Just before advancing into the timber, an unknown New York soldier recalled the calm which sweeps over a battlefield just before the moment of the opening volley. "There is always at such time a lull in the din of battle batteries change places, the part-attacking and the attacked seem nerving themselves for the shock. The charging column was formed beyond rifle range, and received orders to fix bayonets, and not to fire until ordered to do so."[90] All that remained for General Bartlett was to issue the simple yet critical command, "Forward, march."

As Bartlett's brigade prepared to plunge into the belt of timber, Wilcox's Alabamians awaited the unsuspecting Bluecoats. Retiring to the environs of Salem Church before Brooks' strike force deployed for battle, Wilcox arrayed his brigade and developed a formidable defensive line along the Salem heights ridge. North of the Plank Road, on his left, Wilcox posted the 14th and the 11th Alabama. South of the Plank Road, he positioned the 10th Alabama, with its left flank resting on the road, and the 8th Alabama protecting his right flank. He instructed the 9th Alabama to form a reserve directly behind the 10th

Alabama. One company of Alabamians was thrown out ahead of the main battle line to establish an outpost at a log school house while another company was sent into the church with orders "to fire from the windows of the gallery."[91] On the Plank Road, was posted a section of North Carolina artillery, known as the Ellis Light Artillery, under Capt. Basil Manly.[92] By 5 o'clock, or shortly after the hour, Maj. Gen. Lafayette McLaws arrived from Chancellorsville with four additional brigades of infantry to support the gallant Alabamians. McLaws deployed the Virginians of "Billy" Mahone on the extreme left of the Confederate line. Between Mahone's right and the left flank of the 14th Alabama, was a brigade of Georgians commanded by Brig. Gen. Paul Semmes. On the right flank of the 8th Alabama, posted in the woods, were the five South Carolina regiments of Brig. Gen. Joseph Kershaw's brigade.[93] Finally, on the extreme right flank of the Confederate line, were the veterans of Gen. William Wofford's Georgia brigade. Now, as the Unionists pushed through the belt of timber, not one but five brigades of Confederate infantry were waiting for them to emerge into the clearing around the church. General Wilcox later recalled, "When the front line of the enemy reached the wood, they made a slight halt; then, giving three cheers, they came with a rush, driving our skirmishers rapidly before them."[94]

According to Major Lessig, "At 5 o'clock he was ordered [by Gen. Bartlett] to push through the woods on the left of the One Hundred and twenty-first New York Volunteers."[95] As the Pennsylvanians surged forward, Captain Haas recalled that "the skirmishers [2nd New Jersey] were in advance of us. As we got in the edge of the woods I saw a few Rebel skirmishers popping at our skirmishers."[96] Moving slowly into the timber, Lessig reported that as the Pennsylvanians advanced "we came on our skirmishers, who fell back to our rear."[97] Another soldier recalled that as the men "moved into the wood, which seemed to be mostly second growth and thickly grown up with underbrush of the oak variety. I can remember now a strange sort of quiet in the ranks. I had no idea, nor do I think anyone near me had any premonition of any impending calamity."[98] Captain Haas instructed his men to "take plenty of room and leave a pace between each file."[99] Normally the soldiers would advance in line of battle elbow-to-elbow. Major Lessig later wrote, "At this time the firing was very heavy on the right, and, as I advanced into the woods, I came on our skirmishers … [and] I enquired of them what was ahead. They could not tell, except that the enemy was in the woods."[100]

Creeping forward, the Pennsylvanians advanced through the underbrush until they glimpsed the Confederate battle line, one hundred yards in front of them. Major Lessig recalled that "in a few minutes I came in sight of their lines, and at once opened a heavy fire on them, at about 100 yards distant [and] commenced to advance my line."[101] Upon seeing the Graycoats, the 8th Alabama in their immediate front, and to their left front, the 7th South Carolina, supported by the 2nd South Carolina, Captain Haas "ordered his men to put in a volley which they did with fine effect I think. At any rate it saved us in some measure for had they got their 1st volley on us I think somebody would have been hurt. And then the circus commenced. We fired as fast as we could and Johnny Reb done the same."[101] An unidentified soldier in the 96th Pennsylvania, writing ten days after the battle, also described this initial point of contact: "The enemy were massed in thick woods *four lines of battle deep*. Against these fearful odds it seemed almost like a sacrifice to oppose them. However, our troops were so flushed with the victory of storming and capturing the Heights [Marye's], that they feared no danger, and were buoyant with hope and confident of success…. It was soon evident that we had stirred up a 'bee-hive,' for a

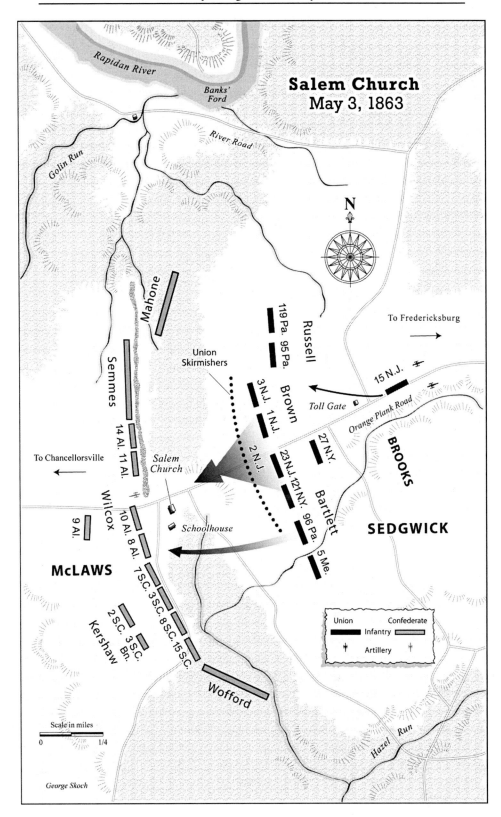

Salem Church
May 3, 1863

N

Rapidan River

Banks'
Ford

River Road

Golin Run

To Fredericksburg

Mahone

119 Pa. 95 Pa.

Russell

15 N.J.

Semmes

Union
Skirmishers

3 N.J. 1 N.J.

Brown

Toll Gate

Orange Plank Road

BROOKS

14 Al. 11 Al.

2 N.J.

27 N.Y.

To Chancellorsville

Salem
Church

23 N.J. 121 N.Y.

Bartlett

SEDGWICK

Wilcox

9 Al.

10 Al. 8 Al.

Schoolhouse

96 Pa. 5 Me.

McLAWS

7 S.C. 3 S.C. 8 S.C. 15 S.C.

2 S.C. 3 S.C.
3 S.C. Bn.

Kershaw

Wofford

Hazel Run

Union	Confederate
Infantry	
Artillery	

Scale in miles

0   1/4

George Skoch

perfect swarm rose up and fired into our lines."[102] Writing twenty years after the battle, W. L. Fagan of the 8th Alabama captured the opening moments of this engagement. "From the field they advanced up the wooded slope towards the church, cheering at every step. The expectant Confederates waited until thirty yards separated the lines, when the Tenth and Eighth Alabama emptied their muskets. This concentrated volley, delivered at short range, did not check the enemy, and as they advanced the Tenth Alabama gave way."[103]

As the 96th Pennsylvania emerged from the belt of timber, pushing back the skirmishers of Company K, 8th Alabama in the process, the Schuylkill Countians halted and fired another decimating volley into the ranks of the Alabamians in their front. Lt. Col. Hilary Herbert, the historian of the 8th Alabama, in his graphic narrative described the initial exchange of fire with the 96th Pennsylvania. "The enemy return[ed] our fire first by volley and then promiscuously.... For a few moments everywhere along the line the enemy are staggered, but in our front do not retreat. The battle seems hanging in the balance, and the second line of the enemy, pressing close behind the first, near the Church, the momentum is such to break our lines."[104] At this moment, recalled one Pennsylvanian, "the fire opened upon all sides and the battle raged with the most intense fury."[105] The anonymous *Amicus Curae* described the deadly engagement in the clearing around the church yard. "The fire of musketry at this point exceeded anything I ever heard; it was here that the gallant Ninety-sixth performed prodigies of valor. The manner of their charge, the determined manner in which they unflinchingly braved the storm of iron and lead, elicited from the commanding General encomiums of the highest praise."[106] As the firing intensified, Major Lessig, on horseback, moved to the regiment's left flank, where elements of Kershaw's brigade concentrated their fire on the left wing of the 96th Pennsylvania.[107]

W. A. Johnson of the 2nd South Carolina, in a lengthy memoir first appearing in the Atlanta *Journal*, recalled that "the Federals came pouring through the woods right up to our lines, and when they were fired into were close up, so that when our lines fired on them they fell thick and fast."[108] Another member of the 2nd South Carolina, John Coxe, wrote, "The Federals came up the slope with a rush and a great shout.... When they got to the road a solid volley from the Alabamians and an oblique front fire from our regiment, only a few steps from them, so wiped them out that few got away.... In that little old road the Federal dead and wounded lay side by side and across each other.... We found we had engaged with a full Pennsylvania regiment, and that it had been sent forward as preliminary to a greater and more general assault."[109] At this point, casualties were beginning to mount within the ranks of the Schuylkill Countians as they struggled to maintain their advanced position from the deadly fire from front and flank.

In the two combat actions of May 3, Companies B and H sustained the highest number of casualties within the ranks of the 96th. Lieutenant John VonHollen's company suffered one killed, five wounded while five other soldiers were counted as missing. Captain Samuel Russsell's company lost six killed, ten wounded and six others among the missing. Thomas Houck of Company A, was wounded in the battle. Five weeks later, only twenty-two years old, he would die due to the gunshot wound to his shoulder, which he received at Salem Church. Upon the death of Sergeant Houck, the *Miners' Journal* reported that "the country loses a brave soldier and sterling patriot, and the community a good citizen."[110] Lieutenant Alexander Allison, of Company C, was mortally wounded in the engagement, while his brother, Corp. John Allison was killed in the battle. As with the death of Sergeant Houck, the *Miners' Journal* also eulogized the Allison brothers. "The death of Lt. Allison and his brother is deeply regretted. Their kind dispositions and fine soldierly qualities made many warm friends who mourn their loss."[111] The lieutenant was 26 years old while his brother was three years his junior. The following year, older brother George Allison, serving with the 56th Pennsylvania, would be killed in the fighting at Spotsylvania. And finally, a fourth brother, James, 28 years old, soldiering with the renowned 48th Pennsylvania, would be killed in action in late June of 1864. In 1907, a memorial honoring their mother, Agnes Allison, was erected in the Presbyterian Cemetery in Port Carbon.[112]

Major Lessig was in fact concerned about the oblique fire of Kershaw's South Carolina brigade enfilading his left wing. Perhaps, Lessig was overly cautious regarding his endangered left flank because he believed, incorrectly, that his regiment was unsupported beyond that point. Not until after the engagement did he learn that the 5th Maine, to the left of the 96th, stood firm against Kershaw's South Carolinians. While inspecting the situation on his left, Lessig noticed significant combat action developing on his right flank which compelled him to rush toward the far right wing of his regiment in order to ascertain the tactical situation unfolding at that moment.[113] As Lessig moved through the woods, Colonel Upton, commanding the 121st New York, led his command forward, collapsing the 10th Alabama in his path and temporarily breaking the Confederate line of battle. Driving between Salem Church on his right and the stubborn 8th Alabama on his left, Upton's New Yorkers "never flinched at all, but poured a volley into them that filled the road with their dead, and took a great many prisoners."[114] As the men of the 121st New York delivered several destructive volleys, the 8th Alabama, refused its left wing by executing a backward half wheel, enabling the Confederates to level enfilading fire against the exposed left flank of the Empire State men. W. L. Fagan, recalled that "the 8th Alabama, without moving from position, poured in a continuous flank fire, from which the Federals recoiled."[115] Within five minutes, however, the 9th Alabama, 350 soldiers strong, pushed through the shattered 10th Alabama, pressed back the 121st New York and restored the integrity of the Confederate line. Not only did the 9th Alabama close the breach, the regiment, commanded by Maj. Jeremiah Williams, spontaneously ignited a Confederate countercharge which proved to be the turning point of the battle.[116]

In his narrative of the battle, Major Lessig recalled that he "rushed to the right of my regiment, and found that the whole line on the right was falling back, and that we alone were holding our position."[117] Captain Haas, too, recognized the emergency developing on the regiment's right wing and recalled that "one of my men came to me and said the Rebs were flanking us. I told the Major and he said all we had to do was to attend to the fellows ahead of us."[118] Haas and Lieutenant Luckenbill respectively, recorded in their diaries the destructive rifle fire that the Alabamians trained upon the brave, hearty Pennsylvanians. According to Captain Haas, "the enemy fired volley after volley at us," while Luckenbill recorded in his journal that "the fire was getting so hot, the right wing broke, and we had to fall back."[119] Fearing that the Pennsylvanians might be cut off and captured Major Lessig issued the order to withdraw. "Finding that the whole Regiment must be taken if I did not at once fall back, I gave the order to do so."[120]

Observing the sudden turn of events, Captain Haas stated, "So, of course we were compelled to retreat and then a terrible skedipper ensued. We ran back toward the main road, the Enemy following us."[121] Continuing his recollection of the retreat, Major Lessig recounted that "at the edge of the woods [western side of the woodlot] we faced about and delivered our fire on the enemy as they advanced upon us, and then fell back."[122] Captain Haas later recorded the following in his pocket diary. "We retreated back to the woods and to the road ... a perfect rout ensued."[123] From the belt of timber, the retreat became a foot race between the charging Secessionists and the refugees of the VI Corps. In a memoir written after the war, Lieutenant Colonel Herbert, commanding the 8th Alabama, stated that his men rushed forward "through the woods, and into the fields, driving the enemy's lines over one another, and as they mingle pell mell in the open field, high above the Confederate yell are heard the voices of officers and men shouting, 'take good aim boys!' 'Hold your muskets level, and you'll get a Yank!'"[124]

Seizing upon the shift in momentum provided by the counterattack of the 9th Alabama, the other four regiments of Wilcox's brigade charged forward intent upon driving the Bluecoats from the field and achieving a resounding victory over the VI Corps. Edmund Patterson of the 9th Alabama described the decisive moment when the Alabamians launched their counter assault. "With a wild yell the brigade moved forward at the same time the whole Yankee line was driven back in confusion, and the day was won."[125] According to Lewis Luckenbill the refugees of the 96th Pennsylvania "retreated some distance and found a line of battle again and rested there overnight."[126] Major Lessig later recalled the end of the battle in a letter written shortly after the engagement.

> A picture of a battle cannot be painted; no one can form any idea of it at a distance; all is smoke, dust and noise.
> To add to the horrors of the night the woods took fire and continued to burn for some time. We could not rescue some of our wounded, but a great many were in the hands of the enemy. At about 10 o'clock I was relieved and then fell back to where our Brigade was laying.[127]

The Battle of Salem Church proved to be an overwhelming victory for the Confederates and a singular defeat for the VI Corps. For the exhausted, vanquished soldiers of the 96th Pennsylvania, May 3 was the most challenging day of their military service to this point in the war. The day opened with the skirmish along the rail line of the RF&P and culminated in a twenty-minute fusillade with the 8th Alabama at Salem Church. In the course of the afternoon engagement, eleven Schuylkill Countians were killed in the battle, thirty-four sustained wounds during the furious fire fight.[128] Conversely, the Pennsylvanians killed five soldiers and wounded forty-five men—out of 500 officers and enlisted engaged—of the 8th Alabama.[129] In the wild, confusing retreat from the battlefield, however, eleven more Schuylkill Countians were captured. Any assessment of the regiment's casualties, and an examination of the toll exacted upon the Secessionists, affords only a small glimpse into the combat effectiveness of the 96th Pennsylvania at the railroad engagement in the morning and the battle in the church yard in the afternoon. Other factors, too, should be evaluated, such as weather conditions, terrain, generalship and the experience of close quarters combat, in order to form any conclusions about the combat performance of the 96th Pennsylvania in these engagements.

First and foremost, the Pennsylvanians started their longest day when they were roused at 1 a.m. and repositioned along the Bowling Green Road. Six hours later, the Schuylkill Countians skirmished with Hoke's Tarheels and withstood considerable Confederate artillery fire. This action, while it added to the regiment's casualty list, enabled Major Lessig to gain invaluable combat leadership experience. His command performance during the railroad skirmish was personally commended by General Brooks. "Bully" Brooks also mentioned this minor action by the 96th Pennsylvania in his official after-action report. Bartlett, too, in his report praised Lessig and his regiment for its conduct in this engagement. Lessig's leadership of the regiment during this action, commanding the Pennsylvanians in a highly exposed position without immediate support, no doubt underscored, especially with the soldiers, his ability to command the regiment in combat. His withdrawal from the field, executed with consummate skill and conducted under heavy fire from Confederate artillery, validated him as a worthy successor to Colonel Cake.[130]

This interesting photograph depicts soldiers from Company C of the 96th Pennsylvania Volunteers. Color bearer George Foltz can be seen in the middle of the front row directly beneath the American flag. The location and date of this image are unknown (Ronn Palm collection).

As the day progressed, the unseasonably warm weather, coupled with the heavy knapsacks borne by the soldiers, along with the march from below Fredericksburg to Salem Church, tired the men in the ranks. The stress of the morning engagement, along with the ponderous movement in line of battle in the afternoon, only served to further fatigue the exhausted soldiers as they prepared to assail Wilcox's Alabamians at Salem Church. In addition to the warm May weather and the debilitating experiences endured during the day, the terrain further handicapped the Bluecoats in the afternoon engagement. The strip of woods running along a north-south axis on the ridge where Salem Church stood, posed a significant obstacle for the generals in charge of the operation and their subordinate officers. The woodlot and underbrush screened the Confederates from the view of their attackers. General Sedgwick, "Bully" Brooks and General Bartlett erroneously believed that a lone Confederate brigade, spotted early in the afternoon by a Signal Corps observer and subsequently by Sedgwick and his staff, stood between the VI Corps and Chancellorsville. Unknown and unforeseen by the Bluecoats, the prominent line of timber masked the concentration of the Confederates along the Salem Church ridge. The dry leaves on the ground within the thicket of trees also posed an unanticipated obstacle for the attackers.[131]

Not only did the woodlot and underbrush impede the movement and visibility of the Federal regiments, but the deadly volley of Rebel musketry, produced an unexpected threat to the safety of the soldiers. While not specifically mentioned by the Pennsylvanians, the woods in their sector were set on fire by Union artillery. John Hartwell of the 121st New York described the scene in a letter written two weeks after the battle. "As we came to the woods we got over a brush fence which is the most common here. A little before we came near the woods some shells burst near this fence which set it on fire ... the fire was on the left of our regt."[132] James Cronkite later recalled the incident in a history of the 121st New York written twenty-five years after the battle. "We gladly welcomed the night that closed the day's conflict. But as darkness came over the scene a lurid flame, kindled by the fire of our batteries, was consuming the dry leaves and underbrush in the wood in which our helpless wounded lay. Many of them, it was feared, were burned alive."[133] With the deadly fire of Confederate buck and ball in their front and the woods ablaze along their line, it is little wonder that the men of the 96th Pennsylvania were fixed in place along the western edge of the woodlot. In sum, the obstacles of nature impeded the advance of the Schuykill Countians, but the heavy musketry, delivered at short range by the Alabamians, fixed the Pennsylvanians in place and prevented them from advancing to support "Upton's Regulars." The short, compact field of fire further enhanced the effectiveness of the Confederate smoothbore muskets.

Brooks' failure to determine the relative strength of the Confederate infantry blocking the road to Chancellorsville was merely the first of many mistakes made by the commanding officers of the VI Corps in this operation. In hindsight, the lengthy delay devoted to advancing Brooks's division to the head of the VI Corps column, along with the decision to send two brigades (Bartlett's and Brown's) along with two additional regiments (from Russell's brigade) against the Secessionists at Salem Church, rather than deploying two full divisions, proved to be an additional error leading the strike force toward defeat rather than victory. In addition to screening the concentration of the Confederate infantry at Salem Church, the woodlot also handicapped the individual regiments during the battle. From available reports, diaries, and contemporary letters, evidence suggests that General Bartlett, in order to command his brigade, never entered the timber and remained on the eastern edge of the woods. Major Lessig, in his lengthy letter describing the events of the campaign, stated that at approximately five o'clock Bartlett ordered him, presumably while standing east of the wood lot, to "push through the woods" on the left of Upton's regiment the 121st New York. Subsequently, Bartlett reappears, according to Major Lessig, when he meets the Pennsylvania major at the eastern side of the timber during the retreat. "I came to the edge of the woods," recalled Lessig, where "General Bartlett ... ordered me to retire with my men."[134]

Bartlett's absence on the line of battle, along with the underbrush and the blinding smoke, caused by the small arms fire, essentially constricted mobility, compromised visibility and severed communication between regimental commanders and their superior officer during the battle. As a result, the various regiments waged individual engagements against Wilcox's well prepared, heavily defended position. Subsequently, the various elements of Bartlett's brigade, suffering from significant handicaps, and lacking unit cohesion, were essentially doomed to fail in this blind attempt to break through the determined Alabamian defenders at Salem Church. In his report, General Bartlett summarized many of these conditions which led to Federal defeat. "Nothing could surpass the gallantry with which my troops threw themselves against the enemy's well-selected position. They were exhausted by fatigue and want of sleep, yet their enthusiasm carried them beyond all consideration of self, and made heroes of every officer and man. It was the first time they were ever ordered to hold a position which they were unable to do; it was the first time they had ever retired in the face of an enemy."[135] Like Bartlett, Major Lessig, in his official report, underscored fatigue as a major factor in the setback suffered by the 96th Pennsylvania. "The men were entirely worn out and without spirit having been nearly sixteen hours under arms, the greater portion under a burning sun."[136]

Valor, bravery and courage, however, exhibited by many of the soldiers at Salem Church, could not overcome the handicaps and hardships which they confronted throughout the course of the long day under arms. The Battle of Salem Church, according to the accounts written by participants, culminated in an exchange of rifle fire that lasted just twenty minutes. For this brief period, with fifty yards or less separating Reb from Yank, volley after volley was fired by the respective combatants. This furious fusillade, recalled an unknown member of the 96th Pennsylvania, "was one perfect continuous shower of lead—miniature messengers of death that made the air musical with fear."[137] After the battle, Captain Haas related that his Company G was "within 15 paces of their rifle pit," where the 8th Alabama was in line of battle.[138] A New York soldier in Bartlett's brigade reported that "after firing two rounds our Regiment advanced into the road, when the Rebs, in the pits poured a volley into us, mowing us down like grass. We held the road about fifteen minutes, when having fired nearly all our cartridges, we were ordered to fall back; which we did in good order."[139] In describing this climactic scene of the battle, Adjutant Morse of the 121st New York stated in his memoir, "No mortal could stay and live where we were, and the line moved back and retreated in confusion."[140] Even after the high tide of the battle crested, the men of the 96th Pennsylvania, demonstrating their coolness and courage, were reluctant to disengage completely. According to *Amicus Curae*, "the men halted, and taking deliberate aim decimated the ranks very effectively [of] the advance of the foe."[141]

Courage defined the combatants of both sides, but especially the Bluecoats. Like Greek warriors of the ancient world, the soldiers in Blue and Butternut stood toe-to-toe under conditions which tested the combat limits of the participants. A New York soldier described the terror and severity of the battle in the clearing surrounding Salem Church in a letter to his brother. "The contest was a very severe one. Regiments that had often faced showers of lead and walked up to the enemy, with gleaming bayonets pointed at their own hearts, as if destruction seemed inevitable, declared that the firing during the action eclipsed anything that they ever heard in point of noise and destruction.... The engagement lasted about 20 minutes."[142] While the soldiers withstood the crash of muskets and the chaos of combat, the officers, too, demonstrated their bravery on the battlefield. After the engagement, *Amicus Curae* noted, "Too much cannot be said in behalf of the conduct of all the officers of the regiment. The daring and intrepid dash of Major Lessig was commended in terms of the most exalted praise."[143] Finally, General Bartlett also recognized Lessig's leadership upon the tactical field. In his report he offered the following recommendation regarding the Pennsylvania major. "W. H. Lessig, commanding Ninety-sixth Pennsylvania Volunteers, exhibited his fine ability to command. His true fighting qualities are unsurpassed. His bravery, so often proved, was once more the incentive to noble action on the part of his regiment, and his promotion to colonelcy would be the least reward he merits."[144]

In addition, *Curae* wrote that the three VI Corps generals in the chain of command above Major Lessig "complimented him in the most eloquent style for his unexampled gallantry and daring, recommending that he be commissioned as Colonel of the regiment."[145] In the same letter, too, *Curae* reiterated comments made by Lessig concerning his subordinates and General Bartlett's assessment of the 96th Pennsylvania.

> The Major speaks with feelings of pride about the manner in which the line officers conducted themselves, and the very valuable aid they gave him in urging the men to do their whole duty. General Bartlett says, "he believes it [the 96th Pennsylvania] to be one of the best if not *the best fighting regiment representing the Keystone State*."[146]

Finally, Dr. Bland also offered testimony concerning the courage of the Pennsylvanians at Salem Church. "The First Division performed prodigies of valor and I believe no one regiment on the ground conducted itself more gallantly than the gallant 96th. I say this from personal observation, and with feelings of pride, both national and State. The officers have behaved most splendidly."[147]

While courage defined the role of many of the soldiers at Salem Church, the issue of cowardice also received treatment in the post battle writings of the Pennsylvanians. At the end of his official report, Major Lessig included the following statement. "I am sorry to say that the conduct of second Lt. Thomas H. Reed (Company E) was cowardly and disgraceful, and I therefore recommend that he be dishonorably discharged the service of the United States."[148] Writing after the war a New Yorker, who served with Bartlett's brigade, stated that "nothing can be more distressing to a good soldier than to have it said that his behavior in action was not manly or valorous…. The fear that one's bearing and general conduct may discredit him with his associates and lose him the consideration of his superiors" was keenly felt by the soldiers.[149] Another incident of potential cowardice, arose earlier in the morning during the skirmish at the railroad. Peter Fries, of Company H, misinterpreted the actions under fire of a new soldier who joined the 96th Pennsylvania after the Battle of Antietam. In a letter to his sister, Private Daniel Faust, related the details of his initial experience in combat.

> On Sunday May 3 we was engaged on an old railroad and we was laying so close together an officer give us orders for some of us to come to the other side and I got up to cross the railroad and the fellow that was laying aside me had not heard the command and thought I was going to run and he up with his gun and was just ready to shoot me and he quick turned his head around toward the enemy and a ball come and took him right through the head and killed him instantly. He never moved after it hit him. His name was Peter Freece.[150]

Lt. John Von Hollen, in a letter written from Georgetown Seminary Hospital two weeks after the battle, informed Lieutenant Colonel Filbert about the skulkers and cowards in Company B. "2nd Lieutenant Louis [Lewis] Luckenbill was much afraid of being hit and so was Sgt. Huber. Sgt. Bonewitz is a brave soldier and [Sgt.] F.A. Snyder and so was the whole Company, with the exception of 3 or 4. I suppose you know who they are."[151]

In addition to these instances of individual cowardice, for reasons that had their roots beyond the battlefield, the 96th Pennsylvania was also maligned by a few members in other regiments of Bartlett's brigade. Writing eleven days after the battle, Adam Rice of the 121st New York, criticized the performance of the Schuylkill Countians at Salem Church. "The 96th Pennsylvania, did not honor themselves a great deal. I have seen it stated in the papers, that the 96th led the brigade. I assure you that it did lead it in the retreat. It never was known to fight well but once, and that was at Crampton's Gap…. The 96th Pennsylvania fired two volleys and run."[152] Captain Kidder of the 121st New York stated the case more bluntly. In a letter to his wife, Kidder opined that the 96th Pennsylvania was a "cowardly Regiment."[153] Surgeon Holt, of the same regiment, offered the most critical commentary after the 121st New York was assigned to Bartlett's brigade. "With the 96th Pa. we were ever at variance. From the first, our boys could not endure the Saerkrout illiterate lunk heads, and they appeared to equally despise us. They were cowards; and like all other cowards, were braggadocios and abusive."[154]

While courage and cowardice emerged as significant themes after the Battle of Salem Church, criticism of the VI Corps commanders was also prominent in soldier correspondence. Although the Bluecoats admired "Bully" Brooks for his bravery under fire, the men lamented his failure to utilize Union artillery, prior to the assault, to adequately develop the position and strength of the Confederate force in their front. The Pennsylvania

2nd Lt. Thomas H. Reed, Company E. Promoted from sergeant March 19, 1863. Discharged September 27, 1863 (collection of James Reed).

regimental historian, Samuel P. Bates, stated the following concerning "Bully" Brooks: "Without stopping to shell the woods or develop the enemy's strength, Brooks' Division was pushed forward, on the very heels of the skirmishers, until it came suddenly upon three divisions of the rebel army drawn up in ambush awaiting the advance of the Union column."[155] Captain Haas, in a letter to his brother, offered his opinion of Brooks's generalship.

> While we rested before going into the fight Hexheimer [sic] wanted to shell the woods with his Battery but General Brooks, not knowing that the Rebs had received reinforcements from Lee, thought the infantry could easily press them out of the woods. I do not mean this as a reflection on. Gen. Brooks as I believe him to be an able General.[156]

Amicus Curae was in agreement with Captain Haas in his critique of generalship when he wrote, "Without shelling the woods, or taking Any precautionary steps, our troops were marched into the thicket."[157] Finally, a New York officer stated, "Salem Church where *'Bully Brooks'* ordered us in without shelling the woods, and the result was that we came out almost perfectly annihilated."[158] Even "Bully" Brooks realized that Salem Church was, in effect, his Waterloo. Watching the Bluecoats come tumbling back through the fields after the Confederate counter attack, Brooks turned to a staff officer and said, "Twenty-five years in the army, Mr. Wheeler, and ruined at last."[159]

While "Bully" Brooks received most of the criticism for the defeat at Salem Church, "Uncle" John Sedgwick, too, was also held accountable by the men of the VI Corps. A soldier serving with the 121st New York stated, "Without a view to censure, I must say that some of our Generals, either Brooks or Sedgwick, committed a great error, in the crowding of our forces into that Hell-hole on Sunday afternoon without first ascertaining the strength and position of the enemy."[160] In contrast, both in the writings of the soldiers, and in the official reports, General Bartlett was soundly praised for his conduct of the battle. Sedgwick, in his report, attested to "the skill and personal gallantry of Brigadier General Bartlett," while "Bully" Brooks commended Bartlett for his "able and skillful manner," and stated that his confidence in him was unlimited.[161] Despite the praise from his superiors above him, and those he commanded below him, Bartlett's decisions upon the tactical field should be closely scrutinized by anyone studying the Battle of Salem Church.

Like the soldiers he commanded and sent into battle, General Bartlett also confronted a number of handicaps and obstacles in the course of the engagement at Salem Church. The initial deployment upon the tactical level should essentially serve as the starting point in any review of Bartlett's performance. The battlefield was divided from east to west by the Orange Plank Road and from north to south with the long strip of woods. Bartlett elected to anchor the center of his battle line with an untested and untried regiment, the 23rd New Jersey.[162] Given the critical posting of the 23rd New Jersey, a better attack formation might have been to replace the Jersey men with the veteran 16th New York regiment, with 410 effectives, followed by another experienced organization, the 27th New York Volunteers. Both of these regiments also featured seasoned commanding officers with significant combat experience. The 23rd New Jersey should have been assigned to the rear of the attack column and given orders to follow the brigade at close support.

Perhaps Bartlett halted his brigade east of the wood line to reconnoiter the terrain and ascertain the position of the Confederates before issuing the order to commit his brigade to battle. "Bully" Brooks, however, insisted that Bartlett not delay his attack and push his men through the woods against the Alabamians. Ironically, Upton's assault, with the 121st New York, surged beyond Salem Church. As a result, the 23rd New Jersey on the right, and the 96th Pennsylvania on the left, needed to advance to support the courageous but exposed men of Upton's regiment. Neither the Jerseyans or the Pennsylvanians were able to move forward to support "Upton's Regulars." Subsequently, Bartlett, to bolster Upton's sortie, double-quicked the 16th New York into the action by moving them north of the Plank Road and swing them around the stalled 23rd New Jersey. Despite getting a fresh regiment to the front of his battle line, the impact of the 16th New York to support Upton was minimized due to the physical location of Salem Church, which effectively limited the field of fire of Colonel Seaver's men. While these decisions by Bartlett did not lose the Battle of Salem Church, for the veterans of his brigade, the inability to adequately support Upton and the endangered 121st New York resulted in significant casualties to that regiment. Unlike Gaines' Mill and Crampton's Gap, which featured open farm fields advantageous to Union infantry fire, the terrain around Salem Church reduced Bartlett's field of vision and handicapped him as a commander. The belt of woods at Salem Church, however, reduced the ability to view the movement of the regiments, constricting maneuver and significantly reducing Bartlett's role from tactical administrator to spectator once his brigade entered the timber.[163]

Retreating from the woods at Salem Church, Bartlett instructed Lessig to retire to a crest of ground where the Federal artillery was posted. There the New Yorker hoped to reform his brigade of retreating refugees. As the Bluecoats fell back, Lessig, with two companies of his command, occupied a house near the Plank Road. The Pennsylvanians took the "featherbeds and mattresses [sic] off of the beds, ... [and] ... made a perfect fort of it, and from the windows ... soon compelled the enemy to fall back ... night found us in possession of the house and part of the battlefield, and my gallant little band holding the advanced post."[164] After checking the Graycoat advance, Lessig's Unionists fell back to where the brigade had reformed. Later in the evening, after the musket fire had died out, Bartlett invited the Pennsylvania major to have supper with him. The pair enjoyed a "sumptuous" feast of hardtack and coffee. As the tired Bluecoats settled down to sleep on their arms that night, several things were abundantly clear. The fighting that raged across Salem heights during the late afternoon was most decisive. There would be no linkage with Hooker's battered forces at Chancellorsville. From the rumbling of wagon wheels, Sedgwick knew that Lee was plotting his destruction. Aware by now that he had run into something considerably stronger than a mere rearguard, he spent the night forming a perimetrical defense line. For the Unionists the day had been a long and difficult one. May 4, however, gave promise of being even harder.

At 3 a.m. the Schuylkill County men were awakened and told to draw ammunition. One hour later the Pennsylvanians found themselves in line of battle, supporting a battery of artillery.[165] As the gray pre-dawn hours gave way to a warm morning sun, a Butternut cannonade assailed Howe's Second Division line, posted in rear of Marye's Heights. The artillery barrage signaled the start of the Confederate counterattack to regain Fredericksburg. Upon learning of the fall of Fredericksburg, later that day, Sedgwick issued instructions in regard to the Graycoat attack that was sure to come. Sedgwick urged his troops, holding a horseshoe shaped battle line ten miles in length, "that a regiment must do the work of a brigade."[166] Anxiously the Unionists awaited the attack. A nervous Bluecoat recalled the vigil this way:

> All the afternoon we watched the Rebels moving through the woods on our front, and every now and then uttering the Rebel Yell, at times apparently forming into lines of battle and preparing for attack. It was one of the most anxious six or seven hours that I ever spent.[167]

Finally, after a day of delay and confusion, Lee's Secessionists were positioned to assault Sedgwick's VI Corps.

Lee planned to hurl Rebel columns against three separate sectors of Sedgwick's battle line. The attack, however, was a disjointed, poorly coordinated effort by the Graycoats. According to Captain Haas the 96th Pennsylvania "moved around in different directions a great many times during the day.... During the afternoon several attacks were made on our lines but the batteries drove them back very promptly."[168] Sedgwick's line had been shaken but not demolished. Lee, anxious to exploit his gains, ordered a night attack. In the darkness the Confederate artillery shelled Banks' Ford, attempting to seal off that exit, while the infantry groped about in the dense fog. While Lee's voltiguers probed the countryside in search of the Bluecoat line, Sedgwick planned his withdrawal across the Rappahannock.[169]

After nightfall Sedgwick issued orders for a withdrawal. The details of the retrograde movement, which called for a skilled engineer officer, were entrusted to John Newton, commanding the Third Division. Newton first constructed a rifle pit on the high ground in front of Banks' Ford. After that defensive line was established, he coordinated the laying of a pontoon bridge across the Rappahannock. After Newton completed his work, Sedgwick ordered the withdrawal of his weary soldiers.[170] Bartlett's brigade, upon learning of the order to retreat, started for Banks' Ford at the double quick. In a letter written one week after the battle Captain Haas recalled the retreat:

> As soon as dark came, we formed, called the skirmishers in and then retreated to Banks Ford. The Rebs shelled us as we retired but did not follow closely. About 11 p.m. we came near the river and occupied a long rifle pit formed 3 lines of Battle and posted our cannon. I fervently wished the Rebs would have attacked us here.[171]

Throughout the night the Secessionist batteries shelled the Bluecoats. During the bombardment Bartlett's brigade acted as a rear guard, covering the removal of the VI Corps across the Rappahannock. At 2 a.m. Bartlett recalled his skirmishers and supervised the passage of his brigade to the north side of the Rappahannock. After marching a mile from the river, the refugees of the 96th Pennsylvania went into camp. The men in the ranks lay down upon the ground and quickly fell asleep. The rain, that pelted the men shortly after daybreak, was their biggest worry.

Early the next morning, as Bartlett's brigade rested from the arduous fighting of the previous two days, the 96th Pennsylvania was ordered down to Scott's Ford to relieve the men of the 23rd New Jersey, who were having trouble dismantling the pontoon bridge. Sedgwick personally instructed Lessig that if his Pennsylvanians could not get the pontoons out of the water, they were to destroy the bridge.[172] The Pennsylvanians, after a period of intense labor, managed to drag the pontoons ashore. For the next three days they performed picket duty at the bridgehead. During this interval several members of the 96th Pennsylvania encountered their Rebel counterparts at the ford. On May 7, according to Jerome Miller, "four Rebel officers came down to the River with a flag of truce and said we should come and get our wounded next day."[173] Lewis Luckenbill, who heard the exchange between the rebel officers and Major Lessig, recorded in his diary that the major "told them to call tomorrow morning at eight, then he would have a boat there to go acrossed on."[174] Captain Haas noted in his pocket diary that he and Maj. Lessig "went to the River edge and had a talk with the Rebels. They belong to the 8th Alabama and the 16th Georgia."[175] After leaving Scott's Ford, they joined the VI Corps columns which were marching back to their old winter camps at White Oak Church. The campaign for Chancellorsville was over.

In a remarkably short time the Army of the Potomac settled back into its old routine. The demoralization that had swept through the army after the December battle at Fredericksburg did not recur at the close of Hooker's campaign. The Bluecoats, although downhearted, were not demoralized. The soldiers were more bewildered, rather than sullen, concerning the outcome of the campaign. Perhaps one brigade historian explained the state of mind of the Bluecoats best when he noted that the soldiers were "puzzled to know how they had been defeated without fighting [a] decisive battle."[176] Daniel Faust expressed the positive state of mind that most Bluecoats had at the end of the campaign. "We had a nice little dual with them [the Confederates] and I think if we had stuck to it a little longer we would have whipped them severely."[177] Major Lessig also proclaimed that "the army is not demoralized, and will fight again just as well as ever."[178] Two weeks after the battle, Erasmus Reed reported that "the men all seem to be in good spirits."[179] After Chancellorsville, the soldiers were convinced that their combat performance was not the reason for the failure of the Army of the Potomac. Soldier commentaries focused on the failure of Union commanders upon the battlefield. Perhaps the most pointed criticism of the Union high command came from the pen of Captain Haas. "The fact is that if our generals had half the energy and ability the C.S.A. have, a few short months would settle the C.S.A. [If] … we do not soon do better, I will quit the service and go to China to serve under the new Mandarin."[180]

The fighting at Fredericksburg and Salem Church, on May 3, marked Lessig's first opportunity to commend the 96th Pennsylvania in battle. His conduct that day, and throughout the entire operation, must be accorded high marks. Lessig, a fearless soldier, was fortunate in his initial command assignment in that he led veteran troops into battle. The Pennsylvanians were seasoned volunteers with substantial battlefield experience. Lessig did not need to worry about them fleeing the firing line at the crucial moment. Throughout the day Lessig exhibited the traits necessary for a successful regimental commander. Twice that day he boldly led his unit into battle. In both instances his regiment performed well under adverse conditions. At Salem Church Lessig carefully watched his flanks, maintained his position, and withdrew his regiment when he realized that the right wing of the Federal line was deteriorating. Lessig's leadership clearly defined him as the regiment's commander and the men in the ranks realized that he was a very capable officer.[181]

In the final analysis the Chancellorsville campaign, although a Unionist setback, clarified many things for the Bluecoats. The soldiers of the 96th Pennsylvania learned that they had found a good battlefield commander in Major Lessig. The Bluecoats also realized that "Uncle" John Sedgwick was as competent a corps commander as there was in the Army of the Potomac. The men in the ranks also sensed that the army had somehow come of age at Chancellorsville. There was a feeling that the Army of the Potomac was a professional army now in everything but name.[182] The untested volunteers of 1861 were now seasoned veterans and justifiably proud of their accomplishments. Captain Haas offered the following summary of the Chancellorsville campaign.

> Hooker's Army is back to their old camps—all is just as it was before the fight, only we are minus about 15,000 men. The newspapers may claim a great victory, but I know something too. If we do not have a force of 300,000 men, it is no use knocking; give me that force and in 30 days I will take Richmond and destroy the Rebel Armies. This way of doing things is sheer nonsense.[183]

Remarkably the spirit of the Bluecoat army had not been broken during "Fighting Joe" Hooker's campaign. But as Captain Haas stated, changes needed to be made in order to defeat the Confederates.

IX

"The Sixth Corps has come!"

The march from Scott's Ford back to the White Oak Church encampment was dreary for the veterans of the 96th Pennsylvania. Tired and dejected, soaking wet and covered with mud, the Greek Cross men tramped along the muddy farm lanes once again in pelting rain. Some of the Unionists, fed up with the war and ready to quit, fell out of the marching column and pillaged the countryside. For a week the provost marshal had squads of cavalry combing Stafford County in search of these lawless soldiers. For most of the 96th, the mood fell short of unruly, but the soldiers were downcast about the failed Chancellorsville campaign. Two weeks after the withdrawal of the soldiers to the north side of the Rappahannock, Edward Henry expressed his opinion concerning the Union war effort in a letter to his sister.

> I am very sorry to hear of the difficulty in the allotment rolls and hope it may soon be adjusted to the satisfaction of both parties but it is too true what you say in regard to men at home living off the blood of their fellow men who are out doing the [fighting?] they think no more of us than they would of a dog which I hear from those who have been home on leave.[1]

George Foltz, a color bearer with Company C, echoed the captain's criticism in a letter to his brother.

> I am very glad to hear that the government is gowing to Inforce the Conscript Law. It is near time Fore the North to doe something to settle this war. I am in Hopes that there will soon be five hundred thousand men called out as we will have now Army unless they come out as the Report is that our Army we be Redused three hundred Thousand by the middle of Jun as the two years mens will be out. And the Nine months men will be out the following month.[2]

For some veterans, mustering out after their terms of service expired would be enough to raise individual spirits. What the whole Army of the Potomac needed, though, was a decisive victory over the Army of Northern Virginia.

By mid–May the sullen mood of the troops slowly gave way to anticipation. The expiration of the terms of service of the 16th and 27th New York regiments, both two year units, was cause for an informal celebration within Bartlett's brigade.[3] After the departure of the two New York regiments, the 95th Pennsylvania Volunteers, known as "Gosline's Zouaves," joined Bartlett's brigade. The transfer of the Pennsylvania Zouave troops, from the Third Brigade, First Division, VI Corps, brought the Second Brigade up to fighting trim. The shifting of soldiers, however, was not limited to the combat veterans. Officers, too, were transferred to other posts during this period. The chronic poor health of the First Division commander, Major General Brooks, along with his outspoken criticism of General Burnside, and with his dismal defeat at Salem Church, led to his removal from the field.[4] Into his place stepped Horatio G. Wright, a West Pointer who had seen very limited action up to this point in the war.

Like his chief, John Sedgwick, Horatio Wright was a Connecticut native and a graduate of West Point in the class of 1841.[5] Although Wright had not distinguished himself by the spring of 1863, he showed promise as a general officer. A year later, U.S. Grant stated, in a letter to Henry Halleck, that "Gen. Wright is one of the most meritorious officers in the service, and with opportunity will demonstrate his fitness for any position."[6] The subsequent commander of the Army of the Potomac, George Meade, described Wright as "an excellent officer."[7] A combat soldier serving with the 2nd Vermont believed that Wright possessed "Napoleon-like shrewdness."[8] And finally, a Rhode Island officer remarked that after the death of Sedgwick "the Sixth Corps was under the command of Major General Horatio G. Wright, an officer distinguished both for gallantry and ability."[9] James Treichler, of the 96th Pennsylvania, stated that "Gen. Wright was a good officer … but never … another Sedgwick."[10]

As May turned into June, Sedgwick encouraged his corps to maintain their drilling regimen and to keep active with other sports and games. Cockfights and horse races were welcome entertainment for the Union veterans.[11] No doubt, the relaxed atmosphere of the post–Chancellorsville period was a welcome respite for the battle weary Bluecoats. The lull in the fighting, however, was short lived. On June 4, Hooker's observation balloons spotted the movement of Secessionists on the south side of the Rappahannock.[12] Lee had reorganized his army and was marching his troops northwestward for a thrust down the Shenandoah Valley, shifting the war from the line of the Rappahannock to more favorable ground north of the Potomac. It was an offensive aimed at achieving grand objectives, and to Joseph Hooker the movement of Lee's army caused considerable distress. Not knowing how to interpret Lee's maneuver, Hooker decided to probe the enemy's strength. Two days later, the 96th Pennsylvania, for the third time in six months, marched to the Rappahannock, stopping for the night along the bluff at Franklin's Crossing.[13]

Later the next day, just after 7 p.m., they crossed to the south side of the river and formed a line of battle near the Bernard House. For several days the unit remained in that sector engaged in digging rifle pits that extended one mile along the Union line. Captain Haas informed his brother about the conditions he experienced on the picket line. "This morning we were sent to the front to picket, and I can tell you now that it

Maj. Gen. Horatio G. Wright, commander, VI Corps Army of the Potomac and later the Army of the Shenandoah (author's collection).

is very nasty. Their sharpshooters are hid in buildings on the outskirts of this town and fire at us constantly. Son of a b____h shot seven of our pickets yesterday, at one post and has been shooting all morning again."[14] When not working on the rifle pits, the Pennsylvania troops were annoyed by the enemy sharpshooters in the Deep Run area. Toward evening on June 10, generals Hooker, Sedgwick, Wright, Newton and Bartlett rode up and down the line inspecting the rifle pit and no doubt discussing the possibility of an advance.[15] Later that evening, the soldiers of the 96th were relieved and recrossed the Rappahannock. Hooker was finally convinced that Lee intended to strike a blow somewhere north of the Potomac.[16] Lincoln advised Hooker to follow Lee, stick to his flank, and "fret him and fret him."[17]

While the Pennsylvanians awaited marching orders from Hooker, a small group representing the ladies of Pottsville arrived to present the regiment with a beautiful battle flag. On the afternoon of June 11, the soldiers were ordered to form in a hollow square to formally receive the banner. General Bartlett accepted the colors, offering an eloquent speech, which in the ears of one listener was "indicative of soldier, scholar and statesman he has already proven himself to be."[18] The next morning, Bartlett's brigade was ordered to perform picket duty along the Rappahannock.[19] During this duty the troops fished and swam in the river. At night they were treated to the music of a Rebel band which, according to Captain Haas, "played some fine pieces."[20]

June 12 was a delightful day along the Rappahannock. Lieutenant Luckenbill's company was assigned to picket duty near a fine brick farm house, "a magnificent place … with a beautiful grove in the front of the house and a beautiful flower garden." The men of Luckenbill's Company B posted themselves along the river and noticed that "the Rebs have their [pickets] on the opposite bank. There is only the distance of the river between [us] about 30 yards."[21] A few Confederate pickets swam the river and exchanged papers, tobacco and coffee with the Pennsylvanians. The following day, however, the mood quickly changed. Captain Haas reported that the "General Officer of the Day came around and gave me hell—ordered me to alter the posts. Told me the whole Army had moved."[22] During the day, Hooker's headquarters ordered Sedgwick to reorganize his command on the north bank of the Rappahannock. Hooker's chief of staff, Daniel Butterfield, notified Sedgwick that he was not to begin his movement until after dark. At 10 p.m., according to Henry Keiser, the men on the picket line were told to quietly withdraw and rendezvous back at the regiment's camp.[23] Orders to march were now issued to the Army of the Potomac.

That evening Major Lessig recalled his picket line and reunited with the balance of Bartlett's brigade at White Oak Church.[24] By this time, Sedgwick's staff had completed the complicated logistics of moving the VI Corps—the largest in Hooker's command— to meet the foe. At this time the corps was comprised of thirty-six infantry regiments, eight batteries of artillery, and a cavalry complement, totaling about 18,000 men. That night the troops under Bartlett learned that the VI Corps was to act as the rear guard. After Sedgwick's troops destroyed the immense quantities of stores that the Army of the Potomac could not transport, the soldiers began their march northward. The darkness of the night was made worse by heavy rain, which turned the road into a sticky mire. A soldier recalled that several comrades tumbled headlong down a steep embankment only to receive a snide comment—"Have you a pass to go down there?"—from several soldiers who witnessed the accident.[25] Throughout the night, braving the elements, the men pushed on.[26]

Potomac Creek Bridge, Stafford County, Virginia. In 1862 President Abraham Lincoln viewed this bridge and stated, on May 28, "That man Haupt has built a bridge five hundred feet long and one hundred feet high, across Potomac Creek, on which loaded trains are passing every hour, and upon my word, gentlemen, there is nothing in it but cornstalks and beanpoles." The 96th Pennsylvania crossed Potomac Creek at the outset of the Gettysburg Campaign (Library of Congress).

At 1 a.m. on June 14, the night punctuated by "roaring thunder and flashing lightning," the men marched toward the bridge spanning Potomac Creek.[27] The thirteen miles to Potomac Creek, however, proved to be arduous as the "men stumbled over stones and fallen trees ... breaking their legs and arms."[28] Upon reaching Potomac Creek, the 96th waited until early in the evening for the rest of Bartlett's brigade to reunite with them. At 8 p.m., the soldiers were once again on the march tramping eight miles, finally stopping at 2 a.m. at Stafford Court House. Captain Haas recorded in his diary that "this was the most tiresome march I ever made. Suffered much from loss of sleep. 'Hard time.'"[29] The march of the VI Corps that day, however, proved to be more grueling than the opening night of the campaign. Oppressive heat, dusty roads and the army's trains impeded the movement of the corps throughout the day. According to surgeon Stevens, "All day long the trains crowded by, four and five wagons abreast; the drivers shouting and lashing their beasts to their greatest speed. No one who has not seen the train of an army in motion, can form any just conception of its magnitude, and the difficulties attending its movements. It was said that the train of the Army of the Potomac, including artillery ... if placed in a single line, the teams ... would extend over seventy miles."[30]

The next day, the entire Army of the Potomac was on the road again. The Virginia tidewater experienced a debilitating heat wave that June, making the march one of the worst that the soldiers ever endured. The sun was blistering hot, roadside springs and brooks were scarce, and the Graycoats had filled many of the local wells with stones. Dust formed an opaque cloud as the Unionists tramped along the country lanes.[31] Captain Haas noted that "a great many men were sun-struck—at least one hundred men in our Division were taken so."[32] In a postwar memoir another Bluecoat confirmed the rigors of this march:

> The men at length began to fall from exhaustion. One after another, with faces burning with a glow of crimson, and panting for breath, would turn to the surgeons of their regiments, and receive passes to the ambulances and a draught from the surgeon's flask…. The spectacle along the road-side became appalling. Regiments became like companies and companies lost their identity; men were dying with sunstroke, and still the march was continued.[33]

Finally, at nightfall, Wright halted the First Division in the vicinity of Dumfries allowing the stragglers to rejoin their regiments. But it was the heat and humidity, not the army's ponderous train, which afflicted the soldiers that day.[34]

According to one foot soldier, the march of the VI Corps on June 15 was "the most trying march of the Army of the Potomac."[35] Lieutenant Luckenbill recorded in his diary that this was "the hottest day of all. Men fell out of the ranks, dead, sun struck. The road sides were lined with men that had given out. When the regiment halted [at 6 p.m. in Dumfries] the whole regiment did not number over 80 men."[36] Captain Haas noted in his diary that the 96th "marched all day to make 12 miles in all from Stafford [Court House]…. I laid in the woods for one hour in a creek … slept sound and solid."[37] Little did the weary veterans know that their labors had not ended after that arduous march. For the next two weeks long marches punctuated by brief halts would be the rule. During this period overnight encampments were of short duration because the VI Corps commanders sought to move the men early in the morning, affording the soldiers some rest during the hottest part of the day. One regimental historian recalled one of those sleepless nights: "At two o'clock in the morning, the shout passed along the line, 'fall in! fall in!' And so, without coffee, we rolled our blankets and fell into line."[38]

Early on the morning of June 16, the 96th took up its line of march long before daylight. Like the previous day the heat was oppressive. All extra garments—overcoats, underclothing and suits—were quickly thrown away. Only a rest at Occoquan Creek revitalized the weary soldiers as they plunged into the cool water.[39] Once resumed, the march was sluggish, delayed by an artillery train blocking the passage of the infantry. "Teams of troops continually clogged the way, occasioning the most vexatious delays. I don't know as I could explain it, but it is a fact, nevertheless, that it tires a soldier more to have to stand still half of the time than it does to march straight along without interruption. I had rather march fifteen miles in reasonable time, than spend the same time marching five."[40] General Sedgwick, scolded his troops for their slow marching pace, but the rumor of the rapid march of Lee through Maryland and into Pennsylvania, probably had a more profound effect on the troops as they quickened their gait.[41] That evening, as the soldiers rested near Fairfax Station, the troops were rewarded with a ration of whiskey for their efforts. That night, too, Captain Haas recorded in his diary, "News that the 'Rebs' are in Pennsylvania great sensation."[42]

For the next ten days the VI Corps encamped in the vicinity of Fairfax Court House while Hooker's cavalry conducted movements to ascertain Lee's intentions. While Hooker collected reports of Lee's movements, the 96th tried to gather information from Rebel prisoners and Washington newspapers. About all the Pennsylvanians could learn, however, was that Lee's army continued to push northward while the Yanks rested. The former adjutant of the 96th Pennsylvania, now Bartlett's aide de camp, Matt Richards, summarized their state of mind:

> We are in a great state of uncertainty what the rebs intend to do. Whether to make their main advance on Penna. Or to pitch towards Washington.

Without question this is the most fascinating image in regard to the photographic documentation related to the 96th Pennsylvania Volunteers. According to the diary of Captain Haas, the photograph was composed near Fairfax Court House June 25, 1863: "We had our photographs taken in a group." Maj. Lessig is featured in the left center of the photograph leaning against the tree with his right arm. The other officers are unidentified. The name of the photographer is unknown (collection of Douglas Sagrillo).

> If they pitch towards Washington we have no doubt whatever but that we will repulse them very badly and if they go towards Penna. We will be after them there. In fact we are ready to fight them every where and anywhere North whenever they want to go or to be whipped. They give us the advantage of being on the defensive and whenever they do that we can whip them always.[43]

Despite the difficult conditions endured by the soldiers during the long marches, morale actually enjoyed a resurgence. Many of the Bluecoats believed that moving the war away from Fredericksburg, where the Confederates enjoyed many advantages, might yield an opportunity to offer battle on terms and conditions of their choosing. "The report is here that Lee is not far from here with a great force but I think he will draw out of it for long. We are on equal footing with him here. He handt got the forts and rifle pits to get in like at Fredericksburg. I feel quite at home since I am away from the Rappahannach. I was tired of that place, it looked awful dangerous there and I hope we never need go there any more."[44]

Without question, however, the news of the "rebel invasion" elicited animated reactions from the veterans of the VI Corps. Many soldiers believed that the presence of the Confederates in south central Pennsylvania might result in a concerted response from the administration to undertake sterner measures to bring the war to an end. Writing to his brother, Daniel Faust stated, "I saw in the paper that the rebs was in Pa. and that is the best thing that happened yet. I would like to hear if they would go through half of the state and let the people find out what war is and then I think we would get more help here and this thing would be over."[45]

Despite the surge in morale, there was a loss of confidence in Hooker and his generalship during the period that the VI Corps was encamped near Fairfax Court House. Misperception concerning "Fighting Joe's" reaction to Lee's opening gambit perhaps contributed to the notion that Lee was a superior general to any officer who commanded the Army of the Potomac.[46] A New York soldier in Bartlett's brigade thought that "when we crossed the [Rappahannock] river the last of April with the odds so much in our favor that there was no chance for Lee, but he has proved himself the first general of the day."[47] In any case, the VI Corps soldiers viewed the next battle as a pivotal event, perhaps even a turning point, toward determining the outcome of the war. Surgeon Holt, of the 121st New York, expressed this line of thought in a letter to his wife. "This, to me, appears to be the culminating point in the rebellion. Lee and his generals are risking their all upon a single [roll of the] die. If successful, Heaven knows what a disgraceful compromise may be made—if unsuccessful, the last hard blow will be struck."[48]

Finally, on June 26, the anxious Pennsylvanians were instructed to dismantle their shelter tents and resume the march. At first the movement progressed smoothly. The troops, stripped to light marching orders, their excess baggage having been sent to Washington, pressed forward with a wonderful spirit along the uneven roads. By early afternoon the misty drizzle of the morning had turned into a pelting rainstorm.[49] Several members of the 96th, who fell out of ranks during this march, were escorted off to Richmond by the Rebel guerrilla parties who aggressively patrolled this area. After marching eighteen miles, the regiment camped for the night near Dranesville. Evan Gery recounted the day in his diary. "Were aroused at 2 a.m. and made coffee. At 4 a.m. we took up the line of march to reach Dranesville, 15 miles away, at 12. Rested a half hour, two miles before we got to Dranesville, waiting for stragglers to rejoin us. I was out for cherries and got quite a mess. Made 17 miles today. Have orders to march at 3 a.m. tomorrow."[50]

Late the next afternoon, as the band played "Maryland! My Maryland!," the VI Corps crossed the Potomac. Jerome Miller recorded the moment in his diary. "Crossed the Potomac at 5 1/2 p.m. They had 64 pontoons across the Potomac and 11 over Goose Creek. Marched back one mile from the river and camped. It was drizzling all day."[51] Captain Haas, recognized the significance of the moment when he penciled the following account of the river crossing in his pocket diary. "Arrived at Edwards' Ferry at 10 a.m. Loudoun County is the best I have seen in Virginia. Maryland is looking nice from this side. Sugar Loaf stares us in the face. Crossed the Potomac ... and camped in a large field at 6½ p.m."[52] Later that day Stuart's cavalry reached Dranesville, only to find the smoldering camp fires of the Greek Cross Corps. Quickly he realized that Hooker had managed to maneuver his army between the cavalry and the main columns of Lee's army. Although Hooker was handling the army skillfully, the strategy was not impressing his superiors, Secretary of War Stanton and General Halleck. Throughout the entire movement from the Rappahannock to the Potomac that pair refused to cooperate with Hooker, whom they did not want to command the Union army in the next battle. Shortly after Hooker got his army loosely concentrated near Frederick, Maryland, he asked to be relieved of his command. On the evening of June 28, Lincoln appointed George Gordon Meade, a

Pennsylvanian, to replace Hooker.[53] James Treichler, in his lengthy memoir, was the only member of the 96th Pennsylvania who offered any commentary on Meade. "Gen. Meade's fitness for this position was as yet problematical. He had shown great ability as a Corps Commander—cautious but firm—Modest but never Arrogant."[54]

On the same day that Meade received his appointment, the VI Corps continued its advance northward from the vicinity of Poolesville, Maryland. That evening Meade formulated his grand strategy. He proposed, following the President's edict, to protect Washington and Baltimore and "to compel the enemy to loose his hold on the Susquehanna, and meet me in battle at some point."[55] Next, Meade instructed his engineers to study the Maryland topography and establish a defensive line along which the Bluecoats could concentrate if Lee crossed South Mountain. To guard the approaches to Baltimore and Washington,

Maj. Gen. George G. Meade, commander, Army of the Potomac (author's collection).

the army's engineers recommended that Meade deploy his infantry and artillery behind Big Pipe Creek, extending from Manchester on the right flank to Middleburg on the left. Late in the day, June 30, Meade issued his famous Pipe Creek Circular, assigning the various army corps their positions along the proposed Pipe Creek line. The orders, naturally, were tentative. The Pipe Creek line would be adopted only if developments did not dictate fighting elsewhere. In fact, within twenty-four hours the Pipe Creek line would become obsolete.

While Meade planned his strategy, the 96th Pennsylvania tramped northward along the Maryland roads. On June 28, the Pennsylvanians passed through Barnesville in the morning and camped near Hyattstown in the evening. Evan Gery made the following entry in his diary describing the day's activities. "Rose at 3 a.m. made our coffee and marched through Poolesville and Barnesville, Md., before resting near the latter place. We passed Hyattstown and along the right of Sugarloaf mountain where we had a skirmish last summer. We camped one mile beyond Hyattstown after covering 20 miles this day."[56] The next morning they marched through Monrovia, New Market, Ridgeville and Mount Airy, stopping for the night near New Windsor. The hard work that day was rewarded with a grand cherry feast in the evening. On June 30, the VI Corps marched through Westminster and tramped a total of seventeen miles before bivouacking for the night near Manchester.[57] Meade sent his largest corps there because Lee's advance had reached York, and Manchester was directly between York and Baltimore. On the surface, Meade's disposition of Sedgwick's VI Corps at Manchester appeared logical. The posting of the Greek Cross Corps, on the army's right flank, was actually a poor logistical decision. It is clear that in his anxiety to prevent Lee from maneuvering his troops between

Washington and the Unionist forces, Meade was overly concerned with the vulnerability of his right flank. Hence, he instructed Sedgwick, who commanded almost twenty percent of Meade's infantry, to move his corps to Manchester, a relatively inaccessible place eight miles northeast of Westminster. According to Edwin Coddington, Meade should have realized that the signs of impending battle were pointing toward Gettysburg. Meade should also have kept the Greek Cross Corps at Westminster and covered the area around Manchester with Gregg's cavalry division.[58] While Meade finalized his deployment, the Unionists, who were "very tired and footsore," slept soundly in the Maryland countryside.[59]

The last two days of June brought more marching through Maryland. With the advent of Meade to command the army, the pace of the campaign accelerated. Starting just after 5:30 in morning on June 29, and finishing about five o'clock in the afternoon the following day, the 96th Pennsylvania tramped 40 miles. Beginning at Hyattstown, the regiment marched to Monrovia, then New Market, crossed the Baltimore & Ohio Railroad, struck the Baltimore Pike, marched to Ridgeville, and finally headed for Westminster. Subsequently, the column recrossed the railroad at Mount Airy and reached Jewsburg at 6 p.m. where the exhausted Bluecoats went into camp.[60] The following day, the march started at 7 o'clock in the morning but rain slowed the progress of the column. About noon the 96th reached Westminster, "a beautiful town," recently evacuated by elements of Jeb Stuart's cavalry. That evening, at 6 o'clock, the 96th Pennsylvania camped near Bixler's mill located one mile from Germantown and two miles from Manchester. Henry Keiser remarked that "the citizens along our line of march seemed very pleasant."[61] As the Pennsylvanians bivouacked that evening, Captain Haas noted in his diary that "three prisoners brought in." Clearly, the enemy was close at hand—both literally and figuratively.[62]

On Wednesday morning July 1, a while a furious battle erupted across the farm fields west of Gettysburg, the soldiers of the 96th enjoyed a leisurely day in camp near Manchester, Maryland. Evan Gery spent the morning foraging for cherries.[63] Lieutenant Luckenbill and Captain Haas held company inspections, but rumors of heavy cannonading toward Gettysburg filtered through the camp.[64] Another rumor was documented by Evan Gery. "A [premature] report reached camp that our men [Union army under Ulysses S. Grant] have captured Vicksburg [Mississippi]."[65] At 9 o'clock, the soldiers were ordered to break camp and to march back towards Westminster and continue on to Taneytown. Subsequently, Sedgwick received two more orders directing him to reroute his corps, via Littlestown, and continue to Gettysburg using the Baltimore Pike. Moving the enormous VI Corps through the Maryland countryside, in the darkness, posed a number of challenges for the commanding officers. Poor leadership by a local guide, uncertainty concerning the best road for the column to use, and changes in orders complicated the movement of the corps. A Maine soldier stated that "about eleven o'clock, the command was halted; and after a tarry of about one hour, the information was received that they had *taken the wrong road*. This was tough. By the time that the right road was discovered, the boys were mostly asleep; and the starting up and turning of them around to retrace their steps, caused much strong language. The night's march was one of the most severe of the campaign."[66] Not until daylight the next morning was the VI Corps able to redirect its line of march and take the final steps on the road to Gettysburg.

As daylight on July 1 faded, and the flag that floated over VI Corps headquarters was furled, a dust-covered courier galloped up to Sedgwick's tent and delivered dispatches from General Meade. As Sedgwick shuffled through the papers, he learned of the fighting that had occurred earlier in the day at Gettysburg. The I and XI Corps had been broken and forced to retreat as the Secessionists captured the town. The balance of the Army of the Potomac was concentrating just south of Gettysburg, with plans of resuming the battle in the morning. How soon, Meade wanted to know, could the VI Corps be at Gettysburg? Suddenly, the evening of July 1, 1863, which had promised to be peaceful for the big VI Corps, was transformed into a logistical nightmare. After pondering his situation, Sedgwick turned to the courier and said, "[Tell] General Meade that my corps will be at Gettysburg at four o'clock tomorrow [afternoon]."[67]

Earlier in the day Meade instructed Sedgwick to have his corps on the outer periphery of operations, near Manchester, so as to be ready to move in any direction at a moment's notice. Later in the afternoon, Meade ordered Sedgwick's corps to march to Taneytown that night, after sending the VI Corps trains, except for ambulances and ammunition wagons, to Westminster. By evening all of those orders had been countermanded. After news of the fighting reached VI Corps headquarters, the nature and tempo of Sedgwick's operations changed dramatically. Instead of marching to Taneytown, which some Bluecoats had already begun to do, Meade ordered Sedgwick to head his VI Corps immediately toward Gettysburg by the shortest route. To hasten this movement, Meade authorized Sedgwick to stop all trains which might be in his way, or force them off the road. Clearly Meade desired the immediate presence of Sedgwick's corps at Gettysburg. As Meade's courier departed Sedgwick's tent, the headquarters bugler sounded his tune, followed by a crashing drum roll. Not tattoo, as the soldiers expected, but the sharp notes of assembly.[68]

Other army corps made grueling marches during the Gettysburg campaign, but the circumstances attending that of the VI Corps made this march famous. Needed in a hurry at Gettysburg, the corps marched from 10 p.m. on the night of July 1 until 5 p.m. the next afternoon, covering a distance of thirty-two miles, with only a few short rests. On and on the Bluecoats trudged, at first through darkness and then continuing through the heat of the hot July sun. The broken white limestone with which the Baltimore Pike had been originally paved had been ground by long use into a powder, which created choking dust. Many Unionists fainted and within a short time the ambulances were full. To inspire the men the bands alternated the shrill of fifes with the roll of drums. Never before had the Bluecoat bands played on the march, except when the army entered a town or village. Soon the soldiers heard the booming of cannon in the distance, confirming the persistent rumors that a great battle was being fought.[69]

Determined to arrive at Gettysburg in time for the battle, General Bartlett wore the Second Brigade to the point of exhaustion on July 2. Footsore men tried to drop out of ranks, but Upton made examples of a few stragglers, by firing upon them, and the rest of the weary men resumed their march. According to Maurus Oestreich, the 96th crossed the state line dividing Maryland and Pennsylvania at twenty minutes past eight o'clock in the morning and marched through the village of Littlestown.[70] Captain Haas recalled that the Schuylkill Countians "took the [Baltimore] Pike to Littlestown and Gettysburg. Rumor that a big battle [taking] place at Gettysburg that General Reynolds had been killed. Passed through Littlestown, a nice place. Ladies cheering and waving their kerchiefs."[71] Private Keiser described the festive scene at Littlestown as the 96th Pennsylvania marched through the village.

> At ten a.m. we passed through Littlestown. The Citizens along the line of march could not do enough for us. Most every household standing ready with water buckets dealing out water to the boys as we marched along, and the Stars and Stripes hanging out in all directions. It made us feel as if we were home once more, and the citizens of Southern Pennsylvania, through their kindness to the soldiers have put new life into us.[72]

As the Unionists pushed northward, traces of the previous day's fighting passed in grim review. Ambulances laden with Federal wounded creaked along the Baltimore Pike bound for field hospitals. As they marched over the ridges the men could see a valley in the distance filled with smoke. They could also hear the roar of the cannon. At Meade's headquarters, staff officers anxiously awaited the arrival of the VI Corps. Finally a signal officer noticed a column moving toward the Union rear along the pike. The sighting caused consternation. There was speculation that Stuart's troopers might be attempting a flanking maneuver against the Federal rear. Officers gazed intently through their field glasses at the column advancing slowly up the pike. About 2 o'clock in the afternoon a Union officer said, "It is not cavalry, but infantry. There is the flag. It is the Sixth Corps! The Sixth Corps has come!"[73] As the Greek Cross troops crossed Rock Creek cheers rolled down the Union line.

As Longstreet's divisions stepped off, at 4 p.m., and started on that memorable assault toward Little Round Top, Devil's Den, the Wheatfield and the Peach Orchard, Bartlett's brigade reached the battlefield at Gettysburg. At last, the long, dusty march, covering thirty-two miles was over. Perhaps realizing the significance of the moment, six men in the 96th Pennsylvania recorded the exact time when the Schuylkill Countians reached Gettysburg. Four soldiers noted that the column arrived at 4 p.m. Captain Haas marked 4:30 in his diary while Henry Keiser noted the regiment's arrival at 5 p.m. In a letter written seven weeks after the battle, Adjutant Richards recalled that the Second Brigade reached the battlefield at 5 p.m. James Treichler, in a letter published in the *National Tribune*, more than fifty years after the battle, also stated that the 96th Pennsylvania reached Gettysburg at 5 p.m.[74] After resting for a short period, the VI Corps veterans saw a lone figure riding down over a hill toward them, swinging his hat wildly. As Martin T. McMahon, Sedgwick's Chief of Staff, approached the troops he shouted, "The general [Sedgwick] directs the corps toward the heavy firing."[75] Immediately the Bluecoats of Gen. Frank Wheaton's brigade sprang to their feet, pushed down fences, and headed west along Wheatfield Road, nearly a mile away. Although they had just finished an exhausting forced march, the soldiers were in high spirits. One volunteer described the temperament of the troops, as they advanced to support their comrades:

> Drums beat, colors were flying,–it was a season of rejoicing. The long weary miles were forgotten. On to the contest was the thought and spirit which now inspired the men. The Johnnies were met, they were out of their usual entrenchments, and now an opportunity was presented for a fair test of strength and ability.[76]

About 6 p.m., Bartlett's brigade advanced, in line of battle, going into position behind Gen. Samuel Crawford's Pennsylvania Reserves. Captain Haas recorded in his diary that the 96th Pennsylvania, with about 350 men, "Went into action at 6 p.m., charged forward several times and, at dark, rested behind a stonewall for the night … the groans of the wounded filled the night air—they laid very thick."[77] Wounds notwithstanding, the 96th was then ordered to advance to the right, somewhat in front of Little Round Top. The Pennsylvanians formed a line of battle behind a stone wall, facing west, with their left flank on the Wheatfield Road and the right flank extending north toward the Weikert farm house. Upton's New Yorkers deployed to the left and rear of the 96th and positioned themselves on Little Round Top's north slope, in support of an artillery battery. The 95th Pennsylvania and the 5th Maine formed lines behind the 96th Pennsylvania. As evening fell across the battlefield, and the roar of the cannon fell silent, the groans of the wounded drifted eerily through the night air. That night the soldiers of the 96th Pennsylvania slept on their arms, and waited for the dawn. Daylight was sure to bring a renewal of the second day's fighting.[78]

Friday, July 3, a bright, clear day, was ushered in by the crackle of skirmishing along the Federal lines. During the day Bartlett's brigade maintained its position in the Little Round Top sector. Throughout the morning they strengthened the hastily erected breastworks of the previous evening, while "missiles of death" plowed the ground in front of them. At 1:10 p.m. a Confederate artillery barrage, the most intensive Rebel shelling of the war, swept the Union line along Cemetery Ridge.[79] Although the cannonade continued for nearly two hours, its significance was not entirely clear to the troops of the 96th. They did not know that at the conclusion of the bombardment, Lee would send 12,000 infantry across a mile of open fields to assault the Union center. Captain Haas dismissed the artillery fire with a simple one line statement in his diary, "Shelling very heavy at our line all day."[80] Throughout the afternoon as the fury swirled around a clump of trees, the focal point of the Confederate attack on Cemetery Ridge, the veterans of Bartlett's brigade remained in reserve near Little Round Top. Through the sounds of battle and the enormous number of wounded passing their position, the VI Corps troops waited nervously for the order to attack.[81] That order, however, never came. Meade attempted to determine a point to strike the Confederates but found that Longstreet's men held a line of battle "in force" and were still full of fight. Darkness ended the battle on July 3. Captain Haas characterized the day in his diary by stating: "All in all, our success was very brilliant."[82]

Viewing the battlefield after sunrise, Henry Keiser noted in his diary that "the field is covered with dead and wounded. There must be fearful fighting on the right judging from the very heavy firing, sometimes coming down the line pretty near to us. We were shelled occasionally during the day, but none of our Company were hurt."[83] Late in the day, about 6:30 p.m., according to Lieutenant Luckenbill, the 96th Pennsylvania supported General Crawford's division, ordered by General Sykes to clear the area known as Devil's Den of any lingering Confederates. Luckenbill recorded in his diary that the "Penna. Reserves made a splendid charge and drove the Rebs back, [and] took a nice lot of prisoners."[84] Captain Haas also noted this operation in his diary. "In the evening the third Division made a charge and advanced our line. Also, the Pennsylvania Reserves. They took the 15th Georgia [General Benning's brigade] prisoners."[85] Captain Samuel Russel, commanding Company H, echoed Haas' sentiments. In a letter written the following day, he proclaimed, "Our success yesterday was most complete. We repulsed the rebels at every attack…. The men are in splendid spirits. We will wind up the rebel army before they reach the Potomac."[86]

As darkness closed in on July 3, except for the occasional crack of a sharpshooter's rifle, the tumult of combat gave way to the moans of the wounded who lay among the dead "thick as fallen leaves of autumn."[87] The Union soldiers, after long forced marches and three days of nerve-wracking battle, sagged from fatigue, were in need of rest and food. Longstreet's assault, often referred to as "Pickett's Charge," had failed to break through the Federal line at the copse of trees, but the Yanks of the VI Corps wondered if they would have to spearhead a counterattack. Heavy rain the following day, coupled with Lee's withdrawal, preempted a Union assault.

The "Glorious Fourth" brought quiet and tranquility to Cemetery Ridge. Early in the morning, after the night's rain subsided, the 96th and the 5th Maine, supported a reconnaissance movement by Sykes' Regulars.[88] During this operation Captain Haas noted that "the carnage of the field … is horrible. The Regulars must have suffered considerably. Took a walk over the battlefield. Our loss was heavier than theirs…. At 10½ a.m., advanced to the Wheat Field and supported a reconnaissance made by the 2nd Brigade, of Sykes Regulars. Found the Enemy in force about 1 mile in the rear of his old position. He opened up with shell on our advance…. Our men gathered great quantities of arms all day from the advanced picket line."[89] At noon they were relieved by the Pennsylvania Reserves. That night, as the soldiers tried to sleep, another heavy evening rainstorm drenched the Pennsylvanians. While the soldiers battled the elements, Meade discussed with Sedgwick further details concerning the pursuit of Lee's army.

Before dawn on the morning of July 5, Sedgwick roused his men of the VI Corps. With the approval of Meade, he took the entire Greek Cross Corps, instead of just a division, turning the movement into a pursuit of Lee's troops as well as a reconnaissance.[90] The columns of the VI Corps did not get underway until almost noon, and moved at times in line of battle, a formation not conducive to a rapid advance. Captain Haas described the initial pursuit of Lee's army in his pocket diary. "The whole Corps seemed to move and halted in [Rose's] Wheat Field until 1 p.m., when we moved forward. I think the 'Rebs' have gone…. Moved forward by columns and line of battle at times, skirmishing along. Major [Lessig] and Company A took 2 of the 47th Alabama. Found that the Rebs left all their hospitals and wounded fall into our hands."[91] As they moved to overtake the foe, the horrible stench from the dead overwhelmed the combat veterans. Private Keiser graphically described the grimness of war and the suffering of those who were "hors de combat" in his diary:

> Every barn we passed was converted into a Rebel hospital and had the red flag floating over it. While we were halting near one (a large barn full of wounded Rebs) I ran over to see how it looked. It was sickening to look at. The barn floor and every place in the barn where a person could be layed was filled with wounded Rebels, and outside the barn, on the southside, I seen a pile of hands, feet, legs and arms, at least two feet high.[92]

In contrast to the thunderous fury of the fighting at Gettysburg, the skirmishing on July 5 near Fairfield was unremarkable. In fact, the warfare that day was so passive that Captain Haas' fondest memory of the day was not of battle, but of watching the Confederate wagon trains wind their way through Fairfield Gap. No doubt this scene caused the hearts of the men of the 96th to swell with pride. Although the Schuylkill County regiment had been held in reserve during the Battle of Gettysburg, the troops had the satisfaction of knowing that they had defended their native soil from the Confederate invaders. That night the tired soldiers slept on their arms in line of battle.[93]

Shortly after noon on July 6 Meade abandoned any thought he had of pursuing of Lee by way of Fairfield Gap because of what Sedgwick had told him about the formidable nature of the mountain passes.[94] A small Confederate force could keep Bluecoat columns in check for a long time. Furthermore, information from other sources led Meade to believe that Lee had already reached Hagerstown. Accordingly, Meade instructed Sedgwick to withdraw most of the VI Corps from Fairfield to Emmitsburg. Starting after 11 p.m., the VI Corps marched through the night on muddy roads arriving at Emmitsburg at three o'clock the next morning. Henry Keiser stated that the soldiers endured "a very hard march.... At daylight ... we halted a short distance from the town."[95] This movement effectively ended active pursuit of Lee's Graycoats by the Greek Cross Corps. In fact, a review of Sedgwick's operations of July 4 to 6, makes clear that the VI Corps commander had no intention of precipitating a battle with Lee's rear guard. Even after receiving Meade's instructions early on July 6 to probe the Confederate defenses more vigorously, Sedgwick permitted the stiffening of Rebel resistance to slow the forward movement of his corps. Edwin Coddington, in his classic work on the Battle of Gettysburg, argues that "at any time between noon of the 5th and noon of the 6th, while the Southern army was in motion and its defenses were not yet set, Sedgwick might have caused a renewal of a general engagement if he had dashed ahead and led a slashing attack upon Lee's rear guard."[96] Instead, Sedgwick exercised extreme caution when Mr. Lincoln would have applauded even modest aggression.

The torrential rain that soaked the Pennsylvanians throughout July 7 made all of the roads, except the pikes, impassable. Countless wagons and artillery pieces stalled in the mud, and it took time and effort to pull them out. Even after reaching Emmitsburg, and heading south toward Frederick, the rain returned with a vengeance, turning the roads into muddy quagmires. At Emmitsburg, Captain Haas noted that the Confederates burned some of the dwellings but also observed that the "institute buildings [were] very fine."[97] During the day, the soldiers churned through the mud tramping through the villages of Franklinville and Mechanicstown (now Thurmont) where the "ladies sang, waving flags."[98] Marching past the Catoctin Furnace, the VI Corps veered off the Frederick Road (present day U.S. Route 15) at Lewiston, and headed toward Hamburg Pass, intent upon crossing over the Catoctin Mountain.[99] The unyielding elements alone, however, did not stop the Bluecoats. Late that night, some of the Schuylkill Countians reached the summit of Catoctin, but the VI Corps artillery train, stuck in the mud, blocked the road and virtually made it impassable for the infantry. Exhausted and out of rations, the Pennsylvanians camped in the woods on the mountain and waited for the rain to stop. Although morning brought daylight, the rain continued to soak the soldiers. About 10 o'clock, when the stragglers reached the summit the regiment reorganized and continued down the western slope of the mountain. Captain Haas described the hardships of this march. "Horrible marching. Commenced to rain and continued all night. Regiments got lost. Artillery jammed up and things were awfully mixed up. Marched along until 10 1/2 p.m., when I camped in the woods with 3 of my men. Thousands of men went and laid down in the rain.... All suffered from hunger, fatigue and exposure. Distance made 25 miles."[100]

In the morning, after the Second Brigade formed on the mountain's summit, the troops marched down the western slope toward the village of Belleville, once again through ankle deep mud. Henry Keiser recalled that "we marched until 4 p.m. when we encamped near Middletown. This march from the [Catoctin] mountain was a fearful one most of the way. I stopped several times to wash the mud out of my shoes."[101] The regiment went into camp, about a mile east of Middletown on the National Road, early in the afternoon. Finally, as the soldiers stopped for the day, so, too, did the rain. Toward South Mountain, the men heard the booming of artillery and the clash of cavalry. Somewhere Unionists were fighting Confederates. The 96th Pennsylvania, however, continued to battle the elements.

Once again, on July 9, the Pennsylvanians were awake before dawn and moving forward in column by 5 a.m. Moving through Middletown, the Bluecoats crossed South Mountain at Turner's Gap and stopped for the day upon reaching Boonsboro. After daybreak on July 10, the Schuylkill Countians marched toward Hagerstown and stopped about a mile beyond Beaver Creek. After briefly supporting a battery, the 96th was assigned picket duty along Antietam Creek. Picket firing on the right of the line, extending toward Funkstown, was brisk throughout the afternoon.[102] Early the next morning, marching on the National Road, the regiment moved toward the right flank. The Pennsylvanians formed in line at the picturesque stone bridge spanning the Antietam at ten o'clock and rested briefly while orders were issued to Major Lessig. Subsequently, Lieutenant Luckenbill and Captain Haas led their respective companies across the bridge and occupied the rifle pits abandoned earlier in the morning by the Confederates.[103] Crossing the mill race bridge and the Claggett's Mill bridge, the Schuylkill Countians fanned out in skirmish formation and pushed out into the farm fields. Evan Gery recorded in his diary that the squad of men he was with "drove the rebels from a house, [and] captured two men and two horses."[104] Captain Haas reported that he ordered "out skirmishers. They drove the Rebs back to the woods. Took one prisoner of Munford's 2nd Virginia Cavalry. Firing lively. I fired some three or four shots…. Moved into the skirmish line and supported a

Claggett's Mill located on Antietam Creek, near Funkstown, Maryland. The lithograph created by the distinguished battlefield artist Edwin Forbes is dated July 12, 1863. The scene depicts the VI Corps crossing the stone bridge in pursuit of Lee's army after the Battle of Gettysburg. The bridge still stands as a mute witness to the VI Corps soldiers who crossed the Antietam heading back to Virginia. Today the narrow country lane is known as Poffenberger Road (Library of Congress).

section of artillery."[105] Late in the afternoon, Companies B and G returned across the bridge, rejoined the regiment, and went into camp for the night near Funkstown.

On the foggy Sabbath morning of July 12, the VI Corps advanced toward Funkstown with orders to take possession of the Antietam Creek crossing and to gain control of the high ground beyond the bridge.[106] With alacrity the Greek Cross Corps executed the movement and secured the territory after exchanging brisk musket fire with Graycoat pickets. Two days later, after learning from the troops holding the picket line that the enemy had retreated, H.G. Wright initiated a reconnaissance movement to probe the Butternut entrenchments. The 96th Pennsylvania supported Wright's operation. The Bluecoats moved forward to the enemy's rifle pits only to find that "the bird had flown."[107] With the completion of a pontoon bridge and an ebbing of the rain swollen Potomac, Lee's army had crossed the river during the night of July 13–14 to the safety of Virginia. Upon learning that Lee's troops had eluded him, General Meade wrote: "I start to-morrow to run another race with Lee."[108]

Although the Battle of Gettysburg was over the campaign was shifting from Pennsylvania to the Loudoun Valley of Virginia. Sergeant Boland informed a friend in Pottsville that the 96th Pennsylvania "followed them up by zigzag marches through the state of Maryland. We hemmed them in at Williamsport, Md. General Meade made a great error in not giving them battle."[109] After Gettysburg Meade proclaimed that "the commanding general looks to the army for greater efforts to drive from our soil every vestige of the ... invader."[110] Lincoln was aghast upon reading Meade's statement. In response, Lincoln drafted a letter—which he never sent—to the army commander. "I do not believe you appreciate the magnitude of the misfortune involved in Lee's escape. He was within your easy grasp, and to have closed upon him would ... have ended the war."[111] Despite Meade's failure to destroy Lee's army, the soldiers of the Army of the Potomac recognized Meade's success at Gettysburg. Perhaps, at last, they had found their general. Erasmus Reed told his brother, "Every body seems to have confidence in our Leader. General Meade has gained for himself a position of confidence of the army of the Potomac second to none."[112]

X

"O how I do wish that them Irish drunkerts would get drafted"

After Gettysburg, there was a distinct shift in soldier attitude concerning the prosecution of the war. The successes achieved by General Meade at Gettysburg and General Grant at Vicksburg proved to be enormous strategic victories for the Union armies. In the summer of 1863, the alignment of military policy and political objectives shaped the direction of the war in the year to come. More importantly, however, the soldiers embraced the war policies and political objectives. The conservative democratic generals, prominent in the Army of the Potomac earlier in the war, were slowly being supplanted by new officers whose generalship supported the policies articulated by Lincoln and the Republicans. In addition, the soldiers perceived that they were beginning not only to win the war on the battlefield, but also to emerge victorious in regard to the political battles behind them which previously divided the home front in Pennsylvania. By 1863, the volunteers who left Schuylkill County in the autumn of 1861 were combat veterans who supported emancipation as a war aim. Furthermore, they recognized that in order to defeat the Confederacy, they would also need to influence Republican victories at the ballot box as well. As the war slowly changed in 1863, so too, did the soldiers approach to achieving victory on the battlefield. Calling upon citizens in Schuylkill County to vote Republican and accept the war aims of the Lincoln administration afforded the soldiers institutional support in their struggle against the Confederacy. They recognized, too, that the Army of the Potomac could no longer just cross a river, fight a battle, and retreat to the safety of its camp grounds. The soldiers understood that morale, discipline and training, coupled with leadership upon the tactical field were essential in order to turn a volunteer army into a professional fighting force. As a result, harsh military measures, such as executing deserters, were necessary to build the army into a formidable military instrument. By the autumn of 1863, the war was far from over but the road to Appomattox started during the winter encampment at Brandy Station.[1]

For the exhausted soldiers of the 96th Pennsylvania, the long, arduous Gettysburg campaign was finally over. For Captain Haas, so too was his service as an infantry officer in the Army of the Potomac. Haas' military career abruptly changed on the afternoon of July 11 during a brisk skirmish along Antietam Creek. Late in the day, as Company G was supporting a section of artillery, Captain Haas struck two men under his command with his sword "for disobedience of orders," knocking them both to the ground.[2] Henry Keiser described the incident in his diary. "Just before the regiment started back Capt. J. W. Haas had a misunderstanding or difficulty with Jacob Nice…. He struck Nice on the head with his sword haft knocking him insensible. This raised my 'dander' and I said more than I should have said. I got a similar blow from the Captain. I tried to shoot him, but he was too quick for me. We both have fearful cuts in our heads, and bled like pigs."[3] The incident clearly alienated the men of Company G from Captain Haas and as a result he was quickly reassigned to inactive duty in Schuylkill County.[4] During the summer of 1863, however, Schuylkill County was experiencing civil unrest and related violence due to the *Conscription Act*. Upon returning to Pottsville, Haas was charged with insuring that drafted men in Schuylkill County reported to their assigned rendezvous sites in Harrisburg and Philadelphia. The draft was unpopular throughout Pennsylvania. In the coal region, conscription turned violent requiring the presence of the 10th New Jersey Volunteers to perform temporary duty in Schuylkill County in order to maintain order and prevent unlawful acts.

In late October 1862, Governor Andrew Curtin advised the Secretary of War, Edwin Stanton, about the potentially explosive situation regarding draft resistance in Schuylkill County. "I think the organization to resist the draft in Schuylkill, Luzerne and Carbon Counties is very formidable.... They will not permit the drafted men, who are willing to leave, and yesterday forced them to get out of the cars. I wish to crush the resistance so effectually that the like will not occur again. One thousand regulars would be most efficient, and I suggest that one [regiment] be ordered from the army.... I am getting volunteer troops ready."[5] Reports such as Curtin's convinced the authorities in Washington to commit Union troops, reassigned from the Army of the Potomac, to the coal region in order to enforce the draft and prevent violence from spreading throughout Schuylkill County.

By the summer of 1863, Gen. William Whipple, charged with overseeing the draft in Philadelphia, issued a report to Gen. James B. Fry in Washington stating that based upon his sources he was setting forth "the true state of things in Schuylkill County, Pa." Given the facts as he understood them, Whipple recommended that the draft "be postponed in that district [10th Congressional] for the present, and, when it is undertaken, that the whole district be drawn at Pottsville, and in the presence of at least a regiment of infantry and a battery of artillery."[6] In short, Whipple firmly believed that only a strong military presence in Schuylkill County would enable the draft to be "enforced here firmly, but judiciously, [and] it will go far toward correcting a state of lawlessness which existed here for the past few years and which has made the name of the miner a terror to all law-abiding citizens."[7] General Darius Couch, head of the Department of the Susquehanna, also advocated stationing a significant military force in the coal region. Couch warned that "the ignorant miners have no fear of God, the state authority or the devil. A strong military power under the general government alone keeps matters quiet."[8]

In addition to Whipple's call to arms, the local provost marshal, Charlemagne Tower, also urged the authorities in Washington to send troops to Schuylkill County in the belief that a significant military presence would prevent further disruption of the draft in the coal region.[9] Traditional interpretations of the events associated with draft resistance in Schuylkill County have concluded that the Irish miners were chiefly responsible for the unlawful incidents that swept through the region during the war. Fred Shannon, who examined these events in great detail, concluded that by the summer of 1863 "the rebellious element was entirely too strong for the small force at the disposal of the provost marshal."[10] In reality, as other historians have persuasively argued, the threat to the disruption of the draft by the Irish mine workers was grossly overstated by political and military officials. The civil unrest in the anthracite region was not in response to conscription but instead proved to be a separate issue centered on labor organization by the Irish miners in the coal fields. One historian suggested that "draft resistance and labor organization were concurrent but separate issues, each arising from specific historical conditions."[11] In sum, the Irish miners were not disloyal to the Union or unpatriotic. Unfortunately, influential individuals in Schuylkill County drew a thick line connecting labor activism with treason and held the Irish miners responsible for causing all of the problems in the coal region.[12]

At the center of this controversy was the district's provost marshal, Charlemagne Tower. An entrepreneur with considerable investments in coal lands, Tower used the conscription law to wage war against the labor activism of the Irish miners. The labor issues between coal operators and the miners had little or no impact upon the unrelated matter of draft resistance in Schuylkill County.[13] As a result, one historian concluded that "the provost marshal's power extended far beyond the draft."[14] In addition, local mine owners, such as Charles Albright, unhesitatingly equated labor activism with treason and disloyalty. In a lengthy letter to Lincoln, Albright stated that "since the commencement of the draft a large majority of the coal operatives have been law-defying, opposing the National Government in every possible way, and making unsafe the lives and property of the Union men. They are so numerous that they have the whole community in terror of them. They dictate the prices for their work, and if their employers don't accede they destroy and burn coal breakers, houses, and prevent those disposed from working. They resist the draft, and are organized into societies for this purpose.... These men are mostly Irish and call themselves 'Buckshots.'"[15]

Albright successfully and succinctly directly associated labor organization and disloyalty with the Irish miners. Furthermore, he convincingly argued that the issues of hostility and violence in the coal region were caused by a vast conspiracy attributed to the "Buckshots," also known as the Molly Maguires. The documentary evidence, however, clearly supports the conclusion that Charlemagne Tower used his position and influence to develop a standing army in the coal region to support mine owners in their war against the labor organizers rather than to quell any resistance to the draft. The Irish miners were not disrupting the draft in Schuylkill County in the summer of 1863, but they were causing problems for the coal operators who used all of the means available to them to crush the unwanted labor agitation.[16]

Beginning in the late spring of 1863, a persistent rumor swept through the camp of the 96th Pennsylvania to the effect that the regiment might be recalled from Virginia to perform provost duty in the coal region. In his diary one soldier wrote that "it was rumored about camp that Capt. Charlemagne Tower and Col. Henry L. Cake would come for the regiment to do provost duty in Schuylkill and Luzerne Counties."[17] The Gettysburg campaign, however, intervened and quickly ended the possibility of transferring the regiment to prevent draft resistance. Several months later, reports and rumors again surfaced suggesting that the 96th would be sent home to relieve the 10th New Jersey, currently performing provost duty in Schuylkill County.[18] Another Pennsylvanian recorded in his diary, "There is a great talk of us going to Pottsville ... to enforce the draft, and that the request had been sent to Gov. Curtin."[19] And finally, a few days later, he noted that "our Colonel [Lessig] had [received] a letter from Gov. Curtin stating that he had sent the papers in regard to sending us to Pottsville, to the Secretary of War for his approval."[20] In mid–August, Edward Henry characterized the situation in Schuylkill County as it appeared to a veteran soldier. "I hear there are some stiff times at home on account of the draft. If the old 96th was there they would not play with them as they do with the Sunday soldiers.... Schuylkill Co. is a disgrace to the state and the instigators of this disturbance should pay for it."[21]

The prospect of returning to Schuylkill County for provost duty, along with the upcoming election in Pennsylvania, afforded several officers in the 96th Pennsylvania a convenient opportunity to express their political opinions. In particular, they directed their commentary toward the Copperheads: the anti-war Democrats they perceived as generally responsible for the political unrest in Schuylkill County. An officer submitted the following statement to the *Miners' Journal*, published in the October 2 issue of the weekly newspaper. He wrote, "We fully appreciate the importance of the coming election.... We had better lose a battle in the field than that you lose the contest at home.... We are taking good care of the enemy in the front, do you at home take care of them in our rear. I can conceive of nothing that would tend to dishearten and demoralize the Pennsylvania troops now in the field, more than the defeat of [Governor] Curtin."[22] Seizing upon previous editorials in the *Miners' Journal*, several soldiers publicly expressed their dislike of the Copperheads; who they likened to the venomous snake of the same name. The soldiers believed that the Copperheads were a more significant problem, more so than draft resistance, in regard to defeating the Confederacy.

The issues encompassing the draft and the upcoming election proved to be very significant to the soldiers of the 96th Pennsylvania. Both issues received commentary in their letters and diaries throughout the spring and summer of 1863. Writing to his brother Fred in early June, Captain Haas offered the following opinion regarding the draft. "Draft and make them come. 4 weeks drilling is enough. A man can learn to load and shoot in 1 week and 3 weeks is enough to learn him to go ahead. He will learn to retreat himself."[23] Daniel Faust, perhaps offering the perspective of the German soldiers in the regiment, stated, "O how I do wish that them Irish drunkerts would get drafted so they would get out here ... [where] they have to be all temperance."[24] While the draft drew some commentary from the Pennsylvanians, the fall election received substantial treatment in their correspondence. In addition, the soldiers also took aim at another issue, a long term problem concerning the Union war effort, the influence of Copperheads in Schuylkill County.

Beginning after the Chancellorsville campaign and continuing into late summer, the Pennsylvanians, through their correspondence, impressed upon their families and friends in Schuylkill County, the significance of the upcoming election. Captain Haas, writing to his brother Fred, stated that "I am almost convinced that we will never subdue the Rebels unless the Government quits this dilly dallying and makes a fuss over Copperheads and goes to work in earnest."[25] Captain Isaac Severn published his opinion concerning Copperheads in the *Miners' Journal*. "We have, to day, been two years in the service of our country and feel that we have a right to take an interest in the affairs of good old, loyal, Pennsylvania, even if absent. The war is not yet over, because all were not *true* patriots of the Curtin stamp. Copperheads appeared (but another name for traitors) and by word and deed encouraged the rebel lion."[26] And finally, a soldier in Company H published the following statement in the county's weekly newspaper against

Copperheads who were so opposed to President Lincoln's emancipation proclamation, and for those who have made themselves the dupes of designing demagogues, who teach them that they can be loyal and yet lay every obstacle in the way of the Government and its rightfully constituted authorities.... Now let me say one word in reference to those miserable Miscreants; those Copperheads, yes those traitors, right In our midst, and in the whole North. They have not only by their base treason prolonged the war and needlessly sacrificed thousands of our bravest soldiers, but daily are inviting those Southern devils right into our borders, and worst of all, into our ranks.[27]

The reelection of the "War Governor," Andrew Curtin, and the elimination of the influence of the Copperheads upon war policy were two home front battles that the soldiers believed they needed to win in order to march on to ultimate Union victory. Letters to the *Miners' Journal*, for example, served as important outlets for the soldiers to articulate their views on these matters. The soldiers, too, perceived Gettysburg as a significant turning point in the war. To the rank and file, Gettysburg symbolized much more than a tactical battlefield victory achieved on Northern soil. Despite the fact that Lee's army had not been destroyed at Gettysburg, morale was extremely high within the ranks of the Army of the Potomac. While the great achievement at Gettysburg was significant to the soldiers, the Pennsylvanians understood that a victory at the ballot box would sharpen their bayonets even more in the next battle. Erasmus Reed expressed his views concerning these issues in a letter to his brother.

The army as far as I can see is in fine spirits. Everybody seems willing to go through any hardships for the sake of winding up the war. The tide of battle has turned against the rebels … you at home also have a vigorous campaign in prospect. I mean the coming election. It is not necessary for me to advise you in regard to it, because without doubt you are on the right side, and that is for Curtain, of course. If there are any of our connections who are not sure for Curtain, use your influence in converting them and get their votes polled in the Loyal box…. There is a certain Party in our state who seem to dread the results of a vote in the army.[28]

Captain Severn, of Company C, publicly encouraged everyone in Schuylkill County to support the war effort and the soldiers in the field by returning Curtin to the governor's chair.

I believe that all Pennsylvania soldiers are in favor of the re-election of Andrew G. Curtin. He has been from the very beginning of this wicked rebellion, the firm and unflinching supporter of the Union, and a faithful protector of Pennsylvania's sons…. Should he be defeated, it will be a calamity for the soldier as well as the country…. We think there is a necessity for using all exertions to bring out the strength of the friends of the government.

In this coming election … we still number upwards of 300 voters, all, I believe, Curtin men … we feel very anxious about this election, and would like to take an active part in it.[29]

The leadership of General Meade, along with the great victory at Gettysburg, the surge in morale in the army and political victories at home, aligning the soldiers with Lincoln's national strategy, would yield decisive victory for the Unionists. Despite unity in the ranks behind Lincoln's war policy, the autumn of 1863 would prove to be a series of indecisive operations returning the war to central Virginia for the winter. The war, however, was about to enter a different phase. Unrelenting combat, rather than intermittent, warfare would characterize the spring of 1864.

Throughout the balance of July, the VI Corps, along with the rest of the Army of the Potomac, slowly moved back into Virginia in the final phase of the Gettysburg campaign. On July 19, while the VI Corps bands played "Oh Carry Me Back to Ole Virginia," the Bluecoats crossed into the land of "Dixie" via a pontoon bridge at Berlin, Maryland.[30] After a week of grueling marches made over rough roads, the VI Corps finally halted.

On July 25 Sedgwick established an encampment in the hills just west of Warrenton, where the Pennsylvanians enjoyed their first days of rest since the week long encampment near Fairfax Court House.[31] They quickly settled into a pleasant camp routine. After they spent a few days picking wild blackberries, and swimming in a nearby river, the war seemed very far away. During this time, stationed near New Baltimore, the men performed light outpost duty, participated in regimental drills, read newspapers and letters or slept away their hours.[32] This interlude was broken only by two unrelated incidents, the first on August 14, when Bartlett's brigade assembled for the execution, by firing squad, of a deserter from the 5th Maine.[33]

After the Chancellorsville campaign and continuing through the Gettysburg campaign, desertion emerged as an alarming problem within the Army of the Potomac. In order to curb the rate of desertion in late summer, deserters were subjected to court-martial and military executions conducted in the presence of an entire Union division. Of the army's

Capt. Isaac E. Severn, Company C. Promoted from first lieutenant November 1, 1862. Mustered out with regiment October 21, 1864 (collection of James F. Haas, United States Army Heritage and Education Center).

267 reported military executions, 147 were carried out due to desertion. Earlier in the war, soldiers were opposed to such harsh measures.[34] In late summer of 1863, however, they no longer stood against military executions; especially when the soldier was deemed a deserter, which they equated with cowardice. The 96th Pennsylvania was plagued with desertion throughout 1863.[35] Soldier diaries and letters reveal a number of men who deserted and evaded capture by the provost marshal. Thomas Jewett, of Company D, 5th Maine, however, was arrested in Washington and charged with "leaving his post in the face of the enemy," as his comrades struggled in the timber against Kershaw's brigade at Salem Church. He was subsequently tried and convicted by court martial.[36] Jewett was sentenced to death "with musketry" by a firing squad on August 14. The firing squad was assembled from men selected by lottery from the ranks of the 96th Pennsylvania.

On August 12, the soldiers of the 96th Pennsylvania were informed at dress parade that a private serving with the 5th Maine was scheduled to be executed by firing squad in two day's time. Henry Keiser recorded the following entry in his diary. "A deserter from the 5th Maine is to be shot tomorrow and our Company is to furnish two of the firing party. Our officers decided that we should draw lots to decide who would be the unlucky ones. The boys did not like the idea of shooting one of our own men, but it was so decreed, and had to be."[37] The following day, the men drew lots in each company to determine the individual soldiers who would be assigned to the firing squad. In Company B, John Reed and Israel Reed drew the tickets for the unwanted duty.[38] Sgt. William Buck and Pvt. Joseph Workman were chosen for the same grim task from Company G.[39] The execution was scheduled for the afternoon, at a large field near Warrenton, with the entire First Division present to witness the macabre spectacle.

According to Lieutenant Luckenbill, the 96th Pennsylvania left camp "at half past ten [and] … moved out the turnpike towards Warrenton, marched about 2 miles, where we met the other three brigades of our division."[40] Henry Keiser noted that "the Division formed in a hollow square … the 2nd [Brigade] on the left … leaving an open space at one side."[41] Edward Henry, in a letter to his sister, described the scene that the soldiers witnessed that afternoon. "We had to wait but a short time when an open wagon containing the prisoner and the chaplain [Adams of the 5th Maine] were escorted around the square. The band playing a funeral dirge the prisoner was seated on his coffin … as composed as though going on parade … he spoke to the shooting party and told them he forgave them as they were but doing their duty…. He read a few verses from his Bible and said his soul would soon be in heaven."[42] Finally, Luckenbill recorded his impression of the execution of Private Jewett. "His coffin was placed on the ground, at 1 he took his seat on the coffin and the 20 men counted ten paces in front of him. They preached a short prayer, at 10 minutes past 1, he was blindfolded and 12 minutes past one he fell dead."[43] Another soldier recalled that "immediately following the discharge of musketry, the command closed ranks, broke into column, marched past the body of the culprit who lay just as he fell, that all might read the lesson of the results which follow treachery and desertion."[44] Private Henry concluded that "it was a sad sight and I hope it will serve [as] a warning to other[s]."[45]

The other exciting event featured the dash and boldness so often associated with Civil War exploits. In early September, near Warrenton, the 96th Pennsylvania was stationed in a region of Virginia patrolled by Col. John Mosby and his famous "Rangers" of the 43rd Battalion Virginia Cavalry.[46] Although Mosby was wounded in an engagement with the 2nd Massachusetts Cavalry on August 24, his band of guerrillas continued their raids against the Army of the Potomac. While camped at New Baltimore, General Bartlett established his headquarters in the, "home of a Southern lady with several accomplished daughters."[47] According to one of Upton's "Regulars," Bartlett's headquarters was "in the yard of a mansion about six hundred yards from our camp." The brigade band was camped nearby the general's tent. Subsequently, Confederate cavalry learned about the location of Bartlett's headquarters and determined to undertake a daring raid with the intent of capturing General Bartlett. They planned to conduct the operation on the night of September 4. That evening, several soldiers from the 96th Pennsylvania were performing picket duty, charged with protecting the general from just such a guerrilla attack.[48]

At 2 a.m. a squadron of cavalry, with orders to capture Bartlett, boldly rode up to the picket post. The guard ordered the troopers to halt, dismount, and give the countersign. The guerrilla leader responded by drawing his revolver, shooting the picket guard, and galloping up the road, followed by his comrades, in search of Bartlett's tent. The guerrillas then fired upon a group of officer's tents, which was pitched in an orchard. Bartlett, aroused by the gun fire, sprang out of bed, seized his revolver, and dashed out of his tent and fired upon his would be captors "in his nether garments."[49] An eyewitness, however, stated that "General Bartlett, ready and intrepid soldier that he was, had seized his revolver instead of his pants and fought his would be captors in the uniform nature had furnished him."[50] The former adjutant of the 96th Pennsylvania, Mathias Richards, also fired upon the raiders. According to the historian of the 121st New York, "His revolver spoke more than once in welcome to the raiders and in loud tones than did that of the General, who the next day lamented the smallness of his weapon."[51] Aside from wounding a couple of Pennsylvania soldiers, the Graycoats made off with the brigade battle flag. For the Confederates, it was an exciting raid with little significant achievement. For the Unionists the affair provided hearty laughter.[52]

The episode was chronicled by several soldiers in the 96th Pennsylvania. Lieutenant Luckenbill noted in his diary that "the enemy cavalry made a dash on the Headquarters of General Bartlett.... The long roll was immediately rolled and the camp aroused. By the time we got up out of bed and grabbed our clothes and swords, the firing was in front all around headquarters.... General Bartlett was in the yard behind trees, firing from behind."[53] Henry Keiser recorded in his journal that "a band of guerillas, about 30 in number made a dash at Gen. Bartlett's Headquarters ... he escaping through the backdoor, in his night clothes ... the Rebs were driven back by Co. F.... They had two men wounded."[54] The raid, however, amused the soldiers who marveled at the boldness demonstrated by the Rangers but considered the affair to be poorly executed.[55] While the daring raid failed in its objective, the episode successfully captured the imagination of the flamboyant chief of cavalry Jeb Stuart. Three days later, he composed an official report of the operation and proclaimed the "affair, though only partially successful, as highly creditable to the daring and enterprise of [Benjamin Franklin] Stringfellow and his band."[56]

Along with a shift in soldier attitudes in regard to the prosecution of the war in the summer of 1863, autumn brought a change in commanders to the soldiers of the Second Brigade. For the first time in over a year, General Bartlett would no longer lead the men in combat. Bartlett was transferred to command a division in the V Corps. As a result of his transfer, Col. Emory Upton, a rising star in the Army of the Potomac, was promoted to command the brigade. Born on a farm near Batavia, New York, in 1839, Emory Upton was regarded as one of the "Boy Generals" of the Civil War. After briefly attending Oberlin College, Upton enrolled at West Point and graduated from the Military Academy in the spring of 1861. He ranked eighth in a class of forty-five cadets.[57] Commissioned a second lieutenant, he served on Gen. Daniel Tyler's staff during the First Bull Run Campaign. Subsequently, he commanded an artillery battery in the VI Corps. In October 1862, he was appointed colonel of the 121st New York Volunteers. Upton was an unwavering supporter of the Union and an ardent abolitionist. The distinguished cavalry officer James Harrison Wilson penned the following character sketch of Upton.

> His life was pure and unselfish in the highest degree, and yet it was controlled by a patriotic sleepless ambition, accompanied by an ardent love for the profession of arms, which from their earliest dawn, filled him with the resolve to acquire military fame. His courage was both physical and moral, and therefore of the highest type. In the hour of battle he was as intrepid a man as ever drew a saber. He gave loyal and unquestioning support to his superior officers, and especially to those who were in chief command.... Upton was as good an artillery-officer as could be found in any country, the equal of any cavalry commander of his day, and ... the best commander of a division of infantry in either the Union or rebel army.[58]

Chaplain Hall of the 16th New York told his wife, "Upton is a Republican, a despiser of McClelland & all treason & is a true man."[59] Surgeon Stevens simply characterized him as "the young, ambitious, Colonel Upton."[60]

Within a few weeks of his promotion, Upton was afforded an opportunity to lead his new brigade in battle. At daybreak, November 7, Sedgwick's Right Wing (the V and VI Corps) tramped down the Fayetteville Road toward the bridgehead at Rappahannock Station, a depot on the Orange & Alexandria Railroad.[61] As the Federal troops arrived at the river, the V Corps deployed in a line of battle east of the railroad line, while the VI Corps (temporarily under Wright) positioned themselves to the west of the tracks. One Unionist, peering cautiously at the Secessionist works, recalled the prelude to battle in a letter written shortly after the affair.

> Rappahannock Station is a vile place to approach for attack—a plain, long and wide with a small hill only for a mile or more till you come to the river bank, which is quite high, naturally a strong position made more so by two redoubts … with rifle pits extending a great distance above & below.[62]

Near sunset, with the shadows lengthening along the river bank, Brig. Gen. David A. Russell requested permission from General Wright to attack the enemy with his First Division. Russell, confident in the battle tested character of his troops, believed he could successfully assault the Confederate position. After listening to Russell's appeal, Wright concurred with him.[63]

Within five minutes, Russell assembled a double skirmish line and issued the command, "Forward, double-quick." Col. Peter C. Ellmaker's brigade led the assault against the Confederate entrenchments. Emory Upton's brigade, positioned several hundred yards behind Ellmaker's, was detailed as additional support. The Bluecoat attack, according to one Federal officer, "astonished and bewildered" the enemy.[64] Ellmaker's brigade, after encountering stiff resistance from the 8th and 9th Louisiana regiments, cleared the redoubts of Secessionists. As the Bluecoats secured the center of the Confederate line, the Tarheels of the 6th and part of the 57th North Carolina, poured a flanking fire into Ellmaker's four regiments.[65] With Ellmaker's brigade being somewhat disorganized and under heavy fire from Col. Archibald Godwin's North Carolinians, Russell ordered Upton's brigade into the fight.

Upon receiving Russell's order, Upton prepared to attack Colonel Godwin's Tarheels with the 5th Maine and his own regiment, the 121st New York. The 95th and 96th Pennsylvania regiments were instructed to support Upton's assault. Prior to the attack, Upton told his troops: "Men … your friends at home and your country expect every man to do his duty on this occasion. When I give the command to charge, move forward. If they fire upon you, I will move six lines of battle over you and bayonet every one of them. Some of us have got to die, but remember you are going to heaven."[66] With that, Upton's men advanced with "unexampled

Col. Emory Upton, 121st New York Volunteers, subsequently promoted to brigadier general. Commanded the 2nd Brigade, 1st Division, VI Corps (author's collection).

coolness, steadiness, and bravery" against the Graycoats.[67] Without firing a shot, Upton's troops broke Godwin's line by executing a textbook bayonet assault. According to Upton, the Tarheels "fought stubbornly," but being outnumbered they quickly surrendered.[68] After Upton's successful attack, the 95th and 96th Pennsylvania regiments advanced to the redoubts. Lessig's Schuylkill Countians secured the bridge, while the Zouave regiment took charge of the prisoners. Almost immediately the Federal troops recognized the importance of the battle. The fight at Rappahannock Station, one of the most decisive actions of the war, instilled tremendous pride in the Army of the Potomac. Indeed, Walter Taylor, one of Lee's staff officers, did not exaggerate when he called the action at Rappahannock Station "the saddest chapter in the history of [the] army [of Northern Virginia]."[69]

For the 96th, the Battle of Rappahannock Station proved to be a very long day, but a bloodless ordeal. Rising at 4 a.m., the Pennsylvanians cooked coffee, drew rations, and made final preparations before starting in marching column for Rappahannock Station. After ten miles, the Pennsylvanians discovered "the Rebels entrenched on the north bank of the Rappahannock."[70] According to Dr. Bland, "The day was clear, cool and a bracing air.... The orders were to take possession of the Station and go into camp."[71] About 2 o'clock, the Pennsylvanians halted in the woods, in line of battle, and deployed skirmishers in their front. Henry Keiser recalled that the regiment "advanced under a heavy artillery fire, driving in their skirmishers. The shells burst all around us.... Our Regiment advanced to within several hundred yards of the Rebel works when we were ordered to lie down behind a small knoll."[72] As the soldiers advanced, Lieutenant Luckenbill noted that "the shells would all strike the ground in front of our lines and bounce over us ... one man was wounded of our Company, Corporal Edward J. Jones ... by a piece of shell."[73]

Surgeon Bland recalled the scene as the battle opened in a detailed letter published in the *Miners' Journal.*

> The line of skirmishers were ordered to advance. The columns of infantry were in line of battle. The sight was magnificently grand. The clear, blue sky—the clear, cold air that nerved every man to action, rendered the picture one for an artist.... Rapid firing now commenced along the whole line of skirmishers. Pop, pop went the muskets, when all at once the boom of cannon was heard, which announced that the battle had begun.[74]

Under the cover of darkness, the Bluecoats, led personally by Colonel Upton, executed a bayonet charge, routed the Confederates from their rifle pits and captured 1,200 prisoners. A week after the battle, a North Carolinian reported the details of the battle in a letter printed in the Richmond *Examiner.* "Although the odds were greatly against us ... our men received the shock as brave men only do ... being thus so greatly outnumbered, [we] were compelled to yield. Some surrendered; others rushed to the pontoon [bridge] and escaped; some others ... plunged into the [Rappahannock] river below and swam across a few being drowned."[75] Once inside the Confederate field fortifications, Upton brought the 96th forward to hold the bridge.[76] Lieutenant Luckenbill recalled that "the battle continued till a-while after dark, after they were acrossed the river the 96th occupied the rifle pits this side of the river. Company G and B [were] sent to the river to guard their bridge [and] to keep them from destroying it."[77] Surgeon Bland, who observed the initial phase of the battle, proudly stated that "the gallant 96th, ever true to her colors and her hard earned prestige, were prominent in the fight. Under the leadership of the dashing Col. Lessig, we took and held the enemy's bridge, and were the first to cross the river, capturing two prisoners and killing one, who refused to halt."[78]

After the swift and decisive action at Rappahannock Station, Meade took two weeks to rebuild the Orange and Alexandria Railroad for a supply line and meticulously plan his next move. By November 9, Lee's army had withdrawn beyond the Rapidan River, where the Graycoats established a new line, covering a thirty-mile front, extending from Clark's Mountain on the western flank to Mine Run and Liberty Mills on the eastern flank. Meade, believing that he should assume the initiative, conceived a bold plan to dislodge Lee's Confederates. He proposed to march his army downstream, well beyond the enemy's right, cross at Germanna and Ely's Fords, and execute a fast march west along the Orange Turnpike for a blow against the eastern flank of the Butternuts before Lee could bring up his other corps in support. The success of the operation rested on the ability of the Bluecoats to move swiftly and avoid detection by the Confederate outposts. The plan, however, did not allow for muddy lanes, causing slow marching, or a miscalculation in the number of pontoons needed to bridge a river. Delays of this sort usually proved fatal to the plans of Civil War generals.[79]

Problems immediately beset Meade's carefully crafted battle plan. On November 24, the day prescribed for the Bluecoat advance, rain swelled the rivers and mired the roads. Due to the weather, the operation was postponed another two days.[80] Finally, on November 26, at seven o'clock in the morning, as the Second Brigade band played "Yankee Doodle," "Hail to the Chief" and "Hail, Columbia," orders were read to the soldiers informing them that once again the Army of the Potomac was undertaking a movement to strike the Confederates.[81] The 96th Pennsylvania, along with a section of artillery, formed the rear guard of the VI Corps. Reaching Brandy Station at noon, the soldiers received orders allowing them to cook coffee, but Lieutenant Luckenbill reported that some of the Bluecoats seized the opportunity to charge upon an unsuspecting sutler and rob him of his goods. The march toward the Rapidan River that day was slow and tedious. Artillery caissons stuck in the mud, roads choked with wagons and infantry soldiers all contributed to the slow advance of the VI Corps column. Luckenbill wrote in his diary, "Every few steps we were delayed by the teams, the roads awfully cut up here it went very slow."[82] After crossing Mountain Run, referred to by the soldiers as Muddy Run, the Bluecoats plodded along until midnight, having marched ten miles, when they went into camp. That night, one soldier wryly remarked, "Our Thanksgiving dinner that day consisted of fat raw pork, hard bread, and cold water."[83]

For the soldiers of the 96th Pennsylvania, November 27 proved to be as challenging as Thanksgiving Day. After an early breakfast, Evan Gery reported in his diary that the Schuylkill Countians "pulled a few wagons out of the mud and up the hill. Teams were hitched and we resumed the march. Teams became stuck every now and then, but at 7 a.m. we got onto the [Germanna] plank road."[84] At approximately 10 o'clock, Upton's brigade reached Jacobs Ford, on the Rapidan River, only to find that the pontoon bridge had already been dismantled by the engineers. Subsequently, the 96th marched down the river to Germanna Ford, when they crossed the Rapidan and advanced, at the double-quick, to support the III Corps which according to Henry Keiser was "hotly engaged." Lieutenant Luckenbill recalled that "we marched out and formed line of battle in the rear of the [Third] brigade [Neill's] of the 6th Corps. Terrible musketry, several charges made battle continued until after dark, when the fight ceased [and] we were ordered to build small fires and make some coffee and lay under arms all night."[85] Rather than rest from the rigors of the day, the soldiers "were routed up at midnight and marched about four miles to the left and joined the right of the 2nd Corps about 4 a.m."[86] As the sun rose the next morning, the Pennsylvanians reached the vicinity of Robertson's Tavern. To the veterans of Upton's brigade, all indications pointed toward a battle unfolding in the wilderness surrounding Mine Run.[87]

After a slow, disjointed march, conducted in darkness, Upton's brigade connected with the extreme right flank of the II Corps at daybreak. After a hasty breakfast, "a detail for our brigade," recalled Evan Gery, "was organized for skirmishing. I was on the skirmish line. We advanced about two miles and found the rebels in force opposite us, very strongly entrenched across Mine Run."[88] Another soldier recalled that "about eight o'clock we were deployed into line of battle, and advanced toward a piece of woods called the Wilderness. And indeed it was a wilderness—truly and well named—a wild forest, twelve miles square, featuring only an occasional opening, and with only passable roads or paths through it. It was with the greatest difficulty that any sort of line could be kept; indeed, it was most terrible marching."[89] Although the VI Corps was in position to launch an assault, the formidable earthworks held by the Confederates along with the rain and extremely cold weather compelled the Union high command to postpone the scheduled attack until the following day. According to surgeon Stevens, "The night was spent by both parties in throwing up earthworks, and the morning revealed several strong lines of rifle pits on the rebel side of the stream."[90]

The next day, November 28, Meade found that Lee had pulled his entire army behind Mine Run, and now looked across the stream at the Federals from behind a formidable line of defenses. After personally reconnoitering the Confederate works—a seven-mile line of entrenchments whose approaches had been cleared for overlapping fields of fire—Meade remained determined to break through the Confederate line. After speaking with his corps commanders at Robertson's Tavern, it was agreed that Warren would mass on Lee's right flank, while Sedgwick would attack the Confederate left, a sector which Meade believed offered a good chance for success. On the night of November 29, General Meade ordered "Uncle John" Sedgwick "to make a sudden and determined attack upon the enemy's left, under a concentrated fire from our batteries."[91]

In preparation to support this assault, Upton's brigade marched in the darkness a mile toward the Union right flank, which Sedgwick established as the staging area for the attack. One Bluecoat recalled that "the dense thicket and a gentle eminence concealed the corps from the view of the rebels, who were but a few yards distant."[92] At 8 o'clock, Lieutenant Luckenbill noted that a "terrible cannonading commenced all along the line and continued for almost one hour."[93] Evan Gery recorded in his diary that "the rebels were unaware of this move. We were to charge along the entire line … at 9, with the band adding their best music as we moved."[94] As the hour for the attack drew near, Henry Keiser recounted the battle plan in his diary. "The intention was to charge the Rebel breastworks, a very strong position, Mine Run running between us, with a steep hill on the other side, with trees cut down with limbs all pointing, toward us and pointed…. I felt that I certainly would get killed, or at least badly wounded…. I never had such a feeling before and I really believe that I would have been shot."[95] Just before 9 a.m., Sedgwick received an order from Meade to suspend the attack. Later that day the Bluecoats withdrew to their original position. A relieved Union infantry soldier proclaimed that the withdrawal from Mine Run proved to be "one of the greatest battles never fought."[96]

Tuesday, December 1, was a bitterly cold day. Soldiers who had discarded their great-coats, to lighten their marching load during the advance to Mine Run, now suffered terribly from the cold weather. Pickets, performing outpost duty, were found frozen to death.[97] Realizing that further offensive movements were impractical, Sedgwick abandoned the Mine Run line and retreated across the Rapidan at Germanna Ford. Within a few days the 96th established a fine winter camp along the Hazel River, near Welford's ford, on the Major's farm near Brandy Station.[98] Quickly the Bluecoats began the task of building log huts to protect themselves from the harsh winter weather that was approaching. "The troops burrowed into the earth and built their little shelters," recalled a Federal brigadier, "and the officers and men devoted themselves to unlimited festivity, balls, horse races, cockfights … and other games such as only soldiers can devise."[99]

Meade's withdrawal from Lee's Mine Run front, accomplished with surprising skill, effectively ended all infantry operations for 1863. On both sides of the Rapidan the two armies entered into winter quarters, beginning what would be a five month rest. As the autumn fighting subsided, the military and political leaders of both sides could sit back and reflect upon the changing character of the conflict. The northern press and many politicians in Washington openly criticized Meade, referring to his Mine Run campaign as a failure. From this point forward the public and military leaders were not going to tolerate battlefield reverses. Grant's decisive victory at Chattanooga ensured that. By the third winter of the conflict the Federal war objective was clear. It was made so by policy and action, implemented by competent field commanders, manpower and material supremacy. Emancipation had become an irrevocable commitment. In 1864, military conquest of the Confederacy would be relentlessly pursued. Nevertheless, the bloody battles of 1863, the continued efforts by the Confederacy to seek foreign recognition, and the upcoming election year in the North promised that 1864 would be a year of uncertainty. All of this, however, meant little to the Civil War volunteer. For him there was the grim reality of another winter encampment to endure.[100]

The winter of 1863 was different from the two previous ones because General Meade, normally cranky, suddenly became liberal by allowing officers to bring their wives to camp on extended visits. Many wives, in fact, availed themselves of Meade's noble gesture. During the celebration of Washington's birthday, the dance floors of the ballrooms constructed by the Bluecoats overflowed with officers in gaudy uniforms and women in puffy, hoop skirts. Unfortunately for the soldiers in the ranks, they never had the opportunity to experience the gaiety of the dances. Instead, they were often assembled in an open field and marched past a reviewing stand where their military strength was admired by the officers' ladies. In the Second Brigade of the First Division of the VI Corps, however, an amusement hall was built and a minstrel troop provided entertainment for the soldiers. The troops of Upton's brigade also erected a chapel, much to the delight of the regimental chaplains. While these projects no doubt absorbed the idle hours of a majority of the volunteer Bluecoats, the officers of the units found other avenues to expend their time and energies. The field officers of the 96th, not overburdened by military paperwork, found the time to pursue their favorite winter encampment pastime: regimental politics.[101]

In December 1863, Maj. William H. Lessig, who commanded the regiment, launched yet another futile plot to secure his colonel's eagle. At this time, the 96th did not have the minimum number of men present for duty as required for a colonelcy appointment. Learning of this technicality, Lessig decided to settle for the lieutenant colonelcy, with

Captain Haas, who had been detailed out of the regiment for recruiting purposes, returning to the unit in Lessig's vacated major slot. Haas' return, however, presented Lessig with a unique problem. In order for Haas to receive the appointment as regimental major, Lessig would need to discredit Captains Russell and Boyle, both of whom held seniority over the former captain of Company G. It was now up to Lessig to set his plot in motion.[102]

In typical fashion, the commander of the 96th wasted no time in composing and forwarding a most disparaging letter to Governor Curtin. Lessig's missive vehemently attacked the character of the two senior captains, both original line officers of the regiment. The epistle stated:

> I have the honor to transmit the following reasons why Captains [James] Russell [Co. E] and [John] Boyle [Co. D] should not be appointed to the vacant position of Major of the 96th Regt. Penna. Vols.
> 1st I consider both incompetent and inefficient as field officers.
> 2nd The quarrelsome and troublesome disposition of the one and the eccentricities of the other would render them both unfit for the position and it would be an injury to the Regiment and impair its efficiency.
> I trust that upon the perusal of these reasons that your excellency will commission Captain Haas for that position and confer a favor to the Regiment as well as myself.[103]

Lessig's scheme, however, did not meet with the approval of Governor Curtin. Upon learning that the "War Governor" refused to commission Haas, his hand-picked choice as the regimental major, Lessig campaigned hard to insure that neither Russell nor Boyle was given the honor. After much bitter wrangling, meetings between the officers, and pressure from Lessig, a compromise was reached in this divisive and volatile issue. Finally, in mid–January, Lessig notified Governor Curtin that he was "withdrawing all former recommendations, [as] I believe the best interests of the service will be promoted by the favorable return within."[104] The "favorable return within" referred to a petition, signed by all of the line officers, to Curtin, requesting that Levi Huber, the captain of Company B, be promoted to the grade of major. The line officers were "convinced that this will end all dispute and prove agreeable to all interested as well as promote the good of the service."[105]

Although Huber received his commission as major, overwhelmingly approved by the line officers, his elevation to a staff position was not in accordance with the seniority system. Clearly Russell and Boyle, and to a lesser extent Haas,

Capt. Lamar Hay, original captain of Company A. Discharged on surgeon's certificate December 27, 1862 (Heber Thompson, *The First Defenders*, 1910).

were at the highest rungs of the promotional ladder. The ratification of Huber as major, subsequently approved by Curtin, was clearly a gesture on the part of Lessig to maintain some element of harmony within his command.[106] Whatever the motivation of Lessig throughout this scheme, one thing is certain: the plot was typical of Civil War regimental promotions. Cake and Lessig controlled the field officer promotions, elevating personal friends against accepted military regulations, engineering the dismissal of officers they disliked, and preventing others from attaining promotions justly deserved. Assessing motivation in these promotional schemes, however, is hazardous at best. In the case of Cake, the attainment of a colonel's eagle was translated into a successful post-war political and business career.[107] Lessig, too, later promoted to the rank of colonel but never mustered in that grade, used his military service after the war to receive a political appointment.[108]

After the defeat of Lessig's ambitious promotional plot, resulting in the elevation of Levi Huber, the 96th regiment devoted its energies to surviving the winter encampment near Brandy Station. No doubt, the troops had learned much about winter quarters from their two previous encampments. Immediately the streets, walks and parade of the camp were laid out with military precision. The huts, built of logs, were large enough to house four Yanks. Although the quarters might appear cramped, at least to the modern reader, one Unionist described the huts as being "very comfortable and cosy [sic] and pleasant."[109] As soon as the camp was complete, the old winter encampment diversions began to emerge from the veterans.

A theme that connects the observations of the rank and file and officer corps of the 96th Pennsylvania focuses upon impressions of the pervasiveness of debauchery in Union camps. Letters and diaries, especially concerning the officers, reveal the consumption of intoxicants, which often led to physical altercations. Pay day in camp, seasonal holidays and rewarding the men with a ration of whiskey often led to disruptive behavior and at times severe military justice for infractions. Theft of property, from another soldier or from the regimental sutler, also resulted in harsh measures for the man found guilty of such crimes. The issue is not that depraved men flocked to the colors while the moral and righteous ones stayed at home, or that the army was the devil's own instrument for making sinners out of the upright Bluecoats. There is nothing contaminating about an army uniform, and many Bluecoats emerged from the service as righteous as when they enlisted. Perhaps the degeneration of the moral standards of many Yanks resulted from the removal of many accustomed civilian restraints and associations. The desire to escape boredom, and the inadequacy of religious facilities combined to erode the moral value system.[110]

One of the most common evils of camp life was profanity. The *Articles of War* forbade the use of profanity and, in the case of officers, prescribed a fine of one dollar for each offense. Little attention, however, was paid to the prohibition, and officers, far from enjoining their men, seem to have set an unwholesome example in the frequent use of oaths in their speech. Captain John T. Boyle, Company D, related in a letter to Lieutenant Colonel Filbert, how Lieutenant Colonel "Lessig swore terribly, when [Henry] Royer's [captain of Company H] resignation came back accepted."[111] Statements in the journals and letters of the soldiers suggest that such outbursts were common among the officer corps of the 96th. Captain Haas' diary and more often, his letters, present significant usage of profane language. Religiously inclined soldiers sometimes rebuked comrades for their blasphemy, but this practice usually led to peer ridicule. The type of profanity used in the camp of the Pennsylvanians is revealed in some detail in their letters and diaries. "Hell" and "damn" were the most common expletives. "God dam" and "son of a bitch" were close seconds.[112] Although the historian Bell Wiley asserts in his study of the social life and customs of the Union soldier that "the drift toward swearing was so strong that it drew in many good men," the written legacy of the 96th Pennsylvania Volunteers does not support Wiley's conclusion.[113] God-fearing men such as Lewis Martin, Peter Filbert, Francis Boland and Daniel Faust wrote dozens of letters without using profanity in their missives. Although the evidence, as it pertains to the Schuylkill Countians, does not support Wiley's generalization, it is accepted that profanity, primarily the pedestrian type, could be heard in most Union camps.

Gambling, another favorite diversion, was hardly less prevalent than swearing. The peak of gambling came on payday when clusters of soldiers could be found attempting to double their greenbacks through games of chance. The principal gambling medium was cards and the favorite game was poker, commonly called "bluff," and played in several variations. Other card games included *vingt-et-un*, faro, and seven-up or "old-sledge." Crap-shooting was also popular. In the 96th regiment pitching pennies and tiddly winks were favorite pastimes. The most common dice game seems to have been chuck-a-luck, also called sweat, which was a contest played by rolling three dice on a board or cloth marked off into numbered squares. Horse racing and cockfighting were also popular, but neither drew the following of cards or dice. Whatever the form of gambling, the stakes were usually small. Due to the sparse references to gambling in the journals and letters of the 96th Pennsylvania volunteers, it is difficult to assess the extent of gambling within the officer corps and the ranks.[114]

Along with swearing and gambling, the consumption of alcoholic beverages proved to be the most prolific problem in camp.[115] Whiskey was a great favorite, but gin, "lemonade," brandy, wine, and—among the German and Irish troops of the 96th Pennsylvania—beer were consumed in copious quantities.[116] Excessive drinking disturbed regimental officers, such as Lieutenant Colonel Filbert, who expressed concern that intoxicating liquor exacerbated the problem of discipline. Filbert especially disdained the drinking habits of the field officers. In the evening the line officers could usually be found in Cake's tent, most emerging from the marquee, at a late hour, well "hived."[117] Lieutenant Luckenbill described a "merry" Christmas in camp when General Bartlett presented the 96th Pennsylvania a gift of ale. His diary entry on Christmas Day stated the following:

> General Bartlett presented the regiment to a bail of ale in the afternoon. The regiment was formed in front of regimental headquarters and the ale issued to the men. When they got half through issuing the ale they got to laughing and rolled on the bail and made the ale fly—had a little jollification in the evening.[118]

Tom Houck informed his brother Joe, as early as Christmas Day in 1861, that the camp of the 96th Pennsylvania "was cursed with a plague. It is liquor. More than half the Regiment is drunk. They are fighting in all the streets. The guard house is full."[119]

Within the 96th Pennsylvania drinking, although a problem in camp, did not impair the efficiency of the regiment in combat. For most of the soldiers drinking was a matter of opportunity and a mechanism to cope with the monotony of camp life. Holidays, such as Christmas, and the arrival of the paymaster were harbingers of increased alcoholic consumption. Efforts of officers, chaplains, and civilian reformers to combat drinking in the army often were paralleled by temperance activities of the soldiers themselves. Many regiments had temperance associations which solicited abstinence pledges and generally worked to restrict liquor. In the spring of 1864, a temperance movement in the 5th Maine was said to have spread to numerous other organizations in the Army of the Potomac.[120] How the 5th Maine's temperance movement affected the 96th Pennsylvania is not known. At the very least, this movement and other attempts to curb drinking among the soldiers appears to have had little impact upon the problem.

One of the most notorious of soldier temptations was the association of Bluecoats with lewd women. Prostitution was most rampant in the cities frequented by soldiers. Because of its prominence as a military center, Washington became a mecca for whores and camp followers. During the winter encampments of 1862–1863 and 1863–1864, the Bluecoats were encamped far from the bordellos of Washington. This geographical problem, though, did not preclude prostitution near the Pennsylvanians' camp. In a letter home in March of 1863, Captain Haas described a bawdy house near the Union line.

> There is a house on the picket line where three women live, their men are in the Rebel Army. Our men say they wash for hard tack and ____ for soft bread. I know by their figure that a strong Union sentiment is developing itself in their bosoms.[121]

While prostitution and venereal infection were problems that plagued the Union army, reference to immoral women and venereal disease are almost non-existent within the letters and diaries of the Schuylkill County volunteers.[122]

The forces of corruption, no matter how pervasive, were always resisted by some. Religion was the usual medium of opposition.[123] The religion practiced by the 96th was practical and unobtrusive, marked by attending weekly sermons delivered by the regimental chaplain, Samuel F. Colt. Occasionally Colonel Cake addressed the volunteers, urging them to pursue moral and upright lives.[124] Presumably both Colt and Cake sought to inculcate the Protestant ethic values of industry, piety, sobriety, thrift, and self-improvement through self-discipline. The Irish-Catholic of mid-nineteenth century, however, possessed cultural values that were in many ways antithetical to the Puritan ethic. To many Irish, the practice of self-discipline, self-denial, and investment in the future seemed pointless since others possessed all of the wealth and power. Although confronted with this Protestant-Catholic gulf, Chaplain Colt was able to minister to the spiritual needs of the soldiers. Statements in the letters and diaries of the soldiers attest to his popularity. Clement Potts, in a letter to his Dear Auntie, offered this commentary in regard to Chaplain Colt. "This afternoon I was over and heard Mr. Colt preach a very good sermon. I think a good deal of him."[125] Surgeon Nugent, too, thought highly of Rev. Colt. In a letter to his wife he stated, "Mr. Colt, our Chaplain, is a very interesting preacher, a man of letters and a polished gentleman. The services are generally well attended. All the Companies save the Catholic are generally represented pretty well. There are two Companies composed mostly of Catholics who of course never grace the meetings with their presence."[126] Apparently Colt's integrity, sympathy and sincere interest in the spiritual needs of the troops made for a successful chaplaincy.

Forms of worship varied, but the usual Sunday service consisted of Scripture reading, songs and a sermon. The heart of Sunday services was the sermon, usually delivered by Chaplain Colt. Religious worship was often conducted outdoors. Aside from worship, the publication and distribution of religious literature was an important aspect of promoting the spiritual welfare of the soldiers. Hymn books, testaments and scriptural selections were made available by the American Bible Society and other organizations. Religious tracts, however, were by far the most common form of scriptural literature dispensed to the volunteers. Unfortunately, the letters and diary entries of the Pennsylvanians do not make reference to any religious tracts. In fact, the Pennsylvanians rarely mentioned religious literature of any kind in their correspondence. The lack of data regarding the religious habits and practices of the 96th Pennsylvania precludes any conclusive statement concerning the impact of religion upon combating misdeeds in camp.[127]

While not nefarious, anti–black feeling in the army was, at the very least, an undesirable attitude toward the changing status of black. One who reads the letters and diaries of Union soldiers encounters frequent antipathy toward the Southern black. Expressions of prejudice range from blunt statements manifesting intense hatred to belittling remarks concerning the intelligence, dress, and demeanor of the "darkies." Many Bluecoats professed dislike of the slaves because they found them lazy and shiftless. Occasionally Union troops found fault with the blacks as liars and thieves, but more frequently their dislike was based on what they regarded as "insolence or sauciness." The factor, however, that probably contributed most to anti-slave sentiment among the rank and file was the association of slaves with the war itself. At first the war was fun, but after a while it became a grim and wearisome chore. In time the slaves who flocked to the Union lines, known to the Bluecoats as "contrabands," became scapegoats on whom the Federal soldier could vent his hatred of the war.[128]

Denunciations of the Blacks were more frequent and more violent after unsuccessful military operations. According to the historian Bell Wiley, "The peaks of anti–Negro feeling in the Army of the Potomac seem to have been reached in the wake of McClellan's repulse before Richmond in the summer of 1862 and Burnside's bloody failure at Fredericksburg the following winter."[129] Wiley's contention can be supported by a bizarre passage in a letter written by Captain Haas to his brother Fred, during the 1862–1863 winter encampment along the Rappahannock.

> On the other side of the river [Rappahannock] some of the sixth corps pickets have been doing quite a business of trading with the "rebs." The "Modus Operandi" is as follows, one of our picket goes to a "reb" picket and says, "How many sheep will you give me for a nigger?" Mr. Reb says, "two." Yank says, "get your sheep," and has a bully feed for the boys, ingenious ain't, but it is true.[130]

Such exchanges were typical of the disparagement of the Southern slaves. Prejudice and hostility frequently manifested themselves in this type of cruelty.

It is clear that many Yanks regarded the Southern blacks "as belonging to a lower physical class than the whites."[131] But the broad picture of soldier-slave relations had its bright spots. Many Yanks were favorably disposed toward the slaves and sympathized with their plight. Stories heard in the North of suffering under slavery aroused the deep sympathy of humanitarians. Initially, however, the soldiers of the 96th did not support a war aim of slave emancipation. By 1863, as Lincoln's political strategy evolved, the soldiers emerged as staunch supporters of the President and stalwart Republicans. In his memoir, James Treichler recalled the shift in attitude which took place during the winter encampment at White Oak Church. "When the Army became active again [spring 1863] and the south threatened the homes of the north by Invasion, this feeling [of not waging a war of slave liberation] Subsided and Judgment prevaled and the morale became strong again."[132] Another VI Corps veteran addressed the friendly relations between Yanks and blacks in a post-war memoir.

> Our northern soldiers had, by ... [1864], begun to look upon slavery in its true light. They had also learned that the negroes were their friends. It required a long schooling to teach them this lesson, but it was thoroughly learned at last. We heard now no jeering and hooting when a negro or wagon load of negroes went by. The soldiers treated them with the greatest kindness, and aided them in every way to get off to the north.[133]

Indeed many Yanks testified to the piety, intelligence and eloquence of the black. Evidence of these virtues tended to promote good will between the Federal soldier and the Southern black.

In his detailed narrative history, surgeon Stevens recalled that "many pleasant recollections cluster around the old camp at Brandy Station, which will never be effaced from the memory of the soldiers of the Army of the Potomac."[134] Unlike the first winter of the war near Alexandria and the previous winter at Fredericksburg, the encampment at Brandy Station featured several significant differences. First, recognizing the importance of hearth and home, the sprawling Union camp featured better infrastructure and well constructed, "comfortable, cosy and pleasant" huts for the soldiers. The individual camps were laid out according to regulations and company streets were "wide and neatly turnpiked." Most importantly, wooden walkways were constructed in each camp such that "one could step from any tent and traverse the entire encampment upon this walk."[135] In mid–January, nine men from the 96th Pennsylvania were detailed to erect a handsome log quarters for Major Lessig. Company G furnished the manpower to construct a corduroy sidewalk in front of the officer's quarters and along the company street.[136] In addition to building comfortable quarters with connecting walkways, the enterprising Yankees also constructed an opera house or entertainment hall, a chapel and a bridge connecting Upton's brigade with the rest of the VI Corps across Hazel River. Both the opera house and the chapel drew large audiences throughout the winter.[137]

Most importantly, however, as surgeon Stevens noted, "our camp near Brandy Station ... was the most cheerful winter we had passed in camp."[138] What differentiated the winter at Brandy Station from the winter at Camp Northumberland and White Oak Church was the presence of women resident in the camp throughout the winter. Major Lessig's wife was at Brandy Station during the month of February. Lieutenant Luckenbill recorded in his diary that "General Pleasanton, Col. McMahon, Colonel Upton and other with ladies rode through our camp."[139] Henry Keiser noted in his journal that "Colonel Upton inspected the camp, four ladies accompanying him, three in wagons and one on horseback."[140] Another officer later recalled the impact that the ladies had on the Brandy Station encampment.

> A new feature during our stay in that camp, was presented by the presence of many ladies in various commands, wives of both officers and men.... There were several ladies in our regiment; and certainly their presence carried much cheer, not only to their own companies, but to all of the boys. One could not help noticing the feeling of refinement which a single lady would exert over the entire command.[141]

As the winter near Brandy Station progressed, a variety of regimental issues confronted Lieutenant Colonel Lessig and his field officers. The first matter, pertaining to the field and staff officers, centered on the brigade band. After the discharge of the 96th Pennsylvania's musicians, the Pottsville Cornet Band, at the close of the Peninsula Campaign, it became incumbent upon the line officers of each regiment of the Second Brigade to fund the brigade band. To insure the continued services of the band, the fee, totaling in excess of one hundred sixty dollars, was quickly raised. Following on the heels of the cost for the brigade band was the unresolved issue concerning the post fund and sutler Gee. In order to settle this squabble, which plagued the regiment virtually from its inception, Lieutenant Colonel Lessig issued Regimental Order Number Sixty-nine, calling for convening a Council of Administration.[142] Presumably Lessig wanted the Council, composed of Captains Boyle, Huber and Severn, to review the existing problem and render a decision that would resolve the matter in a satisfactory fashion. It is not known, however, whether or not some agreement between the council and sutler Gee was reached. Perhaps the sudden movement of the VI Corps in late February disrupted the proceedings causing the council of administration to delay its decision indefinitely.

In late February a cavalry officer in the Army of the Potomac, Judson "Kill Cavalry" Kilpatrick, received permission from the War Department to conduct an ambitious raid upon Richmond.[143] Designed strictly as a cavalry operation, with the purpose of crippling supply and communication lines between the Rapidan and the James, disrupting the rebel government, and freeing the Union captives being held in large numbers in Richmond, the plan grew to include the support of infantry. On February 27 Sedgwick's VI Corps left its winter quarters and ponderously marched toward the Rapidan. The Greek Cross Corps, along with George A. Custer's cavalry, was entrusted with the task of creating a diversion that would give Lee the impression that his left flank was in danger of being turned. By February 28, Sedgwick's Bluecoats reached Robertson's River, where they built a bridge, and crossed for an overnight bivouac.[144] Custer and his command rode southward, after the flamboyant cavalry commander told Sedgwick to withdraw if he did not return by March 2. For two days the Union troops remained in position enduring icy rain and heavy mud awaiting Custer's return. On March 1, after Sedgwick reported Custer's safe return a day earlier than planned, the VI Corps withdrew from the south bank of Robertson's River as the rapidly rising stream threatened to isolate the Greek Cross troops.[145] After several sleepless nights and a twenty-three mile march over muddy lanes, the VI Corps returned to its winter campsites. The Bluecoat feint had been well executed and indeed quite successful. Kilpatrick's raid, however, was in the words of Sedgwick, "a great failure."[149]

During the second week of March, the boredom and monotony of camp life near Brandy Station was broken by the arrival of a soldier from the west. During the last week of the month U.S. Grant arrived at his new headquarters in Culpeper, Virginia. A veteran of the Second Brigade remarked, "General Grant was now in command of the army, and it was believed that when the army moved, it would be to some purpose."[150] The soldiers were eager "to try again the troublesome and difficult road which led 'on to Richmond.'"[151] In six weeks the Army of the Potomac would break camp at Brandy Station, march toward the river crossings and plunge into the wilderness. The final deadly act of the long war was about to begin.

XI

"The skirmishers were sent out ahead"

The winter encampment at Brandy Station witnessed a season of change within the Army of the Potomac. General Meade reorganized the army by consolidating the five corps into three. He appointed a new commander of the cavalry corps. Senior generals were transferred and replaced. In addition to these appointments, the new lieutenant general Ulysses S. Grant would accompany the Army of the Potomac in the upcoming spring campaign. Grant's presence with the army signaled a significant change in the conduct of future operations. Combat would become continuous rather than sporadic. In order to prepare for the renewal of battle, Grant issued orders to the army commanders to rigorously prepare the soldiers for the next offensive. Beginning in late March and continuing through April the veterans of the Army of the Potomac trained in target shooting, battalion drill, skirmish exercises and use of the bayonet in combat. In addition to preparing for battle physically, the soldiers also reaffirmed their commitment to defeating the Confederates on the battlefield. The former adjutant of the 96th spoke for the soldiers in a letter to Dear Sophie. "When the orders come we will obey them, and that if the orders lead us into a fight we will find it out when the fight commences, and that when the fight is over, we will likely know who is whipped."[1]

As the blustery March winds whipped through the camp of the 96th Pennsylvania, the Army of the Potomac and the whole Federal army were on the verge of a significant manpower problem. The service of 455 volunteer infantry regiments, almost half of the units in the entire Union army, would soon expire. The authorities in Washington realized that the war could not be won unless a substantial percentage of veteran volunteers consented to reenlist. The government, relying mostly on the ideal of the "Union cause" and the allegiance of the volunteers, could offer only a handful of meager inducements to reenlist: a four-hundred-dollar bounty (plus whatever sum a man's own city or county might be offering), a thirty-day furlough, the right to call oneself a "veteran volunteer," and a chevron that could be worn on the sleeve. If three-fourths of the men in any regiment reenlisted, the regiment could go home as a unit for a thirty-day furlough and retain its regimental number, its organization and its flag. In addition, the veteran volunteers would be privy to a share of the bounty money. (Adding state and Federal bounties together, a soldier who reenlisted stood to get about $700.) To persuade the volunteers to reenlist the Washington administrators engaged in a high profile advertising campaign and issued orders to the various regiments to detail the benefits that a "veteran volunteer" would receive.[2]

In his diary, Henry Keiser noted that the initial reenlistment offer was not enthusiastically received by the soldiers. "The officers are again trying to get us to reenlist but

212

the fish do not seem to bite very well."[3] Nevertheless, the opportunity to return home for a month, rather than a cash bounty, induced some men to reenlist. The 96th Pennsylvania, Lieutenant Luckenbill noted in his diary, "re-enlisted some two hundred veterans in the regiment today."[4] Reenlistments continued throughout the winter. Erasmus Reed reported to his family that "if 2/3 of an old Regiment reenlists they will be sent North to be recruited up to the required number."[5] For the veterans from Schuylkill County, the decision to reenlist was an easy choice. As one Bluecoat stated, "Reenlist? Yes. What tempted those men? Bounty. No. The opportunity to go home … the soldiers heart yearned for that place…. It was reenlistment—furlough—home."[6] Although at least half of the men whose time was about to expire refused to stay with the army, 26,767 volunteers in the Army of the Potomac did reenlist by the end of March.[7] To the War Department that meant that the Army of the Potomac would not be severely crippled just when Grant was starting to use it. In fact, upon his arrival Grant would tighten the army's administration, assess the rank and file and prepare the soldiers to face the foe. Near the end of April Grant informed Halleck, "The Army of the Potomac is in splendid condition and evidently feel like whipping somebody."[8] But before the lieutenant general reached Virginia, the soldiers continued to enjoy the splendid encampment spent near Brandy Station.

When Grant first arrived in Virginia, stories quickly appeared in the newspapers that "a letter from the Army of the Potomac says that an order has been issued directing that all ladies within the lines shall leave as early as practicable, and that no more passes shall be granted to such visitors."[9] General Grant disapproved of these stories and refused to take them seriously. In fact, Grant sought to prepare the Army of the Potomac for the field. After Grant took command, the 96th Pennsylvania engaged in endless regimental and brigade drills and much target practice. A circular from Meade's headquarters decreed that every soldier should be made to load and fire his weapon under supervision of an officer, as "it is believed there are men in this army who have been in numerous actions without ever firing their guns."[10] (Evidently this instruction was mandated by the ordnance officers who had collected hundreds of discarded muskets containing anywhere from two to a dozen unexploded cartridges. In the heat of battle the Bluecoats failed to notice that they had not pulled the trigger, reloaded a weapon that had not been fired, or forgot to cap their musket, thus pulling the trigger to no effect.) Grant was determined to improve the combat effectiveness of the

1st Lt. Frank W. Simpson, Company A. Promoted from first sergeant May 1, 1864. Transferred to 95th Pennsylvania October 18, 1864 (Ronn Palm collection).

army. Baseball games and horse races which amused the men during the month of March were replaced in April by a heavy tactical training regimen.[11]

The diaries of the soldiers, especially the entries in late April, while the army was encamped at Brandy Station, chronicle the drilling and training the soldiers received during this period. In the last two weeks of April, the Pennsylvanians participated in two significant reviews, drilled by company, battalion or regiment, seven times and were inspected four times, once by General Wright. In addition, the soldiers drilled in target shooting, an uncommon practice during the Civil War.[12] Henry Keiser noted in his diary that his company "had target shooting this forenoon. Our Company [G] put eight balls into a board sixteen inches square."[13] The drills the soldiers conducted, too, were not merely a series of parade ground evolutions. Lieutenant Luckenbill reported that Upton's brigade, in one instance, formed "in front of camp and deployed and skirmished through the woods to the Picket line and back again."[14] In addition, Luckenbill recorded in his diary that Company B participated in target practice on two occasions in April. Finally, James Treichler stated in his memoir that the Schuylkill Countians also conducted bayonet exercises. "We certainly had the advantage when it came to a fight with the bayonets [sic]; as the previous winter while at Brandy Station we had spent all our time when the weather would permit, in drill, and prided ourselves as being quite handy in that exercise."[15]

Along with drilling and training came the grand reviews. The military reviews of 1864 lacked the old McClellan touch. The pomp and flourish of the McClellan era was supplanted by the business-like marshaling of the troops before the new lieutenant general. On April 18, the 96th Pennsylvania, along with the rest of the VI Corps, was reviewed by Grant. According to one eyewitness Grant was mounted on a fine chestnut colored

horse and was in full military dress for the occasion. Unlike McClellan and Hooker, he did not appear to care whether anyone cheered him or not. The soldiers of the 96th Pennsylvania dutifully recorded the event in their diaries, but the grand review in front of Grant did not receive the commentary in their journals that the review the previous April, in the presence of Hooker and Lincoln, had. Imperceptibly, however, Grant brought a new spirit to the Army of the Potomac. Determination supplanted indifference. The training and drilling lessons learned in April would prove invaluable in May when the fighting commenced. As the soldiers readied themselves for the upcoming campaign, the War Department and General Meade carried out several reassignments in command.[16]

In late March, the reorganization of the Army of the Potomac was announced to the officers and soldiers. Most impor-

Lt. Gen. Ulysses S. Grant (author's collection).

tantly, Grant consolidated the army's five corps into three. Winfield S. Hancock commanded the II Corps, Gouverneur K. Warren the V Corps, and "Uncle" John Sedgwick retained command of the VI Corps. On April 30, when Sedgwick signed his "consolidated morning report," the VI Corps consisted of three divisions, containing eleven brigades, with some 24,413 effectives. Horatio G. Wright—upon whom Sedgwick relied with such confidence that he designated Wright as his successor—commanded the First Division. The First and Second Brigades were led, respectively, by Colonels Henry W. Brown and Emory Upton, while the Third and Fourth brigades were commanded by Brigadier Generals David A. Russell and Alexander Shaler. Brig. Gen. George Washington Getty assumed command of the Second Division, while Brig. Gen. James B. Ricketts was named to command the Third Division. On April 28, after all of the command reshuffling had been completed, Sedgwick relaxed at a sumptuous dinner given by an influential local Unionist John Minor Botts. All of the generals, including Grant, attended the affair. It was to be the last function on the social circuit for the winter encampment. All that remained was for Grant to issue marching orders.[17]

Early on the morning of May 2, the soldiers of the 96th Pennsylvania received orders to cross Hazel River and rejoin the main body of the Army of the Potomac. Once across the river, the pontoon bridge was taken up and the army began to move. On the afternoon of May 3, the supply wagons began to move, jolting clumsily toward the lower crossings of the Rapidan, Germanna and Ely's Fords, destined for the clearings at Chancellorsville. At 5 a.m., on May 4, the 96th, along with the other regiments in the VI Corps, formed into marching column and started toward Germanna Ford. Slowly, almost ponderously, the huge VI Corps began its march toward the river crossings. No doubt the soldiers knew, too, that the march to Germanna Ford signaled the beginning of the long awaited spring campaign. Indeed, the Pennsylvanians must have experienced a wide range of emotions as they tramped away from Brandy Station. The sky was clear, with a gentle spring breeze, and the woodlands shimmered with new green leaves, while the dogwood glistened in the morning light. Yet, surrounded by all of this natural beauty, death was lingering several miles away in an area known as the Wilderness; an area of second growth timber extending twelve miles from east to west and six miles from north to south. Here, within two days the two armies would clash in a violent, confusing battle. As Bruce Catton so eloquently stated, "The Army of the Potomac was beginning its last campaign; the curtain was going up on the terrible final act of the war."[18]

The Union cavalry took the lead, moving down through the camps to the Rapidan crossings. The infantry followed, singing songs and the brigade bands playing as the soldiers marched toward Germanna Ford. As the sun rose, the day grew warm. Many recruits, who had loaded themselves down with excessive equipment, discarded their overcoats in roadside ditches, figuring they would not need them again.[19] Straggling developed as many soldiers struggled to carry great loads on their backs. Upton's brigade tramped through Brandy Station at 6:30 and passed through Stevensburg at ten o'clock. Henry Keiser noted that "up to this place we traveled the same road which we travelled last fall to Mine Run."[20] A little past noon Grant crossed the Rapidan River at Germanna Ford, where he dismounted in front of an abandoned farmhouse and sat on the porch to watch Sedgwick's VI Corps go by. According to Keiser, the 96th Pennsylvania reached the Rapidan River at 3 p.m. and, "crossed on a pontoon bridge at Germania Ford."[21] Two miles below the ford, on the Germanna Plank Road, the VI Corps went into bivouac for the night. As the soldiers rested from their sixteen mile march from Brandy Station, Sedgwick sought his orders for the next day's march.[22]

At first light Grant planned to march his Bluecoats to the key road intersections in the Wilderness. Hancock, and the II Corps, were to make the longest march—a quick tramp south from Chancellorsville and then west, crossing the Brock Road at Todd's Tavern, across the Po River at Corbin's Bridge, and stopping in the vicinity of Shady Grove Church on the Catharpin Road. Warren was to take the V Corps southwest from Wilderness Tavern, and plant the vanguard of his column on the Plank Road at Parker's Store. Sedgwick, whose Greek Cross Corps was to make the shortest march, was instructed to advance from Wilderness Tavern and move his infantry west on the Orange Turnpike and await developments. Upon the columns reaching their objectives, Hancock was to extend his right to make contact with Warren's left, and the V Corps in turn was to make firm contact with Sedgwick. During this complicated operation, Burnside's IX Corps was expected to reach Germanna Ford, ready to reinforce any part of the Unionist line should a general engagement develop. On paper, the plan appeared sound. All that remained was to engage the enemy in battle.[23]

In the early morning grayness of May 5, Sedgwick's Bluecoats advanced in accordance to Grant's instructions. Shortly after 8 a.m. musket firing began in the area that was assigned to Warren's V Corps. As Warren maneuvered his brigades into position

This dramatic photograph depicts the last soldiers of the VI Corps to cross the Rapidan River at Germanna Crossing May 4, 1864. Gen. Sedgwick's VI Corps crossed using the pontoon bridges in the scene between 1 and 6p.m., headed toward the Wilderness, where Gen. Warren's V Corps was engaged. The photograph was composed by Timothy O'Sullivan (Library of Con-

south of the Orange Turnpike, Sedgwick's troops marched to support the right flank of the V Corps. Wright's division, the vanguard of Sedgwick's column, however, was slowed by heavy skirmish fire delivered by the 1st North Carolina Cavalry, as well as sharpshooters from Walker's "Stonewall Brigade."[24] Henry Keiser recalled in his diary the opening scene of the battle for the Pennsylvanians. "At 5 o'clock we got up, cooked coffee, and started off at six. The skirmishers were sent out ahead, and we advanced in a line of battle into the Wilderness … we advanced for two miles through the awfullest brush, briars, grapevines, etc. I ever was in. We soon met the enemy and the Battle of the Wilderness began."[25]

Not until 3 p.m. did Wright's division make contact with the V Corps, which was already engaged straddling the Orange Turnpike, and extend Warren's line north of the turnpike. Upon reaching Warren's area, Wright quickly deployed his division. Upton's brigade formed on the left of Wright's line, several hundred yards north of the turnpike. Brown's brigade anchored the center of the First Division line, while Russell's brigade held the right flank. As the 96th prepared to advance its battle line, the 18th Massachusetts, part of General Bartlett's V Corps brigade, came up from behind them and fired a volley into the ranks of the regiment, mistaking the Keystone troops for Graycoats. Several men of the unit were wounded in this tragic incident, which was not an infrequent occurrence in Civil War battles. Henry Keiser recalled the harrowing experience in his pocket diary.

> While in this position, the 39th [18th] Massachusetts coming up in our rear, mistook us for Rebels and fired a volley into us, wounding two of Company B. The balls struck all around me. Two balls passing down right by my breast as I turned to my right side to see what troops were coming, as we could hear them coming through the brush. As luck would have it for us, they, in their excitement, fired to[o] high.[26]

But the shock of this incident did not destroy the integrity of the regiment as a fighting force. Quickly, Lessig reorganized his line and stabilized the regiment, in a position behind a ridge. The carnage from the fighting that had taken place several hours before, in the V Corps sector, could be seen everywhere. A Federal officer noted in his report that "the ground … was strewn with wounded of both sides, many of whom must have perished in the flames, as corpses were found partly consumed."[27] Despite the horrors of the human wreckage that confronted the Pennsylvanians, the regiment, along with the other elements of Upton's brigade, maintained its position on the extreme left of the VI Corps.

In the evening, as the skirmish line firing died down, the sound of axes felling trees could be heard as the soldiers worked feverishly to construct log breastworks. Henry Keiser recalled that "four men of each Company were detailed to cut and carry timber to build rifle-pits tonight. The Rebels kept up a brisk fire all night in our front, but none of our Regiment were hurt."[28] Although the Greek Cross Corps had not made its weight felt, in the offensive against Ewell's left flank, the VI Corps did blunt an attack by two Confederate brigades and checked any further advance. It proved to be a workmanlike day for the VI Corps. Their efforts, although spirited, fell short of Grant's expectations. To insure success the next day, Grant instructed Meade's Chief of Staff, A. A. Humphreys, to send identical orders to Hancock, Warren and Sedgwick: "The attack ordered for tomorrow will begin at 5 a.m., instead of 4:30 a.m."[29]

At dawn Upton's brigade learned that the order for the early morning attack had been countermanded. Instead of fighting, the five-brigade front of Sedgwick's VI Corps spent the day shifting to the right, to make room for Griffin's division of the V Corps, and engaging the enemy in skirmish fire.[30] Lewis Luckenbill recorded in his diary that "half past four this morning the fighting was renewed. Heavy fighting all along the lines. 10:30 they shot grape and canister. We lay three lines deep behind a slope of a hill. Continued skirmish fire all day."[31] At 7 p.m., however, the relative calm that had characterized Sedgwick's sector throughout the day gave way to the thunderous fire of the Georgia brigade under the command of Gen. John B. Gordon. Just before nightfall, Gordon's brigade, supported by Gen. Robert Johnston's brigade of North Carolinians, launched a furious assault against Sedgwick's right flank. Suddenly the woods behind the Union right were littered with demoralized infantrymen and the noise of gunfire crackled closer to VI Corps headquarters.

The chaos and confusion on the Union right flank called for immediate action. Sedgwick ordered elements of Upton's and Morris' brigades to check Gordon's attack and restore order to that sector of the field. Upton instructed Col. James Duffy to lead the 121st New York and the 95th Pennsylvania, toward the imperiled area.[32] After dispatching his former regiment and Gosline's Zouaves, Upton decided to leave his main line, consisting of the 96th Pennsylvania and the 5th Maine, under the command of Col. William H. Penrose and personally lead the Bluecoats into battle.[33] Because of the dense forest undergrowth, the musket fire that swept across his line of advance, and the Unionists fleeing from the Confederate onslaught, Upton's operation broke down, forcing the colonel to reform his command in a set of rifle pits near Sedgwick's headquarters. Upton subsequently redeployed the two regiments in a line of trenches to the right of Morris' brigade, where he consolidated his position, as darkness again engulfed the Wilderness.[34]

The furious combat in the Wilderness resulted in just a few casualties for the 96th Pennsylvania. In the two-day battle the regiment lost one man killed, seven wounded and two captured or missing.[35] Death and dying, however, would exact a heavy toll on the Schuylkill County regiment during the course of the Overland campaign. The Wilderness proved to be just the first in a series of bloody battles which would blaze a trail from the Rapidan River near Fredericksburg to the James River outside Richmond. Throughout this ordeal the Pennsylvanians would confront the Butternuts time and again in a series of grueling battles. Along with the brutal battles, the soldiers would undertake a series of exhausting marches. When not battling the foe or recovering from the demanding movements of the army, they also contended with the elements and exposed themselves to other risks associated with campaigning in the Wilderness. James Treichler related an incident in his memoir which perhaps frightened one Schuylkill Countian more than the Secessionists.

> Co. H was one of the Color Companies locating it in the center of the Regiment.—at the right of this Company on the elevated ground stood a small Cedar tree with a goodly sized branch extending out over it.—The bullets were flying fast and thick and it was almost impossable to stand up at any length of time without being Plunked.—Among this foliage an enormous Black-snake was concealed from view.—A bullet or more bullets had no doubt cut this limb until the weight of the reptile caused it to break and precipitate mister Snake upon sergent H[ughes]. The sergent jumped and scampered around in much fright paying no attention to the Bullets.
>
> The snake took to the grass and disappeared from view. The Sergent thought he could stand a few bullets, but when they commenced shooting Snakes it was time to stampede. This goes to show how trifles sometimes effect men under trying circumstances.[36]

After two days of fighting and practically no sleep the men of the 96th Pennsylvania were unspeakably weary. Although the soldiers needed rest, combat, not calm, would characterize the third day of fighting. The morning fog of May 7, coupled with the heavy smoke from the brush fires in the Wilderness, rendered any type of visual reconnaissance impossible for the Army of the Potomac. Shortly after dawn, as Grant tried to assess his position and plan the army's next move, companies B and G of the 96th Pennsylvania were detailed as skirmishers along the VI Corps front.[37] Although Company G failed to make contact with the picket outposts, the detachment captured three members of the 26th Georgia. Some of the Bluecoats also fell prey to the same fate at the hands of the Confederates. Jerome Miller recorded in his diary that "early this morning our Company [G] and Co. B were sent out as skirmishers, and stayed out all day and night. Evan M. Gery was taken prisoner a while before dark."[38]

Pvt. David P. Thompson, Company H. Discharged on surgeon's certificate December 22, 1862 (Ronn Palm collection).

While companies B and G performed skirmish duty, the balance of the 96th constructed rifle pits along the VI Corps line. Sometime after breakfast Grant remarked to his staff that it looked like a drawn battle. Consequently, he forced Lee to come out from behind his entrenchments and wage a stand-up fight in the open country.

After talking with his staff officers, Grant ordered Meade to "make all preparations during the day for a night march to take position at Spotsylvania C.[ourt] H.[ouse] with one army corps, at Todd's Tavern with one, and another near the intersection of the Piney Branch and Spotsylvania road with the road from Alsop's to Old Court House."[39] Shortly after dark, on May 7, Sedgwick's VI Corps was ordered to pull out of line and proceed toward Spotsylvania Court House, situated south and east of the Wilderness at another strategic crossroad. According to Lieutenant Luckenbill, withdrawing and reorganizing the regiment from skirmish duty to marching column in the darkness added to the confusion accompanying the movement of the army. "At one o'clock at night we received orders to withdraw our skirmish lines and reassemble out in a field…. When we arrived there [we] could not find the Major [Lessig]. Waited about one and a half hours…. Marched off and struck the road [to the] Pike."[40] James Treichler recalled the difficulties soldiers and staff officers encountered during this difficult night march. "The night was so dark that it was impossible to see any thing; we were obliged to feel our way and keep in touch with the file next to us. A staff officer led the way through the wilderness with compass in hand, lighting a match now and then to know that we were following the right direction."[41]

Sedgwick's foot soldiers followed Warren's V Corps column by way of Chancellorsville and the Piney Branch Church Road to where it met the Brock Road. The march that night was a difficult one intended to carry out Grant's plan of moving to the left. Near dawn, as the exhausted Unionists of the VI Corps tramped toward the historic ruins of the Chancellor House, the men glimpsed the grim reality of the 1863 battle. According to a Maine veteran, the soldiers saw "large numbers of skeletons ... in the woods ... Union soldiers, where a leg or an arm showed itself ... reported as 'missing,' without enough earth to cover their bones."[42] According to Private Keiser, the 96th Pennsylvania was "on the road all last night, but did not make much headway. At daylight we passed over the old battlefield at Chancellorsville, and at 8 a.m. we stopped long enough [near Piney Branch Church] to cook coffee."[43] The sultry weather, dust and weariness of the Unionists caused many men to straggle. Compounding the problem of marching weary troops on a long forced march, along inadequate farm lanes, was a massive traffic jam at an obscure crossroads where Todd's Tavern was situated. After a delay of several hours, the road was finally cleared and the Yanks pushed on toward Spotsylvania.[44] As the march resumed, a brigade band struck up an old camp ditty, "Aint I Glad to Get Out of the Wilderness."

About 6:30 p.m., after a ragged march hindered by trees felled in the path of the Unionists, Sedgwick's troops formed a line of battle supporting the left of Warren's position.[45] As the 96th Pennsylvania wheeled into line, they noticed that a Rebel force was approaching their right flank. Quickly, Lessig's regiment, along with Gosline's Zouaves, was ordered to cut-off the advance of the oncoming Graycoats. Private Keiser recalled the movement of the 96th in his diary.

> We cut across an open field at a double-quick ... and got there before the Rebels, but in doing so
> we had to pass within rifle range of the Rebel breast-works and the bullets "zipped" past us thick
> and fast.[46]

Unfortunately, the efforts of the 96th Pennsylvania and the other Union regiments were not rewarded as Sedgwick's attack faltered in the darkness. As nightfall engulfed the Virginia countryside, the soldiers of the 96th Pennsylvania entrenched. The long night march and ensuing battle yielded only grim prospects for the Bluecoats once daylight returned. What the tired Unionists needed was a day of rest. Grant, however, wanted to continue his advance.[47]

May 9 was a day of preparation, during which Grant learned that Lee's Graycoats, entrenched as they were at Spotsylvania Court House, effectively blocked his line of march. Grant, after carefully reviewing the military situation, issued orders for a Bluecoat assault. The advent of nightfall and a change in the tactical deployment of Lee's forces spelled a missed opportunity for the Unionists and rendered a morning attack meaningless. During the day, while Hancock's II Corps maneuvered into position for an assault that was eventually canceled, the combat continued to smolder along the VI Corps front. On Warren's left, Sedgwick's corps strengthened its position, digging trenches and building gun emplacements while the Secessionists opposite them did the same. Throughout the morning a lively skirmish fire crackled up and down the line of the Greek Cross Corps. Undaunted by this rifle fire, Sedgwick personally conducted a reconnaissance of the VI Corps line where the exposure to the sharpshooters fire was greatest. Upon reaching an exposed angle between the V and VI Corps, Sedgwick sought to re-deploy the

14th New Jersey to develop a clear field of fire for a section of Battery A, 1st Massachusetts Light Artillery. While issuing his orders Sedgwick derided the accuracy of the Graycoat riflemen, stating that "they couldn't hit an elephant at this distance." Suddenly the burly general from Cornwall Hollow fell dead with a sharpshooter's bullet in his brain. Upon learning of the death of Sedgwick, Grant twice asked his aide, Colonel Horace Porter, "Is he really dead?"[48]

As word spread about Sedgwick, the Bluecoats of the VI Corps were shocked and saddened. After being embalmed, the general's body lay in state on a rustic bier over which the Unionists built a bower of evergreens.[49] In the 96th Pennsylvania, Private Keiser noted Sedgwick's passing in his diary with a rather straightforward statement: "Heard that Gen. Sedgwick, our Corps Commander, had been shot in the head by a Rebel sharp-shooter, killing him instantly."[50] Writing years after the war, James Treichler stated, "Early on the morning of the 9th of May, Gen. Sedgwick while placing his Artillery was killed by a Rebel sharp shooter. He was of jovial disposition and ready to take or perpetrate a joke with his Officers and even with the men in the ranks ... we knew he was reckless and brave, but the thought he would be killed never occurred to us.... The Sixth Corps had lost its Commander—The Army of the Potomac had lost a brilliant and courageous soldier."[51] Although the death of Sedgwick was a tragic event, the soldiers did not have time to properly mourn the fallen leader. Grant, still looking for a soft spot in Lee's line, issued orders for Wright and Warren to probe the center of the Confederate line the next day. The assault Grant originally intended, however, never materialized. Instead, Emory Upton revolutionized Civil War tactics through a bold and daring attack against the enemy entrenchments.[52]

The sudden, unexpected death of Sedgwick stunned the soldiers of the VI Corps and caused a series of promotions to fill the void left by the fall of the gallant "Uncle John." General Wright, Sedgwick's hand-picked successor, assumed the duties as chief of the VI Corps. Wright's promotion left open his former position as head of the First Division of the VI Corps. The vacancy was filled by another promising Union officer, David Allen Russell. Born in 1820, in Salem, New York, Russell graduated from West Point, near the bottom of his class, in 1845.[53] In late January 1862, he was promoted colonel of the 7th Massachusetts Volunteers. Nelson Hutchinson, the historian of the 7th Massachusetts, stated that Russell was a "sterling officer and man!" In addition, Hutchinson proclaimed, "as a colonel, he had no equal; as

Brig. Gen. David A. Russell. Commanded 1st Division, VI Corps. Killed in action at 3rd Battle of Winchester, September 19, 1864 (author's collection).

a leader of a brigade he was superb; and, as a division commander, brilliant and almost unequalled."[54] In late November of that year, he was appointed brigadier general and commanded the Third Brigade in the First Division of the VI Corps. He greatly distinguished himself a year later in the planning and executing the daring assault at Rappahannock Station. By the spring of 1864, Russell was a rising star in the VI Corps and the Army of the Potomac.[55]

The tactical problem that confronted Grant at Spotsylvania was easy enough to identify. The old-style linear assault, soldiers advancing in line of battle with elbow touching elbow, on an entrenched position could no longer be successfully executed. The evolution of trench warfare, coupled with the development of rifle muskets, rendered defensive works virtually impregnable.[56] According to Gen. Andrew A. Humphreys, fieldworks of this nature perhaps quadrupled the strength of a defensive line. Commenting on the Confederate position at Spotsylvania, Meade's chief of staff declared that the entrenchments were constructed "in a manner unknown to European warfare, and, indeed, in a manner new to warfare in this country."[57] For three miles the log-and-dirt breastworks of Lee's troops were studded with cannon at critical points. Traverses at right angles to provide cover against enfilading fire from artillery, and head logs afforded riflemen a protective slit through which they could take aim at attacking soldiers. Where there were woods in front of the line, trees were slashed to deny concealment for two hundred yards or more, and where ever the ground was open, timber barricades, called abatis, or chevaux-de-frise were erected within easy musket range, bristling with sharpened stakes to slow the attackers, allowing the defenders to fire at them. Grant realized the grim prospects of carrying these works by a frontal assault, but decided that it was an attack that must be made.

The military situation at Spotsylvania hardly favored a Bluecoat attack. The fundamental problem involved in a linear attack, the formation commonly used during the Civil War, was that long, thin lines presented an easy target for troops on the defensive. Before the introduction of the easily loaded rifle musket this was unimportant, because the enemy could fire its smoothbore pieces with deadly accuracy only when the attackers were within a distance of 100 to 125 yards. During the Civil War, however, the widespread use of the fast-loading rifle musket, which was longer ranged and more accurate than the smoothbore, rendered the linear attack an assaulting formation little short of murder. The defensive riflemen could begin firing when the attackers were approximately 500 yards away, and discharge eight or ten volleys in five minutes. Learning that his corps was going to make an assault on the Confederate works, Emory Upton viewed the proposed operation as his first opportunity to make an important reform in the field of tactics where, at least in his opinion, the army most needed improvement. Upton believed strongly that he had conceived a plan that, if properly executed, would allow the Yankees to break through the Rebel entrenchments. On the afternoon of May 10, Upton presented his proposal.[58]

Upon returning from an examination of the Confederate fortifications, Upton reported to his new division commander, Brig. Gen. David Russell, how the Bluecoats could breach the Rebel entrenchments. Upton believed that in order to successfully storm an entrenched position, the attacking troops had to move quickly. To stop and fire a volley, standard procedure at that time, was to lose the element of surprise and incur substantial casualties. Upton advocated that the strike force attack on a narrow front, four lines deep, without pausing to fire their weapons until a penetration into the Confederate works had been gained. Achieving a break in the Confederate defenses, the first line of Bluecoats would fan out left and right to widen the gap, while the second line would plunge straight ahead to deepen it, supported by the third and fourth waves, which would form the reserve and be called upon as needed. Russell liked what he heard and took Upton to see Wright, who also endorsed the operation. Grant and Meade listened to the proposal, too, and thought so highly of the plan that they told Wright to give Upton twelve regiments to use in his attack, and arrange to have a full division standing by ready to exploit whatever success was achieved.[59]

During the Civil War, important tactical changes most often came from brigade or regimental commanders who were close to the fighting and knew first-hand the effect of rifle fire and entrenchments, which greatly enhanced the ability of defensive troops to break an attack. Upton, although unwilling to abandon completely the firepower that a linear attack offered, believed that due to the devastating effects of rifles and entrenchments, it was more important to come to grips quickly with the enemy than achieve maximum firepower. In time Upton developed the idea of attacking enemy works in column formation. He realized his plan restricted the firepower of the assaulting column, while greatly exposing the attacking troops to flanking fire. The advantages to Upton's proposal, however, were great. By initiating their charge from close up, the attackers reduced the number of volleys they would receive while the weight of the column would force an opening in the enemy's lines which could be exploited to create flanks where none had existed. Further, the column would put enough men through the enemy lines to enable the attackers to hold their gains. Several officers suggested tactical changes, but Upton's plan was accepted because of his past accomplishments and reputation. Now it was Upton's responsibility to execute and lead the assault.[60]

Early in the morning of May 10, Upton met with Martin T. McMahon, the VI Corps chief of staff. McMahon pulled from his pocket a list of twelve regiments and asked, "What do you think of that for a command?" Upton replied, "Golly, Mack, that is a splendid command. They are the best men in the army." McMahon then told Upton that he was to use these hand-picked troops to conduct his attack in column. The chief of staff added, Upton ... if you do not carry [the enemy works] you are not expected to come back, but if you carry them I am authorized to say that you will get your stars." To that Upton responded, "Mack, I will carry those works. If I don't I will not come back." As Upton rode away from the meeting, the young colonel turned to McMahon and shouted, "I'll carry those works. They cannot repulse those regiments."[61]

After speaking with McMahon, Upton and Russell, along with Capt. Ranald S. Mackenzie of the Engineers, met at the jump-off point for the attack, the edge of a belt of pines 150 yards from the rebel works, where the group examined the terrain. The point of attack for the operation was a point along the western face of a salient which Ewell's corps had constructed to deny the Federals possession of some high ground. To get to the enemy's works the Bluecoats would have to cross a field which sloped up toward the salient which the Rebels called the "Mule Shoe."[62] In this case, the distance between the Union staging area and the Confederate line was, according to Upton "about 200 yards."[63] Other eyewitnesses, many of whom participated in the celebrated charge, estimated the distance from the pine woods, used as the staging point for the attack, to the Confederate fortifications to be as little as 100 to a maximum of 300 yards from the line of timber.[64]

Given the available documentation, the distance between the Unionists and the Confederates was most likely between 125 to 150 yards. In front of the salient were heavy lines of abatis, with the sharpened stakes pointing toward the Federals. The main Confederate trench line was a dozen paces beyond the formidable abatis. Enhancing the Graycoat lines of logs and banked-up earth were heavy traverses, mounds of dirt running back at right angles from the main embankment, built at frequent intervals to provide protection from enfilade fire. The Mule Shoe itself was 1,300 yards deep and 1,150 yards wide in the vicinity of the McCoull house, located within the "Mule Shoe."

In his official report, dated September 1, 1864, Emory Upton stated that the Confederate "position was in an open field about 200 yards from a pine wood," where he formed his division for the assault.[65] Other eyewitnesses, however, recorded different estimates of the distance between the edge of the pine forest and the Confederate field fortifications. Three postwar accounts state that the distance from the pine trees to the entrenchments was as little as one hundred yards. Henry Keiser of the 96th Pennsylvania judged, from his vantage point in the front rank, that "the Rebels were about two hundred yards away." In the same entry in his diary, however, Keiser later recorded that his regiment "had to charge across an open field about 150 yds. wide."[66] Two soldiers serving

with the 121st New York stated that it appeared to them that the distance between the vanguard of the attack column and the Confederate line was 300 yards.[67] Another soldier, also in the front rank with the 5th Maine, recorded that the field between the Unionists and Graycoats was 250 yards.[68] James Treichler, in his detailed memoir, recalled that "between these works and the starting point was an open field sloping to the works of probably Four hundred yards."[69] Several Confederate soldiers, too, noted the distance between their position and the pine forest in their immediate front. An artillerist with the 3rd Richmond Howizters stated that "immediately in our front, and 300 yards from our line of works, was a body of piney woods."[70] A member of the 44th Georgia recalled that "we constructed a line of breastworks in the edge of an old pine field. In our front was a broom-sedge field, gradually sloping to a branch some two hundred and fifty yards away."[71] Finally, an infantry soldier serving with the 4th Georgia noted that "we threw up breastworks on the edge of a small clearing which sloped gently to a dense thicket about two hundred yards in front."[72]

Capt. Edwin L. Severn, Company K. Promoted from first lieutenant, Company C, March 19, 1864. Discharged from service August 17, 1864, for wounds received at Spotsylvania, Virginia, May 10, 1864 (National Museum of Health and Medicine).

Upton's estimate of the distance, along with the observation made by the soldier serving with the 4th Georgia, positioned at the point of the salient, both concluded that the span of ground separating the opposing forces was 200 yards.[73]

Awaiting Upton's attack were Maj. Gen. Edward Johnson's "Stonewall Division" and part of Maj. Gen. Robert E. Rodes' division. Twenty-two guns provided artillery support for these first-rate troops of General Ewell's Second Corps. To be sure, the Confederate position was an imposing one. (As Upton and his lieutenants surveyed the situation, Ewell, the one-legged general, was strengthening his position by constructing a second line along the southern base of the salient.) The vanguard of Upton's strike force would crash into the three Georgia regiments commanded by the capable George P. Doles, whose brigade was positioned on a slight knoll, offering the Butternuts an open field of fire. In this sector of the Confederate works, the line bulged out slightly from the principal Confederate position forming a salient, the target of Colonel Upton's proposed attack.[74]

Doles commanded four Georgia regiments, one of which, the 21st Georgia, was on detached duty in Southside Virginia. He arrayed the remaining three regiments from left to right as follows: 44th Georgia, 4th Georgia and 12th Georgia. One company of the 21st Georgia was also assigned a position within the brigade line. According to a member of the 44th Georgia, the three regiments, at the start of the campaign numbered 1,567 officers and men. The deadly fighting in the Wilderness, principally the engagement of May 5, exacted a toll of approximately 210 Georgians killed and wounded. On May 10, the three Georgia regiments, and one company of the 21st Georgia, would defend the Confederate line, which would become known as Doles' Salient, with approximately 1,350 muskets. To the left of the Georgians was the North Carolina brigade under Junius Daniel and four guns of the 3rd Richmond Howitzers, commanded by Capt. Benjamin Smith. Extending Doles' line to the right was the vaunted "Stonewall Brigade," composed of five stalwart and distinguished Virginia regiments of infantry led by Brig. Gen. James "Stonewall Jim" Walker.[75]

About 8 o'clock, shortly after the meeting between Martin McMahon and Emory Upton, artillery fire erupted along the lines. This deadly artillery exchange was merely a prelude to the bloody encounter later in the afternoon. According to one Bluecoat, who endured the battery fire, "During all the battles in the Wilderness, artillery had been useless … but now all the artillery on both sides was brought into the work. It was the terrible cannonading of Malvern Hill with the fierce musketry of Gaines Mill combined, that seemed fairly to shake the earth and skies."[76] Lieutenant Luckenbill noted in his diary that at "quarter after 8 artillery commenced to play on each other. At ten they sent a shell into the woods where we lay. At 10:30 a shell exploded in our lines. Wounded Capt. Ed. Severn Co. K, Lt. Mackay Co. B, Corporal Brennan and three other men of Company K…. Terrible cannonading…. Heavy firing all along the line."[77] Henry Keiser reported that the shell which struck Company K wounded seven men. Adding further in his diary he stated, "This afternoon our Regiment was moved behind the brow of a hill to protect us from the enemy shells. Our batteries succeeded in silencing their guns in our immediate front."[78] The artillery round which exploded within the ranks of Company K, however, was quite simply a missile of death. Surgeon Bland later reported that "the shot wounded seven men, four of whom died in a few hours." One of the severely wounded soldiers was the 27-year-old captain of Company K, Edwin Severn.[79]

In the darkness of the pine forest, Capt. Edwin L. Severn of the 96th Pennsylvania awaited the services of one of the VI Corps surgeons. Earlier in the morning, he had been wounded, "by the explosion of case-shot, fired from the guns of the enemy while the command [was] resting in line of battle." Captain Severn's injury to his right shoulder required immediate medical attention. According Dr. Bland, who had previously served as the surgeon of the 96th Pennsylvania and was currently acting as the VI Corps Medical Inspector, "A portion of the shell had passed through the top of the shoulder, carrying with it a considerable portion of the clavicle and superior part of the scapula."[80] The surgeon then conferred with several other medical officers, and they reached a unanimous conclusion to remove the arm at the shoulder joint. After Bland selected a surgical team, he began the operation under the light of a half dozen candles. By Civil War medical standards, the operation went exceedingly well. Three weeks later, Severn was sent north and placed in the Officer's Hospital in Georgetown. For the young captain the Civil War was over. For the 96th Pennsylvania, however, the terrors of Spotsylvania were just beginning.

XII

"Forward, double quick! Charge!"

Only six days into the spring campaign and it was apparent to many participants that the traditional offensive tactics were no match for the formidable field fortifications shielding Lee's army from the futile Bluecoat assaults. No longer could an attacking force close within musket range, deliver a series of volleys, rush the defenders, and overpower them in hand-to-hand combat. Consequently, an innovative idea emerged, principally developed by Colonel Upton, advocating that an attack, made in column, without the soldiers firing their muskets until they breached the enemy's line, offered a better opportunity for success. In addition, once the strike force was physically inside the enemy's works, the bayonet was to be used extensively and officers anticipated hand-to-hand fighting of the highest intensity. Bayonet charges, while infrequent, were not a radical idea in the Army of the Potomac. The first highly publicized bayonet charge was achieved by the brigade of Hancock "the Superb" at Williamsburg. Subsequently, General Slocum's division over-ran a Confederate brigade with a well executed bayonet assault at Crampton's Gap. Gen. Andrew A. Humphreys conducted a bayonet charge at Fredericksburg, but his men failed to reach the stone wall, protecting the Confederate defenders, below Marye's Heights. The most dramatic and successful bayonet attack, planned and executed by David Russell and Emory Upton, was at Rappahannock Station in early November 1863. Now, in early May 1864, Russell and Upton were once again asked to collaborate and test the tactical lessons they learned from their previous experiences.[1]

The twelve hand-picked regiments presented by McMahon to Upton for the operation included a number of veteran units familiar with attacking across open fields, breaching defensive positions and executing bayonet charges. Most of the twelve regiments on McMahon's list had participated in successful bayonet charges during their service with the VI Corps. Four regiments, the 6th Maine, 43rd New York, 49th Pennsylvania and 5th Wisconsin, had executed a gallant bayonet charge, during the Battle of Williamsburg, under the command of "Hancock the Superb." In a telegram to the Secretary of War, sent immediately after the battle, General McClellan wrote that "Hancock has taken two redoubts and repulsed Early's brigade by a real charge with the bayonet, taking 1 colonel and 150 prisoners, killing at least 2 colonels and as many lieutenant colonels and many privates."[2] The official casualty reports state that Hancock's brigade sustained 82 killed and wounded while Early's Confederates suffered 287 in killed, wounded and captured. While Hancock's charge brought him fame, and received significant coverage in the newspapers, the bayonet attack as a military tactic received scant attention from Union generals. Further, bayonet charges as a tactical innovation, would evolve slowly over time, but would emerge as a specialty tactic in the ranks of the VI Corps.[3]

Four months after the bayonet attack at Williamsburg, Henry Slocum's division executed a similar charge, on a larger scale, at Crampton's Gap. In this engagement the 5th Maine and the 96th Pennsylvania, part of Bartlett's brigade, were instrumental in this successful assault. In his after-action report, Bartlett recounted that once he issued "the command ... to 'Charge,' ... our whole line advanced with cheers, rushing over the intervening space to the stone wall and routing the enemy."[4] Also involved in this battle, playing a minor role in the attack at the base of South Mountain, was the 95th Pennsylvania, assigned to Gen. John Newton's Third Brigade. In his official report, Newton stated, "After a fusillade of about one hour and a half ... the order to charge was given, in which the ... infantry of the division ... were engaged. The charge was short and decisive, and the enemy was driven from his stronghold in a very few moments."[5] In both instances, Williamsburg and Crampton's Gap, the bayonet charge was conducted in similar style delivering resounding success to the attackers and vanquishing the defenders. Each assault was also similar in regard to formation, terrain and tactical approach by the field commanders to achieve maximum results. Hancock and Slocum initially deployed their men in the standard linear battle line and double-quicked across the fields to close on the enemy. After the Bluecoats were within close proximity to the Confederate defenders, the Unionists delivered several volleys before charging with fixed bayonets and routing the Secessionists with cold steel. Each bayonet assault resulted in heavy casualties for the vanquished Confederates and relatively modest losses for the victorious Bluecoats. In both engagements, the bayonet charges achieved decisive results for the Yankees and demoralized the Graycoats. At Crampton's Gap, Slocum's division sustained 511 killed and wounded while the Butternuts lost about 1,100 in killed, wounded and captured.[6]

Late in the morning on May 3, 1863, elements of the VI Corps, prepared to finish the bayonet assault which the gallant men of Andrew Atkinson Humphreys aborted during the bitter December battle at Fredericksburg. The terrain at Fredericksburg was remarkably similar to the ground Slocum's division encountered at Crampton's Gap in September 1862. There was a wide open field which sloped gently toward a long stone wall situated at the base of Marye's Heights which commanded the battlefield at Fredericksburg as South Mountain did at Crampton's Gap. Two Confederate brigades, Mississippians under Gen. William Barksdale and Louisianans commanded by Gen. Harry Hays, blocked the advance of two divisions of the VI Corps. To break the thin line of Graycoats standing defiantly against the Unionists, the VI Corps commanders determined to conduct a series of coordinated frontal assaults culminating in a bayonet charge to dislodge the Secessionists. Unlike the charge at Williamsburg and the attack at Crampton's Gap, where the Bluecoats initially deployed in a conventional line of battle, at Fredericksburg a column formation four regiments deep would be utilized for the operation.[7]

Below Fredericksburg, Gen. Albion Howe arrayed his division for the impending assault. In his official report, Howe stated, "I opened my artillery fire with full force, and advanced two columns under [Gens. Thomas] Neill and [Lewis] Grant, with the bayonet, upon Cemetery Hill."[8] The assault, conducted with nine regiments, successfully broke through the Confederate line, routing the 17th Mississippi in the process. A Vermont soldier recalled the charge in a postwar memoir. "The order was to move at double-quick across the plain, push straight up the heights, and carry the works at the point of the bayonet. At [the] signal the storming columns started together ... [and] advanced over three quarters of a mile [across] … open ground, commanded … by the enemy's batteries; driving the enemy's infantry from their breastworks at the base of the hill."[9]

Along the narrow streets of the old colonial town, Col. George Spear aligned four additional regiments intent upon striking the left flank of the Confederate line. While standing in column, a tactical change from the linear formation, along William Street, Colonel Spear issued specific orders concerning the conduct of the attack. One participant recorded that, the tactical movement was planned as follows: "both regiments [61st Pennsylvania and 43rd New York] … were to charge the rebel works. Neither regiment was to do any firing, both to rely on the cold steel and move double quick."[10] A soldier serving with the 43rd New York recalled the details of the charge in a letter written two weeks after the battle.

> We had first to take the caps off the guns, so that the men should not fire, for on the bayonet alone were they to depend…. We fairly astounded them and before they recovered from their astonishment at seeing a handful of men spring in among them, the bayonet and butt of the gun were doing their terrible work.[11]

To the left of Colonel Spear's column, Col. Hiram Burnham, commanding the "Light Division," arrayed his Bluecoats for an assault against the infamous stone wall at the base of Marye's Heights. Prior to the assault, Col. Thomas Allen, commanding the 5th Wisconsin, addressed the men: "When the order 'Forward' is given, you will start at double quick—you will not fire a gun—you will not stop until you get the order to halt! *You will never get that order!*"[12] According to the historian of the 6th Maine, "The men rushed forward at double-quick, with arms a port."[13] A soldier in the 5th Wisconsin recalled that "shot, shell and canister tore through the ranks of the gallant storming party, but without stopping to return a shot, the band of heroes rushed on, surmounted the stonewall, where they bayoneted some of the foe and scattering the others like chaff."[14] Finally, writing after the war, Adjutant Charles Clark of the 6th Maine described the climax of the battle. "There was a hand to hand fight at this point of short duration, and the enemy was routed. It is not true that bayonets were never crossed during the war. They were used at the stone wall, by our men, and after the battle it was found, by actual count, that forty of the enemy had been bayoneted here."[15] Casualties in this engagement were virtually equal, but once again a well-executed bayonet assault proved to be an efficient, successful and formidable tactic for the attackers.[16]

The tactical assaults conducted by the soldiers of the VI Corps at the Second Battle of Fredericksburg introduced several new features to improve the capability and enhance the success of the bayonet charges. First, the men were arranged in column, rather than battle line, prior to starting the attack. Next, the soldiers were specifically instructed to remove the caps from their rifle muskets, insuring that the men could not discharge their weapons. In addition, the advance across the field, although swept by Confederate fire, was made at the double-quick, without stopping, reducing the time the defenders had to load and deliver volleys in order to disrupt the oncoming columns. Finally, the soldiers were told that once they breached the Confederate position to anticipate hand-to-hand fighting and to use the bayonet to finish the assault. Adjutant Clark of the 6th Maine later stated, "I do not think that the Sixth Maine fired a single musket until we were inside the enemy's line of works. Our success was glorious…. In … less than five minutes which elapsed from the time we started upon the charge until our flag floated in victory over the heights which had been thought impregnable."[17] Despite the overwhelming success of the assault, converging fire inflicted significant casualties upon the Bluecoats as they plowed their way across the field toward the Confederate position. Perhaps a young, innovative tactician could further refine the technique of the evolving bayonet charge in the next battle.[18]

Six months after the Battle of Second Fredericksburg, Emory Upton was afforded an opportunity to plan and execute another bayonet charge against Confederate field fortifications at Rappahannock Station. In this engagement, Upton, in charge of a brigade, collaborated with Gen. David Russell, temporarily commanding the First Division of the VI Corps. Together, the two enterprising officers believed a unique opportunity arose to successfully storm the Confederate works defended by the Louisiana brigade under Harry Hays and a brigade of Tarheels commanded by Col. Archibald C. Godwin. Initially, General Wright, temporarily commanding the VI Corps, "hesitated in ordering the assault of so strong a position."[19] Upton and Russell, however, convinced Wright that he was wrong and the VI Corps chief relented and authorized, "the assault with part of the troops of his [Russell's] division, the rest being held ready to re-enforce the storming party."[20] Like the attack at Marye's Heights, the soldiers' weapons were uncapped and the advance was made at the double-quick. In addition to these technical matters, Upton and Russell incorporated several new features in this operation designed to enhance the opportunity for success by the strike force.[21]

Preceding the assault, General Wright ordered the Union artillery "to keep up a rapid and continuous fire till the attacking force reached the works." Also, prior to the opening of the artillery bombardment, a strong Bluecoat skirmish line was ordered to advance and clear the field of Secessionists which might impede the advance of the principal attack force. According to General Russell, "The advance was made in gallant style, and driving in the skirmishers of the enemy, our skirmish line at once occupied and held a position at the foot of the hill upon which were situated the two redoubts."[22] Near dusk, Upton and Russell pushed forward and positioned their respective brigades for the final assault. In this movement, Upton reported that his brigade "advanced at quick time to within 30 yards of the [Confederate] works."[23] Using the cover of darkness to conceal the attack, Upton issued explicit orders to the men of the 5th Maine and the 121st New York "to charge the enemy at the double-quick, without firing."[24] Cleveland Campbell of the 121st New York recalled the climatic moments of the battle in a letter written two weeks after the engagement.

> Col. Upton in command of the line. Double columns were formed; muskets were loaded the step changed to double-quick. Fifty rods from the works the columns were deployed; twenty-five rods farther [a] halt was ordered; knapsacks were unslung; "forward, double quick, march," shouted the colonel, and the two regiments had, in five minutes more, accomplished their work without firing a shot and thanks to the darkness with slight loss.[25]

The bold and courageous charge at Rappahannock Station earned plaudits for both Russell and Upton. In his report, General Wright stated, "To Brigadier-General Russell is due the credit of leading his troops gallantly to the attack, and of carrying, I believe, the first intrenched position of importance during the war on the first assault."[26] In turn, General Russell commended Upton. In his after-action report, Russell wrote, "Colonel Upton ... led ... the assault upon the rifle-pits with unexampled coolness, steadiness, and bravery. At the bayonet's point they overcame the enemy everywhere, and resistance was speedily over."[27] The assault resulted in the Unionists capturing 103 commissioned Confederate officers and 1,200 enlisted men. Conversely, the Bluecoats suffered 328 casualties in the heroic endeavor.[28] As a result of this magnificent achievement, Russell and Upton, along with the Union high command, recognized the potential of such assaults. No doubt, Russell and Upton hoped that they could employ the tactical lessons learned at Rappahannock Station on a future battlefield. At Spotsylvania, on May 10, 1864, they were afforded the opportunity to collaborate again and employ the tactical innovations that served them so well the previous autumn.

The tactical planning that unfolded during the day of May 10, developed primarily by a handful of Union officers, was remarkable in its attention to detail. The careful selection of the staging and the choreographing of the role each infantry unit was to play in the attack, underscored the thorough preparation given to the assault. Identifying Doles' salient, on the western face of the Mule Shoe as the point of attack, was also critical to the success of the operation. Several additional features, related to terrain, added to the initial observations by officers such as Captain Mackenzie, that the sector of the Confederate line defended by the Georgians of Brig. Gen. George Doles was the most promising military target. This segment of the Mule Shoe, although strongly defended by veteran combat soldiers, was lightly supported by artillery. Only Capt. Benjamin Smith's battery, consisting of four guns, of the 3rd Richmond Howitzers, guarded the approach to Doles' salient. Striking the point of the salient, too, would prevent the Secessionist infantry from delivering converging fire upon Upton's column as it moved at the double-quick across the field toward the Confederate field fortifications. In addition, the pine forest, with its ravines, afforded the Unionists a natural staging area where they could concentrate for the assault in proximity to the Confederate line without being detected. Furthermore, in order to insure that his strike force was concealed from view by the enemy, Upton sent out a reinforced skirmish detail to clear the field between the Confederate works and the Union staging area. Inexplicably, Doles did not attempt to push the Yankee skirmishers back toward the pine forest and regain control of the field in his front. This subtle movement, often overlooked in significance in accounts of the battle, was critical to the initial success of the attack. Concealing his division from observation and controlling the ground between the lines enabled Upton to retain the element of surprise and afforded his column clear passage across the field.[29]

Late in the afternoon, on May 10, the twelve regiments selected for the assault, assembled at the staging area concealed in the pine woods opposite Doles' salient. As the Bluecoat officers studied the Rebel works, Upton explained his plan of attack. According to one officer, he "left nothing to chance, and trusted nothing to mere luck, but provided for everything."[30] The young colonel explained that the success of the assault depended upon speed and precision. After quickly charging across the ground separating Yankee from Confederate, and breaching the rebel entrenchments, the Bluecoats needed to move swiftly to overwhelm the gun crews of the Confederate artillery before they could swing into action. Having shown the individual unit commanders their objectives on a map, as well as pointing out specific terrain features, Upton ordered them to bring their troops forward, one unit at a time, to avoid attracting attention to the concentration of Bluecoats, and form as instructed for the impending assault. The attack was rescheduled for 6 p.m., one hour before sunset and two before dark.[31]

Historians who have studied Upton's assault, generally agree, although based on very little evidence, that his strike force numbered approximately 5,000 men in the twelve hand-picked regiments. An exhaustive search of contemporary letters and diaries, however,

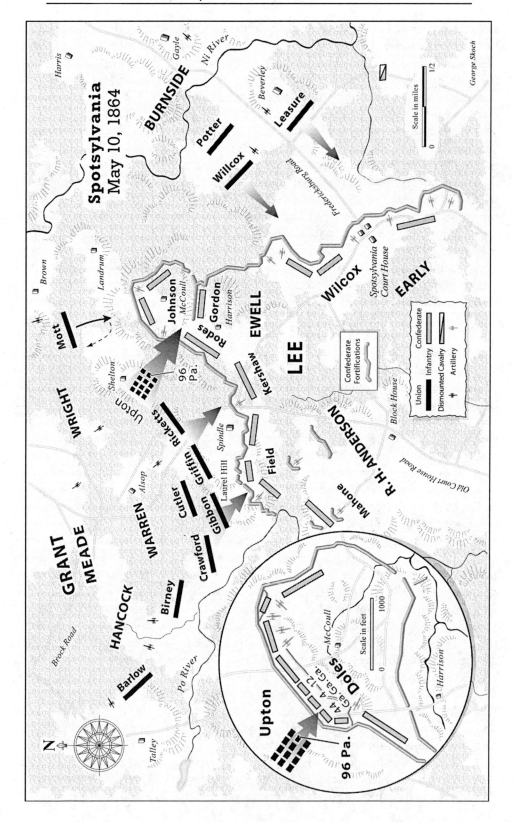

Spotsylvania
May 10, 1864

reveals unofficial strength reports for ten regiments of Upton's command. After examining and evaluating the contemporary accounts, and some postwar reports, the documentation reveals that Upton's division numbered less than 4,500 men rather than the accepted figure of 5,000 muskets.[32] While the evidence points in this direction, only by a thorough examination of the official morning reports, most likely submitted May 1, 1864, along with a careful review of the casualty rolls from May 5 to 9, can a precise strength report for Upton's command be compiled and documented. Regardless of the number of men assigned to him for the assault, however, Upton was confident he could lead the men to victory in the dramatic charge he sought to undertake. On the eve of the Battle of Rappahannock Station, Upton revealed to his brother his understanding of the relationship between the soldier in the ranks and the officer at the head of the column.

> No soldier in the world can equal the American, if properly commanded.... He only wants a general who can call out his good qualities, or one who comprehends his nature. I think our generals betray in some instances total ignorance of human nature. They fail to appeal to the emotions or passions of their men.... I have never seen them ride along the lines and tell each regiment that it held it *to the last*. I have never heard them appeal to the love every soldier has for his colors or to his patriotism. Neither have I ever seen a general thank his troops after the action for the gallantry they have displayed.
>
> My brief experience has taught me the value of a few words.[33]

As the regiments massed at the staging area, near the Shelton house, Upton divided them into three lines, four regiments deep. The 121st New York, on the right front of the first line, and the 96th Pennsylvania, in the center of the front line, were instructed to wheel to their right as soon as they gained the enemy works, and charge the Confederate batteries. The 5th Maine, on the front left of the first wave of attackers, was to change front to left and open an enfilading fire upon the enemy. The second line of three regiments was to halt at the entrenchments and concentrate their fire to the front. The third line of attackers was to support the second wave. The fourth line, composed of three Vermont regiments, was instructed to advance to the edge of the wood used as the staging area, lie down, and be prepared to advance through a breach, if the assault was successful, or to meet a counterattack if it was not. At 5 p.m. the Bluecoats were ordered to unsling their knapsacks. The time for the attack was near.[34]

From the perspective of the infantry soldiers, the hours prior to the assault were spent getting into position, enduring Confederate artillery fire and managing the stress and tension associated with impending combat. The men of the 96th Pennsylvania, veteran soldiers with significant battlefield experience, were well suited to spearhead Upton's strike force from the front rank. Lieutenant Colonel Lessig had the confidence of the rank and file, due principally to his leadership of the regiment at Salem Church the previous May and later in the early autumn at Rappahannock Station. Henry Keiser described the events preceding the infantry charge. "The Rebels shelled us considerably this forenoon. One shell struck a stack of Company K, wounding several men. This afternoon our Regiment was moved behind the brow of a hill to protect us from the enemy shells. At 5 o'clock this evening we had orders to pile our knapsacks and placed William Buck to guard them. We were marched a short distance ... to form a charging line, and were ... the first Regiment to get into position."[35]

After stowing their knapsacks, the Bluecoats sheltered themselves from the Confederate artillery fire in a ravine running through the pine forest. Before 5:30 p.m., the regiments formed for the assault, twenty paces apart, and given instructions to lie down and await further orders. The 5th Maine, still commanded by Col. Clark Edwards, was now, according to its commanding officer, a "small battalion of about two hundred" muskets.[36] The 96th, commanded by Lieutenant Colonel Lessig, numbered at most 400 men, with only seven of its ten companies in the strike force.[37] Three companies, H, I and K, were assigned skirmish duty which proved to be as perilous as being part of the storming column.[38] The 121st New York, Upton's "Regulars," prepared for the attack with 420 enlisted men and officers.[39] The first three regiments forming the vanguard of Upton's column numbered about 950 combat veterans. General Doles arrayed 1,350 Georgians, behind formidable field fortifications, 150 yards away from the lead elements of Upton's highly trained soldiers. Just before 6 p.m., Wright's aide Henry R. Dalton instructed Upton to begin his attack as soon as he finalized his preparations. While Upton waited anxiously to advance, tension mounted for the Bluecoats. Although the soldiers were aligned to advance, problems arose which delayed the start of the attack.[40]

Even before Upton's anticipated assault started, things began to unravel. To Upton's left, Gen. Gershom Mott's Fourth Division of the II Corps, ordered to support Upton's operation, broke and ran to the rear under the weight of Confederate artillery fire. No one, however, informed Upton of this reversal of fortune. On Upton's right, an attack by the V Corps of General Warren, supported by Hancock's II Corps, was repulsed with heavy losses, and failed to draw Confederates away from the point of attack selected for Upton's column. Furthermore, General Ewell was becoming increasingly suspicious of Federal activity, especially the Union skirmishers who appeared, "particularly active and spiteful."[41] At 6 p.m., three Union artillery batteries—McCartney's, Cowan's and Rhodes's—opened on the stretch of works held by Doles' brigade. One of General Wright's staff noted in his diary that the VI Corps "batteries are firing hell bent."[42] Finally, Meade decided that he could not afford to wait any longer and ordered Upton to undertake the attack. A Union officer waved a handkerchief overhead. The artillery ceased firing and Upton rode to the head of his column. It was approximately 6:30 p.m. The men rose up. In front of the Bluecoats was an open field, controlled by a heavy presence of VI Corps skirmishers. As James Treichler peered at the Confederates from the pine forest he observed that "this point [was] a very strong Salient … a densely wooded prominance [sic] standing out from the main line in defiance."[43] Henry Keiser observed that the Confederates were posted behind "strong Rifle-pits with head-logs for protection."[44] A member of the 5th Maine, writing shortly after the battle, recalled the moment just prior to the charge. "All was now ready, the enemy in front still unconscious of the terrible storm soon to break forth."[45]

As the Unionists awaited the order to advance, Upton directed all attackers to fix bayonets and ordered the men in the three regiments constituting the front ranks of the column to cap and load their weapons. Only the Yankees in the first line, however, were allowed to cap their muskets. (To "cap" a Civil War musket was to put a copper percussion cap on its nipple so that it could instantly be fired. With their weapons uncapped, the Bluecoats could not fire as they charged and would have to keep advancing toward the Confederate entrenchment where they could cap their pieces for close-range firing.) Upton emphasized that he wanted all of the regimental commanders to shout the command "forward" constantly. He admonished the soldiers not to cheer, nor stop and assist a wounded comrade until they reached the enemy's works. Now everything was in readiness. The clash of arms about to begin. Upton, astride his horse, turned to his command and shattered the stillness of the pine forest when he shouted, "Attention, battalions! Forward, double quick! Charge!"[46]

Although Upton sought to inspire, exhort and subsequently praise his men, secrecy characterized his actions prior to the assault on the evening of May 10. It is clear that Upton understood that maintaining the element of surprise would ultimately emerge as a critical factor in the eventual success or failure of his bold operation.[47] As a result, he took several precautions to prevent the enemy from detecting his division massing for the attack in the pine forest. Taking advantage of the pine trees, which concealed his strike force from the Confederates, Upton, moved his men into position along the woods road leading from the Shelton house, and ordered each regiment to lie down on the ground prior to the attack. A soldier in the 121st New York later recalled that his regiment "formed under cover of the woods, without being observed."[48] A color bearer with the 5th Maine noted in his diary that his regiment, "lay close to the ground waiting for orders."[49] A soldier in the ranks of the 49th Pennsylvania recalled, "We are laying low, and not a word is spoken above a whisper in our ranks. We see the duty we are expected to perform, and orders are quietly passed along the line in a whisper."[50] After Upton aligned his command in column for the attack, he carefully reviewed the tactical plan with the individual commanders and issued instructions to them concerning his expectations regarding their leadership and responsibilities during the operation. Finally, near 6 o'clock, according to Upton "all the preparations were completed ... the lines rose, moved noiselessly to the edge of the woods, and then, with a wild cheer and faces averted, rushed for the works."[51]

The exact time that the Bluecoats surged forward and emerged from the pine forest is also difficult to determine given the varying accounts in contemporary sources. In his report, Upton does not state a specific time when he issued the command to move forward, but suggests the column advanced at ten minutes past 6 o'clock.[52] Two reliable and observant staff officers, Theodore Lyman and Oliver Wendell Holmes, Jr., both noted the time in their respective records of the events of May 10. In a letter written that same day, Lyman stated, "At 6.30 Upton, with a heavy column of picked men, made a most brilliant assault with the bayonet, at the left of the Sixth Corps."[53] Holmes, scribbling notes in his pocket diary, recorded that the "Attack begins now 6.35."[54] Several historians have accepted the start of the attack, alluded to in Upton's report, but not explicitly stated, as 6:10 p.m.[55] Another historian, however, accepted Holmes's observation, as stated in his diary.[56] Adding credibility to Holmes's statement was his position as an officer serving on General Wright's VI Corps staff. Four soldiers in the 96th Pennsylvania, all of whom participated in the charge, noted different statements in their diaries concerning the exact time that the attack commenced. Jerome Miller recorded in his diary that the men moved forward at 7 p.m., while Henry Keiser recalled that "at 6 o'clock p.m., all being in readiness, the command to charge was given."[57] Writing several decades after the battle, James Treichler recalled from memory that "at 6 o.c. p.m. the artulery opened fire upon the works and in Twenty minutes we were upon the open field."[58] Lieutenant Luckenbill wrote in his diary, "At 6 o'clock our Boys all formed line of battle in front of rebel works under heavy fire of muskets to charge the works.... At about 6:30 the order was given to charge the works."[59] Evaluating the evidence, given the statements from participants and observers, it is most likely that Upton issued his command to advance at the bottom of the hour of 6 o'clock or a few minutes later.

One Bluecoat, in a post-war memoir, recalled his thoughts upon hearing Upton's order to attack.

> I felt my gorge rise, and my stomach and intestines shrink together in a knot, and a thousand things rushed through my mind. I fully realized the terrible peril I was to encounter. I looked about in the faces of the boys around me, and they told the tale of expected death. Pulling my cap down over my eyes, I stepped out.[60]

With a yell, contrary to Upton's orders, the three lead regiments surged out of the pine forest across the plain and up the slope toward the Confederate works. Quick as lightning, a sheet of flame burst from the Rebel entrenchments, a leaden hail swept the ground over which the Yankees advanced, while canister from Butternut artillery crashed through the Unionist ranks at every step. Upon seeing the Bluecoats streaming out of the woods, an artilleryman with the 3rd Richmond Howizters issued a warning to his battery mates. "Make ready, boys—*they are charging!*"[61] One Bluecoat in the 96th recalled the start of the charge. "About 6:30 the order was given. Forward. Off we started under heavy artillery fire and terrible musketry.... Had orders not to fire a shot."[62] Another Bluecoat in the forefront of the attack recalled that the column crossed the field "at a double-quick, receiving terrible punishment from the rebels on our left. The rebels behind the breastworks ... having nothing to trouble them could rake us at their pleasure."[63] Henry Keiser stated that the Schuylkill Countians "started on the full run with a cheer." He also noted, too, that "many a poor fellow fell pierced with Rebel bullets before we reached the rifle-pits."[64] Double-quicking across the field, a soldier with the 5th Maine later recalled that the Confederate artillery and small arms fire caused his regiment, after it forced its way through the abatis, especially the left of the column, to crowd the regiment into the path of the 96th Pennsylvania.[65] Despite the delay involved in breaking through the tangled abatis, erected just in front of the Confederate entrenchments, men of all three leading regiments mounted the enemy parapet within five minutes of the jump-off. Upon ascending the parapet of the Confederate works, the Bluecoats "fired a volley and went over them with a yell."[66]

Prior to the assault, the 96th Pennsylvania was assigned to the center of the first line of the attack column. Three companies from the 96th (H, I and K) were detailed to perform skirmish duty. As a result, only seven companies actually formed in line for the attack. In his diary, Luckenbill later recalled, "Out of 7 companys we went in with 248 men."[67]

2nd Lt. Amos Forseman, Company D. Promoted from first sergeant November 21, 1862. Discharged October 21, 1864 (courtesy Patriotic Order Sons of America).

Emerging from the pine forest with a "wild cheer," the Bluecoats hustled across the open field at the double-quick, "under heavy artillery fire and terrible musketry." A soldier in the 5th Maine later recalled that "the rebs behind breastworks at the left, having nothing to trouble them, could rake us at their pleasure."[68] Another soldier at the forefront of the attack later stated that as his regiment "leaped forward from their place of concealment, and dashed forward with a yell of defiance. A murderous fire of musketry and artillery opened ... but not a man faltered while seeing his comrades fall thick and fast, but pressed on."[69] Reaching the Confederate entrenchments in a matter of minutes, they surmounted the parapet and crashed into the ranks of the 4th Georgia deployed in the middle of Doles' brigade. As the lead elements of the 96th poured over the field fortifications, Henry Keiser recalled the initial contact with the Georgians. "We started on the full run with cheers ... with instructions to reserve our fire until we jumped the rifle-pits, which proved lucky for us, as most of the Rebel guns were empty while

Corp. James Jerome Miller. Wounded at Spotsylvania, Virginia, May 10, 1864. Transferred to Veteran Reserve Corps October 17, 1864 (courtesy George Hay Kain).

ours were loaded, and they were at our mercy."[70] As they surged into the rifle-pits, a soldier in the 6th Alabama witnessed the initial clash between Billy Yank and Johnny Reb. "On they came without stopping to fire (some falling upon the very top of the breastworks) until they got within bayoneting distance of Doles' men. They then delivered their fire with telling effect in the ranks of our boys. Two Companies of the 4th Ga. Being overcome in this way, surrendered, those of them who could not escape—This gave the Yankees a foot-hold—a starting point—and very soon the entire brigade was whipped, and forced to surrender their works."[71]

Enduring a heavy frontal fire, the three lead regiments of Upton's column surged over the log breastworks and into the Rebel rifle pits. The initial encounter of attacker and defender at the fortifications was quick, violent and deadly. In his after-action report, Colonel Upton described the moment when the Bluecoats clambered up the fortifications and fired at point blank range into the Georgians. "Through a terrible front and flank fire the column advanced quickly gaining the parapet. Here occurred a deadly hand-to-hand conflict. The enemy sitting in their pits with pieces upright, loaded, and with bayonets fixed, ready to impale the first who should leap over, absolutely refused to yield the ground. The first of our men who tried to surmount the works fell pierced through the head by musket-balls. Others, seeing the fate of their comrades, held their pieces at arms length and fired downward, while others, poising their pieces vertically, hurled them down upon their enemy, pinning them to the ground."[72]An officer of the 121st New York jumped on top of the parapet and shouted, "Come on, men," then pitched forward, shot dead.[73] As the Pennsylvanians clambered over the parapet, they engaged the Rebels in ferocious hand-to-hand combat. Private Pat O'Donnell successfully mounted the Secessionist works only to become pinned to the parapet by a Rebel bayonet. Moments after his peculiar imprisonment, O'Donnell was set free.[74] Henry Keiser recorded in his diary that "when those who were left reached the pits we left them have it. They were very stubborn, and the bayonets and clubbed muskets were used freely before the pit was fully in our possession. We captured, killed or wounded the big majority of the first pit."[75]

Once over the parapet the lead elements of Upton's strike force encountered the Confederate defenders as they swarmed into the rifle pits. Jumping into the rifle-pit, a New York soldier later wrote that "we carried the works after a sharp hand to hand conflict in which the bayonett was freely used until the rebels broke & ran. We followed them & drove them from their second line of works & held them thare for near an hower or a parte of them."[76] Upton also graphically described the hand-to-hand fighting, which he closely observed, in his after-action report. "The struggle lasted but a few seconds. Numbers prevailed, and, like a resistless wave, the column poured over the works, quickly putting hors de combat those who resisted, and sending to the rear those who surrendered."[77] Henry Keiser, in his detailed journal, recounted this phase of the engagement. "When those who were left reached the pits we left them have it. They were very stubborn, and the bayonets and clubbed muskets were used freely before the pit was fully in our possession. We captured, killed or wounded the big majority of the first pit. We sent the prisoners to the rear and went for the second pit."[78]

Capt. Isaac Severn, wife and child. The captain and his family sat for this portrait in front of a.m. Allen, photographer, Pottsville, Pennsylvania (MOLLUS Mass. Collection, United States Army Heritage and Education Center).

From the perspective of a soldier who served with the 44th Georgia, Upton's storming column "came on us with a yell and never made any halt. Our men did all in their power to repel the assault, but the enemy outnumbered us ten to one. Numbers prevailed; they ran upon our works and killed and captured a large number of our brigade.... We were simply overwhelmed and forced to retire, *every man for himself*."[79] The initial confrontation between the lead elements of Upton's strike force and Doles' Georgia brigade, was vicious, swift and decisive for the Bluecoats. Not only were the Georgians overpowered and compelled to withdraw to a second line of works, many of the Graycoats were captured at this point in the attack. A soldier with the 4th Georgia recalled, "The battle is not yet decided. It is the bloodiest day of the War.... Our Brigade has suffered more than any in the army, having lost more than A thousand men; about 500 in killed and wounded—the balance prisoners."[80]

In a graphic letter, written almost a month after the battle, a soldier with the 12th Georgia described the moment the 96th scaled the earthen parapet of the salient and engaged the men of Doles' Brigade inside the Mule Shoe. "As soon as the enemy made a breach in the line," wrote Irby Scott, "they poured through and turning to the right & left commenced pouring a fire right down the line and also passing in our rear. We remained in the ditch until I saw the enemy shooting & capturing men within forty yards of us. Some of us ran taking the risks of being shot while others remained and were taken prisoners."[81] Levi Smith of the 44th Georgia recorded in his diary that "about one half hour before sun[down], the enemy made a charge on Gen. Doles' Brigade and forced a passage through the 4th Ga. Regt. after which the 12th and 44th were flanked.... Bravely they fought at the point of their bayonets."[82] Many of the Bluecoats of the 96th Pennsylvania, who tried to surmount the works, fell pierced through the head by musket balls. James Treichler recalled the charge in his memoir. "[With] heads down we dashed for the enemies works; and gained them in spite of the deadly fire; with a rush the first column went over and the deadly work began. In a very short time the bayonet decided the contest."[83] According to Upton's report, the struggle was furious but lasted only a few moments before the Confederate brigade retreated to a second line of rifle pits. "Numbers prevailed and, like a resistless wave, the column poured over the works, quickly putting hors de combat those who resisted, and sending to the rear those who surrendered."[84]

As the shattered Confederates sought refuge in the second line of rifle pits, Upton ordered his ranks forward. As the first wave of Upton's attackers turned to the right and left, at the breach in the Rebel works, the second and third lines of Bluecoats pressed forward and stormed the enemy's second line of entrenchments. Quickly the lead elements of Upton's column secured the gap in the Graycoat works, the 121st New York captured several pieces of artillery, manned by Capt. Benjamin Smith's 3rd Company Richmond Howitzers, while rendering two other Napoleons inoperable. At this point, many Confederates were either captured or shot down. A soldier serving with the 44th Georgia later recalled this phase of the battle in a letter to his mother composed the day after the engagement. "Our Brigade [Doles] fought until two of their lines were in our works. We fell back 75 or 100 yards, rallied, turned on & charged them out again & drove them back with great slaughter. We lost several killed, great many wounded, most of them thrust with bayonets & nearly all prisoners, I mean in the Brigade."[85] Pushing forward, the Schuylkill Countians overwhelmed the 4th Georgia and prepared to assail the Confederates rallying in the second rifle pit 200 yards to their front. Henry Keiser recorded the details of this final phase of the battle in his diary.

> We sent the prisoners to the rear and went for the second pit, about 75 yards away, carried that and some of our troops were closing in on the third pit, where they had artillery in position when our support, not giving us the aid expected of them, we were flanked and had to get back, losing all we had gained and leaving our dead and wounded in the enemies hands, all owing to the supporting Regiments not attending to their duty.[86]

In his diary, Lieutenant Luckenbill noted, "Carried two entrenchments.... Captured a great many prisoners. Our support did not come up. We held the works till after dark.

Finding we had no support and the rebs were coming in on our flank we were obliged to fall back to our old position."[87] To this point, the assault unfolded precisely as Upton had planned: the enemy's line was broken, the gap widened and held by the first line of Union attackers. The second and third wave of Upton's column were advancing toward the second line of rifle pits where the Graycoats were attempting to reform and stem the tide of oncoming Unionists. The ultimate success or failure of Upton's breakthrough, however, depended upon the ability of Gershom Mott's division of the II Corps to support the attack. Mott's once proud division, however, had lost its fighting edge in the Wilderness. Compounding the loss of *esprit de corps* in Mott's division was the artillery fire that initially slowed his advance and eventually broke his ranks. As dusk settled over the salient, Upton realized that his command would have to fight its way out of the Rebel rifle pits with the same fervor the troops displayed in mounting the parapet and driving Doles' Georgians across the Mule Shoe to a second line of entrenchments.[88]

Sweeping Doles' Georgians from the western face of the salient enabled the first line of Yankees to reorganize quickly and moved forward with the next phase of the operation. Unfortunately for the vanguard of Upton's column, the ability to move swiftly along the Confederate line was compromised by the height of the traverses. As a result, the ground inside the Mule Shoe vacated by Doles' refugees, quickly filled with the second and third wave of Upton's storming column. Adding to the congestion, too, was the hundreds of Confederate prisoners being escorted toward the Union line. A soldier serving with the 5th Maine, also observed that the influx of Yankees into the Mule Shoe, and the exodus of Butternut prisoners from the salient to the rear, caused chaos and confusion for the combatants. In his detailed diary, William Morse of the 5th Maine recalled that "the rebel line on the flank not being able to readily distinguish much through the smoke thought it was Yanks being driven back, so [they] poured lead into our own men as fast as they could load and fire."[89] One of the artilleryman with the 3rd Richmond Howitzers also noted "that everything was in the direst confusion—all company organization was entirely broken up."[90] A soldier with the 49th Pennsylvania, on the right flank of the second line, described the scene he witnessed as he leaped into the rifle pit of the Mule Shoe. "The column was in much confusion," wrote Captain Hutchinson, "for they had encountered a terrible fire of artillery and musketry, and had a hand-to-hand fight in the works … just inside the rebel works … our wounded were working their way, painfully, to the rear. The struggle had been short, but severe; and our men cheered, in unwonted enthusiasm, as they sent their thousand captured rebels to the rear. For a few minutes there was a quiet—a sort of lull in conflict—and then, from the front, and both flanks, the enemy rushed upon the bold Yankees who had penetrated their works with tremendous force and in overpowering numbers."[91]

At this point in the operation, with two lines of his assault column within the confines of the Mule Shoe, the Bluecoats had already achieved many of the objectives Upton outlined in his original plan. The Yankees had successfully stormed the Confederate works and overpowered Doles' Georgians. The 121st New York successfully seized the four artillery pieces of the 3rd Richmond Howitzers and compelled the right wing of Junius Daniel's North Carolina brigade to retreat while capturing a number of the brave Tarheels in the process.[92] On the left of Upton's storming column, the 5th Maine drove back the 2nd and 33rd Virginia regiments of the Stonewall Brigade and pushed on toward the next rifle pit.[93] The veterans of the Stonewall Brigade, however, reformed along a line running perpendicular to the earthworks, and according to General Walker, "poured an oblique fire on [the] foe as they advanced."[94] In the middle of Upton's first wave, the men of the 96th vanquished the Georgians of Doles' brigade, quickly reorganized, and pushed south inside the works toward the next rifle pit. While Doles' men sought to reorganize and prevent the Yankees from achieving further gains, the Schuylkill Countians pressed on with the bayonet attack. Henry Keiser recalled the advance across the field in his graphic diary entry of May 10. "About 75 yards away [we] carried that [rifle pit] and some of our troops were closing in on the third pit, where they had artillery in position."[95] Lieutenant Luckenbill simply noted in his diary that the 96th "carried two entrenchments."[96] Having successfully stormed the western face of the salient, routed Doles' Georgians and pursued them an additional seventy-five yards, the Union high tide was about to crest. In fact, the tide of battle was about to recede for the jubilant Bluecoats. The

1st Lt. Thomas Burns, Company K. Promoted from first sergeant April 4, 1864. Transferred to 95th Pennsylvania October 18, 1864 (Ronn Palm collection).

Confederates, although dazed by the onslaught, were mounting a massive counterattack designed to reclaim the lost ground inside the salient and reestablish the western face of the Mule Shoe.

With his entire division engaged, Upton could not achieve further gains without reinforcements. In his detailed report, Upton stated, "The column of assault had accomplished its task.... The impulsion of the charge being lost, nothing remained but to hold the ground. I accordingly directed the officers to form their men outside the works and open fire."[97] As the battle waned, reinforcements to exploit the opening in the Confederate line, created by Upton's strike force, failed to move forward. Lieutenant Luckenbill astutely noted in his diary, "We held the works till after dark. Finding we had no support and the rebs were coming in on our flank we were obliged to fall back to our old position."[98] Henry Keiser recorded in his diary that "when our support, not giving us the aid expected of them, we were [soon] flanked and had to get back, losing all we had gained and leaving our dead and wounded in the enemies hands, all owing to the supporting Regiments not attending to their duty."[99] In his diary, writing in his native German, Maurus Oestreich summarized the participation of the 96th Pennsylvania in Upton's famous charge. No doubt his thoughts reflected the sentiments of his comrades in arms who undertook the perilous mission.

Our 96th Pennsylvania Volunteers was among those making the charge. They did what they were ordered to do and went into a deadly hail of bullets and drove the rebs out of the rifle pits and took several hundred prisoners, but as they had no support, they had … to fall back again, and all was wasted. The many killed and wounded had done their duty for nothing. Our regiment lost half of their number.[100]

With his command committed, Upton was more than three quarters of a mile in front of the main Union line, with no prospect of any support. Realizing that Mott's advance had broken down, Upton sought to consolidate his force to meet the impending Confederate counterattack. Butternut reinforcements were quickly moving toward the breach from other sectors of the salient. The second wave of Unionist attackers, clinging to a battery of guns at the second trench, abandoned their trophies and double-quicked back to the main Rebel rifle pit. When a Confederate battery enfiladed his lines from the left, Upton pleaded for men from the 121st New York to rush it, saying, "Are there none of my old regiment here?"[101] Failing to halt the rush of Graycoats toward the breach, Upton ordered the Federal line officers to regroup the remnants of the assault column outside the works and to continue to fire upon the enemy. Upton then rode back toward the Union line to call forward the three Vermont regiments remaining in reserve, but found that "they had already mingled in the contest and were fighting with a heroism which has ever characterized that elite brigade."[102] At the edge of the pine-wood Upton met General Russell, who ordered the young colonel to withdraw his remaining troops from the Rebel works. The advent of night-fall and the inability of Mott's division to get into the fight compelled Russell to issue the withdrawal order. Shielded by the darkness, the survivors retreated to the safety of the Union line. Retreating from the Mule Shoe meant that many of the Bluecoats, wounded in the engagement, would likely fall into the hands of the enemy. Henry Keiser recorded a poignant episode regarding the withdrawal in his diary.

> Just after getting back to the first pit taken Henry Remberger, of our Company, jumped clear over the rifle-pit as pale as a sheet. He was shot a little to the left of the navel. I told him to lean on me and I would take him out, but he said he must rest first. Just then an officer directed a lot of us to the left, and I had to leave him. Shortly after that, Lewis Romich seen him and washed off his wound, but could not move him.[103]

As Upton's Bluecoats struggled to maintain, and possibly widen, the breach in the Secessionist line, the Confederates sought to mount a counterattack aimed at restoring the status quo and driving the Yankees from their works. John Worsham, serving with the 21st Virginia of Col. William Witcher's Brigade, positioned to the rear of Doles' Georgians, observed in his memoir that "the breastworks occupied by Doles' Brigade and a company of Richmond Howitzers, just to the left of the Stonewall Brigade of our division, were captured by the enemy; but troops near-by were hurried to that point, and as soon as they could be formed in line, the order was given to charge, and drive the Yanks out!"[104] Responding to the emergency, General Ewell rode to the threatened sector of the Mule Shoe to reorganize the demoralized Confederates and personally took charge of the chaotic situation. Halting behind the 45th North Carolina, of Junius Daniel's brigade, Ewell shouted, "Don't run, boys. I will have enough men here in five minutes to eat up every damned one of them!"[105] Rallying Daniel's brigade, Ewell then sought to bring forward the Alabama brigade commanded by Gen. Cullen Battle, Gen. Stephen D. Ramseur's brigade of North Carolinians and Gen. Robert Johnston's Tarheels. Finally, Brig. Gen. John B. Gordon, commanding a brigade of Georgians was thrust into the fray.[106]

A soldier serving with the 45th North Carolina recalled the perilous situation his regiment faced upon the rout of Doles' Georgia brigade. In a post-war memoir Cyrus

Watson captured the critical moments of the engagement. "The enemy poured through the breach, captured quite a number of men on the extreme right of our brigade; forced the brigade to retire to avoid enfilading fire, and caused the temporary loss of ... [four] pieces of artillery. Our brigade slowly fell back firing as it retreated, the enemy advancing and taking possession of our abandoned guns ... the enemy massing in great numbers in our front. It seemed even to the eye of a private soldier that a dangerous crisis was upon us.... Presently we heard a yell up the line in our rear as we stood, and Battles Brigade of Alabamians were seen coming to our support.... We raised a yell and dashed forward."[107] In his diary, J. W. Roberts, of the 6th Alabama, chronicled the exciting counter charge. "The Yankees ... fell upon Daniel's right flank and rear—he being on Dole's left—and his men were soon driven from their works—This gave them possession of a half mile of fortifications—and several pieces of Artillery—This must be recovered speedily or the day is lost—Gordon's and Battle's Brigade are ordered forward—and assist each other in regaining the lost ground—The Yankees fought with unusual desperation."[108]

Withdrawing from the Mule Shoe proved to be as deadly as attacking the salient. In a letter written six days after the battle, Major Levi Huber of the 96th, stated that Upton's "desperate charge upon the enemy's entrenchments" resulted in the Unionists carrying three lines of Confederate works, but "the enemy brought a cross fire of musketry and artillery upon us from our right and left flanks, and, unfortunately for our cause we had to retire."[109] The retreat across the field to the safety of the pine forest proved to be a perilous journey. A brigade of North Carolinians under Gen. Robert Johnston sought to smite the invaders as they retreated. A Tarheel serving with the 23rd North Carolina described the final closing scene of the action in a postwar memoir. "Our brigade was double-quicked by the right flank in column," recalled Captain Turner, "from behind a pine thicket where it had been resting and concealed.... We met and drove the enemy back across the breastworks and regained several pieces of artillery which were still in position. Some of the Confederate gunners who, concealed the cannon pits, had escaped capture, now sprung out and used the guns very effectively on the retreating Federals."[110] General Walker, commanding the Stonewall Brigade, described the role of his command in a postwar account. "The triumph of the victors was of short duration ... the enemy was driven back pell-mell at a double quick, and as they recrossed our works and the open space to seek the friendly gloom of the pine forest, they had a few moments before left in such gallant array, they were shot down until the ground was covered with their dead and wounded."[111]

According to Irby Scott, soldiering with the 12th Georgia, Doles' reorganized brigade "drove the enemy back and retook our works about dusk."[112] Asbury Jackson of the 44th Georgia stated that Doles' brigade "fought until two of their lines were in our works, we fell back 75 or 100 yards, rallied, turned on & charged them out again & drove them back with great slaughter. We lost several killed, great many wounded, most of them thrust with bayonets & nearly all prisoners."[113] Levi Smith, also in the 44th Georgia, recorded in his diary, "About two hundred and five of the Georgia boys were captured. Bravely they fought at the point of their bayonets."[114] Another Graycoat, serving with the 4th Georgia, recalling the particulars of the battle the following morning, stated that "170 Yankees are lying dead inside our works to-day—many bayoneted. It was the most desperate fight that has occurred yet. Doles now commands 450 men."[115] While the Confederates reclaimed their lost ground as darkness ended the fighting, both sides were bloodied in this brief, tenacious and deadly engagement. In his report Colonel Upton summarized the operation from his saddle as the commander of this classic infantry charge. "Our officers and men accomplished all that could be expected of brave men. They went forward with perfect confidence, fought with unflinching courage, and retired only upon the receipt of a written order, after having expended the ammunition of their dead and wounded comrades."[116]

As they scrambled back to the pine forest, the exhausted troops of the 96th slumped to the ground. During Upton's furious assault, the Pennsylvanians suffered staggering casualties. Captain Edward Thomas, commanding Company A, was killed during the assault, along with thirty-one other Pennsylvanians. Five line officers along with one hundred eight non-commissioned Schuylkill Countians were wounded.[117] Thirty-nine soldiers were believed, according to Lieutenant Colonel Lessig's report in the *Miners' Journal*, to be either captured or missing. Total casualties for the twelve regiments numbered about 1,000 in killed, wounded, captured and those reported missing.[118] The three regiments from Upton's brigade lost approximately fifty percent of their combat strength. As the Unionists rested around the evening campfires, the surgeons began their grizzly work. Lending an eerie touch to the groans of the wounded was a Confederate band off in the distance playing "Nearer, My God, to Thee." A soldier serving with the 44th Georgia recalled, "The sound of this beautiful piece of music had scarcely died away when a Yankee band over the line gave us the 'Dead March.'"[119]

Upon his return to the main Federal line, Upton immediately visited Russell at VI Corps headquarters. Upton was disappointed that the breakthrough at the salient had not produced dramatic success. Depressed, he muttered about the casualties his command sustained and the lack of support from Mott's division. (Later that evening, at Meade's headquarters, Wright stated, "General, I don't want Mott's men on my left; they are not a support; I would rather have no troops there!")[120] Although Upton was not pleased with the outcome of his daring operation, Grant was moderately impressed with the young colonel's partial success. Grant noted Upton's tactics and advised Meade to formulate plans to renew the tactical offensive of May 10. Meade's staff immediately went to work to plan a hammer-like blow against the enemy. After much wrangling, Meade's subordinates proposed a three-pronged assault against the Confederate salient. At dawn, Hancock's II Corps was instructed to attack the apex of the salient Upton-style, while Burnside's IX Corps launched an assault against the salient's eastern face in concert with pressure from Warren's V Corps and Wright's VI Corps against the western side of the Mule Shoe. Grant believed that if a corps of infantry rushed the salient at daybreak, following Upton's tactical break through, they could overrun the parapet before the musket and artillery fire could check their assault. Then, with the apex of the salient breached, the support troops could achieve success against the flanks of the Mule Shoe. With the salient broken, Lee's army would be cut in half. In the aftermath of Upton's operation, a cavalry officer serving as an orderly at Grant's headquarters, overheard the lieutenant general say to General Meade, "A brigade today—we'll try a corps tomorrow."[121]

XIII

"O God, what a sight"

The ghastly combat waged during the Battle of Spotsylvania Court House, which lasted two weeks, resulted in the Army of the Potomac sustaining 18,400 casualties.[1] Upton's assault, conducted on the evening of May 10, totaled in approximately 1,000 Bluecoats killed, wounded, captured or missing. The front rank of the strike force, 5th Maine, 96th Pennsylvania and 121st New York, suffered 464 casualties in the deadly encounter. Despite the perceived success of the operation, the casualty rolls offered grim testimony regarding the cost of Union soldiers to gain victory over the Confederates at Spotsylvania. The unrelenting grueling combat, resulting in enormous casualties, left the soldiers wondering how long they could continue to endure the headlong tactics of Upton style assaults. Although the men were seasoned combat veterans, could they continually summon the courage to conduct frontal assaults or would the horrors of Spotsylvania cause the men to question the basic assumptions of soldiering and the course of the war under General Grant. After the bloody Battle of Fredericksburg Lincoln confided to his secretary William Stoddard that "no general yet found can face the arithmetic."[2] In Ulysses S. Grant Lincoln found that general. The question remained after Spotsylvania, could the rank and file of the army survive the deadly human subtraction.

The British military historian C. F. Atkinson, writing in his study of Grant's Virginia campaign, concluded that Upton's May 10 operation was "one of the classic infantry attacks of military history."[3] A VI Corps staff officer noted in his pocket diary that Upton's attack was "a brilliant magnificent charge."[4] Colonel Wainwright, the observant, opinionated artillery commander of the V Corps, recorded in his journal that the Union assaults conducted on May 10 accomplished very little, "except Upton's, which was very brilliant, as he carried the works at the point of the bayonet without firing a shot, and brought out 900 prisoners."[5] Theodore Lyman, a member of General Meade's staff, wrote in his diary, "At 6:30 Upton, with a heavy column of picked men, made a most brilliant assault with the bayonet, without firing a shot, carried the breastworks in the face of cannon and musketry, and took 900 prisoners."[6] Writing in his colorful memoir, decades after the battle, James Treichler of the 96th Pennsylvania stated, "This engagement is recorded in History as one of the most brilliant charges of the War."[7] While historians and soldiers praised Upton, admired his courage and unanimously agreed that the attack was "brilliant," the infantrymen who carried out the operation drew different conclusions. A New York officer, writing a day after the battle stated, "I hardly know *what* to think of the wholesale slaughter in storming breastworks so well manned and stubbornly defended. *I don't believe it pays.*"[8] Despite the ghastly, bloody Battle of May 10, the soldiers who survived Upton's celebrated charge emerged with a renewed sense of confidence in their commanders and commitment to their cause.

Bravery characterized the soldiers of both sides in the charge upon the Mule Shoe. The aftermath of the battle, however, focused on the vanquished of the both sides: the killed, wounded, missing and soldiers captured during the engagement. Colonel Upton's hand-picked command, totaling twelve regiments, suffered 283 killed, 1,066 wounded and 211 missing in action.[9] The total loss, sustained in approximately ninety minutes of fighting was 1,560 or about thirty-three percent of his strike force. The Confederates also sustained significant casualties in the struggle for the Mule Shoe. A detailed casualty list of Doles' Brigade, including the lone company of the 21st Georgia, was published five weeks after the battle in the Milledgeville *Southern Recorder*.[10] This extraordinary document, encompassing the entire front page of the newspaper, chronicles the casualties in Doles' Brigade from May 5 through May 21. During that period, which included the Wilderness fighting and the Spotsylvania actions, the Georgians suffered enormous losses. The official reports state that 125 were killed, 357 wounded and 475 listed as missing or captured. In addition, a soldier serving with the 32nd North Carolina, positioned to the left of Doles' Brigade, recorded that in his regiment 231 soldiers were captured in the engagement.[11] In his personal diary, Marsena Patrick, the Provost Marshal of the Army of the Potomac, noted in the last sentence of his entry for May 10 as follows: "I should also say, that 6' Corps avenged the loss of their Leader by a desperate assault upon the enemy, capturing 913 men & 37 officers."[12]

Pvt. William M. Lashorn, Company D. Transferred to Veteran Reserve Corps (MOLLUS Mass. Collection, United States Army Heritage and Education Center).

Although not entirely clear, and also incomplete in many instances, especially regarding the Confederates engaged, the documentary evidence indicates that Upton's assault exacted an extremely heavy toll on the Bluecoats only to achieve a temporary breakthrough within the vaunted Confederate Mule Shoe.[13] In fact, official casualty rolls compiled by Colonel Edwards, of the 5th Maine, and Lieutenant Colonel Lessig, of the 96th Pennsylvania, reflect slightly higher losses than the casualty returns published in the *Official Records*.[14] Similarly, an unofficial report published in the Little Falls *Journal*, submitted by 1st Lt. Joseph Heath of the 121st New York, differs significantly with the returns listed in the *Official Records*.[15] The 96th suffered nearly a casualty per minute in this savage, ferocious hand-to-hand struggle. At the end of the battle, 32 Schuylkill Countians were dead, 113 were wounded and 39 were classified as missing or captured.[16] By the end of the battle, only two other Union regiments, the 121st New York and the 49th Pennsylvania, suffered more casualties. The "brilliant" tactical assault, planned and executed by

Upton, achieved little but added greatly to the ever-growing casualty rolls of the VI Corps and the Army of the Potomac. And yet, the bloody engagement of May 10 was merely the opening act in a series of dramatic battles that would collectively become known as the Spotsylvania Campaign.

Upton's classical military attack, proved to be brilliant in its conception, planning and initial execution. The operation featured several tactical innovations, principally developed by Upton through his previous battlefield experiences and his quest to reduce casualties while pressing the tactical offensive.[17] Swiftly moving substantial numbers of men across a field, ordering the men not to discharge their weapons while conducting the charge, and finally overpowering the enemy at the point of the bayonet proved to be an effective tactic in 1862 and 1863. But it was not a viable offensive tactic in Virginia in May of 1864 against heavily fortified Confederate field fortifications. At Crampton's Gap, Second Fredericksburg and Rappahannock Station, entire divisions executed bayonet assaults against weakly held positions featuring only two brigades of Confederate defenders. In all three of these instances, Confederate artillery proved to be of little support to the Graycoat infantry standing on the defensive. Furthermore, unlike the situation at Spotsylvania, where the Secessionists could quickly move troops to respond to a Union assault, there were no reserves available in the other engagements to support the beleaguered defenders.

The bayonet attack, which proved an effective tactic in 1862 and 1863 was rendered obsolete in Virginia by the spring of 1864. The extensive development of field fortifications, featuring several lines of works affording defense in depth, coupled with the ability of the Confederates to utilize interior lines and respond quickly to threatened sectors, essentially ended the effectiveness of bayonet charges as a practical offensive tactic. At Spotsylvania, on the evening of May 10, Upton's bayonet assault successfully broke through the outer Confederate line, overwhelmed one brigade—composed of just three regiments—temporarily captured four artillery pieces and sent about 950 prisoners to the rear but an considerable cost to the attackers. Ultimately, Upton's masterful attack must be judged a failure despite the careful planning and excellent execution and exemplary leadership by the field officers. The entire episode, conceived to deliver a resounding victory with minimal casualties, only served to lengthen the casualty rolls in Grant's evolving operations in Virginia. Finally, Upton's famous charge had virtually no impact on the outcome of the bloody battles constituting the Spotsylvania campaign.[18]

Throughout the afternoon of May 11 a persistent drizzle dampened the troops holding the entrenchments around Spotsylvania. During the night the Bluecoats moved into position for the assault scheduled at daybreak. At 4:30 a.m. the next morning, there was enough light to turn the rain clouds from black to gray, and visibility increased to the point where the troops could see the outlines of objects. Slowly the rainfall gave way to heavy ground fog; a natural phenomenon that would mask the impending assault of the Yankees. Suddenly the rain stopped and the lead elements of Hancock's II Corps doublequicked out of the woods toward the apex of the salient. Within minutes the Unionists cleared their path of entangling abatis and mounted the Rebel parapet. Quickly the Bluecoats captured two general officers, upward of 3,000 prisoners, thirty-two stands of colors and an important half-mile segment of trench in the very heart of Lee's line. By all ordinary military standards, this major breakthrough in the Rebel works, accomplished against modest resistance, portended a decisive victory for the Federals. Ultimate victory on this day, however, rested just beyond the grasp of the Unionists. As suddenly as the

Federal soldiers overwhelmed the Graycoats, a partial paralysis struck the troops of the II Corps. The mob of captured enemy soldiers, coupled with the mass of disorganized Bluecoats spilling across the Rebel parapet, slowed the momentum of Hancock's assault. Then, a savage Confederate counterattack repulsed the wave of Yanks pouring through the breach at the apex of the salient, forcing the Unionists back to the initial line of captured Rebel trenches. At 6 a.m. Meade ordered Warren's V Corps and Wright's VI Corps to Hancock's support.[19]

In the pine forest, where the 96th Pennsylvania was posted, the Bluecoats tried to boil water for coffee over smoky, sputtering fires. The arrival of a mounted officer interrupted their breakfast. He read a congratulatory order from Grant regarding the fine work executed by the II Corps earlier in the morning.[20] Upon learning that the Unionists under Hancock had captured a Rebel division and twenty cannon the Yankees gave a rousing cheer. Then the Greek Cross men learned that they were going into battle to support the II Corps, which was still heavily engaged at the salient. According to Emory Upton, his brigade was positioned in the rear of the VI Corps. Not until 7 a.m. did Upton's brigade deploy along the right flank of the Greek Cross Corps' line of battle. Shortly afterward, the brigade was ordered to march behind the VI Corps to support the wavering right flank of the II Corps line. Upton immediately set his brigade in motion, at the double-quick, toward a point along the salient that was forever after to be known as the "Bloody Angle" to the Bluecoat veterans.[21]

Upton galloped ahead of his mobile field command in order to reconnoiter the situation on the right flank of the II Corps. Stopping his mount on a slight elevation, the newly appointed brigadier general—he had been promoted by Grant "for gallant and meritorious services," in the charge of May 10—could see that the II Corps troops were exchanging furious rifle fire along a "V" shaped protrusion on the western face of the salient; just to the right of this angle was the focal point of Upton's May 10 assault.[22] After carefully reviewing the tactical situation, Upton moved to the head of his column and instructed Gosline's Zouaves to "take a steady step" toward the crest of ground he had just stood on observing the battle. Returning to the slight elevation, Upton "saw that the flank of the [II Corps] troops had been turned and that they had been compelled to abandon the entrenchments to the point where I then stood."[23] A moment later, as the 95th Pennsylvania reached the crest of ground in front of the salient, the unit received a fearful volley from a Confederate battle line occupying the Rebel works. At this point Upton ordered the head of the 95th Pennsylvania to lie down and open fire while the body and tail of the column, still advancing at the double-quick, swung around to the left and anchored their left flank. In a postwar memoir, one Unionist recalled the fearful rifle fire that raked the Bluecoats as they hugged the muddy crest of ground for protection: "I can-not imagine how any of us survived the sharp fire that swept over us at this point— a fire so keen that it split the blades of grass all about us, the minies moaning as they picked out victims by the score."[24]

In an attempt to inspire the courageous men of his command, Upton sent an aide, most likely Captain Fish of the 121st New York, to order up the brigade band, posted about a mile in the rear. Band members, as previously noted, were usually stationed at field hospitals and assisted the wounded during a battle. Subsequently, the musicians were found and sent forward at the double quick. Upon reaching Upton's position a few of the bandsmen issued some wry remarks regarding their unforeseen assignment. One musician stated, "We didn't enlist to play in a fight," while another opined, "[I] don't see what the general wants to get us up here to get killed for." Maneuvering the band within sight of the brigade, hotly engaged with the enemy, Captain Fish used the undulating terrain to shelter the bandsmen and reported to Upton for further orders. At this point, however, given the intensity of the engagement, Upton countermanded his previous order for music from the brigade band and granted permission for the musicians to retire to a less dangerous position. Captain Fish returned to inform the bandsmen of Upton's decision only to find that "not a "horn" was to be seen." Looking across the field, through the rain, Captain Fish spotted "the coattails of some two or three (the others were probably in advance of them) were seen flapping in the breeze, as they disappeared over the horizon." Many of the bandsmen, since the return home of the 16th and 27th New York regiments, were musicians from the 96th Pennsylvania. Another soldier, who witnessed the skedaddle of the musicians stated, "Well … no wonder, thems Pennsylvania."[25]

As the 95th Pennsylvania, cheered on by Upton, cleared the abatis in front of their position and stormed the Rebel works, the 96th Pennsylvania struggled to come to the support of Gosline's Zouaves. Emerging from a belt of woods into a muddy field, the unit received a deadly volley at close range. Lessig immediately ordered his regiment to lie down. Initially slowed by the rifle fire, Lessig soon rallied his unit and advanced the troops a short distance to support the 95th Pennsylvania.[26] Disregarding the heavy fire, the Gosline's Zouaves clambered over the parapet at the Bloody Angle. Only a determined effort by the proud Butternuts turned back the charge of the Zouaves. While the 95th Pennsylvania received a murderous volley from the Graycoats, Upton, the only mounted officer within the vicinity of the angle, realigned the other elements of his brigade. Within a short time, the 5th Maine and 121st New York were sandwiched between Gosline's Zouaves on the left flank and the 96th Pennsylvania on the right of the line. Once in position Upton described the fighting in his official report. "At this point where our line diverged from the works the opposing line came in contact, but neither would give ground and for eighteen hours raged the most sanguinary conflict of the war."[27]

At this point the Unionists held one side of the "V" shaped Bloody Angle, while the enemy clung desperately to the other side. At the apex of the Bloody Angle, the sector held by Upton's brigade, the Union and Confederate soldiers were face-to-face. Fighting at arm's length across the parapet, the combatants were embroiled in a struggle that lasted sixteen hours. Throughout the day, in the midst of a drenching rainstorm, the opposing troops poured rifle fire into each other's lines. Down in the trenches, dead and wounded soldiers were trampled out of sight by their comrades filling their vacant post along the line. Suddenly the fighting at the Bloody Angle turned white hot. The Confederates counterattacked and regained their lost trenches at the angle. Upton, realizing the peril to his brigade and the advantage gained by the enemy, bravely cheered his troops, hat in hand, and pleaded with his men to "hold this point."[28]

About 9:30 in the morning, Upton's brigade of the VI Corps was ordered forward to support the right flank of the beleaguered II Corps.[29] Little did the soldiers of the 96th Pennsylvania know that morning, as they moved forward, that the fighting would again be conducted at close quarters. Unlike the assault of May 10, however, which ended in approximately ninety minutes, the combat of May 12 would last seven agonizing hours. Initially, Upton ordered forward the 95th Pennsylvania and then the 121st New York and the 5th Maine, both regiments deploying to the right of the Zouaves. Finally, the Schuylkill

Countians moved into position and secured the brigade's right flank. Henry Keiser recalled the opening moments of the engagement in his diary. "We went in on the right in a thick woods and ran into a line of Rebels and received a heavy volley at close range. We had orders to lie down close."[30] Most likely, the "heavy volley" which staggered the Pennsylvanians, came from Brig. Gen. Nat Harris' Mississippians, or Brig. Gen. Samuel McGowan's brigade of South Carolinians. Firing into the unsuspecting ranks of the 96th Pennsylvania, in order to strengthen their position at what the soldier's would later call the "Bloody Angle," the Confederates solidified their line as the Yankees massed for an assault in their front. Thomas Roche, serving with the 16th Mississippi, described the scene at approximately 10 a.m. in front of the "Bloody Angle." "Just then the Federals made their third desperate charge on our front. This time they were met by the stern front of the Mississippians and South Carolinians, who strove to rival each other in acts of courage. The enemy continued steadily to advance. The contest grew in fierceness. Reeling to and fro, and shattered terribly by the murderous fire from our works, he stubbornly pressed on, almost up to the muzzles of our guns when he began to give way."[31]

A Bluecoat serving in Upton's brigade, writing after the war, described the importance of the desperate close quarters fighting waged across the parapet at the "Bloody Angle." According to this veteran, Upton's brigade was thrust into the fray.

> [We] went into action on the "double quick," under a galling and severe fire, and took position to the right of a point known as the "angle," so called, was strengthened by a huge breast-works of logs and earth, and was held by a force of Mississippi and South Carolina troops. The rain was pouring in torrents, yet the men readily obeyed the order to lie down in the mud and commence firing.[32]

A soldier with the 121st New York recalled the chaotic scene near the "Bloody Angle" in a postwar memoir. "The fog, rain and mist loaded with smoke, obscured our view partially. The enemy's fire came from our right and front, but we were partially protected by their works and we kept up a continuous fire.... Where we were the works were V-shaped, the point or bottom of the V being toward us. We held the works from the point down the left side of the V as it faced us, and the Rebs held the right side."[33] After the initial volley from the Confederates, Lieutenant Luckenbill noted in his diary that "our Brigade rallied reformed and fell back behind their first line of works now in our possession and kept up a terrific fire of musketry and artillery all day."[34]

According to General Harris, commanding the Mississippians defending the

John Bennett (MOLLUS Mass. Collection, United States Army Heritage and Education Center).

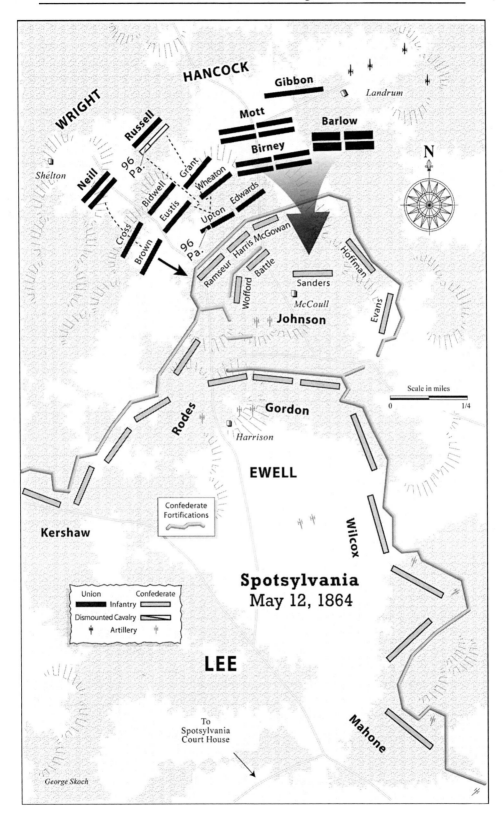

WRIGHT

HANCOCK

Gibbon

Landrum

Russell

Mott

Barlow

Neill

96 Pa.

Grant

Birney

Shelton

Bidwell

Wheaton

Eustis

Edwards

Cross

Upton

Brown

96 Pa.

McGowan

Harris

Ramseur

Battle

Hoffman

Wofford

Sanders

McCoull

Evans

Johnson

Rodes

Gordon

Harrison

EWELL

Confederate
Fortifications

Wilcox

Kershaw

Scale in miles

0   1/4

Union   Confederate

Infantry

Dismounted Cavalry

Artillery

Spotsylvania
May 12, 1864

N

LEE

Mahone

To
Spotsylvania
Court House

George Skoch

Mule Shoe, "A cold, drenching rain fell during the greater portion of the day and night and the trenches were filled with water."[35] While the rain hindered and restricted troop movement, it did not prevent the combatants from exchanging incessant rifle fire at close range. Hour after deadly hour the soldiers loaded and fired their weapons fighting desperately and in many instances within a few feet of each other. A soldier with the 16th Mississippi later wrote that "the firing from the enemy at this point was terrible in its fierceness … [no] human could apparently survive it. The Federals on the right would quickly throw their guns over the traverse without exposing the head or body, and fire into this pit, the bullets striking with a dull, sickening thud into the dead bodies that were piled within it."[36] A member of McGowan's brigade, serving with the 1st South Carolina, recalled that "not for a *moment* during that *day and night* did the firing cease. Sometimes the Yankees would put their rifles over the works and fire on our men as we crouched down, but they could not get at us. Nothing but a pile of logs separated us."[37] Outside the Mule Shoe, hugging the ground, the 96th persevered against the elements and continued to battle the Secessionists.

For the courageous men of the 96th Pennsylvania, the day proved to be a harrowing experience. For hours the men hugged the muddy ground and exchanged fire at close range with the Confederate defenders inside the Mule Shoe. Lieutenant Luckenbill recorded the following thoughts about the Battle of the "Bloody Angle." "Heavy rain falling nearly all day. Mud a foot deep. There we were firing as fast as they could load the line of battle right in front of us."[38] Henry Keiser recalled the intensity of the combat that day in his diary. "We received a continual shower of lead over the pits so that the Rebels did not have much [of a] chance to raise and fire at us … but we kept up the fire and we were covered with mud from head to foot."[39] In his memoir, James Treichler described the grim fighting at the Bloody Angle.

> In this engagement our Brigade occupied a position close to this salient (or bloody angle as it was sometimes called) in a depreshion to the right. The works we were confronting, were still occupied by the enemy, who were compelled to keep close to them and well under cover, on account of our troops occupying the works on the left, who were thus able to direct their fire, on account of the angle, close to the rear of the works, and kept a constant and study [steady] fire all day from fireing into us, or attempting to get away. We lost but very few men during the day, and they were mostly picked off by sharp-shooters.[40]

All day the battle raged back and forth across the lines at the "Bloody Angle." Maurus Oestreich noted in his diary, "Not for a second has this fearful battering stopped. Hundreds of men get wounded and killed in a few hours."[41] According to James Treichler, pack mules were used to bring ammunition to the soldiers. "Two cases of ammunition were strapped together and thrown over the back of the mule and brought to our rear, and broken open and each man supplied himself as needed. I used five guns during the day; when one became too hot or dirty for use, I picked up another from among those strewn in plenty over the ground around us."[42] The last line of Keiser's diary entry stated that "I fired one hundred and sixty rounds at the 'Angle' today. My right arm being almost useless tonight from the re-bound [recoil] of my rifle."[43] A soldier in the 5th Maine described the furious nature of the engagement in his diary.

> At this point we seemed much of the time to have no organization. Not only were companies mixed together, but regiments and brigades. We would sometimes lose ground little by little; we

were up to the works several times during the day, but when the rebs would concentrate their fire on us we would gradually lose ground till we would be, perhaps three or four rods from the works, then we would press forward and gain them again.[44]

Brig. Gen. Lewis Grant, commanding the Vermont brigade, stated, "Several times during the day the rebels would show a white flag about the works, and when our fire slackened jump over and surrender."[45] Lieutenant Luckenbill recalled such an incident in his diary. "About 2 p.m. they raised a white flag. The command was then given to cease firing and about 30 prisoners came over."[46] Henry Keiser also recorded a similar situation during the fighting at the angle in his journal. "Today a captain and twelve of his men jumped up in all the fire, and ran into our lines (our boys not firing on them). As they passed by me the Captain said, "The Devil couldn't stand it in there." They were covered with mud and blood."[47]James Treichler, however, remembered a different version of events concerning the Confederates waving a white surrender flag. "Soon after we had relieved the charging troops in the morning, they succeeded in playing a ruse upon us by raising a white flag and asking to surrender. We ceased firing at once; they then raised and fired over the trenches, a deadly volley of musketry into our ranks … but in their excitement, they fired to high and but a few were killed or wounded."[48]

Tactically, the situation was deteriorating rapidly for the Federals at the Bloody Angle. Troop fatigue was fast becoming a factor in how long they could maintain their positions. Casualties, rapidly thinning the ranks of the combat troops, were posing a dilemma for Union generals. Also, there was a limit to how long the Yankees could simply trade rifle fire with the enemy without either side achieving some sort of limited victory. In an attempt to break through the Confederates holding the Bloody Angle, Upton ordered forward two brass fieldpieces from Battery C, 5th United States Artillery. The guns came splashing up through the mud and the rain to the Union line and were wheeled about within rods of the entrenched Confederate infantry. The gunners sent double charges of canister plowing through the enemy's ranks with horrifying re - sults. Not satisfied with the initial havoc they had wrought, the gun crews ran the fieldpieces forward by hand until they touched the very parapet, and then they resumed firing. Within moments, however, with the cannoneers and drivers either dead or wounded, the two brass pieces lay quiet with their muzzles projecting defiantly over the enemy's works and their wheels half sunk in the mud. With the guns silent, Upton's brigade withdrew slightly from the breastworks but maintained a lively fusillade.[49]

Pvt. Thomas Holloran, Company K. Transferred to 95th Pennsylvania October 18, 1864 (courtesy Michael Cavanaugh).

As the morning turned to afternoon, the rifle fire continued across the Bloody Angle. Upton instructed his brigade to concentrate its fire against the top logs of the breastworks and the adjacent traverses which were eventually "splinted like brush-brooms, while the oak abatis in front was completely shot away."[50] The rifle fire that missed this target— and there many Federal soldiers with poor aim—passed harmlessly over the heads of the Confederates only to destroy a grove of trees within the salient. Late in the afternoon, Upton's exhausted brigade was relieved and sent to the rear. In a postwar article on the fighting at the Bloody Angle, one of Upton's Bluecoats recalled his physical condition at the end of the day's battle:

> Our lips were incrusted [sic] with powder from "biting cartridge." Our shoulders and hands were coated with mud that had adhered to the butts of our rifles ... [and we needed to fall] back a short distance to rearrange our shattered ranks and get something to eat, which we were sadly in need of when darkness came on we dropped of exhaustion.[51]

One of Wright's staff officers, in trying to describe the fighting at the Bloody Angle after the battle wrote: "I never expect to be fully believed when I tell what I saw of the horrors of Spotsylvania, because I should be loath to believe it myself were the case reversed."[52] Before dawn the Butternuts abandoned the Mule Shoe and assumed a new position behind a freshly constructed line of entrenchments at the base of the salient.

Although the battle inflicted modest casualties upon the 96th Pennsylvania, the engagement was characteristic of Grant's evolving campaign. In eight days of constant combat, from May 5 through May 12, the 96th suffered 35 killed in action, 133 wounded and 45 missing, or men presumed dead or captured by the Confederates.[53] According to Jerome Miller of Company G, the 96th lost about twenty men in the deadly encounter at the "Bloody Angle."[54] Lieutenant Luckenbill recorded losses of two men killed, thirteen wounded and four missing in his diary that day.[55] The Schuylkill County regiment left Brandy Station with 420 men and now numbered slightly more than 200. Grant's relentless campaign was exacting a heavy toll upon the Unionists as well as the Confederates. Despite the enormous casualties in the VI Corps, morale remained high and the soldiers were confident in their cause and their commanders. One soldier stated: "We have been fighting like fury ... and are now nearly worn out, as you may well imagine, but we keep up good cheer and feel 'bully,' confident of ultimate victory."[56] Another Bluecoat informed his readers at home that "so far as we can learn our cause goes bravely on. We have already gained large advantages, and we are able to hold it, and follow it up, we believe. The army is well satisfied with Grant's plans and movements thus far, and is giving him its most entire confidence."[57]

Throughout this deadly affair both sides were locked in an intractable tactical situation from which neither could or would loosen his respective grip. It was a form of warfare neither side ever imagined or experienced in this war. A Bluecoat with the 5th Maine later recalled, "When our regiment was relieved it was about four rods from the works, but all were in line of battle and every man seemed to be doing his best. The men were wet and covered with mud, and the hours were long, but the fighting was stubborn.... The bullets whistled all night, as the fighting at that contested point was kept up until 3 a.m., when the rebs at this point fell back and moved back a little farther and lay down among the dead bodies of rebs who had fallen in the fight of last Tuesaday, and still lay unburied."[58] At the end of the day, about 10 p.m., the Pennsylvanians camped in the pine woods, near the spot where they formed for attack on May 10. Lieutenant Luckenbill recorded in his diary, "We fell in and marched to the right in pine woods. Heavy rain falling. Lay in line of battle all night without any fires. Cold all wet. Very disagreeable…. Heavy picket firing all night along the line."[59]

Early the next morning, Federal patrols reported the retreat of the Graycoats. Union burial details then performed their somber business at the angle. In order to bury the dead, the labor parties simply turned the breastworks upon the corpses lying in the trenches.[60] This prompted one Pennsylvanian to remark, "the unfortunate victims [had] unwittingly dug their own graves." Maurus Oestreich, of the 96th Pennsylvania, witnessed the carnage at the Bloody Angle on May 13. In his journal he wrote the following:

> The rebels have left their works, so on the 13th we went to look at what was left, and O God, what a sight, fearful to pen in my book that a person may read it after the War is over! Thousands of dead bodies are seen and the trenches are filled with them, 4 and 5 on top of each other, and sometimes the lowest on the bottom are wounded and alive, yet were covered with mud and smothered. Trees of 1 and 2 feet thick are shot off by musket bullets, and the wounded and dead bodies which had fallen in the first charge at the commencement of the battle were shot to pieces by the 1/2 inch and mashed. Stacks of wood and trenches were no stronger in withstanding our brave soldiers' bullets and artillery batteries. I have seen so much that I can't nor will put it in this book. I will seal this in my memory by myself. God, have mercy on those who started this cruel war.[61]

For the Bluecoats of the VI Corps, the abandoned Confederate Mule Shoe revealed the horrors of Spotsylvania. A Vermont officer recalled, "I was at the angle the next day. The sight was terrible and sickening, much worse than the Bloody Lane (Antietam). There a great many dead men were lying in the road and across the rails of the torn down fences, and out in the cornfield; but they were not piled up several deep and their flesh was not so torn and mangled at the 'angle.'"[62] Lieutenant Luckenbill recorded his recollections of the dead at the dreaded Mule Shoe in his diary. "Found many of our men dead on the field. All carried out and buried near the entrenchments…. Went over the battlefield. A terrible sight. Dead and wounded piled on top of each other from both sides who have been lying here three four days ago. Awful smell. Trees all cut down and smashed from bullets. The greatest sight I ever witnessed."[63] Henry Keiser recalled that "at one o'clock today we left the woods and halted where we had made the charge and gathered some of our dead, who were swollen and bloated so that they could scarcely be recognized…. We buried them in one trench, first placing a blanket underneath and one on top, placing a board of a cracker box, with the name, Company and Regiment marked thereon, at the head of each."[64]

According to a soldier serving in the 2nd Vermont, he overheard General Russell refer to the Battle of the "Bloody Angle" as "a regular bull-dog fight," which he never before witnessed until the armies reached Spotsylvania.[65] The same soldier stated that he visited the battlefield the morning after the Confederates abandoned the Mule Shoe. In a letter he stated, "I visited the place the next morning, and though I have seen horrid scenes since this war commenced, I never saw anything half so bad as that. Our men layed piled one top of another, nearly all shot through the head. There were many among them that I knew well, five from my own company. On the rebel side it was worse than ours. In some places the men were piled four or five deep, some of whom were still alive. I turned away from that place, glad to escape from such a terrible, sickening sight."[66] A New York officer reported to his wife that "after eight days of the hardest fighting the world has ever witnessed, I have an opportunity of telling you that I am still alive and as yet unhurt…. No tongue can describe the horrors of the scene around me. Dead and dying men by scores and hundreds lie piled upon each other in promiscuous disorder. God has seen fit so far to spare me, for which I truly feel thankful. I cannot even attempt to give you a *slight* idea of this field of death. All around you lie the unmistakable evidences that death is doing its most frightful work."[67]

Another Bluecoat in Upton's brigade published a graphic report of the human misery he observed in the vicinity of the Mule Shoe after the Battle of the "Bloody Angle." His lengthy essay essentially concluded that the high number of casualties was the price of vanquishing the Confederacy.

> As soon as daylight appeared I visited the place, and there beheld a sight never before witnessed by one who has been on many a hard fought battlefield…. Within' the redoubt, which was partially filled with water and mire from the rain of the previous day, lay the enemy three and in some places *four deep!* In every conceivable form. Some with their arms off, others with their heads nearly severed from their bodies, proving that our mortar shells must have done terrible execution. Beneath this mass of, what were once, human beings, I could discern now and then some poor wretches who yet retained some life, but who were being crushed by the weight of dead above them and being suffocated by the filth and water they were lying in. That awful sight can never be forgotten by those who witnessed it. If one was inclined to any sympathy for those miserable infatuated beings who had just perished, he would have but to look behind him and see the thickly strewed forms of many a gallant Union soldier, whose death will cause so much anguish in his quiet home in the North, to believe that the punishment, though terrible, was just, and with your correspondent exclaim, "May this be the fate of all the enemies of our country."[68]

During the next week, the Army of the Potomac fought a battle of some sort every day. Other than engaging in routine picket duty, the 96th Pennsylvania during this period was relatively inactive. On May 14, however, the regiment, along with the balance of Upton's brigade, which numbered less than 800 Bluecoats, was ordered to cross the Ny River and seize Myers Hill, to the left and front of Warren's V Corps.[69] On the march toward Myers Hill, Henry Keiser of Company G, temporarily captured a rebel major. In his diary he recorded particulars of the exciting event.

> At about 4 p.m. we again advanced, but had not gone far when a short distance ahead, I seen a Rebel hat lying on the edge of a gully washed out along the edge of a woods. I says to John Gloss, the man to my right, "There is a Rebel hat, and the Reb is not far off." I soon seen the top of a Reb's head, who was sitting down in the gully. I brought my rifle to bear on him, and asked his to surrender. He jumped up holding his hands above his head and said, "For God's sake don't shoot." … not one minute after he was taken to the rear, we ran into two full lines of Rebs, and I tell you, we were not slow in getting back, each one for himself. I was very nearly taken, but "halt you Yankee Son of a ____," did not stop me. I got over the stream by crossing on a submerged log, and got wet to the knees. A poor excited soldier jumped into the stream right below me … and all that could be seen after were a few bubbles. During the skedaddle the Rebel Major got away.[70]

As Upton's soldiers reached Myers Hill, the young brigadier general discovered that a regiment of regulars had already carried the position. After relieving these troops, Upton's attention was drawn to a hill about 800 yards on his right where a regiment of Confederate infantry was forming. The presence of Upton's brigade south of the Ni River on the high ground where the Myers farm house (one soldier described it as a mansion) was situated, posed a threat to the Confederates and hence resulted in a tactical response.[71] After confirming the presence of Graycoat cavalry on his left and the movement of enemy soldiers on his right, through the lookout posted atop the mansion on Myers Hill, Upton sent a message to Wright explaining to the VI Corps commander that he could not hold his position without the support of another brigade. Not having a brigade to spare, the leader of the Greek Cross Corps dispatched the 2nd and 10th New Jersey Volunteers to Upton's active sector. As Upton waited, his command constructed a breastwork of fence rails along a perimeter in front of the house and out buildings. After being reinforced by the New Jersey regiments, Upton ordered the 96th forward with instructions to push the enemy off the distant hill that they occupied. After receiving Upton's directive to advance against the Rebels—Upton was concerned that the enemy's sharpshooters might occupy the wooded area nearest the mansion—Lessig ordered his regiment to form a line of battle. As they assembled for their advance, the company commanders checked the alignment of the troops, while the junior officers and sergeants took their positions in the rear of the formation to act as file closers.[72]

According to Upton, "About 4 p.m. the lookout [posted on the top of the Myers farm house] discovered [enemy] infantry skirmishers on the hill," 800 yards in the distance.[73] Two brigades of Confederate infantry, General Harris' Mississippians, bloodied from the day-long Battle of May 12, and Gen. Ambrose Wright's Georgians, virtually unscathed thus far in the campaign. Subsequently, in response to the sighting of Confederate infantry, Upton directed Lieutenant Colonel Lessig to move the 96th Pennsylvania forward and occupy a point of woods across the field from the base of Myers hill, in order to secure that area from being infiltrated by Confederate sharpshooters.[74]As the 96th Pennsylvania advanced in line of battle, General Meade and General Wright rode up to the Myers farm house where Upton invited them to watch the action unfold in the fields below the high ground. Lessig quickly led his regiment across the farm field but upon entering the woods the Pennsylvanians encountered two veteran Confederate brigades forming to charge Upton's weakly held and lightly supported position. It was at this point Henry Keiser stumbled upon the Confederate major—most likely one of Wright's Georgians—who had moved forward to the edge of the woods to ascertain a better view of the Union position. Before advancing his entire regiment further into the woods, Lessig decided to develop additional intelligence concerning the presence and strength of the Confederates massing in the forest.

Viewed from his command post on Myers hill, Upton related the opening scene of the brief skirmish in his after-action report. "Colonel Lessig had scarcely entered the wood before he encountered two brigades of infantry, forming to charge our position. He [Lessig and the 96th Pennsylvania] immediately fell back, while at the same time the Ninety-fifth Pennsylvania and Tenth New Jersey were ordered forward. They were barely in position when the enemy's column emerged from the wood."[75] Lieutenant Luckenbill recorded that it was a "cloudy rainy [day]. Very muddy. Arrived at the front. Our regiment sent out to skirmish the pine woods. Established a line away from our works several miles. The rebels charged and drove us back."[76] A soldier in General Wright's Georgia brigade wrote a graphic account of the battle four days after the engagement. "Proceeding about a mile, line of battle was formed and the brigade advanced to find the enemy and assault his breastworks…. On the line pressed, through thick bushes, over the fence, into the orchard just before the enemy's works…. Exchanging a few rounds with the enemy the Brigade rushed upon the foe. On, over the entrenchments we went, the Yankees fleeing like frightened deer before us."[77] A soldier with the 3rd Georgia later stated that the fighting lasted only twenty minutes. "Our loss was," he added further, "for the length of time engaged very severe, being seventy-eight men killed and wounded."[78]

Upon entering the woods on the far side of the field across from Upton's position, Lessig's unit stumbled upon two full enemy brigades. Realizing the great peril that confronted his regiment, Lessig ordered his troops to retreat—along with the two companies of the 2nd New Jersey who were supporting the reconnaissance movement—to the crude line of works in front of the mansion. As the Pennsylvanians withdrew from the woods, Upton pushed forward the 95th Pennsylvania and the 10th New Jersey, in order to block the advance of the oncoming Graycoats. As the two Union regiments deployed in the field in front of the mansion, a squadron of Confederate cavalry, with a battery of horse artillery, galloped onto the field to the left of the house, unlimbered, and opened fire, enfilading the Union line. Maurus Oestreich described the engagement in greater detail. "Our brigade was out on the skirmish line and…. At 4 p.m. we were driven back by three lines of the rebel battle line. In order to get out of there we had to retreat at double quick, for the rebels had flanked us on both sides, nearly surrounding the whole cavalry and some battery pieces there, intending to take us all prisoners before dark by surprise."[79] Unable to effectively halt the determined Butternuts, Upton instructed his command to abandon its position on Myers Hill. Commenting on the retreat after the war, one Bluecoat had this to say: "Some of our men jumped into [the Ny River and tried to wade] across, but the water was too deep and they were fished out, wetter and wiser men."[80] That evening, after reorganizing his command, Upton marched his brigade back across the river and reoccupied the abandoned position atop Myers Hill.[81]

Given the situation, and reluctance to advance without further intelligence, Lessig decided to send a scout into the woods in order to develop additional information regarding enemy strength. According to a soldier in Upton's brigade, "A bright little fellow, some thirteen years of age, a stray waif in the army, who had been a sort of waiter around head-quarters begged for the privilege of going saying he, "was'nt afrad, they couldn't hit him."[82] Lessig acquiesced, gave the youngster a horse and "away the little fellow galloped within shooting distance of the enemy, where he halted, and coolly surveyed the situation, until several shots admonished him of his dangerous position." Immediately, he rode back, waving his cap, to Lieutenant Colonel Lessig and reported that he saw "lots of them in the woods." As Lessig sought to complete his mission, suddenly the woods erupted with the sound of musketry. A soldier with the 121st New York recalled the opening sights and sounds of the engagement. "While we were attending to the enemy in front the 96th Pennsylvania moved out in line of battle and advanced toward the woods. We expected to continue this advance, but the 96th had scarcely disappeared in the woods when they met the enemy, and immediately the battle broke out."[83]

Upton reported total casualties, killed, wounded and missing at "about 100." According to Henry Keiser, the 96th Pennsylvania was "scattered in all directions" by the overpowering attack of the Georgians.[84] A New York officer, however, captured the affair in amusing fashion in a letter to his wife. "An advance is made of about thirty or forty rods when we come flying back in all sorts of a hurry. Every man for himself. Here we had *another* run for sweet life. Plenty of grape and canister, minie balls and shot help us over the ground…. From the fact that we ran *so well* and after the command to *advance*, it is henceforth to be known as 'Upton's Run!'"[85]

For six days after the engagement at Myers' Hill the 96th Pennsylvania marched and countermarched behind the Union lines. Finally, on May 20 the fighting around Spotsylvania stopped and the Army of the Potomac began pushing south, past Lee's flank. As the long march for the James River was resumed, the spirits of the men in the ranks rose dramatically. There had been continuous fighting or marching for more than two weeks. The Bluecoats had neither taken off their clothing or had an unbroken night's rest since they crossed the Rapidan. Losses had been staggering. Many brigades—Upton's among them—were no bigger than regiments, and many units were down to normal company strength. The army moved south from Spotsylvania Court House, having lost 33,000 men in the Wilderness fighting and the bloody Spotsylvania campaign. In this time, the army averaged 2,000 Unionists either killed, wounded or missing every twenty-four hours. Instead of pulling back for a breathing spell—the option McClellan or Hooker might have chosen—Grant's army tried once more to march around Lee's flank and force the Butternuts to fight a pitched battle in open country.[86]

XIV

"There was hope in the air"

During the last ten days of May, the Army of the Potomac executed a series of marches to get around Lee's flank. A rash of little firefights for river crossings and little known road intersections proved indecisive. During this period the only war-like propensity displayed by the 96th Pennsylvania was the destruction of a strip of railroad track on May 25 along the Virginia Central Railroad near Noel's Station. Lieutenant Luckenbill stated that the men "burned the ties and bent the rails a good distance."[1] Another Bluecoat recalled the details of this process in a postwar history. "We would form on the uphill side of the track, and taking hold and lifting turn the track completely over, and removing the ties stack and cord them, setting fire to the piles, the rails on top of the ties thus piled…. Then we would take the rails off the piles and wind them around trees or stumps."[2] Destroying the railroad was an integral part of Grant's operations along the North Anna River. Unable to pierce Lee's formidable breastworks at North Anna, Grant abandoned the endeavor and marched his army southeast toward Hanover town, where the Bluecoats planned to cross the Pamunkey River.

Upon crossing the Pamunkey, Grant found Lee's troops dug in behind the headwaters of an insignificant stream called Totopotomoy Creek. The chance of breaking Lee's defensive line here looked as grim as it had several days earlier along the south bank of the North Anna River. Consequently, Grant opted once more to slip past Lee's right flank. As May came to a close the Unionists were once more marching around the Confederates. Learning of Grant's intentions, Lee again shifted his forces to block the advance of the oncoming Yankees. This time Lee chose to form his defensive line around an unobtrusive tavern, situated at a relatively quiet crossroads known locally as Cold Harbor.[3]

As the month of May ended, the Schuylkill Countians were nearly out of rations and many of them needed rest. Rather than allowing the exhausted soldiers to rest from the tiring marches, commanders ordered the 96th to conduct a reconnaissance mission in the vicinity of Mechanicsville. Rations finally reached the famished soldiers that night. Henry Keiser recalled that "the boys were up most all night cooking and eating."[4] Writing from camp on the last day of the month Erasmus Reed penned a quick letter to his folks at home. "Our line of battle now is near and around Mechanicsville, and there is considerable fighting all along the lines. I expect we will [be]siege Richmond again shortly…. Our Army is today as strong or stronger than it was when we started from winter quarters…. There has been fighting more or less every single day this month."[5] The morrow would bring more marching and more fighting.

The opening act of the Battle of Cold Harbor for the 96th Pennsylvania took the form of a long march. Early in the morning on June 1, the Schuylkill Countians left their encampment near Atlee's Station and started toward the strategic crossroads at Cold Harbor. According to Henry Keiser, "It was very hot and dusty, and we were all played out."[6] Diary entries by Henry Keiser and Lewis Luckenbill indicate that the 96th marched at 6 a.m. and arrived at Cold Harbor at 2 o'clock in the afternoon. Other soldiers in Upton's brigade, however, recorded that the Bluecoats reached "Cool Arbor" as early as 11 a.m. Upton, in his detailed report, states that the brigade reached Cold Harbor at 11 a.m. While some soldiers recorded a different hour regarding the exact time the brigade reached Cold Harbor, there is considerable agreement concerning the time when the Bluecoats arrayed for battle.[7] Between four and five o'clock, Upton's brigade deployed in line and prepared to attack the Graycoats. The Schuylkill Countians formed the fourth line in Upton's deep tactical formation, posted in front of eighteen pieces of Union artillery. Henry Keiser recorded the scene in his pocket diary. "At 4 p.m. our Regiment and the balance of the old Brigade were placed in line of battle about 30 yards in front of three batteries, as a support to the 2nd [Connecticut] Heavies who were ordered to make a charge across a swamp."[8]

Upon reaching Cold Harbor early in the afternoon, Wright's exhausted foot soldiers relieved General Sheridan's beleaguered troopers. After marching all morning, Upton's brigade arrived opposite the Confederate works, and went into position in the middle of the Union line, flanked by "Baldy" Smith's XVIII Corps—just called up from Butler's Army of the James operating at Bermuda Hundred—to their right. After a great deal of delay—primarily on the slowness of Smith's corps in getting into position—late in the afternoon the Unionists launched an assault. Upton formed his command into a column of four lines, the newly arrived 2nd Connecticut Volunteer Heavy Artillery—a former artillery regiment converted to infantry—comprising the first three lines. A detachment from the 121st New York formed as skirmishers in front of the Connecticut men, while the balance of that unit, the 95th and 96th Pennsylvania and the 5th Maine formed the fourth attack line. The last line of Upton's troops were instructed to act as a rear or provost guard during the assault and to allow only wounded troops to pass to the rear of the Union line.[9]

Not knowing the relative strength of the opposing troops, a brigade of North Carolinians commanded by Brig. Gen. Thomas L. Clingman, Upton's brigade was ordered forward. About 6:30 p.m., the 2nd Connecticut attacked Clingman's North Carolinians in an assault which constituted a forlorn hope. Seeing the Heavies move forward, the Union artillery roared to life hurling missiles against the Tarheels. The "Heavies," as they jauntily referred to themselves, marched in close order across the field to meet the enemy, Henry Keiser recalled that they went into battle "like old veterans."[10] As the 2nd Connecticut began its assault, under the supervision of its big, burly, red-faced commander, Col. Elisha S. Kellogg, the Rebels opened fire. Within moments the 1,800 Connecticut men were caught "in a sheet of flame, sudden as lightning, red as blood—so near that it seemed to singe the men's faces."[11] In a few minutes two hundred of the Nutmeg men were shot down. Kellogg, after shouting the command, "About face," was struck twice in the head by rifle fire and fell dead. Upton, seeing the Connecticut men milling around like sheep in front of the Rebel works, galloped to the regiment and tried to regroup the demoralized soldiers. Initially Upton, the battlefield tested professional soldier, sought to rally the green troops, this being the 2nd Connecticut's first full scale experience under fire. Realizing that they were trapped, frightened, and pinned down—due to a Confederate counterattack—Upton gradually withdrew the unit to its original line of breastworks. After reorganizing the "Heavies" behind the Union line, Upton ordered the Nutmeg troops to continue firing. A Connecticut company commander, fearful that the enemy might overrun his sector of the line sent word to Upton of his concern. To that notion Upton replied, "If they [the Confederates] come, catch them on your bayonets, and pitch them over your heads!"[12]

As the Connecticut men advanced, Lieutenant Luckenbill recalled the impact the artillery had on the soldiers formed in reserve in front of the guns. The lieutenant reported, "Heavy skirmishing going on in our front. Cannons playing on us hard as they could fairly lifting us from the ground. Terrible fighting. Captured 50 prisoners in one lot and 171 in another. Adjutant John Hannum right arm blown off."[13] Henry Keiser also recorded his thoughts concerning the artillery fire. "The Batteries in our rear … kept up a furious canonading. Our own, as well as the Rebel, shells flew around us like hail. One piece in the Battery directly in our rear exploded its shells right in our midst. The Adjutant's left arm was knocked off at the shoulder, and A.[braham] Dreibelbies' right foot was shattered by a shell from this piece."[14] According to Captain Boyle, "On this day Lieutenant John T. Hannum, of Company D, acting adjutant, received a mortal wound, of which he died on the 7th. He was an intelligent man and a good soldier."[15] For two hours the 2nd Connecticut fought valiantly against Clingman's North Carolinians. As the Heavies struggled to pierce the Confederate line, the 96th Pennsylvania moved forward to support the beleaguered Nutmeg men.

In order to bolster the wavering line of the 2nd Connecticut, the 96th Pennsylvania along with the 121st New York and 5th Maine would need to advance across an open field 300 yards to reach the position the Heavies were gallantly trying to hold. Henry Keiser recalled that "the shells flew around us like hail…. [A] Battery directly in our rear exploded…. We were advanced under fire, a short distance, halted and laid down."[16] Another Bluecoat stated that "the Rebel fire was very effective and it seemed to us from where we stood that our poor fellows would all get shot. The ground over which … [we advanced] was covered with men."[17] Darkness finally ended the fighting. Martin McMahon, serving on Gen. Wright's VI Corps staff, graphically recalled the grim scene which greeted the men of Upton's brigade the next morning. "The field in front of us … was indeed a sad sight…. The 2d Connecticut Heavy Artillery, a new regiment eighteen hundred strong, had joined us but a few days before the battle. Its uniform was bright and fresh; therefore its dead were easily distinguished where they lay. They marked in a dotted line an obtuse angle, covering a wide front, with its apex toward the enemy."[18]

After the 2nd Connecticut repulsed the Confederate counter-attack, the 96th Pennsylvania relieved them in the front line of Upton's position. As night cloaked the hot and windless battlefield, the tired Bluecoats tried to sleep on their arms in the trenches. As darkness came and the rifle fire died away along the line, the foot soldiers evaluated the gains they had achieved during the day. They had successfully driven Lee's troops out of Cold Harbor and tightened their grip on the vital crossroads. Unionist casualties, however, tempered Yankee achievements. During the evening Grant's lieutenants urged him to renew the assault at first light. Wright reported that if he and Hancock could not attack promptly at dawn, "I may lose what I have gained."[19] The next morning, as dawn heralded the coming of day, the soldiers remained behind the hastily erected breastworks. Along Upton's sector the 121st New York relieved the 96th Pennsylvania. As the Pennsylvanians retired to the rear, the continuous musketry of the previous day prompted Lieutenant Colonel Lessig to remark that his regiment "had fired 90,000 rounds of ammunition."[20]

The assault, proposed by Grant's lieutenants for June 2, however, failed to materialize. The inability of the Bluecoats to successfully march through the tangled woodlands, down narrow, dusty lanes in pitch-darkness to their assault positions, coupled with the bone-weary fatigue of the Yankees, rendered a morning attack impossible. An afternoon assault was also postponed. During this period of quiescence, while Grant pondered his strategy, Lee sought to bolster his sagging forces. Not only was Lee concerned about the constant battle stress on his troops due to Grant's savage attacks, but the Confederate commander desperately needed to replenish his ranks with fresh foot soldiers and replace general officers killed or wounded in the preceding battles. While Lee wrestled with his staff work, Grant, determined to break through the Confederate position, ordered an attack for June 3. That night the battered VI Corps, in line along the Richmond road, tried to get some rest, but the weary 96th Pennsylvania was denied sleep as it relieved Gosline's Zouaves on the skirmish line. As the grayness of first light grew brighter, they could see the cunningly and elaborately constructed breastworks of the Rebels. (The Confederate line ran from the Chickahominy swamps to the Totopotomy.) The works were constructed in an intricate angular fashion so that cross-fires protected all possible avenues of approach. The ground over which the Unionists were to advance was deceptive. The Confederate works—running along an uneven chain of low hills and ridges—did not appear to be particularly formidable. They were, however, ideal for defensive purposes. Just before dawn the rain stopped and the sky grew brighter. Suddenly, a gigantic crash of artillery, like a thunderclap, broke the morning quiet and signaled the beginning of the battle.[21]

Lieutenant Luckenbill recalled that daybreak on June 3 brought "terrible musketry and cannonading."[22] The soldiers of the 96th Pennsylvania were near the front of the Second Brigade's position. A New York veteran reported that "we were in the trenches when Generals Wright and Russell, and some staff and engineer officers passed along the line of works and attracted considerable attention from our men as well as from the Rebels who frequently sent lead messages to them as they exposed themselves. They spent considerable time in the trenches to the left of us talking with General Upton. Shortly after they went away, word was passed along that the order to charge had been countermanded at this place. Generals Russell and Upton deeming the position too strong to be taken."[23] Throughout the day, the Bluecoats improved their field works and dodged the Confederate sharpshooters. Lieutenant Luckenbill recalled that "our outer works and first line of the Rebels are only about 25 yards apart. Great many dead laying on the field unburied of the 2nd Conn. of our Brigade. All black. Awful bad smell."[24] Henry Keiser noted in his diary that "we are only thirty yards from them. The Rebel sharp-shooters tried hard to "pink" Yankee heads all day but we kept our heads low while digging. Some of our boys paid them back in their own coin. Several of our regiment were killed and wounded."[25] The 96th Pennsylvania suffered three men killed and about twelve wounded at Cold Harbor.[26]

For the next nine days the armies sniped at each other from behind the breastworks at Cold Harbor. Only a brief two hour cease fire on June 7 interrupted the relentless combat. Along most of the Union line the assault of June 3 was stopped before it ever had an opportunity to develop. The Army of the Potomac's major offensive, the culmination of a month-long campaign against the Confederates, dissolved into a series of disjointed fights along the Federal front. Throughout the day heavy rifle fire in front of the VI Corps pinned down Wright's troops. Emory Upton, in his report of the Cold Harbor operations, simply stated that "another assault was ordered, but being deemed impracticable along our front was not made."[27] After trying to pierce the Rebel breastworks for five hours without success, Meade formally suspended the assault. The carnage on the field effectively demonstrated the folly of another frontal attack. Nearly 8,000 Federal soldiers were either killed or wounded in the charge. One of Wright's aides best expressed the views of the Bluecoats about the battle when he wrote: "I never heard anyone who was engaged there express a wish to see Cold Harbor again."[28]

In a letter to Lieutenant Colonel Filbert dated June 5, John Von Hollen of the 96th Pennsylvania remarked that "the whole of Spotsylvania County is full of graves, theirs as well as ours."[29] Cold Harbor was beginning to resemble Spotsylvania. After six days of fighting a flag of truce was accepted between the combatants to begin at 4 p.m. and end two hours later. A surgeon with the 121st New York described the ghastly scene in a letter to his wife. "Between the lines (a distance of not greater than thirty rods) … lay wounded and dead, who could not be reached for removal, and here the ground was a complete sepulcher. Scores of putrid bodies defiled the air. It was a strange sight."[30] Another Bluecoat described the grim end suffered by the wounded who could not reach the safety afforded by the earthworks. "They had exhausted their water supply, and sucked their moist clothing to get the rain and dew from it. They had scooped out holes in the ground to shelter themselves, and put moist clay in their mouths to prolong life. Imagine, if you can, their horrible predicament, lying on a bullet-swept field, without [the] ability to crawl, their wounds infested with maggots, and existing five days or more before being succored, and you can get some idea of the horrors of war."[31] During the truce Yank and Reb exchanged pleasantries as the dead were buried and the wounded brought in. Henry Keiser recorded the scene in his diary. "Our boys and the Jonnies were on friendly terms with each other, exchanging papers, shaking hands, and having a general talk together. But as soon as the two hours were up, each man jumped behind his 'dirt pile.'"[32]

Upon leaving the Cold Harbor entrenchments the 96th Pennsylvania was both relieved and demoralized. They were delighted to vacate the Cold Harbor trenches where for two weeks they had received only four hours sleep per night and lived in constant fear of the marksmanship of Rebel sharpshooters. They, too, were saddened at the loss of the 5th Maine regiment whose term of service expired shortly after the horrors of Cold Harbor.[33] But most of all, the regiment suffered staggering losses in killed and wounded during Grant's Overland Campaign. Of the 420 Pennsylvanians who crossed the Rapidan only 70 or 80 marched south from the Cold Harbor trenches. The carnage prompted Private Edward Henry of Company D to issue the following proposal regarding the resolution of the war to his sister: "The rebels said they were as tired of the war as we are but are willing to fight it out. We have been reinforced by the 9th, 10th and 18th army corps and if Richmond does not go up this time we might as well knock off and call it a draw game."[34]

From Cold Harbor Upton's brigade marched to the James River and bivouacked on the northside of the river, across from Fort Powhatan, near former President Tyler's mansion. On June 17 the Bluecoats moved to Wilson's Wharf where they boarded transports for Bermuda Hundred. At Bermuda Hundred the Pennsylvanians got their first glimpse of United States Colored Troops, attached to Butler's Army of the James. After chasing a detachment of black cavalry, in a good natured fashion, Upton's Bluecoats marched to Point of Rocks. Upon reaching the latter place, Upton's brigade occupied an elaborate network of trenches constructed by Butler's troops. On June 19, Upton's foot soldiers crossed the Appomattox via a pontoon bridge and advanced toward the Petersburg front. After arriving at Petersburg, Wright's VI Corps was ordered into the trenches facing the city south of the Appomattox. Four days before, the Federals of the XVIII Corps had bungled a splendid opportunity to seize the Graycoat works protecting Petersburg, and indeed the important rail center itself. By June 19 the two armies were fixed in position behind complex networks of entrenchments just below the Petersburg city limits. Now Grant had what he wanted least: a siege.[35]

Failing to capture the "Cockade City," Grant prepared to besiege the endangered rail center of the Confederacy. Before the immobility of siege warfare was accepted, however, Grant sought to cripple the network of railroads that converged on Petersburg from the deep south. Two of these rail lines—of minor importance—the Federals already held: the short spur that went east to the terminus at City Point—Grant's new supply base—and a longer line that angled southeast to Norfolk. The two lines that were still in operation—the Petersburg & Weldon Railroad that ran south to the blockade runners' port of Wilmington and the Southside Railroad that went to Lynchburg—were vital to the survival of Lee's army. From the time that Grant's army crossed the James River until the Appomattox Campaign, the Union high command sought to sever these two lifelines to Lee's Army of Northern Virginia. On June 25, Lieutenant Colonel Lessig led a reconnaissance detachment of 200 Bluecoats toward the line of The Petersburg & Weldon Railroad.[36]

Upon reaching the railroad, the Yankees found the line of tracks heavily guarded by a strong Rebel skirmish line. One member of the reconnoitering party reported that the Unionists "discovered working parties, with a strong guard, engaged in repairing the track destroyed last week by our infantry."[37] Three days later, perhaps acting in part on Lessig's intelligence, Wright's Corps marched to Reams' Station, on the Petersburg & Weldon Railroad, just beyond the Union left flank, with instructions to support Wilson's cavalry and destroy a section of the track. Three days later the Bluecoats were back in the Petersburg entrenchments. As Grant's forces strengthened their works around Petersburg, Lee sought to relieve the pressure along the line of fortifications. To accomplish that objective, Lee ordered Jubal Early, whose troops were advancing down the Shenandoah Valley, to make warlike demonstrations against Washington. Lee hoped that Early's forces would prove such a nuisance that a substantial number of Federals would be shifted to the Valley theater of operations to drive off the advancing enemy. Lee's gambit provoked an immediate response from Grant. On July 9, Grant ordered Wright's First Division to board transports for Washington.[38]

Arriving at City Point on July 10, the 96th Pennsylvania, along with the 121st New York, boarded the *Tappahannock*. Prior to boarding the transport, the 121st New York was assigned to the starboard side of the vessel while the 96th Pennsylvania was sent to the port side of the boat. The Pennsylvanians, however, boarded the vessel first and decided, against orders, to occupy the starboard side of the ship. The soldiers of the 121st New York, immediately objected to the slight shown them by the Schuylkill Countians. Tempers flared and the situation escalated quickly leading to a "pretty lively rough and tumble fight."[39] Lieutenant Colonel Lessig immediately responded to the situation by drawing his sword. Lessig then ordered the soldiers to stand down and threatened to separate the parties with his sword "if he was not instantly obeyed."[40] Thomas Yeoman of the 121st New York, picked up his musket, pointed his gun at Lessig and threatened to "blow a hole through him."[41] Soon other officers separated the protagonists and restored order. Subsequently, Lessig got into an argument with one of his officers, placed him under arrest and sent him below decks for the remainder of the journey. John Ingraham of the 121st New York stated that "the boys are all down on the Col. of the 96th."[42] Surgeon Slocum of the New York regiment attributed the disagreement to a keg of ale smuggled on board the *Tappahannock* by the Pennsylvanians. The diaries of the Schuylkill Countians are curiously silent on this unfortunate incident.

Early in the afternoon on July 12, the fat-sided steamers and transports ascended the Potomac and docked near the Seventh Street wharf. As soon as the longshoremen secured the heaving lines, the gangplanks were slung to the wharf, and lines of Unionists in ragged, sun-bleached uniforms clomped ashore. As soon as the Yankees formed a marching column on the dock, the soldiers tramped up Seventh Street, past the Smithsonian Institution and the Patent Office, toward Fort Stevens. As the troops surged forward the people who crowded the sidewalks to glimpse the spectacle exclaimed, "It is the old Sixth Corps!"[43] A member of the Second Brigade recalled, "As we passed along we were greeted with clapping of hands, waving of handkerchiefs, and many remarks such as 'Bully for you,' 'Hurrah for the 6th Corps.'"[44] The blacks, too, were very demonstrative as they saluted the Bluecoats and praised the arrival of for dem red cross sojers. Wee's all saved now."[45] As Upton's brigade, along with the First Division, tramped toward Fort Stevens, Early's veterans were massing for an assault.

Fort Stevens, a formidable earthwork near Rock Creek, was a link in the chain of forts that protected Washington from invasion. Twenty-four hours prior to the arrival of Wright's VI Corps, Fort Stevens, and indeed all of the earthworks in the Washington defense perimeter, were manned by troops from the Invalid Corps, heavy artillerists, War Department clerks and a sprinkling of untested militia. Now it was the focal point of Early's attack. As the VI Corps reached the threatened fort, puffs of white smoke from the rifles of Rebel skirmishers could be seen across the green meadows and fields of corn. As soon as Wright ascertained the situation, the VI Corps commander ordered one of his veteran brigades out in front of the earthwork to drive off the foe. Early, realizing that he was outnumbered, ordered his soldiers to withdraw. For the veterans of the VI Corps, the affair—a short, decisive skirmish with modest casualties—was important for only one reason. They fought the battle—if it can be called that—under the watchful eye of Abraham Lincoln. For a short time the tall man in the frock coat and stovepipe hat watched the operation from the fort's parapet. The next day, Wright's VI Corps started out in pursuit of Early's weary veterans.[46]

Wright's pursuit of Early was not a vigorous one. After fording the Potomac River, the VI Corps marched through Leesburg and Snicker's Gap coming to rest at the banks of the Shenandoah River. During the advance to the Shenandoah there was much straggling due to the oppressive heat, and as one brigade surgeon confessed, to the "bad whiskey from Washington."[47] Arriving at the Shenandoah, the VI Corps suffered from very low morale. The series of sluggish, aimless marches caused many to question the prosecution of the war by their generals in the field and the authorities in Washington.

All of this confusion prompted one Union veteran to remark that "the Sixth Corps was, in army parlance, 'about played out.'"[48] A few days rest alongside the Monocacy, however, rested the exhausted Bluecoats and restored their spirits. Although the criticism muttered by the soldiers quickly dissipated, their comments were certainly not without a certain degree of merit. Grant, too, felt that there was a problem with Federal leadership in the Shenandoah Valley. On August 1, Grant ordered Sheridan to go up to the Monocacy and take control of all of the troops in that theater of operations. After assigning "Little Phil" to the Shenandoah Valley, Grant wired Halleck that he was instructing Sheridan to "put himself south of the enemy and follow him to the death."[49]

By mid–August, the Army of the Shenandoah, the name given to Sheridan's new command—composed of Wright's VI Corps from the Army of the Potomac, Crook's VIII Corps from David Hunter's old Army of West Virginia, and Emory's XIX Corps from Louisiana—had marched more than a third of the way up the Valley. As the Bluecoats advanced, they maneuvered Early into a strong defensive position behind Fisher's Hill, located twenty miles or more south of Winchester. Believing that Early's position was too strong to be carried by an assault, Sheridan withdrew his army down the fertile Shenandoah Valley. During the six weeks after Sheridan took command, he did little more than guard the lower end of the Shenandoah Valley. Evidently Sheridan shared the War Department's belief that "Old Jube's" army was more than twice as big as it really was. A combination of Early's clever feints and a high degree of "McClellanism"—too much preparation and not enough fighting—on the part of Sheridan paralyzed his command. At last Grant came up from Petersburg, and after visiting with Sheridan, ordered him to strike.[50]

As Sheridan prepared to meet Early's troops in battle, the 96th Pennsylvania rested in its camp near Berryville, Virginia. Daniel Faust, taking advantage of the opportunity to write a letter to his sister, informed her of the destruction of the Shenandoah Valley by the Bluecoats.

> This army since we are in the Shenandoah Valley has butchered thousands of sheep. We have mutton almost every day. Almost every farmer has from a hundred and fifty head of sheep and we clean them out as we go. We have also taken a great many horses off those farmers. One of our fellows asked an old farmer how he liked the Yanks. He said he used to like them but he didn't any more for they took everything he had.[51]

On September 19, five days after Faust wrote to his sister, the Unionists prepared to engage Early's forces at Winchester. Long before sunrise Sheridan's cavalry splashed cross Opequon Creek and drove back the Confederate outposts, and pushed on in an attempt to develop enemy strength. At dawn the VI Corps forded the Opequon, pushed on toward Early's Graybacks. The orders for the tramp that morning, however, had somehow gone awry and a massive traffic jam ensued along the Berryville Pike. By noon, Sheridan's line of battle was rolling forward. The VI Corps was advancing promptly, supported by one of Emory's divisions on their right flank. As they marched into battle, however, a gap developed between the right of the VI Corps and the left of the XIX Corps where the Berryville Pike made a slight turn to the left. Seeing this opening the Rebels launched a furious counterattack. Upton, grasping the situation immediately, shifted the lead elements of his brigade, and instructed his men to lie down in a protecting woods, to await the Confederates pouring into the gap. When the trap was filled, he had his Unionists inflict a devastating fire upon the unsuspecting Butternuts. The surprise rifle fire, Upton reported, "caused the enemy to retire in great disorder."[52] According to Upton's modern biographer, the quick, decisive action by the young brigadier general at the Third Battle of Winchester, or Opequon Creek, probably averted disaster for the Federal army. The 96th Pennsylvania, however, was not involved in any of this high drama. They had been detailed to guard wagon trains by order of their commanding general, who stated "to permit further sacrifice from the Ninety-sixth on the last day of its service, would be murder."[53]

On September 22, their term of service expired, the few remaining soldiers of the 96th Pennsylvania turned their backs on the Shenandoah Valley and marched toward Harpers Ferry, destined for Pottsville. The men from the regiment who still had service time remaining—two full companies—merged with Gosline's Zouaves to form the 95th-96th Pennsylvania battalion. The one hundred or so veterans then began their trip home under Lieutenant Colonel Lessig. Five days later they reached Pottsville, where they were greeted by an enthusiastic crowd. The arrival of their train at the depot was heralded by roman candles, rockets and "other pyrotechnical displays."[54] Upon their return to Pottsville, on September 26, 1864, 120 veterans stepped off the train from Harrisburg that evening. The residents of Pottsville, however, were unaware, until a few hours before the train arrived, that the troops were returning home that night. As a result, "an *impromptu* welcome in which the heart should bear a prominent part," was hastily arranged by the grateful citizens. An eyewitness recalled the scene which unfolded that evening as the people of Pottsville gathered "to welcome with her whole soul, our brave boys back from their three years of honorable service."[55] The soldiers, approximately 120, marched from the railroad station to the Union Hotel, where they were formally welcomed home. A local newspaper reporter summarized their three-year absence best when he wrote:

> The regiment came back with one hundred and twenty men. Three years before it left Pottsville a thousand strong. The bullet and disease had done their work, and many who left here in full health and vigor, fill graves in Virginia hills.[56]

In late September 1864, as the veterans of the 96th Pennsylvania returned to Pottsville, one thing was becoming clear to them and to the soldiers still engaged in active operations: At long last, Confederate resistance was beginning to subside. Victories by Sheridan's Army of the Shenandoah at Winchester, Sherman's seizure of Atlanta and Farragut's success at Mobile Bay indicated that the Southern Confederacy was beginning to crumble. Although the three year volunteers of the 96th Pennsylvania did not share in the decisive victories by Sheridan's troops in the Shenandoah Valley,

Maj. Gen. Philip H. Sheridan, commander, Army of the Shenandoah (author's collection).

Field officers of the 96th Pennsylvania after muster out in Philadelphia, Pennsylvania, October 25, 1864. Back row: third from left, Capt. Company F, Edward J. Philips; sixth from left, Capt. Company H, Samuel R. Russell. Front row, from left: unidentified, Maj. Levi Huber, Lt. Col. William Lessig, Dr. Daniel W. Bland and Quartermaster John Schweers. The men in the back row are unidentified. The photographic firm was Wenderoth and Taylor, 912, 914 and 916 Chestnut Street, Philadelphia (collection of Douglas Sagrillo).

two full companies from the unit did remain with Sheridan's army to share in ultimate Federal victory and control of the Shenandoah Valley. Throughout the balance of Sheridan's Shenandoah Valley Campaign companies E and G of the disbanded 96th Pennsylvania marched into battle with Gosline's Zouaves, thus forming the 95th-96th Pennsylvania Battalion. During the Valley Campaign the 95th-96th Pennsylvania battalion performed mainly skirmish duty. In November, after Early's defeat at Cedar Creek, Wright's Greek Cross Corps was ordered back to the Richmond-Petersburg front. Upon arriving at City Point, Wright's corps was ordered to support the movement of Warren's V Corps to cripple the Petersburg and Weldon Railroad. In the eyes of the Bluecoats the raid was an overwhelming success. After disabling one of Lee's most valuable supply lines, Grant called a halt to further operations and the Unionists went into winter quarters. That winter witnessed a distinct rise of confidence in the Bluecoats. "There was hope in the air," wrote a VI Corps veteran. "All were beginning to feel that the next campaign would be the last, and most of the army now recognized … that emancipation had been the end."[57]

The winter encampment of 1864–1865 was quite different from the three previous winter encampments endured by the Bluecoats. Grant, unlike his predecessors, did not merely use the relative quiescence of the Virginia winter to rebuild his army and await the rebirth of spring. The Lieutenant General continued offensive movements throughout the winter, further tightening his grip on the Richmond-Petersburg front. By late March, after spending the winter fixing Lee's army in place, Grant was ready to launch what he hoped would be his final offensive against the Graycoat entrenchments. On March 29, Grant unleashed his legions against Lee's ever lengthening entrenchments south and west of Petersburg. Four days after the start of the Bluecoat offensive, the VI Corps smashed through the middle of the Butternut entrenchments and pushed the Secessionists out of their camps, seizing artillery pieces and capturing prisoners in the process. After breaking through the Confederate line, a Bluecoat of the Second Brigade stated: "Then, and there the long-tried and ever faithful soldiers of the Republic saw DAYLIGHT!"[58] Then the whole corps looked up and down the Petersburg lines—broken forever—and sent up a wild shout which was "worth dying to hear." A week after the big breakthrough by the VI Corps at Petersburg, Lee met Grant at Appomattox. On April 9, Henry Keiser entered the following passage in his diary:

> This afternoon an officer on horseback, waving his hat, ... came tearing from the front, yelling the glorious news that, "General Lee had surrendered the entire Army of Northern Virginia to General Grant." Such cheering, shouting and rejoicing as there was throughout the entire Army of the Potomac was never heard or seen in America.[59]

After the war, the volunteers of the 96th Pennsylvania and the 95th-96th battalion resumed their civilian lives. Colonel Cake continued his interest in state and local politics and the anthracite coal industry. He established the Philadelphia Coal Company and engaged in the mining and shipping of anthracite coal quickly gaining a reputation as an unsavory coal operator. On more than one occasion Cake angered the local coal entrepreneurs. He tried to regulate coal prices in the volatile post Civil War market by sending his miners into the colliery at higher wages, in an attempt to garner quick profits, while the other operators suffered through strikes and work stoppages. Although Cake was regarded by his business peers as somewhat of a maverick, he was able to secure enough political support to win election to the United States House of Representatives. Cake served his district in the Fortieth and Forty-first Congresses. His tenure in Congress can best be characterized as unremarkable. Most of the legislation Cake introduced in Congress reflected his close connection to the anthracite coal industry. When not speaking about anthracite coal related legislation, he was spearheading a proposal to have Congress award his old army command, the First Defenders battalion, a special medal for being the first troops to arrive in Washington after Lincoln's initial call for volunteers. Cake's pleading, however, after a careful review by the Committee on Military Affairs, was rejected. After his second term in Congress, Cake returned to Schuylkill County and continued his business pursuits in the coal industry.[60]

While Cake rose to prominence in the House of Representatives, his former staff officers forged their own post-war careers. After military service, William Lessig followed Greeley's advice and headed west. Almost immediately he met with good fortune. U.S. Grant, after becoming President, appointed Lessig Surveyor General of Colorado. During this period, Lessig forged a successful and influential career. Between 1870 and 1880, Lessig amassed substantial real estate holdings and improved his financial condition considerably. Marital problems and failing health, however, eventually proved to be Lessig's downfall.

Although Jacob Frick did not achieve prominence and wealth commensurate with Lessig, he did establish a modest business and became active in the affairs of Civil War veterans.[61] After the war Frick returned to Pottsville and engaged in the manufacture of wire coal screens for the coal industry. While he was active in veterans affairs—primarily helping individual veterans or their spouses in obtaining pension benefits—he was not active in the reunions and meetings of the 96th Pennsylvania veterans. No doubt Frick's allegiance was to the 129th Pennsylvania, the nine-month volunteer unit he commanded as colonel. During his tenure as colonel of the 129th Pennsylvania, Frick established himself as a brave and gallant officer. For his heroic service at the Battle of Fredericksburg and Chancellorsville he earned the Medal of Honor, which was finally awarded in 1892. During the Gettysburg campaign he commanded the 27th Pennsylvania Volunteer Militia and prevented a Confederate brigade under Gen. John B. Gordon from seizing the bridge spanning the Susquehanna River, between Columbia and Wrightsville.[62]

Like Frick, Filbert achieved moderate success in the business world after the Civil War. Upon returning to his home in Pine Grove, Filbert started a milling business, which was eventually destroyed by fire. He later managed the mercantile firm of Miller, Filbert and Company. Filbert's quest for reinstatement of his lieutenant colonel's commission after the war proved to be his most important pursuit. In May 1869, he received notification that President Andrew Johnson recommended to the Governor of Pennsylvania that Filbert's discharge be overturned and he be recommissioned in the grade of lieutenant colonel. For Filbert, this proved to be his vindication.[63]

The most interesting incident, upon returning to civilian life, however, involved the former captain of Company G, Jacob W. Haas. In April of 1865, Haas and William Lessig decided to travel to the western Pennsylvania oil fields to pursue a business venture. Their trip, however, turned into an exciting escapade full of tense situations. After spending the night in a hotel near Lewisburg, Pennsylvania, Haas, who bore an uncanny resemblance to John Wilkes Booth, attracted suspicion that he was in fact the fugitive the authorities were desperately seeking to apprehend. For several hours, Haas and Lessig barricaded themselves in a hotel room in order to prevent an angry mob from capturing them. Fortunately, another Schuylkill County resident, familiar with the men, identified the pair, enabling Lessig and Haas to continue upon their journey. Subsequently, Haas was taken into custody in Phillipsburg by a detail of troopers serving with the 16th Pennsylvania Cavalry. Lessig and Haas eventually convinced Lieutenant McDougall that they were former Union army officers and not Lincoln's assassin Booth and an accomplice. Having been issued a safe conduct pass, they continued on their trip. Finally, a third encounter proved to be the most harrowing of all. A mob near Clarion gathered, detained the two men and would not accept the authenticity of the "safe conduct" pass issued by the officer of the 16th Pennsylvania Cavalry. A rope was soon brandished by one of the men in the mob and the situation quickly escalated from misidentification to a hangman's noose. Once again, however, the pair were able to calm the angry mob and secure a third party to identify them. Later that same day, Booth was apprehended in Virginia and Haas' misadventure came to an end. After the war he wrote several versions of this tension-filled tale relating his strange experience as John Wilkes Booth's double. The captain of Company G died in Shamokin in 1914.[64]

While Cake, Lessig, Frick and Filbert resumed their civilian lives, so too, did the veterans of the 96th Pennsylvania Volunteers. For many years the Civil War veterans from Schuylkill County did nothing to commemorate their military service. In fact, not until September 1886, did a reunion of the regiment, to memorialize the unit's participation in the Battle of Crampton's Gap, take place. This gathering of veterans, which included a grand parade through the streets of Pottsville, also gave impetus to related meetings and projects to memorialize the regiment's service. Chief among those affairs was a long term project to erect a monument, on the Gettysburg battlefield, to honor the unit's participation in that important engagement. Soon after the 1886 reunion, the 96th Association, a delegation of 96th Pennsylvania veterans appointed to raise funds for the monument, achieved their goal. That group then selected a local craftsman, Richard Collins, to carve a suitable monument to commemorate their service. In April 1888, Collins unveiled his creation at his marble yard located on Minersville Street. In early summer the monument was ready to be transferred from Pottsville to Gettysburg.[65]

Prior to shipping the memorial, the veterans of the regiment engaged in a series of announcements in the *Miners' Journal*, extolling the importance of the dedication scheduled for late June. The veterans organized a parade to coincide with the removal of the monument from Collins' marble yard to the railroad station. They also arranged a special train to transport them and their families, along with any other interested parties to Gettysburg to witness the unveiling of the monument. The 96th Association also ensured, by calling upon financial resources within the community, that all veterans of the regiment, regardless of their financial situation, would be able to attend. Finally, on June 20, with "nearly every surviving member of the Ninety-Sixth ... present," the veterans entrained for Gettysburg. The next day, in the presence of 148 veterans, Henry Royer, former captain of Company H, delivered the dedicatory address. After rendering a historical sketch of the unit's service, Royer closed his oration by stating: "The camp fire begins to smolder in the embers. One by one the lights are going out. The Ninety-sixth will soon, very soon, be at rest." Indeed, Royer's sad words ultimately proved prophetic

Monument honoring the 96th Pennsylvania on the battlefield at Gettysburg. This monument, known as the "sharp-shooter," was designed by August Zeller and sculpted by George Schreader, and is slightly north and west of Little Round Top on Wheatfield Road. The monument was dedicated on June 21, 1888 (MOLLUS Mass. Collection, United States Army Heritage and Education Center).

Photograph depicting veterans of the 96th Pennsylvania Volunteers posing in front of the "sharp-shooter" monument at Gettysburg. Most likely, this photograph was taken the same day the monument was dedicated, June 21, 1888 (MOLLUS Mass. Collection, United States Army Heritage and Education Center).

as the gray-bearded veterans passed through the Gilded Age and into the cemeteries of Pottsville and the surrounding towns. The Crampton's Gap reunion and the Gettysburg dedication proved to be the post-war high tide for the veterans of the 96th. In time all that remained of the Pennsylvania Volunteers were the lengthy historical sketches by Boyer and Boyle, official sources, other minor unit sketches and the letters and diaries of a few members of the regiment scattered across the United States.[66]

Any assessment of the 96th Pennsylvania Volunteers must take into account a variety of factors. Casualty figures, although revealing, afford only a narrow window through which to view their combat service. According to Col. William F. Fox, who carefully compiled regimental losses for the Union armies, the 96th Pennsylvania qualified as one of the "Three Hundred Fighting Regiments." Fox's distinguished and highly regarded work, "includes every regiment in the Union Armies which lost over 130 in killed and died of wounds during the war."[67] The 96th Pennsylvania sustained 132 officers and men killed in action or died of wounds received in battle. Two hundred ninety-seven soldiers were wounded in combat during the regiment's term of service. Eighty-seven men subsequently died of disease. Eighty-two soldiers were captured and sent to Confederate prisons. One source states that approximately 150 men were marked on company rolls as deserters.[68] Henry Royer, in his address at Gettysburg upon the dedication of the 96th's monument summarized the regiment's service. "Your muster rolls ... bear, in all, the names of eleven hundred and forty-nine men, including musicians and teamsters; while the loss from disease and battle reaches the enormous aggregate of four hundred fifty-seven."[69]

Like the casualty rolls, the names of the battles in which the regiment participated, emblazoned on the flag of the unit, also stand as mute testimony to the military service of the Schuylkill Countians. The battles from Gaines' Mill to Cold Harbor, and the men who fought so gallantly, constitute the historical record and legacy of the 96th Pennsylvania Volunteers. Courage in combat and commitment to the cause of Union defined the volunteers-turned-soldiers from Schuylkill County, Pennsylvania. Historians have stated that the Civil War was America's second revolution. Like the soldiers of Washington's war, the patriots from Pennsylvania played a role in forging the freedom which came to define the Civil War. Upon enlisting, the War Democrats from Schuylkill County sought to reunify North and South. In the course of their three-year service, however, soldier attitudes toward the prosecution of the war changed from reunification to emancipation. By 1864, the War Democrats, through their experience on the battlefield, evolved into staunch Lincoln men who sought complete victory over the Confederacy. Their collective experience in combat had a direct impact upon their changing attitudes toward the prosecution of the war.

Without question the engagement of Gaines' Mill was one of the most important battlefield actions during the 96th's term of service. This battle not only marked the initial confrontation between the soldiers of the 96th Pennsylvania with elements of the Army of Northern Virginia, but also signaled Cake's first field command under fire. While engaged on June 27, 1862, within one hundred yards of their counterparts in gray, the 96th Pennsylvania acquitted itself well against the Tarheels of the 20th North Carolina. Cake's command that day, at least on the tactical level, was competent and responsive to the rigorous demands of combat. Despite the regiment's initial inability to advance and misinterpretation of orders upon withdrawing, the Schuylkill Countians performed as well as many veteran units upon the field that day. The inadvertent crossing of the unit to the south side, while the balance of Bartlett's brigade fired a holding volley on the north side, detracted slightly, however, from the regiment's achievements at Gaines' Mill. While soundness, not brilliance, characterized Cake's command abilities on June 27, steadfastness, not elan, marked the actions of the 96th Pennsylvania.

McClellan's Maryland Campaign afforded the 96th Pennsylvania its next battlefield opportunity. On September 14, 1862, the Bluecoats from Pennsylvania, veterans of the Seven Days' fighting, were eager to pitch into the flank of Lee's army. At Crampton's Gap the unit received its grand opportunity. Cake's tactical leadership on September 14, as at Gaines' Mill, was marked by forthrightness and competence. At all times throughout the day he displayed adequate qualities as a regimental commander. During the battle he maintained control of his unit, led the 96th without incident to the deployment area and exhibited adroit leadership throughout the assault. The regiment, eager to dislodge the Graycoats, advanced aggressively, not recklessly, against the foe. In quick fashion the massive Bluecoat onslaught vanquished the brave but out-manned Secessionists. This battle, for the Schuylkill Countians, started as a close quarters fire fight, within fifty yards of the enemy, and culminated in a bayonet charge. In retrospect, the 96th Pennsylvania's victory at Crampton's Gap proved to be the regiment's most significant military accomplishment.

While the action at Crampton's Gap marked the end of Cake's military career in battle, the engagements of Second Fredericksburg and Salem Church signaled the command debut of William Lessig. Commanding the regiment in the grade of lieutenant colonel, he displayed considerable military talents as a tactical leader during his first combat action. The battle of early morning May 3, 1863, affords important insight into Lessig's military command style. While he not only displayed intrepid personal courage that day, he tempered his charismatic leadership with sound and cautious tactical command when it was needed most. After advancing against the Graycoats at Fredericksburg, Lessig led his unit, with only a brief rest, into a fierce engagement at Salem Church. After committing the 96th Pennsylvania to battle at Salem Church, he soon realized that impending disaster loomed in front of the Bluecoats. Correctly, Lessig sought to extricate his command before a Butternut counter attack engulfed the crumbling Unionist line and sealed the route of retreat for the Yankees. Lessig's judicious tactical decision enabled the lieutenant colonel to maintain the combat integrity of his regiment. Like Gaines' Mill, and the initial encounter with the 10th Georgia at Crampton's Gap, the combat action at Salem Church proved to be another fire fight at close quarters with the 8th Alabama. On May 3, Lessig and his command performed at peak efficiency under difficult conditions. Two battles, sandwiched around a relatively difficult march, attested to the mettle of the rank and file of the 96th Pennsylvania. Arguably, Lessig's initial venture into battle as commander of the 96th was the unit's most difficult day under arms.

The military operations at Spotsylvania, May 10 and 12, 1864, proved to be quite unlike the stand up fire fights of Gaines' Mill, Crampton's Gap, Second Fredericksburg and Salem Church. Upton's assault of May 10, carried the bayonet assault forward with a new delivery of a time honored Civil War tactic. The charge, spearheaded by the 96th Pennsylvania against a strongly fortified Confederate position, was one of the most important tactical exercises of the war. Upton's assault, although unsuccessful, played an important role in regard to Grant's evolving grand tactical decisions during the balance of fighting in the Virginia Theater. Judged by that standard the attack was not a waste of Schuylkill County soldiers on Confederate entrenchments. Although Upton's assault suggested that Union success might be achieved on a grander scale, Grant eventually abandoned frontal attacks in favor of turning the Secessionists' flanks. Upton's assault, however, had not gone unnoticed. Two days later Grant again unleashed an Upton-style attack, on a larger scale only to meet with initial success. This second assault also found the 96th Pennsylvania at the vortex of rifle fire. Once again the Yankees were going to test the deadly Butternut fortifications.

The May 12, 1864, attack by the Bluecoats against the Confederate field fortifications at Spotsylvania resulted in ghastly fighting at a point along the entrenchments known as the Bloody Angle. As in Upton's assault, the Bluecoats of the 96th Pennsylvania on May 12 could not breach and exploit the Graycoat entrenchments at the "Bloody Angle." In sum, the day, indicated that the determining factor in the success of future operations would not be the availability of force but coordination of force. The 96th Pennsylvania Volunteers, however, would not be part of Grant's operations along the Richmond-Petersburg front. The fighting at the "Bloody Angle" was, in effect, the last major action in which the unit participated.

In the final analysis, the unit fought five major engagements, acquitting itself in fine fashion in each of the battles. In four instances, the Pennsylvanians waged stand-up fire fights within one hundred yards, or closer, of their counterparts in gray. In two instances, they executed bayonet charges bringing them into hand-to-hand combat between attacker and defender. Cake and Lessig proved to be capable tactical officers, both able to inspire their command and adjust to changing battlefield conditions. Both also exhibited command competence—a trait not always displayed by untrained military men—and reliability during battle. Thus, the 96th Pennsylvania takes its place within the history of the

Army of the Potomac. Although they did not reach Appomattox the Pennsylvanians helped pave the way for the Army of the Potomac to emerge victorious. While they did not share in the conquest of the Confederacy during their period of service, the Schuylkill Countians helped fashion the hard hand of war that the Union would wield to end the conflict.

After forging a reputation as a dependable, steadfast, although unspectacular unit at Gaines' Mill, so did the regiment discharge its duties throughout the balance of its term of service. It is clear, that the veterans regarded Crampton's Gap as their most important combat action. The possession of the battlefield on September 14, 1862, by the Pennsylvanians—the only time they held the ground previously defended by Graycoat infantry—proved to be a tangible standard of success. Setbacks on the battlefield, as at Salem Church and later at Spotsylvania, did not demoralize the Pennsylvanians. The various attacks by the 96th Pennsylvania, storming of Confederate entrenchments and executing bayonet charges, did not deter them from performing their duty. Heroism in combat greatly defined the term of service of the Schuylkill Countians. Evaluated by that standard, the regiment contributed significantly to eventual Union victory.

Perhaps, the modern reader has been surprised to learn that Civil War era tactical doctrine advocated close quarters combat with rifle muskets culminating in a bayonet charge. In fact, tactics in the Civil War changed very little throughout the four years of bloody battles. In their book, *Attack and Die*, Perry Jamieson and Grady McWhiney stated that "offensive tactics, which had been so successfully used by Americans in the Mexican War, were much less effective in the 1860's because an improved weapon—the rifle—had vastly increased the strength of the defenders."[70] Another historian, Earl Hess, concluded in his study that "McWhiney and Jamieson see nearly all characteristics of Civil War military operations as influenced by the use of the rifle musket. Everything from high casualties to the lack of decisive battles … are ascribed to the potency of the weapon."[71] The idea of the rifle influencing tactics in the Civil War overlooked an important element, according to Dr. Hess: "the range at which combat actually took place."[72] A small but growing group of historians have examined this issue and "based on research in official reports … [they concluded] that infantry combat normally took place at ranges far less than five hundred yards and similar to or only slightly more than the range of smoothbore muskets."[73] In sum, the rifle musket did not revolutionize Civil War operations because the weapon was not used at long range, its principal technological advancement over a smoothbore musket. The parabolic trajectory of the bullet made the Civil War rifle difficult to use effectively at long range. As a result, Civil War "officers and men alike believed that it was more decisive to engage the enemy at ranges of 100 yards or less."[74]

The combat experience of the 96th Pennsylvania Volunteers, however, runs contrary to the thesis put forward in their landmark study by McWhiney and Jamieson. Quite simply, the rifle musket of the Civil War did not influence or revolutionize the tactical approach to warfare exercised in the Civil War. The revolutionary technology introduced by the rifle has proven to be a long held myth in Civil War writings. Given the highly documented actions of the 96th Pennsylvania in these engagements, it is clear that in fact their combat experience aligns closely with recent studies of Civil War tactics. Historians such as Paddy Griffith, Brent Nosworthy and Earl Hess convincingly argue that Civil War infantry fights were conducted at a range of 50 to 150 yards as the respective sides blazed away until they expended their ammunition.[75]

In his study, Nosworthy concludes that although the range of the rifle musket was far greater than the old fashioned smoothbore, "much of the fighting nevertheless occurred at ranges equal to or only slightly more than that found during previous wars.... This forces the conclusion that although the average range at which the opposing sides exchanged fire was indeed *slightly greater than in previous wars*, at the same time it was *considerably less than what modern readers have come to expect*."[76] In addition to the close quarters combat, the 96th Pennsylvania also executed several bayonet charges which proved to be a highly practiced infantry tactic in the Civil War. Like the unchanging tactics concerning the advent of the rifle musket, the bayonet charge sought to rely on the "threat of shock and cold steel, rather than trying to overpower one's opponent with a withering fire."[77] Also, the bayonet tactic underwent further development and innovation during the war as a method of achieving tactical success while reducing casualties to achieve objectives.

Military operations and battlefield exploits alone, however, do not reveal the complete history of the 96th Pennsylvania. The other component of the unit's history lies in the social experience of the young men from Schuylkill County who responded to Lincoln's call for volunteer soldiers. Their tribulations on the march, their views on the war effort, their thoughts concerning the boredom of camp life, their observations of the Southern slave and Dixie, their attitudes toward religion and their opinion of military drill and discipline form an integral part of the history of the 96th regiment. The infantry volunteers from Schuylkill County proved to be a courageous group of citizens-turned-soldiers. Many pointed with pride to their volunteer enlistment and willingness to serve during the war as a sign of their loyalty to the Union. Certainly their strong sense of duty and devotion to country explain a great deal about the motivation behind Bluecoat enlistments. The troops from Schuylkill County also displayed a will and inner strength to endure the hardships of the battlefield and the campground with grit and determination. The fighting quality of the regiment never waned. Unit morale, although it fluctuated during the war, never dwindled into despair.

On the battlefield, the 96th Pennsylvania made notable contributions to Union operations and the eventual victory of the Army of the Potomac over the Army of Northern Virginia. Perhaps the resilience of the regiment in camp and under fire can be attributed to the strength and character of the volunteers from the anthracite coal fields of Schuylkill County. Those coal miners turned warriors forged the historical record of the 96th Pennsylvania Volunteers. Their conduct in crisis, their character and their vitality spelled hope for the nation's future. After the war they would just as proudly join the ranks of the veterans who formed the Grand Army of the Republic. Their descendants can point with pride to the role played by the 96th in the four year struggle of the American Civil War. Perhaps their service was best described by one of the foremost combat soldiers of the war. After the war, at a gathering of veterans, Emory Upton was asked about the volunteers from Schuylkill County who served under him in the Second Brigade of the VI Corps.

> Upon one occasion one of the members [of the 96th Pennsylvania] said to General Upton, "Why was it you always called on the Ninety-sixth Regiment?" "Why," he said, "we called on you because we could depend on you. It was not very much, perhaps, to your comfort, but it was very much to the service, because we could always depend upon the Ninety-sixth Regiment."[78]

Appendix: Roster and Muster Roll Sources

For anyone seeking additional information concerning someone who served in the 96th Pennsylvania Volunteers there exist a number of excellent sources, all of which present detailed rosters with a wealth of information regarding each soldier in the regiment. The original muster rolls of the regiment can be found in RG 19 Department of Military and Veterans' Affairs, Civil War Muster Rolls and Related Records, 1861–1866, Pennsylvania State Archives, Pennsylvania Historical & Museum Commission, Harrisburg. See Group 2, Carton 74–75. These rolls have also been converted to microfilm. See Microfilm Roll 4029.

Another basic source for soldier information is the roster compiled by Samuel P. Bates and published in his monumental work *History of Pennsylvania Volunteers, 1861–5.* See volume III, pages 382–410. There is a roster for each Company A–K. The descriptive company rolls list the names of the members alphabetically, rank held, date mustered into service, term of enlistment, and a brief annotation concerning the soldiers' service. See this link to an online version of Bates' roster at https://archive.org/stream/history ofpennsyl03bate#page/382/mode/2up.

County histories can also prove to be rewarding sources with a wealth of information. Fortunately, there is an excellent county history where a researcher can find a brief history of the 96th Pennsylvania Volunteers and company rosters. *History of Schuylkill County, Pa.: With Illustrations and Biographical Sketches of Some of Its Prominent Men and Pioneers.* See pages 138–144. Following the company rosters are detailed lists of casualties for the battles of Crampton's Gap, Salem Church and Spotsylvania followed by a mortuary record. An online version of this book can also be found at https://archive.org/stream/historyofschuylk00newy#page/138/mode/2up.

Another unique source for 96th Pennsylvania rosters can be found in an obscure volume published under the title *Memorial of the Patriotism of Schuylkill County in the American Slaveholder's Rebellion,* edited by Francis B. Wallace. The company rosters are listed on pages 112–127 and the casualties can be found on pages 410–415. An online version of this book can also be found at https://archive.org/stream/memorialofpatrio 00wall#page/112/mode/2up.

The Pennsylvania Historical and Museum Commission also holds in RG 19 Series 19.65 registers of each Pennsylvania Civil War regiment. The 96th Pennsylvania rolls can be found in volume 8. These registers list the name of the soldier by company, his rank, where he enlisted, date of muster in to service, term of service and remarks for each soldier. This register can be found online at http://www.phmc.state.pa.us/bah/dam/rg/di/ r19-65RegisterPaVolunteers/r19-65Regt096/r19-65Regt096%20pg%201.pdf.

Finally, another useful source for muster rolls is the *Miners' Journal* newspaper, which was published weekly. Rosters for the following companies were published in the *Miners' Journal*: Company A, January 25, 1862; Company C, December 21, 1861; Company D, April 5, 1862; Company E, November 30, 1861; Company G, December 21, 1861; Company H, December 28, 1861; Company K, January 11, 1862. The rosters for companies D, G and K also include the name of the town the soldier was from. For an online version of the *Miners' Journal* see http://digitalnewspapers.libraries.psu.edu/Olive/APA/CivilWar/ ?skin=civilwar&AW=1485726060662&AppName=2#panel=browse.

Chapter Notes

Abbreviations

CWH—*Civil War History*
CWT—*Civil War Times*
CWTI—*Civil War Times Illustrated*
FC—Mrs. Marion Fernsler Collection
GDAH—Georgia Department of Archives and History
GKC—George Hay Kain Collection
GNMP—Gettysburg National Military Park
HCWRTC—Harrisburg Civil War Round Table Collection
HEC—United States Army Heritage & Education Center
HSSC—Historical Society of Schuylkill County
IHS—Indiana Historical Society
JHC—James F. Haas Collection
LC—Library of Congress
MOLLUS—Military Order Loyal legion United States
PH—*Pennsylvania History*
PHMC—Pennsylvania Historical and Museum Commission
PHSSC—Publications of the Historical Society of Schuylkill County
RNB—Richmond National Battlefield
RTC—Randy Treichler Collection
SC—Schoff Collection
UDC—United Daughters of the Confederacy
VTL—Virginia Tech Library
WCL—William Clements Library
WDC—William Dick Collection

Introduction

1. Richard J. Sommers, *Richmond Redeemed: The Siege at Petersburg* (Garden City, New York: Doubleday and Company, 1981), ix.

2. William F. Fox, *Regimental Losses in the American Civil War 1861–1865* (Albany, New York: Albany Publishing Company, 1889), 286.

3. Bruce Catton, *Mr. Lincoln's Army* (Garden City, New York: Doubleday and Company, 1951), 230; Stephen Ambrose, *Upton and the Army* (Baton Rouge, Louisiana: Louisiana State University Press. 1964), 31; Brian K. Burton, *Extraordinary Circumstances: The Seven Days Battles* (Bloomington, Indiana: University Press, 2001), 121–122; Timothy Reese, *Sealed with their Lives: The Battle for Crampton's Gap* (Baltimore, Maryland: Butternut and Blue, 1998), 134–140; Stephen Sears, *Chancellorsville* (New York: Houghton Mifflin, 1996), 382; Gordon Rhea, *The Battles for Spotsylvania Court House and the Road to Yellow Tavern May 7–12, 1864* (Baton Rouge, Louisiana: Louisiana State University Press, 1997), 171–175.

4. Samuel P. Bates, *History of Pennsylvania Volunteers, 1861–5* (Harrisburg, Pennsylvania: B. Singerly, State Printer, 1870), vol. III, 382–389; John T. Boyle, "An Outline Sketch of the Ninety-Sixth Pennsylvania Volunteers," Philadelphia *Weekly Times*, July 17, 1886; Henry C. Boyer, "At Crampton's Pass. The Ninety-Sixth Pennsylvania Regiment Under Fire," Shenandoah *Evening Herald*, August 31, September 2–3, 1886; Henry Royer, "Dedication of Monument 96th Regiment Infantry," *Pennsylvania at Gettysburg: Ceremonies at the Dedication of the Monuments* (Harrisburg, Pennsylvania: William Stanley Ray, State Printer), vol. 1, 515–517.

5. Lesley J. Gordon, *A Broken Regiment: The 16th Connecticut's Civil War* (Baton Rouge, Louisiana: Louisiana State University Press, 2014), 3; John J. Pullen, *The Twentieth Maine: A Volunteer Regiment in the Civil War* (Dayton, Ohio: Morningside House, 1991); Warren Wilkinson, *Mother, May You Never See The Sights I Have Seen: The Fifty-Seventh Massachusetts Veteran Volunteers in the Last Year of the Civil War* (New York: Harper & Row, 1990); Salvatore G. Cilella, *Upton's Regulars: The 121st New York Infantry in the Civil War* (Lawrence, Kansas: University Press, 2009).

6. Leslie Anders, *The Eighteenth Missouri* (Indianapolis, Indiana: Bobbs Merrill Company, 1968), viii.

7. James M. McPherson, *Ordeal by Fire: The Civil War and Reconstruction* (New York: Alfred A. Knopf, 1982), ix.

8. Wayne Smith, "Pennsylvania and the American Civil War: Recent Trends and Interpretations," *Pennsylvania History* (July 1984), vol. 51, no. 3, 215.

9. Edwin A. Glover, *Bucktailed Wildcats: A Regiment of Civil War Volunteers* (New York: Thomas Yoseloff, 1960); Edward J. Hagerty, *Collis' Zouaves: The 114th Pennsylvania Volunteers in the Civil War* (Baton Rouge, Louisiana: Louisiana State University Press, 1997); Dennis W. Brandt, *From Home Guards to Heroes: The 87th Pennsylvania and Its Civil War Community* (Columbia, Missouri: University of Missouri Press, 2006).

10. Sommers, *Richmond Redeemed*, xi.

11. Bell I. Wiley, *The Life of Billy Yank: The Common Soldier of the Union* (Baton Rouge, Louisiana: Louisiana State University Press, 1952), 11.

12. Johhn Keegan, *The Face of Battle: A Study of Agincourt, Waterloo and the Somme* (New York: Viking Press, 1976); See also, Marvin Cain, "A 'Face of Battle' Needed: An Assessment of Motives and Men in Civil War Historiography," *Civil War History*, vol. 28 (March 1982), 5–27.

Chapter I

1. The quotation concerning recruitment was found in Peter A. Filbert, Diary, August 17, 1862, Filbert Papers, Harrisburg Civil War Round Table Collection, United

States Army Heritage & Education Center. Perhaps this entry in Filbert's journal might have been the text of a handbill, or a recruiting poster, distributed throughout Pine Grove.

2. The company nickname of Filbert's unit was found in the lengthy sketch of the 96th Pennsylvania rendered by John T. Boyle, "Outline Sketch," July 17, 1886. The election of Filbert to captain of the Pine Grove Sharpshooters, and Ernest T. Ellrich to first lieutenant is recorded in Filbert, Diary, September 2, 1861, Filbert Papers, HCWRTC, HEC.

3. The biographical profile of Peter Filbert was gleaned from family data provided by Mrs. Mary Filbert, Auburn, Pennsylvania. Filbert's service file, located in Record Group 94, Adjutant General's Office—Compiled Union Service Records, National Archives, provided data concerning his three months' military service.

4. Boyle, "Outline Sketch," July 17, 1886; Bates, *Pennsylvania Volunteers*, vol. III, 382.

5. A variety of sources were consulted to develop Cake's biographical sketch. Chief among them is his obituary column, "Colonel H. L. Cake Dead at Northumberland," which was published in the Pottsville *Miners' Journal*, August 28, 1899; U.S., Congress, House, *The Biographical Directory of the American Congress, 1774–1971* (Washington, D.C., 1971), 690; *The National Cyclopaedia of American Biography* (New York, 1945), vol. V, 352; U.S., Congress, House, *Congressional Directory for the Second Session of the Forty-First Congress of the United States of America* (Washington, D.C., 1869), 40; Cake's militia involvement is documented in the sketch of the National Light Infantry by Edmund McDonald, "The First Defenders," Philadelphia *Weekly Press*, March 24, 1886; Pottsville *Miners' Journal*, August 28, 1899. My character sketch of Cake is based on several primary documents and an important secondary source, a journal article by former Assistant State Historian of Pennsylvania, Marvin W. Schlegel, "The Workingmen's Benevolent Association: First Union of Anthracite Miners," *Pennsylvania History*, vol. X (October 1943). Schlegel takes great care in his article to paint a picture of Cake which portrays the Schuylkill County colonel as a maverick anthracite colliery operator. Schlegel characterizes Cake as a treacherous and unscrupulous mine owner. The Cake who emerges from the narrative·forming the Schlegel article is a rather headstrong, domineering, unsavory character. Cake's personality is also attacked in Jacob G. Frick to Samuel Randall, Letter, March 4, 1887, Isaac Severn Papers, Historical Society of Schuylkill County. This letter describes the friction between Frick and Cake. Several letters of Peter Filbert, especially the undated epistle, probably written in either late September or early October of 1862, from Filbert to Oliver Duff Greene, Filbert Papers, HCWRTC, HEC, best conveys the adverse relationship between Filbert and Cake. Perhaps the most indicting statement of Cake's personality was made by Jacob G. Frick when he cited Cake, "as the meanest of White men." See the letter of Jacob G. Frick to John Filbert, Esquire, May 29, 1866, Filbert Papers, HCWRTC, HEC; McDonald, "The First Defenders," Philadelphia *Weekly Press*, March 24, 1886; Bates, *Pennsylvania Volunteers*, vol. I, 226–227; Boyle, "Outline Sketch," July 17, 1886. See also "Sentiments of a True Democrat," Lewistown *Gazette*, June 18, 1862.

6. U.S., Department of State., *Compendium of the Enumeration of the United States, as Obtained at the Department of State, from the Returns of the Sixth Census* (Washington, D.C.: Dept. of State, 1841), 26, 136; An-

thony F. C. Wallace, *St. Clair: A Nineteenth Century Coal Town's Experience with a Disaster Prone Industry* (New York: Alfred A. Knopf, 1987), 3–6.

7. Bates, *Pennsylvania Volunteers*, vol. III, 382; *Ibid.*, 226.

8. The arrival of the various infantry companies, at Camp Schuylkill, can be traced in Bates, *Pennsylvania Volunteers*, vol. III, 382; Boyle, "Outline Sketch," July 17, 1886. The exact order of arrival, by company, at Camp Schuylkill, is imperative in order to determine officer seniority of the line captains; see also "Schuylkill in the War: Historical Sketch of the Ninety-sixth Pennsylvania Volunteers," Pottsville *Standard*, July 23, 1886.

9. The order of arrival of the second wave of companies at Camp Schuylkill is also documented in Bates, *Pennsylvania Volunteers*, vol. III, 382; Boyle, "Outline Sketch," July 17, 1886; The nickname of Company G, "The Hamburg Light Infantry," was found in the Pottsville *Miners' Journal*, December 7, 1861.

10. Bates, *Pennsylvania Volunteers*, vol. III, 382; "Schuylkill in the War," Pottsville *Standard*, July 23, 1886; Boyle, "Outline Sketch," July 17, 1886; Francis B. *Wallace, Memorial of the Patriotism of Schuylkill County, in the American Slaveholder's Rebellion* (Pottsville, Pennsylvania: Benjamin Bannan, 1865), 112–113; According to the U.S., War Department, *Revised Regulations for the Army of the United States, 186* (Philadelphia, Pennsylvania: George W. Childs, 1862), 11, the prescribed method of commissioned officer promotion was based upon the seniority principle. Article IV, Section 19 states: "All vacancies in established regiments and corps, to the rank of colonel, shall be filled by promotion according to seniority, except in case of disability or other incompetency." Francis A. Lord, *They Fought for the Union* (New York: Bonanza Books, 1960), 230, also sheds some light on the seniority system of promotion, as it pertained to volunteer regiments; Bates, *Pennsylvania Volunteers*, vol. I, 226.

11. The biographical sketch of Jacob G. Frick is based on information gleaned from Boyle, "Outline Sketch," July 17, 1886; The quotation describing Frick's physical appearance was found in Samuel P. Bates, *Martial Deeds of Pennsylvania* (Philadelphia, Pennsylvania: T.H. Davis, 1876), 58–59.

12. *Ibid.*; The biographical sketch concerning Lewis J. Martin was drawn from his obituary printed in the Pottsville *Miners' Journal*, September 20, 1862; See also Pottsville *Miners' Journal*, September 27, 1862; Bates, *Pennsylvania Volunteers*, vol. III, 382.

13. John T. Boyle, "The Ninety sixth Reg't. Its Origin and Early Organization. A Brief History of the Several Companies—Whence they Came and When they Went Into Camp Schuylkill," *Schuylkill Republican*, September 18, 1886; Henry Keiser, Diary, September 23, 1861—September 29, 1861, Keiser Papers, Harrisburg Civil War Round Table Collection, United States Army Heritage & Education Center, Carlisle, Pennsylvania.

14. Boyle, "Outline Sketch," July 17, 1886; The procedures for examining surgeons are clearly outlined in Lord, *They Fought for the Union*, 14; The quotation concerning the attending doctor's and the recruiting officer's statement, both required on the "volunteer enlistment" form, was located in John D. Billings, *Hard Tack and Coffee, or the Unwritten Story of Army Life* (Boston, Massachusetts: George M. Smith & Company, 1888), 200; These same statements are paraphrased in Lord, *They Fought for the Union*, 14.

15. Records of the Department of Military and Veterans' Affairs, Registers of Pennsylvania Volunteers,

1861–1865, RG-19, Pennsylvania State Archives, vol. 8, 365–395. I surveyed companies A, C and E to determine the average age of the soldiers who enrolled in 1861.

16. Benjamin A. Gould, *Investigations in the Military and Anthropological Statistics of American Soldiers* (New York: United States Sanitary Commission, 1869), 88; see also Wiley, *Billy Yank*, 303.

17. Boyle, "Outline Sketch," July 17, 1886.

18. My sketch of the pre-Civil War coal trade in Schuylkill County was developed from several sources. See William Gudelunas, Jr., "Nativism and the Demise of Schuylkill County Whiggery: Anti-Slavery or Anti-Catholicism," *Pennsylvania History*, vol. 45 (July 1978), 225–226, 235; *History of Schuylkill County, Pa.* (New York: W. W. Munsell, 1881), 58; Clifton K. Yearley, Jr., *Enterprise and Anthracite: Economics and Democracy in Schuylkill County, 1820–1875* (Baltimore, Maryland: Johns Hopkins University Press, 1961), 165.

19. Boyle, "Outline Sketch," July 17, 1886. Total number reported concerning ethnicity 1,042.

20. *Ibid.* It is unknown where Boyle gleaned his data regarding ethnicity and occupation. Boyle reported on 1,085 men and their occupations.

21. Christian B. Keller, "Pennsylvania and the Germans During the Civil War: A Brief History and Comparative Analysis," *The Virginia Magazine of History and Biography*, vol. 109, no. 1 (2001), 37–42.

22. Susannah Ural Bruce, "'Remember Your Country and Keep Its Credit': Irish Volunteers and the Union Army, 1861–1865," *Journal of Military History*, vol. 69 (April 2005), 333. Anyone interested in German soldiers from Pennsylvania—Pennsylvania Dutch and German-Americans—should start with *Damn Dutch: Pennsylvania Germans at Gettysburg*, by David Valuska and Christian Keller (Mechanicsburg, Pennsylvania: Stackpole Books, 2004).

23. Keiser, Diary, September 21–30, 1861, Keiser Papers, HCWRTC, HEC; Boyle, "Ninety-Sixth Reg't," *Schuylkill Republican*, September 18, 1886; See also Pullen, *The Twentieth Maine*, 14; Bruce Catton, *This Hallowed Ground: The Story of the Union Side of the Civil War* (Garden City, New York: Doubleday, 1956), 26.

24. My description of the training of volunteer infantry soldiers was based on material in the following sources: Lord, *They Fought for the Union*, 26, 28–30; Pullen, *Twentieth Maine*, 33–35; Wiley, *Billy Yank*, 49–50; Gregory A. Coco, *The Civil War Infantryman: In Camp, On the March, and in Battle* (Gettysburg, Penna.: Thomas Publications, 1996), 17–21; Mark A. Weitz, "Drill, Training and the Combat performance of the Civil War Soldier: Dispelling the Myth of the Poor Soldier, Great Fighter," *Journal of Military History*, vol. 62, no. 2 (April 1998), 272–277. For anyone wishing to examine the training manual literature used during the Civil War, see the following sources Silas Casey, *Infantry Tactics*, 3 vols. (New York: D. Van Nostrand, 1862), William J. Hardee, *Rifle and Light Infantry Tactics*, 2 vols. (Richmond, Virginia: J. W. Randolph, 1861), Winfield Scott, *Infantry Tactics*, 3 vols. (New York: Harper and Brothers, 1861).

25. Pullen, *Twentieth Maine*, 35; Lord, *They Fought for the Union*, 28–30; Wiley, *Billy Yank*, 49–54, all offer insight into the basic training of Civil War volunteer soldiers. Catton also offers an interesting picture of volunteer training in, *This Hallowed Ground*, 43.

26. John T. Boyle, "The Ninety-sixth Reg't," September 18, 1886.

27. Lord, *They Fought for the Union*, 26, renders a recapitulation of the steps preceding the firing of a Civil War musket.

28. The possibility of a raw recruit firing the ramrod from his musket is discussed in Pullen, *Twentieth Maine*, 33; The following data, concerning regimental formation, was extracted from the Pottsville *Miners' Journal*, October 26, 1861. "According to military usages, the arrangement of the companies on military parade or in line of battle is as below."

Number	1	6	4	9	3	8	5	10	7	2
Letter	A	F	D	I	C	H	E	K	G	B

29. Rowland Berthoff, "The Social order of the Anthracite Region, 1825–1902," *Pennsylvania Magazine of History and Biography*, vol. 89 no. 3 (July 1965), 261–270; Grace Palladino, *Another Civil War: Labor, Capital, and the State in the Anthracite Regions of Pennsylvania 1840–68* (Chicago, Illinois: University of Illinois Press, 1990), 72, 90.

30. Keller, "Pennsylvania and Virginia Germans During the Civil War," 42–43; Kevin Kenny, "Nativism, Labor and Slavery: The Political Odyssey of Benjamin Bannan, 1850–1860," *Pennsylvania Magazine of History and Biography*, vol. 118, no. 4 (October 1994), 357–361.

31. Cake's frequent absenteeism from Camp Schuylkill, during the autumn of 1861, is fully documented in Filbert, Diary, Filbert Papers, HCWRTC, HEC. There are also references in the Pottsville *Miners' Journal*, noting Cake's absence from Camp Schuylkill. For one example see Pottsville *Miners' Journal*, November 2, 1861, "Col. Cake in Philadelphia on business connected with his regiment." Cake seemed to have a penchant for leaving the regimental camp to conduct business, always connected with the regiment, elsewhere. A letter in Cake's service file, Record Group 94, Adjutant General's Office—Compiled Union Service Records, National Archives, dated November 29, 1861, written to General Slocum stated: "The settlement of business connected with the reorganization of my regiment renders it necessary for me to go on to New York … for four (4) days."

32. Bannan's article endorsing Cake is in the Pottsville *Miners' Journal*, September 28, 1861; Charlemagne Tower was the successful Democratic Party candidate for district attorney of Schuylkill County in 1853. He was also, at that time, reaping a handsome profit from his anthracite coal land speculative purchases. At the outbreak of the Civil War he organized the Tower Guards, a militia company, in response to Lincoln's call for volunteer soldiers. In 1863 Tower served as the Provost Marshal of Schuylkill County, becoming a key figure in the draft riots which plagued the anthracite coal region.

33. Cake's pre-war activities, at least those pertaining to militia pursuits, are documented in McDonald, "The First Defenders," March 24, 1886. This article, too, offers a glimpse into Cake's personality.

34. Anyone wishing to explore Pennsylvania Civil War politics would be wise to begin with the fine article on the "War Governor" by Rebecca Gifford Albright, "The Civil War Career of Andrew Gregg Curtin, Governor of Pennsylvania," *Western Pennsylvania Magazine of History*, vol. 47 (October 1964), continued in vol. 48 (January 1965) and concludes in vol. 48 (April 1965). To gain an understanding of the dynamics of Schuylkill County politics it is necessary to read the article by Gudelunas, "Nativism and the Decline of Schuylkill County Whiggery," 225–236. In the election, Reilly garnered 6,687 ballots to Cake's 5,490 votes, giving the former a 1,197 vote victory in the general election. Cake did, however, fare quite well

with the volunteer soldier votes of the county. In that voter bloc, Cake secured a 72% share as opposed to Reilly's 28%. Unfortunately for Cake, of the 12,177 votes cast in the election, the Bluecoats who voted constituted only 4% of the entire electorate. The county voting returns can be located in the Pottsville *Miners' Journal*, issue of October 12, 1861. The returns for the soldiers were found in the Pottsville *Miners' Journal*, November 16, 1861. Because Cake's regiment had not yet received their new unit ordinal number, the company returns were listed under the heading: "25th Pennsylvania Volunteers."

	Cake	Reilly
Co. E Captain James E. Russell	5	—
Co. H Captain Charles D. Hipple	4	—
Co. I Captain Isaac M. Cake	6	—
Co. B. Captain Peter A. Filbert	15	2
	30	2

35. Frick to Samuel Randall, Letter, March 4, 1887, Severn Papers, HSSC, tells of Frick's disenchantment with the regimental staff officers of the 96th Pennsylvania; Filbert to Oliver Duff Greene, Letter, probably written in late September or early October, 1862, Filbert Papers, HCWRTC, HEC, relates the political polarization which transpired within the regimental staff of the 96th Pennsylvania Volunteers.

36. Boyle, "Outline Sketch," July 17, 1886; Bates, *Pennsylvania Volunteers*, vol. III, 382; Documentation concerning the cannon of the Good Intent Light Artillery can be found in the Pottsville *Miners' Journal*, September 7, 1861 and October 19, 1861.

37. Biographical information on William H. Lessig was found in several sources: Filbert to Oliver Duff Greene, undated letter, Filbert Papers, HCWRTC, HEC; Boyle, "Outline Sketch," July 17, 1886; Article on the misfortune of William Lessig, Denver *Post*, October 28, 1903 and obituary column in the Denver *Times*, March 2, 1910; The transfer of Beaton Smith's company is documented in Bates, *Pennsylvania Volunteers*, vol. III, 382, and in Boyle, "Outline Sketch," July 17, 1886.

38. Keiser, Diary, October 18, 1861, Keiser Papers, HCWRTC, HEC, tells of the young private's "escape" from Camp Schuylkill, into Pottsville, for a night on the town. This activity, which was quite popular among the more adventurous and spirited Bluecoats, was referred to as "running the guards."

39. The camp stove is documented in the Pottsville *Miners' Journal*, October 26, 1861.

40. The presentation of the flag by A. L. Gee, to the regiment, is described in the Pottsville *Miners' Journal*, October 19, 1861.

41. All of the infantry calls are listed, with music for both drum and bugle, in Casey, *Infantry Tactics*, I, 227ff; I relied upon several sources to describe the daily routine of the 96th Pennsylvania. Clement Potts to his brother, December 15, 1861, Clement Potts Papers, Historical Society of Schuylkill County, Pottsville, Pennsylvania, listed the daily calls and the corresponding times:

Roll Call	6–6:30 AM
Breakfast	7
Drill	8–9:30
Division Drill	10–12
Dinner	Noon
Drill	2–2:30 PM
Drill	3–5
Supper	6
Roll Call	8
Lights Out	8:15

Regimental Order #67, dated February 15, 1864, altered the daily calls slightly:

Reveille will be beaten at	6:15 AM
Breakfast	7
Sick Call	7:30
Police Call	8
Guard Mounting	8:30
Dinner	Noon
Tattoo	8:30 PM
Taps	9:30

This document was located in the Severn Papers, HSSC. Although it is dated 1864, it offers documentation of the calls actually sounded by the Pennsylvanians. For an excellent summary and description of the various calls, see Wiley, *Billy Yank*, 45–46; The signal which headed the official list of calls, but not used by the 96th Pennsylvania, was a preliminary one known as the "assembly of the buglers."

42. Wiley, *Billy Yank*, 46–47.

43. *Ibid.*, 47–48.

44. Boyle, "The Ninety-sixth Reg't.," September 18, 1886. See also Weitz, "Drill, Training and the Combat performance of the Civil War Soldier," 272–277.

45. Boyle, "The Ninety-sixth Reg't.," September 18, 1886.

46. Boyle, "Outline Sketch," July 17, 1886; Wallace, *Memorial of the Patriotism of Schuylkill County*, 108–112; The full text of Curtin's speech can be found in *Ibid.*, 112.

47. The unedited text of Cake's spirited talk can also be found in *Ibid.*, 110–111.

48. *Ibid.*, 112.

49. Boyle, "Ninety-Sixth Reg't," September 18, 1886. See also *Miner's Journal*, October 26, November 2, November 9 and November 16, 1861.

50. For further details concerning the flags carried by the 96th Pennsylvania see Richard A. Sauers, *Advance the Colors!* (Harrisburg, Pennsylvania: Sowers Printing Company, 1991), vol. 2, 325–327; Presumably the rank and file enlisted for the same reason as other northern Bluecoats: patriotism. Both Wiley, *Billy Yank*, 17 and Lord, *They Fought for the Union*, 3, suggest patriotism as the motivating force behind volunteer enlistment; The figure representing the strength of the 96th regiment was taken from Wallace, *Memorial of the Patriotism of Schuylkill County*, 127.

51. Filbert, Diary, November 7, 1861, Filbert Papers, HCWRTC, HEC; Keiser, Diary, November 7 and 8, 1861, Keiser Papers, HCWRTC, HEC.

52. The story of George Foltz joining the 96th Pennsylvania Volunteers can be found in, J.W. Conrad, "Proceedings and Speeches made at the Transfer of Battle Flags to the Historical Society of Schuylkill County December 14, 1913," vol. V, no. 2 (1932), *Publications of the Historical Society Schuylkill County*, 21.

53. Robert M. Sandow, "The Limits of Northern Patriotism: Early Civil War Mobilization in Pennsylvania," *Pennsylvania History,* vol.70, no.2 (Spring 2003), 203.

54. C. D. Hipple, Letter, November 19, 1861, *Miners' Journal*, November 30, 1861; James I. Robertson, *Soldiers Blue and Gray* (Columbia, South Carolina: University of South Carolina Press), 1988, 6–8.

Chapter II

1. My description of the 96th Pennsylvania's trip to Washington was taken from a letter in the Pottsville

Miners' Journal, signed "NINETY-SIXTH," dated November 16, 1861. All quotations cited are from that very graphic letter.

2. *Ibid.*

3. *Ibid.*

4. *Ibid.*

5. Pottsville *Miners' Journal*, November 16, 1861.

6. Bates, *Pennsylvania Volunteers*, vol. III, 382; Boyle, "Outline Sketch," July 17, 1886.

7. Charles D. Hipple, Letter, November 19, 1861, Pottsville *Miners' Journal*, November 30, 1861.

8. Boyle, "Outline Sketch," July 17, 1886.

9. Francis Boland to John Brislin, Letter, November 11, 1861, John Brislin Papers, Historical Society of Schuylkill County, Pottsville, Pennsylvania.

10. Clement Potts to his Mother, Letter, November 7, 1861, Clement Potts Papers, Historical Society of Schuylkill County, Pottsville, Pennsylvania.

11. Bates, *Pennsylvania Volunteers*, vol. III, 382; Boyle, "Outline Sketch," July 17, 1886.

12. The organization of Slocum's Brigade, Franklin's Division, is recorded in Bates, *Pennsylvania Volunteers*, vol. III, 382, see the ff marked by a +; The genesis of Slocum's brigade of Franklin's Division can be traced in, U.S., War Department, Potomac, Army of the, *Letter of Secretary of War Transmitting Report on the Organization of the Army of the Potomac, and of Its Campaigns in Virginia and Maryland, Under Command of George B. McClellan, July 26, 1861—Nov. 7, 1862* (Washington, D.C.: Government Printing Office, 1864), as of October 15, 1861, 13, as of March 13, 1862, 16.

13. For a biography of Franklin see, Mark A. Snell, *From First to Last: The Life of Major General William B. Franklin* (New York: Fordham University Press, 2002); Ezra J. Warner, *Generals in Blue: Lives of the Union Commanders* (Baton Rouge, Louisiana: Louisiana State University Press), 159–160.

14. George B. McClellan, *McClellan's Own Story: The War for the Union, The Soldiers Who Fought it, the Civilians Who Directed it and His Relation to it and to Them* (New York: Charles L. Webster & Company, 1887), 138.

15. Newton M. Curtis, *From Bull Run to Chancellorsville: The Story of the Sixteenth New York Infantry together with Personal Reminiscences* (New York: G. P. Putnam's Sons, 1906), 291.

16. Thomas W. Hyde, *Following the Greek Cross: or, Memories of the Sixth Army Corps* (Cambridge, Massachusetts: Riverside Press, 1897), 116–117.

17. For a recent biography of Slocum see, Brian C. Melton, *Sherman's Forgotten General: Henry W. Slocum* (Columbia, Missouri: University of Missouri Press, 2009); Warner, *Generals in Blue*, p.451–453.

18. Harry W. Pfanz, *Gettysburg: Culp's Hill & Cemetery Hill* (Chapel Hill, North Carolina: University of North Carolina Press, 1993), 89–92.

19. Frank A. Haskell, *The Battle of Gettysburg* (Boston, Massachusetts: Houghton Mifflin, 1958), 60.

20. Alpheus S. Williams, *From the Cannons Mouth: The Civil War Letters of Alpheus S. Williams* (Detroit, Michigan: Wayne State University Press, 1959), 141.

21. Harrison, Letter, [December 30, 1862], Rochester *Union & Advertiser*, January 10, 1862.

22. George W. Bicknell, *History of the Fifth Regiment Maine Volunteers* (Portland, Maine: Hall L. Davis, 1871), 66.

23. Maj. Lyon, Letter, [June 1, 1862], Rochester *Union & Advertiser*, June 9, 1862.

24. Curtis, *From Bull Run to Chancellorsville,* 292.

25. John T. Boyle to Peter Filbert, Letter, January 26 [?], 1863, War Between the States Memorabilia (November 2002).

26. Washington Nugent, Letter, January 8, 1862, in *My Darling Wife…: The Letters of Washington George Nugent, Surgeon Army of the Potomac,* ed. by Maria Allen (Cheshire, Connecticut: Ye Olde Book Bindery, 1994), 91.

27. Boland to Brislin, Letter, November 19, 1861, Brislin Papers, HSSC.

28. McClellan, *McClellan's Own Story*, 229.

29. My description of the Grand Review is taken from Curtis, *From Bull Run to Chancellorsville*, 80–81.

30. Lewis J. Martin to his Mother, Letter, November 23, 1861, Lewis Martin Papers, William Schoff Collection, William Clements Library, University of Michigan, Ann Arbor, Michigan; See also Shelby Foote, *The Civil War: A Narrative, vol. I; Fort Sumter to Perryville* (New York: Random House, 1958), 153–154.

31. The details concerning Private Johnson were ascertained in C. B. Fairchild, *History of the 27th Regiment N. Y. Vols.* (Binghamton, New York: Carl & Matthews, 1888), 26.

32. Keiser, Diary, December 13, 1861, Keiser Papers, HCWRTC, HEC; The Johnson execution is also discussed in Martin to his mother, December 17, 1861, Martin Papers, SC, WCL; There is also an excellent description and personal reaction to the shooting in the Potts correspondence. See Potts to his Brother, Letter, December 15, 1861, where he states that "it was the most horrible sight I ever seen." and that he "did not think that their [sic] were such hard hearted men to shoot another in cold blood," Potts Papers, HSSC.

33. Nugent to My darling Wife, Letters, December 15 and 17, 1861, in *My Darling Wife*, 83.

34. Martin to My Dear Folks at Home, Letter, December 17, 1861, Martin Papers, SC, WCL.

35. Potts to brother, Letter, December 15, 1861, in Potts Papers, HSSC.

36. *Miners' Journal*, January 25, 1862.

37. James Augustine to dear friend, Letter, December 5, [1861], Augustine Papers, William Kerman Collection, Harrisburg Civil War Round Table Collection, United States Army Heritage & Education Center, Carlisle, Pennsylvania.

38. John K. Fernsler, Diary, December 18, 1861, Marion Fernsler Collection, Pottsville, Pennsylvania.

39. Nugent to My Darling Wife, Letter, March 13, 1862 in *My Darling Wife*, p. 103.

40. Boland to [?], [January, 1862], Letter, Brislin Papers, HSSC.

41. Martin to My Dear Folks at Home, Letter, December 27, 1861, Martin Papers, SC, WCL.

42. The data is taken from Wiley, *Billy Yank*, 124; 136–137.

43. U.S., Surgeon General's Office, *Medical and Surgical History of the War of the Rebellion* (Washington, D.C.: Government Printing Office, 1870–1888), Medical Volume, pt. 1, xxxvii, xliii, pt. 2, 3 and pt. 3, 3ff. (Hereafter this source will be cited as *Medical and Surgical History*); W. W. Keen, "Military Surgery in 1861 and 1918," *Annals of the American Academy of Political and Social Science*, LXXX (1918), 12, 18.

44. "Ninety-Sixth" to Dear Journal, letter, January 14, 1862, *Miners' Journal*, January 25, 1862.

45. Patrick McGlenn to John Brislin, Letters, [January 1862], February 17, 1862 and March 5, 1862, in John Brislin Papers, Historical Society of Schuylkill County, Pottsville, Pennsylvania.

46. Potts to his mother, Letter, February 3, 1862, Potts Papers, HSSC.

47. Nugent to My darling Wife, Letter, January 5, 1862, in *My Darling Wife*, p. 89.

48. Potts to his mother, Letter, February 3, 1862, Potts Papers, HSSC.

49. Wallace, *Memorial of the Patriotism of Schuylkill County*, 538–539.

50. Potts to his mother, Letter, February 3, 1862, Potts Papers, HSSC.

51. *Miners' Journal*, February 15, 1862.

52. Leander Stillwell, *Story of a Common Soldier of Army Life in the Civil War 1861–1865* (Kansas City, Missouri: Franklin Hudson Publishing, 1920), 28; Ulysses S. Grant, Testimony before House Select Committee on Government Contracts, October 31, 1861 in *The Papers of Ulysses S. Grant*, ed. John Y. Simon (Carbondale, Illinois: Southern Illinois University Press, 1971), vol.3, 90; Thomas Houck to Beloved Parents, Letter, January 1, 1862, Houck Family Papers, Small Manuscripts Collection, Virginia Polytechnic Institute and State University, Blacksburg, Virginia.

53. Fernsler, Diary, January 7, 1862, FC.

54. Erasmus Reed to Beloved Parents, Letter, January 9, 1862, Erasmus Reed Papers, Indiana Historical Society, Indianapolis, Indiana.

55. Boland to [?], Letter fragment [January 1862], Brislin Papers, HSSC.

56. "Ninety-Sixth" to editor, Letter, January 14, 1862, *Miners' Journal*, January 25, 1862.

57. Potts to brother, Letter, December 15, 1861, in Potts Papers, HSSC.

58. Filbert, Diary, February 13–15, 1862, Filbert Papers, HCWRTC, HEC.

59. *Ibid.*

60. "Ninety-Sixth" to editor, Letter, January 14, 1862, *Miners' Journal*, January 25, 1862.

61. Nugent to My darling Wife, Letter, March 19, 1862, in *My Darling Wife*, 105.

62. Filbert, Diary, March 14 & 26, 1862, Filbert Papers, HCWRTC, HEC.

63. Reed to Beloved Parents, Letter, March 9, 1862, Reed Papers, IHS.

64. Nugent to My darling Wife, Letter, January 5, 1862, in *My Darling Wife*, 80.

65. Boyle, "Outline Sketch," July 17, 1886.

66. Samuel Fisher Colt to the Rev. Samuel Miller, Letter, January 6, 1862, *Miners' Journal*, January 18, 1862.

67. D. Webster Bland to Mrs. John L. Mennig,, Letter, December 11, 1861, *Miners' Journal*, December 21, 1861.

68. The sauerkraut is documented in a letter written by Charles Sailor, the regimental quartermaster, Letter, December 11, 1861, *Miners' Journal*, December 21, 1861; Filbert to his Father, Letter, January 21, 1862, Filbert Papers, HCWRTC, HEC.

69. *Miners' Journal*, March 8, 1862.

70. *Ibid.*

71. The personality differences between Cake and Peter Filbert become quite obvious as one reads through the Filbert correspondence. Filbert to O.D. Greene, September 30, 1862, Filbert Papers, HCWRTC, HEC, clearly outlines the Cake-Filbert differences; Lieutenant Colonel Frick, too, had problems with Colonel Cake. Unfortunately, there is little to document Frick's obvious disenchantment with Cake. One piece of evidence, however, hinting at Frick's dissatisfaction while serving with the 96th Pennsylvania Volunteers, can be found in his military service file, Record Group 94, Adjutant General's Office—Compiled Union Service Records, National Archives. In a letter to Brig. Gen. Seth Williams, dated July 25, 1862, Frick states, "I desire to say that I cannot continue to serve another day in the 96th Pa. Vols. under its present commander and that I cannot any longer be useful there." See also Frick to Samuel Randall, March 4, 1887, Severn Papers, HSSC.

72. Filbert to his Father, March 4, 1862, Filbert Papers, HCWRTC, HEC.

73. *Revised Regulations*, 496.

74. Filbert, Diary, December 9, 1861, Filbert Papers, HCWRTC, HEC.

75. *Ibid.*, December 16, 1861, Filbert Papers, HCWRTC, HEC.

76. *Ibid.*, January 14, 1861, Filbert Papers, HCWRTC, HEC.

77. *Ibid.*, February 21–24, 1862, Filbert Papers, HCWRTC, HEC.

78. Henry Anson Castle, *The Army Mule and Other War Sketches* (Indianapolis, Indiana: Bowen-Merrill Company, 1897), 111.

79. For an excellent article on the Civil War sutler see, Donald P. Spear, "The Sutler in the Union Army," *Civil War History*, vol. 16, no. 2 (June 1970), the quotation can be found on page 122. See also Alfred J. Tapson, "The Sutler and the Soldier," *Military Affairs*, vol. 21, no. 4 (Winter 1957), p. 175–181; Francis A. Lord, *Civil War Sutlers and Their Wares* (New York: Thomas Yoseloff, 1969); and Henry A. Castle, "The Sutler," *Glimpses of the Nation's Struggle* (Saint Paul, Minnesota: H. L. Collins Company, 1898), 4th series, Military Order of the Loyal Legion United States, Minnesota Commandery, 58–65.

80. U. S., Congress, House, *Congressional Globe*, 37th Congress, 2nd Session, CXXIX, 1143; U.S., Sanitary Commission, *Documents of the United States Sanitary Commission* (New York, 1866), Doc. No. 40, 32–33.

81. Lord, *They Fought for the Union*, 130; Spear, "The Sutler in the Union Army," *CWH*, 121–122; Until the Civil War, sutlers were regulated mainly by the *Articles of War* authorized by Congress in 1806. Senator Henry Wilson of Massachusetts, Chairman of the Military Affairs Committee, prompted Congress to pass legislation on March 19, 1862, entitled, "An Act to Provide for the Appointment of Sutlers in the Volunteer Service, and to Define their Duties," U.S., *The Statutes at Large, Treaties, and Proclamations of the United States of America* (Washington, D.C.: Government Printing Office, 1859–1863), vol. XII, 371–373 [1862], known familiarly in the ranks as "Mr. Wilson's Bill." The complete text of Wilson's Bill is in *Statutes at Large*, vol. XII, Chap. XLVII, 371–373; A summary of the bill and a brief record of the debates in Congress is in Frank Moore, ed., *The Rebellion Record: A Diary of American Events, with Documents, Narratives, Illustrative Incidents, Poetry, etc.* (New York: G. P. Putnam, 1862–1867), vol. X, 24–27.

82. *Revised Regulations*, Article XXIII, page 34–36; See also *Ibid.*, Article XXV, 37–38; Spear, "The Sutler in the Union Army," *CWH*, 126–131.

83. *Revised Regulations*, Article XXIII, 34–36; Lord, *They Fought for the Union*, 130–131; *Ibid.*, 240.

84. Filbert to his Brother, March 30, 1863, Letter, Filbert Papers, HCWRTC, HEC, which details the sutler problem. In this letter Filbert states, "When Col. Cake informed us that he had a private contract with the Suttler [sic] and said Suttler [sic] should pay no tax." If this was indeed the situation, the obvious conclusion one would draw was that Cake protected the sutler from paying the tax due the Post Fund.

85. Filbert to his Father, Letter, March 4, 1862, Filbert Papers, HCWRTC, HEC; Filbert to his Father, Letter, September 30, 1862, Filbert Papers, HCWRTC, HEC; Filbert [to O.D. Greene?], undated letter, beginning, "The undersigned has in connection with," Filbert Papers, HCWRTC, HEC.

86. Maurus Oestreich, Diary, "Civil War Centennial Project. Maurus Oestreich: American Citizen, Loyal Catholic, Hessian Born, Union Volunteer, Grand Army of the Republic Veteran, Organ Builder, General Contractor, Musician, Guest Speaker, Devoted Husband, Industrious Father, gifted with many virtues. A Tribute by His Children." translated from German by William Hammeke, Diary, Oestreich Papers, Historical Society of Schuylkill County, Pottsville, Pennsylvania, 5. Maurus Oestreich (pronounced A-strike), was a private in Peter Filbert's Company B. Oestreich was a Catholic immigrant from Hesse (Darmstadt), Germany. A review of the letters and diaries of the 96th Pennsylvania reveals that the famous regimental photograph was composed by a photographic artiste, most likely from Alexandria, on February 26, 1862 at Camp Northumberland. This is one of the most reproduced photographs of the Civil War. See Erasmus Reed to Parents, Letter, February 26, 1862, Reed Papers, IHS; Henry Keiser, Diary, February 27, 1862, Keiser Papers, HCWRTC, HEC.

87. Filbert, Diary, March 9, 1862, Filbert Papers, HCWRTC, HEC.

88. Curtis, *From Bull Run to Chancellorsville*, 90–91.

Chapter III

1. Bicknell, *History of the Fifth Regiment Maine Volunteers*, 76–77.

2. James Treichler, Memoir, Randy Treichler Collection, Three Springs, Pennsylvania.

3. Potts to his Mother, Letter, December 8, 1861, Potts Papers, HSSC.

4. Bruce Catton, *Terrible Swift Sword* (Garden City, New York: Doubleday, 1963), 199–201; Catton, *Mr. Lincoln's Army*, 101; Foote, *Civil War*, vol. I, 263–264.

5. Martin to My Dear Folks, Letter, March 12, 1862, Martin Papers, SC, WCL.

6. For an interesting analysis of McClellan's march to Fairfax Court House see chapter five "Pursuit—After a Fashion," in Russel H. Beatie, *Army of the Potomac: McClellan's First Campaign, March-May 1862* (El Dorado, California: Savas Beatie, 2007), 69–83; Bicknell, *History of the Fifth Regiment Maine Volunteers*, 76–77; Curtis, *From Bull Run to Chancellorsville*, 90–91.

7. Treichler, Memoir, RTC, 6–7.

8. Lewis Luckenbill, Diary, March 10–15, 1862, William Dick Collection, Girard, Pennsylvania; See also a brief passage concerning foraging in Oestreich, Diary, 5, Oestreich Papers, HSSC.

9. Fairchild, *History of the 27th Regiment N. Y. Vols.*, 27; Catton, *Mr. Lincoln's Army*, 104; George T. Stevens, *Three Years in the Sixth Corps: A Concise Narrative of Events in the Army of the Potomac, from 1861 to the Close of the Rebellion, April, 1865* (Albany, New York: S. R. Gray, 1866), 18–21.

10. Nugent to Darling Wife, Letter, March 13, 1862, in *My Darling Wife*, 103; Hyde, *Following the Greek Cross*, 36.

11. McClellan to the Army of the Potomac, March 14, 1862 in *The Civil War Papers of George B. McClellan:*

Selected Correspondence, 1860–1865, ed. by Stephen W. Sears (New York: Ticknor & Fields, 1989), 211.

12. Bicknell, *History of the Fifth Regiment Maine Volunteers*, 78–79.

13. Catton, *Terrible Swift Sword*, 276–277; Catton, *Mr. Lincoln's Army*, 103–107.

14. Foote, *Civil War*, vol. I, 405–406; Catton, *Mr. Lincoln's Army*, 109.

15. Stevens, *Three Years in the Sixth Corps*, 22.

16. Nugent to My Darling Wife, Letter, March 19, 1862 in *My Darling Wife*, 105.

17. Mathias Edgar Richards to Dear Sophie, Letter, March 30, 1862, Richards Papers, United States Army Heritage & Education Center, Carlisle, Pennsylvania.

18. McGlenn to Dear Friend, Letter, April 3, 1862, Brislin Papers, HSSC.

19. Curtis, *From Bull Run to Chancellorsville*, 91; Bicknell, *History of the Fifth Regiment Maine Volunteers*, 78–79.

20. Richards to Brother, Letter, March 2, 1862, and April 5, 1862, Richards Papers, HEC.

21. Edward Henry, Letter, April 13, 1862. Ebay auction February 2, 2009. Typescript copy in author's possession.

22. Fernsler, Diary, April 5, 1862, FC.

23. Luckenbill, Diary, April 5, 1862, WDC.

24. Bicknell, *History of the Fifth Regiment Maine Volunteers*, 80.

25. Keiser, Diary, April 8, 1862, Keiser Papers, HCWRTC, HEC. The torrential downpour at Catlett's Station eventually became a very humorous affair among the veterans of the 96th Pennsylvania. The soldiers remarked in their letters and diaries about other encampments in the rain. The Pennsylvanians did not want to endure another "Catlett's Station."

26. Martin to his folks at home, April 11, 1862, Martin Papers, SC, WCL.

27. Fairchild, *History of the 27th Regiment N. Y. Vols.*, 30; Bicknell, *History of the Fifth Regiment Maine Volunteers*, 82–83.

28. *Ibid.*, 84.

29. Fernsler, Diary, April 14, 1862, FC. Fernsler records the various assignments of the regiment's companies to the three transports in his diary April 23, 1862.

30. Luckenbill, Diary, April 17, 1862, WDC.

31. Fernsler, Diary, April 14, 1862, FC; Luckenbill, Diary, April 17, 1862, WDC; Bicknell, *History of the Fifth Regiment Maine Volunteers*, 84–85.

32. Fairchild, *History of the 27th Regiment N.Y. Vols.*, 31.

33. *Ibid.*

34. *Ibid.*

35. Filbert, Diary, April 18, 1862, Filbert Papers, HCWRTC, HEC.

36. Richards to Dear Sophie, Letter, April 21, 1862, Richards Papers, HCWRTC, HEC.

37. Bicknell, *History of the Fifth Regiment Maine Volunteers*, 85.

38. Curtis, *From Bull Run to Chancellorsville*, 94.

39. Nugent to Darling Wife, Letter, April 24, 1862 in *My Darling Wife*, 114.

40. Martin to Dear Folks at Home, Letter, April 22, 1862, Martin Papers, SC, WCL.

41. Edward Henry to Sister, Letter, April 19, 1862, Henry Papers, United States Army Heritage & Education Center, Carlisle, Pennsylvania.

42. Fernsler, Diary, April 23, 1862, FC.

43. Richards to Dear Sophie, Letter, April 26, 1862, Richards Papers, HEC.

44. Reed to Dear Parents, Letter, April 27, 1862, Reed Papers, IHS.

45. Henry to Dear Sister, Letter, April 19, 1862, Henry Papers, HEC.

46. Houck to Joe, Letter, April 17, 1862, Houck Papers, VTL.

47. Reed to Dear Parents, Letter, April 27, 1862, Reed Papers, IHS.

48. Nugent to Darling Wife, Letter, May 5, 1862 in *My Darling Wife*, 117.

49. Foote, *Civil War*, vol. I, 410; Dwight E. Stinson, Jr., "Eltham's Landing—The End Run that Failed," *Civil War Times Illustrated*, vol. I, no. 10 (February 1963), 38–41.

50. McGlenn to Brislin, Letter, June 3, 1862, Brislin Papers, HSSC.

51. Boland to Brislin, Letter, June 14, 1862, Brislin Papers, HSSC.

52. McClellan, *McClellan's Own Story*, 337.

53. Snell, *From First to Last*, 100.

54. Martin to My Dear Folks at Home, Letter, May 8, 1862, Martin Papers, SC, WCL.

55. Fernsler, Diary, May 6, 1862, FC.

56. William A. Palmer, Jr., *The Battle of Eltham's landing, May 7, 1862*, [West Point, Virginia], 2012.

57. Marker, Letter, May 7, 1862, Rochester *Union and Advertiser*, May 16, 1862.

58. Letter of Officer of Company C, May 8, 1862, *Miners' Journal* May 17, 1862.

59. *Official Records*, vol. XI, Part I, 615.

60. Stinson, "Eltham's Landing," *CWTI*, 38–39; Palmer, *Battle of Eltham's Landing*, 25–28.

61. Stinson, "Eltham's Landing," *CWTI*, 40; Fairchild, *History of the 27th Regiment N. Y. Vols.*, 32–33.

62. Martin to My Dear Folks at Home, Letter, May 8, 1862, Martin Papers, SC, WCL.

63. Letter of Officer of Company C, May 8, 1862, *Miners' Journal* May 17, 1862.

64. *Official Records*, Vol. XI, Part I, 615; *Ibid.*, 623–624.

65. Douglas Freeman, *Lee's Lieutenant's: A Study in Command* vol. I, *Manassas to Malvern Hill* (New York: Charles Scribner's Sons,1942), 193–194, Freeman's chapter examines the rise of John Bell Hood, as a result of his actions at Eltham's Landing; Richard M. McMurry, *John Bell Hood and the War for Southern Independence* (Lexington, Kentucky: University of Kentucky Press, 1982), 37–39.

66. Stinson, "Eltham's Landing," *CWTI*, 40.

67. McMurry, *John Bell Hood*, 39.

68. *Official Records*, Vol. XI, Part I, 615–616; *Ibid.*, 622–624.

69. "The Survivors of the 96th, A Red Letter Day for the Veterans," *Miners' Journal*, September 17, 1886.

70. *Ibid.*

71. *Official Records*, Vol. XI, Part 1, 619–620; A.[ndrew] J. Bennett, *The Story of the First Massachusetts Light Battery Attached to the Sixth Corps* (Boston, Mass.: Deland and Barta, 1886), 36–37.

72. Martin to My Dear Folks at Home, Letter, May 8, 1862, Martin Papers, SC, WCL.

73. Letter of Officer of Company C, May 8, 1862, *Miners' Journal* May 17, 1862; See also "The Battle of West Point: Splendid Victory of General Franklin's Division," New York *Herald*, May 10, 1862. Accompanying this report by the *Herald's* "Special Correspondent," is

an excellent contemporary map depicting the positions of the troops and the naval vessels in the York River.

74. Martin to My Dear Folks at Home, Letter, May 8, 1862, Martin Papers, SC, WCL.

75. "The Battle of West Point: Victory of Gen. Franklin's Division," Philadelphia *Press*, May 12, 1862; Joel Cook, "Our Army Correspondence," Philadelphia *Press*, May 26, 1862.

76. Martin to My Dear Folks at Home, Letter, May 8, 2862, Martin Papers, SC, WCL.

77. Letter of Officer of Company C, May 8, 1862, *Miners' Journal* May 17, 1862; "The Battle of West Point: Splendid Victory of General Franklin's Division," New York *Herald*, May 10, 1862; See also Lewis Luckenbill, Diary, May 7, 1862, WDC; Luckenbill states that his company, "was thrown out to act as a telegraph from the [96th] regiment out to the outer Picketts."

78. McGlenn to Brislin, Letter, June 3, 1862, Brislin Papers, HSSC.

79. John Coxe, "With the Hampton Legion in the Peninsular Campaign," *Confederate Veteran*, vol. 29 (Nov.-Dec. 1921), 442.

80. J.C.S. Thompson, Letter, "Battle of Eltham or West Point," Galveston *Weekly News*, July 2, 1862.

81. Potts to his mother, May 12, 1862, Potts Papers, HSSC; Wiley, *Life of Billy Yank*, 66.

82. E. A. Merritt to Editor, Letter, May 10, 1862, Broome *Republican*, May 20, 1862.

83. "The Fight at West Point," New York *Times*, May 18, 1862; Curtis, *From Bull Run to Chancellorsville*, 97.

84. *Official Records*, Vol. XI, Part I, 625.

85. Boland to Brislin, Letter, June 14, 1862, Brislin Papers, HSSC.

86. Potts to his mother, May 12, 1862, Potts Papers, HSSC.

87. "The Battle at West Point," New York *Times*, May 16, 1862.

88. *Official Records*, Vol. XI, Part I, 618.

89. Boland to Brislin, Letter, June 14, 1862, Brislin Papers, HSSC.

90. Monticello, "Our Army Correspondence," Letter, May 8, 1862, Boston *Journal* May 3, 1862.

91. Luckenbill, Diary, May 8, 1862, WDC; McGlenn to Brislin, Letter, June 3, 1862, Brislin Papers, HSSC.

92. John R. Adams to Editor, Letter, June 10, 1862, Portland *Daily Advertiser*, June 28, 1862.

93. McGlenn to Brislin, Letter, June 3, 1862, Brislin Papers, HSSC.

94. Merritt to Editor, Letter, May 10, 1862, Broome *Republican*, May 20, 1862.

95. Marker to Editor, Letter, May 7, 1862, Rochester *Union and Advertiser*, May 16, 1862.

96. Monticello, "Our Army Correspondence," Letter, May 8, 1862, Boston *Journal* May 13, 1862.

97. Potts to his mother, May 12, 1862, Potts Papers, HSSC.

98. Marker to Editor, Letter, May 7, 1862, Rochester *Union and Advertiser*, May 16, 1862.

99. J[oel] J. S[eaver] to Editor, Letter, May 8, 1862, Malone *Palladium*, May 15, 1862.

100. William Coan, Letter, May 9, 1862, Orleans *Republican*, May 21, 1862.

101. Boland to Brislin, Letter, June 14, 1862, Brislin Papers, HSSC.

102. "The Fight at West Point," New York *Times*, May 18, 1862.

103. Joel J. Seaver to Editor, Letter, May 8, 1862, Malone *Palladium*, May 15, 1862.

104. Luckenbill, Diary, May 11, 1862, WDC.

105. Marker to Editor, Letter, May 20, 1862, Rochester *Union and Advertiser,* May 28, 1862.

106. Foote, *Civil War,* vol. I, 413; McClellan, *McClellan's Own Story,* 337.

107. Stephen Sears, *To the Gates of Richmond: The Peninsula Campaign* (New York: Ticknor & Fields, 1992), 97–99; *Ibid.,* 106–107.

108. Harrison to Editor, Letter, December 30, 1862 [1861], Rochester *Union and Advertiser,* January 10, 1862.

109. Ezra J. Warner, *Generals in Blue: Lives of the Union Commanders* (Baton Rouge, Louisiana: Louisiana State University Press, 1964), 23–24; M. to Editor, Letter, May 27, 1862, Rochester *Union and Advertiser,* June 5, 1862. For biographical sketches of Bartlett see also, George L. Kilmer, "A Hero for the Hour: Some Stories About Gen. Joseph J. Bartlett's Fighting Days," *St. Landry Clarion,* June 24, 1893 and "Washington Gossip," *National Tribune,* November 19, 1885.

110. Isaac Best, *History of the 121st New York State Infantry* (Chicago, Illinois, 1921), 30.

111. Catton, *Terrible Swift Sword,* 305; Foote, *Civil War,* vol. I, 440; Sears, *To the Gates of Richmond,* 114–120.

112. Stevens, *Three Years in the Sixth Corps,* 59.

113. Marker to Editor, Letter, June 2, 1862 in Rochester *Union and Advertiser,* May 28, 1862.

114. Anti Rebel [Wilbur Fisk] to Editor, Letter, May 20, 1862 published in *Green Mountain Freeman,* June 3, 1862.

115. The description of Mechanicsville was taken from Fairchild, *History of the 27th Regiment N. Y. Vols.,* 46.

116. Marker to Editor, Letter, June 2, 1862, Rochester *Union and Advertiser,* June 13, 1862.

117. Curtis, *From Bull Run to Chancellorsville,* 107–108.

118. Bates, *Pennsylvania Volunteers,* vol. III, 383; While working at Gaines' grist mill, the main body of the 96th Pennsylvania was camped in the vicinity of Hogan's House.

119. Robert McAllister, *The Civil War Letters of General Robert McAllister,* edited by James I. Robertson, Jr. (New Brunswick, New Jersey: Rutgers University Press, 1965), 172–173.

120. Catton, *Terrible Swift Sword,* 315.

121. Martin to Dear Folks at home, June 3, 1862, Martin Papers, SC, WCL.

122. "From the Twenty-Seventh," Letter, May 23, 1862 in Rochester *Democrat and American,* June 4, 1862.

123. C.F.P., Letter, May 14, 1862 in Quiner Scrapbook, v.3, p.211, Wisconsin Historical Society.

124. Wiley, *Life of Billy Yank,* 96–98.

125. Stevens, *Three Years in the Sixth Corps,* 59.

126. Bicknell, *History of the Fifth Regiment Maine Volunteers,* 96.

127. McGlenn to John Brislin, June 3, 1862, Brislin Papers, HSSC.

128. McClellan to Stanton, June 7, 1862 in *McClellan's Own Story,* 387–388.

129. Fairchild, *History of the 27th Regiment N. Y. Vols.,* 51.

130. Luckenbill, Diary, June 1, 1862, WDC.

131. Richards to Father, Letter, June 3, 1862, Richards Papers, HEC.

132. Bicknell, *History of the Fifth Regiment Maine Volunteers,* 97; Stevens, *Three Years in the Sixth Corps,* 75.

133. Luckenbill, Diary, June 21, 1862, WDC; Filbert, Diary, June 22, 1862, Filbert Papers, HCWRTC, HEC.

134. *Official Records,* VOL. XI, Part 3, 257.

135. Martin to My Dear Folks at Home, Letter, June 19, 1862, Martin Papers, SC, WCL.

136. Reed to Dear Parents, Letter, May 17, 1862, Reed Papers, IHS.

137. Houck to Joe, Letter, June 12, 1862, Houck Papers, VTL; Oestreich, Diary, HSSC, 11.

138. Richards to Dear Sophie, Letter, April 13, 1862, Richards Papers, HEC.

139. Martin to My Dear Folks at Home, Letter, June 11, 1862, Martin Papers, SC, WCL.

140. John Madison, Letter, [undated] 1862, Carl Madison Collection, Marshall, Virginia.

141. Filbert, Diary, June 20, 1862, Filbert Papers, HCWRTC, HEC; Luckenbill, Diary, June 1, 1862, WDC.

142. Martin to My Dear Folks at Home, Letter, June 16, 1862, Martin Papers, SC, WCL.

143. Richards to Dear Sophie, Letter, April 13, 1862, Richards Papers, HEC.

Chapter IV

1. Sears, *Gates of Richmond,* 183; E. B. Long, *The Civil War Day by Day: An Almanac, 1861–1865* (Garden City, New York: Doubleday, 1971), 231; Joseph P. Cullen, *The Peninsula Campaign, 1862: McClellan and Lee Struggle for Richmond* (Harrisburg, Penna.: Stackpole Books, 1973), 101–103; Sears, *Gates of Richmond,* 200–209; Burton, *Extraordinary Circumstances,* 58–81.

2. Martin to My Dear Folks at Home, Letter, June 25, 1862, Martin Papers, SC, WCL.

3. McGlenn to Brislin, Letter, June 3, 1862, Brislin Papers, HSSC; Boland to Brislin, Letter, June 14, 1862, Brislin Papers, HSSC.

4. John Saylor, "Military History of John Albert Saylor," Memoir, undated, photocopy at Richmond National Battlefield, Richmond, Virginia.

5. Bicknell, *History of the Fifth Regiment Maine Volunteers,* 99.

6. Luckenbill, Diary, June 26, 1862, WDC.

7. Bicknell, *History of the Fifth Regiment Maine Volunteers,* 99.

8. Rev. S. F. Colt to editor *Miners' Journal,* Letter, in Wallace, *Memorial of the Patriotism of Schuylkill County,* 429.

9. Joel Cook, "Our Army Correspondence," Philadelphia *Press,* July 7, 1862.

10. Reed to Dear Parents, Letter, July 6, 1862, Reed Papers, IHS.

11. According to General Franklin's report of operations, June 27-July 2, 1862, *Official Records,* Vol. XI, Part II, 429, where Franklin describes the location of the redoubt this way: "The redoubt was constructed along the crest of a wheat field in front of Smith's division."; Mark M. Boatner, *Civil War Dictionary* (New York: David McKay, 1959), 325; Boyle, "Outline Sketch," July 17, 1886 states 350 men were assigned to this detail; Bates, *Pennsylvania Volunteers,* vol. III, 383, states the detail consisted of 350 men; Luckenbill, Diary, June 26, 1862, WDC, states 30 men from his company were assigned to the construction detail. Filbert, Diary, June 26, 1862, Filbert Papers, HCWRTC, HEC. Capt. Filbert recorded in his diary, "Ordered to report with 30 men, 2 Corp[oral]s, 1 Sargeant to dig redoubts on our picket

line." Cake to Lieut. R. P. Wilson, June 28, 1862, *Official Records,* Vol. XI, Part 2, 455 states 350 men.

12. Joel Cook, "Our Army Correspondence," Philadelphia *Press,* July 7, 1862.

13. Reed to Dear Parents, Letter, July 6, 1862, Reed Papers, IHS.

14. Joel Cook, "Our Army Correspondence," Philadelphia *Press,* July 7, 1862.

15. *Ibid.*

16. Jacob G. Frick, Letter, quoted in J. Merrill Linn, "The Ninth Army Corps, Pennsylvania Reserves," Part 40, Lewisburg *Chronicle,* June 6, 1896; Bates, *Pennsylvania Volunteers,* vol. III, 383–384; Boyle, "Outline Sketch," July 17, 1886; Joel Cook, "Our Army Correspondence," Philadelphia *Press,* July 7, 1862; Reed to Dear Parents, Letter, July 6, 1862, Reed Papers, IHS.

17. Jacob G. Frick, Letter, quoted in J. Merrill Linn, "The Ninth Army Corps, Pennsylvania Reserves," Part 40, Lewisburg *Chronicle,* June 6, 1896.

18. Bates, *Pennsylvania Volunteers,* vol. III, 383–384; Boyle, "An Outline Sketch of the Ninety-Sixth Pennsylvania Volunteers," Philadelphia *Weekly Times,* July 17, 1886.

19. Reed to Dear Parents, Letter, July 6, 1862, Reed Papers, IHS.

20. Sears, *Gates of Richmond,* 210–214; Foote, *Civil War,* vol. I, 484–485; Burton, *Extraordinary Circumstances,* 79–81. The Battle of Beaver Dam Creek is also known as Ellerson's Mill or Mechanicsville.

21. Sears, *Gates of Richmond,* 223–224; Foote, *Civil War,* vol. I, 484–485; Burton, *Extraordinary Circumstances,* 90.

22. E. S., "The Battle of Gaines Hill," New York *Times,* July 3, 1862.

23. Porter to McClellan, telegram, June 27, 1862, McClellan Papers, A-70:28, Library of Congress.

24. Boyle, "Outline Sketch," July 17, 1886; Bates, *Pennsylvania Volunteers,* vol. III, 384; *Official Records,* Vol. XI, Part II, 429; 432–433; *Ibid.,* 446–447; For details concerning the various bridges built by the Union army engineers spanning the Chickahominy see, William J. Miller, "I Only Wait for the River: McClellan and His Engineers on the Chickahominy," *The Richmond Campaign of 1862: The Peninsula & the Seven Days,* ed. Gary W. Gallagher (Chapel Hill, North Carolina: Uni. North Carolina Press, 2000), 44–65.

25. Correspondence on the Woodbury-Alexander bridge with Robert E. L. Krick, historian Richmond National Battlefield.

26. *Official Records,* Vol. XI, Part II,, 447; Bates, *Pennsylvania Volunteers,* vol. III, 384; Wallace, *Memorial of the Patriotism of Schuylkill County,* 423; *Official Records,* Vol. XI, Part II, 455.

27. John Saylor, "Military History of John Albert Saylor," undated, copy at Richmond National Battlefield, Richmond, Virginia.

28. *Ibid.*

29. Reed to Dear Parents, Letter, July 6, 1862, Reed Papers, IHS.

30. *Official Records,* Vol. XI, Part II, 433, 447.

31. *Ibid.,* 447.

32. Wallace, *Memorial of the Patriotism of Schuylkill County,* 426.

33. *Ibid.,* 423.

34. *Official Records,* Vol. XI, Part II, 454–455.

35. Potts to Mother, Letter, July 6, 1862, Potts Papers, HSSC.

36. Wallace, *Memorial of the Patriotism of Schuylkill County,* 423.

37. *Official Records,* Vol. XI, Part II, 454–455.

38. Wallace, *Memorial of the Patriotism of Schuylkill County,* 423.

39. *Ibid.,* 426.

40. Bicknell, *History of the Fifth Regiment Maine Volunteers,* 101.

41. *Official Records,* Vol. XI, Part II, 447.

42. Reed to Dear Parents, Letter, July 6, 1862, Reed Papers, HIS.

43. Burton, *Extraordinary Circumstances,* 122; R. Pryor James, [Report of Casualties], "Casualties in North Carolina Regiments," Raleigh *Register,* July 12, 1862.

44. Maj. William H. Toon, [Official Report of Gaines' Mill], July 12, 1862, *Official Records Supplement,* Vol. 2, 436–439; R. Pryor James, [Report of Casualties], "Casualties in North Carolina Regiments," Raleigh *Register,* July 12, 1862; Toon, *Official Records Supplement,* 437.

45. John Edwards, [Official Report Gaines' Mill], July 5, 1862, *Official Records,* Vol. XI, Part II, 357.

46. Thomas H. Evans, Diary, "'There is no use trying to dodge shot,'" *Civil War Times Illustrated* (August 1967), Vol. 6, no. 5, 44.

47. M. Reed, "Comrade Reed says the 14th U.S. Stood Their Ground at Gaines' Mill," *National Tribune,* April 4, 1901.

48. *Official Records,* Vol. XI, Part 2, 349.

49. *Ibid.,* 447.

50. Curtis, *From Bull Run to Chancellorsville,* 120.

51. C. H. Bentley to Col. Stone, Letter, July 4, 1862, Plattsburgh *Republican,* July 19, 1862.

52. *Official Records,* Vol. XI, Part 2, 447–448.

53. *Ibid.*

54. Wallace, *Memorial of the Patriotism of Schuylkill County,* 423.

55. *Ibid.,* 427.

56. *Official Records,* Vol. XI, Part 2, 455.

57. *Ibid.,* 448.

58. Wallace, *Memorial of the Patriotism of Schuylkill County,* 423.

59. Saylor, "Military History of John Albert Saylor," Memoir, RNB.

60. Wallace, *Memorial of the Patriotism of Schuylkill County,* 423.

61. *Ibid.; Official Records,* Vol. XI, Part 2, 455.

62. Reed to Dear Parents, Letter, July 6, 1862, Reed Papers, IHS.

63. *Official Records,* Vol. XI, Part II, 455.

64. Wallace, *Memorial of the Patriotism of Schuylkill County,* 429.

65. Saylor, "Military History of John Albert Saylor," Memoir, RNB.

66. "The 5th Maine in the Battle," Lewiston *Falls Journal,* July 17, 1862.

67. Wallace, *Memorial of the Patriotism of Schuylkill County,* 427.

68. Luckenbill, Diary, June 27, 1862, WDC; Wallace, *Memorial of the Patriotism of Schuylkill County,* 429–430; *Official Records,* Vol. XI, Part II, 455.

69. Saylor, "Military History of John Albert Saylor, "Memoir, RNB.

70. *Official Records,* Vol. XI, Part II, 455.

71. James Hollister to Editor, Letter, July 5, 1862, *Miners' Journal,* July 12, 1862.

72. Wallace, *Memorial of the Patriotism of Schuylkill County,* 430.

73. Hollister to Editor, Letter, July 5, 1862, *Miners' Journal,* July 12, 1862.

74. *Official Records,* Vol. XI, Part II, 455.

75. *Ibid.*, 448; S. M. Harmon to Aunt, Letter, July 13, 1862, Hornellsville (New York) *Tribune,* July 21, 1862.
76. James J. Hutchinson, Letter, July 14, 1862, "Letter From a Rifleman," Greensboro *Beacon,* August 8, 1862; See also *Voices from Company D: Diaries by the Greensboro Guards, Fifth Alabama Infantry Regiment, Army of Northern Virginia,* ed. by G. Ward Hubbs (Athens, Georgia: University of Georgia Press, 2003).
77. *Official Records,* Vol. XI, Part II, 455; John S. French to Dear Brother, Letter, July 6, 1862, Collection of Dr. Leo Hershkowitz, Queens, New York; Bicknell, *History of the Fifth Regiment Maine Volunteers,* 102; William B. Westervelt, "Battle of Gaines's Mill: Extracts from the Diary of a member of the 27th N. Y.," *National Tribune,* February 27, 1913.
78. Orlando Dunning, "Gaines' Mill: The Battle as Seen by a Participant From the Pine Tree State," *National Tribune,* March 26, 1891.
79. *Official Records,* Vol. XI, Part II, 455.
80. *Ibid.*; Cyrus Stone, Untitled Memoir, Cyrus Stone Papers, Minnesota Historical Society; 10–13.
81. *Official Records,* Vol. XI, Part II, 455; Wallace, *Memorial of the Patriotism of Schuylkill County,* 423.
82. *Official Records,* Vol. XI, Part II, 455.
83. *Ibid.,* 456. Many of the 96th Pennsylvania Volunteers, after firing their sixty rounds, replenished their cartridge boxes from the supply of nearby dead and wounded companions. *Memorial of the Patriotism of Schuylkill County,* 423.
84. *Official Records,* Vol. XI, Part II, 448.
85. Marker to Editor, Letter, July 4, 1862, Rochester *Union and Advertiser,* July 14, 1862.
86. Wallace, *Memorial of the Patriotism of Schuylkill County,* 423–424.
87. *Official Records,* Vol. XI, Part II, 455–456.
88. Luckenbill, Diary, June 27, 1862, WDC; *Official Records,* Vol. XI, Part II, 448; Wallace, *Memorial of the Patriotism of Schuylkill County,* 430. This hospital was a "large house on the brow of the hill overlooking the Woodbury Bridge."
89. Boyle, "Outline Sketch," July 17, 1886.
90. *Official Records,* Vol. XI, Part II, 449.
91. Fernsler, Diary, June 27, 1862, FC.
92. Wallace, *Memorial of the Patriotism of Schuylkill County,* 424.
93. Fernsler, Diary, June 27, 1862, FC.
94. Potts to Dear Mother, Letter, July 3, 1862, Potts Papers, HSSC.
95. Martin to Dear folks at home, Letter, July 5, 1862, Martin Papers, SC, WCL.
96. Richards to Dear Col., Letter, July 5, 1862, Richards Papers, HEC.
97. Wallace, *Memorial of the Patriotism of Schuylkill County,* 424.
98. Potts to Dear Mother, Letter, July 10, 1862, Potts Papers, HSSC.
99. Richards to Dear Col., Letter, July 5, 1862, Richards Papers, HEC.
100. In regard to firing the final volley and last to leave the field see: Fernsler, Diary, June 27, 1862, FC; Oestreich, Diary, HSSC, 13; Cake, after-action report, *Official Records,* Vol. XI, Part 2, 456; Wallace, *Memorial of the Patriotism of Schuylkill County,* 427; "Member of Company A," Letter, [undated], *Miners' Journal,* July 12, 1862.
101. "Return of Casualties in the Union forces at Gaines' Mill, Va., June 27, 1862," *Official Records,* Vol. XI, Part 2, 40; For a list of the casualties by company

see, "The Ninety-Sixth Regiment, P.V., in the Battle before Richmond," *Miners' Journal,* July 26, 1862.
102. *Official Records,* Vol. XI, Part II, 447–448; *Ibid.,* 455.
103. Wallace, *Memorial of the Patriotism of Schuylkill County,* 423.
104. For example see: Bartlett's report, *Official Records,* Vol. XI, Part II, 449; Boyle, "Outline Sketch," July 17, 1886; Wallace, *Memorial of the Patriotism of Schuylkill County,* 424.
105. Bicknell, *History of the Fifth Regiment Maine Volunteers,* 165.
106. Westervelt, "Battle of Gaines's Mill," *National Tribune,* February 27, 1913.
107. Cyrus Stone, "Military Movements of 1862," Memoir, Cyrus Stone Papers, Minnesota Historical Society.
108. Marker to Editor, Letter, September 1, 1862, Rochester *Union & Advertiser,* September 10, 1862.
109. Bates, *Pennsylvania Volunteers,* vol. III, 384.
110. Wallace, *Memorial of the Patriotism of Schuylkill County,* 431; See also *Official Records,* Vol. XI, Part II, 430, Franklin's report states, "On the morning of the 28th of June, finding the enemy in great force at Garnett's [Farm], a new battery in the valley of the river and a battery of heavy guns at Gaines' Hill (sic), I withdrew all the force to the edge of the wood inclosing [sic] Golding's Farm, Slocum's division on the right of the road."
111. William B. Franklin, "Rear-Guard Fighting During the Change of Base," *Battles and Leaders of the Civil War,* edited by Robert Underwood Johnson and Clarence Clough Buel (New York: Century Company, 1887), Vol. 2, 369; Foote, *Civil War,* vol. I, 491–492; Cullen, *Peninsula Campaign,* 122; Burton, *Extraordinary Circumstances,* 148–149; John T. Hubbell, "The Seven Days of George Brinton McClellan," *The Richmond Campaign of 1862,* 37; William Swinton, *Campaigns of the Army of the Potomac* (New York: Charles B. Richardson, 1866), 147; Sears, *To the Gates of Richmond,* 250–251.
112. Keiser, Diary, June 28, 1862, Keiser Papers, HCWRTC, HEC.
113. Wallace, *Memorial of the Patriotism of Schuylkill County,* 431.
114. *Official Records,* Vol. XI, Part II, 434; Cullen, *Peninsula Campaign,* 132; Burton, *Extraordinary Circumstances,* 175–176; *Official Records,* Vol. XI, Part II, 434.
115. Marker to Editor, Letter, July 9, 1862, Rochester *Union and Advertiser,* July 16, 1862.
116. Stevens, *Three Years in the Sixth Corps,* 94–95.
117. Martin to Dear Folks at Home, Letter, July 11, 1862, Martin Papers, SC, WCL.
118. Fairchild, *History of the 27th Regiment N. Y. Vols.,* 70.
119. [Soldier 27th New York] to Dear Standard, Letter, July 2, 1862, printed in Richmond *Daily Whig,* July 8, 186.
120. The destruction of the railroad train is graphically described in Stevens, *Three Years in the Sixth Corps,* 97.
121. Cullen, *Peninsula Campaign,* 133; Sears, *To the Gates of Richmond,* 263–264.
122. Wallace, *Memorial of the Patriotism of Schuylkill County,* 424.
123. Luckenbill, Diary, Diary, June 30, 1862, WDC.
124. *Official Records,* Vol. XI, Part II, 431; *Ibid.,* 434–435; Boatner, *Civil War Dictionary,* 914; *Official Records,* Vol. XI, Part II, 435; Cullen, *Peninsula Campaign,* 148.

125. Keiser, Diary, June 30, 1862, Keiser Papers, HCWRTC, HEC.

126. Richards to Dear Col., Letter, July 5, 1862, Richards Papers, HEC.

127. *Ibid.*

128. Wallace, *Memorial of the Patriotism of Schuylkill County*, 425.

129. *Ibid.*

130. Burton, *Extraordinary Circumstances*, 264–265.

131. Foote, *Civil War*, vol. I, 507; *Official Records*, Vol. XI, Part II, 431.

132. Wallace, *Memorial of the Patriotism of Schuylkill County*, 425. The quotation is from a letter in the Pottsville *Miners' Journal*, dated July 19, 1862, which was later reprinted in Wallace, *Memorial of the Patriotism of Schuylkill County*, 425.

133. Reed to Dear Parents, Letter, July 4, 1862, Reed Papers, IHS.

134. Keiser. Diary, Jul 1, 1862, Keiser Papers, HCWRTC, HEC.

135. Bates, *Pennsylvania Volunteers*, vol. III, 384; *Official Records*, Vol. XI, Part II, 431; Cullen, *Peninsula Campaign*, 159–160.

136. Treichler, Memoir, RTC, 15.

137. Stevens, *Three Years in the Sixth Corps*, 111.

138. George L. Kilmer, "The Army of the Potomac at Harrison's Landing," *Battles and Leaders of the Civil War*, vol. II, 427.

139. Berkeley was the birthplace of President William Henry Harrison.

140. Keiser, Diary, July 1, 1862, Keiser Papers, HCWRTC, HEC.

141. McClellan to the Army of the Potomac, July 4, 1862, *Official Records*, Vol. XI, Part III, 299.

142. Luckenbill, Diary, Diary, July 4, 1862, WDC.

143. Oestreich, Diary, HSSC, 14.

144. Martin to Dear folks at home, Letter, July 5, 1862, Martin Papers, SC, WCL.

145. Keiser and Luckenbill both note in their diaries on July 21 that the regiment received new uniforms and Enfield rifles. Keiser, Diary, July 21, 1862, Keiser Papers, HCWRTC, HEC; Luckenbill, Diary, July 4, 1862, WDC.

146. The legislation caused a great deal of dissatisfaction among the troops; Bates, *Pennsylvania Volunteers*, vol. III, 385.

147. Stevens, *Three Years in the Sixth Corps*, 114.

148. Catton, *Mr. Lincoln's Army*, 149.

149. Marker to Editor, Letter, September 1, 1862, Rochester *Union and Advertiser*, September 10, 1862.

150. Filbert, Diary, August 17 and 19, 1862, Filbert Papers, HCWRTC, HEC.

151. Richards to Dear Col., Letter, July 5, 1862, Richards Papers, HEC.

152. Reed to Dear Parents, Letter, August 11, 1862, Reed Papers, IHS.

153. Henry to Sister, Letter, July 26, 1862, ebay auction February 2, 2009.

154. Filbert to Father, Letter, July 26, 1862, Filbert Papers, HCWRTC, HEC.

155. Fernsler, Diary, July 2, 1862, FC.

156. Filbert to Father, Letter, July 26, 1862, Filbert Papers, HCWRTC, HEC.

157. Martin to Dear Folks at Home, Letter, July 25, 1862, Martin Papers, SC, WCL.

158. Reed to Dear Parents, Letter, August 11, 1862, Reed Papers, IHS.

159. Potts to Dear Mother, Letter, July 10, 1862, Potts Papers, HSSC.

160. Fernsler, Diary, July 13, 1862, FC.

161. *Ibid.*

162. Filbert to his father, July 26, 1862, Filbert Papers, HCWRTC, HEC; Filbert to H. L. Cake, August 1, 1862, Filbert Papers, HCWRTC, HEC.

163. Frick to Brigadier General Seth Williams, July 25, 1862, RG 94, Records of the Adjutant General's Office, NA.

164. *Ibid.*, Bartlett's recommendation can be found on the obverse of Frick's letter to Williams.

165. Filbert to H. L. Cake, August 1, 1862, Filbert Papers, HCWRTC, HEC.

166. Filbert to his brother, March 30, 1863, Filbert Papers, HCWRTC. HEC; According to Bates, *Pennsylvania Volunteers*, vol. III, 389–410, the regimental seniority roster at the end of July appeared like this:

Henry L. Cake	Colonel	
—VACANT—	Lieut. Col.	
Lewis J. Martin	Major	
M. E. Richards	Adjutant	
Peter A. Filbert	Co. B	Sept 23, 1861
John T. Boyle	Co. D	Sept 23, 1861
James E. Russell	Co. E	Sept 23, 1861
Richard E. Budd	Co. K	Sept 23, 1861
Lamar S. Hay	Co. A	Sept 23, 1861
William H. Lessig	Co. C	Sept 23, 1861
Henry Royer	Co. H	Feb. 12, 1862
Jacob W. Haas	Co. G	Mar. 5, 1862
Matthew Byrnes	Co. I	July 15, 1862
Charles Dougherty	Co. F	July 31, 1862

Chapter V

1. Boyle, "Outline Sketch," July 17, 1886.

2. Martin to Dear Mother, Letter, August 10, 1862, Martin Papers, SC, WCL.

3. Stevens, *Three Years in the Sixth Corps*, 124.

4. Martin to Dear Folks at Home, Letter, August 22, 1862, Martin Papers, SC, WCL.

5. Reed to Dear Parents Brothers and Sisters, Letter, August 22, 1862, Reed Papers, IHS.

6. Jacob Haas to his Brother, Letter, August 29, 1862, Haas Papers, Harrisburg Civil War Round Table Collection, United States Army Heritage & Education Center, Carlisle, Pennsylvania.

7. Keiser, Diary, August 15–16, 1862, Keiser Papers, HCWRTC, HEC.

8. Filbert, Diary, August 15–16, 1862, HCWRTC, HEC.

9. Stevens, *Three Years in the Sixth Corps*, 121.

10. Luckenbill, Diary, August 15–16, 1862, WDC.

11. Fairchild, *History of the 27th Regiment N. Y. Vols.*, 83.

12. Stevens, *Three Years in the Sixth Corps*, 121.

13. Luckenbill, Diary, August 18, 1862, WDC.

14. Keiser, Diary, August 15–18, 1862, Keiser Papers, HEC; Luckenbill, Diary, August 18, 1862, WDC.

15. Filbert, Diary, August 19–20, 1862, Filbert Papers, HCWRTC, HEC.

16. Luckenbill, Diary, August 20, 1862, WDC.

17. Keiser, Diary, August 21, 1862, Keiser Papers, HEC.

18. Martin to Dear Folks at Home, Letter, August 22, 1862, SC, WCL.

19. Keiser, Diary, August 22, Keiser Papers, HEC; Curtis, *From Bull Run to Chancellorsville*, 156.

20. Luckenbill, Diary, August 24, 1862, WDC.

21. Filbert, Diary, August 27, 1862, Filbert Papers, HCWRTC, HEC.

22. Keiser, Diary, August 27, 1862, Keiser Papers, HEC.

23. W. B. Franklin, "The Sixth Corps at the Second Bull Run," *Battles and Leaders*, vol. II, 539; Catton, *Terrible Swift Sword*, 424; Boyle, "Outline Sketch," July 17, 1886.

24. McClellan, *McClellan's Own Story*, 513–517.

25. *Official Records*, Vol. XI, Part III, 722.

26. Quoted in Catton, *Mr. Lincoln's Army*, 11.

27. Franklin, "The Sixth Corps at the Second Bull Run," *Battles and Leaders*, vol. II, 540; Curtis, *From Bull Run to Chancellorsville*, 158–159; Bicknell, *History of the Fifth Regiment Maine Volunteers*, 128.

28. Keiser, Diary, August 31, Keiser Papers, HEC.

29. Martin to Dear Folks at Home, Letter, September 3, 1862, Martin Papers, SC, WCL.

30. Keiser, Diary, September 1–2, 1862, Keiser Papers, HEC; Luckenbill, Diary, September 1–2, 1862, WDC.

31. Boyle, "Outline Sketch," July 17, 1886.

32. Quoted in Foote, *Civil War*, vol. I, 663.

33. One Maine veteran commented on the march into Maryland this way: "Like the Israelites of old, we looked upon the land, and it was good." in Hyde, *Following the Greek Cross*, 90.

34. Luckenbill, Diary, September 6, 1862, WDC.

35. Bicknell. *History of the Fifth Regiment Maine Volunteers*, 132–133.

36. Haas, Diary, September 8–9, 1862, Haas Papers, HCWRTC, HEC.

37. Luckenbill, Diary, September 12, 1862, WDC; Boyle, "Outline Sketch," July 17, 1886.

38. Haas, Diary, September 13, 1862, Haas Papers, HCWRTC, HEC.

39. Keiser, Diary, September 11, 1862, Keiser Papers, HEC.

40. Diary, September 8–9, 1862, Haas Papers, HCWRTC, HEC.

41. Filbert, Diary, September 13, 1862, Filbert Papers, HCWRTC, HEC; Boyle, "Outline Sketch," July 17, 1886.

42. Foote, *Civil War*, vol. I, 673.

43. Quoted in *Ibid.*, vol. I, 673–674; Stephen Sears, *Landscape Turned Red : The Battle of Antietam* (New Haven, Conn.: Ticknor & Fields, 1983), 119–120; Franklin's instructions can be found in, *Report on the Organization of the Army of the Potomac*, 191–192; *Official Records*, Vol. II, Part I, 826–827; McClellan, *Papers*, reel 63, LC.

44. McClellan to Ellen, Letter, August 22, 1862, in Sears, *Civil War Papers of George B. McClellan*, 399.

45. Sears, *Landscape Turned* Red, 119.

46. Richard Shannon, [5th Maine], Diary, September 13, 1862, "encamped for the night at Carroll's Manor," Richard Shannon Papers, Colby College, Waterville, Maine.

47. The strength of the Sixth Corps can be found in *Official Records*, Part I, 67.

48. Haas, Diary, September 14, 1862, Haas Papers, HCWRTC, HEC.

49. Joseph J. Bartlett, "Crampton's Pass: The Start of the Great Maryland Campaign," *National Tribune*, December 19, 1889.

50. Filbert, Diary, September 14, 1862, Filbert Papers, HCWRTC, HEC.

51. Ja[me]s H. Rigby to Dear Father, Letter, September 19, 1862, in "Three Civil War Letters of James H. Rigby, A Maryland Federal Artillery Officer," *Maryland Historical Magazine* (June 1962), v.57, 156–157.

52. The Battle of Crampton's Gap has enjoyed a considerable resurgence within the Civil War community in the last generation. As such, several authors and historians have cast critical eyes upon Crampton's Gap and produced a host of studies examining the battle within the past thirty years. See the following monographs: Joseph F. von Deck, "Let Us Burn No More Daylight," *Lincoln Herald* (Spring 1986) vol. 88, no. 1, 19–26; (Summer 1986), vol. 88, no. 2, 43–46; (Fall 1986), vol. 88, no. 3, 97–105; John Michael Priest, *Before Antietam: The Battle for South Mountain* (Shippensburg, Penna., 1992), see chapter 13; Timothy J. Reese, *Sealed with Their Lives: The Battle for Crampton's Gap*; The interested reader should also consult the recent publication of Ezra Carman's magnificent manuscript study "The Maryland Campaign of September 1862." This document, in the manuscript holdings of the Library of Congress, was edited for publication by Dr. Thomas G. Clemens and published by Savas Beatie in 2010. See Ezra A. Carman, *The Maryland Campaign of September 1862, vol. I South Mountain* (New York, 2010). John David Hoptak, *The Battle of South Mountain* (Charleston, South Carolina: History Press, 2011), see chapter four; Brian Matthew Jordan, *Unholy Sabbath: The Battle of South Mountain in History and Memory, September 14, 1862* (El Dorado, California: Savas Beatie, 2012), see chapter nine; D. Scott Hartwig, *To Antietam Creek: The Maryland Campaign of September 1862* (Baltimore, Maryland: Johns Hopkins University Press, 2012), see chapter 14.

53. Hartwig, *To Antietam Creek*, 443.

54. *Official Records*, vol. XIX, Part 1, 817–818.

55. George Neese, *Three Years in the Confederate Horse Artillery* (New York: Neale Publishing Company, 1911), 120.

56. *Official Records*, vol. XIX, Part 1, 826; Hartwig, *To Antietam Creek*, 442–446.

57. H[enry] C. Boyer, "At Crampton's Pass : The Ninety-sixth Pennsylvania Regiment Under Fire," *Shenandoah Herald,* August 31, 1886; J[ohn] T. Boyle, "The Ninety-Sixth at Crampton's Pass," Pottsville *Miners' Journal,* September 30, 1871.

58. *Official Records*, vol. XIX, Part 1, 393.

59. Boyle, "The Ninety-Sixth at Crampton's Pass," Pottsville *Miners' Journal,* September 30, 1871.

60. *Ibid.*

61. *Official Records*, vol. XIX, Part 1, 382. Bartlett, "Crampton's Pass," *National Tribune*, December 19, 1889.

62. *Official Records*, vol. XIX, Part 1, 394;. Bartlett, "Crampton's Pass," *National Tribune*, December 19, 1889.

63. Russell to Father, Letter, September 15, 1862 in Pottsville *Miners' Journal,* October 4, 1862; Boyle, "The Ninety-Sixth at Crampton's Pass," Pottsville *Miners' Journal,* September 30, 1871.

64. *Ibid.*

65. Boyer, "At Crampton's Pass: The Ninety-sixth Pennsylvania Regiment Under Fire," *Shenandoah Herald,* August 31, 1886.

66. Haas, Diary, September 14, 1862, Haas Papers, HCWRTC, HEC.

67. Boyle, "The Ninety-Sixth at Crampton's Pass," Pottsville *Miners' Journal,* September 30, 1871.

68. Boyer, "At Crampton's Pass: The Ninety-sixth Pennsylvania Regiment Under Fire," *Shenandoah Herald,* August 31, 1886.

69. Bartlett, "Crampton's Pass," *National Tribune*, December 19, 1889.

70. *Ibid.*

71. Boyle, "The Ninety-Sixth at Crampton's Pass," Pottsville *Miners' Journal,* September 30, 1871.

72. Bartlett, "Crampton's Pass," *National Tribune*, December 19, 1889.

73. *Ibid.*

74. *Official Records*, vol. XIX, Part 1, 392.

75. George L. Kilmer [27th New York], "McClellan's Reserves: Franklin in the Peninsula Campaign and During the Battle of Antietam," Philadelphia *Weekly Times*, July 29, 1882.

76. Frank Palmer [16th New York] to his Father, Letter, September 22, 1862, Plattsburgh *Republican*, October 4, 1862. See also Cyrus Stone [16th New York] to his Parents, Letter, September 16, 1862, Cyrus Stone Papers, Minnesota Historical Society.

77. Smith Bailey [5th Maine], Diary, September 14, 1862, Smith Bailey Coll., Dartmouth College, Hanover, New Hampshire.

78. *Official Records*, vol. XIX, Part 1, 394; Bartlett, "Crampton's Pass," *National Tribune*, December 19, 1889.

79. Boyer, "At Crampton's Pass: The Ninety-sixth Pennsylvania Regiment Under Fire," Shenandoah *Herald*, September 2, 1886; Boyle, "The Ninety-Sixth at Crampton's Pass," Pottsville *Miners' Journal*, September 30, 1871.

80. Boyer, "At Crampton's Pass: The Ninety-sixth Pennsylvania Regiment Under Fire," Shenandoah *Herald*, September 2, 1886.

81. *Ibid.*

82. *Ibid.*

83. *Official Records*, vol. XIX, Part 1, 389; *Ibid.*, 394.

84. Bartlett, "Crampton's Pass," *National Tribune*, December 19, 1889.

85. Russell to Father, Letter, September 15, 1862 in Pottsville *Miners' Journal*, October 4, 1862.

86. Haas, Diary, September 14, 1862, Haas Papers, HCWRTC, HEC. See also Boyle, "The Ninety-Sixth at Crampton's Pass," Pottsville *Miners' Journal*, September 30, 1871.

87. Capt. James A. Toomer [16th Virginia], "The 'Virginia Defenders' at the Battle of Crampton's Gap—Recollections of a Participant," in John H. W. Porter, *A Record of Events in Norfolk County, Virginia, From April 19th, 1861 to May 10th, 1862, with a History of the Soldiers and sailors of Norfolk County, Norfolk City and Portsmouth Who Served in the Confederate States Army or Navy* (Portsmouth, Virginia: W. A. Fiske, 1892), 128.

88. Boyer, "At Crampton's Pass : The Ninety-sixth Pennsylvania Regiment Under Fire," Shenandoah *Herald*, September 2, 1886; Boyle, "The Ninety-Sixth at Crampton's Pass," Pottsville *Miners' Journal*, September 30, 1871; Boyer, "At Crampton's Pass : The Ninety-sixth Pennsylvania Regiment Under Fire," Shenandoah *Herald*, September 2, 1886; *Official Records*, vol. XIX, Part 1, 389.

89. Boyle, "The Ninety-Sixth at Crampton's Pass," Pottsville *Miners' Journal*, September 30, 1871.

90. Several secondary sources trace the unit history of the 10th Georgia. John Zwemer, "The Thomson Guards from Georgia's McDuffie County Served the Confederacy to the Bitter End," *America's Civil War* (July 1995): pp. 6, 12 & 79–80; Thomas E. Holley, *Company F, Thomson Guards, Tenth Regiment Georgia Volunteers, Army of Northern Virginia, Confederate States of America: The Officers, the Battles, and a Genealogy of Its Soldiers* (Fernandina Beach, FL), 2000; R. L. Horner, "A History of the 10th Georgia Infantry Regiment During the Civil War, 1861–1865," Thesis (Milledgeville, Georgia: Georgia College, 1993).

91. Bartlett, "Crampton's Pass," *National Tribune*, December 19, 1889.

92. Boyer, "At Crampton's Pass : The Ninety-sixth Pennsylvania Regiment Under Fire," Shenandoah *Herald*, September 3, 1886.

93. *Ibid.*

94. *Ibid.*

95. Boyle, "The Ninety-Sixth at Crampton's Pass," Pottsville *Miners' Journal*, September 30, 1871. See also, Samuel E. Russel to Father, September 15, 1862 in Pottsville *Miners' Journal*, October 4, 1862; Henry [Royer] to Father, September 18, 1862, Norristown *Herald*, September 23, 1862.

96. Boyle, "The Ninety-Sixth at Crampton's Pass," Pottsville *Miners' Journal*, September 30, 1871.

97. *Official Records*, vol. XIX, Part 1, 394.

98. Boyer, "At Crampton's Pass : The Ninety-sixth Pennsylvania Regiment Under Fire," Shenandoah *Herald*, September 3, 1886.

99. In regard to effective strength of the 96th Pennsylvania at Crampton's Gap, two of the sources state that the regiment numbered approximately 400 muskets. See the following, Samuel E. Russel to Father, September 15, 1862 in Pottsville *Miners' Journal*, October 4, 1862, where he states, "very little over 400 strong,"; Boyle, "The Ninety-Sixth at Crampton's Pass," Pottsville *Miners' Journal*, September 30, 1871, states, "the regiment which took into the fight less than four hundred men"; Boyle cites the same effective strength in his historical sketch of the regiment. See John T. Boyle, "An Outline Sketch of the Ninety-Sixth Pennsylvania Volunteers," Philadelphia *Weekly Times*, July 17, 1886; Finally, Henry C. Boyer in his lengthy narrative, "At Crampton's Pass," published in the Shenandoah *Herald*, September 3, 1886, states "we now numbered less than 500" just before the bayonet charge against the 10th Georgia. Also, see Frank Simpson to Friend Cap, Letter, September 19, 1862 in *Miners' Journal* October 4, 1862, where he states after Antietam "Our Regiment numbers 435 men." Finally, Lieut. Col. Filbert's diary entry of December 21, 1862, after the Battle of Fredericksburg, 457 present for duty. Although one contemporary letter, Russel's, and Boyle's article, "Ninety-sixth at Crampton's Pass," indicate the regiment being only 400 strong, it is my contention that the regiment went in to battle at Crampton's Gap with an effective strength between 500–525 men. It seems reasonable given that the regiment finished the Seven Days' battles with approximately 700 men, that illness and sickness further reduced the ranks to near 500 by the time of Crampton's Gap. According to Filbert, the 96th Pennsylvania, numbered 457 after Fredericksburg. A few recruits joined the regiment after Antietam. Therefore, Filbert's strength report aligns with Simpson's post Antietam letter.

100. *Official Records*, vol. XIX, Part 1, 394.

101. Boyle, "The Ninety-Sixth at Crampton's Pass," Pottsville *Miners' Journal*, September 30, 1871.

102. *Official Records*, vol. XIX, Part 1, 877. The number of color bearers wounded and killed along with significant casualties in the companies at the center of the regiment's line of battle supports this conclusion.

103. Boyle, "The Ninety-Sixth at Crampton's Pass," Pottsville *Miners' Journal*, September 30, 1871.

104. *Ibid.*

105. Russel to Father, September 15, 1862 in Pottsville *Miners' Journal*, October 4, 1862.

106. Keiser, Diary, September 14, 1862, Keiser Papers, HCWRTC, HEC.

107. Boyle, "The Ninety-Sixth at Crampton's Pass," Pottsville *Miners' Journal*, September 30, 1871.

108. Treichler, Memoir, RTC, 22.

109. Boyle, "The Ninety-Sixth at Crampton's Pass," Pottsville *Miners' Journal,* September 30, 1871. In his report, *Official Records,* vol. XIX, Part 1, 396, Cake also noted the names of the color bearers who were killed and wounded.

110. Boyle, "The Ninety-Sixth at Crampton's Pass," Pottsville *Miners' Journal,* September 30, 1871.

111. Boyer, "At Crampton's Pass: The Ninety-sixth Pennsylvania Regiment Under Fire," Shenandoah *Herald,* September 3, 1886.

112. Boyle, "The Ninety-Sixth at Crampton's Pass," Pottsville *Miners' Journal,* September 30, 1871.

113. Boyer, "At Crampton's Pass: The Ninety-sixth Pennsylvania Regiment Under Fire," Shenandoah *Herald,* September 3, 1886.

114. Boyle, "The Ninety-Sixth at Crampton's Pass," Pottsville *Miners' Journal,* September 30, 1871.

115. Henry [Royer] to Father, September 18, 1862, Norristown *Herald,* September 23, 1862.

116. Russel to Father, September 15, 1862 in Pottsville *Miners' Journal,* October 4, 1862.

117. Boyle, "The Ninety-Sixth at Crampton's Pass," Pottsville *Miners' Journal,* September 30, 1871.

118. *Ibid.*

119. *Official Records,* vol. XIX, Part 1, 394–395.

120. Boyle, "The Ninety-Sixth at Crampton's Pass," Pottsville *Miners' Journal,* September 30, 1871; Henry [Royer] to Father, September 18, 1862, Norristown *Herald,* September 23, 1862.

121. Lafayette McLaws, "The Capture of Harpers Ferry," Philadelphia *Weekly Press,* September 12, 1888.

122. Boyle, "The Ninety-Sixth at Crampton's Pass," Pottsville *Miners' Journal,* September 30, 1871.

123. *Official Records,* vol. XIX, Part 1, 394.

124. McLaws, "The Capture of Harpers Ferry," Philadelphia *Weekly Press,* September 12, 1888.

125. Haas, Diary, September 14, 1862, Haas Papers, HCWRTC, HEC; Boyle, "The Ninety-Sixth at Crampton's Pass," Pottsville *Miners' Journal,* September 30, 1871.

126. *Ibid.*

127. *Ibid.*

128. Francis E. Pinto, "History of the 32nd Regiment, New York Volunteers, In the Civil War, 1861 to 1863, and Personal Recollections During that Period," (Brooklyn, New York, 1895), 98.

129. *Official Records,* vol. XIX, Part 1, 394.

130. *Ibid.*

131. Bartlett, "Crampton's Pass " *National Tribune,* December 19, 1889.

132. For the alignment of Cobb's brigade see: H. C. Kearney, "Fifteenth Regiment," *Histories of the Several Regiments and Battalions From North Carolina in the Great War, 1861–'65,* ed. by Walter Clark (Raleigh, North Carolina: Nash Brothers, 1901), vol. 1, 740; See his statement, " the Georgia regiments (which formed the right of the brigade); "Gen. Cobb's Brigade at the Battle in Maryland, on Sunday the 14th of September," Athens *Southern Banner,* October 8, 1862; The column states that, "Gen. Cobb immediately ordered up the other two regiments of his command, Cobb's legion and the 16th Ga., accompanying them in person and arrived on the field in ten minutes after the 24th Ga. and 15th N.C. The two regiments last named going into the battle on the left, while the Legion and the 16th Ga. Went in on the right." In his after-action report in *Official Records,* vol. XIX, Part 1, 870, Cobb states, "Two of my regiments

were sent to the right and two to the left…" without further specificity; E[lijah] H[enry] Sutton, [24th Georgia], *Grand Pa's War Stories,* (Demorest, Georgia, 1910) 11–12.

133. *Official Records,* vol. XIX, Part 1, 861.

134. Douglas S. Freeman, *Lee's Lieutenants: A Study in Command,* vol. II, *Cedar Mountain to Chancellorsville* (New York: Charles Scribner's Sons, 1943), 190.

135. Boyle, "The Ninety-Sixth at Crampton's Pass," Pottsville *Miners' Journal,* September 30, 1871.

136. *Ibid.; Official Records,* vol. XIX, Part 1, 394.

137. Henry [Royer] to Father, September 18, 1862, Norristown *Herald,* September 23, 1862.

138. *Official Records,* vol. XIX, Part 1, 394.

139. Treichler, Memoir, RTC, 22.

140. Eli Landers to My Dear Respected Mother, Letter, September 25, 1862, *In Care of Yellow River: The Complete Civil War Letters of Pvt. Eli Pinson Landers to His Mother,* ed. by Elizabeth W. Roberson (Gretna, Louisiana: Pelican, 1997), 96–97.

141. *Official Records,* vol. XIX, Part 1, 395.

142. Boyle, "The Ninety-Sixth at Crampton's Pass," Pottsville *Miners' Journal,* September 30, 1871.

143. For the alignment of Cobb's Brigade see: "Gen. Cobb's Brigade at the Battle in Maryland, on Sunday the 14th of September," Athens *Southern Banner,* October 8, 1862; Henry C. Kearney, "Fifteenth Regiment," *Histories of the Several Regiments and Battalions From North Carolina in the Great War, 1861–'65,* ed. by Walter Clark (Raleigh, North Carolina, 1901), vol. 1, 740.

144. Sutton, [24th Georgia], *Grand Pa's War Stories,* 12.

145. Russel to Father, September 15, 1862 in Pottsville *Miners' Journal,* October 4, 1862.

146. Luckenbill, Diary, September 14, 1862, WDC.

147. Haas, Diary, September 14, 1862, Haas Papers, HCWRTC, HEC.

148. Boyer, "At Crampton's Pass: The Ninety-sixth Pennsylvania Regiment Under Fire," Shenandoah *Herald,* September 3, 1886.

149. Boyle, "The Ninety-Sixth at Crampton's Pass," Pottsville *Miners' Journal,* September 30, 1871.

150. *Official Records,* vol. XIX, Part 1, 861.

151. *Ibid.*

152. David Chandler [15th North Carolina], Letter, to Dear Father and Wife, September 26, 1862, in "Yours Truly Until Death: The Civil War Letters of Private David Ruffin Chandler," ed. by Darrell Wayne Chandler, *Virginia Cavalcade* (Summer 1994), vol. 44, 10–11.

153. Kearney, "Fifteenth Regiment," *Histories of the Several Regiments and Battalions From North Carolina in the Great War, 1861–'65,* vol. 1, 740.

154. Keiser, Diary, September 14, 1862, Keiser Papers, HEC.

155. Treichler, Memoir, RTC, 22.

156. Boyer, "At Crampton's Pass : The Ninety-sixth Pennsylvania Regiment Under Fire," Shenandoah *Herald,* September 3, 1886.

157. Henry [Royer] to Father, Letter, September 18, 1862, Norristown *Herald,* September 23, 1862.

158. Bailey [5th Maine], Diary, September 14, 1862, Smith Bailey Coll., Dartmouth College, Hanover, New Hampshire.

159. Boyle, "The Ninety-Sixth at Crampton's Pass," Pottsville *Miners' Journal,* September 30, 1871.

160. Russell to Father, Letter, September 15, 1862 in Pottsville *Miners' Journal,* October 4, 1862.

161. Henry [Royer] to Father, Letter, September 18, 1862, Norristown *Herald,* September 23, 1862.

162. Luckenbill, Diary, September 14–15, 1862, WDC.

Chapter VI

1. Luckenbill, Diary, September 15, 1862, WDC.
2. Henry [Royer] to Father, Letter, September 18, 1862, Norristown *Herald*, September 23, 1862.
3. Haas, Diary, September 15–16, 1862, Haas Papers, HCWRTC, HEC.
4. Francis Boland, Letter fragment, undated, Brislin Papers, HSSC.
5. *Official Records*, vol. XIX, Part 1, 183.
6. Boyer, "At Crampton's Pass: The Ninety-sixth Pennsylvania Regiment Under Fire," Shenandoah *Herald,* September 3, 1886.
7. Haas, Diary, September 15, 1862, Haas Papers, HCWRTC, HEC.
8. Henry [Royer] to Father, Letter, September 18, 1862, Norristown *Herald*, September 23, 1862.
9. Boyer, "At Crampton's Pass: The Ninety-sixth Pennsylvania Regiment Under Fire," Shenandoah *Herald,* September 3, 1886.
10. Henry [Royer] to Father, Letter, September 18, 1862, Norristown *Herald*, September 23, 1862.
11. Joel Cook, *The Siege of Richmond: A Narrative of the Military Operations of Major-General George B. McClellan During the Months of May and June, 1862* (Philadelphia, Penna.: G. W. Childs, 1862), 288–290.
12. Boyle, "The Ninety-Sixth at Crampton's Pass," Pottsville *Miners' Journal,* September 30, 1871.
13. The regiment left Pottsville in early November for Virginia with 1,139 officers and enlisted men. See Wallace, *Memorial of the Patriotism of Schuylkill County*, 127.
14. Frank Simpson to Friend Cap, Letter, September 19, 1862, *Miners' Journal*, October 4, 1862; Boyer, "At Crampton's Pass: The Ninety-sixth Pennsylvania Regiment Under Fire," Shenandoah *Herald,* September 3, 1886.
15. The Battle of Crampton's Gap, or Crampton's Pass, is referred to as the Battle of the Blue Ridge by many of the Schuylkill Countians. See the Pottsville *Miners' Journal,* September 20, 1862.
16. Haas, Diary, September 19, 1862, Haas Papers, HCWRTC, HEC.
17. *Official Records*, vol. XIX, Part 1, 376–377.
18. Bicknell. *History of the Fifth Regiment Maine Volunteers*, 143.
19. Haas, Diary, September 17, 1862, Haas Papers, HCWRTC, HEC.
20. Fairchild, *History of the 27th Regiment N. Y. Vols.*, 95, describes the ghastly procedures of the surgeons.
21. *Official Records*, vol. XIX, Part 1, 376–377.
22. Boyle, "The Ninety-Sixth at Crampton's Pass," Pottsville *Miners' Journal,* September 30, 1871.
23. Bennett, *The Story of the First Massachusetts Light Battery*, 79.
24. Keiser, Diary, September 17, 1862, Keiser Papers, HCWRTC, HEC.
25. Sears, *Landscape Turned Red*, 271; *Official Records*, vol. XIX, Part 1, 377.
26. Keiser, Diary, September 17, 1862, Keiser Papers, HCWRTC, HEC.
27. Haas, Diary, September 17, 1862, Haas Papers, HCWRTC, HEC.
28. Henry [Royer] to Father, Letter, September 18, 1862, Norristown *Herald*, September 23, 1862; Luckenbill, Diary, September 17, 1862, WDC.
29. Henry [Royer] to Father, Letter, September 18, 1862, Norristown *Herald*, September 23, 1862.
30. Treichler, Memoir, RTC, 23.
31. Keiser, Diary, September 18, 1862, Keiser Papers, HCWRTC, HEC.
32. Haas, Diary, September 18, 1862, Haas Papers, HCWRTC, HEC.
33. Reed to Parents, Letter, September 20, 1862, Reed Papers, IHS.
34. Daniel Faust to Dear Mother, Letter, June 7, 1863, Faust Papers, John J. Cobaugh Coll., Harrisburg Civil War Round Table Collection, United States Army Heritage & Education Center, Carlisle, Pennsylvania; Reid Mitchell, *The Vacant Chair: The Northern Soldier leaves Home* (New York: Oxford University Press, 1993), 142–143; Hess, *The Union Soldier in Battle*, 141; Drew Gilpin Faust, "The Civil War Soldier and the Art of Dying," *Journal of Southern History*, vol. 47, no. 1 (February 2001), 3–38; Drew Gilpin Faust, *This Republic of Suffering: Death and the American Civil War* (New York: Alfred A. Knopf, 2008), 4–60.
35. Keiser, Diary, June 27, 1862, Keiser Papers, HCWRTC, HEC.
36. James Hollister to Editor, Letter, July 5, 1862, *Miners' Journal*, July 12, 1862.
37. *Miners' Journal*, July 5, 12 and 19, 1862; see also casualty list in *Miners' Journal* July 26, 1862.
38. Richards to Father, Letter, July 4, 1862, Richards Papers, HEC.
39. Reed to Dear Brother, Letter, July 6, 1862, Reed Papers, IHS.
40. Henry [Royer] to Father, Letter, September 18, 1862, Norristown *Herald*, September 23, 1862.
41. *Official Records*, vol. XI, Part 2, 456.
42. *Ibid.*
43. Boland to John Brislin[?], Letter fragment, [September ?, 1862] Brislin Papers, HSSC; Earl J. Hess, *The Union Soldier in Battle: Enduring the Ordeal of Combat* (Lawrence, Kansas: University Press of Kansas), 141.
44. [Royer] to Father, Letter, September 18, 1862, Norristown *Herald*, September 23, 1862.
45. Officer of the 96th Pennsylvania, Letter, in *Miners' Journal*, July 12, 1862.
46. *Official Records*, vol. XIX, Part 1, 395. Captain Boyle paid tribute to his comrade John Dougherty with a lengthy poem. See "To the Memory of John Dougherty of Co. F, 96th Regt., P.V., who was killed while gallantly leading his men to the charge at Crampton's Gap, Md., SePart 14, 1862," J[ohn]. T .B[oyle]., *Miners' Journal*, January 24, 1863.
47. Cake to Mrs. Martin, Letter, September 15, 1862, Martin Papers, SC, WCL. Cake's letter of condolence was also published in the *Miners' Journal*, September 20, 1862.
48. *Miners' Journal*, September 20, 1862.
49. For a graphic description of the battlefield and the labors of the surgeons see, Stevens, *Three Years in the Sixth Corps*, 153–154.
50. Haas, Diary, September 20, 1862, Haas Papers, HCWRTC, HEC.
51. Samuel Russel to Dear Father, Letter, September 23, 1862, *Miners' Journal*, October 4, 1862; Frank W. Simpson to Friend Cap, Letter, September 19, 1862, *Miners' Journal*, October 4, 1862.
52. The site of the 96th Pennsylvania encampment, on the Rush Estate, was pinpointed in Boyle, "Outline Sketch," July 17, 1886.

53. In a speech delivered before the survivors of the 96th Pennsylvania regiment, Cake commented on the order from VI Corps Headquarters to fill the field vacancies of lieutenant colonel and major. He stated, "The first duty of a soldier is to obey orders, but when the order was given for the promotion of junior officers over my head, I sent the orderly back upon one occasion with instructions to say that there must be some mistake. I expected to be court martialed but I felt I could no longer put up with those indignities." Quoted in, "The Survivors of the 96th A Red Letter Day for the Veterans," Pottsville *Miners' Journal*, September 17, 1886.

54. The situation surrounding the reassignment of Frick, the death of Martin, and the subsequent lieutenant colonel and major vacancies are discussed in, Filbert to his Father, Letter, September 30, 1862, Filbert Papers, HCWRTC, HEC.

55. Filbert to his father, Letter, August 28, 1862, Filbert Papers, HCWRTC, HEC; Filbert also based his claim to the lieutenant colonelcy on his workload. In a letter home, dated August 8, 1862, Filbert stated, "I am continually acting [the] Major's [Martin] duties. I do the work, he gets the honors." Martin was frequently ill during the winter encampment at Camp Northumberland and throughout much of the Peninsula fighting.

56. Filbert to his father, Letter, August 7, 1862, Filbert Papers, HCWRTC, HEC.

57. Filbert to his father, August 28, 1862, Filbert Papers, HCWRTC, HEC.

58. Filbert to his father, Letter, September 30, 1862, Filbert Papers, HCWRTC, HEC; Filbert, Diary, September 29, 1862, Filbert Papers, HCWRTC, HEC; According to Bates, *Pennsylvania Volunteers*, vol. III, 389–410, the seniority roster at the close of the Maryland campaign appeared like this:

Henry L. Cake	Colonel	
— VACANT—	Lieut. Col.	
—VACANT—	Major	
M. E. Richards	Adjutant	
Peter A. Filbert	Co. B	Sept 23, 1861
John T. Boyle	Co. D	Sept 23, 1861
James E. Russell	Co. E	Sept 23, 1861
Richard E. Budd	Co. K	Sept 23, 1861
Lamar S. Hay	Co. A	Sept 23, 1861
William H. Lessig	Co. C	Sept 23, 1861
Henry Royer	Co. H	Feb. 12, 1862
Jacob W. Haas	Co. G	Mar. 5, 1862
Matthew Byrnes	Co. I	July 15, 1862
Charles Dougherty	Co. F	July 31, 1862

59. Filbert to his Father, Letter, September 30, 1862, Filbert Papers, HCWRTC, HEC.

60. *Ibid.*; Filbert to O.D. Greene, undated letter, Filbert Papers, HCWRTC, HEC.

61. According to Boatner, *The Civil War Dictionary*, 356, Oliver Duff Greene was a native New Yorker and a Union officer c.1833–1904. Greene graduated from West Point in 1854, 26th in a class of 46 cadets. Prior to the war he served on the frontier and in the Kansas border disturbances. At South Mountain and Antietam he was the Adjutant General of the VI Corps. After the war he continued in the Regular Army, retiring as a colonel in 1897; Filbert to Governor A. G. Curtin, Letter, October 13, 1862, Filbert Papers, HCWRTC, HEC.

62. Filbert to O.D. Greene, undated letter, Filbert Papers, HCWRTC, HEC.

63. Filbert, Diary, October 15, 1862, Filbert Papers, HCWRTC, HEC; Filbert to his Father, Letter, September 30, 1862, Filbert Papers, HCWRTC, HEC; Filbert to his

Father, Letter, August 7, 1862, Filbert Papers, HCWRTC, HEC.

64. Filbert to his Father, Letter, September 30, 1862, Filbert Papers, HCWRTC, HEC; Filbert Diary, October 23, 1862, Filbert Papers, HCWRTC, HEC; *Ibid.*, October 31, 1862; Filbert to his Brother, Letter, March 30, 1863, Filbert Papers, HCWRTC, HEC.

65. Filbert, Diary, November 2, 1862, Filbert Papers, HCWRTC, HEC.

66. Filbert to his Brother, Letter, [Late September, 1862], Camp Near Burkittsville, Filbert Papers, HCWRTC, HEC. Henry L. Cake to R. P. Wilson, Letter, November 2, 1862, Filbert service file, Record Group 94, Records of the Adjutant General's Office—Compiled Union Service Records, National Archives; Filbert to O. D. Greene, undated letter, Filbert Papers, HCWRTC, HEC, written in camp near Burkittsville, Maryland.

67. Filbert to his brother, Letter, [Late September, 1862], Filbert Papers, HCWRTC, HEC.

68. *Ibid.*

69. Filbert, Diary, November 11, 1862, Filbert Papers, HCWRTC, HEC; William Borrowe to Whom It Might Concern, Letter, November 2, 1862, Record Group 19, Records of the Department of Military Affairs—Office of the Adjutant General—Records Relating to Civil War Service—Muster Rolls and Related Records, 1861–1865, 96th Pennsylvania Volunteers, Pennsylvania Historical and Museum Commission; Cake to R. P. Wilson, Letter, November 2, 1862, Filbert service file, RG 94, NA.

70. Stanley L. Swart, "The Military Examination Board in the Civil War: A Case Study," *Civil War History*, vol. 16, no. 3 (September 1970), 228.

71. *Ibid.*; Lord, *They Fought for the Union*, 197.

72. *Ibid.*, 197.

73. According to Swart, "The Military Examination Board in the Civil War," *CWH*, 236–237, field grade officers were examined on the following basis: One-sixth of their questions touched on the School of the Soldier, another one-third of the questions dealt with the School of the Company, while the bulk of the questions were drawn from the School of the Battalion.

74. Silas Casey, *Infantry Tactics, for the Instruction, Exercise, and Manoeuvres of the Soldier, a Company, Line of Skirmishers, Battalion, Brigade, or Corps D'Armee* (New York: D. Van Nostrand, 1862).

75. Filbert, Diary, November 13, 1862, Filbert Papers, HCWRTC, HEC.

76. Swart, "The Military Examination Board in the Civil War," *CWH*, 236–237.

77. Allan Nevins, *The War for the Union*: vol. II *War Becomes Revolution 1862–1863* (New York: Charles Scribner's Sons, 1960), 329; T. Harry Williams, *Lincoln and the Radicals* (Madison, Wisconsin: University of Wisconsin, 1941), 181.

78. *Official Records*, Vol. XIX, Part I, 72.

79. Nevins, *War for the Union*, vol. II, 328–330; Catton, *Terrible Swift Sword*, 476; Nevins, *War for the Union*, vol. II, 328–330.

80. Fairchild, *History of the 27th Regiment N. Y. Vols.*, 111.

81. Bicknell, *History of the Fifth Regiment Maine Volunteers*, 159.

82. Filbert, Diary, November 10, 1862, Filbert Papers, HCWRTC, HEC.

83. Keiser, Diary, November 10, 1862, Keiser Papers, HCWRTC, HEC; Marker to Dear Union, Letter, November 10, 1862, Rochester *Union and Advertiser*.

84. Warner, *Generals in Blue*, 47; Boatner, *Civil War Dictionary*, 89.

85. D.M.M. [3rd Vermont] to Editor Freeman, Letter, January 18, 1862 in Lamoille *Newsdealer*, January 24, 1862.

86. George Foltz to Brother John, Letter, October 26, 1862, Greg Coco Collection, Box B-17, Gettysburg National Military Park, Gettysburg Pennsylvania.

87. Warner, *Generals in Blue*, 463; William F. Smith, *Autobiography of Major General William F. Smith, 1861–1864*, ed. by Herbert M. Schiller (Dayton, Ohio: Morningside Bookshop, 1990).

88. Hyde, *Following the Greek Cross*, 117.

89. Stevens, *Three Years in the Sixth Corps*, 186.

90. Bruce Catton, *Never Call Retreat* (Garden City, New York: Doubleday and Company, 1965), 14; William C. Davis, *Stand in the Day of Battle*: vol. II, The *Imperiled Union: 1861–1865* (New York: Doubleday and Company, 1983), 36.

91. Haas, Diary, December 4, 1862, Haas Papers, HCWRTC, HEC.

92. Bicknell, *History of the Fifth Regiment Maine Volunteers*, 162–163.

93. Curtis, *From Bull Run to Chancellorsville*, 219–220. See also Fairchild, *History of the 27th Regiment N. Y. Vols.*, 114; Keiser, Diary, November 11, 1862, Keiser Papers, HCWRTC, HEC; Haas, Diary, December 4, 1862, Haas Papers, HCWRTC, HEC.

94. Bicknell, *History of the Fifth Regiment Maine Volunteers*, 164.

95. Curtis, *From Bull Run to Chancellorsville*, 220.

96. Haas, Diary, December 5, 1862, Haas Papers, HCWRTC, HEC.

97. Bicknell, *History of the Fifth Regiment Maine Volunteers*, 164.

98. *Ibid.*, 166.

99. *Ibid.*, 165. It is evident from the tone of the commentary by Adjutant Bicknell that he did not worship Colonel Cake. Nor did Bicknell have respect for the Pennsylvania colonel's ability to command volunteer troops.

100. Keiser, Diary, December 6, 7 and 8, 1862, Keiser Papers, HCWRTC, HEC.

101. Richards to Sophia, Letter, December 7, 1862, Richards Papers, HEC.

102. Edward J. Stackpole, *Drama on the Rappahannock: The Fredericksburg Campaign* (Harrisburg, Penna.: Stackpole, 1957), 122–123; For a recent comprehensive analysis of the Battle of Fredericksburg see, Frank A. O'Reilly, *The Fredericksburg Campaign: Winter War on the Rappahannock* (Baton Rouge, Louisiana: Louisiana State University Press, 2003).

103. Filbert, Diary, December 11, 1862, Filbert Papers, HCWRTC, HEC.

104. Keiser, Diary, December 11, 1862, Keiser Papers, HCWRTC, HEC.

105. Fairchild, *History of the 27th Regiment N. Y. Vols.*, 11.

106. Filbert, Diary, December 11, 1862, Filbert Papers, HCWRTC, HEC; Stackpole, *Drama on the Rappahannock*, 139–140.

107. Haas, Diary, December 11, 1862, Haas Papers, HCWRTC, HEC.

108. Best, *History of the 121st New York State Infantry*, 41.

109. *Official Records*, Vol. XXI, 526.

110. Haas, Diary, December 12, 1862, Haas Papers, HCWRTC, HEC, gives the timetable of the 96th Penn-

sylvania for that day; See also Filbert, Diary, December 12, 1862, Filbert Papers, HCWRTC, HEC.

111. Keiser, Diary, December 12, 1862, Keiser Papers, HCWRTC, HEC.

112. Haas, Diary, December 12, 1862, Haas Papers, HCWRTC, HEC.

113. Oestreich, Diary, HSSC, 18.

114. Haas, Diary, December 12, 1862, Haas Papers, HCWRTC, HEC.

115. *Ibid.*, December 13, 1862.

116. Stackpole, *Drama on the Rappahannock*, 192–194.

117. Filbert, Diary, December 13, 1862, Filbert Papers, HCWRTC, HEC; It should also be noted that neither Cake, commanding the brigade, or Filbert, in command of the 96th Pennsylvania, filed a report concerning the actions of the regiment at Fredericksburg.

118. Fernsler, Diary, December 13, 1862, FC.

119. Haas, Diary, December 13, 1862, Haas Papers, HCWRTC, HEC.

120. F[rank] E. F[oote] to Dear Journal, Letter, December 15, 1862, *Herkimer County Journal*, December 25, 1862; Best, *History of the 121st New York State Infantry*, 47.

121. Haas, Diary, December 14, 1862, Haas Papers, HCWRTC, HEC.

122. Oestreich, Diary, HSSC, 20.

123. Haas, Diary, December 14, 1862, Haas Papers, HCWRTC, HEC.

124. Filbert, Diary, December 15, 1862, Filbert Papers, HCWRTC, HEC.

125. Haas, Diary, December 16, 1862, Haas Papers, HCWRTC, HEC.

126. Fairchild, *History of the 27th Regiment N. Y. Vols.*, 122.

Chapter VII

1. Williams, *Lincoln and the Radicals*, 236–237; Wiley, *Life of Billy Yank*, 278.

2. Bicknell, *History of the Fifth Regiment Maine Volunteers*, 183–184. See also Fairchild, *History of the 27th Regiment N. Y. Vols.*, 128 on constructing winter huts.

3. Haas, Diary, December 25, 1862, Haas Papers, HCWRTC, HEC.

4. Faust to Mother, Letter, December 26, 1862, Faust Papers, HCWRTC, HEC.

5. Filbert, Diary, December 25, 1862, Filbert Papers, HCWRTC, HEC.

6. Haas, Diary, December 25, 1862, Haas Papers, HCWRTC, HEC.

7. Houck to Brother Joe, Letter, December 26, 1862, Houck Papers, VTL.

8. Oestreich, Diary, HSSC. 22.

9. Faust to Mother, Letter, December 26, 1862, Faust Papers, HCWRTC, HEC.

10. Haas, Diary, December 25, 1862, Haas Papers, HCWRTC, HEC.

11. Bruce Catton, *Glory Road: The Bloody Route from Fredericksburg to Gettysburg* (Garden City, New York: Doubleday, 1952), 94–95; A. Wilson Greene, "Morale, Maneuver, and Mud: The Army of the Potomac, December 16, 1862—January 26, 1863," in *The Fredericksburg Campaign: Decision on the Rappahannock*, ed. by Gary M. Gallagher (Chapel Hill, North Carolina: University North Carolina Press, 1995), 171–227.

12. Treichler, Memoir, RTC, 24.
13. Shelby Foote, *The Civil War: A Narrative*, vol. II, *Fredericksburg to Meridian* (New York: Random House, 1963), 117.
14. Haas to his Brother, Letter, January 3, 1863, Haas Papers, HCWRTC, HEC.
15. Houck to Brother Joe, Letter, December 22, 1862, Houck Papers, VTL.
16. Haas to Brother, Letter, December 18, 1862, Haas Papers, HCWRTC, HEC.
17. John T. Boyle to Peter Filbert, Letter, January 13, 1863, Filbert Papers, HCWRTC, HEC.
18. McGlenn to John Brislin, Letter, March 18, 1862, Brislin Papers, HSSC; McGlenn to John Brislin, Letter, June 3, 1862, Brislin Papers, HSSC.
19. Wiley, *Life of Billy Yank*, 44.
20. Allen C. Guelzo, *Lincoln's Emancipation Proclamation: The End of Slavery in America* (New York: Simon & Schuster, 2004); Wiley, *Life of Billy Yank*, 41–43.
21. *Ibid.*, 281, 41–44.
22. Haas to Brother, Letter, January 3, 1863, Haas Papers, HCWRTC, HEC.
23. Faust to Mother, Letter, January 5, 1863, Faust Papers, HCWRTC, HEC.
24. Reed to family, Letter, January 10, 1863, Reed Papers, IHS.
25. Faust to Mother, Letter, [undated], Faust Papers, HCWRTC, HEC, for his view on the moral issues posed by the Civil War. The letter was most likely written in November, 1863.
26. Catton, *Mr. Lincoln's Army*, 329.
27. Bigelow, *Chancellorsville*, 36.
28. Reed to Parents, Letter, January 27, 1863, Reed Papers, IHS.
29. Haas, Diary, December 1–31, 1862, Haas Papers, HCWRTC, HEC. The diary chronicles his numerous visits to Dr. O'Leary in hopes of receiving a medical discharge.
30. Henry to Sister, Letter, January 15, 1863, CWMisc. Coll, HEC.
31. Boyle to Filbert, Letter, January 13, 1863, Filbert Papers, HCWRTC, HEC.
32. Filbert, "Officer's Casualty Sheet," in his service file, RG 94, Records of the Adjutant General's Office, NA. Filbert was officially discharged December 22, 1862.
33. Filbert, Diary, December 31, 1862, Filbert Papers, HCWRTC, HEC. The table below represents the seniority roster as of Filbert's discharge. Compiled from company and field & staff rosters in Bates, *Pennsylvania Volunteers*, vol. III, 389–410.

Henry L. Cake	Colonel	
—VACANT—	Lieutenant Colonel	
William H. Lessig	Major	
John T. Boyle	Co. D	Sept. 23, 1861
James E. Russell	Co. E	Sept. 23, 1861
Richard Budd	Co. K	Sept. 23, 1861
Lamar S. Hay	Co. A	Sept. 23, 1861
Henry Royer	Co. H	Feb. 12, 1862
Jacob W. Haas	Co. G	March 5, 1862
Levi Huber	Co. G	June 27, 1862
Matt Byrnes	Co. I	July 15, 1862
Charles Dougherty	Co. F	July 31, 1862
Isaac Severn	Co. C	Nov. 1, 1862

34. C. D. Haeseler to Whom It Might Concern, Letter, January 27, 1863, Henry L. Cake service file, Record Group 94, Records of the Adjutant General's Office, National Archives. Haeseler, the colonel's personal physician, offers a detailed analysis of Cake's medical problems.

35. Boyle, "Outline Sketch," July 17, 1886.
36. "Sword, Belt, etc., for Col. Henry L. Cake," *Miners' Journal*, January 17, 1863; "Presentation of a Sword, Belt, etc., to Col. Henry L. Cake," *Miners' Journal*, January 24, 1863.
37. Wiley, *Life of Billy Yank*, 152–153.
38. *Ibid.*, 153–154.
39. Boland to John Brislin, Letter. November 11, 1861, Brislin Papers, HSSC.
40. Haas to his Brother, Letter, December 18, 1862, Haas Papers, HCWRTC, HEC.
41. Wiley, *Life of Billy Yank*, 153–154.
42. Haas, Diary, September 17, 1862, Haas Papers, HCWRTC, HEC. See footnote 1 in the typescript copy of the diary.
43. LeRoy R. to Editor, Letter, February 24, 1862, *Miner's Journal*, March 8, 1862. Songs such as: *Hail Columbia, Katy Dear, Red, White and Blue, The Star-Spangled Banner* and *Gay and Happy Still* were popular tunes.
44. Reed to Parents, Brothers and Sisters, Letter, May 22, 1863, Reed Papers, IHS. See also Fernsler, Diary, March 30, 1862, FC, which states that the regimental band serenaded the colonel at 11PM.
45. Fernsler, Diary, April 2, 1862, FC.
46. Filbert, Diary, April 3, 1862, Filbert Papers, HCWRTC, HEC.
47. Wiley, *Life of Billy Yank*, 157–159.
48. *Ibid.*, 169–170.
49. Haas, Diary, April 5, 1863, Haas Papers, HCWRTC, HEC; There is a fine description of a snowball battle in Stevens, *Three Years in the Sixth Corps*, 183.
50. *Ibid.*, 184.
51. Faust to his Sister, Letter, May 23, 1863, Faust Papers, HCWRTC, HEC.
52. Haas to his Brother, Letter, June 9, 1863, Haas Papers, HCWRTC, HEC.
53. Faust to his Brother, Letter, June 20, 1863, Faust Papers, HCWRTC, HEC.
54. Boland to Dear Sir [John Brislin], Letter, June 14, 1862, Brislin Papers, HSSC.
55. Fernsler, Diary, June 10, 1862, FC.
56. Faust to his Sister, Letter, May 23, 1863, Faust Papers, HCWRTC, HEC.
57. Potts to his Mother, Letter, November 7, 1861, Potts Papers, HSSC.
58. Keiser, Diary, see the statistical data, reprinted below, regarding his correspondence for the year 1862 between entries of December 31, 1862 and January 1, 1863, Keiser Papers, HCWRTC, HEC.

Letters Received in 1862 From:		*Letters Written in 1862* To:	
Miss Sallie	26	Miss Sallie	26
Father Danl. Kiser	12	Father	13
Mother	6	Mother	7
Bro William	5	Bro William	6
Sister Mariah	7	Sister Mariah	7
Sister Elizabeth	7	Sister Elizabeth	6
Bro George	2	Bro George	3
Edw Workman	7	Edw Workman	5
Miss R. Bast	2	Miss R. Bast	2
Henry Wentzel	1	Henry Wentzel	1
J. Zimmerman	1	J. Zimmerman	1
S. B. Cobs	2	S. B. Cobs	4
Chas Shoemaker	1	Edmond Umholtz	1
Tobias Row	1	Levi Ream	1
Levi Ream	1		
Elias Wolf	1		
Total	82		83

59. Haas to his Brother, Letter, June 9, 1863, Haas Papers, HCWRTC, HEC.

60. Filbert to Father, Letter, August 7, 1862 and Filbert to Father, Letter, September 30, 1862, Filbert Papers, HCWRTC, HEC.

61. Martin to Dear Folks at Home Mother and Sister, Letter, May 23, 1862, Martin Papers, SC, WCL.

62. Quoted in Foote, Civil War, vol. II, 128–129.

63. Catton, Glory Road, 98.

64. Ibid.; Foote, Civil War, vol. II, 128; Greene, "Morale, Maneuver, and Mud: The Army of the Potomac, December 16, 1862—January 26, 1863," in The Fredericksburg Campaign, 195.

65. Fairchild, History of the 27th Regiment N. Y. Vols., 134, tells of dismantling the winter cabins.

66. For Burnside's General Order Number 7 see, Official Records, vol. XXI, 127. See also excerpt in Fairchild, History of the 27th Regiment N. Y. Vols., 134.

67. Morse, "The "Rebellion Record" of an Enlisted Man," National Tribune Scrapbook (Washington, D.C., [1909]?), 57.

68. Marker to Dear Union, Letter, January 23, 1863, Rochester Union and Advertiser, January 29, 1863. For another letter offering testimony regarding soldier morale see F.[rank] E.F.[oote] to Friend Stebbins, Letter, January 20, 1863, Herkimer County Journal, February 5, 1863.

69. Keiser, Dairy, January 20, 1863, Keiser Papers, HCWRTC, HEC, states that the Schuylkill Countians began their march at noon; Bicknell, History of the Fifth Regiment Maine Volunteers, 191, states that dinner, the noon meal, was served to the Second Brigade earlier than usual. See also Evan Gery, Diary, January 20, 1863, ed. by George T. Kalbach, Hamburg Item, 1942.

70. Morse, "The "Rebellion Record,"" 56.

71. Bicknell, History of the Fifth Regiment Maine Volunteers, 192–193.

72. Virginius to Editor, Letter, January 30, 1863, Portland Transcript, February 14, 1863.

73. Bicknell, History of the Fifth Regiment Maine Volunteers, 192.

74. Fairchild, History of the 27th Regiment N. Y. Vols., 134.

75. Gery, Diary, January 20, 1863, Hamburg Item, 1942.

76. Fairchild, History of the 27th Regiment N. Y. Vols., 134–135.

77. Ibid., 135.

78. Marker to Editor, Letter, January 23, 1863, Rochester Daily Union & Advertiser, January 29, 1863.

79. Fernsler, Diary, January 21, 1863, FC.

80. Gery, Diary, January 21, 1863, Hamburg Item, 1942.

81. Catton, Glory Road, 104–105, relates the anecdote concerning the issuance of whiskey to the Bluecoats. Morse, "The "Rebellion Record,"" 57 also mentions the ration of whiskey to the soldiers.

82. Bicknell, History of the Fifth Regiment Maine Volunteers, 195.

83. S. to Editor, Letter, January 26, 1863, Malone Palladium, February 5, 1863.

84. Virginius to Editor, Letter, January 30, 1863, Portland Transcript, February 14, 1863. A similar exchange is related briefly by Levi Huber to Peter Filbert, Letter, January 30, 1863, Filbert Papers, HCWRTC, HEC.

85. William F. Smith to William B. Franklin, Official Records, vol. 21, 991.

86. Bicknell, History of the Fifth Regiment Maine Volunteers, 196.

87. Marker to Editor, Letter, January 23, 1863, Rochester Daily Union & Advertiser, January 29, 1863.

88. Bicknell, History of the Fifth Regiment Maine Volunteers, 196.

89. Fairchild, History of the 27th Regiment N. Y. Vols., 135.

90. Ibid., 136.

91. Huber to Filbert, Letter, January 30, 1863, Filbert Papers, HCWRTC, HEC.

92. Treichler, Memoir, RTC, 13.

93. Gery, Diary, January 24, 1863, Hamburg Item, 1942.

94. Treichler, Memoir, RTC, 13.

95. Fairchild, History of the 27th Regiment N. Y. Vols., 136.

96. Bicknell, History of the Fifth Regiment Maine Volunteers, 197.

97. Gery, Diary, January 25, 1863, Hamburg Item, 1942.

98. Treichler, Memoir, RTC, 13.

99. Huber to Filbert, Letter, January 30, 1863, Filbert Papers, HCWRTC, HEC.

100. Morse, "The "Rebellion Record,"" 57.

101. Foote, Civil War, vol. II, 130.

102. Boyle, "Outline Sketch," July 18, 1886.

103. Boyle to Filbert, Letter, January 13, 1863, Filbert Papers, HCWRTC, HEC.

104. Houck to Brother Joe, Letter, February 11, 1863, Houck Papers, VTL.

105. F[rank].E.F[oote]. to Friend Stebbins, Letter, January 20, 1863, Herkimer County Journal, February 5, 1863.

106. Gery, Diary, January 26, 1863, Hamburg Item, 1942. See also Fairchild, History of the 27th Regiment N. Y. Vols., 141.

107. Houck to Brother Joe, Letter, February 11, 1863, Houck Papers, VTL.

108. Foote, Civil War, VOL. II, 130–132.

109. John T. Boyle to Peter Filbert, Letter, January 13, 1863, Filbert Papers, HCWRTC, HEC; Huber to Filbert, Letter, January 30, 1863, Filbert Papers, HCWRTC, HEC.

110. Foote, Civil War, vol. II, 131; Richard Elliott Winslow, General John Sedgwick: The Story of a Union Corps Commander (Novato, Cal.: Presidio Press, 1982), 54–55. See also Stevens, Three Years in the Sixth Corps, 328.

111. Ulysses S. Grant, Personal Memoirs of U.S. Grant (New York: Charles L. Webster & Co., 1886), vol. 2, 771.

112. Martin T. McMahon, In Memoriam: Maj.-Gen. John Sedgwick (Togus, Maine: National Home, 1885), 5.

113. George W. Cullum, Biographical Register of the Officers and Graduates of the U.S. Military Academy at West Point, N. Y. (Cambridge, Mass., Riverside Press, 1891), vol. 1, 683.

114. Stevens, Three Years in the Sixth Corps, 186, 328; See also William Swinton, Campaigns of the Army of the Potomac (New York: Charles Scribner's Sons, 1882), 447.

115. According to Bates, Pennsylvania Volunteers, vol. III, 386, companies C and K did not go to Windmill Point.

116. Boyle, "Outline Sketch," July 18, 1886.

117. Reconstructed from Bates, Pennsylvania Volunteers, vol. III, 390–410, the seniority roster in mid-March appeared like this:

—VACANT—	Colonel	
—VACANT—	Lieut. Col.	
William H. Lessig	Major	
John T. Boyle	Co. D	Sept. 23, 1861
James Russell	Co. E	Sept. 23, 1861
Richard Budd	Co. K	Sept. 23, 1861
Jacob W. Haas	Co. G	March 5, 1862
Matthew Byrnes	Co. I	July 15, 1862
Levi Huber	Co. B	July 30, 1862
Isaac E. Severn	Co. C	Nov. 1, 1862
John Harlan	Co. A	March 1, 1863
James Casey*	Co. F	Sept. 15, 1862
William Davis**	Co. H	March 3, 1863
*First Lieutenant		
**First Lieutenant		

118. Bates, *Pennsylvania Volunteers*, vol. III, 382; *Miners' Journal*, September 7, 1861.

119. *Miners' Journal*, August 9, 1862.

120. *Official Records*, vol. XIX, Part. 1, 395.

121. Haas, Diary, March 14, 1863, Haas Papers, HCWRTC, HEC. Where Captain Haas states, "Passed the evening at Gen. Bartlett's arranging matters with the Major and Adjt. Richards."; Haas to his brother, Letter, March 16, 1863, Haas Papers, HCWRTC, HEC.

122. For capsule summaries, regarding dates of enlistment, promotion, muster and discharge, regarding captain's Boyle, Russell and Budd, see Bates, *Pennsylvania Volunteers*, vol. III, 397, 398 and 408. Personal politics and officer factionalism run throughout the correspondence of officers such as Captain Haas and Lieutenant Colonel Filbert.

123. Foote, *Civil War*, vol. II, 233.

124. New York *Times*, February 19 and March 1, 1863.

125. Winslow, *General John Sedgwick*, 59; Catton, *Glory Road*, 98–99 and Fairchild, *History of the 27th Regiment N. Y. Vols.*, 153, relate incidents concerning baseball games between the 19th Massachusetts—7th Michigan and the 32nd New York—27th New York Volunteers.

126. Houck to Joe, Letter, April 17, 1863, Houck Papers, VTL.

127. Winslow, *General John Sedgwick*, 60.

128. Keiser, Diary, March 8—April 8, 1863, Keiser Papers, HCWRTC, HEC; Gery, Diary, March 8—April 1, 1863, Hamburg *Item*, 1942 Haas, Diary, April 8, 1863, Haas Papers, HCWRTC, HEC; Haas, Diary, March 8—April 1, 1863, Haas Papers, HCWRTC, HEC.

129. *Amicus Curae,* "Letters from our Volunteers," April 21, 1863, *Miners' Journal*, May 2, 1863. It is possible that the letters signed "Amicus Curae" are a variant of the Latin phrase "Amicus Curiae," translated as "friend of the court."

130. *Ibid.*

131. Reed to Dear Parents, Letter, April 3, 1863, Reed Papers, IHS.

132. *Ibid.*

133. "Letter from the 96th Reg., P.V.," March 31, 1863, *Miners' Journal*, April 18, 1863.

134. Houck to Joe, Letter, April 17, 1863, Houck Papers, VTL.

135. Stevens, *Three Years in the Sixth Corps,* 187.

136. For strength of the four corps see Edward J. Stackpole, *Chancellorsville: Lee's Greatest Battle* (Harrisburg, Pennsylvania: Stackpole Company, 1958), 373.

137. Gery, Diary, April 8, 1863, Hamburg *Item*, 1942.

138. Keiser, Diary, April 8, 1863, Keiser Papers, HCWRTC, HEC.

139. J. Jerome Miller, Diary, April 8, 1863, Georg Hay Kain Collection, Emigsville, Pennsylvania.

140. Treichler, Memoir, RTC, 30.

141. The exact site of the VI Corps review was at Gen. Sickles' III Corps headquarters, which was the Fitzhugh family's "Boscobel" estate. See Marsena Patrick, *Inside Lincoln's Army: The Diary of Marsena Patrick, Provost Marshall General, Army of the Potomac*, ed. by David S. Sparks (New York: Thomas Yoseloff, 1964), 231.

142. Bicknell, *History of the Fifth Regiment Maine Volunteers*, 202–203.

143. Morse, "The "Rebellion Record,"" 59.

144. *Curae,* "Letters from our Volunteers," April 21, 1863, *Miners' Journal*, May 2, 1863.

145. Haas, Diary, April 8, 1863, Haas Papers, HCWRTC, HEC. For additional details of the grand review see Jane Hollenbeck Conner, *Lincoln in Stafford* (Stafford, Virginia: Parker Publishing, 2006).

146. Fairchild, *History of the 27th Regiment N. Y. Vols.*, 153.

147. Davis, *Stand in the Day of Battle*, vol. II, 93; U.S., Congress, Joint Committee on the Conduct of the War, *Report of the Joint Committee on the Conduct of the War* (Washington, D.C., 1863–66), *Army of the Potomac*, Part 2, xli.

148. Davis, *Stand in the Day of Battle*, vol. II, 93–94; John Bigelow, Jr., *The Campaign of Chancellorsville: A Strategic and Tactical Study* (New Haven, Connecticut: Yale University Press, 1910), 174–175; Haas, Diary, April 19, 1863, Haas Papers, HCWRTC, HEC.

149. *Ibid.*, April 28, 1863, Haas Papers, HCWRTC, HEC.

150. See Bartlett's official report in the *Official Records*, Vol. XXV, Part I, 579–580.

151. Haas, Diary, April 19, 1863, Haas Papers, HCWRTC, HEC.

152. Haas to Bro. Fred, Letter, May 12, 1863, Haas Papers, HCWRTC, HEC.

153. Letter of Lessig reprinted in Wallace, *Memorial of the Patriotism of Schuylkill County*, 248.

154. Brooks' report can be found in *Official Records*, Vol. XXV, Part I, 566.

155. According to Fairchild, *History of the 27th Regiment N. Y. Vols.*, 163, the pontoon boats were carried by the troops the last mile to the river as it was feared the creaking of the wagon wheels would be heard by the Graycoats.

Chapter VIII

1. *Official Records*, Vol. XXV, Part I, 579–580; *Ibid.*, 591.

2. Gery, Diary, April 28–29, 1863, Hamburg *Item*, 1942; Bates, *Pennsylvania Volunteers*, vol. III, 387.

3. Gery, Diary, April 29, 1863, Hamburg *Item*, 1942; Haas, Diary, April 29, 1863, Haas Papers, HCWRTC, HEC; See also Haas to Brother, Letter, May 12, 1863, Haas Papers, HCWRTC, HEC.

4. Lessig to a friend, Letter, [undated] in Wallace, *Memorial of the Patriotism of Schuylkill County*, 248.

5. See map #34 "Fredericksburg" in Bigelow, *Campaign of Chancellorsville*.

6. *Official Records*, Vol. XXV, Part I, 580; Winslow, *General John Sedgwick*, 68.

7. Haas, Diary, April 30, 1863, Haas Papers, HCWRTC, HEC.

8. *General Orders No. 47* can be found in *Official Records*, Vol. XXV, Part 2, 171; Catton, *Never Call Retreat*, 147. At 6 p.m. on April 30 the 96th Pennsylvania

relieved the 3rd New Jersey on the skirmish line. See *Official Records*, Vol. XXV, Part I, 578.

9. Haas, Diary, April 30, 1863, Haas Papers, HCWRTC, HEC.

10. Haas, Diary, May 1, 1863, Haas Papers, HCWRTC, HEC.

11. Luckenbill, Diary, May 1, 1863, WDC.

12. Haas to bro. Fred, Letter, May 12, 1863, Haas Papers, HCWRTC, HEC.

13. Haas, Diary, May 2, 1863, Haas Papers, HCWRTC, HEC.

14. Theodore A. Dodge, *The Campaign of Chancellorsville* (Boston, Mass.: James R. Osgood and Company, 1881), 164; Winslow, *General John Sedgwick*, 69.

15. Lessig to friend, Letter, [undated], in Wallace, *Memorial of the Patriotism of Schuylkill County*, 248.

16. Bicknell, *History of the Fifth Regiment Maine Volunteers*, 216.

17. *Official Records*, Vol. XXV, Part I, 580.

18. Haas to bro. Fred, Letter, May 12, 1863, Haas Papers, HCWRTC, HEC.

19. Haas, Diary, May 2, 1863, Haas Papers, HCWRTC, HEC.

20. Fairchild, *History of the 27th N. Y. Vols.*, 167.

21. Winslow, *General John Sedgwick*, 71.

22. For recent examinations of Sedgwick's generalship and the operations of the Sixth Corps at Fredericksburg see the following: Stephen W. Sears, *Chancellorsville* (New York: Houghton Mifflin Company, 1996), 181–187; 214–216; 228–229 and 248–251; Philip W. Parsons, *The Union Sixth Army Corps in the Chancellorsville Campaign* (North Carolina: McFarland & Company, 2006); Chris Mackowski and Kristopher D. White, *Chancellorsville's Forgotten Front: The Battles of Second Fredericksburg and Salem Church, May 3, 1863* (El Dorado, California: Savas Beatie, 2013).

23. Jubal Anderson Early, *War Memoirs: Autobiographical Sketch and Narrative of the War Between the States* (Indiana: Indiana University Press, 1960), 205.

24. *Official Records*, Vol. XXV, Part 1, 567.

25. *Ibid.*, 580.

26. Haas to bro. Fred, Letter, May 12, 1863, Haas Papers, HCWRTC, HEC.

27. *Official Records*, Vol. XXV, Part1, 567.

28. *Ibid.*, 567; *Ibid.*, 593; *Ibid.*, 596.

29. *Ibid.*, Vol. XXV, Part1, 580.

30. Haas, Diary, May 3, 1863, Haas Papers, HCWRTC, HEC.

31. Haas to Brother, Letter, May 12, 1863, Haas Papers, HCWRTC, HEC.

32. Lessig, Letter, [undated], in Wallace, *Memorial of the Patriotism of Schuylkill County*, 249.

33. *Ibid.*, 249.

34. *Ibid.*, 249; "Letter from the Ninety-sixth Reg., P.V.," *Miners' Journal*, April 18, 1863. The strength figure is stated in this letter written from White Oak Church.

35. Haas, to bro. Fred, Letter, May 12, 1863, Haas Papers, HCWRTC, HEC.

36. Haas, Diary, May 3, 1863, Haas Papers, HCWRTC, HEC.

37. *Ibid.*,

38. Richard Snowden Andrews, *A Memoir* (Baltimore, Maryland: Sun Job Printing Office, 1910), 85. Andrews' "official report" of this action can be found on pages 81–93. The report was not included in the War Department's publication of the *Official Records*. For a map of the action in the vicinity of Deep Run see Erik F. Nelson, "East of Chancellorsville: Second Fredericks-

burg and Salem Church," *Blue & Gray Magazine* vol. XXX, no. 1 (2013), 13.

39. Fairchild, *History of the 27th Regiment N.Y. Vols.*, 167.

40. *Official Records*, Vol. XXV, Part 1, 580.

41. *Ibid.*, 580; Bicknell, *History of the Fifth Regiment Maine Volunteers*, 217–220.

42. Clark Edwards to Maine, Adjutant General, Official Report, May 9, 1863. Maine Adjutant General's Department, Maine Archives. This report differs from the published after-action report in the *Official Records*, Vol. XXV, Part1, 584–585.

43. Lessig, Letter, [undated], in Wallace, *Memorial of the Patriotism of Schuylkill County*, 249.

44. Luckenbill, Diary, May 3, 1863, WDC.

45. Haas to bro. Fred, Letter, May 12, 1863, Haas Papers, HCWRTC, HEC.

46. Haas to bro. Fred, Letter, May 12, 1863, Haas Papers, HCWRTC, HEC.

47. Lessig, Letter, [undated], in Wallace, *Memorial of the Patriotism of Schuylkill County*, 249.

48. Lee Sherrill, *The 21st North Carolina: A Civil War History, with a Roster of Officers* (North Carolina: McFarland, 2015), 224–225; From left to right the Confederate line ran: 1st North Carolina Sharpshooter Battalion, 57th North Carolina, 21st North Carolina, 54th North Carolina and 6th North Carolina.

49. Eli Coble, [21st North Carolina] Memoir, Dec. 1862—June 1863, trans. by Lee Sherrill, Coble Papers, Greensboro Historical Museum, Civil War Coll.—Mss. Coll. #16, Folder 13.4.

50. John C. Zimmerman to Mrs. M. A. Zimmerman, Letter, May 7, 1863, in *The Fighting 57th North Carolina: The Life and Letters of James Calvin Zimmerman*, ed. by William Hartley and David Zimmerman (Morrisville, North Carolina: Lulu.com, 2006), 78. See also H. C. Jones, Jr., [57th North Carolina] Report, May 13, 1863, in Avery Papers, Southern Hist. Coll., Uni. North Carolina; Unattributed, Report, Gen. Robert Hoke's Brigade, May 13, 1863, Avery Papers, Southern Hist. Coll., Uni. North Carolina.

51. Haas to bro. Fred, Letter, May 12, 1863, HCWRTC, HEC; Andrews, *Memoir*, 85–86.

52. Haas, Diary, May 3, 1863, Haas Papers, HCWRTC, HEC; *Official Records*, Vol. XXV, Part1, 588.

53. Fairchild, *History of the 27th Regiment N.Y. Vols.*, 167.

54. Lessig, Letter, [undated], in Wallace, *Memorial of the Patriotism of Schuylkill County*, 249.

55. Haas, to bro. Fred, Letter, May 12, 1863, Haas Papers, HCWRTC, HEC.

56. The casualties in the 96th Pennsylvania can be found in Bartlett's after-action report. *Official Records*, Vol. XXV, Part 1, 581 and Lessig's report *Official Records*, Vol. XXV, Part 1, 590.

57. Lessig, Letter, [undated], in Wallace, *Memorial of the Patriotism of Schuylkill County*, 249.

58. Haas to bro. Fred, Letter, May 12, 1863, Haas Papers, HCWRTC, HEC.

59. Bicknell, *History of the Fifth Regiment Maine Volunteers*, 219.

60. Lieut. [Marcus] Casler to editor, Letter, May 6, 1863, Herkimer *County Journal*, May 14, 1863.

61. *Amicus Curae*, Letter, May 13, 1863, reprinted in Wallace, *Memorial of the Patriotism of Schuylkill County*, 240–241.

62. Haas to bro. Fred, Letter, May 12, 1863, Haas Papers, HCWRTC, HEC.

63. Oestreich, Diary, HSSC, 26.

64. Marker to editor, Letter, May 6, 1863, Rochester *Daily Union & Advertiser*, May 11, 1863.

65. *Amicus Curae*, Letter, May 13, 1863, reprinted in Wallace, *Memorial of the Patriotism of Schuylkill County*, 241.

66. *Official Records*, Vol. XIX, 396.

67. Jonathan Letterman, *Memoir of Jonathan Letterman, M.D.*, ed. by Bennett A. Clements, *Journal of the Military Service Institution*, vol. 4, no. 15 (September 1883), 10.

68. *Ibid.*, 36–38.

69. Reed to Dear Parents, Letter, May 22, 1863, Reed Papers, IHS.

70. Stevens, *Three Years in the Sixth Corps*, 180–181.

71. Huntington W. Jackson, "Sedgwick at Fredericksburg and Salem Heights," *Battles & Leaders*, vol. III, 229–230.

72. Haas to bro. Fred, Letter, May 12, 1863, Haas Papers, HCWRTC, HEC.

73. *Ibid.*

74. *Official Records*, Vol. XXV, Part I, 581.

75. *Ibid.*, 856–857; *Ibid.*, 855.

76. *Official Records*, Vol. XXV, Part II, 592; *Official Records*, Vol. XXV, Part II, 576–577; Best, *History of the 121st New York State Infantry*, 68; The Battle of Salem Church has received coverage in the following works: Bigelow, *Campaign of Chancellorsville*, 396–401; Stackpole, *Chancellorsville: Lee's Greatest Battle*, 329–338; Happel, *Salem Church Embattled* ([Philadelphia, Penna.: Eastern National Park, 1980]), 25–52; Sears, *Chancellorsville*, 376–386; Ernest B. Furgurson, *Chancellorsville 1863: The Souls of the Brave* (New York: Alfred A. Knopf, 1992), 273–280; Parsons, *The Union Sixth Army Corps in the Chancellorsville Campaign*, 94–110; Mackowski and White, *Chancellorsville's Forgotten Front*, 238–269.

77. *Official Records*, Vol. XXV, Part I, 581.

78. *Ibid.*, 581.

79. For the strength of each regiment see the following: 23rd New Jersey, Joseph G. Bilby, "Seeing the Elephant: The 15th New Jersey Infantry at the Battle of Salem Church," *Military Images* (January/February 1984), 10. See also Joseph G. Bilby, *Three Rousing Cheers: A History of the Fifteenth New Jersey from Flemington to Appomattox* (Hightstown, New Jersey: Longstreet House, 1993).

80. Best, *History of the 121st New York State Infantry*, 29; For the 121st New York I have accepted unit strength of 500 based on the following: Company D was detached in Fredericksburg and did not participate in the battle. Upton's report, *Official Records*, Vol. XXV, Part I, 589, states 453 as does Best, *History of the 121st New York State Infantry*, 72. Adj. F[rancis]. W. Morse, *Personal Experiences in the War of the Great Rebellion* (Albany, New York: Munsell, 1866), 26, states 452. Other sources, however, cite a much higher number of men engaged. "Otsego in the Rebellion: The 121st Regiment," *History of Otsego County, New York* (Philadelphia, Penna.: Everts & Fariss, 1878), 69, states "The total loss of the regiment was 287 out of 540 who entered the engagement. John Hartwell, Diary, May 5, 1863, in *To My Beloved Wife and Boy at Home: The Letters and Diaries of Orderly Sergeant John F. L. Hartwell*. ed. by Ann Hartwell Britton and Thomas J. Reed. (Madison, New Jersey: Fairleigh Dickinson University Press, 1997), 83, "The loss to the regt. is 273 about ½ of the regt." Capt. Galpin, Letter, May 6, 1863, Herkimer *County Journal*, May 14, 1863, "Our regiment lost 273…. We have 307

men this morning." Lieut. Casler, Letter, May 6, 1863, Herkimer *County Journal*, May 14, 1863, "Our killed, wounded and missing amount to 273—half of our number."

81. For the 96th Pennsylvania, "Letter from the Ninety-sixth Reg., P.V.," Letter, March 31, 1863, *Miners' Journal*, April 18, 1863, "350 men fit for duty."

82. Morse, "The "Rebellion Record,"" 61, States "Tuesday our regiment numbered 320 enlisted men."

83. Curtis, *From Bull Run to Chancellorsville*, 249, states "The Sixteenth New York took 30 officers and 380 enlisted men on the campaign."

84. W. A. Johnson, "Salem Church Fight," Richmond *Dispatch*, October 20, 1901.

85. *Official Records*, Vol. XXV, Part I, 586.

86. In his report Brooks stated that "the dense growth of shrubs and trees … concealed the enemy," *Ibid.*, 568.

87. Upton's report, *Ibid.*, 586, states 300 yards in depth; Mrs. Frank Palmer, "Military History : The Sixteenth Regiment," *History of Clinton and Franklin Counties, New York* (Philadelphia, Pennsylvania: J. W. Lewis & Co., 1880), 73; For the official reports see: Bartlett, *Official Records*, Vol. XXV, Part I, 581, states depth to be 30 yards; Seaver, *Official Records*, Vol. XXV, Part I, 586, states depth as 30 yards; and Upton, *Official Records*, Vol. XXV, Part I, 589, states depth to be 300 yards; Also, see, "Captain Basil Manly's Report," commanding 1st North Carolina Artillery, in Fayetteville *Observer*, May 28, 1863. Manly describes a "Dense belt of woods in front of us, about 300 yards in width."; "Otsego in the Rebellion: The 121st Regiment," *History of Otsego County, New York*, 69, describes, "a belt of woods two hundred yards in width."; Finally two contemporary letters by men in the 121st New York state that the depth of the timber was 30 rods. (30 rods equals 165 yards.) See Lieut. Casler, Letter, May 6, 1863, Herkimer *County Journal*, May 14, 1863 and John Hartwell to My Beloved Wife, Letter, May 17, 1863, *To My Beloved Wife and Boy at Home*, 87. "The woods were about 30 rods through to a clearing." The historian Stephen Sears states that the belt of timber was 250 yards in depth. He offers no documentation for this statement. See his *Chancellorsville*, 379; Wyckoff, *History of the 3rd South Carolina*, 108, also accepts the belt of timber as being 250 yards in depth.

88. Capt. Galpin, Letter, May 6, 1863, Herkimer *County Journal*, May 14, 1863.

89. Lieut. Casler, Letter, May 6, 1863, Herkimer *County Journal*, May 14, 1863.

90. Anonymous [16th New York], "Fredericksburg During the Civil War," Schoff Civil War Collection, William Clements Library, University of Michigan.

91. *Official Records*, Vol. XXV, Part I, 858.

92. "Captain Basil Manly's Report," commanding 1st North Carolina Artillery, Fayetteville *Observer*, May 28, 1863.

93. Kershaw's brigade was deployed as follows: From the left to right of the line; 7th, 3rd, 8th and 15th South Carolina. The 2nd and 3rd South Carolina Battalion, posted left to right, supported the first line; J. R. Parrott to editor, Letter, May 10, 1863, Atlanta *Southern Confederacy*, May 19, 1863, states that "our brigade arrived just in time, near the brick church about 4 miles from Fredericksburg on the plank road." All five regiments of Kershaw's brigade have recent regimental histories. Unfortunately, these well researched and judiciously written monographs add very little to the brigade's ac-

tions at Salem Church. See Mac Wyckoff, *A History of the 2nd South Carolina Infantry: 1861–65* (Fredericksburg, Virginia: Sergeant Kirkland's Museum and Historical Society, 1994), 71; Mac Wyckoff, *A History of the 3rd South Carolina Infantry: 1861–65* (Fredericksburg, Virginia: Sergeant Kirkland's Museum and Historical Society, 1995), 108–109; Sam B. Davis, *A History of the 3rd South Carolina Volunteer Infantry Battalion (James Battalion): 1861–1865* (Wilmington, North Carolina: Broadfoot Publishing Company, 2009), 120; Glen Allan Swain, *The Bloody 7th* (Wilmington, North Carolina: Broadfoot Publishing Company, 2014); James B. Clary, *A History of the 15th South Carolina Volunteer Infantry Regiment: 1861–1865* (Wilmington, North Carolina: Broadfoot Publishing Company, 2007), 101.

94. *Official Records*, Vol. XXV, Part I, 858.

95. *Ibid.*, Vol. XXV, Part I, 590.

96. Haas to bro. Fred, Letter, May 12, 1863, Haas Papers, HCWRTC, HEC.

97. *Official Records*, Vol. XXV, Part I, 590.

98. Best, *History of the 121st New York State Infantry*, 68.

99. Haas to bro. Fred, Letter, May 12, 1863, Haas Papers, HCWRTC, HEC.

100. Letter of Lessig in Wallace, *Memorial of the Patriotism of Schuylkill County*, 249.

101. *Ibid.*

101. Haas to bro. Fred, Letter, May 12, 1863, Haas Papers, HCWRTC, HEC.

102. *Amicus Curae*, Letter, in Wallace, *Memorial of the Patriotism of Schuylkill County*, 241.

103. W. L. Fagan, "Battle of Salem Church," Philadelphia *Weekly Times*, July 7, 1883.

104. "Reminiscent Letter from Col. Hilary Herbert," Montgomery *Advertiser*, April 20, 1918, 4; Hilary A. Herbert, "Colonel Hilary A. Herbert's 'History of the Eighth Alabama Volunteer Regiment, C.S.A.,'" ed. by Maurice S. Fortin, *Alabama Historical Quarterly* (1977), vol. 39, nos. 1–4, 101. See especially Chapter XI, "The Battle of Salem Church," pages 96–111; See also Linda L. Green, *First, for the Duration: The Story of the Eighth Alabama Infantry, C.S.A.* (Maryland: Heritage Books, 2008), 50–52; Thomas G. Rodgers, "A Patchwork Outfit From All Walks of Life, the 8th Alabama Became Cohesive Fighting Unit," *America's Civil War* (May 1989), vol. 2, no. 1, 12–15.

105. *Curae*, Letter, in Wallace, *Memorial of the Patriotism of Schuylkill County*, 241.

106. *Ibid.*, 241.

107. *Ibid.*, 249.

108. W. A. Johnson, "Salem Church Fight," Richmond *Dispatch*, October 20, 1901.

109. John Coxe, "In the Battle of Chancellorsville," *Confederate Veteran* (April 1922), vol. XXX, no. 4, 140. Although Coxe attributes this passage to the events of the following day, referred to as the Battle of Banks' Ford, it appears that his narrative more closely aligns with the fighting at Salem Church.

110. For obituary regarding Houck see *Miners' Journal* June 6 and 13, 1863.

111. Obituary for the Allison brothers is in the *Miners' Journal* June 6, 1863.

112. See also, "Schuylkill County's Lydia Bixby: Mrs. Agnes Allison," *Schuylkill County in the Civil War, A Publication of the Historical Society of Schuylkill County* (1961), vol. VII, no. 3, 94–96.

113. Lessig, Letter, in Wallace, *Memorial of the Patriotism of Schuylkill County*, 249; *Official Records*, Vol.

XXV, Part I, 590; Haas to bro. Fred, Letter, May 12, 1863, Haas Papers, HCWRTC, HEC.

114. Lieut. Casler, Letter, May 6, 1863, Herkimer *County Journal*, May 14, 1863; For details concerning the role of Upton's regiment at Salem Church, see Salvatore G. Cilella, Jr., *Upton's Regulars: The 121st New York Infantry in the Civil War* (Lawrence, Kansas: University Press of Kansas, 2009), 160–176.

115. W. L. Fagan, "Battle of Salem Church," Philadelphia *Weekly Times*, July 7, 1883; Herbert, "Colonel Hilary A. Herbert's 'History of the Eighth Alabama Volunteer Regiment, C.S.A.,'" 101; *Official Records*, Vol. XXV, Part I, 858. For unit strength of the 9th Alabama, I have accepted the report of Adj. R. C. Jones. See "List of Casualties," Richmond *Dispatch*, May 18, 1863.

116. Col. J.C.C. Sanders, Official Report, unpublished, May 10, 1863, W.H. Sanders Papers, Department of Archives and History, Montgomery, Alabama; George Clark, *A Glance Backward: Or Some Events in the Past History of My Life* (Texas, 1914[?]), 33–34; Herbert, "Colonel Hilary A. Herbert's 'History of the Eighth Alabama Volunteer Regiment, C.S.A.,'" 101; Unattributed report in E. P. Alexander Papers, So. Hist. Coll., Uni. North Carolina, published in *Official Records Supplement*, Vol. 4, Part I—Reports, 677.

117. Lessig in Wallace, *Memorial of the Patriotism of Schuylkill County*, 249.

118. Haas to bro. Fred, Letter, May 12, 1863, Haas Papers, HCWRTC, HEC.

119. Haas, Diary, May 3, 1863, Haas Papers, HCWRTC, HEC; Luckenbill, Diary, May 3, 1863, WDC.

120. Lessig in Wallace, *Memorial of the Patriotism of Schuylkill County*, 249.

121. Haas to bro. Fred, Letter, May 12, 1863, Haas Papers, HCWRTC, HEC.

122. Lessig in Wallace, *Memorial of the Patriotism of Schuylkill County*, 249.

123. Haas, Diary, May 3, 1863, Haas Papers, HCWRTC, HEC.

124. Herbert, "Colonel Hilary A. Herbert's 'History of the Eighth Alabama Volunteer Regiment, C.S.A.,'" 102.

125. Edmund Patterson, *Yankee Rebel: The Civil War Journal of Edmund DeWitt Patterson*, ed. by John G. Barrett (Chapel Hill, North Carolina: University North Carolina Press, 1966), 102.

126. Luckenbill, Diary, May 3, 1863, WDC.

127. Lessig in Wallace, *Memorial of the Patriotism of Schuylkill County*, 249–250.

128. *Official Records*, Vol. XXV, Part I, 590; In a later report of casualties, 29 men were recorded as missing or captured. See Wallace, *Memorial of the Patriotism of Schuylkill County*, 244.

129. *Official Records*, Vol. XXV, Part I, 806 for casualties in the 8th Alabama. See also "Casualties in 8th Alabama Regiment," Montgomery *Daily Mail*, May 22, 1863.

130. *Official Records*, Vol. XXV, Part I, 567; *Ibid.*, 580–581.

131. *Ibid.*, Vol. XXV, Part I, 581; *Ibid.*, 590; William F. Stevens, [5th Maine], "In Battle and In Prison: A Reminiscence of the War of the Rebellion," *Granite Monthly* (April 1879), vol. 2, no. 7, 216; For an interesting essay exploring the impact of the terrain on the Battle of Chancellorsville, see, Mark E. Neely, Jr., "Wilderness and the Cult of Manliness: Hooker, Lincoln, and Defeat," in *Lincoln's Generals*, ed. by Gabor S. Boritt (New York: Oxford University Press, 1994), 53–77, notes 204–209.

132. Hartwell to My Beloved Wife, Letter, May 17, 1863, *To My Beloved Wife and Boy at Home*, 87.

133. "Otsego in the Rebellion: The 121st Regiment," *History of Otsego County, New York*, 69.

134. Lessig in Wallace, *Memorial of the Patriotism of Schuylkill County*, 249; *Official Records*, Vol. XXV, Part I, 581

135. *Official Records*, Vol. XXV, Part I, 582.

136. *Ibid.*, 590.

137. *Curae*, Letter, in Wallace, *Memorial of the Patriotism of Schuylkill County*, 241.

138. Haas to bro. Fred, Letter, May 12, 1863, Haas Papers, HCWRTC, HEC.

139. Lieut. Casler, Letter, May 6, 1863, *Herkimer County Journal*, May 14, 1863.

140. Morse, *Personal Experiences in the War of the Great Rebellion*, 25.

141. *Curae*, Letter, in Wallace, *Memorial of the Patriotism of Schuylkill County*, 241.

142. William Remmel to Brother, Letter, May 16, 1863, in *Like Grass Before the Scythe: The Life and Death of Sgt. William Remmel 121st New York Infantry* (Tuscaloosa, Alabama: University of Alabama Press, 2007), 37.

143. *Curae*, Letter, in Wallace, *Memorial of the Patriotism of Schuylkill County*, 241.

144. *Official Records*, Vol. XXV, Part I, 583.

145. *Curae*, Letter, in Wallace, *Memorial of the Patriotism of Schuylkill County*, 242.

146. *Ibid.*

147. D. Webster Bland to Dr. Koebler, Letter, May 9, 1863, *Miners' Journal*, May 16, 1863.

148. *Official Records*, Vol. XXV, Part I, 590.

149. Curtis, *From Bull Run to Chancellorsville*, 270.

150. Faust to Sister, Letter, May 7, 1863, Faust Papers, HCWRTC, HEC.

151. John Von Hollen to Filbert, Letter, May 17, 1863, Filbert Papers, HCWRTC, HEC.

152. Adam Clarke Rice to brother, Letter, May 14, 1863, in *The Letters and Other Writings of the Late Lieut. Adam Clarke Rice, of the 121st Regiment, N. Y. Volunteers*, comp. by C. E. Rice (Little Falls, New York: Journal and Courier, 1864), 71.

153. James Kidder to wife, Letter, December 5, 1863, *Subdued by the Sword: A Line Officer in the 121st New York Volunteers* ed. by James M. Greiner (Albany, New York: State University of New York Press, 2003), 95.

154. Holt to wife, Letter, September 5, 1862, *A Surgeon's Civil War: The Letters & Diary of Daniel M. Holt, M.D.*, ed. by James M. Greiner, *et. al.* (Kent, Ohio: Kent State University Press, 1994), 13–14.

155. Bates, *Pennsylvania Volunteers*, vol. III, 387; See also Bicknell, *History of the Fifth Regiment Maine Volunteers*, 233–234; Curtis, *From Bull Run to Chancellorsville*, 291.

156. Haas to bro. Fred, Letter, May 12, 1863, Haas Papers, HCWRTC, HEC.

157. *Curae*, Letter, in Wallace, *Memorial of the Patriotism of Schuylkill County*, 241.

158. Holt, *A Surgeon's Civil War*, 105.

159. Camille Baquet, *History of the First Brigade, New Jersey Volunteers from 1861 to 1865* (Trenton, New Jersey: MacCrellish and Quigley, 1910), 250.

160. Rice to brother, Letter, May 14, 1863, in *The Letters and Other Writings of the Late Lieut. Adam Clarke Rice, of the 121st Regiment, N. Y. Volunteers*, 71.

161. *Official Records*, Vol. XXV, Part I, 562; *Ibid.*, 569.

162. For further details concerning the 23rd New Jersey at Salem Church see Baquet, *History of the First Brigade*, 237–255.

163. Bartlett's detailed report discusses the obstacles and disadvantages he faced at Salem Church. See *Official Records*, Vol. XXV, Part I, 579–583.

164. Letter of Lessig in Wallace, *Memorial of the Patriotism of Schuylkill County*, 250.

165. *Ibid.*

166. Martin T. McMahon, *General John Sedgwick: An Address Delivered Before the Vermont Officers' Reunion Society at their Sixteenth Annual Meeting at Montpelier, Novol. 11, 1880* (Togus, Maine, 1885), 175.

167. Mason Whiting Tyler, *Recollections of the Civil War: With Many Original Diary Entries and Letters Written from the Seat of War and with Annotated References*, William S. Tyler, ed. (New York: G. P. Putnam's Sons, 1912), 87.

168. Haas to bro. Fred, Letter, May 12, 1863, Haas Papers, HCWRTC, HEC.

169. Freeman, *Lee's Lieutenants*, vol. II, 631; Foote, *Civil War*, vol. II, 312.

170. Huntington W. Jackson, "Sedgwick at Fredericksburg and Salem Heights," *Battles and Leaders*, vol. III, 231–232; Winslow, *General John Sedgwick*, 83; Fairchild, *History of the 27th Regiment N. Y. Vols.*, 172; *Official Records*, Vol.XXV, Part I, 582.

171. Haas to his Brother, Letter, May 12, 1863, Haas Papers, HCWRTC, HEC.

172. Letter of Lessig in Wallace, *Memorial of the Patriotism of Schuylkill County*, 250.

173. Miller, Diary, May 7, 1863, GKC.

174. Luckenbill, Diary, May 7, 1863, WDC.

175. Haas, Diary, May 7, 1863, Haas Papers, HCWRTC, HEC.

176. Catton, *Glory Road*, 215.

177. Faust to Sister, Letter, May 23, 1863, Faust Papers, HCWRTC, HEC.

178. Lessig in Wallace, *Memorial of the Patriotism of Schuylkill County*, 250.

179. Reed to Parents, Letter, May 22, 1863, Reed Papers, IHS.

180. Haas to his Brother, Letter, June 9, 1863, Haas Papers, HCWRTC, HEC.

181. *Official Records*, Vol. XXV, Part I, 583.

182. Catton, *Glory Road*, 236.

183. Haas to bro. Fred, Letter, May 12, 1863, Haas Papers, HCWRTC, HEC.

Chapter IX

1. Henry to his Sister, May 20, 1863, Henry Papers, CWMisc Coll., HCWRTC, HEC.

2. Foltz to Brother, Letter, March 22, 1863, Coco Coll., GNMP.

3. Fairchild, *History of the 27th Regiment N. Y. Vols.*, 175; Bicknell, *History of the Fifth Regiment Maine Volunteers*, 233; Bates, *Pennsylvania Volunteers*, vol. III, 387.

4. Warner, *Generals in Blue*, 47; Catton, *Glory Road*, 109.

5. Warner, *Generals in Blue*, 575; "William W. Bergen, "The Other Hero of Cedar Creek: The "Not Specially Ambitious" Horatio G. Wright," *The Shenandoah Valley Campaign of 1864*, ed. by Gary W. Gallagher (Chapel Hill, North Carolina: University North Carolina Press, 2006), 85–133.

6. Grant to Halleck, Letter, May 20, 1864, *The Papers of Ulysses S. Grant*, vol. 10, 469.

7. George Meade to Wife, Letter, July 15, 1864, *Life and Letters of George Gordon Meade* (New York: Charles Scribner's Sons, 1913), vol. 2, 213.

8. Wilbur Fisk to Editor *Green Mountain Freeman*, October 4, 1864, in *Anti-Rebel: The Civil War Letters of Wilbur Fisk*, ed. by Ruth and Emil Rosenblatt (Croton-on-Hudson, New York, E. Rosenblatt, 1993), 261.

9. Elisha H. Rhodes, "The Second Rhode Island Volunteers at the Siege of Petersburg," *Personal Narratives of Events in the war of the Rebellion* (Rhode Island, 1915), 7th Series, no. 10, 6.

10. Treichler, Memoir, RTC, 44; Gery, Diary, May 23, 1863, Hamburg *Item*, 1942.

11. Winslow, *General John Sedgwick*, 89; See also diaries of Gery, Luckenbill and Miller for the month of May, 1863.

12. Winslow, *General John Sedgwick*, 90–91; For a brief summary of Lee's "objectives," see Bruce Catton, *Never Call Retreat* (Garden City, New York: Doubleday and Company, 1965), 160.

13. Haas, Diary, June 5–7, 1863, Haas Papers, HCWRTC, HEC.

14. Haas to Bro. Fred, Letter, June 9, 1863, Haas Papers, HCWRTC, HEC; Haas, Diary, June 8–9, 1863, Haas Papers, HCWRTC, HEC.

15. Luckenbill, Diary, June 10, 1863, William Dick Coll.

16. Noah A. Trudeau, "False Start at Franklin's Crossing," *America's Civil War* (July 2001), vol. 14, no. 3, 32–37 and 86.

17. Basler, *Collected Works*, vol. 6, 257.

18. Wallace, *Memorial of the Patriotism of Schuylkill County*, 494–495; Haas, Diary, June 11, 1863, Haas Papers, HCWRTC, HEC; Keiser, Diary, June 11, 1863, Keiser Papers, HCWRTC, HEC; See also Pottsville *Miners' Journal* issue of March 5, 1864.

19. Haas, Diary, June 12, 1862, Haas Papers, HCWRTC, HEC; Elements of Pender's Division of A.P. Hill's Third Army Corps were opposite the pickets of the 96th Pennsylvania. In his diary, Captain Haas noted the presence of the 14th Georgia, of Thomas' Third Brigade. A search of Edwin B. Coddington's "Order of Battle," outlining the Army of Northern Virginia, contained in his work, *The Gettysburg Campaign: A Study in Command* (New York: Charles Scribner's Sons, 1968), 575–595, failed to reveal any North Carolina units with the ordinal numbers of 29 and 49. Obviously, Captain Haas was in error when he reported the presence of these two regiments along the Rappahannock.

20. Haas, Diary, June 12, 1862, Haas Papers, HCWRTC, HEC.

21. Luckenbill, Diary, June 12–13, WDC.

22. Haas, Diary, June 13, 1863, Haas Papers, HCWRTC; Stevens, *Three Years in the Sixth Corps*, 222.

23. Keiser, Diary, June 13, Keiser Papers, HEC.

24. Haas, Diary, June 13, 1863, Haas Papers, HCWRTC, HEC; Luckenbill, Diary, June 12–13, 1863, WDC.

25. Stevens, *Three Years in the Sixth Corps*, 223.

26. For a comprehensive examination of the march of the VI Corps to Gettysburg see, David A. Ward, "'Sedgwick's Foot Cavalry': The March of the Sixth Corps to Gettysburg," *The Gettysburg Magazine* (July 2000), no. 22, 43–65.

27. Luckenbill, Diary, June 14, 1863, WDC.

28. Stevens, *Three Years in the Sixth Corps*, 222.

29. Haas, Diary, June 14, 1863, Haas Papers, HCWRTC, HEC.

30. Stevens, *Three Years in the Sixth Corps*, 223.

31. *Ibid.*, 226.

32. Haas, Diary, June 15, 1863, Haas Papers, HCWRTC, HEC.

33. Stevens, *Three Years in the Sixth Corps*, 226.

34. John W. Schildt, *Roads to Gettysburg* (Parsons, West Virginia: McClain Printing Company, 1963), 90; Bicknell, *History of the Fifth Regiment Maine Volunteers*, 236.

35. Stevens, *Three Years in the Sixth Corps*, 227.

36. Luckenbill, Diary, June 15, 1863, WDC.

37. Haas, Diary, June 15, 1863, Haas Papers, HCWRTC, HEC.

38. Stevens, *Three Years in the Sixth Corps*, 227.

39. *Ibid.*; See also Haas, Diary, June 16, 1863, Haas Papers, HCWRTC, HEC, where he states "Swam in the Occoquan."

40. Fisk, *Anti-Rebel*, 105.

41. Haas, Diary, June 16, 1863, Haas Papers, HCWRTC, HEC.

42. *Ibid.*

43. Richards to Annie, Letter, June 19, 1863, Richards Papers, HEC.

44. Faust to brother, Letter, June 20, 1863, Faust Papers, Cobaugh Coll., HCWRTC, HEC; See also Ward, "Sedgwick's Foot Cavalry," *Gettysburg Magazine*, 44–45.

45. Faust to brother, Letter, June 20, 1863, Faust Papers, Cobaugh Coll., HCWRTC, HEC; See also Ward, "Sedgwick's Foot Cavalry," *Gettysburg Magazine*, 48.

46. *Ibid.*, 50–51.

47. Delevan Bates to Father, Letter, June 17, 1863, *Civil War Letters of Delevan Bates*, ed. by William S. Saint, Jr. (Illinois, 1988), http://www.usgennet.org/usa/ne/topic/military/CW/bates/genbate1.html.

48. Holt to Dear Wife, Letter, June 19, 1863, *A Surgeon's Civil War*, 113.

49. Best, *History of the 121st New York State Infantry*, 86; Haas, Diary, June 26, 1863, Haas Papers, HCWRTC, HEC. Stevens, *Three Years in the Sixth Corps*, 235.

50. Gery, Diary, June 26, 1863, Hamburg *Item*, 1942.

51. Miller, Diary, June 27, 1863, GKC.

52. Haas, Diary, June 27, 1863, Haas Papers, HCWRTC, HEC.

53. Schildt, *Roads to Gettysburg*, 281; Alanson A. Haines, *History of the Fifteenth Regiment, New Jersey Volunteers* (New York: Jenkins & Thomas, 1883), 75; Catton, *Glory Road*, 275, makes clear the wishes of Halleck and Stanton in regard to Hooker's leadership of the Army of the Potomac.

54. Treichler, Memoir, RTC, 39. See also Stevens, *Three Years in the Sixth Corps*, 238.

55. Quoted in Glenn Tucker, *High Tide at Gettysburg: The Campaign in Pennsylvania* (Dayton, Ohio: Morningside Bookshop, 1973), 90.

56. Gery, Diary, June 28, 1863, Hamburg *Item*, 1942.

57. Schildt, *Roads to Gettysburg*, 318–319; *Ibid.*, 379–380.

58. Coddington, *The Gettysburg Campaign*, 356.

59. Haas, Diary, June 30, 1863, Haas Papers, HCWRTC, HEC.

60. Gery, Diary, June 26, 1863, Hamburg *Item*, 1942.

61. Keiser, Diary, June 13, Keiser Papers, HCWRTC, HEC.

62. Haas, Diary, June 29–30, 1863, Haas Papers, HCWRTC, HEC.

63. Gery, Diary, July 1, 1863, Hamburg *Item*, 1942.

64. Luckenbill, Diary, July 1, 1863, WDC; Haas, Diary, July 1, 1863, Haas Papers, HCWRTC, HEC.

65. Gery, Diary, July 1, 1863, Hamburg *Item*, 1942.

66. Bicknell, *History of the Fifth Regiment Maine Vol-*

unteers, 242; Garry Adelman, "The Third Brigade, Third Division, Sixth Corps at Gettysburg," *The Gettysburg Magazine* (July 1994), no. 11, 92–93.

67. Tucker, *High Tide at Gettysburg*, 204–205; James W. Latta, "Dedication of Monument 119th Regiment Infantry September 22, 1888," in Pennsylvania, Gettysburg Battlefield Commission, *Pennsylvania at Gettysburg: Ceremonies at the Dedication of the Monuments Erected by the Commonwealth of Pennsylvania to Major General George Gordon Meade, Major General Winfield Scott Hancock, Major General John F. Reynolds and to Mark the Positions of the Pennsylvania Commands Engaged in the Battle* (Harrisburg, Pa., 1904), vol. 2, 652. (Hereafter this source will be cited as *Pennsylvania at Gettysburg*.)

68. Coddington, *The Gettysburg Campaign*, 325–326; Tucker, *High Tide at Gettysburg*, 205.

69. Coddington, *The Gettysburg Campaign*, 357; Tucker, *High Tide at Gettysburg*, 207–208; Winslow, *General John Sedgwick*, 100.

70. Oestreich, Diary, HSSC, 31.

71. Haas, Diary, July 2, 1863, Haas Papers, HCWRTC, HEC.

72. Keiser, Diary, July 2, 1863, Keiser Papers, HCWRTC, HEC.

73. Quoted in Charles Carleton Coffin, *Four Years of Fighting: A Volume of Personal Observation with the Army and Navy* (Boston, Mass.: Ticknor and Fields, 1866), 286. See also Tucker, *High Tide at Gettysburg*, 209–210; Winslow, *General John Sedgwick*, 101; Sedgwick and his staff preceded the vanguard of the VI Corps column to Gettysburg. The brigade at the head of the column was the Third Brigade, Third Division commanded by Brig. Gen. Frank Wheaton. Regimental commanders Kohler, 98th Penna. and Moody 139th Penna. reported that their regiments reached Gettysburg at 3 p.m. See *Official Records*, Vol. XXVII, Part 1, 686, 688.

74. Haas, Diary, July 2, 1863, Haas Papers, HCWRTC, HEC; John W. Busey and David G. Martin, *Regimental Strengths at Gettysburg* (Hightstown, New Jersey: Longstreet House, 1982), 72, state that as of June 30, 1863 the 96th Pennsylvania reported 356 men for duty. Subsequently, the authors believe, due to their calculations, that 308 soldiers were actually engaged in the battle at Gettysburg. See also brief statement of Capt. Haas, "They [96th Penna.] number about 350 muskets fit for duty." *Miners' Journal*, July 25, 1863. Determining how far the VI Corps marched from Manchester, Maryland to Gettysburg, Pennsylvania, is difficult to measure exactly. Of the six diarists in the 96th Pennsylvania who chronicled the campaign, one recorded 30 miles, four stated that the march was 32 miles, Adj. Richards recalled the march being 35 miles, while two stated that they tramped 36 miles. Retracing the march from the regiment's camp, east of Manchester, by automobile, places the total distance at 32 miles. Samuel R. Russel to Mother, Letter, July 4, 1863, *Miners' Journal*, July 11, 1863; Richards to Brother, Letter, August 24, 1863, Richards Papers, HEC; James M. Treichler, "End of the Battle" Charge of a Brigade of the Sixth Corps at Gettysburg," *National Tribune*, May 4, 1916.

75. Quoted in Winslow, *General John Sedgwick*, 103.

76. Bicknell, *History of the Fifth Regiment Maine Volunteers*, 243–244.

77. Haas, Diary, July 2, 1863, Haas Papers, HCWRTC, HEC.

78. *Official Records*, Vol. XXVII, Part I, 671; New York (State), *Monuments Commission for the Battlefields of Gettysburg and Chattanooga, Final Report on the Bat-*

tlefield of ettysburg, ed. by William F. Fox (Albany, N.Y., 1900), vol. II, 516–517 (Hereafter this source will be cited as *New York at Gettysburg*.); Maine, Gettysburg Commission, *Maine at Gettysburg: Report of Maine Commissioners Prepared by the Executive Committee* (Portland, Maine, 1898), 355 (Hereafter this source will be cited as *Maine at Gettysburg*.); *Pennsylvania at Gettysburg*, vol. I, 516–517; Keiser, Diary, July 2, 1863, Keiser Papers, HCWRTC, HEC.

79. Luckenbill, Diary, July 3, 1863, WDC; Keiser, Diary, July 3, 1863, Keiser Papers, HCWRTC, HEC.

80. Haas, Diary, July 3, 1863, Haas Papers, HCWRTC, HEC.

81. Bicknell, *History of the Fifth Regiment Maine Volunteers*, 246; *Official Records*, Vol. XXVII, Part I, 636, 671.

82. Haas, Diary, July 3, 1863, Haas Papers, HCWRTC, HEC.

83. Keiser, Diary, July 2, 1863, Keiser Papers, HCWRTC, HEC; *Official Records*, Vol. XXVII, Part I, 654.

84. Luckenbill, Diary, July 3, 1863, WDC.

85. Haas, Diary, July 3, 1863, Haas Papers, HCWRTC, HEC.

86. Samuel R. Russel to Mother, Letter, July 4, 1863, *Miners' Journal*, July 11, 1863.

87. Dispatch from Carleton [C.C. Coffin] near Gettysburg, July 3, [1863], in Boston *Morning Journal*, July 7, 1863. See also Haas, Dairy, July 3, 1863, Haas Papers, HCWRTC, HEC.

88. *Maine at Gettysburg*, 367.

89. Haas, Diary, July 4, 1863, Haas Papers, HCWRTC, HEC.

90. Coddington, *The Gettysburg Campaign*, 549–550.

91. Haas, Diary, July 5, 1863, Haas Papers, HCWRTC, HEC.

92. Keiser, Diary, July 5, 1863, Keiser Papers, HCWRTC, HEC; Andrew A. Humphreys, *From Gettysburg to the Rapidan: The Army of the Potomac July 1863, to April, 1864* (New York: Charles Scribner's Sons, 1883), 2–3.

93. Coddington, *The Gettysburg Campaign*, 549–550; Haas, Diary, July 5, 1863, Haas Papers, HCWRTC, HEC; For an excellent analysis of Meade's pursuit of Lee see, A. Wilson Greene, "From Gettysburg to Falling Waters," in *The Third Day at Gettysburg and Beyond*, ed. by Gary W. Gallagher (Chapel Hill, North Carolina: University North Carolina Press, 1994), 161–201; John W. Schildt, *Roads from Gettysburg* (Chewsville, Maryland: Schildt, 1979); Eric Wittenberg, David J. Petruzzi and Michael F. Nugent, *One Continuous Fight: The Retreat from Gettysburg and the Pursuit of Lee's Army of Northern Virginia, July 4–14, 1863* (New York: Savas Beatie, 2008). See also Peter C. Vermilyea, "Maj. Gen. John Sedgwick and the Pursuit of Lee's Army After Gettysburg," *Gettysburg Magazine* (July 2000), no. 22, 113–128.

94. Coddington, *The Gettysburg Campaign*, 550–551.

95. Keiser, Diary, July 6–7, 1863, Keiser Papers, HCWRTC, HEC.

96. Coddington, *The Gettysburg Campaign*, 551.

97. Haas, Diary, July 7, 1863, Haas Papers, HCWRTC, HEC.

98. *Ibid*.

99. Schildt, *Roads from Gettysburg*, 85–87; Bicknell, *History of the Fifth Regiment Maine Volunteers*, 248–251.

100. Haas, Diary, July 7, 1863, Haas Papers, HCWRTC, HEC.

101. Keiser, Diary, July 5, 1863, Keiser Papers, HCWRTC, HEC.

102. Gery, Diary, July 10–11, 1863, Hamburg *Item*, 1942.

103. Haas, Diary, July 11, 1863, Haas Papers, HCWRTC, HEC; Luckenbill, Diary, July 11, 1863, WDC. For a map locating Claggett's Mill see *Atlas to Accompany the Official Records of the Union and Confederate Armies*, Plate XLII Map 5. See also, Helen Ashe Hays, *The Antietam and Its Bridges: The Annals of an Historic Stream* (New York: G. P. Putnam's Sons, 1910), 109–120.

104. Gery, Diary, July 11, 1863, Hamburg *Item*, 1942.

105. Haas, Diary, July 11, 1863, Haas Papers, HCWRTC, HEC.

106. Haas, Diary, July 12, 1863, Haas Papers, HCWRTC, HEC, 96th skirmished opposite the 1st South Carolina of Col. Abner Perrin's brigade.

107. Haas, Diary, July 14, 1863, Haas Papers, HCWRTC, HEC.

108. Meade, *Life and Letters of George Gordon Meade*, vol. II, 134.

109. Boland to John Brislin, Letter, September 2, 1863, Brislin Papers, HSSC.

110. *Official Records* Vol. XXVII, Part III, 519.

111. Lincoln to Meade, Letter, July 14, 1863, *Collected Works of Abraham Lincoln*, vol. 6, 327–328.

112. Reed to Brother, Letter, September 21, 1863, Reed Papers, IHS.

Chapter X

1. Isaac E. Severn to Editor, Letter, September 23, 1863, *Miners' Journal*, October 2, 1863; See also Samuel R. Russel, Letter, September 23, 1863, *Miners' Journal*, October 2, 1863; Henry to Sister, Letter, May 20, 1863, Henry Papers, HEC; Reed to Brother, Letter, September 21, 1863, Reed Papers, IHS; See also John J. Hennessy, "I Dread the Spring: The Army of the Potomac Prepares for the Overland Campaign," *The Wilderness Campaign*, ed. by Gary W. Gallagher (Chapel Hill, North Carolina: University North Carolina Press, 1997), 66–105.

2. Haas, Diary, July 11, 1863, HCWRTC, Haas Papers, HEC.

3. Keiser, Diary, July 11 and 22, 1863, Keiser Papers, HCWRTC, HEC.

4. Luckenbill, Diary, July 11, 1863, WDC; Miller, Diary, July 11, 1863, GKC; Gery, Diary, July 11, 1863, Hamburg *Item*, 1942.

5. Curtin to Stanton, Correspondence, October 23, 1862, *Official Records*, Vol. XIX, Part 2, 473.

6. Whipple to Fry, Report, July 23, 1863, *Official Records*, Series III, Vol. III, 562.

7. *Ibid.*, 674.

8. Couch's statement is quoted in, Jim Zbick, "Coalfields' Perfect Hell," *America's Civil War* (March 1992), vol. 4, no. 6, 25.

9. Tower to Fry, Correspondence, June 10, 1863, *Official Records*, Series III, Vol. III, 330–332.

10. Fred A. Shannon, *The Organization and Administration of the Union Army, 1861–1865* (Massachusetts, 1965), vol. 1, 222.

11. Palladino, *Another Civil War*, 117.

12. Kevin Kenny, *Making Sense of the Molly Maguires* (New York: Oxford University Press, 1998), 95; Arnold Shankman, "Draft Resistance in Civil War Pennsylvania," *Pennsylvania Magazine of History and Biography* (April 1977), vol. 101, no. 2, 197; Arnold Shankman, *The*

Pennsylvania Antiwar Movement, 1861–1865 (New Jersey 1980); Leo L. Ward, "'It Was Open, Defiant Rebellion,'" *Civil War* (March/April 1991), vol. 9 no. 2, 56–63. See also Timothy J. Orr, "'A Viler Enemy in Our Rear': Pennsylvania Soldiers Confront the North's Antiwar Movement," in *The View From the Ground: Experiences of Civil War Soldiers*, ed. by Aaron Sheehan-Denn (Lexington, Kentucky: University of Kentucky Press, 2007), 171–198.

13. Priscilla Long, *Where the Sun Never Shines: A History of America's Bloody Coal Industry* (New York: Paragon House, 1989), 94–95.

14. Kenny, *Making Sense of the Molly Maguires*, 95.

15. Albright to Lincoln, Correspondence, November 9, 1863, *Official Records*, Series III, Vol. III, 1008–1009.

16. Palladino, *Another Civil War*, 112–113.

17. Gery, Diary, May 28, 1863, Hamburg *Item*, 1942. See also Miller, Diary, May 28, 1863, GKC.

18. Faust to Sister, Letter, September 26, 1863, Cobaugh Coll., Faust Papers, HCWRTC, HEC.

19. Keiser, Diary, September 24, 1863, Keiser Papers, HCWRTC, HEC.

20. *Ibid.*

21. Henry to Sister, Letter, August 14, 1863, Henry Papers, HEC.

22. Isaac E. Severn to Editor, Letter, September 23, 1863, *Miners' Journal*, October 2, 1863; See also Samuel R. Russel, Letter, September 23, 1863, *Miners' Journal*, October 2, 1863.

23. Haas to Brother, Letter, May 12, 1863, Haas Papers, HCWRTC, HEC. See also Foltz to Brother, Letter, March 22, 1863, Coco Coll., GNMP.

24. Faust to Sister, Letter, September 26, 1863, Cobaugh Coll., Faust Papers, HCWRTC, HEC.

25. Haas to Brother, Letter, June 9, 1863, Haas Papers, HCWRTC, HEC.

26. Severn to Editor, Letter, September 23, 1863, *Miners' Journal*, October 2, 1863.

27. A Soldier from Company H to editor, Letter, September 9, 1863, under heading "Listen to a Soldier of the 96th Regiment," *Miners' Journal*, September 19, 1863.

28. Reed to Brother, Letter, September 21, 1863, Reed Papers, IHS.

29. Isaac E. Severn to Editor, Letter, September 23, 1863, *Miners' Journal*, October 2, 1863; See also Samuel R. Russel, Letter, September 23, 1863, *Miners' Journal*, October 2, 1863.

30. Wiley, *Life of Billy Yank*, see footnote 51, 397–398.

31. Stevens, *Three Years in the Sixth Corps*, 268–269.

32. Bates, *Pennsylvania Volunteers*, v.III, 388.

33. Bicknell, *History of the Fifth Regiment Maine Volunteers*, 253.

34. Gerald F. Linderman, *Embattled Courage: The Experience of Combat in the American Civil War* (New York: Free Press, 1987), 174. Regarding desertion see also Ella Lonn, *Desertion During the Civil War* (Gloucester, Massachusetts: P. Smith, 1966); Robert I. Alotta, *Stop the Evil: A Civil War History of Desertion and Murder* (California: Presidio Press, 1978); Jason Mann Frawley, "Voting with Their Feet: Union Desertion in the Army of the Potomac, 1861–1865," Thesis (Statesboro, Georgia: Georgia Southern University, 2003).

35. See for example Luckenbill, Diary August 17, 1863; September 6, 1863; September 10 and 13, 1863, WDC. Luckenbill's diary gives details concerning the desertion of Jacob Huber and Joseph Minnig of Company B. According to Bates, *Pennsylvania Volunteers*,

vol. III, 393–394, after Gettysburg the following men deserted from Company B. Jacob Bast, July 2, 1863; Reuben Fertig, July 16, 1863; James Keesy, July 2, 1863.

36. Cilella, *Upton's Regulars*, 209–211.

37. Keiser, Diary, August 13, 1863, Keiser Papers, HCWRTC, HEC.

38. Luckenbill, Diary, August 13, 1863, WDC.

39. Miller, Diary, August 13, 1863, GKC; Gery, Diary, August 13, 1863, Hamburg *Item*, 1942.

40. Luckenbill, Diary, August 14, 1863, WDC.

41. Keiser, Diary, August 14, 1863, Keiser Papers, HCWRTC, HEC.

42. Henry to Dear Sister, Letter, August 14, 1863, Henry Papers, HEC.

43. Luckenbill, Diary, August 14, 1863, WDC. For additional accounts of the execution see Holt, *A Surgeon's Civil War*, 131; Casler to Editor, Letter, August 15, 1863, Herkimer *County Journal*, August 27, 1863.

44. Bicknell, *History of the Fifth Regiment Maine Volunteers*, 255.

45. Henry to Dear Sister, Letter, August 14, 1863, Henry Papers, HEC.

46. Jeffry D. Wert, *Mosby's Rangers* (New York: Simon & Schuster, 1990), 96–97.

47. Best, History of the 121st *New York State Infantry*, 94.

48. Bates, *Pennsylvania Volunteers*, v.III, 388.

49. *Official Records*, Vol. XXIX, Part I, 102–103.

50. Best, *History of the 121st New York State Infantry*, 93–95.

51. *Ibid.*

52. Bicknell, *History of the Fifth Regiment Maine Volunteers*, 255–256.

53. Luckenbill, Diary, September 5, 1863, WDC.

54. Kesier, Diary, September 5, 1863, Keiser Papers, HCWRTC, HEC.

55. James Cox to Editor, Letter, September 8, 1863, Herkimer *County Journal*, September 17, 1863.

56. Stuart to R. E. Lee, September 7, 1863, Report, *Official Records*, Vol. XXIX, Part I, 102–103.

57. Stephen E. Ambrose, *Upton and the Army* (Baton Rouge, Louisiana: Louisiana State University Press, 1964), 16–53; Warner, *Generals in Blue*, 519–520.

58. Peter S. Michie, *The Life and Letters of Emory Upton: Colonel of the Fourth Regiment of Artillery, and Brevet Major-General, U.S. Army* (New York: D. Appleton and Company, 1885), see the introduction by James Harrison Wilson, xi–xii, xv–xvi, xxvi–xxvii.

59. Franklin Hall to Wife, Letter, February 24, 1863, "Spared to Each Other: The Civil War Correspondence of Frank and Fanny Hall," ed. by Don Wickman, Kent-Delord House Museum, Plattsburgh (New York, 2001) http://www.kellscraft.com/civilwarcontent.html.

60. Stevens, *Three Years in the Sixth Corps*, 286.

61. Jeff Wert, "Rappahannock Station," *Civil War Times Illustrated*, vol. XV, no. 8 (December 1976), 4–8 and 40–46.

62. Oliver Wendell Holmes, Jr., to Charles Whittier, Letter, November 10, 1863, Oliver Wendell Holmes, Jr., Papers, Library of Congress.

63. Wert, "Rappahannock Station," *CWTI*, 42–43; Winslow, *General John Sedgwick*, 122–123; Martin F. Graham and George F. Skoch, *Mine Run: A Campaign of Lost Opportunities, October 21, 1863—May 1, 1864* (Lynchburg, Virginia: H. E. Howard, 1987), 15–29.

64. *Official Records*, Vol. XXIX, Part I, 592–594; *Ibid.*, 588–589.

65. Douglas Southall Freeman, *Lee's Lieutenants: A*

Study in Command, vol. III *Gettysburg to Appomattox* (New York: Charles Scribner's Sons, 1944), 264–267.

66. Best, *History of the 121st New York State Infantry*, 102.

67. *Official Records*, Vol. XXIX, Part I, 589.

68. *Ibid.*, 592.

69. Walter H. Taylor, *Four Years with General Lee* (New York: D. Appleton & Co., 1877), 116. See also Freeman, *Lee's Lieutenants*, vol. III, 192.

70. Keiser, Diary, November 7, 1863, Keiser Papers, HCWRTC, HEC.

71. Bland to Koehler, Letter, November 13, 1863, *Miners' Journal*, November 21, 1863.

72. Keiser, Diary, November 7, 1863, Keiser Papers, HCWRTC, HEC.

73. Luckenbill, Diary, November 5, 1863, WDC. The description of the battle can be found under the date of November 5 in Luckenbill's diary. He telescoped Nov 5–7 under one entry.

74. Bland to Koehler, Letter, November 13, 1863, *Miners' Journal*, November 21, 1863.

75. John Paris [54th North Carolina] to editor, Richmond *Examiner*, Letter, November 10, 1863, printed in Greensboro *Patriot*, November 20, 1863.

76. *Official Records*, Vol. XXIX, Part I, 593.

77. Luckenbill, Diary, November 5, 1863, WDC.

78. Bland to Koehler, Letter, November 13, 1863, *Miners' Journal*, November 21, 1863.

79. Foote, *Civil War*, vol. II, 873; Boatner, *Civil War Dictionary*, 552; Jay Luvaas and Wilbur S. Nye, "The Campaign that History Forgot," *Civil War Times Illustrated*, vol. VIII, no. 7 (November 1969), 11–42; Graham and Skoch, *Mine Run*, 15–29.

80. Foote, *Civil War*, vol. II, 874–875; Davis, *Stand in the Day of Battle*, vol. II, 318–319; Winslow, *General John Sedgwick*, 131; Graham and Skoch, *Mine Run*, 44–60.

81. Luckenbill, Diary, November 26, 1863, WDC; Gery, Diary, November 26, 1863, Hamburg *Item*, 1942.

82. Luckenbill, Diary, November 26, 1863, WDC.

83. Bicknell, *History of the Fifth Regiment Maine Volunteers*, 282–283.

84. Gery, Diary, November 27, 1863, Hamburg Item, 1942.

85. Luckenbill, Diary, November 27, 1863, WDC.

86. Keiser, Diary, November 28, 1863, HCWRTC, HEC.

87. Bicknell, *History of the Fifth Regiment Maine Volunteers*, 282–284; Stevens, *Three Years in the Sixth Corps*, 295.

88. Gery, Diary, November 30, 1863, Hamburg *Item*, 1942. See also Luckenbill, Diary, November 30, 1863, WDC.

89. Bicknell, *History of the Fifth Regiment Maine Volunteers*, 284.

90. Stevens, *Three Years in the Sixth Corps*, 295; *Official Records*, Vol. XXIX, Part I, 797.

91. *Ibid.*, 797.

92. Stevens, *Three Years in the Sixth Corps*, 295.

93. Luckenbill, Diary, November 30, 1863, WDC.

94. Gery, Diary, November 30, 1863, Hamburg *Item*.

95. Keiser, Diary, November 30, 1863, HCWRTC, HEC.

96. Quoted in Clark B. Hall, "Season of Change: The Winter Encampment of the Army of the Potomac December 1, 1863—May 4, 1864," *Blue & Gray Magazine* (April 1991), vol. IV, no. 4, 11.

97. Winslow, *General John Sedgwick*, 131.

98. Boyle, "Outline Sketch," July 17, 1886.

99. Quoted in Foote, *Civil War*, vol. II, 889.

100. Foote, *Civil War*, vol. II, 888; The Federal war objective is cogently summarized in Long, *Civil War Day by Day*, 441, 451; Boland to Friend, Letter, September 2, 1863, Brislin Papers, HSSC; Reed to brother, Letter, September 21, 1863, Reed Papers, IHS.

101. Bruce Catton, *A Stillness at Appomattox* (New York: Doubleday and Company, 1953), 1–2; Winslow, *General John Sedgwick*, 139; For a detailed description of the amusement hall, see Bicknell, *History of the Fifth Regiment Maine Volunteers*, 297.

102. William H. Lessig to Governor A. G. Curtin, December 2, 1863, RG 19, Records of the Department of Military Affairs, 96th Pennsylvania Volunteers, PHMC.

103. *Ibid.*

104. *Ibid.*

105. *Ibid.* According to Bates, *Pennsylvania Volunteers*, vol. III, 390–410, the seniority roster in mid-January, 1864, appeared like this:

—VACANT—	Colonel	
—VACANT—	Lieut. Col.	
William H. Lessig	Major	
John T. Boyle	Co. D	Sept 23, 1861
James E. Russell	Co. E	Sept 23, 1861
Jacob W. Haas	Co. G	Mar. 5, 1862
Levi Huber	Co. B	July 30, 1862
Isaac Severn	Co. C	Nov. 1, 1862
John Harlan	Co. A	March 1, 1863
Samuel R. Russell	Co. H	May 1, 1863
Edward J. Phillips	Co. F	Jan. 9, 1864
William Cusack	Co. I	[Jan. 20, 1864]
Edwin L. Severn	Co. K	[Mar. 19, 1864]

106. On regimental harmony in January, 1863, among the field and staff officers of the 96th Pennsylvania see Boyle to Peter Filbert, January 13, 1863, Filbert Papers, HCWRTC, HEC.

107. See the obituary of Cake, "Colonel H.L. Cake Dead at Northumberland," Pottsville *Miners' Journal*, August 28, 1899.

108. Obituary of Lessig by Elizabeth Kelly, "Gen. Lessig, Once Social Lion, Dead," Denver *Post*, July 19, 1910.

109. Bicknell, *History of the Fifth Regiment Maine Volunteers*, 291.

110. Wiley, *Life of Billy Yank*, 247–248.

111. Boyle to Peter Filbert, Letter, January 13, 1863, Filbert Papers, HCWRTC, HEC; Bates, *Pennsylvania Volunteers*, vol. III, 404, lists Henry Royer resigning January 13, 1863.

112. For examples of swearing see Haas, Diary, under the following dates: March 7, 1862, September 14, 1862, December 4, 1862, December 5, 1862, Haas Papers, HCWRTC, HEC.

113. Wiley, *Life of Billy Yank*, 248.

114. *Ibid.*, 249–250; Haas, Diary, April 10–11, 1863, Haas Papers, HCWRTC, HEC; In regard to pitching pennies, see *Ibid.*, April 10, 1863, Haas Papers, HCWRTC, HEC.

115. Wiley, *Life of Billy Yank*, 252–254.

116. Haas Diary, December 25, 1862, Haas Papers, HCWRTC, HEC. See also Faust to his sister, September 26, 1863, Faust Papers, HCWRTC, HEC.

117. Filbert, Diary, November 27, 1862, HCWRTC, HEC.

118. Luckenbill, Diary, December 25, 1863, WDC.

119. Houck to Joe, Letter, December 21, 1861, Houck Papers, VTL.

120. Portland, Maine *Transcript*, April 23, 1864.

121. Haas to his brother, March 16, 1863, Haas Papers, HCWRTC, HEC.

122. For an interesting sketch of Civil War prostitution see Margaret Leech, *Reveille in Washington* (Garden City, New York: Garden City Publishing Company, 1945), 260–269.

123. Wiley, *Life of Billy Yank*, 262–268.

124. Filbert, Diary, January 26, 1862, Filbert Papers, HCWRTC, HEC.

125. Potts to his mother, Letter, March 23, 1862, Potts Papers, HSSC.

126. Nugent to Darling Wife, Letter, December 15, 1861, *My Darling Wife*, 78.

127. Wiley, *Life of Billy Yank*, 269–274.

128. *Ibid.*, 109–112; See also Leon Litwack, *Been in the Storm so Long: The Aftermath of Slavery* (New York: Alfred A. Knopf, 1979).

129. Wiley, *Life of Billy Yank*, 112.

130. Haas to his brother, Letter, March 16, 1863, Haas Papers, HCWRTC, HEC.

131. Wiley, *Life of Billy Yank*, 113.

132. Treichler, Memoir, RTC, 39.

133. Stevens, *Three Years in the Sixth Corps*, 273–274.

134. Stevens, *Three Years in the Sixth Corps*, 302. The 96th Pennsylvania camped on the Major farm.

135. Bicknell, *History of the Fifth Regiment Maine Volunteers*, 291.

136. Keiser, Diary, January 19, 1864 and December 20, 1863, Keiser Papers, HCWRTC, HEC.

137. Bicknell, *History of the Fifth Regiment Maine Volunteers*, 293; Stevens, *Three Years in the Sixth Corps*, 300–301.

138. Stevens, *Three Years in the Sixth Corps*, 300.

139. Luckenbill, Diary, February 2, 1864, WDC.

140. Keiser, Diary, February 12, 1864, Keiser Papers, HCWRTC, HEC.

141. Bicknell, *History of the Fifth Regiment Maine Volunteers*, 291; See also Stevens, *Three Years in the Sixth Corps*, 300.

142. "Regimental Order Number 69," February 25, 1864, Severn Papers, HSSC.

143. Foote, *Civil War*, vol. II, 907–916, has a good analysis of the Kilpatrick—Dahlgren raid.

144. *Official Records*, Vol. XXXIII, 616–628.

145. *Ibid.*

149. Quoted in Winslow, *General John Sedgwick*, 141.

150. Bicknell, *History of the Fifth Regiment Maine Volunteers*, 301.

151. *Ibid.*, 300.

Chapter XI

1. Mathias Richards, Letter, [date unknown], quoted in Hall, "Season of Change," *Blue & Gray Magazine*, 60.

2. Catton, *This Hallowed Ground*, 317–318; *Official Records*, Series III, Vol. V, 650; Catton, *A Stillness at Appomattox*, 33–34; See also the copy of "Special Orders No. 7," in compliance with G. O. No. 376, War Department, November 21, 1863 in the Severn Papers, HSSC.

3. Keiser, Diary, January 3, 1864, Keiser Papers, HCWRTC, HEC.

4. Luckenbill, Diary, January 3, 1864, WDC.

5. Reed to Parents, Letter, December 24, 1863, Reed Papers, IHS.

6. Bicknell, *History of the Fifth Regiment Maine Volunteers*, 296.

7. Catton, *A Stillness at Appomattox*, 35; See also *Official Records*, Vol. XXXIII, 776.
8. Grant to Halleck, Letter, April 26, 1864, *Papers of Ulysses S. Grant*, vol. 10, 357.
9. "The Army of the Potomac," New York *Times*, March 11, 1864.
10. *Official Records*, Vol. XXXIII, 908.
11. Bicknell, *History of the Fifth Regiment Maine Volunteers*, 298.
12. See Keiser, Diary, April 18 to May 1, 1864 HCWRTC, HEC and Luckenbill, Diary, April 18 to May 1, 1864, WDC.
13. Keiser, Diary, April 28, 1864 HCWRTC, HEC.
14. Luckenbill, Diary, April 8, 1864, WDC.
15. Treichler, Memoir, RTC, 50.
16. *Official Records*, Vol. XXXIII, 907; Catton, *A Stillness at Appomattox*, 46; Keiser, Diary, April 18, 1864, Keiser Papers, HCWRTC, HEC; Winslow, *General John Sedgwick*, 148; Catton, *A Stillness at Appomattox*, 53.
17. Winslow, *General John Sedgwick*, 145–146; Boatner, *Civil War Dictionary*, 48, J. J. Bartlett was transferred to a brigade command in the V Corps; Warner, *Generals in Blue*, 575–576; *Ibid.*, 416–417; *Ibid.*, 170–171; *Ibid.*, 403–404.
18. Catton, *Grant Takes Command*, 179.
19. Catton, *A Stillness at Appomattox*, 59.
20. Keiser, Diary, May 4, 1864, Keiser Papers, HCWRTC, HEC.
21. *Ibid.*
22. Winslow, *General John Sedgwick*, 151; Catton, *Grant Takes Command*, 181.
23. *Ibid.*, 183–184.
24. Robert Garth Scott, *Into the Wilderness with the Army of the Potomac* (Bloomington, Indiana: Indiana University Press, 1985), 53–54, 69; Edward Steere, *The Wilderness Campaign* (Harrisburg, Penna.: Stackpole Company, 1960), 243–244; *Official Records*, Vol. XXXVI, Part I, 665–666; Scott, *Into the Wilderness*, 93, 95; In regard to the advance to Warren's position, Upton stated in his report that the First Division marched, "by the right of wings, it being impossible to march in line of battle on account of the dense pine and nearly impenetrable thickets which met us on every hand."; *Official Records*, Vol. XXXVI, Part I, 665.
25. Keiser, Diary, May 5, 1864, Keiser Papers, HCWRTC, HEC.
26. *Ibid.*
27. *Official Records*, Vol. XXXVI, Part I, 665–666; Gordon C. Rhea, *The Battle of the Wilderness May 5–6, 1864* (Baton Rouge, Louisiana: Louisiana State University Press, 1994), 178–180.
28. Keiser, Diary, May 6, 1864, Keiser Papers, HCWRTC, HEC.
29. *Official Records*, Vol. XXXVI, Part II, 415.
30. Rhea, *Battle of the Wilderness May 5–6*, 318–320.
31. Luckenbill, Diary, May 6, 1864, WDC.
32. *Official Records*, Vol. XXXVI, Part I, 666; Steere, *Wilderness Campaign*, 445.
33. Colonel William H. Penrose commanded the 15th New Jersey Volunteers, First Brigade, First Division, VI Army Corps. Due to confusion along the battle line of May 5, 1864, Penrose placed his unit under the command of Upton. Upon Upton moving with the 95th Pennsylvania and the 121st New York to the right of the Federal line, Penrose, as the senior officer, assumed command of the rest of Upton's brigade; Scott, *Into the Wilderness*, 95.
34. Rhea, *Battle of the Wilderness May 5–6*, 422–425.

See also Keiser, Diary, May 6, 1864, Keiser Papers, HCWRTC, HEC; Luckenbill, Diary, May 6, 1864, WDC; *Official Records*, Vol. XXXVI, Part I, 666; Stevens, *Three Years in the Sixth Corps*, 313.
35. *Official Records*, Vol. XXXVI, Part I, 126.
36. Treichler, Memoir, RTC, 57.
37. Keiser, Diary, May 7, 1864, Keiser Papers, HCWRTC, HEC.
38. Miller, Diary, May 7, 1864, GKC.
39. *Official Records*, Vol. XXXVI, Part II, 481.
40. Luckenbill, Diary, May 8, 1864, WDC.
41. Treichler, Memoir, RTC, 43.
42. Bicknell, *History of the Fifth Regiment Maine Volunteers*, 307.
43. Keiser, Diary, May 8, 1864, Keiser Papers, HCWRTC, HEC.
44. Catton, *Grant Takes Command*, 209; Winslow, *General John Sedgwick*, 168; Joseph P. Cullen, "Spotsylvania," *Civil War Times Illustrated*, vol. X, no. 2 (May 1971), 6.
45. *Official Records*, Vol. XXXVI, Part I, 666–667; Winslow, *General John Sedgwick*, 169.
46. Keiser, Diary, May 8, 1864, Keiser Papers, HCWRTC, HEC.
47. Winslow, *General John Sedgwick*, 170; Catton, *Grant Takes Command*, 217; Gordon C. Rhea, *The Battles for Spotsylvania Court House and the Road to Yellow Tavern May 7–12, 1864* (Baton Rouge, Louisiana: Louisiana State University Press, 1997), 83–85.
48. For a full account of Sedgwick's death see, Winslow, *General John Sedgwick*, 173–174; See also Hyde, *Following the Greek Cross*, 192–193; G. Norton Galloway, "Death of Sedgwick," Philadelphia *Weekly Times*, March 1, 1884; G. Norton Galloway, "Death of the Gallant Sedgwick," Philadelphia *Weekly Times*, January 8, 1881 and January 15, 1881; Martin T. McMahon, "The Death of General John Sedgwick," *Battles and Leaders of the Civil War*, vol. 4, 175; Catton, *A Stillness at Appomattox*, 109; Rhea, *The Battles for Spotsylvania Court House*, 92–95. The Grant quote can be found in Horace Porter, *Campaigning with Grant* (New York: The Century Company, 1897), 90.
49. Winslow, *General John Sedgwick*, 175.
50. Keiser, Diary, May 9, 1864, Keiser Papers, HCWRTC, HEC.
51. Treichler, Memoir, RTC, 54–55.
52. Catton, *Grant Takes Command*, 219.
53. A. D. Slade, *That Sterling Soldier: The Life of David A. Russell* (Dayton, Ohio: Morningside, 1995); Warner, *Generals in Blue*, 416–417; Cullum, *Biographical Register of the Officers and Graduates of the U.S. Military Academy*, 3rd ed., vol. II, 1891; Stevens, *Three Years in the Sixth Corps*, 284; Charles S. Wainwright, *A Diary of Battle: The Personal Journals of Colonel Charles S. Wainwright, 1861–1865*, ed. by Allan Nevins (New York: Harcourt, Brace & World, 1962), 465.
54. Nelson V. Hutchinson, *History of the Seventh Massachusetts Volunteer Infantry* (Taunton, Massachusetts: Regimental Association, 1890), 22–23.
55. A. B. Hutchinson, "History of the 49th Pennsylvania," *Bellefonte Republican*, July 14, 1869; G. Norton Galloway, *The Ninety-fifth Pennsylvania Volunteers ("Gosline's Zouaves") in the Sixth Corps* (Philadelphia, Penna.: Collins, 1884), 36.
56. Catton, *Grant Takes Command*, 220; Rhea, *The Battles for Spotsylvania Court House*, 161; Foote, *Civil War*, vol. III, 204.
57. Andrew A. Humphreys, *The Virginia Campaigns*

of '64 and '65: The Army of the Potomac and The Army of the James (New York: Charles Scribner's Sons, 1883), 117.

58. Herman Hattaway and Archer Jones, *How the North Won: A Military History of the Civil War* (Urbana, Illinois: University of Illinois Press, 1983), 559; Catton, *Grant Takes Command*, 220; Stephen E. Ambrose, *Upton and the Army*, 29; Marion D. Joyce, "Tactical Lessons of the Civil War," *Civil War Times Illustrated* (February 1964), vol. 2, no. 10, 42–46; John K. Mahon, "Civil War Infantry Assault Tactics," *Military Affairs* (Summer 1961), vol. 25, no. 2, 57–68; Catton, *A Stillness at Appomattox*, 112.

59. Foote, *Civil War*, vol. III, 208; Stephen E. Ambrose, "A Theorist Fights: Emory Upton in the Civil War," *Civil War History* (December 1963), vol. 9, no. 4, 350–353.

60. Ambrose, *Upton and the Army*, 29–31. See also Rhea, *The Battles for Spotsylvania Court House*, 161–163. See also Gregory A. Mertz, "Upton's Attack: And the Defense of Doles' Salient, Spotsylvania Court House, Va., May 10, 1864," *Blue & Gray Magazine* (August 2001), vol. XVIII, no. 6, 10.

61. Best, *History of the 121st New York State Infantry*, 135–136.

62. Jeff Wert, "Spotsylvania: Charge on the Mule Shoe," *Civil War Times*, vol. XXII, no. 2 (April 1983), 14–15; Foote, *Civil War* vol. III, 208; Catton, *A Stillness at Appomattox*, 113; Rhea, *The Battles for Spotsylvania Court House*, 163–167.

63. *Official Records*, Vol. XXXVI, Part I, 667.

64. Bicknell, *History of the Fifth Regiment Maine Volunteers*, 313; Hartwell, Diary, May 10, 1864, in *To My Beloved Wife and Boy at Home*, 226.

65. *Official Records*, Vol. XXXVI, Part I, 667.

66. Keiser, Diary, May 10, 1864, Keiser Papers, HCWRTC, HEC.

67. Hartwell, *To My Beloved Wife and Boy at Home*, 226; F. W. Foot to Mother, Letter, May 29, 1864, unknown newspaper in http://dmna.ny.gov/historic/reghist/civil/infantry/121stInf/121stCWN4.pdf.

68. "The Charge of the 10th of May," Portland *Transcript*, June 11, 1864.

69. Treichler, Memoir, RTC, 59.

70. White, *Contributions to a History of the Richmond Howitzer Battalion*, 243. See also "Third Company Richmond Howitzers—The Battery Captured—Heavy Losses," Richmond *Daily Dispatch*, May 16, 1864.

71. Thomas, *History of the Doles-Cook Brigade*, see page 478, 44th Georgia history, which states, "some two hundred fifty yards away."

72. *Ibid.*, 77, 4th Georgia history which states, "about two hundred yards in front."

73. For additional estimates concerning the distance between the pine forest and the Confederate position see: Stevens, *Three Years in the Sixth Corps*, 331; Bicknell, *History of the Fifth Regiment Maine Volunteers*, 313; Robert S. Westbrook, *History of the 49th Pennsylvania Volunteers* (Altoona, Penna.: Altoona Times, 1898), 189; See also "Fifth Maine Regiment," in *Maine at Gettysburg* (Portland, Maine, 1898), 381, which states that the field was "not more than 10 rods in width,"; Col. Clark S. Edwards, "War Reminiscences," No. 19, unknown Bethel, Maine newspaper 1897, states, "Between us and the enemy was an open field of fourteen or fifteen rods in width"; Mertz, "Upton's Attack," *Blue & Gray,* accepts 200 yards as the distance on p. 11, but reduces the distance to 150 yards on p. 12; Matter, also accepts the distance as 200 yards, see his, *If It Takes All Summer*, 156.

74. Rhea, *The Battles for Spotsylvania Court House*, 169–170. See also William D. Matter, *If It Takes All Summer: The Battle of Spotsylvania* (Chapel Hill, North Carolina: University of North Carolina Press, 1988), 156–169; W. S. Dunlop, *Lee's Sharpshooters; or, The Forefront of Battle* (Little Rock, Arkansas: Tunnah & Pittard, 1899), 444; William J. Seymour, *The Civil War Memoirs of Captain William J. Seymour: Reminiscences of a Louisiana Tiger* (Baton Rouge, Louisiana: Louisiana State University Press, 1991), 119–120; Edward Porter Alexander, *Fighting for the Confederacy: The Personal Recollections of General Edward Porter Alexander*, ed. by Gary W. Gallagher (Chapel Hill, North Carolina: University of North Carolina Press, 1989), 372.

75. Irby Scott to Loved Ones at Home, Letter, June 8, 1864, in *Lee and Jackson's Bloody Twelfth*, ed. by Johnnie P. Pearson (Knoxville, Tennessee: University of Tennessee Press, 2010), 165; Asbury H. Jackson to Mother, Letter, May 11, 1864, Edward Harden Papers, Perkins Library, Duke University; Gerald J. Smith, "The Hard-Fighting 44th Georgia Suffered Some of the Heaviest Losses of any Regiment in the Civil War," *America's Civil War* (March 1996), vol. 9, no. 1, 24; "The Fourth Ga. Regt.—Albany Guards," Albany *Patriot*, May 26, 1864, states that the 4th Georgia went in to the Battle of the Wilderness with a strength of 400 men and sustained 26 killed and 102 wounded. See also Scott T. Glass, "An Analysis of Unit Cohesion in the 44th Georgia Infantry," Thesis (Fort Leavenworth, Kansas, 1999); and Richard O. Perry, "Twelfth Regiment, Georgia Volunteer Infantry in the Civil War," Thesis (Athens, Georgia: University of Georgia, 1967); A recent study of Confederate strength during the Overland Campaign concluded that Doles' brigade numbered 1,365. See Alfred C. Young, *Lee's Army During the Overland Campaign: A Numerical Study* (Baton Rouge, Louisiana: Louisiana State University Press, 2013), 110.

76. Stevens, *Three Years in the Sixth Corps*, 329.

77. Luckenbill, Diary, May 10, 1864, WDC.

78. Keiser, Diary, May 10, 1864, Keiser Papers, HCWRTC, HEC.

79. *Medical and Surgical History of the War of the Rebellion*, Vol. III, 615.

80. *Ibid.*

Chapter XII

1. Mertz, "Upton's Attack," *Blue & Gray*, 10–11. See also Earl J. Hess, *Civil War Infantry Tactics: Training, Combat, and Small-Unit Effectiveness* (Baton Rouge, Louisiana: Louisiana State University Press, 2015), 182–183 and Neal Meier, "Civil War Tactics: The Last Hurrah,"" *Blue & Gray Magazine* (February 1998), vol. XV, no. 3, 22–24, 26–30.

2. *Official Records*, Vol. XI, Part. I, 448–449.

3. *Ibid.*, Vol. XI, Part I, 450 for the Union casualties and *Ibid.*, Vol. XI, Part I, 569 for the Confederate casualties.

4. *Official Records*, Vol. XIX, Part I, 389.

5. *Ibid.*, 396.

6. Confederate casualties can be found in *Official Records*, Vol. XIX, Part I, 843 and the Union casualties are enumerated in *Official Records*, Vol. XIX, Part I, 843.

7. Mackowski and White, *Chancellorsville's Forgotten Front*, 183–224; Parsons, *The Union Sixth Army Corps in the Chancellorsville Campaign*, 65–93.

8. *Official Records*, Vol. XXV, Part I, 599.

9. George G. Benedict, *Vermont in the Civil War: A History of the Past Taken by the Vermont Soldiers and Sailors in the War for the Union 1861–5* (Burlington, Vermont: Free Press Association, 1886), vol. 1, 362.

10. A. T. Brewer, *History of the Sixty-first Pennsylvania Volunteers 1861–1865* (Pittsburgh, Penna., Art Engraving & Printing Company, 1911), 54.

11. John Ahern to Editor, Letter, [May 1863], Albany *Evening Journal,* [May, 1863] at http://dmna.ny.gov/historic/reghist/civil/infantry/43rdInf/43rdInfCWN2.pdf

12. E. B. Quiner, *The Military History of Wisconsin* (Chicago, Illinois: Clarke & Company, 1866), 514.

13. Charles A. Clark, *Campaigning With the Sixth Maine* (Des Moines, Iowa: Kenyon Press, 1897), 33.

14. Quiner, *The Military History of Wisconsin,* 514.

15. Clark, *Campaigning With the Sixth Maine,* 33.

16. Union casualties can be found at *Official Records,* Vol. XXV, Part I, 190–191 while Confederate casualties are listed at *Official Records,* Vol. XXV, Part I, 806–807.

17. Clark, *Campaigning With the Sixth Maine,* 34.

18. *Official Records,* Vol. XXIX, Part I, 585–586.

19. *Ibid.,* 585.

20. *Ibid.,* 586.

21. *Ibid.,* 592–593; Morse, Diary, November 7, 1863, "The "Rebellion Record,"" 71; Quiner, *The Military History of Wisconsin,* 518; Clark, *Campaigning With the Sixth Maine,* 46.

22. *Official Records,* Vol. XXIX, Part I, 588.

23. *Ibid.,* 592.

24. *Ibid.,* 593.

25. Cleveland Campbell to Editor, Letter, November 20, 1863, *Cherry Valley Gazette* [November 1863] in http://dmna.ny.gov/historic/reghist/civil/infantry/121stInf/121stCWN4.pdf.

26. *Official Records,* Vol. XXIX, Part I, 586.

27. *Ibid.,* 589.

28. For casualties see *Ibid.,* 589–590.

29. Mertz, "Upton's Attack," *Blue & Gray,* 11.

30. Michie, *The Life and letters of Emory Upton,* xvi.

31. Rhea, *The Battles for Spotsylvania Court House,* 168; Wert, "Spotsylvania: Charge on the Mule Shoe," *CWT,* 15; Foote, *Civil War,* vol. III, 208; Ambrose, *Upton and the Army,* 30–31.

32. For unit strength see the following: 5th Maine (200), Bicknell, *History of the Fifth Regiment Maine Volunteers,* 315 and *Maine at Gettysburg,* 381; 96th Pennsylvania (420), Edward Henry to Dear Sister, Letter, June 1, 1864, HEC; 121st New York (420), J.H. Heath to Editor, Letter, May 20, 1864, Herkimer *County Journal,* June 2, 1864; 49th Pennsylvania (474), Westbrook, *History of the 49th Pennsylvania Volunteers,* 197; 6th Maine (195), *Maine at Gettysburg,* 427; 77th New York (400), "The 77th—List of Killed and Wounded," *The Saratogian,* May 19, 1864; 5th Wisconsin (351), "From the Fifth Regiment—Its part in the Late Battles—List of Casualties," Letter, May 11, 1864, Wisconsin *State Journal,* May 19, 1874; 2nd Vermont (452), George G. Benedict, *Vermont in the Civil War,* v.1, 115. 800 present for duty May 1, 1864 minus 348 Wilderness casualties = 452; 5th Vermont (255), Benedict, *Vermont in the Civil War,* v.1, 196–197. 500 as of May 1, 1864 minus 245 Wilderness casualties = 255; 6th Vermont (355), Benedict, *Vermont in the Civil War,* v.1, 223. 550 as of May 1, 1864 minus 195 Wilderness casualties = 355. It should be noted, too, four companies of the 49th Pennsylvania (A, D, E and G) were part of the skirmish operation. Three companies of the 96th Pennsylvania (H, I and K) were assigned

as skirmishers. P. R. Simmons, 5th Maine, "The Charge of the 10th of May," Portland *Transcript,* June 11, 1864, states that Upton's strike force numbered 4,000.

33. Upton to Brother, Letter, November 6, 1863, in Michie, *The Life and Letters of Emory Upton,* 79–80.

34. *Official Records,* Vol. XXXVI, Part I, 667; Bicknell, *History of the Fifth Regiment Maine Volunteers,* 314; Best, *History of the 121st New York State Infantry,* 128–129.

35. Keiser, Diary, May 10, 1864, Keiser Papers, HCWRTC, HEC.

36. Bicknell, *History of the Fifth Regiment Maine Volunteers,* 315.

37. Henry to Dear Sister, Letter, June 9, 1864, Henry Papers, C. W. Misc. Coll., HEC.

38. Levi Huber to Editor, Letter, May 16, 1864, in *Miners' Journal,* May 28, 1864.

39. J. H. Heath to Editor, Letter, May 20, 1864, in Herkimer *County Journal,* June 2, 1864; Cronkite, "Otsego in the Rebellion: The 121st Regiment," *History of Otsego County, New York,* 75.

40. Rhea, *The Battles for Spotsylvania Court House,* 168–169.

41. James A. Walker, ""The Bloody Angle": The Confederate Disaster at Spotsylvania Court-House, May 12, 1864," by which the "Stonewall Brigade" was annihilated," *Southern Historical Society Papers,* Vol. 21, 234; *Official Records,* Vol. XXXVI, Part I, 1072.

42. Holmes, *Touched With Fire,* 112.

43. Treichler, Memoir, RTC, 59.

44. Keiser, Diary, May 10, 1864, Keiser Papers, HCWRTC, HEC.

45. P. R. Simmons to Editor, "The Charge of the 10th of May," Portland *Transcript,* June 11, 1864.

46. *Official Records,* Vol. XXXVI, Part I, 667; Catton, *A Stillness at Appomattox,* 113; Foote, *Civil War,* vol. III, 208; Best, *History of the 121st New York State Infantry,* 128–130; Stevens, *Three Years in the Sixth Corps,* 331.

47. *Official Records,* Vol. XXXVI, Part I, 667. See also Keiser, Diary, May 10, 1864, Keiser Papers, HCWRTC, HEC; Luckenbill, Diary, May 10, 1864, WDC.

48. Foot to Mother, Letter, May 29, 1864, [unknown newspaper] in http://dmna.ny.gov/historic/reghist/civil/infantry/121stInf/121stCWN4.pdf.

49. Morse, "The 'Rebellion Record,'" 78.

50. Westbrook, *History of the 49th Pennsylvania Volunteers,* 191.

51. *Official Records,* Vol. XXXVI, Part I, 668.

52. *Ibid.,* 667–668.

53. Lyman, *Meade's Headquarters, 1863–1865,* 109.

54. Holmes, *Touched With Fire,* 112.

55. The historians who have examined the charge have generally accepted the time frame Upton puts forth in his report. Mertz, "Upton's Attack," *Blue & Gray,* 23 and Matter, *If It Takes All Summer,* 162, interpreted Upton's report to mean that the advance started forward at 6:10 PM.

56. Rhea, *The Battles for Spotsylvania Court House,* 169, accepts the time as cited by Oliver Wendell Holmes, Jr., 6:35 p.m. It is my belief that Holmes's account is most precise. He served on Gen. Wright's VI Corps staff.

57. Miller, Diary, May 10, 1864, GKC; Keiser, Diary, May 10, 1864, Keiser Papers, HCWRTC, HEC.

58. Treichler, Memoir, RTC, 60.

59. Luckenbill, Diary, May 10, 1864, WDC.

60. Best, *History of the 121st New York State Infantry,* 129.

61. William S. White, *Contributions to a History of*

the Richmond Howitzer Battalion (Richmond, Virginia: Carlton McCarthy & Company, 1883), 244.

62. Luckenbill, Diary, May 10, 1864, WDC.

63. Morse, Diary, May 10, 1864, "The "Rebellion Record,'" 78.

64. Keiser, Diary, May 10, 1864, HCWRTC, HEC.

65. Morse, Diary, May 10, 1864, "The 'Rebellion Record,'" 78.

66. F. W. Foot [121st New York] to his Mother, unknown newspaper, in http://dmna.ny.gov/historic/reghist/civil/infantry/121stInf/121stCWN4.pdf

67. *Ibid.*

68. Morse, "The "Rebellion Record,'" 78.

69. "The Charge of the 10th of May," Portland *Transcript*, June 11, 1864.

70. Keiser, Diary, May 10, 1864, Keiser Papers, HCWRTC, HEC.

71. Roberts, "The Wilderness and Spottsylvania, May 4–12, 1864," 69.

72. *Official Records*, Vol. XXXVI, Part 1, 668.

73. J.[ohn] M. Lovejoy to Editor, Letter, "Spottsylvania: A Sketch of the Grand Charge of 12 Regiments on the 'Angle,'" *National Tribune*, May 26, 1887.

74. *Official Records*, Vol. XXXVI, Part I, 668.

75. Keiser, Diary, May 10, 1864, Keiser Papers, HCWRTC, HEC.

76. Hartwell, *To My Beloved Wife and Boy at Home*, 227.

77. *Official Records*, Vol. XXXVI, Part I, 668.

78. Keiser, Diary, May 10, 1864, Keiser Papers, HCWRTC, HEC.

79. Thomas, *History of the Doles-Cook Brigade*, 478–479.

80. J.A.H. to Dear _____, Letter, May 11, 1864, *The Confederate Union*, May 31, 1864.

81. Scott to Loved Ones at Home, Letter, June 8, 1864, in *Lee and Jackson's Bloody Twelfth*, 165.

82. Levi J. Smith, Diary, May 10, 1864, United Daughters of the Confederacy Collection, Georgia Department of Archives and History, Atlanta, Georgia.

83. Treichler, Memoir, RTC, 60.

84. *Official Records*, Vol. XXXVI, Part I, 668.

85. Asbury Jackson to Mother, Letter, May 11, 1864, Edward Harden Papers, Perkins Library, Duke University.

86. Keiser, Diary, May 10, 1864, Keiser Papers, HCWRTC, HEC.

87. Luckenbill, Diary, May 10, 1864, WDC.

88. Ambrose, *Upton and the Army*, 32–33; Foote, *Civil War*, vol. III, 209; Wert, "Spotsylvania: Charge on the Mule Shoe," *CWT*, 20–21.

89. Morse, "The "Rebellion Record,'" 78.

90. White, *Contributions to a History of the Richmond Howitzer Battalion*, 245.

91. Hutchinson, "History of the 49th Pennsylvania," Chapter XVI, Bellefonte *Republican*, August 25, 1869.

92. White, *Contributions to a History of the Richmond Howitzer Battalion*, 244–245.

93. Morse, "The "Rebellion Record,'" 78.

94. *Official Records*, Supplement, vol. 6, 679.

95. Keiser, Diary, May 10, 1864, Keiser Papers, HCWRTC, HEC.

96. Luckenbill, Diary, May 10, 1864, WDC.

97. *Official Records*, Vol. XXXVI, Part I, 668.

98. Luckenbill, Diary, May 10, 1864, WDC.

99. Keiser, Diary, May 10, 1864, Keiser Papers, HCWRTC, HEC.

100. Oestreich, Diary, HSSC, 47.

101. Best, *History of the 121st New York State Infantry*, 132.

102. *Official Records*, Vol. XXXVI, Part I, 668; Wert, "Spotsylvania: Charge on the Mule Shoe," *CWT*, 20–21; Ambrose, *Upton and the Army*, 33.

103. Keiser, Diary, May 10, 1864, Keiser Papers, HCWRTC, HEC.

104. John H. Worsham, *One of Jackson's Foot Cavalry* (New York: Neale Publishing, 1912), 211.

105. *Histories of the Several Regiments and Battalions from North Carolina in the Great War 1861-'65*, ed. by Walter Clark (Raleigh, North Carolina: Nash Brothers, 1901), vol. 3, 47–48.

106. Rhea, *The Battles for Spotsylvania Court House*, 171.

107. *Histories of the Several Regiments and Battalions from North Carolina in the Great War 1861-'65*, vol. 3, 47.

108. John W. Roberts, "The Wilderness and Spottsylvania, May 4–12, 1864," ed. by Albert H. Roberts, *The Florida Historical Quarterly* (October 1932), vol. 11, no. 2, 69.

109. Levi Huber to Editor, Letter, May 16, 1864, *Miners' Journal*, May 28, 1864.

110. *Histories of the Several Regiments and Battalions from North Carolina in the Great War 1861-'65*, vol. 2, 242.

111. *Official Records*, Supplement, vol. 6, 679.

112. Scott to Loved Ones at Home, Letter, June 8, 1864, in *Lee and Jackson's Bloody Twelfth*, 165.

113. Jackson to Mother, Letter, May 11, 1864, Edward Harden Papers, Perkins Library, Duke University.

114. Smith, Diary, May 10, 1864, UDC Coll., GDAH.

115. J.A.H. to Dear _____, Letter, May 11, 1864, *The Confederate Union*, May 31, 1864.

116. *Official Records*, Vol. XXXVI, Part I, 668.

117. *Official Records*, Vol. XXXVI, Part I, 144, gives the casualty statistics relative to the 96th Pennsylvania and Upton's brigade.

118. The casualty totals in the *Official Records* differ slightly from the figures stated in the Pottsville *Miners' Journal*, May 28, 1864.

119. Henry W. Thomas, *History of the Doles-Cook Brigade Army of Northern Virginia, C.S.A.* (Atlanta, Georgia: Franklin Printing, 1903), 479.

120. Quoted in Catton, *Grant Takes Command*, 222; Ambrose, *Upton and the Army*, 33–34; Theodore Lyman, *Meade's Headquarters, 1863–1865: Letters of Colonel Theodore Lyman from the Wilderness to Appomattox*, ed. by George Agassiz (Boston, Mass.: Atlantic Monthly Press, 1922), 110.

121. Luman Harris Tenney, *War Diary of Luman Harris Tenney 1861–1865* (Cleveland, Ohio: Evangelical Publishing House, 1914), 115. In regard to Upton's assault on May 10 and especially to Hancock's grand assault two days later, Grant sent a telegram to Halleck on the late afternoon of May 12, 1864. "We have destroyed and captured one division (Johnson's), one brigade (Doles'), and one regiment entire of the enemy." *Official Records*, Vol. XXXVI, Part I, 4.

Chapter XIII

1. *Official Records*, Vol. XXXVI, Part I, 149.

2. William O. Stoddard, *Inside the White House in War Times* (New York: Charles L. Webster & Co., 1890), 178–179.

3. C. F. Atkinson, *Grant's Campaigns of 1864 and 1865: The Wilderness and Cold Harbor (May 8—June 3, 1864)* (London: Hugh Rees, 1908), 265.

4. Oliver Wendell Holmes. Jr., *Touched With Fire: Civil War Letters and Diary of Oliver Wendell Holmes, Jr.*, 1861–186, ed. by Mark De Wolfe Howe (New York: Fordham University Press), 113.

5. Wainwright, *Diary of Battle*, 363–364.

6. Lyman, *Meade's Headquarters, 1863–1865*, 109.

7. Treichler, Memoir, RTC, 60.

8. Holt, *A Surgeon's Civil War*, 186.

9. *Ibid.*, Vol. XXXVI, Part I, 144–145.

10. E. Saulsbury to Editor, Letter, May 29, 1864, "Casualties in Doles' Brigade," [Milledgeville, Ga.], *The Southern Recorder*, June 14, 1864.

11. Francis Boyle [32nd North Carolina], Diary, May 10, 1864, Southern Historical Collection, Uni. of North Carolina.

12. Marsena Patrick, *Inside Lincoln's Army*, ed. by David S. Sparks (New York: Thomas Yoseloff, 1964), 371. See also Holmes, *Touched with Fire*, 113, states there were 950 prisoners and Lyman, *Meade's Headquarters, 1863–1865*, 109, states that Upton "took 900 prisoners."

13. *Official Records*, Vol. XXXVI, Part I, 144–145.

14. C[lark] S. Edwards to Editor, Letter, May 29, 1864, Portland *Transcript*, June 25, 1864.W.H. Lessig to Editor, *Miners' Journal*, May 28, 1864.

15. J.H. Heath to Editor, Letter, May 20, 1864, *Little Falls Journal*, [unknown date] in http://dmna.ny.gov/historic/reghist/civil/infantry/121stInf/121stCWN4.pdf

16. *Official Records*, Vol. XXXVI, Part I, 144.

17. Upton to Sister, Letter, November 15, 1863, in Michie, *Life and Letters of Emory Upton*, 85–86.

18. Matter, *If It Takes All Summer*, 166; Earl J. Hess, *Trench Warfare Under Grant & Lee: Field Fortifications in the Overland Campaign* (Chapel Hill, North Carolina: University North Carolina Press, 2007), 54–58.

19. Catton, *Grant Takes Command*, 224; Catton, *A Stillness at Appomattox*, 124; Catton, *Grant Takes Command*, 227; Cullen, "Spotsylvania," *CWTI*, 9.

20. Best, *History of the 121st New York State Infantry*, 144.

21. Letter of Emory Upton quoted in G. Norton Galloway, "Capture of the Salient," Philadelphia *Weekly Times*, November 18, 1882.

22. Quoted in Foote, *Civil War*, vol. III, 210.

23. Letter of Upton to Galloway, quoted in Galloway, "Capture of the Salient," Philadelphia *Weekly Times*, November 18, 1882.

24. G. Norton Galloway, "Hand-to-Hand Fighting at Spotsylvania," *Battles and Leaders*, vol. IV, 171.

25. Bicknell, *History of the Fifth Regiment Maine Volunteers*, 322; James A. Davis, "Music and Gallantry in Combat During the American Civil War," *American Music* (Summer 2010), vol. 28, no. 2, 141–172.

26. Keiser, Diary, May 12, 1864, Keiser Papers, HCWRTC, HEC.

27. *Official Records*, Vol. XXXVI, Part I, 669.

28. Galloway, "Hand-to-Hand," *Battles and Leaders*, vol. IV, 171.

29. *Official Records*, Vol. XXXVI, Part I, 669.

30. Keiser, Diary, May 12, 1864, Keiser Papers, HCWRTC, HEC.

31. Thomas T. Roche [16th Mississippi], "The Bloody Angle: A Participant's Description of the Fiercest Combat of the War," Philadelphia *Weekly Times*, September 3, 1881.

32. Bicknell, *History of the Fifth Regiment Maine Volunteers*, 318.

33. Best, *History of the 121st New York State Infantry*, 144.

34. Luckenbill, Diary, May 12, 1864, WDC.

35. *Official Records*, Vol. XXXVI, Part I, 1092.

36. Roche [16th Mississippi], "The Bloody Angle." For another graphic account of the battle written by a soldier in the 16th Mississippi see, "Gen. N. M. Harris' Brigade," Meridian *Daily Clarion*, June 13, 1864. Casualties listed by regiment and broken down by company for Harris' Brigade can be found in the Meridian *Daily Clarion*, June 13, 1864.

37. J. R. McMahon [1st South Carolina] to Editor, Letter, May 14, 1864, Columbia *Guardian,* May 26, 1864.

38. Luckenbill, Diary, May 12, 1864, WDC.

39. Keiser, Diary, May 12, 1864, Keiser Papers, HCWRTC, HEC.

40. Treichler, Memoir, RTC, 53.

41. Oestreich, Diary, HSSC, 48.

42. Treichler, Memoir, RTC, 53. Galloway, "Hand-to-Hand," *Battles and Leaders*, vol. IV, 171 also mentions using pack mules to haul ammunition.

43. Keiser, Diary, May 12, 1864, Keiser Papers, HCWRTC, HEC.

44. Morse, "The "Rebellion Record,"" 80.

45. Grant quoted in Humphreys, *The Virginia Campaign of '64 and '65*, 99–100.

46. Luckenbill, Diary, May 12, 1864, WDC.

47. Keiser, Diary, May 12, 1864, Keiser Papers, HCWRTC, HEC.

48. Treichler, Memoir, RTC, 53; For these surrender incidents, see also Robert K. Krick, "An Insurmountable Barrier Between the Army and Ruin: The Confederate Experience at Spotsylvania's Bloody Angle," in *The Spotsylvania Campaign*, ed. by Gary W. Gallagher (Chapel Hill, North Carolina: University North Carolina Press, 1998), 106–108.

49. Galloway, "Hand-to-Hand," *Battles and Leaders*, vol. IV, 171–172; Catton, *A Stillness at Appomattox*, 125–126.

50. Emory Upton to G. Norton Galloway, Letter, quoted in Galloway, "Capture of the Salient," Philadelphia *Weekly Times*, November 18, 1882.

51. Galloway, "Hand-to-Hand," *Battles and Leaders*, vol. IV, 174.

52. Hyde, *Following the Greek Cross*, 200–201.

53. Levi Huber to Editor, Letter, May 16, 1864, *Miners' Journal*, May 28, 1864.

54. Miller, Diary, May 12, 1864, GKC.

55. Luckenbill, Diary, May 12, 1864, WDC.

56. Heath to Editor, Letter, May 20, 1864, Little Falls *Journal*, [unknown date], in http://dmna.ny.gov/historic/reghist/civil/infantry/121stInf/121stCWN4.pdf

57. "From the Fifth Regiment—Its part in the Late Battles—List of Casualties," Letter, May 11, 1864, Wisconsin *State Journal*, May 19, 1874.

58. Morse, "The "Rebellion Record,"" 80.

59. Luckenbill, Diary, May 12, 1864, WDC.

60. Keiser, Diary, May 13, 1864, Keiser Papers, HCWRTC, HEC, offers a fascinating description of the burial procedures. See also Galloway, "Hand-to-Hand," *Battles and Leaders*, vol. IV, 174.

61. Oestreich, Diary, HSSC, 48.

62. Humphreys, *The Virginia Campaign of '64 and '65*, 100.

63. Luckenbill, Diary, May 13, 1864, WDC.

64. Keiser, Diary, May 13, 1864, Keiser Papers, HCWRTC, HEC.

65. Wilbur Fisk to Editor, Letter, May 9, 1864, *Green*

Mountain Freeman, May 31, 1864, page 2. The letter is also printed in Fisk, *Anti-Rebel: The Civil War Letters of Wilbur Fisk,* 221.

66. *Ibid.*

67. Holt to Wife, Letter, May 13, 1864, *A Surgeon's Civil War,* 188.

68. P.R. Simmons, "Terrible Effects of Musketry," Portland *Transcript,* June 11, 1864.

69. *Official Records,* Vol. XXXVI, Part I, 670.

70. Keiser, Diary, May 13, 1864, Keiser Papers, HCWRTC, HEC.

71. For accounts of the engagement at Myers Hill see: Gordon C. Rhea, *To the North Anna River: Grant and Lee May 13–25, 1864* (Baton Rouge, Louisiana: Louisiana State University Press, 2000), 78–87 and Mackowski and White, "Maneuver and Mud," *Blue & Gray Magazine,* 21.

72. *Official Records,* Vol. XXXVI, Part I, 670; Ambrose, *Upton and the Army,* 35; Keiser, Diary, May 14, 1864, Keiser Papers, HCWRTC, HEC.

73. *Official Records,* Vol. XXXVI, Part I, 670.

74. Best, *History of the 121st New York State Infantry,* 150; Rhea, *To the North Anna River,* 78–87.

75. *Official Records,* Vol. XXXVI, Part I, 670.

76. Luckenbill, Diary, June 1, 1864, WDC.

77. Unknown Soldier to Editor, Letter, May 18, 1864, Macon *Daily Telegraph,* May 31, 1864.

78. James M. Folsom, *Heroes and Martyrs of Georgia: Georgia's Record in the Revolution of 1861* (Georgia, 1864), 79.

79. Oestreich, Diary, HSSC, 49.

80. Best, *History of the 121st New York State Infantry,* 150.

81. *Official Records,* Vol. XXXVI, Part I, 670. For a tactical map of the Myers Hill engagement see Chris Mackowski and Kristopher D. White, "Maneuver and Mud: The Battle of Spotsylvania C. H. May 13–20, 1864," *Blue & Gray Magazine* vol. XXVII, no. 6 (2011), 15.

82. Bicknell, *History of the Fifth Regiment Maine Volunteers,* 323.

83. Best, *History of the 121st New York State Infantry,* 150; Rhea, *To the North Anna River,* 78–87.

84. Keiser, Diary, May 15, 1864, Keiser Papers, HCWRTC, HEC.

85. Holt, Diary, May 14, 1864, *A Surgeon's Civil War,* 189.

86. Catton, *A Stillness at Appomattox,* 131–132.

Chapter XIV

1. Luckenbill, Diary, May 25, 1864, WDC. See also Keiser, Diary, May 25, 1864, Keiser Papers, HCWRTC, HEC.

2. Best, *History of the 121st New York State Infantry,* 152–153.

3. *Official Records,* Vol. XXXVI, Part I, 670; Joseph P. Cullen, "A Detour on the Road to Richmond," *Civil War Times Illustrated,* vol. III no. 10 (February 1965), 16–23; For further details concerning VI Corps operations at North Anna River see Rhea, *To the North Anna River* and J. Michael Miller, "The North Anna Campaign," *Blue & Gray Magazine* (2015), vol. XXXI, no. 6.

4. Keiser, Diary, May 30, 1864, Keiser Papers, HCWRTC, HEC.

5. Reed to [Family], Letter, May 31, 1864, Reed Papers, IHS.

6. Keiser, Diary, June 1, 1864, Keiser Papers, HCWRTC, HEC.

7. *Ibid.* recorded 2 P.M.; Luckenbill, Diary, June 1, 1864, WDC, stated 2 P.M.; Isaac E. Severn, Diary, June 1, 1864, Severn Papers, HCWRTC, HEC, Captain Company C, 2 P.M.; *Official Records,* Vol. XXXVI, Part I, 671; Upton in his report stated that the second brigade reached Cold Harbor at 11 A.M.; [Alfred G. Bliss] to editor, Letter, June 6, 1864, Winsted Connecticut *Herald,* June 10, 1864, wrote "Cool Arbor about 11 A.M."; Hartwell, *To My Beloved Wife and Boy at Home,* 235, stated noon; Lewis Bissell to Father, Letter, June 2, 1864 in *The Civil War Letters of Lewis Bissell,* ed. by Mark Olcott and David Lear (Washington, D.C.: Field School Educational Press, 1981), 245, recorded 2 p.m.

8. Keiser, Diary, June 1, 1864, Keiser Papers, HCWRTC, HEC.

9. Catton, *A Stillness at Appomattox,* 149–152; Gordon C. Rhea, *Cold Harbor: Grant and Lee May 26—June 3, 1864* (Baton Rouge, Louisiana: Louisiana State University Press, 2002), 238–243. See also Louis J. Baltz, *The Battle of Cold Harbor 27—June 13, 1864* (Lynchburg, Virginia: H. E. Howard, 1994), 86–91; Ernest B. Furgurson, *Not War But Murder: Cold Harbor 1864* (New York: Alfred A. Knopf, 2000), 99–106; Ambrose, *Upton and the Army,* 36; John Niven, *Connecticut for the Union* (New Haven, Conn.: Yale University Press, 1965), 249: Keiser, Diary, June 1, 1864, Keiser Papers, HCWRTC, HEC.

10. Keiser, Diary, June 1, 1864, Keiser Papers, HCWRTC, HEC.

11. Theodore F. Vaill, *History of the Second Connecticut Volunteer Heavy Artillery* (Winsted, Conn.: Winsted Printing Company, 1868), 62.

12. *Ibid.,* 66; Richard W. Smith, *The Old Nineteenth: The Story of the Second Connecticut Heavy Artillery in the Civil War* (Lincoln, Nebraska: iUniverse, 2007), 122–131. Niven, *Connecticut for the Union,* 249–251;

13. Luckenbill, Diary, June 1, 1864, WDC.

14. Keiser, Diary, June 1, 1864, Keiser Papers, HCWRTC, HEC.

15. Boyle to Filbert, Letter, June 5, 1864, Filbert Papers, HCWRTC, HEC.

16. Keiser, Diary, June 1, 1864, Keiser Papers, HCWRTC, HEC.

17. Best, *History of the 121st New York State Infantry,* 155.

18. Martin T. McMahon, "Cold Harbor," *Battles and Leaders,* vol. 4, 218–219.

19. Quoted in Catton, *Grant Takes Command,* 260.

20. Best, *History of the 121st New York State Infantry,* 157.

21. Foote, *Civil War,* vol. III, 286–287; Catton, *A Stillness at Appomattox,* 157–160.

22. Luckenbill, Diary, June 3, 1864, WDC.

23. Best, *History of the 121st New York State Infantry,* 157–158.

24. Luckenbill, Diary, June 3, 1864, WDC.

25. Keiser, Diary, June 3, 1864, Keiser Papers, HCWRTC, HEC.

26. For casualties see, Wallace, *Memorial of the Patriotism of Schuylkill County,* 351.

27. *Official Records,* Vol. XXXVI, Part I, 671.

28. Hyde, *Following the Greek Cross,* 214.

29. John Van Hollen to Filbert, Letter, June 5, 1864, Filbert Papers, HCWRTC, HEC.

30. Holt to Wife, Letter, June 10, 1864, *A Surgeon's Civil War,* 201.

31. Best, *History of the 121st New York State Infantry,* 158–159.

32. Keiser, Diary, June 8, 1864, Keiser Papers, HCWRTC, HEC.

33. The 5th Maine's term of service expired June 22, 1864.

34. Henry to his sister, Letter, June 9, 1864, Henry Papers, HEC.

35. Best, *History of the 121st New York State Infantry*, 162–163; For a brief examination of Butler's failure to capture Petersburg June 8–9 see, Edward G. Longacre, "The Petersburg Follies," *Civil War Times Illustrated*, vol. XVIII, no. 9 (January 1980), 4–9, 34–41.

36. Catton, *Grant Takes Command*, 296; Pottsville *Miners' Journal*, July 2, 1864; David F. Cross, *A Melancholy Affair at the Weldon Railroad* (Shippensburg, Pennsylvania: White Mane, 2003); Edwin C. Bearss and Bryce A. Suderow, *The Petersburg Campaign: The Eastern Front Battles June—August 1864* (El Dorado, California: Savas Beatie, 2012), 132–199.

37. Faust to his Mother, July 3, 1864, Faust Papers, HCWRTC, HEC.

38. Catton, *A Stillness at Appomattox*, 257–258; Catton, *Grant Takes Command*, 311.

39. Quoted in Cilella, *Upton's Regulars*, 325.

40. *Ibid.*

41. *Ibid.*

42. John Ingraham to Brother, Letter, July 11, 1864, in *John J. Ingraham's Civil War Letters 1862–65* (Dolgeville, New York: Dolgeville-Manheim Historical Society, 1990).

43. Stevens, *Three Years in the Sixth Corps*, 372.

44. Best, *History of the 121st New York State Infantry*, 170.

45. *Ibid.*

46. Stevens, *Three Years in the Sixth Corps*, 373–374; Catton, *A Stillness at Appomattox*, 64–266.

47. Quoted in Catton, *A Stillness at Appomattox*, 267.

48. Stevens, *Three Years in the Sixth Corps*, 384.

49. *Official Records*, Vol. XXXVII, Part I, 271; *Ibid.*, Vol. XXXVII, Part II, 374, 408.

50. Catton, *Grant Takes Command*, 360; Catton, *Never Call Retreat*, 389; Catton, *A Stillness at Appomattox*, 295; Keiser, Diary, August 21, 1864, Keiser Papers, HCWRTC, HEC. It is possible that the skirmish at Summit Point, August 21, 1864, was the last time in battle line formation for the Schuylkill Countians.

51. Faust to his Mother, Letter, September 14, 1864, Faust Papers, HCWRTC, HEC.

52. Catton, *A Stillness at Appomattox*, 296–297; Ambrose, *Upton and the Army*, 40.

53. *Pennsylvania at Gettysburg*, vol. I, 517.

54. Wallace, *Memorial of the Patriotism of Schuylkill County*, 370. Keiser, Diary, September 22, 1864, Keiser Papers, HCWRTC, HEC.

55. "Spirited Reception of the Veteran Ninety-sixth Regiment," *Miners' Journal*, October 1, 1864.

56. Wallace, *Memorial of the Patriotism of Schuylkill County*, 370.

57. Hyde, *Following The Greek Cross*, 238;.Catton, *A Stillness at Appomattox*, 300; Bates, *Pennsylvania Volunteers*, vol. III, 389; Keiser, Diary, September 22, 1864, Keiser Papers, HCWRTC, HEC; Faust, *Historical Times Illustrated Encyclopedia of the Civil War*, 260; Foote, *Civil War*, vol. III, 563; Jeffry D. Wert, *From Winchester to Cedar Creek: The Shenandoah Campaign of 1864* (Carlisle, Penna.: South Mountain Press., 1987), 143.

58. Vaill, *History of the Second Connecticut Volunteer Heavy Artillery*, 159.

59. Keiser, Diary, April 9, 1865, Keiser Papers, HCWRTC, HEC.

60. "Col. H.L. Cake Dead at Northumberland," Pottsville *Miners' Journal*, August 28, 1899; Schlegel, "Workingmen's Benevolent Association," *PH*, 249, 254, 258; *Biographical Directory of the American Congress*, 690; *Congressional Directory*, 40; *Congressional Globe*, 41st Cong., 2nd Session, 1870, vol. 42, pt. 3, 2757–2758.

61. Kelly, "Gen. Lessig, Once Social Lion Dead," Denver *Post*, July 19, 1910; "Gallant Soldier's Sorrows," Denver *Post*, October 28, 1903.

62. Bates, *Pennsylvania Volunteers*, vol. IV, 184–186; *Official Records*, Vol. XXI, 137; "Gen. Order No. 11," January 25, 1863, Severn Papers, HEC; Bates, *Pennsylvania Volunteers*, vol. IV, 186; Wilbur S. Nye, *Here Come the Rebels!* (Baton Rouge, La.: Louisiana State University Press, 1965), 286–295; Bates, *Pennsylvania Volunteers*, vol. IV, 1263–1266.

63. See Filbert's service file, RG94, Records of the Adjutant General's Office, NA; Biographical data concerning Peter Filbert provided by Mrs. E. Stuart Filbert; Thomas M. Vincent to the Govol. of Pa., May 24, 1869, RG19, Records of the Department of Military Affairs, 96th Pennsylvania Volunteers, PHMC.

64. "Booth's "Double": Jacob W. Haas," *Schuylkill County in the Civil War*, 111–112.

65. "The Survivors of the 96th," Pottsville *Miners' Journal*, September 14, 1886; "The 96th's Reunion," Pottsville *Miners' Journal*, September 15, 1886; Pottsville *Miners' Journal*, June 1, 1888; *Ibid.*, May 3, 1888; *Ibid.*, June 2, 1888; *Ibid.*, June 11, 1888 ; *Ibid.*, June 14, 1888; *Ibid.*, June 20, 1888.

66. Henry Royer, "Dedication of Monument 96th Regiment Infantry, June 21, 1888," in *Pennsylvania at Gettysburg*, vol. 1, 515–523; See also, Pottsville *Miners' Journal*, June 22, 1888.

67. Fox, *Regimental Losses in the American Civil War*, 122. For the 96th Pennsylvania see page 286.

68. For casualties see Wallace, *Memorial of the Patriotism of Schuylkill County*, 410–415; Boyle, "An Outline Sketch of the Ninety-Sixth Pennsylvania Volunteers," Philadelphia *Weekly Times*, July 17, 1886; Bates, *History of Pennsylvania Volunteers*, vol. III, 390–410.

69. Henry Royer, "Dedication of Monument 96th Regiment Infantry June 21, 1888," *Pennsylvania at Gettysburg*, vol. I, 517–518.

70. Grady McWhiney and Perry D. Jamieson, *Attack and Die: Civil War Military Tactics and the Southern Heritage* (Tuscaloosa, Alabama: University of Alabama Press, 1982), xv; See also John K Mahon, Civil War Infantry Assault Tactics," *Military Affairs*, vol. 25, no. 2 (Summer 1961), 57–68.

71. Earl J. Hess, *Civil War Infantry Tactics*, xii.

72. *Ibid.*

73. *Ibid.* See also Earl J. Hess, *The Rifle Musket in Civil War Combat: Reality and Myth* (Lawrence, Kansas: University of Kansas Press, 2008).

74. *Ibid.*

75. Brent Nosworthy, *The Bloody Crucible of Courage: Fighting Methods and Combat Experience of the Civil War* (New York: Carroll and Graf, 2003); Paddy Griffith, *Rally Once Again: Battle Tactics of the American Civil War* (Great Britain, 1989).

76. *Ibid.*, 592.

77. *Ibid.*, 607.

78. Conrad, "Proceedings and Speeches Made at Transfer of Battle Flags to The Historical Society of Schuylkill County, December 14, 1913," *PHSSC*, 22.

Bibliography

Manuscript Sources

DIARIES, LETTERS AND MEMOIRS

Augustine, James. Letter. December 5, 1861. Augustine Papers. William Kerman Collection, Harrisburg Civil War Round Table Collection, United States Army Heritage & Education Center, Carlisle, PA.

Boland, Francis, and Patrick McGlenn. Letters. November 1861—September 1863. Manuscript Collection, Historical Society of Schuylkill County, in the John Brislin Papers. Original manuscript letters, most of which were written by Francis Boland. Typescript copies of these letters can also be found in the Harrisburg Civil War Round Table Collection, United States Army Heritage & Education Center, Carlisle Barracks, PA.

Faust, Daniel. Letters. September 1862—September 1864. Photocopies of the original manuscript letters. Harrisburg Civil War Round Table Collection, United States Army Heritage & Education Center, Carlisle Barracks, PA. See also Faust Family Correspondence. Grand Valley State University, Allendale, MI. Original manuscript letters in the Civil War and Slavery Collection.

Fernsler, John., Diary. November 13, 1861—February 25, 1863. Original manuscript pocket diary in leather case. Collection of Mrs. Marion Fernsler, Pottsville, PA.

Filbert, Peter A., Diary and Letters. September, 1861— December 30, 1862. Collection of Mrs. Mary Stuart Filbert, Auburn, PA. A handwritten transcription of this diary and photocopies of the original manuscript letters are in the collection of the United States Army Heritage and Education Center, Carlisle Barracks, PA. Harrisburg Civil War Round Table Collection.

Foltz, George W. Letters. October 1862—May 1864. Typescript copies of manuscript letters. Gettysburg National Military Park, Gettysburg, PA. Gregory Coco Collection.

Gery, Evan. Diary. January 1863—May 1864. Gery's 1863 diary published, with annotations, in the Hamburg Pennsylvania *Item*, 1942. Typescript copy of 1864 diary January—June courtesy of Edward Reinsel, Missoula, MT.

Haas, Jacob W., Diary and Letters. March, 1862—July 16, 1863. Collection of Mr. James F. Haas, Harrisburg, PA. Typescript excerpts of this diary can be found in the manuscript holdings of the United States Army Heritage & Education Center, Carlisle Barracks, PA. Harrisburg Civil War Round Table Collection. It should also be noted that this journal constitutes only volume II of Captain Haas' diary. It is possible that volume one resides with another Haas family member.

Henry, Edward. Letters. November 1861—June 1864 United States Army Heritage and Education Center, Carlisle Barracks, PA. Civil War Miscellaneous Collection. Photocopies of original manuscript letters.

Houck, Thomas G. Letters and Diary. November 1861—May 1863. Typescript copies of letters and diary. Virginia Polytechnic Institute and State University, Blacksburg. Civil War Small Manuscripts Collection.

Keiser, Henry. Diary. "Diary of Henry Keiser of Lykens, Pennsylvania, Company G, 95th & 96th Pennsylvania Volunteers, War of the Rebellion, 1861 to 1865." September 23, 1861—July 20, 1865. Collection of Mr. Ronald Keiser, Baltimore, MD. This extensive diary also includes a detailed muster roll of Company G, battles and skirmishes in which Company G was engaged, annotated entries listing the casualties sustained by Company G, and an itinerary of the movements of the 96th Pennsylvania Volunteers. Two federal libraries hold copies of this important manuscript source: The United States Military Academy Library, West Point, NY, and the United States Army Heritage & Education Center, Carlisle Barracks, PA. Harrisburg Civil War Round Table Collection.

Luckenbill, Lewis. Diary. September 1861—September 1862 and March 1863—September 1864. Typescript of the original pocket diaries. William Dick Collection, Girard, PA. Typescript photocopy of the diary also at United States Army Heritage & Education Center, Carlisle Barracks, PA. Northwest Corner Civil War Round Table Collection.

Madison, John. Letters. November 1861—July 1862. Original manuscript letters. Collection of Carl Madison, Marshall, VA. Photocopies and transcripts of the letters at the Historical Society of Schuylkill County, Pottsville, PA.

Martin, Lewis J. Letters. September 1861—September 1862. Original manuscript letters in the James S. Schoff Civil War Collection. William L. Clements Library, University of Michigan.

Miller, J. Jerome. Diary. January 1863—June 1864. Original manuscript pocket diaries in leather cases. George Hay Kain Collection, Emigsville, PA.

Oestreich, Maurus. Diary. "Civil War Centennial Project. Maurus Oestreich: American Citizen, Loyal Catholic, Hessian Born, Union Volunteer, Grand Army of the Republic Veteran, Organ Builder, General Contractor, Musician, Guest Speaker, Devoted Husband, Industrious Father, gifted with many virtues. A Tribute by His Children." Translated from German by William Hammeke. November 9, 1861—June, 1864. Collection of the Rev. Emil C. Oestreich. Copies of this diary can be found at the Historical Society of Schuylkill County, Pottsville, PA, and the United States Army Heritage and Education Center, Carlisle Barracks, PA, Harrisburg Civil War Round Table Collection. Also, a copy was deposited at the Historical Society of Pennsylvania, Philadelphia.

Potts, Clement. Letters. November 1861—July 1862. Potts Family Papers. Manuscript Collection. Original manuscript letters. Historical Society of Schuylkill County, Pottsville, PA.

Reed, Erasmus. Letters. November 1861—July 1864. Typescript copies of the original manuscript letters. Indiana Historical Society, Indianapolis. Sesquicentennial History Project Collection. These letters were also published in the South Bend [Indiana] *Tribune*, 1962.

Risheill, Reuben. Diary. 1861–1864. Digital copy of original pocket diaries in leather cases. Virginia Sesquicentennial of the American Civil War and the Fairfax Sesquicentennial Committee. James I. Robertson, Jr. Civil War Sesquicentennial Legacy Collection. Donated for reproduction by Mark Wegner.

Richards, M. Edgar. Letters. November 1861—February 1864. Original manuscript letters. United States Army Military Heritage & Education Center, Carlisle Barracks, PA. Civil War Miscellaneous Collection.

Saylor, John. "Military History of John Albert Saylor." Typescript. Undated. Copy at Richmond National Battlefield, Richmond, VA.

Severn, Isaac. Diary. January, 1864—December, 1864. United States Army Heritage and Education Center. Original pocket diary in leather case. Also, miscellaneous documents in the Historical Society of Schuylkill County, Pottsville, PA.

Treichler, James M. Memoir. Typescript headed at top of first page, "Capt. James M. Treichler, Ellston, Iowa 1861–1865." Randy Treichler Collection, Three Springs, PA.

Other Published Sources, 96th Pennsylvania Volunteers

Bates, Samuel P. *History of Pennsylvania Volunteers, 1861–5.* 5 vols. Harrisburg, PA: B. Singerly, 1869–1871. Vol. III, 382–410.

Boyer, Henry C. "At Crampton's Pass. The Ninety-Sixth Pennsylvania Regiment Under Fire. Its Gallant Charge Over Rough Ground and Under Galling Fire to Achieve a Triumph of Distinction." Shenandoah *Evening Herald*, August 31, 1886; September 2, 1886; September 3, 1886.

Boyle, John T. "The Ninety-Sixth at Crampton's Pass." Pottsville *Miners' Journal*, September 30, 1871.

_____."Ninety-Sixth Reg't." *Schuylkill Republican*, September 18, 1886.

_____. "An Outline Sketch of the Ninety-Sixth Pennsylvania Volunteers." Philadelphia *Weekly Times*, July 17, 1886.

Brandt, Randolph D. "Stars and Stripes in All Directions." *Living History* 4 (Winter 1985): 22–25, 45.

"Colonel H. L. Cake Dead at Northumberland." Pottsville *Miners' Journal*, August 28, 1899.

Delaney, James. "At Petersburg: The Work Done by the Sixth Corps for Its Capture." *National Tribune*, April 16, 1891.

History of Schuylkill County, Pa. with Illustrations and Biographical Sketches of Some of Its Prominent Men and Pioneers. New York: W.W. Munsell Company, 1881. Chap. XXIV "Histories of the Ninety-Third and Ninety-Sixth Regiments," 138–144.

Kelly, Elizabeth. "General Lessig, Once Social Lion, Dead." Denver *Post*, July 19, 1910.

Nugent, Washington George. *My Darling Wife…: The Letters of Washington George Nugent, Surgeon Army of the Potomac.* Edited by Maria Randall Allen. Cheshire, CT: Ye Olde Book Bindery, 1994.

Pennsylvania. Gettysburg Battlefield Commission. *Pennsylvania at Gettysburg: Ceremonies at the Dedication of the Monuments Erected by the Commonwealth of Pennsylvania to Major General George Gordon Meade, Major General Winfield Scott Hancock, Major General John F. Reynolds and to Mark the Positions of the Pennsylvania Commands Engaged in the Battle.* Harrisburg, PA: William Stanley Ray, State Printer, 1904. Vol. 1, Henry Royer, "Dedication of Monument 96th Regiment Infantry June 21, 1888," 515–523.

"Proceedings and Speeches Made at the Transfer of Battle Flags to the Historical Society of Schuylkill County December 14, 1913." *Publications of the Historical Society of Schuylkill County*, Vol. V, no. 2 (1932), 15–25.

Sauers, Richard A. *Advance the Colors! Pennsylvania Civil War Battle Flags.* Harrisburg, PA: Capitol Preservation Committee, 1991. Vol. 2, 325–327.

"Schuylkill in the War: Historical Sketch of the Ninety-sixth Pennsylvania Volunteers." *Pottsville Standard*, July 23, 1886.

"Survivors of the 96th. A Red Letter Day for the Veterans." Pottsville *Miners' Journal*, September 17, 1886.

Treichler, James M. *Crimson Fields: Civil War Biography of Captain James Madison Treichler.* Edited by Don Treichler. Roseville, CA: 2012.

_____. "End of the Battle. Charge of a Brigade of the Sixth Corps at Gettysburg." *National Tribune*, May 4, 1916.

Wallace, Francis B. *Memorial of the Patriotism of Schuylkill County, in the American Slaveholder's Rebellion, Embracing a Complete List of the Names of all the Volunteers from the County During The War; Patriotic Contributions by the Citizens; List of the Names of Those Who Fell in Battle or Died by Disease; Descriptions of the Part Taken in Various Engagements by our Regiments, With Casualties; Chronological Record of the Principal Events of the Rebellion; Biographical Sketches of Prominent Officers and of Surgeons from the County, &c., Accompanied by a Plate of Portraits of Generals and Colonels From this County, and a Map of the Southern States with the Battle Fields Marked.* Pottsville, PA: Benjamin Bannan, 1865.

Ward, David A. "Amidst a Tempest of Shot and Shell: A History of the Ninety-sixth Pennsylvania Volunteers." New Haven, CT: Southern Connecticut State University, 1988.

_____. "Of Battlefields and Bitter Feuds: The 96th Pennsylvania Volunteers." *Civil War Regiments: A Journal of the American Civil War* 3, no. 3 (1993): 1–32.

Other Manuscript Sources

Anonymous. [16th New York]. "Fredericksburg During the Civil War." Schoff Civil War Collection. William Clements Library. University of Michigan.

Bailey, Smith. [5th Maine]. Diary, June 1862—May 1863, Smith Bailey Coll. Dartmouth College Library, Hanover, NH.

Bates, Samuel P. Collection. Pennsylvania Historical and Museum Commission. Harrisburg, PA.

Franklin, William B. Papers. Manuscript Division, Library of Congress, Washington, D.C.

French, John S. [5th Maine] Letters. Dr. Leo Hershkowitz Collection. Queens, NY.

Howland, Joseph. [16th New York] Papers. New York Historical Society.

Latta, James William. [119th Pennsylvania] Diaries, 1862–1865. Manuscript Division, Library of Congress, Washington, D.C.

Sanborn, Fred. Manuscript. [5th Maine] "Narrative and Scrapbook of the 5th Maine Regiment's Participation in Spotsylvania, Cold Harbor, etc." Manuscript Division, Library of Congress, Washington, D.C.

Sedgwick, John. Collection. University of Connecticut, Storrs.

Stone, Cyrus R. [16th New York] Letters and memoir. Minnesota Historical Society, Minneapolis.

Whittier, Charles A. [Sedgwick's staff] Manuscript. Typescript. "Reminiscences of the War, 1861–1865, or Egotistic Memoirs, C.A.W., Feb. 13, 1888 M.[assachusetts]   Milit.[ary]   Hist.[orical] S[ociet]y." Boston Public Library, Boston, MA.

Newspapers

Herkimer County (NY) *The Journal and Courier*
Malone (NY) *Palladium*
New York *Herald*
New York *Times*
New York *Tribune*
Philadelphia *Weekly Press*
Philadelphia *Weekly Times*
Portland (ME) *Transcript*
Pottsville (PA) *Miners' Journal*
Pottsville (PA) *Standard*
Rochester (NY) *Democrat and American*
Rochester (NY) *Union and Advertiser*
Shenandoah (PA) *Evening Herald*
Washington D.C. *National Tribune*

Government Publications

Maine. Gettysburg Commission. *Maine at Gettysburg: Report of Maine Commissioners* Prepared by the Executive Committee. Portland, ME: [Lakeside Press], 1898.

New York (State). Monuments Commission for the Battlefields of Gettysburg and Chattanooga. *Final Report on the Battlefield of Gettysburg.* Edited by William F. Fox. Albany, NY: J.B. Lyon, 1900.

United States. *The Statutes at Large, Treaties, and Proclamations of the United States of America.* Edited by George P. Sanger. By authority of Congress. Washington, D.C.: Government Printing Office, 1859–1869.

U.S. Congress. *Biographical Directory of the American Congress, 1774–1971, the Continental Congress, September 5, 1774, to October 21, 1788, and the Ninety-first Congress, March 4, 1789 to January 3, 1971,* inclusive. Lawrence F. Kennedy, chief compiler. Washington, D.C.: Government Printing Office, 1971.

U.S. Congress. *Congressional Globe.* Register of Debates in Congress: Comprising the Leading Debates and Incidents of the [number] Session of the [section] Congress. Washington, D.C.: Government Printing Office, 1861–1865.

U.S. Surgeon General's Office. *Medical and Surgical History of the War of the Rebellion (1861–1864).* 6 vols. Washington, D.C.: Government Printing Office, 1870–1888.

U.S. War Department. *Army of the Potomac. Letter of the Secretary of War, Transmitting Report on* the Organization of the Army of the Potomac, and of Its Campaigns in Virginia and Maryland, Under the Command of Maj. Gen. George B. McClellan, From July 26, 1861 to November 7, 1862. By George B. McClellan. Washington, D.C.: Government Printing Office, 1864.

U.S. War Department. *Atlas to Accompany the Official Records of the Union and Confederate Armies.* Published under the direction of the secretaries of war, by Maj. George B. Davis, et al. Washington, D.C.: Government Printing Office, 1891–1895.

U.S. War Department. *Revised Regulations for the Army of the United States, 1861.* Philadelphia, PA: George W. Childs, 1862.

U.S. War Department. *The War of the Rebellion: A Compilation of the Official Records of the Union and Confederate Armies.* 70 Vols. in 128 Parts. Washington, D.C.: Government Printing Office, 1880–1901.

Primary Sources

BOOKS

Adams, John Ripley. *Memorial and Letters of Rev. John R. Adams, D.D., Chaplain of the Fifth Maine and One Hundred and Twenty-First New York Regiments During the War of the Rebellion, Serving From the Beginning to its Close.* [Cambridge, MA] Priv. Print. [University Press: J. Wilson and Son], 1890.

The Annals of the War, Written by Leading Participants, North and South. Philadelphia, PA: The Times Publishing Company, 1879.

Baquet, Camille. *History of the First Brigade, New Jersey Volunteers, from 1861–1865.* Trenton, NJ: MacCrelish & Quigley, 1910.

Bates, Samuel P. *Martial Deeds of Pennsylvania.* Philadelphia, PA.: T.H. Davis & Company, 1876.

Battles and Leaders of the Civil War. Edited by Robert Underwood Johnson and Clarence Clough Buel. 4 vols. New York: The Century Company, 1887.

Benedict, George G. *Vermont in the Civil War, a History of the Part Taken by the Vermont Soldiers and Sailors in the War for the Union, 1861–5.* Burlington, VT: Free Press Association, 1886. 2 vols.

Bennett, A. J. *The Story of the First Massachusetts Light Battery Attached to the Sixth Corps.* Boston, MA: Deland and Barta, 1886.

Best, Isaac O. *History of the 121st New York State Infantry.* Chicago, IL: James H. Smith, 1921.

Bicknell, George W. *History of the Fifth Regiment Maine Volunteers.* Portland, ME: Hall L. Davis, 1871.

Bissell, Lewis. [2nd Connecticut Vol. Heavy Artillery] *The Civil War Letters of Lewis Bissell.* Edited by Mark Olcott and David Lear. Washington, D.C.: Field School Educational, 1981.

Blake, Henry N. *Three Years in the Army of the Potomac.* Boston, MA: Lee and Shepard, 1865.

Carman, Ezra A. *The Maryland Campaign of September 1862: Vol. I South Mountain.* Edited by Thomas G. Clemens. El Dorado, CA: Savas Beatie, 2010.

Casey, Silas. *Infantry Tactics.* 3 vols. New York: D. Van Nostrand Company, 1862.

Castle, Henry Anson. *The Army Mule and Other War Sketches.* Indianapolis, IN: The Bowen-Merrill Company, 1897.

The Civil War Letters of General Robert McAllister. Edited by James I Robertson. New Brunswick, NJ: Rutgers University Press, 1965.

Clark, Walter. *Histories of the Several Regiments and Battalions from North Carolina in the Great War 1861–'65.* Raleigh, NC: Nash Brothers, 1901. 5 vols.

Coffin, Charles Carleton. *Four Years of Fighting: A Personal Observation with the Army and Navy from the First Battle of Bull Run to the Fall of Richmond.* Boston, MA: Ticknor & Fields, 1866.

Cook, Joel. *The Siege of Richmond: A Narrative of the Military Operations of Major-General George B. McClellan During the Months of May and June, 1862.* Philadelphia, PA: George W. Childs, 1862.

Correspondence of John Sedgwick, Major General. Edited by Henry Sedgwick. 2 vols. New York: DeVinne, 1902–1903.

Cullum, George W. *Biographical Register of the Officers and Graduates of the U. S. Military Academy at West Point, N.Y. From Its Establishment, in 1802 to 1890.* Cambridge, MA: Riverside Press, 1891. 2 vols.

Curtis, Newton Martin. *From Bull Run to Chancellorsville: The Story of the Sixteenth New York Infantry together with Personal Reminiscences.* New York: G.P. Putnam's Sons, 1906.

Dodge, Theodore A. *The Campaign of Chancellorsville.* Boston, MA: James R. Osgood, 1881.

Doubleday, Abner. *Chancellorsville and Gettysburg.* New York: Charles Scribner's Sons, 1882.

Fairchild, C.B. *History of the 27th Regiment N. Y. Vols. Being a Record of its More Than Two Years of Service in the War for the Union, From May 21st 1861, to May 31st, 1863, With a Complete Roster, and Short Sketches of Commanding Officers, Also, a Record of Experience and Suffering of Some of the Comrades in Libby and Other Rebel Prisons.* Binghamton, NY: Carl & Matthews, 1888.

Fisk, Wilbur. [2nd Vermont Vols.] *Anti-Rebel: The Civil War Letters of Wilbur Fisk.* Edited by Emil Rosenblatt. Croton-on-Hudson, NY: Emil Rosenblatt, 1983.

Fox, William F. *Regimental Losses in the American Civil War.* Albany, NY: Albany Publishing Company, 1889.

Galloway, G. Norton. *The Ninety-Fifth Pennsylvania Volunteers ("Gosline's Pennsylvania Zouaves") in the Sixth Corps.* Philadelphia, PA: [Collins] Printer, 1884.

Grant, Ulysses S. *Personal Memoirs of U.S. Grant.* 2 vols. New York: Charles L. Webster & Company, 1886.

Haines, Alanson A. *History of the Fifteenth Regiment, New Jersey Volunteers*. New York: Jenkins and Thomas, 1883.

Hardee, William J. *Rifle and Light Infantry Tactics*. 2 vols. Philadelphia, PA: J.B. Lippincott Company, 1863.

Hartwell, John F.L. [121st New York Vols.] *To My Beloved Wife and Boy at Home: The Letters and Diaries of Orderly Sergeant John F. L. Hartwell*. Edited by Ann Hartwell Britton and Thomas J. Reed. Madison, NJ: Fairleigh Dickinson University Press, 1997.

Holt, Daniel M. [121st New York Vols.] *A Surgeon's Civil War: The Letters & Diary of Daniel M. Holt, M.D.* Edited by James M. Greiner, Janet L. Coryell and James R. Smither. Kent, OH: Kent State University Press, 1994.

Humphreys, Andrew A. *From Gettysburg to the Rapidan: The Army of the Potomac July, 1863 to April, 1864*. New York: Charles Scribner's Sons, 1883.

_____. *The Virginia Campaigns of '64 and '65: The Army of the Potomac and the Army of the James*. New York: Charles Scribner's Sons, 1883.

Hyde, Thomas W. *Following the Greek Cross; or, Memories of the Sixth Army Corps*. Boston, MA: Houghton Mifflin & Company, 1894.

Ingraham, John. [121st New York Vols.] *John J. Ingraham's Civil War Letters 1862–65*. Dolgeville, NY: Dolgeville-Manheim Historical Society, 1990.

Kidder, John S. *Subdued by the Sword: A Line Officer in the 121st New York Volunteers*. Edited by James M. Greiner. Albany, NY: State University of New York Press, 2003.

Lyman, Theodore. *Meade's Headquarters, 1863–1865: Letters of Colonel Theodore Lyman from the Wilderness to Appomattox*. Edited by George Agassiz. Boston, MA: Atlantic Monthly, 1922.

McClellan, George B. *McClellan's Own Story: The War for the Union, the Soldiers Who Fought it, the Civilians Who Directed it and His Relation to It and to Them*. New York: Charles L. Webster & Company, 1887.

McMahon, Martin T. *General John Sedgwick: An Address Delivered Before the Vermont Officers' Reunion Society at their Sixteenth Annual Meeting at Montpelier, November 11, 1880*. Rutland, VT: Tuttle & Company, 1885.

_____. *In Memoriam: Maj.-Gen. John Sedgwick*. Togus, ME: National Home, 1885.

Meade, George. *The Life and Letters of George Gordon Meade, Major-General United States Army*. New York: Charles Scribner's Sons, 1913.

Meade's Headquarters, 1863–1865: Letters of Colonel Theodore Lyman from the Wilderness to Appomattox. Edited by George Agassiz. Boston, MA: Massachusetts Historical Society, 1922.

Michie, Peter S. *The Life and Letters of Emory Upton: Colonel of the Fourth Regiment of Artillery, and Brevet Major-General, U. S. Army*. New York: D. Appleton and Company, 1885.

Morse, Francis W. [121st New York Vols.] *Personal Reminiscences in the War of the Great Rebellion from December 1862 to July 1863*. Albany, NY: W. W. Munsell, 1866.

Morse, William E.H. [5th Maine Vols.] "The "Rebellion Record" of an Enlisted Man." *The National Tribune Scrap Book*. Washington, D.C., 1909[?].

Palfrey, Francis Winthrop. *The Antietam and Fredericksburg*. New York: Charles Scribner's Sons, 1882.

Patrick, Marsena. *Inside Lincoln's Army: The Diary of Marsena Patrick, Provost Marshall General, Army of the Potomac*. Edited by David S. Sparks. New York: Thomas Yoseloff, 1964.

Pinto, Francis E. "History of the 32nd Regiment, New York Volunteers, In the Civil War, 1861 to 1863, and Personal Recollections During that Period." Brooklyn, NY, 1895.

Porter, Horace: *Campaigning with Grant*. New York: Century, 1906.

Remmel, William. *Like Grass Before the Scythe: The Life and Death of Sgt. William Remmel, 121st New York Infantry*. Edited by Robert P. Bender Tuscaloosa: University of Alabama Press, 2007.

Rice, Adam Clarke. *The Letters and Other Writings of the late Lieut. Adam Clarke Rice, of the 121st Regiment, New York Volunteers*. Little Falls, NY: Journal & Courier, 1864.

Ropes, John Codman. *The Army Under Pope*. New York: Charles Scribner's Sons, 1881.

Schaff, Morris. *The Battle of the Wilderness*. Boston and New York: Houghton, Mifflin, 1910.

Slocum, Charles Elihu. *The Life and Services of Major General Henry Warner Slocum*. Toledo, OH: Slocum, 1913.

Stevens, George T. *Three Years in the Sixth Corps: A Concise Narrative of Events in the Army of the Potomac, from 1861 to the Close of the Rebellion, April, 1865*. Albany, NY: S.R. Gray, 1881.

Stine, J.H. *History of the Army of the Potomac*. Philadelphia: Rogers Printing Company, 1892.

Sutton, Elijah Henry. [24th Georgia] *Grandpa's Civil War Stories*. Demorest, GA: Banner Print, [1910].

Swinton, William. *Campaigns of the Army of the Potomac: A Critical History of Operations in Virginia, Maryland, and Pennsylvania, from the Commencement to the Close of the War, 1861–5*. New York: Charles B. Richardson, 1866.

Thomas, Henry W. [12th Georgia]. *History of the Doles-Cook Brigade Army of Northern Virginia, C.S.A.* Dayton, OH: Morningside Bookshop, 1988.

Tyler, Mason Whiting. *Recollections of the Civil War: With Many Original Diary Entries and Letters Written from the Seat of War and with Annotated References*. Edited by William S. Tyler. New York: G.P. Putnam's Sons, 1912.

Vaill, Theodore F. *History of the Second Connecticut Volunteer Heavy Artillery: Originally the Nineteenth Connecticut Volunteers*. Winsted, CT: Winsted Printing Company, 1868.

Wainwright, Charles S. *A Diary of Battle: The Personal Journals of Colonel Charles S. Wainwright, 186–1865*. Edited by Allan Nevins. New York: Harcourt, Brace & World, 1962.

Webb, Alexander S. *The Peninsula: McClellan's Campaign of 1862*. New York: Charles Scribner's Sons, 1881.

Westbrook, Robert S. *History of the 49th Pennsylvania Volunteers*. Altoona, PA: Altoona Times, 1898.

Welch, Emily Sedgwick. *John Sedgwick, Major-General: A Biographical Sketch*. New York: The DeVinne Press, 1899.

Westervelt, William B. [27th New York Vols.] *Lights and Shadows of Army Life: From Bull Run to Bentonville*. Marlboro, NY: C. H. Cochrane Printer, 1886.

Wiley, Samuel T. *Biographical and Portrait Cyclopedia of Schuylkill County: Comprising a Historical Sketch of the County*. Philadelphia, PA: Rush, West and Company, 1893.

Primary Sources

ARTICLES

Bartlett, Joseph J. "Crampton's Pass: The Start of the Great Maryland Campaign," *National Tribune*, December 19, 1889.

Bigelow, John, Jr. "The Battle of Marye's Heights and Salem Church." *Papers of the Military Historical Society of Massachusetts*, vol. III, 240–314.

Bowen, James L. "In Front of Fredericksburg." Philadelphia *Weekly Times*, December 2, 1882.

_____. "Marching to Gettysburg: How the Sixth Corps Tramped From the Rappahannock Into Pennsylvania." Philadelphia *Weekly Times*, May 27, 1882.

_____. "The Sixth Corps at Gettysburg." Philadelphia *Weekly Times*, June 24, 1882.

Dunning, Orlando. "Gaines' Mill: The Battle as Seen by a Participant From the Pine Tree State." *National Tribune*, March 26, 1891.

Fagan, W.L. "Battle of Salem Church." Philadelphia *Weekly Times*, July 7, 1883.

Feather, A.G. "Cold Harbor." Philadelphia *Weekly Times*, September 12, 1885.

_____. "The Mine Run Campaign." Philadelphia *Weekly Times*, August 6, 1887.

Franklin, W.B. "Notes on Crampton's Gap and Antietam." *Battles and Leaders of the Civil War*, vol. II, 591–597.

_____. "Rear-Guard Fighting During the Change of Base." *Battles and Leaders of the Civil War*, vol. II, 366–382.

_____. "The Sixth Corps at the Second Bull Run." *Battles and Leaders of the Civil War*, vol. II, 539–541.

Galloway, G. Norton. "At Spotsylvania." Philadelphia *Weekly Times,* January 15, 1881.

_____. "Battle of Gaines' Mill." Philadelphia *Weekly Times*, February 21, 1885.

_____. "Battle of the Wilderness." Philadelphia *Weekly Times*, February 16, 1884.

_____. "The Bloody Angle." Philadelphia *Weekly Press*, August 10, 1887.

_____. "Capture of the Salient." Philadelphia *Weekly Times*, November 18, 1882.

_____. "Death of Sedgwick." Philadelphia *Weekly Times*, March 1, 1884.

_____. "Death of the Gallant Sedgwick." Philadelphia *Weekly Times*, January 8, 1881, and January 15, 1881.

_____. "Hand-to-Hand Fighting at Spotsylvania." *Battles and Leaders of the Civil War*, vol. IV, 170–174.

_____. "Through the Wilderness." Philadelphia *Weekly Times*, January 8, 1881.

Graham, H.C. "Battle of Gaines' Mill." Philadelphia *Weekly Times*, December 8, 1883.

Hall, Henry Seymour. "Personal Experience Under General McClellan." *Papers of the Kansas Commandery, Military Order of the Loyal Legion of the United States*, 1–22, no. 10 [n.p.], [1894].

Herbert, Hilary. "Colonel Hilary A. Herbert's 'History of the Eighth Alabama Volunteer Regiment, C.S.A.'" Edited by Maurice S. Fortin. *Alabama Historical Quarterly* (1977) 39, nos. 1–4.

Holt, Daniel. "In Captivity." *Civil War Times Illustrated* 18, no. 5 (August 1979): 34–39.

Jackson, Huntington W. "Sedgwick at Fredericksburg and Salem Heights." *Battles and Leaders of the Civil War*, vol. III, 224–232.

Kilmer, George L. "The Army of the Potomac at Harrison's Landing." *Battles and Leaders of the Civil War*, vol. II, 427–428.

_____. "McClellan's Reserves. Franklin in the Peninsular Campaign and During the Battle of Antietam." Philadelphia *Weekly Times*, July 29, 1882.

_____. "Slocum at Gaines' Mill." Philadelphia *Weekly Times*, April 17, 1886.

_____. "Slocum's Soldiers." Philadelphia *Weekly Times*, April 16, 1887.

Mark, Penrose G. "The Controversy as to the Time the Sixth Corps Arrived at Gettysburg." Philadelphia *Weekly Times*, June 10, 1882.

McMahon, Martin T. "The Death of General John Sedgwick." *Battles and Leaders of the Civil War*, vol. IV, 175.

Nevin, R. B. "Fort Stevens." Philadelphia *Weekly Times*, October 3, 1885.

Orr, Robert L. "Marye's Heights." Philadelphia *Weekly Press*, January 19, 1887.

Roche, Thomas T. "The Bloody Angle." Philadelphia *Weekly Times*, September 3, 1881.

Slater, J.S. "The Fray at Gaines' Mill." Philadelphia *Weekly Times*, January 26, 1884.

Smith, William Farrar. "Franklin's Left Grand Division." *Battles and Leaders of the Civil War*, vol. III, 128–138.

Westervelt, William B. "Battle of Gaines's Mill: Extracts from the Diary of a Member of the 27th N. Y." *National Tribune*, February 27, 1913.

Secondary Sources

BOOKS

Ambrose, Stephen A. *Upton and the Army*. Baton Rouge, LA: Louisiana State University Press, 1964.

Baltz, Louis J. *The Battle of Cold Harbor May 27–June 13, 1864*. Lynchburg, VA: H. E. Howard, 1994.

Bearss, Edwin C., and Bryce A. Suderow. *The Petersburg Campaign: The Eastern Front Battles June–August 1864*. El Dorado, CA: Savas Beatie, 2012.

Bigelow, John, Jr. *The Campaign of Chancellorsville: A Strategic and Tactical Study*. New Haven, CT: Yale University Press, 1910.

Boatner, Mark Mayo. *The Civil War Dictionary*. New York: David McKay, 1959.

Burton, Brian K. *Extraordinary Circumstances: The Seven Days Battles*. Bloomington, IN: Indiana University Press, 2001.

Catton, Bruce. *The Coming Fury*. Garden City, NY: Doubleday, 1961.

_____. *Glory Road: The Bloody Route from Fredericksburg to Gettysburg*. Garden City, NY: Doubleday, 1952.

_____. *Grant Takes Command*. Boston, MA: Little, Brown, 1968.

_____. *This Hallowed Ground: The Story of the Union Side of the Civil War*. Garden City, NY: Doubleday, 1956.

_____. *Mr. Lincoln's Army*. Garden City, NY: Doubleday, 1951.

_____. *Never Call Retreat*. Garden City, NY: Doubleday, 1965.

_____. *A Stillness at Appomattox*. Garden City, NY: Doubleday, 1953.

_____. *Terrible Swift Sword*. Garden City, NY: Doubleday, 1963.

Cilella, Salvatore G. *Upton's Regulars: The 121st New York Infantry in the Civil War*. Lawrence, KS: University Press of Kansas, 2009.

Coddington, Edwin B. *The Gettysburg Campaign: A Study in Command*. New York: Charles Scribner's Sons, 1968.

Cullen, Joseph P. *The Peninsula Campaign, 1862: McClellan and Lee Struggle for Richmond*. Harrisburg, PA: Stackpole, 1973.

Davis, William C. *The Imperiled Union, 1861–1865*, vol. 1 *Deep Waters of the Proud*. New York: Doubleday, 1982.

_____. *The Imperiled Union, 1861–1865*, vol. 2 *Stand in the Day of Battle*. New York: Doubleday, 1983.

Dowdey, Clifford. *The Seven Days: The Emergence of Lee*. Boston, MA: Little, Brown, 1964.

Dyer, Frederick H. *A Compendium of the War of the Rebellion*. New York: Thomas Yoseloff, 1959.

Faust, Drew Gilpin. *This Republic of Suffering: Death and the American Civil War*. New York: Alfred A. Knopf, 2008.

Foote, Shelby. *The Civil War: A Narrative*, vol. I. *Fort Sumter to Perryville*. New York: Random House, 1958.

_____. *The Civil War: A Narrative*, vol. II. *Fredericksburg to Meridian*. New York: Random House, 1963.

_____. *The Civil War: A Narrative*, vol. III. *Red River to Appomattox*. New York: Random House, 1974.

Freeman, Douglas S. *Lee's Lieutenants: A Study in Command*. 3 vols. New York: Charles Scribner's Sons, 1942–1944.

Furgurson, Ernest B. *Chancellorsville 1863: The Souls of the Brave*. New York: Alfred A. Knopf, 1992.

_____. *Not War But Murder: Cold Harbor 1864*. New York: Alfred A. Knopf, 2000.

Gallagher, Gary W. ed. *The Fredericksburg Campaign: Decision on the Rappahannock*. Chapel Hill: University North Carolina Press, 1995.

_____. *The Richmond Campaign of 1862: The Peninsula & the Seven Days*. Chapel Hill: University North Carolina Press, 2000.

_____. *The Shenandoah Valley Campaign of 1864*. Chapel Hill: University North Carolina Press, 2006.

_____. *The Spotsylvania Campaign*. Chapel Hill: University North Carolina Press, 1998.

_____. *The Wilderness Campaign*. Chapel Hill: University North Carolina Press, 1997.

Graham, Martin F., and George F. Skoch. *Mine Run: A Campaign of Lost Opportunities, October 21, 1863–May 1, 1864*. Lynchburg, VA: H. E Howard, 1987.

Griffith, Paddy. *Rally Once Again: Battle Tactics of the American Civil War*. Ramsbury, U.K.: Crowood, 1989

Guelzo, Allen C. *Lincoln's Emancipation Proclamation: The End of Slavery in America*. New York: Simon & Schuster, 2004.

Happel, Ralph. *Salem Church Embattled*. [Fredericksburg], Va.: Eastern National Park and Monument Association, 1980.

Hartwig, D. Scott. *To Antietam Creek: The Maryland Campaign of September 1862*. Baltimore, MD: Johns Hopkins University Press, 2012.

Hattaway, Herman, and Archer Jones. *How the North Won: A Military History of the Civil War*. Urbana, IL: University of Illinois Press, 1983.

Henderson, William D. *The Road to Bristoe Station: Campaigning With Lee and Meade, August 1 - October 20, 1863*. Lynchburg, VA: H. E. Howard, 1987.

Hess, Earl J. *Civil War Infantry Tactics: Training, Combat, and Small-Unit Effectiveness*. Baton Rouge, LA: Louisiana State University Press, 2015.

_____. *The Rifle Musket in Civil War Combat: Reality and Myth*. Lawrence, KS: University Press of Kansas, 2008.

_____. *Trench Warfare Under Grant & Lee: Field Fortifications in the Overland Campaign*. Chapel Hill, NC: University North Carolina Press, 2007.

_____. *The Union Soldier in Battle: Enduring the Ordeal of Combat*. Lawrence, KS: University Press of Kansas, 1997.

Historical Times Illustrated Encyclopedia of the Civil War. Edited by Patricia M. Faust. New York: Harper & Row, 1986.

Hoptak, John David. *The Battle of South Mountain.* Charleston, SC: History, 2011.

Jordan, Brian Matthew. *Unholy Sabbath: The Battle of South Mountain in History and Memory, September 14, 1862.* El Dorado, CA: Savas Beatie, 2012.

Linderman, Gerald F. *Embattled Courage: The Experience of Combat in the American Civil War.* New York: Dial, 1987.

Litwack, Leon F. *Been in the Storm So Long: The Aftermath of Slavery.* New York: Alfred A. Knopf, 1979.

Long, E.B. *The Civil War Day by Day: An Almanac, 1861–1865.* Garden City, NY: Doubleday and Company, 1971.

Lord, Francis. *Civil War Sutlers and Their Wares.* Cranbury, NJ: Thomas Yoseloff, 1969.

_____. *They Fought for the Union.* New York: Bonanza, 1960.

McPherson, James. *Battle Cry of Freedom: The Civil War Era.* New York, New York: Oxford University Press, 1988.

_____. *Ordeal by Fire: The Civil War and Reconstruction.* New York: Alfred A. Knopf, 1982.

McWhiney, Grady, and Perry D. Jamieson. *Attack and Die: Civil War Military Tactics and the Southern Heritage.* Tuscaloosa, AL: University of Alabama Press, 1982.

Mackowski, Chris, and Kristopher D. White. *Chancellorsville's Forgotten Front: The Battles of Second Fredericksburg and Salem Church, May 3, 1863.* El Dorado, CA: Savas Beatie, 2013.

Matter, William D. *If It Takes All Summer: The Battle of Spotsylvania.* Chapel Hill, NC: University North Carolina Press, 1988.

Mitchell, Reid. *Civil War Soldiers: Their Expectations and Their Experiences.* New York: Viking, 1988.

_____. *The Vacant Chair: The Northern Soldier Leaves Home.* New York: Oxford University Press, 1993.

Murfin, James V. *The Gleam of Bayonets: The Battle of Antietam and the Maryland Campaign of 1862.* New York: Thomas Yoseloff, 1965.

Nevins, Allan. *The War for the Union.* New York: Charles Scribner's Sons, 1971. 4 vols.

Niven, John. *Connecticut for the Union: The Role of the State in the Civil War.* New Haven, CT: Yale University Press, 1965.

Nosworthy, Brent. *The Bloody Crucible of Courage: Fighting Methods and Combat Experience of the Civil War.* New York: Carroll and Graf, 2003.

Nye, Wilbur Sturtevant. *Here Come The Rebels!* Baton Rouge, LA: Louisiana State University Press, 1965.

O'Reilly, Frank A. *The Fredericksburg Campaign: Winter War on the Rappahannock.* Baton Rouge, LA: Louisiana State University Press, 2003.

Palladino, Grace. *Another Civil War: Labor, Capital, and the State in the Anthracite Regions of Pennsylvania 1840–68.* Champaign, IL: University of Illinois Press, 1990.

Palmer, Jr., William A. *The Battle of Eltham's Landing, May 7, 1862.* [West Point, Virginia]: 2012.

Parsons, Philip W. *The Union Sixth Army Corps in the Chancellorsville Campaign.* Jefferson, NC: McFarland, 2006.

Priest, John Michael. *Before Antietam: The Battle for South Mountain.* Shippensburg, PA, 1992.

Pullen, John J. *The Twentieth Maine: A Volunteer Regiment in the Civil War.* Dayton, OH: Morningside House, 1991.

Reese, Timothy J. *Sealed with Their Lives: The Battle for Crampton's Gap, Burkittsville, Maryland, September 14, 1862.* Baltimore, MD: Butternut & Blue, 1998.

Rhea, Gordon C. *Battle of the Wilderness May 5–6, 1864.* Baton Rouge, LA: Louisiana State University Press, 1994.

_____. *The Battles for Spotsylvania Court House and the Road to Yellow Tavern May 7–12.* Baton Rouge, LA: Louisiana State University Press, 1997.

_____. *Cold Harbor: Grant and Lee May 26—June 3, 1864.* Baton Rouge, LA: Louisiana State University Press, 2002.

_____. *To the North Anna River: Grant and Lee May 13–25, 1864.* Baton Rouge, LA: Louisiana State University Press, 2000.

Robertson, James I., Jr. *Soldiers Blue and Gray.* Columbia, SC: University South Carolina Press, 1988.

Schildt, John W. *Roads from Gettysburg.* [Parsons, WV: McLain], 1979.

_____. *Roads to Gettysburg.* Parsons, WV: McLain, 1978.

Scott, Robert Garth. *Into the Wilderness with the Army of the Potomac.* Bloomington, IN: Indiana University Press, 1985.

Sears, Stephen W. *Chancellorsville.* New York: Houghton Mifflin, 1996.

_____. *Landscape Turned Red: The Battle of Antietam.* New Haven, CT: Ticknor and Fields, 1983.

_____. *To the Gates of Richmond: The Peninsula Campaign.* New Haven, CT: Ticknor and Fields, 1992.

Shankman, Arnold. *The Pennsylvania Antiwar Movement, 1861–1865.* Madison, NJ: Fairleigh Dickinson University Press, 1980.

Smith, Richard W. *The Old Nineteenth: The Story of the Second Connecticut Heavy Artillery in the Civil War.* Lincoln, NE: iUniverse, 2007.

Slade, A. D. *That Sterling Soldier: The Life of David A. Russell.* Dayton, OH: Morningside, 1995.

Snell, Mark A. *From First to Last: The Life of Major General William B. Franklin.* New York: Fordham University Press, 2002.

Sommers, Richard J. *Richmond Redeemed: The Siege at Petersburg.* Garden City, NY: Doubleday, 1981.

Stackpole, Edward J. *Chancellorsville: Lee's Greatest Battle.* Harrisburg, PA: Stackpole, 1958.

_____. *Drama on the Rappahannock: The Fredericksburg Campaign.* Harrisburg, PA: Stackpole, 1957.

Steere, Edward. *The Wilderness Campaign.* Harrisburg:, PA Stackpole, 1960.

Tucker, Glenn. *High Tide at Gettysburg: The Campaign in Pennsylvania.* Dayton, OH: Morningside Bookshop, 1973.

Warner, Ezra J. *Generals in Blue: The Lives of the Union Commanders.* Baton Rouge, LA: Louisiana State University Press, 1977.

Wert, Jeffry D. *From Winchester to Cedar Creek: The Shenandoah Campaign of 1864.* Carlisle, PA: South Mountain, 1987.

_____. *Mosby's Rangers.* New York: Simon & Schuster, 1990.

_____. *The Sword of Lincoln: The Army of the Potomac.* New York: Simon & Schuster, 2005.

Wiley, Bell Irvin. *The Life of Billy Yank: The Common Soldier of the Union.* Baton Rouge, LA: Louisiana State University Press, 1952.

Williams, T. Harry. *Lincoln and the Radicals.* Madison, WI: University of Wisconsin, 1941.

Winslow, Richard Elliott. *General John Sedgwick: The Story of a Union Corps Commander.* Novato, CA: Presidio, 1982.

Wittenberg, Eric, David J. Petruzzi and Michael F. Nugent. *One Continuous Fight: The Retreat from Gettysburg and the Pursuit of Lee's Army of Northern Virginia, July 4–14, 1863.* El Dorado, CA: Savas Beatie, 2008.

Yearley, Clifton. *Enterprise and Anthracite: Economics and Democracy in Schuylkill County, 1820–1875.* Baltimore, MD: Johns Hopkins University Press, 1961.

Young, Alfred C. *Lee's Army During the Overland Campaign: A Numerical Study.* Baton Rouge, LA: Louisiana University Press, 2013.

Secondary Sources

ARTICLES

Albright, Rebecca Gifford. "The Civil War Career of Andrew Gregg Curtin, Governor of Pennsylvania." *Western Pennsylvania Magazine of History* 47 (October 1964): 323–341; vol. 48 (January 1965), 19–42; vol. 48 (April 1965): 151–173.

Ambrose, Stephen E. "A Theorist Fights: Emory Upton in the Civil War." *Civil War History* 9, no. 4 (December 1963): 341–364.

Beers, Paul A. "Andrew Gregg Curtin—A Profile." *Civil War Times Illustrated* VI, no. 2 (May 1967): 13–20.

Cain, Marvin. "A 'Face of Battle' Needed: An Assessment of Men and Motives in Civil War Historiography." *Civil War History* 28 (March 1982): 5–27.

Cullen, Joseph P. "The Battle of Chancellorsville." *Civil War Times Illustrated* VIII, no. 2 (May 1968): 4–50.

_____. "The Battle of the Wilderness." *Civil War Times Illustrated* X, no. 1 (April 1971): 4–12, 43–47.

_____. "Cedar Creek." *Civil War Times Illustrated* VIII, no. 8 (December 1969): 5–9, 42–48.

_____. "Cold Harbor." *Civil War Times Illustrated* II, no. 7 (November 1963): 11–17.

_____. "A Detour on the Road to Richmond: When Grant Faced Lee Across the North Anna." *Civil War Times Illustrated* III, no. 10 (February 1965): 16–23.

_____. "Sheridan Wins at Winchester." *Civil War Times Illustrated* VI, no. 2 (May 1967): 5–11; 40–44.

_____. "The Siege of Petersburg!" *Civil War Times Illustrated* IX, no. 5 (August 1970): 4–50.

_____. "Spotsylvania." *Civil War Times Illustrated* X, no. 2 (May 1971): 5–9; 46–48.

Faust, Drew Gilpin. "The Civil War Soldier and the Art of Dying." *The Journal of Southern History* 67, no. 1 (February 2001): 3–38.

Gudelunas, William. "Nativism and the Decline of Schuylkill County Whiggery: Anti-Slavery or Anti-Catholicism." *Pennsylvania History* 45 (July 1978): 225–236.

Hall, Clark B. "Season of Change: The Winter Encampment of the Army of the Potomac December 1, 1863–May 4, 1864." *Blue & Gray Magazine* IV, no. 4 (April 1991): 8–22, 48–62.

Keen, W.W. "Military Surgery in 1861 and 1918." *Annals of the American Academy of Political and Social Science* LXXX (November 1918): 11–22.

Keller, Christian B. "Pennsylvania and the Germans During the Civil War: A Brief History and Comparative Analysis." *The Virginia Magazine of History and Biography* 109, no. 1 (2001): 37–86.

Levin, Bernard. "Pennsylvania and the Civil War." *Pennsylvania History* 10, no. 1 (January 1943): 1–10.

Luvaas, Jay, and Wilbur S. Nye. "The Campaign that History Forgot." *Civil War Times Illustrated* VIII, no. 7 (November 1969): 11–42.

Mackowski, Chris, and Kristopher D. White. "Maneuver and Mud: The Battle of Spotsylvania C. H. May 13–20, 1864." *Blue & Gray Magazine* XXVII, no. 6 (2011): 6–26, 42–50.

Mahon, John K. "Civil War Infantry Assault Tactics." *Military Affairs* 25, no. 2 (Summer 1961): 57–68.

Mertz, Gregory A. "Upton's Attack: And the Defense of Doles' Salient, Spotsylvania Court House, Va., May 10, 1864." *Blue & Gray Magazine* XVIII, no. 6 (Summer 2001): 6–25, 46–52.

Miller, J. Michael. "The North Anna Campaign." *Blue & Gray Magazine* XXXI, no. 6 (2015): 6–28, 40–50.

Nelson, Erik F. "East of Chancellorsville: Second Fredericksburg and Salem Church." *Blue & Gray Magazine* XXX, no. 1 (2013): 6–30, 39–50.

Reese, Timothy J. "Howell Cobb's Brigade at Crampton's Gap." *Blue & Gray Magazine* XV, no. 3 (Winter 1998): 6–21, 47–56.

Sandow, Robert M. "The Limits of Northern Patriotism: Early Civil War Mobilization in Pennsylvania." *Pennsylvania History* 70, no. 2 (Spring 2003): 175–203.

Schlegel, Marvin W. "The Workingmen's Benevolent Association: First Union of Anthracite Miners." *Pennsylvania History* X (October 1943): 243–267.

"Schuylkill County in the Civil War." *Publications of the Historical Society of Schuylkill County* VII, no. 3 (1961): 12–124.

Shankman, Arnold. "Draft Resistance in Civil War Pennsylvania." *Pennsylvania Magazine of History and Biography* 101, no. 2 (April 1977): 190–204.

Smith, Wayne. "Pennsylvania and the American Civil War: Recent Trends and Interpretations." *Pennsylvania History* 51, no. 3 (July 1984): 206–231.

Spear, Donald P. "The Sutler in the Union Army." *Civil War History* 16, no. 2 (June 1970): 121–138.

Stinson, Dwight E., Jr. "The Battles of South Mountain." *Civil War Times Illustrated* I, no. 5 (August 1962): 12–15.

_____. "Eltham's Landing—The End Run That Failed." *Civil War Times Illustrated* I, no. 10 (February 1963), 38–41.

Sutherland, Daniel E. "Getting the 'Real War' into the Books." *The Virginia Magazine of History and Biography* 98, no. 2 (April 1990): 193–220.

Swart, Stanley L. "The Military Examination Board in the Civil War: A Case Study." *Civil War History* 16, no. 3 (September 1970): 227–245.

Vermilyea, Peter C. "Maj. Gen. John Sedgwick and the Pursuit of Lee's Army After Gettysburg." *Gettysburg Magazine* 22 (July 2000): 113–128.

von Deck, Joseph F. "Let Us Burn No More Daylight." *Lincoln Herald* 88, no. 1 (Spring 1986): 19–26; 88, no. 2 (Summer 1986): 43–46; vol. 88, no. 3 (Fall 1986): 97–105.

Ward, David A. "'Sedgwick's Foot Cavalry': The March of the Sixth Corps to Gettysburg." *The Gettysburg Magazine* 22 (July 2000): 43–65.

Ward, Leo L. "'It Was Open Defiant Rebellion.'" *Civil War: The Magazine of the Civil War Society* 9, no. 2 (March/April 1991): 56–63.

Weitz, Mark A. "Drill, Training and the Combat Performance of the Civil War Soldier: Dispelling the Myth of the Poor Soldier, Great Fighter." *The Journal of Military History* 62, no. 2 (April 1998): 263–289.

Wert, Jeff. "Duped in the Mountains of Virginia." *Civil War Times Illustrated* XVII, no. 8 (December 1978): 4–11; 41–44.

_____. "One Great Regret: Cold Harbor: A Federal Army Went Down Before a Sheet of Flame." *Civil War Times* XVII, no. 10 (February 1979): 22–35.

_____. "Rappahannock Station." *Civil War Times Illustrated* XV, no. 8 (December 1976): 4–8; 40–46.

_____. "The Snicker's Gap War." *Civil War Times* XVII, no. 4 (July 1978): 30–40.

_____. "Spotsylvania: Charge on the Mule Shoe: Emory Upton's Fight for a Brigadier's Star." *Civil War Times* XXII, no. 2 (April 1983): 12–15; 19–21.

Index

Numbers in **bold italics** indicate pages with illustrations

African Americans 52, 55, 56, 61, 192

Alabama troops: Battle's Brigade 242, 243; Wilcox's Brigade 159, 160, 161–62, 166; 5th Infantry 69; 6th Infantry 237, 243; 8th Infantry 140, 161, 162, 164, 165, 166, 169, 174, 275; 9th Infantry 165, 166; 10th Infantry 161–62, 165; 11th Infantry 161; 14th Infantry 161; 26th Infantry 69; 47th Infantry 188

Albright, Charles 194

Alexandria, VA 40, 41, 43, 86, 87

Allison, Alexander 164–65

Allison, George 165

Allison, James 165

Allison, John 165

Alvord, Jacob 124

Anderson, Andrew 105

Anthony, Joseph 10, **79**

Antietam, MD, battle of 110–12

Antietam Creek, MD 192–93

Army of the Shenandoah 267

Atlanta *Journal* 164

Augustine, James 28

Banks' Ford, VA 173–74

Bannan, Benjamin 15–16, 135

Bartlett, Joseph J. 45–46, 54, 64, 65, 57, 71, 72, 82, 90–1, 92, 94–95, 96, 97, 110, 138, 141–42, 148, 149, 153, 154, 155, 157, 160, 167, 168, 170, 171–72, 178, 185, 199, 207; Bartlett's brigade 62, 63, 64, 69, 70, 73, 76, 86, 88, 104, 112, 115, 123, 139–40, 141, 151, 154, 157, 160, 161, 168–69, 174–76, 185, 186–87, 198–99

Bates, Samuel P. 171, 279

bayonet attacks 227–231, 247

Belle Plain Landing, VA 123–24, 138

Bennett, John **250**

Bermuda Hundred, VA 264–65

Bland, D. Webster 12, **29**, 32, 62, 146, 170, 201, 225–26

Bocam, Louis 32

Boland, Francis 23, 45, 51, 52, 60, 109, 114, 137

Boland, Michael 113

Bonewitz, Daniel 170

Boyer, George 104

Boyer, Henry 93–94, **94**, 96, 97–98, 106, 107, 109, 110

Boyle, John T. 10, 11, 13, 18, 25, 88, 92, 98–99, 100, 101, 102, 103, 104, 105, 117, 118, 131, 133, 142, 145, 205, 206

Brandy Station, VA 204, 206, 210, 212

Brennan, Andrew 225

Brick House Landing, VA 45–47

Brooks, William T.H. 118, 120–1, **121**, 141, 146–47, 152, 153, 154, 155, 157, 169–60, 161, 162, 167, 168, 171, 176–77

Buck, William 198, 233

Budd, Richard 10, 19, 45

Burkittsville, MD 92–93

Burns, Thomas 241

Burnside, Ambrose E. 120, 121–22, 124, 129, 130, 138, **139**, 143

Cake, Henry L. 7, **8**–9, 10, 11, 15–16, 19, **30**, 32–33, 36–37, 64, 67–68, 69–70, 71, 72, 74, 80–82, 91, 92, 93, 94, 95–96, 97, 98, 100, 101, 102–3, 104, 105, 107, 109, 110, 113–14, 115–19, 124, 125, 127, 129, 131, 134, 142, 144–45, 158, 270, 274, 282n5, 283–84n34

Cake, Isaac 10, 79, **80**, 137

Camp Bland, VA 60

Camp Franklin, VA 24, 26–27

Camp Haeseler, VA 78, 80

Camp Martin, VA 44

Camp Northumberland, VA 27–34, **33**, **36**, 40–1

Camp Nugent, VA 80

Camp Richards, VA 55–56

Camp Schuylkill, PA (Lawton's Hill) 9–10, 11–12, 14–16, 17, 18, 19, 37

Camp Slocum, VA 38

Camp Wilder, DC 23

Casey, James 103

Catlett's Station, VA 41, 42–43, 122, **123**

Chancellorsville, VA, battle of *see* Fredericksburg, VA, second battle of; Salem Church

Charles City Courthouse, VA 85

Cheeseman's Creek, VA 44

Chickahominy River, VA 54–57, 61–62, 71, 73, 85

Claggett's Mill, MD **190**

Cobb, Howell 92

Cold Harbor, VA, battle of 260–64

Colt, Samuel F. 17, 31–32, 51, 60, 208

Connecticut troops: 2nd Heavy Artillery 261–62

Crampton's Gap, MD, battle of 89–108, 228, 274, 294n99

Curtin, Andrew G. 15, 18–19, 115, 117, 145, 193, 194–196, 205, 206

Dana, Napoleon J.T. 47

Douden, James N. 10

Dougherty, John 93, 102, **103**, 114, 134

Duane's Bridge, VA 61–62

Early, Jubal A. 153, 265, 266

Ellmaker, Peter C. 200

Ellrich, Ernest 67, **68**, 114

Eltham's Landing, VA, engagement at 46–53

Emancipation Proclamation 131–32

Emmitsburg, MD 189

Ewell, Richard S. 242

executions, military 27, 197–98

Fair Oaks, VA 55

Fairfax Courthouse, VA 38–39, 86–87, 180

Fairfield, PA 188–89

Faust, Daniel **129**, 131–32, 136, 137, 170, 174, 182, 195, 267

Fernsler, John 28–30, **42**, 44, 45, 71, 80, 127, 136, 137, 140

Fesig, Arthur S. 133

Fifth Army Corps 62, 63, 64, 65, 234

Filbert, Peter A. 7–8, 9, 31, 32–33, 34, 37, 43, 79, 80, 81–82, 84, 85–86, 89, 91, 107, 115–19, 120, 125,

126–27, 128–29, 133–34, 136, 137, 138, 271
Fisher, Henry 105
Foltz, George W. *20*, 121, 176
Foresman, Amos *236*
Fort Davidson, VA 63, 73
Fort Ellsworth, VA 86
Fort Lyon, DC 86, 88
Fort Monroe, VA 44, 86
Fort Stevens, DC 266
Fourth Army Corps 91
Franklin, William B. 24, *25*, 37, 45, 47, 53, 62, 87, 94–95, 111, 122, 125, 126, 143
Franklin's Crossing, VA *148*, 149–50, 177
Fredericksburg, VA 121–22, *158*, 228–30; battle of 124–27; second battle of 153–59, 173
Freece, Peter 170
Frick, Jacob G. 10, *11*, 12, 14, 16, 17, 18, *30*, 31, 37, 43, 59, 61, 62, 79, 82, 86, 116, 270–1
Fries, Peter 170

Gaines' Mill, VA, battle of 62–73, 274
Gee, A.L. 34–37, 81–82, 211
Georgia troops: Cobb's Legion 104, 106; Doles' Brigade 225, 238, 246; Gordon's Brigade 242; Wright's Brigade 257; 3rd Infantry 257; 4th Infantry 224, 225, 237, 239; 10th Infantry 91, 92, 97, 98, 100–1, 102, 103, 105, 106, 109, 275; 12th Infantry 225, 239, 243; 15th Infantry 187; 16th Infantry 104, 105, 106, 107, 109, 174; 21st Infantry 225, 246; 24th Infantry 104–5, 106; 26th Infantry 219; 44th Infantry 224, 225, 238, 239, 243, 244
Germanna Ford, VA 215, *216*
Gery, Evan 139, 140, 142, 143, 146, 147, 182, 183, 184, 190, 202, 203, 219
Gettysburg Campaign 177–91
Gordon, John B. 218
Goulding's Farm, VA 74
Grant, Ulysses S. 211, 212, 213, *214*, 215, 219, 221, 222, 223, 224, 245, 263, 267
Greene, Oliver D. 117

Haas, Jacob H. 85, *86*, 89, 90, 94, 96, 103, 106, 109, 111, 112, 115, 122–24, 125, 126, 127, 129, 130, 131, 133, 135, 136–37, 145, 146, 148, 149, 151–52, 153, 155, 157, 159, 162, 165–66, 169, 171, 173, 174, 175, 177–78, 179, 180, 181, 182, 184–86, 186–87, 188, 189, 190–1, 192–93, 195, 205, 206, 208, 209, 271
Haley, John 12
Halloran, Thomas *253*
Hampton, Wade 47
Hannum, John 133, 262

Harley, Otho 93–94
Harpers Ferry, WV 89, 90, 111
Harrisburg *Telegraph* 113
Harrison's Landing, VA 78–80, 84, 85
Hay, Lamar S. 9, 10, 95, 117, *205*
Henry, Edward 42, 44, 133, 176, 195, 198, 264
Hill, Ambrose P. 62
Hill, Daniel H. 64–65
Hipple, Charles D. 10, 21, 73
Hollister, James 68–69
Holmes, Oliver W. 235
Holt, Willis 103
Hood, John B. 47
Hooker, Joseph *143*, 145–46, 147, 148–49, 151, 152, 177, 178, 182
Houck, Thomas 30, 129, 130, 142–43, 147, 164, 207
Howe, Albion P. 122, 153, 173
Howland, Joseph 65, 70
Huber, David 170
Huber, Levi 142, 205–6, 243
Huger, Benjamin 61, 76
Hughes, John M. 218
Hyde, Thomas 24

James River, VA 74, 78, 79, 80, 264
Jewett, Thomas 197–98
Johnson, Joseph S. 102
Johnson, William 27
Johnston, Joseph E. 46, 49, 52–53, 54
Jones, Edward 201
Jones, Thomas 12

Keiser, Henry 27, 42, 74, 76, 77, 78, 86–87, 88, 89, 101, 107, 112, 113, *120*, 124, 125, 126, 137, 146, 147, 187, 184, 186, 187, 189, 192–93, 197, 199, 201, 202, 210, 212–13, 214, 215, 217, 220, 224, 225, 233, 234, 235, 236, 237, 238, 239, 241, 242, 250, 252, 253, 255, 256, 257, 258, 260, 261, 262, 263, 264, 270
Kilpatrick, Hugh J. 211

Lashorn, William M. *246*
Lee, Robert E. 60, 62, 74, 83, 88, 180, 182, 263, 265
Lessig, William H. 16, 98, *100*, 108, 117, 134, 145, 149–50, 151, 152, 153, *154*, 154–55, 156, 157, 160, 162, 164, 165, 166–67, 168, 169, 173, 174, 175, 178, 188, 190, 204–6, 210, 211, 219, 244, 257, 258, 263, 265, 266, 270, 274–75
Light, Samuel B. *136*
Lincoln, Abraham 40, 119–20, 147, 178, 191, 245, 266
Little Falls *Journal* 246
Littlestown, PA 185–86
Louisiana troops: Hays' Brigade 230; Washington Artillery 157; 8th Infantry 200; 9th Infantry 200
Lowe, Thaddeus 59

Luckenbill, Lewis 42, 43, 51, 57, 61, 68, 70, 76, 78, 85, 86, 88, 106, 108, 109, 165, 166, 170, 174, 178, 180, 187, 190, 198, 199, 201, 202, 203, 207, 210, 213, 214, 218, 219, 225, 235, 236, 239–40, 241, 250, 252, 254–55, 258, 260, 261, 262, 263
Lyman, Theodore 235, 245

Mackay, Michael 225
Madison, John *58*, 58–59, 80
Magruder, John B. 61
Maine troops: 3rd Infantry 140; 5th Infantry 24, 25, 43, 47, 51, 67, 69, 70, 72, 73, 88, 95, 140, 154, 155–56, 160, 165, 187, 188, 197, 200, 208, 218, 224, 228, 230, 233, 234, 235, 236, 237, 240, 245, 246, 249, 252–53, 254, 261, 262, 264; 6th Infantry 227, 229; 7th Infantry 61, 121
Malvern Hill, VA 77, 78
Manassas, VA: first battle of 41–42; second battle of 87–88
Manassas Junction, VA 41–42
Manchester, MD 183–84, 185
Martin, Lewis J. 9, 10–11, *12*, 27, 28, 38, 43, 45, 46, 48, 56, 59, 60, 71, 74, 78, 80, 84, 85, 88, 93, 94, 97, 98, 101, 102, 114, 115, 117, 137, 138
Maryland Campaign 1862 88–115
Maryland troops, CSA: 1st Battery 155
Massachusetts troops: 1st Battery 48, 64, 221; 7th Infantry 221; 18th Infantry 217; 19th Infantry 48
McClellan, George B. 24, 38, 39–41, *41*, 45, 52, 57, 58, 60, 62, 74, 75, 78, 79, 84, 87, 88, 90, 112, 119–20
McDowell, Irvin 37, 40
McGlenn, Patrick 28, 41, 45, 48–49, 51, 56–57, 60, 131
McLaws, Lafayette 91, 92, 103, 162
McMahon, Martin 144, 223, 227, 262
McMichael, Barney 114
McMinzie, Solomon 100, 101, 102
Meade, George G. 182–83, *183*, 184, 185, 188, 189, 191, 202, 203, 213, 214–15, 219, 223, 234, 244, 258, 264
Mechanicsville, VA 55, 60–1
Milledgeville *Southern Recorder* 246
Miller, Jerome 147, 174, 182, 219, 235, *237*, 254
Mine Run Campaign 202–4
Mississippi troops: Harris' Brigade 250, 252, 257; 16th Infantry 250, 252; 17th Infantry 228
Mosby, John 198–99
Moyer, Edwin 113
Mud March 138–42
Munford, Thomas T. 91, 92

Myers Hill, VA 256–58

Neill, Thomas H. 202
Nester, George 113
New Baltimore, VA 198–99
New Jersey troops: Brown's
    brigade 160, 161, 168; 1st Battery
    77; 2nd Infantry 160, 257; 10th
    Infantry 193, 194, 257; 23rd In-
    fantry 160, 172, 174
New York *Times* 51, 52, 62, 135, 146
New York *Tribune* 135
New York troops: 1st Lincoln Cav-
    alry 27; 16th Infantry 24, 25, 44,
    47, 64, 65, 67, 70, 72, 73, 95, 123,
    140, 160, 161, 172, 176, 199; 18th
    Infantry 47, 104; 27th Infantry
    24, 25, 43, 45–46, 47, 54, 67, 69,
    70, 73, 79, 95, 98, 125, 156, 160,
    172, 176; 31st Infantry 47, 152;
    32nd Infantry 47, 104; 43rd In-
    fantry 227, 229; 54th Infantry
    23; 77th Infantry 121; 121st In-
    fantry 125, 127, 160, 162, 165, 168,
    170–1, 172, 182, 187, 199, 200, 218,
    224, 230, 233, 234, 235, 238, 239,
    242, 245, 246, 249, 250, 258, 261,
    262, 264, 265–66
Newport News, VA 86
Newton, John 46, 47, 63, 122, 153,
    159, 173
Nice, Jacob 192–93
North Carolina troops: Cling-
    man's Brigade 261; Daniel's
    Brigade 225, 240; Ellis Light Ar-
    tillery 162; Godwin's Brigade
    230; Ramseur's Brigade 242;
    Robert Johnston's Brigade 218,
    242, 243; Rowan Artillery 47; 1st
    Cavalry 217; ; 1st Sharpshooter
    Battalion 156; 6th Infantry 47,
    200; 15th Infantry 104, 105, 106–
    7, 109; 20th Infantry 65, 274;
    23rd Infantry 243; 32nd Infantry
    246; 45th Infantry 242–43; 57th
    Infantry 156, 200
Nugent, Washington 27, 28, 31, 39,
    41, 44–45, 80, 208
Ny River, VA 256, 258

Oberrender, John S. 133
O'Donnell, Pat 238
Oestreich, Maurus 78, 126, 127,
    129, 157, 185, 241–42, 252, 255,
    258
Old Tavern, VA 61
Oliver, Thomas 100, 101
Orange & Alexandria Railroad, VA
    41, 42
Ortner, William 102

Peninsula Campaign 40–78
Pennsylvania troops: Good Intent
    Light Artillery 16, 145; Hamburg
    Light Infantry 10; National Light
    Infantry 8–9, 10; Pennsylvania
    Reserves 186, 187, 188; Pine
    Grove Sharpshooters 7, 9; Wash-

ington Light Infantry 8; 6th
    Cavalry 92; 10th Infantry 7, 8;
    16th Cavalry 271; 25th Infantry
    8, 9, 10, 11, 98; 27th Militia 271;
    48th Infantry 165; 49th Infantry
    227, 235, 240, 246; 52nd Infantry
    16; 56th Infantry 165; 61st In-
    fantry 229; 95th Infantry 47, 176,
    187, 200, 201, 218, 220, 228, 248,
    249, 258, 261, 263, 268; 95th-
    96th Infantry 269, 269; 129th In-
    fantry 79, 86, 271
Pennsylvania troops, 96th In-
    fantry: alcohol in 129, 137, 206,
    207–8, 266; average age of sol-
    diers 12; casualties 273; cow-
    ardice 170–1; desertions 142–43,
    197; diet 32; drilling 14, 17–18, 31,
    213–14, 286n71; end of service
    268; equipment 23, 30, 37, 78;
    ethnicity of soldiers 12–13, 14;
    flags 17, 18–19, 98, 178; furlough
    issues 132–33; gambling 207;
    Gettysburg monument 272–73;
    gifts from Schuylkill County
    residents 19, 23, 32; group pho-
    tographs 30, 33, 36, 53, 93, 167,
    181, 269, 273; health 28–29, 34,
    58, 80, 146, 159; issues with Sut-
    ler 34–37, 80–82, 211; letter writ-
    ing 136–38; morale 58–59, 129–
    31, 142, 181, 196; motivation for
    enlisting 20–21; music and songs
    32, 135–36; muster rolls 279–80;
    mustered into service 12; news-
    paper reading 135; occupations
    of soldiers 13; organization 9–11;
    profanity use 206–7; prostitu-
    tion use 208; recreation 136; reli-
    gion 31, 208–9; reunions 271–73;
    training 11, 14–15, 17–18, 31; vet-
    eran reenlistments 212–13; views
    on African Americans 209–10;
    views on Emancipation Procla-
    mation 131–32, 192
Petersburg, VA 265, 269–70
Petersburg & Weldon Railroad
    265, 269
Philadelphia *Inquirer* 73, 113, 135
Philadelphia *Press* 48, 61, 73, 110,
    113, 135
Pope, John 83, 85, 87, 88
Porter, Fitz John 62, 63
Potomac Creek, VA 179
Potomac Creek Bridge, VA *179*
Potomac River 182, 191
Potts, Clement 27, 28, 31, 49–50,
    51, 52, 64, 71, 72, 78, 80, 137, 208
Pottsville, PA 9, 18–19, 20, 22
Pottsville Cornet Band 10, 17, 19,
    27, 32, 79, 135, 211, 268
Pottsville *Miner's Journal* 15, 22,
    27–28, 31, 48, 69, 77, 113, 114, 135,
    148, 164, 195, 196, 201, 244

Rapidan River, VA 202, 204, 215,
    216
Rappahannock River, VA 121, 123,

124, 125, 138, 140–1, 149, 151, 177,
    178
Rappahannock Station, VA 200–1,
    230–1
Reed, Erasmus 30, 31, 44, 58, 61,
    62, 63, 77, 80, 84–85, 112, 132,
    133, 147, 158–59, 174, 191, 196,
    213, 260
Reed, Israel 198
Reed, John 198
Reed, Thomas H. 170, *171*
Reilly, Bernard 16
Remberger, Henry 242
Rich, Jonas M. 113–14
Richards, Mathias E. 10, 42, 43,
    44, 55, *57*, 58, 59, 61, 71, 76, 79,
    113, 145, 180–1, 186, 199
Richmond *Examiner* 201
Romick, Lewis C. 113, 242
Royer, Henry 101, 102, *105*, 107,
    108, 109–110, 112, 114, 134, 206
Russell, David A. *221*, 222, 230,
    242, 244, 255, 263; Russell's
    brigade 149, 151, 152, 160, 168
Russell, James E. 10, 12, *101*, 102,
    106, 107–8, 145, 205
Russell, Samuel 96, 115, 164, 187

Salem Church, VA, battle of 159–
    73, 275
Sargent, McCoy 112
Sauerbrey, E.E. 113
Savage's Station, VA 74, *75*
Saylor, John 60, 63, 67, 68
Schuylkill County, PA: anti-war
    sentiment in 195–96; draft issues
    193–94; immigrants in 9; Irish
    miners in 193–95; Molly
    Maguires in 194; politics 15–16
Schweers, John 134, *135*
Second Army Corps 112, 247–48;
    Mott's division 234, 240, 244
Sedgwick, John 29, 143–44, *144*,
    149, 151, 152, 153, 159, 167, 171–72,
    173, 175, 177, 178, 180, 185, 188,
    189, 203, 204, 211, 215, 217, 220–1
Severn, Isaac 195, 196, *197*, *224*,
    225–26, 238
Shamo, John 136
Shenandoah Valley, VA 267–69
Sheridan, Philip 267, *268*
Simpson, Frank 115, *213*
Sixth Army Corps 53, 55, 74, 76,
    85, 87, 89–90, 111, 120–1, 122,
    125–26, 215; Light Division 153,
    159; photographs of officers 53
Slocum, Henry W. 24, 25–26, *26*,
    31, 40, 42, 47, 54, 55, 75, 88, 92,
    94, 95–96, 109, 110, 120, 143;
    Slocum's division 62, 63, 74, 75,
    76, 77, 85, 90, 104–5, 107, 111
Smith, Beaton 9–10, 16, 117–18
Smith, Gustavus W. 46
Smith, William F. 74, 90, 121, *122*,
    143
Soldier's Retreat 23
South Carolina troops: Hampton's
    Legion 47, 49; Kershaw's

Brigade 160–1, 165; McGowan's Brigade 250, 252; 1st Infantry 252; 2nd Infantry 162, 164
Spotsylvania, VA, battle of 219, 226, 231–59, 275
Strausser, William 113
Stuart, Jeb 91

tactics 276–77
Tennallytown, DC 89
Texas troops Hood's Brigade 47; 1st Infantry 49
Thomas, Edward 244
Thompson, David P. *219*
Torbert, Alfred T.A. 96, 97
Tower, Charlemagne 15, 194, 283*n*32
Treichler, James 38, *77*, 101, 107, 112, 141, 142, 147, 177, 183, 209–10, 214, 218, 219, 224, 234, 235, 239, 245, 252, 253
Treon, Frank 112
Tritt, Susan 103–4

United States Regular Army: Sykes' Division 62, 64, 69, 188; 3rd Artillery 65; 3rd Infantry 71;

Battery C, 5th Artillery 253; 12th Infantry 65
Upton, Emory 199, *200*, 221, 248; at Bloody Angle 248–56; Spotsylvania assault 222–26, 231–47; Upton's Brigade 200, 202, 203, 204, 210, 215, 217, 256–58, 261, 262, 263, 264, 265, 267–68

Vermont troops: Vermont Brigade 242, 253; 2nd Infantry 177, 255; 3rd Infantry 62, 121; 6th Infantry 146
Virginia Central Railroad 260
Virginia troops: Chew's Battery 91; Portsmouth Battery 91; Walker's Brigade 225, 240–1, 243; Witcher's Brigade 242; 1st Richmond Howitzers 224; 2nd Cavalry 91, 92, 190; 2nd Infantry 240; 3rd Richmond Howitzers 225, 231, 236, 239, 240; 12th Cavalry 91, 92; 16th Infantry 91, 92, 96; 21st Infantry 242; 32nd Infantry 91; 33rd Infantry 240
Von Hollen, John 106, 164, 170, 264

Warrenton, VA 197, 198
Washington, DC 23–24, 188, 266
Wheaton, Frank 186
White Oak Church, VA 122, 127, 128, 132–33, *133*, 144, 148, 174, 176, 178
Whiting, W.H.C. 46–47
Wilderness, VA, battle of 215–19
Williamsburg, VA 44, 45, 85, 227
Wilson, R.P. 127
Winchester, third battle of 267–68
Windmill Point, VA 144
Wisconsin troops: 5th Infantry 227, 229
Wolf, Daniel 12
Woodbury's Bridge, VA 62, 63
Workman, Joseph 198
Wright, Horatio G. *177*, 191, 200, 215, 221, 223, 230, 244, 258, 262, 263, 266

York River, VA 45, 86
Yorktown, VA 44, 45, 85–86

Ziegler, Charles 102